# SCRIPTURE, CREED, THEOLOGY

# Scripture, Creed, Theology

### Lectures on the History of Christian Doctrine in the First Centuries

## Robert L. Calhoun

*Edited and with an Introduction by George A. Lindbeck*

CASCADE *Books* · Eugene, Oregon

SCRIPTURE, CREED, THEOLOGY
Lectures on the History of Christian Doctrine in the First Centuries

Cascade Books
An Imprint of Wipf and Stock Publishers
199 W. 8th Ave., Suite 3
Eugene, OR 97401

www.wipfandstock.com

ISBN 13: 978-1-55635-494-6

*Cataloging-in-Publication data:*

Calhoun, Robert Lowry, 1896–1983.

Scripture, creed, theology : lectures on the history of Christian doctrine in the first centuries / Robert L. Calhoun ; edited with an introduction by George A. Lindbeck.

lxx + 438 p. ; 23 cm. Includes bibliographical references and index.

ISBN 13: 978-1-55635-494-6

1. Theology, Doctrinal—History. I. Lindbeck, George A. II. Title.

BT21.2 .C35 2011

Manufactured in the U.S.A.

# Contents

# Abbreviations

*ACO*      *Acta Conciliorum Oecumenicorum.* Edited by Edward
           Schwartz, continued by Johannes Straub. Berlin: de
           Gruyter, 1925–

ACW        Ancient Christian Writers

*ANF*      *Ante-Nicene Fathers.* 10 vols. Edited by Alexander Roberts
           and James Donaldson, revised by A. Cleveland Coxe.
           Peabody: Hendrickson, 1995.

CCSL       Corpus Christianorum, Series Latina

CSEL       Corpus Scriptorum Ecclesiasticorum Latinorum

GCS        Griechischen christlichen Schriftsteller der ersten
           Jahrhundert

LFC        Library of Fathers of the Holy Catholic Church

LHCD       *Lectures on the History of Christian Doctrine*, by Robert L.
           Calhoun. See footnote 1 of chapter 1 for remarks about
           the history of this text.

*JThST*    *Journal of Theological Studies*

*JTh*      *Journal of Theology*

LCC        Library of Christian Classics

LST        *Lectures in Systematic Theology*, by Robert L. Calhoun.
           Recorded, condensed, and mimeographed by R. H. Smith.
           Available from Yale Divinity School Library. 1954.

*NPNF1*    *Nicene and Post-Nicene Fathers.* 1st series. 10 vols. Edited
           by Philip Schaff. Peabody: Hendrickson, 1995.

NPNF2    *Nicene and Post-Nicene Fathers.* 2nd series. 14 vols. Edited by Philip Schaff and Henry Wace. Peabody: Hendrickson, 1995.

PL       *Patrologia Latina*

ZNW      *Zeitschrift für die neutestamentliche Wissenschaft*

# Introduction

# Calhoun as Historical Theologian

*By George A. Lindbeck*

It has been a half-century or more since the Yale professor Robert Lowry Calhoun, yielding to the urgings of colleagues, friends, students, and publishers, agreed to prepare his *Lectures on the History of Christian Doctrine* for publication. Now, more than four decades after his retirement in 1965 and a quarter century since his death in 1983 at the age of eighty-six, this agreement is fulfilled for the half of these lectures that cover the period from the New Testament to the eve of the Middle Ages. The importance of these seven centuries for the later history of Christian doctrine down to the present and the reasons Calhoun never got beyond them in his preparatory work are described in the last section of this introduction.

The first two sections sketch his towering reputation and considerable influence during his teaching career. Both his reputation and his influence were almost entirely the product of orally delivered lectures that he never published and that nevertheless significantly affected mainline Protestant theology and practice in ways that historians of American religious thought have heretofore overlooked. The third section, by far the longest, examines the sources of the unusual theological appeal of his *Lectures on the History of Christian Doctrine* in their original setting; and the fourth suggests reasons for thinking that they are abundantly worth reading even today. The fifth and last section deals with, in addition to what has already been mentioned, the procedures followed in preparing the lectures in this book for publication.

## A Forgotten Reputation

Calhoun's reputation was immense but ephemeral. It grew from his teaching and other undocumented activities and scarcely at all from his writings. As is not unusual in such cases, even his name is now often unknown to Yale Divinity School faculty of the younger generation—not to mention their students—and few if any are aware that he taught ministerial, doctoral, and college students at Yale for close to a record length of time, from 1923 until he retired in 1965. In his own day, in contrast, he was famous far and wide. Reports of his preternatural brilliance began penetrating the hinterland from the early 1930s onward; I heard them almost immediately upon entering a Midwestern college the year before Pearl Harbor. It was in the 1940s and 1950s, however, that Calhoun's reputation reached its height. He was then customarily linked with H. Richard Niebuhr and Roland Bainton as one of the three giants who contributed most to making Yale Divinity School the major center at that time of university ministerial and theological studies in North America. (Union Seminary in New York was generally regarded as Yale's only real rival, but Union was not an integral part of a university.)

Nor was Calhoun's fame confined to those interested in religion. It was also stellar among undergraduate students of philosophy, as scarcely anyone still active in the University now remembers. As was true elsewhere, it was Calhoun's lecturing in particular that made him a legendary reputation in Yale College. For more than a quarter century he taught a yearlong survey of the history of philosophy that regularly attracted a hundred or more undergraduates. Nor were only the young enthusiastic. There were those in the university faculty at large who credited not only his undergraduate but also his graduate teaching—especially his Plato seminar—for contributing substantially to the revival of philosophy at Yale that began in the thirties. Yet the history of philosophy survey was the one most famous for its difficulty. Calhoun called it an "advanced" introductory survey; and in addition to the undergraduates, PhD students who sat for a doctoral examination in the field automatically took it even when they had had what was elsewhere considered good undergraduate preparation. One of these, Virginia Corwin, who did her dissertation under Calhoun and was head of the religion department at Smith until her retirement, tells of the time the undergraduate final was exactly the same as the PhD qualifying examination in the history of philosophy.

The undergraduates, to be sure, were graded more leniently; yet only the brightest and best survived—as I know from being a teaching assistant for Calhoun in that same course rather more than a decade later. In retrospect, I find myself dumbfounded that he was able to attract so many from the college into what for most was a murderously difficult course.

The impression Calhoun made on many of us did not fade as we grew older. Like others who have had a chance to sample great teaching throughout the world, I think of him as the greatest lecturer I have either heard or heard of. He was simultaneously both enthralling and intellectually demanding, not only occasionally but for three hours a week in yearlong courses that went for a full thirty weeks. Furthermore, it was possible to sit in on the same course year after year without being bored, for his was a questioning mind: he regularly found fresh ways of reading and explaining the texts that he dealt with. Albert Outler, who studied and taught at Yale before his long and distinguished career at Perkins School of Theology of Southern Methodist University, sat through the history of doctrine course twice while he was a graduate student and once after joining the YDS faculty. Calhoun lectured steadily and without notes, yet in such a way that one thought of him as thinking through every sentence and paragraph as he spoke. Nevertheless, when transcribed word for word, those sentences and paragraphs—indeed, whole lectures—read as if they had been polished for publication. Let me borrow from Virginia Corwin once again, this time a quotation:

> No student who has become a teacher can remember [Calhoun's lectures] without a stab of envy.... The thought of someone gone centuries ago—St. Augustine, for example, or Origen—takes shape before the mind, every essential detail in place ... the line and structure of the whole dominate, and the part is held in true proportion.... This extraordinary effect of clarity is not achieved by sacrificing a [thinker] or his conceptions to a scheme of one's own.... Students know that they are watching a master teacher who is also an austerely honest historian, testing the theses of other scholars by reading the sources in their original language, by controlling the less well-known writings and personal letters, and making his independent report. He protests that he knows but little of the domain he traverses, but the listener is not deceived. ... The response can only be one of keen pleasure.[1]

---

1. Corwin, "To Recall in Gratitude," 1–7. The quoted material is excerpted and reordered from 1–2.

It was not only Calhoun's lectures, however, that made him a great teacher. "An ill-defined question thrust into a lecture is treated with kindness beyond its deserts, rephrased and presented at its best before it is answered respectfully."[2] Or, to cite a complaint from Roland Bainton: "[Calhoun] is equally self-giving to all inquirers. He will do anything for someone in front of him, though he finds it hard to work for the general public or posterity. A student, after a class ending at ten o'clock, would come with a question. Bob would discuss it with him until noon, take him to lunch and bring him back for further elucidation into the middle of the afternoon. Some of us have wished that he might do for the masses what he does for the man, but if Bob thinks about it he would probably answer that he leaves it to the man to minister to the masses. [He] teaches our generation largely through those whom he has taught."[3]

Yet Calhoun's reputation, great though it once was, is now rarely mentioned. Even those of us who are most heavily indebted to him rarely have occasion or opportunity to acknowledge our debts. We aren't asked how he has influenced us; and when we try to document our borrowings from him, we are baffled. In part this silence is because of the difficulty of footnoting oral communications; but Calhoun also had the disconcerting habit whenever he was asked of citing a half-dozen or so sources for every idea we thought was original with him. Perhaps he had too good a memory, and that is why he had virtually no specialized scholarship to his credit despite his prodigiously broad and by no means shallow learning.[4] Most scholarly books, he would tell us, are redundant because in their search for originality, they ignore or forget so much of what is already known that they lose perspective and balance. Not surprisingly, he thought of the classroom as the main locus of his job of transmitting the heritage and instilling a proper sense of what constitutes responsible scholarship. Such a legacy, however, although of central importance in the educational process, is bound to be largely anonymous; it resists public display and goes largely unrecorded.

Another now largely forgotten dimension of Calhoun's reputation was national and international. He was active in the Federal and its suc-

2. Ibid.

3. Bainton, "Tribute to Robert Calhoun."

4. The only exception to this lack of specialized publication, I think it would be fair to say, is a long and youthful but still impressive essay on "Plato as Religious Realist," 195–251.

cessor the National Council of Churches as well as in the World Council as a theological consultant, a giver of addresses, and a drafter of major reports. Some say he was better able than other theologians to explain Americans to Europeans. Even Karl Barth, whom he respected but for the most part did not agree with, is reported to have been impressed by his knowledge of patristic sources—more recent theology appears not to have entered into their discussions.[5] I, like others who studied under him, was only vaguely aware of his extramural fame at the time it was at its height in the 1940s and 1950s when I was his student, and I have done little to investigate it since. All I know is that I long kept meeting people before my retirement both here and abroad for whom Calhoun was a notable figure—not because they had ever met, heard, or read him, but simply because of his reputation.

## PAST INFLUENCE

Calhoun's reputation as a teacher and lecturer accounts for the eagerness with which the publication of his *Lectures on the History of Christian Doctrine* was once awaited. According to the rumors—undocumented as far as I know—that circulated at Yale, publishers competed to get their hands on the *Lectures* because they expected these would become a widely used textbook. The source of their eagerness, as could be expected, was Calhoun's stellar reputation as a superb lecturer and excellent scholar whose difficult yearlong lecture course in the history of doctrine had became standard fare, not only for those enrolled in doctoral programs but also for ministerial candidates from what were then the dominant American Protestant denominations at what was widely regarded as the foremost divinity school in the country.

Some of the explanation for Calhoun's appeal has already been quoted from Virginia Corwin. She emphasized the intellectually aesthetic awe and delight that came from hearing a great scholar and great lecturer put on an ever-changing but cumulative series of masterful performances day after day and week after week. These qualities would be attractive in our day also, but something more is needed to explain the special impression he made at midcentury. Perhaps it will help if I tell the story of one undergraduate in his history of philosophy course for which I was a teaching assistant in the late forties.

5. Leith, *Crisis in the Church*, 11.

M.,[6] as I shall call him, was a philosophy major, a professed atheist, and came from a semi-observant Jewish family. Calhoun was, he thought, the most brilliant human being he had ever encountered. More than that: Calhoun's intellectual breadth, balance, and objectivity seemed stunning to this student. He did a more persuasive job of giving a synoptic overview of the thought of Plato and Aristotle, of Spinoza and Kant, not to mention other great philosophers, than they presumably could have done for themselves; and he did this not by bowdlerizing or translating into modern conceptualities, but in terms they themselves would have recognized as fair to what they were seeking to say. M. found himself first a Platonist, then an Aristotelian, later a Spinozist, and finally a Kantian (he never became a Hegelian, for although the course included Hegel, there were limits to Calhoun's sympathies). At the end of the year, M. was left with one great question: what did Calhoun himself believe? As a Congregationalist clergyman, this great professor was assumed to be a theist of some sort, but of what kind and for what reasons? M. decided that the way to find out was to enroll at the Divinity School, which he proceeded to do for a year after he completed his BA. It was an enjoyable year, he later told me, not least because he never felt excluded, as had happened not infrequently while he was in Yale College. And Calhoun, the believer, was in evidence in the chapel talks he gave from time to time, as did all members of the YDS faculty.

Most significantly for M., the Divinity School helped to reconnect him with his Jewish roots. He left Yale and went on to write his PhD dissertation on Martin Buber and teach until his retirement from a major university. Throughout his life, however, Calhoun remained an enigma to him. He was baffled by Calhoun's ability to engage such a student as himself in a personally meaningful search for the truth and yet be so objective that scarcely any hint of his theistic and Christian commitments appeared in his philosophy course. Or, at the Divinity School, how did he manage to be so evenhanded as not to offend such a Jew as himself and—this is my own addition—to be acceptable to everyone from Unitarians to Eastern Orthodox Christians including, perhaps most remarkably, the Protestant liberals, who were in the majority in the student body, and who

---

6. M. and I remained in touch until his death some years ago; and while I never had the opportunity to check the accuracy of this account with him, we talked enough about the past for me to think he would have basically agreed with it.

thought of Calhoun as one of their own despite his for them puzzling respect for—among other things—the Nicene and Chalcedonian creeds?

Part of the answer to this question is that Calhoun was so good an expositor that he didn't need to be a controversialist; he didn't need to intrude his own opinions or convictions in order to fascinate. Yet it must be added, I suppose, that impartiality and objectivity were more highly regarded in those days than in ours. The hermeneutics of suspicion had not yet received a name; and while two world wars and the irrationality of Nazism and Communism had already undermined the Enlightenment version of rationality, there was still a widespread belief that objectivity could be asymptotically approached, and that historians like Calhoun, who were both comprehensive and balanced and seemed to come closest to seeing things clearly and whole, were more reliable guides in the search for the truth than the ideologically biased advocates on the right or left. Yet Calhoun did not produce disciples. Perhaps one could say that his students never found out enough about what he believed or why he believed it to become his followers. Yet whatever their own convictions, whether staunchly secular or deeply religious, they tended to develop, as I earlier said, a Calhounian sense of intellectual responsibility; a belief that scholars are obligated to be respectful, fair, and indeed charitable in their understanding of others.

Yet in combination with his subject matter, Calhoun's influence on attitudes did have consequences for theological orientation. Although he never directly discussed ecumenism in any of his history of doctrine classes as far as I know, he did mention the ecumenical importance of the study of historical theology in the only explicitly methodological essay on that subject he ever published.[7] Four decades ago Robert Cushman, who was then the dean of Duke Divinity School, penned some lines that are in effect though not in form a personal confession of what happened to him when he was a student at YDS. "Professor Calhoun's distinctive contribution," he wrote, "was to explore pre-modern deposits of philosophical and Christian wisdom" at a time when theological studies in the American mainline denominations and the universities, not least at Yale, were "heavily weighted on the side of sciences of religion and post-Kantian thought."

---

7. Calhoun, "Role of Historical Theology," 444–54, especially 453ff. In this article as I read it, Calhoun treats historical theology as denotatively though not connotatively synonymous with the history of Christian thought and views the history of Christian doctrine as central to though not exhaustive of the former.

No other single individual, Cushman implied, did more to open a way in the last century "for sympathetic rediscovery of classical Christian positions both Catholic and Protestant." Calhoun thereby "mightily helped doctrinally illiterate children of liberal American Christianity in the thirties and forties to recover a critical comprehension of the well-nigh unsearchable riches of inherited Christian wisdom." He "not only prepared the ground" for informed encounter with the neo-orthodox theology that "liberal American religious thought was ill-prepared to receive," but also equipped American theologians (including Cushman) "to enter into responsible discussion with their counterparts in the world ecumenical movement," and thus fulfill "the role Providence [has assigned] as their theological and ecclesiastical vocation in the mid-twentieth century and, seemingly, for the foreseeable future."[8]

The foreseeable future quickly arrives and then vanishes. Cushman wrote close to fifty years ago at the beginning of an outburst of ecumenical zeal and optimism that is now almost unimaginable even to those who lived through it. Vatican II together with the ecumenism represented by the World Council of Churches brought changes and opened dialogues that swept Catholics, Protestants, and Orthodox into what seemed for a few years to be unstoppable advances toward church unity. *Ressourcement*, the return by divided Christians to the common sources of the faith, was chiefly responsible for whatever substance these advances had, but the enthusiasm that inflated their significance, vastly reinforced by mass-media sensationalism, came from the *aggiornamento*—the updating of the churches that would, so it was supposed, overcome the ancient and supposedly obsolete divisions of Christians from one another as well as from the modern world. Dean Cushman, as could be expected from a former student of Calhoun's, focused on *ressourcement*, going so far as to hint in the above quotation that his teacher's role in helping Protestants recover "the well-nigh unsearchable riches of inherited Christian wisdom" was providentially arranged. As I happen to have been one of those whose ecumenism benefited from Calhoun's instruction, it would be ungrateful not to acknowledge the debt a good many of us owe to him for having given us a sympathetic, nonpartisan grounding in Christian doctrinal traditions as a whole. Nothing like it was available anywhere else in North America. Without his teaching, such Yale alumni as Albert

8. Cushman, Introduction, vii–viii.

Outler, my wife Violette Lindbeck, and I would have found our years in Rome at the Second Vatican Council much more bewildering and much less fruitful than they were. Historians who want to know the theological background of North American Protestant ecumenism during those heady years would benefit from consulting, among other things, this volume of Calhoun's *Lectures on the History of Christian Doctrine.*

## Sources of Strength

It was not long, however, before that era ended. Theological concerns shifted radically in the time between 1965, when Calhoun retired, and the memorial service for him at Yale Divinity School in February 1984, a few months after his death. My own experience was not atypical: students who focused on doctrinally oriented ecumenism diminished to a trickle while those chiefly interested in topics of which I knew pitifully little, such as liberation theologies and death of God manifestoes, increased to a flood. This shift was naturally accompanied by a loss of enthusiasm for the sort of history of doctrine that Calhoun had practiced. Another kind of case than that advanced by Dean Cushman is needed to explain and support the present pertinence of Calhoun's work.

### Testimonies

Fortunately the two *in memoriam* speakers who are most important for our purposes, Professors Hans Frei and William Christian, were unswayed by these fluctuating fashions. Both had studied under Calhoun and were by this time generally thought of as Yale's leading theologian and philosopher of religion respectively. Their memories of him centered on what they took to be his abiding strengths—which, if they were right, are as deserving of consideration now as when he was alive.[9]

Hans Frei's task was to explain Professor Calhoun's role as an historian of doctrine (or, as he was officially titled, historical theologian). This was a difficult assignment. Ever since the Enlightenment, the history of Christian doctrine has been widely seen as a mixture of incompatibles, of fish and fowl, and hence illegitimate within a university setting. Traditionalists viewed the development of doctrine as ultimately guided by the Holy Spirit and thus requiring faith as well as reason for its investigation. For liberals, in contrast, doctrinal developments can be studied in

9. Frei, "In Memory of Robert L. Calhoun," 8.

a strictly historical fashion only insofar as they are accessible apart from faith. Calhoun belonged in neither of these two camps, for he sought to reconcile methodological liberalism more liberal than that of the liberals with doctrinal substance that was basically traditional. In contrast to theologically liberal historians and indeed to most people down to the present day, Calhoun did not think that the modern critical outlook is a liberal monopoly. It can be used in defense of tradition as well as against it, and also against liberalism no less than in its defense. Frei believed Calhoun was successful in his reconciliation of liberal method and traditional substance: "What is so clear in retrospect is the distinctive harmony of liberalism and Christian traditionalism without detriment to either, in Professor Calhoun's thinking."[10]

Frei's explanation of this thesis was brief, as befitted an *in memoriam* occasion, but it prompted much of the content of this introduction and needs to be recalled in detail. He began by noting that those of us, including himself, who had been Calhoun's students from the late 1930s through the early 1960s had badly misunderstood him. We knew that so-called neo-orthodoxy had increasingly affected Yale along with other mainline Protestant seminaries during most of that period, and that Calhoun had become less liberal theologically though more liberal politically (as was generally true of those influenced by neo-orthodoxy). What was assumed to be evident, however, was that he remained theologically to the left not only of Karl Barth but also of the three very different figures who in those days were considered most representative of North American neo-orthodoxy: Reinhold Niebuhr and Paul Tillich of Union in New York City;

---

10. Frei's next sentence reads, "He made a transition from liberalism to a post-liberal pattern of thought. . . ." (8). This comment has sometimes been interpreted as saying that harmonizing liberalism and Christian traditionalism produced a "post-liberalism" different from both of these apparent contradictories, but what this post-liberalism would amount to is not clear. As far as I know, Frei did not employ this hyphenated word except on this occasion, and Calhoun never used it. In any case, it should not be confused with another terminological innovation, unhyphenated "postliberalism." This latter term first appeared in print with one of its present standard meanings in 1984, but it gained currency only later. For its original sense, see Lindbeck, *Nature of Doctrine*, 135. This page contains a summary description of postliberal theology (which, however, presupposes acquaintance with previous portions of that book). As there summarized, postliberal theology is compatible with Frei's and Calhoun's "generous orthodoxy" and with what Frei called the "harmony of liberalism and Christian traditionalism" in Calhoun's thought, but it neither implies nor is implied by the latter. This compatibility is contested at length (and in my opinion unsuccessfully) in DeHart's *Trial of the Witnesses*.

and at Yale, Reinhold's brother H. Richard Niebuhr, a colleague and close friend of Calhoun. That was enough to identify Calhoun as basically a liberal. Neo-orthodoxy had come to define orthodoxy, and we took disagreement with the former as proof of liberalism.

Frei told us that he had come to see that we had been deeply mistaken. While it was true that methodological liberalism was a major factor in Calhoun's thinking, it was not this element that substantively separated him from the neo-orthodox as well as from liberals in general. Rather, as has already been mentioned, it was Christian traditionalism that did so. This recognition came as a jolt. Calhoun had often been labeled liberal, and he had done this himself, but he had never been called a traditionalist by either himself or others. Yet Frei showed us in a few tightly packed minutes that the evidence for his former teacher's traditionalism pervaded his work. He also implied that much of what we had thought of as liberal because it was not neo-orthodox was in fact traditional, but few got the message despite abundant indications to that effect in what he said:

> [Calhoun] taught us to use the time-honored orthodox term "doctrine" once again with ease, and not even to be afraid of the word "dogma." In his lectures . . . "orthodoxy" was a matter of broad consensus within a growing and living tradition with wide and inclusive perimeters. His theological teaching was above all *generous*, confident that divine grace and human reflection belonged together and that the revelation of God in Christ was no stranger to this world, for the universe was providentially led, and human history was never, even in the instances of the greatest follies, completely devoid of the reflection of the divine light. And therefore church and world, the Christian community and the broad, infinitely varied life of culture belonged naturally together. Music, poetry, sports, the day's work in the shop, on the farm or in the study—none of it is foreign to the service of the same God whose name is praised and exalted in the church. It was quite natural, then, for Calhoun . . . to be equally a part of the academic, yes, the increasingly secular academic community and to be fully a part of the church. . . . [His ecumenical] service was the practical companion piece to what, in the classroom, was a solid doctrine of the church which included liberal views but also the older Protestant heritage and, back of that, the Augustinian *Civitas dei* with its vision of a transcendent kingdom of tensed and always incomplete presence here on earth. . . .

[I]n his doctrine of God he was not at all averse to a philosophical and religious use of the traditional theistic proofs—ontological, cosmological, and teleological. How could that be? In large part because in his theory of knowledge he was a critical realist (in contrast to Richard Niebuhr's critical idealism). The God we worship is not simply a transcendental subject, not simply the *ground* of our intuitions about God present in our responses to him. The God we worship is an overpoweringly real and objective majestic presence, the One beyond the many, who is at the same time Creator, Judge, and Redeemer. God is *there* in his own right, independent and prior to all that we say and do, and therefore rightly to be worshipped. . . . . Critical realism in the doctrine of the knowledge of God served Calhoun in making the transition from liberalism, not to neo-orthodoxy, but to a view closer to traditional orthodoxy, without abandoning his liberal convictions. It was reflected in the doctrine of God and many others, and it provided a common ground for knowledge of the real God in nature and in revelation.

. . . We talk today of the distinctiveness of religious or Christian language use. Calhoun didn't use those terms, but he would have understood them and understood in a richer way than we often do. He knew full well that the pattern of ancient philosophical thought, chiefly Hellenic and Hellenistic, and then the whole course of the history of Western philosophy has its own integrity and autonomy, apart from the roles it has had in Christian thought. But more than many others he also showed that philosophy found a home in the history of Christian doctrine, and not to the detriment of the integrity of that history. In contrast to Adolph [*sic*] von Harnack as well as some conservative historians of doctrine, he believed that the Greeks were there right from the inception of Christian thought, and that they and their philosophical successors were fitly there. They contributed to the construction of the building. He would have agreed with Schleiermacher that Christianity, when freed from unwarranted fears of secular thought and from a hopeless passion for ideal linguistic purity, has right from the beginning been a "language-shaping" force and not a shapeless receptacle for every bit of new vocabulary that needs purification from time to time. [Instead of this,] Calhoun went about the business of showing how the one great, continuing tradition was built with the aid of . . . countless cultural contributions then and now.

What he did, then, was to hand on to his students in the pulpit as well as in the classroom the vision of a living, integral and open-ended Christian tradition, a strong tradition. He is a powerful link in a long, unbroken pedagogic chain, an unforgettable example to those of us who follow after him with gratitude.[11]

Frei singled out in these concluding remarks those aspects of Calhoun's work that provide much help to those in large part unfamiliar even at second hand with Calhoun's vision of the two-thousand-year history of Christian thought. Frei delivered his only as-yet-unquoted reference earlier in his talk well before the last paragraph, even though it was of climactic importance. It reads as if it were a blurb for the present volume written a quarter century ahead of time, for the case in favor of Calhoun's historical vision may be as strong or stronger now than it was in 1984.

Looking over his great *Lectures in* [sic] *the History of Christian Doctrine,* the publication of which is finally in preparation, one rediscovers the marvelously panoramic setting which served as the chrysalis of his generous, liberal orthodoxy.[12]

Frei himself can be regarded as both heir and transposer of Calhoun's historical vision. He was closer theologically to Calhoun than to his primary academic mentor, H. Richard Niebuhr, and it is further remembered that he talked at times as if Calhoun's example had in important ways correctively balanced Barth's impact. It has even been suggested that after Barth, Calhoun was the Christian thinker who had most influenced him. It is difficult to know how much to trust undocumented memories,[13] but these points are consistent with the *in memoriam* remarks we have considered. In part because of this, it makes sense (even if one disregards undocumented memories) to see Frei's contribution to the theological understanding of Christian faith in the present situation as an extension into modern times of the combination of liberalism and traditionalism characteristic of Calhoun's contribution to the historical understanding of that same faith in premodern settings.

11. Frei, "In Memory of Robert L. Calhoun," 8–9.

12. Ibid., 9.

13. These memories are at this point entirely my own as far as I know. They originated in part in the recollections of others who are no longer with us and can neither validate nor invalidate what I recall.

Such has been said for the purposes of an introduction to indicate what was unique in Calhoun's history of Christian doctrine that made it into the cradle or chrysalis of an orthodoxy that was also generous and liberal. He was among those who turned away from prewar liberalism after World War I; but unlike the others, he moved "not to neo-orthodoxy but to a view closer to traditional orthodoxy without abandoning his liberal convictions."[14] He came to recognize through his historical work that traditionalisms and not only liberalisms can be generous (as well as ungenerous) in their interactions with one another and with the world at large. Thus "Calhoun agreed with [the liberal] Schleiermacher that Christianity has right from the beginning been a 'language-shaping' force," and disagreed with the later and, in his day, supremely influential liberal historical theologian, von Harnack, for whom Christianity had been "a shapeless receptacle for every bit of new vocabulary" from which it needs to be purged from time to time.[15] In opposition both to Harnackian liberal versions of the Reformation *sola Scriptura* as well to modern conservative ones, "Calhoun went about the business of showing how the one great, continuing tradition was built with the aid of . . . countless cultural contributions then and now." It was this, to repeat, that enabled him "to hand on to his students . . . the vision of a living, integral and open-ended Christian tradition"[16] that was liberal in its inclusiveness and, as also needs to be emphasized, traditional in its undergirding: "[W]ithin a growing and living tradition with wide and inclusive perimeters . . . orthodoxy was a matter of a wide consensus."[17]

A second and shorter memorial talk, this one by Professor Christian, dealt with Calhoun's work from a philosophical perspective, though not without appreciation for his work on doctrine. After explaining that his "outrageous expectations surprised [his students] into doing better than their best" for "he really thought we knew more than we did,"[18] Christian spoke of a Plato seminar in which Calhoun yielded to the pleading of his students and shared with them why he was philosophically a sort of Platonist (although of an unfamiliar kind). "He argued, to us very impres-

---

14. Ibid., 9.
15. Ibid., 9.
16. Ibid., 9.
17. Ibid., 8.
18. Christian, "In Memory," 11.

sively, that more sense could be made of the methods of modern science on Plato's principles than Aristotle's" or Kant's.[19] The lesson above all that he learned was this:

> There have been philosophers who have thought that the value of the history of philosophy is only that it tells us the mistakes of the past. But [Calhoun] was not one of them. He thought that some philosophers who lived in bygone ages should be listened to with respect. Indeed on some points it might turn out that they were right.
>
> At one point nearly forty years ago [the late 1940s] he had been in Chicago as a visiting professor. I asked him what he thought of it. He said with an air of surprise and puzzlement, "Those people don't know the Enlightenment is over." . . . The point was that the Enlightenment had happened, and a good thing too. But much had happened since then, and much had happened before that. The long conversation that has been going on since Thales should not, in its admissions policy so to speak, restrict its participants to those of a certain epoch and, perhaps, particularly not to those of the Enlightenment. One might say that he was an enlightened man, but not a man of the Enlightenment. He lived, and taught, by a different light.[20]

Others were waiting to speak; and there was no time to describe the puzzlingly "different light" by which Professor Calhoun "lived, and taught." Yet something must be said about this light that led him both to agree with the general belief that it was "a good thing . . . the Enlightenment had happened" even while he also held, in opposition to widespread scholarly opinion, that this era was now out of date. This was true not only in such areas as mathematics and the natural sciences; the new methods of critical inquiry initiated by Kant's three *Critiques* could be helpfully (as well as unhelpfully) employed in philosophy and theology also. What had been disastrous were not the new insights but the blindly dismissive attitude

19. Ibid., 11. Calhoun preferred Plato to Kant not least because the latter was epistemologically an idealist, whereas Plato's principles were consistent with the critical realism that Calhoun argued is presupposed, though at times unwittingly, by science in general as well as by ordinary commonsense knowledge as a whole. He nevertheless considered Kant the most influential of modern philosophers, as is clear from his extensive treatment of Kant in his stenographically recorded *Lectures on the History of Philosophy* (*LHP*). Copies marked "For private circulation only" can be consulted in the Yale Divinity School Library.

20. Ibid., 11.

toward much that was best in premodern thought. A. O. Lovejoy, whom Calhoun rated more highly than any other historian of ideas, diagnosed the basic problem this way:

> Assuming human nature to be a simple thing, the Enlightenment also, as a rule, assumed political and social problems to be simple, and therefore easy of solution. Rid man's mind of a few ancient errors, purge his beliefs of the artificial complications of meta-physical "systems" and theological dogmas, restore to his social relations something like the simplicity of the state of nature, and his natural excellence would, it was assumed, be realized, and mankind would live happily ever after.[21]

### Liberal or Traditionalist?

The methodological dependence of theology on the Enlightenment that Calhoun deplored was more widespread than he seemed to think. Those beginning their studies in places like Yale Divinity School generally came from liberal churches or colleges and were habituated to taking as authoritative such sources as the *Encyclopedia Britannica* treatment of "Liberalism, Theological" in the edition current both long before and well after Calhoun's retirement. According to this entry, theological liberalism "is a form of religious thought that establishes religious inquiry on the basis of a norm other than the authority of tradition."[22] The alternative basic norm may be reason, as it was for Kant, or religious experience understood with the help of Kant's critical analysis of reason, as it was for Schleiermacher, but it was generally assumed in both cases that that the results would be contrary to tradition. Liberal methods were counted on to support liberal conclusions, and the reverse was expected of traditional methods. That is why theological conservatives were warned against attending places like Yale, and why liberals ignored conservative scholars on the grounds that they already knew the latter's methodological mistakes.

---

21. Lovejoy, *Great Chain of Being*, 9.

22. "Liberalism, Theological," in *Encyclopedia Britannica*. The author, interestingly enough, was a professor at the University of Chicago. While John Locke (d. 1704) comes first in his account of distinctively modern liberal theology, he does acknowledge the preeminent influence of Kant and Schleiermacher on nineteenth- and twentieth-century developments.

Calhoun's perspective was distinctly different from this generally accepted view, for he did not regard critical thinking whether Kantian or Schleiermacherian as necessarily anti-traditional:

> Toward the end of the 18th century, a new theological method and temper came into being. . . . [To it] Kant affixed the label *critical,* and that term continues to serve better than any other to identify the essential difference between newer and older theologies, whether affirming or dissenting from traditional norms . . . [T]hinkers as diverse as Schleiermacher and Ritschl, on the one hand, Kierkegaard and Barth, on the other, display the characteristic effects of Kant's fresh analysis of the grounds and limits of human knowledge . . . [L]iberalism, romantic or moralistic, and dialectical "neo-orthodoxy" are modes of thought essentially different from both patristic, scholastic, or confessional theologies, and from the pre-Kantian rationalisms of all kinds. A full examination of the newer modes of theology would . . . [bring] the story down to the present decade. But here we must content ourselves with a glance at the new critical principle as Kant began its formulation, and at the first . . . full-scale system of liberal Protestant dogmatic [viz., Schleiermacher's theology] in which the principle has been applied.[23]

There were both advantages and disadvantages in thus ending the course in history of doctrine with Kant and Schleiermacher. It was with them more than anyone else that the methodological shift from old to new ways of doing theology took place. So great were the changes they wrought that all major later developments were classified at Yale as "Contemporary Theology" and assigned to teachers other than Calhoun. The final factor contributing to his reticence was this curricular division that barred the history of doctrine (also known as historical theology) from covering

23. Calhoun, *LHCD* (1948), 525. In the pre-Vatican II days when Calhoun delivered these lectures, he was unable to think of any magisterially approved Roman Catholic theologians in whom "The critical method and orientation have found [a] natural place" (ibid.); that is, who were seriously engaged either pro and con with what Bernard Lonergan among others called Kant's "Copernican turn to the subject"; cf. Lonergan, *Subject.* Needless to say, the situation has changed since Vatican II. Fergus Kerr has recently written a book, *Twentieth-Century Catholic Theologians,* in which perhaps all ten authors with whom he deals qualify as critical theologians by Calhoun's criteria as much as do Kierkegaard and Barth, although for somewhat different reasons. Moreover, most and perhaps all of them are in good standing with the Roman curia, including, not surprisingly, Joseph Ratzinger, whom Kerr evaluates on the basis of his scholarly works written prior to his becoming Pope Benedict XVI.

the period after around 1800 (which period, not coincidentally, was the heyday of liberalism). Developments after this date except for Roman Catholic trends through 1870 were classified as contemporary rather than historical and were the province of systematic and dogmatic theology—which functioned as two names for the same discipline.

Most people thought Calhoun's resistance to transgressing disciplinary boundaries (which applied not only to theology but also to such other cognate areas as scriptural studies) was excessive, and complaints were not unknown. Dissertation writers dealing with "newer modes of theology" murmured *sotto voce* that even when he clearly knew more about a thesis topic than anyone else and was endlessly helpful in unofficial ways, he refused to act as director. He did this for what to them was the implausible reason that he was not an expert in the field. His faculty colleagues, on the other hand, were not surprised: they agreed with the complainers that his ability to read quickly, broadly, and at the same time retentively was unparalleled, but they also knew of his insistence that the task of "bringing the story down to the present decade" belonged to dogmaticians and systematicians and not to him.[24]

In accordance with this rule, he ended his history of doctrine with a lecture on Schleiermacher,[25] whose life straddled 1800, and whom he like many others regarded as the initiator and the architect of what can be conveniently described as "mediating liberalism"—though he generally called it simply "liberalism." Its seeming solution to the problem of reconciling liberalism and Christian traditionalism helped to make it far more popular in religious circles; and for that reason, it was a far greater challenge to Christian traditionalism than purebred Enlightenment liberalism had ever been. From its beginnings until the Great War of 1914–1918, mediating liberalism dominated the theological *avant garde* of Protestantism and remained strong on the grassroots level for decades afterward—not to mention the persistence of its influence in new forms down to the present. Nothing that happened after its beginnings, how-

---

24. Ibid., 525 contains the quoted phrases.

25. Ibid., 525–37. The lecture of which this is a transcript consists mostly of what Calhoun considered an excessively hurried summary of Schleiermacher's *Christian Faith*, "the first—and thus far the only—full-scale system of liberal Protestant dogmatic" (525). Unfortunately there are no transcripts of more satisfactory versions of this lecture delivered in other years such as Calhoun might have been willing to revise for publication or to have quoted at length.

ever, fell within Calhoun's teaching area, and we are chiefly dependent on what he had to say about Schleiermacher for his understanding of later developments. It was Schleiermacher's view of "the job of the theologian [that] . . . has come to be associated with liberal Protestant thought."[26]

In Calhoun's discussions of Schleiermacher, he seemed to take for granted that we knew that a key axiom of liberal anti-traditionalism rested on the fallacy of denying the antecedent.[27] Fortunately for students who had never taken a course in logic, Calhoun's way of teaching the history of doctrine taught them to recognize this fallacy even when they didn't know its technical name. His way of plotting the story of doctrinal development provided plenty of evidence that there are often good reasons for traditional beliefs that are quite different from the discredited ones that had once been persuasive. Thinking otherwise came to seem in student bull sessions as I remember them no less silly than doubting the traditional belief, old as the race, that the sun will continue to rise and set as long as sun and earth endure just because the ancients falsely supposed that the rising and setting resulted from the sun's rotation around the earth rather than the earth's rotation on its axis. This astronomical example was too simplistic an analogy for Calhoun to use, but we were more simpleminded than he was.

It should not be supposed, however, that Mr. Calhoun had no help in resisting anti-traditionalism. Those enrolled for divinity degrees were not eligible to take his courses until their second year; and by that time, from the 1930s on, they had been assured by their fellows (especially those who took courses from H. Richard Niebuhr, a recent addition

---

26. See below, chapter 1, page 4.

27. Those who took logic in high school or college (as seminary students were told they ought to do in Calhoun's day) will remember such textbook examples of this fallacy as "if human, then mortal; not human, therefore not mortal" (i.e., if $p$, then $q$; not $p$, therefore not $q$). The valid form of *modus tollens* is the inverse; i.e., the denial of the consequent: "if human, then mortal; not mortal, therefore not human" (if $p$ then $q$, not $q$, therefore not $p$). The supposition in liberal instances of this fallacy is that modern critical disproofs of traditional grounds ($p$) for traditional beliefs ($q$) also disprove those beliefs and thus clear the way for other beliefs favored by nontraditional and presumptively better arguments. What is overlooked is that there may be many—perhaps very many—critically valid ways of grounding these same beliefs. Calhoun had a talent for turning blundering queries into intelligent questions by answering them as if he were simply articulating more clearly what we already knew. It was in some such way that I (and I suppose many of his other students) learned of the anti-traditionalist affinity for the fallacy of denying the antecedent.

to the faculty) that liberalism in general was out of date. The future belonged to the dialectical or crisis theologies from Europe that came to be called neo-orthodox in their American versions. For this rapidly strengthening *avant garde,* the truly dangerous liberalism was not that of the original Enlightenment that had rejected the Christian doctrinal heritage as a whole, but the mediating variety that sought to reconcile tradition and modernity and in the process perverted what it retained. It was the latter that was far and away the more popular and powerful. It dominated mainline Protestantism intellectually even if not numerically throughout the world from the late nineteenth century until at least the Great War of 1914, and its influence remained strong in North America long after that.

As mentioned earlier, Calhoun, like others, traced the beginnings of what were still in his day the dominant forms of mediating liberalism to Friedrich Schleiermacher (1768–1834).[28] This great German theologian sought to reconcile traditionally Pietist forms of Christian experience with what Calhoun, in agreement with almost every competent judge of the matter including Karl Barth, regarded as an intellectually and in some respects, experientially impressive conjoining of the Kantian Enlightenment with late eighteenth-century Romanticism. Whatever one thinks of the original character of this mediating liberalism (of which more later), its offshoots had become enmeshed well before 1900 in what Calhoun viewed as a Western culture in which earlier Enlightenment optimism had been reshaped and intensified by the unscientific misuse of Darwinism in the work of such philosophers as Herbert Spencer (1820–1903). Here is some of what his students heard about the consequences in 1947:

> [These thinkers] enshrined "the struggle for existence" and the mechanisms of "natural selection" among the basic principles of the world we live in ... [The ethic] of the secular way of life ... was the quest for success, measured especially in terms of possessions and power. To this end [paradoxically], a whole gamut

28. "Mediating liberalism" is a neologism that has the advantage of distinguishing the liberalism stemming from Schleiermacher (1768–1834), with which Calhoun was chiefly concerned, from other forms of what is technically termed mediating theology. The latter embraces not only the thought of Schleiermacher and those influenced by him (which was generally regarded in Calhoun's day as ending with the rise of neo-orthodoxy after World War I), but also previous efforts to reconcile modernity with Christianity that go back as far as John Locke (1632–1704).

of virtues [of which Christians approve] was called for: industry, sobriety, thrift, and many more. Its cult was imperialistic nationalism replete with ritual, emotional appeal, and a genuine call for self-devotion [for self-sacrifice on behalf of the nation]. . . . The mode of thought which served as a kind of theology for this secular religion was evolutionary naturalism. . . . Evolution was king, and all would be well.

The outcome in 1914 and thereafter has been a harsh judgment on such naïve optimism. First came war. . . . Then came depression. . . . War and depression combined to spawn more virulent forms of neo-paganism. Thence came World War II, ending in universal [nuclear] dread. . . . For this unhappy crisis much of so-called Christianity must of course share the blame.[29]

Calhoun did not exempt conservative Christians from blame, but his audience knew that it was mostly liberal Christianity he had in mind. It was this that was the chief provider of religious reinforcement to the "naïve optimism" that was at the heart of the debacle. It was liberal Christians who had taken the lead in minimizing the sinfulness of human beings and maximizing their ability to perfect themselves and their society and thus usher in the Kingdom of God on earth. Moreover, the liberals did this in a period when the mainline Protestant churches in which they were dominant were generally regarded as immensely influential in three leading world powers: Britain, Germany, and the United States. Calhoun was only belatedly disenchanted with this liberalism that did not come under attack in America until well after World War I. In the 1930s, however, he finally wrote of the disastrous consequences of the replacement of faith in God by faith in cultural progress in all "forms of liberalism and of the 'social gospel' within the churches which identify the Kingdom of God with a cultural ideal or an improved social order."[30]

<hr />

29. Calhoun, *LHCD* (1948), 24–25.

30. Calhoun, "Dilemma of Humanitarian Modernism," 71. The "disastrous results" could be made to include the bloody suppression of the Philippine effort to gain independence after the United States dispossessed Spain at the beginning of the twentieth century. I am indebted for the quotation (though not for the example I have added) to Thelen, *Man as Sinner*, 132. Calhoun's remark, it should be noted, was not motivated by political conservatism. When he wrote this, he was, as Thelen puts it, "moving politically to the left, theologically to the right" (ibid., 129), as were all the former theological liberals whom she classifies as "realistic" or "neo-orthodox" in her book (Ibid., 6–7 with special attention to n. 14).

As student memories faded of the character and consequences of Protestant liberalism's captivity to the culture of the prewar period, Calhoun decided after his retirement not to publish the bulk of what he had said on these topics. The major exception he made concerned the effects of that culture on biblical interpretation as manifest, for example, in the "tendency, prevalent at the turn of the century, to find in the gospels the story of a modern-minded religious leader."[31] This exception sharpens the question to be next addressed as to why his students thought of him as liberal even though those outside Yale classified him as neo-orthodox.[32]

## Calhoun as a Liberal

Hans Frei suggested in his *in memoriam* remarks, it will be recalled, that Calhoun's traditionalism had resemblances to liberalism that made him seem more liberal than the neo-orthodox (including his friend and colleague, H. Richard Niebuhr), but that this same traditionalism made him closer to traditional orthodoxy than were the neo-orthodox. The first lecture in this volume provides some of the support for this analysis: "Before entering into detail, it will be well to remind ourselves of different ways of envisioning the theological enterprise in relation to God's revelatory activity, on the one hand, and human religious experience, on the other."[33] There are three such ways—liberal, neo-orthodox, and traditional—and while Calhoun does not expressly say as much, his traditional way brackets neo-orthodoxy on both left and right: it is both more liberal and more orthodox than the latter. In outlining the differences and similarities between liberal experiential and traditional revelational positions, he made Schleiermacher the paradigmatic representative of liberalism:

> It seemed to him that religion as the rationalists of the eighteenth century had understood and attacked it, was misconceived. They had tried to identify it with a particular set of doctrines or with a particular set of morals, pronouncements of the intellect or guidelines for the will. . . . [He] undertook to defend the validity of theology upon a new ground by urging that its task is the elaboration of the content of religious experience.[34] The emphasis

31. See below, chapter 2, page 20.

32. Ibid. Thelen is one example among others.

33. See below, chapter 1, page 2.

34. In Schleiermacher's own words, theology "is based entirely on the inner experience of the believer; its only purpose is to describe and elucidate that experience." *Christian Faith*, 428.

now is not upon an objective act of God but upon the personal experience of human beings. Schleiermacher had no intention at any time of denying the presence and activity of God; that was an indispensable presupposition. But it seemed to him that all one could know of God, and all that one could intelligently talk about as a theologian was what happened in God's presence . . . . And so theology is concerned in the first instance not with revelation, but rather with religion. . . .

I myself am inclined to welcome especially the reaction of those who say revelation is the chief concern of the theologian: God, but God speaking to man, God as he is known to human beings in his presence, judgment, and mercy. It seems to me that the primary emphasis must be placed where the traditional view placed it: upon the impact of God on man. At the same time Schleiermacher's insights simply cannot be brushed aside. . . . [T] he human response to that impact familiarly called religious experience, is inseparable from the account of God's self-revelation.[35]

One of the reasons that it was easy to think of Calhoun as liberal was that intentionally or not, he made Schleiermacher's view of theology seem more attractive than was the traditional position that he said was his own. As Calhoun indicated more fully elsewhere than in the present volume, Schleiermacher's stress on religious experience appealed first of all to the religiously and romantically inclined for whom eighteenth-century rationalism was affectively barren; second, to the modern-minded for whom experientialism's presumed independence of tradition warranted making it an authoritative basis for theology (or "religious inquiry," as the *Britannica* article put it); and third, to the devotees of the Enlightenment for whom religious experience when independent of tradition was a permissible foundation provided that modern critical reason was treated as a coequal authority. In the long run, however, the greatest of all attractions was the compatibility, according to Schleiermacher and his followers, of cherished Christian traditions with religious experience.

The Christian shares in the religiousness common to all human beings. . . . [He] knows, however, two further moments: he is not only creature, but is also sinner. . . . Yet he is not only sinner, he is also aware of salvation through Jesus Christ. He doesn't know himself as sinner until he has been saved. . . . Now Jesus Christ becomes for him redeemer because he, first and alone of human-

35. See below, chapter 1, page 5.

> kind, had perfect God-consciousness.... made accessible to those
> who associate themselves with him in faith, as a community.[36]

Everything in this summary is reconcilable with the church's historic faith. To be sure, some central doctrines are not included, most notably the Trinitarian ones, but these are not rejected.[37] The first sentence would have troubled Barth, for whom "[r]eligion is declared to be of man's making: it is human, all too human," and is in no sense God's self-revelation,[38] but the Barthian view of religion and religious experience was for Calhoun an unfortunate modern reaction against liberalism. The so-called dialectical position was untraditional as well as illiberal, opposed to the scripturally defensible (though not explicitly stated) view that religiousness, even though susceptible to demonic distortions, originates initially in response to the general revelation referred to in such texts as "the heavens declare the glory of God" (Ps 19:1), and "what can be known about God is plain [also to those 'who suppress the truth'] . . . in the things that have been made" (Rom 1:19–20). Equally without warrant are objections to such concepts as "God-consciousness" on the grounds that they are untraditional, for untraditionality was also characteristic of much of the conceptuality of the ancient creeds at the time they were formulated. Neither could traditionalists protest against the "two further moments," sin and salvation, nor against the affirmation that Jesus Christ, "first and alone of humankind," had perfect consciousness of God. More objections to these clauses would have come from Calhoun's liberal students, for they were in the majority, than from the scattered minority of conservatives.[39] The most widespread disagreement would have been

36. See below, chapter 1, page 4.

37. Schleiermacher, for example, considered the doctrine of the Trinity dispensable and relegated it in *Christian Faith* to an appendix; but instead of denying it outright, he reinterpreted it in a way compatible with his highly christocentric theological analysis of Christian piety—and also, as he painstakingly and learnedly sought to demonstrate, with traditional Trinitarianism. Even if one thinks his attempt was unsuccessful, one should not confuse his position with that of either ancient Arianism or modern Unitarianism.

38. See below, chapter 1, page 5.

39. The only sizable number of those studying for the ministry who not only came from but remained in a conservative evangelical denomination was Southern Baptists. That was possible in those days because congregational autonomy and independence meant more in the Southern Baptist Convention than it does in 2010. Other non-Roman churches in which theological liberalism was rare at that time were sparsely represented—I as a Lutheran was in this category. The liberal wings of the mainline Protestant denominations supplied the great majority of students.

with the statement that a sinner "doesn't know himself as sinner until he has been saved," but that was a problem for Arminian conservatives just as much as for the few liberals who shared the Arminian dislike of the traces of Calvinistic Augustinianism in Schleiermacher's work—a dislike Calhoun did not share.

Here then was an apparently successful reconciliation of liberalism with traditionalism, of anti-traditional experientialism with traditional-sounding theological conclusions. Calhoun, it seemed, should have approved of this combination, and yet he disagreed. Moreover, he gave no reasons for holding that the liberal failure to treat religious experience as human response to God's self-revelation disqualified it from serving as the basis of theology. This position was doubly puzzling in view of his approving references *qua* historian to the originally Lutheran Pietist reaction against the "arid dogmatic theology" of seventeenth-century Protestant scholasticism; to the Moravian revitalization of this Pietism; and to the fact that "[t]hrough John Wesley in England and Friedrich Schleiermacher in Germany, this Moravian re-emphasis of 'religion of the heart' spread into wider and wider spheres of influence."[40] It sounded to his hearers as if he thought that while Trinitarianism when rightly understood and practiced was preferable to the "unitarianism of the Second Person" (to borrow a phrase from his colleague, H. Richard Niebuhr) that characterized Schleiermacher's version of christocentric, feeling-suffused piety, the latter was nevertheless better than the rationalistic Trinitarian orthodoxy that had come to be identified with Christian traditionalism in the eighteenth century.

Finally, in reference to scholarship, Calhoun reminded his classes that the study of religion, of the Bible, of Christianity, and of Christianity's relation to other religions benefited greatly from the liberal emphasis on religious experience.[41] His treatment of worship in this volume,[42] for example, draws extensively on Rudolf Otto's classic analysis of the experience of the numinous in *Das Heilige* (1917). Given all these commend-

40. Calhoun, *LHCD* (1948), 23; on Wesley, 502–11. As Calhoun makes clear, the role of religious experience in Wesley's thought was not at all the same as in Schleiermacher's. Nevertheless, he thought that there were affinities between the liberalism that developed in nineteenth- and twentieth-century Methodism and the liberalism that was influenced more directly by Schleiermacher.

41. Calhoun, *LHCD* (1948), 23.

42. See below, chapter 1, esp. pages 8–13.

able characteristics, even conservatives (or evangelicals, as they probably would now be called) found themselves wondering whether religious experience of the right kind wasn't a better grounding for theology than the revelational objectivity their teacher favored. And he, with his passion for getting students to make up their own minds, seemed satisfied with this outcome.

Calhoun's resistance to anyone's becoming his disciple seems almost ludicrous in retrospect, though that is not the way it was experienced. After his semester-long seminar on Schleiermacher (which he gave every year or two), students were uncertain whether he thought the latter's masterpiece, *The Christian Faith,* "was the most important work of Reformed theology since the *Institutes* . . . [or] the most destructive aberration from the Reformed theological tradition to which the contemporary Christian mind has been made victim." All they were sure of was that he thought that "[b]oth judgments can find strong reasons."[43] When pleas to resolve such uncertainties were especially urgent, he responded on occasion that he was an historian and not a theologian.[44] Officially this was true and also, to repeat, he did tend to overestimate us. Yet what we chiefly understood him to be saying was that we should make up our own minds. He was acutely aware that we were much too likely to be swayed by his opinions just because they were his and not because of their intrinsic worth. He was also probably not unaware that his uncommunicativeness about his own convictions enhanced his reputation for objectivity; and this reputation in turn made understandable why those who knew or suspected that they radically disagreed with him trusted his reliability as an historian as fully as did the rest of us.

43. Calhoun, *LHCD* (1948), 525.

44. This self-description was exaggerated but there was also some truth in it. Only toward the end of Calhoun's teaching career did he briefly function as a professional theologian when, in the absence of anyone else to do the job, he briefly taught the course in systematic theology. The one available copy of student notes from this course was never reviewed by Calhoun; and the notes are much less satisfactory than those from his lectures on the history of doctrine and of philosophy. Nevertheless, even though they cannot be relied on for details, they make evident that in conformity with his own principles, Calhoun had had little practice in publicly formulating his own personal theological convictions and opinions. See Robert H. Smith's compilation and condensation of his extensive (but often confusing and sometimes clearly erroneous) notes on Calhoun's 1954 *Lectures in Systematic Theology.* These notes were mimeographed with Calhoun's permission but without his reading or corrections. Copies are available for reading in the YDS library.

It would be wrong, however, to conclude that these factors were the only reason for Calhoun's favorable treatment of the liberalism with which he disagreed. He was also motivated, some of his students came to suspect, by the indiscriminateness of the neo-orthodox reaction against prewar liberalism. Dialectical theologians tended to lump together Schleiermacher's *Christian Faith,* for example, with the insanely optimistic and complacent *Kulturprotestantismus,* as the Germans termed it, that dominated much of the Protestant establishment in America as well as elsewhere before World War I. Schleiermacher could not be blamed for this later development, as Calhoun thought Barth was inclined to do—a complaint that Calhoun modified when Barth's view of Schleiermacher became more nuanced.[45] This lack of discrimination (in which Emil Brunner was a worse offender than Barth) created a climate so unfavorable to Schleiermacher's version of liberalism that students were unlikely to develop enduring attachments to it no matter how appealing their teacher made it seem. The message that most of them thought they heard was that uncritical rejection of liberalism was to be resisted just as much as uncritical acceptance of neo-orthodoxy; and this evenhandedness, they were accustomed to thinking, was a mark of liberalism rather than traditionalism.

In addition to Calhoun's evenhanded treatment of such controversial figures as Schleiermacher, it was often difficult for his students even to guess what he personally believed from his teaching. He would persuade students that Athanasius out-argued the Arians and that the Nicene and Chalcedonian creeds were more successful than any alternatives in formulating internally consistent and comprehensively applicable guidelines for interpreting the many very different biblical references to the issues with which they dealt. This persuasiveness, however, would not resolve their uncertainties as to whether he was himself a Trinitarian or a Unitarian, or whether he personally believed that Jesus Christ incarnate is a single and indivisible person who is both fully God and fully human. Their questions on such matters might have been answered if they listened to his chapel talks or came to know such addresses as the one he delivered at the Oberlin Faith and Order Conference in 1957 on

45. See below, chapter 1, pages 3–6. According to my undocumented memories, Calhoun viewed Schleiermacher's hopes for the church's progress within history as influenced though not constituted by Enlightenment utopianism, much as could also be said of Jonathan Edwards' expectations of the millennium.

"Christ and the Church."[46] In the absence of data like this, however, it was possible to think of him as an excellent scholar who was superbly fair in communicating what he knew, whether favorable or unfavorable, about the teachings of a religion that, for all one could tell, was not his own. Even some of the not inconsiderable number of students who were indebted to him for helping them to settle their doubts about the biblical basis of the early creeds continued to think of him as a liberal such as they no longer were. Why else would he be so reticent about his own theology, and so averse to telling even those who asked his guidance what they should believe? Creedlessness and liberalism, after all, often go hand in hand.

## Methodological Agnosticism

Historical studies were for Calhoun a this-worldly enterprise with a perspective limited to empirical aspects of reality. Not that he ignored the actions of the triune God, Father, Son, and Holy Spirit, in creating, saving, and guiding the world and all that is within it. Nevertheless, it was the incontestably this-worldly actuality of belief in the realities affirmed by faith that was historically relevant, not the truth or falsity of what was believed. Concern about the truth or falsehood was the business of such other disciplines as theology. This position of Calhoun's that history (as well as other empirical disciplines in the soft and hard sciences) should be methodologically agnostic was rare during his teaching career but began to be expressed by the time he retired. Calhoun, however, was not one to refer students to his own writings, and few ever read the comments on methodology in his article on the role of historical theology. If they did, their impressions of his liberalism were likely to be reinforced.

> Whereas the historian's end term is always, in principle, some actual happening in time and space, within history, theological beliefs claim an origin partly beyond history . . . . With the validity of this claim to divine origin, historical theology as such cannot properly deal. That is a task for systematic theology and philosophy of religion [or as is now usually said, philosophical theology]. Yet the history of theology cannot be written at all without continually presupposing this claim as one of its facts.[47]

46. Calhoun, "Christ and the Church," 52–78.

47. Calhoun, "Role of Historical Theology," 444–54. Calhoun's opinions as expressed in this brief article of nine pages do not entirely correspond to my undocumented

This neutrality *qua* historian regarding the truth or falsity of claims to the divine origin of theological beliefs made it possible to think of Calhoun's historical methodology as more inclusive and therefore more liberal than that of the liberals. It was more liberal because in the first place, it was not only open methodologically to the liberal belief that doctrines have a divine origin insofar as they are expressively true reflections of authentic religious experience but also to the traditional belief that they are based on God's revelatory acts and thus objectively true. Moreover, in a further degree of inclusiveness, this methodology is compatible with antireligious as well as religious convictions. Calhoun's neutrality about conflicting beliefs within a religion as well as between the religious and irreligious arguably exceeded in methodological agnosticism that of any historical theologian before him.

Calling this neutrality methodologically agnostic was not Calhoun's idea, but it seemed appropriate in the 1960s when Peter Berger popularized the application of this term to all "empirical disciplines [that] . . . view religion *sub specie temporis*, thus leaving open the question of how it might also be viewed *sub specie aeternitatis*."[48] For Calhoun, however, neither this term nor the more pallid phrase "methodological neutrality" signified immunity from religious or nonreligious predispositions. On the contrary, he held that personal involvement in religion deepens and enlarges understanding of the subject matter, and that religious folk are capable both of worse misuse and of greater objectivity regarding doctrines than are the nonreligious:

> Theological doctrines, unlike battles and treaties, have their primary locus in religious devotion, in the deepest loyalties of particular men and communities. One who does not share a particular set of these loyalties may find it difficult to understand them at all. One who does share a particular set of them may find it difficult to deal fairly with any others, especially others that conflict with these. The right balance between objectivity and personal commitment is not easy to define nor to maintain. . . .

memories of his later views, but none of the differences as I recall them were materially important. As could be expected, the texts cited from the article are all compatible with what I think of as his later positions. And in any case, the article is the only explicitly methodological discussion, published or unpublished, that we have from him.

48. Berger, *Sacred Canopy*, 180. Berger called his treatment of religion methodologically "atheistic," but he should have named it "agnostic" in view of what he says about "leaving open" questions concerning God's perspective (i.e., *sub specie aeternitatis*).

> The historian of doctrine becomes himself almost unavoid-
> ably, if not an adherent of some particular dogma, then at least
> a practitioner of tacit affirmation or denial concerning the fun-
> damental character of all dogma. And if his attitude is negative,
> his understanding of the dogmas he treats is likely to stop at the
> sociological level.[49]

Not that sociology and other secular studies are of no use to historical theology.[50] As Calhoun noted in a lecture in this volume, "the entire secular environment of nature and of history, of thoughts, actions
and developments both religious and nonreligious" is germane to the
development of doctrine.[51] In other words, Christian theology in this
traditional understanding is *not* isolated from all that is non-Christian.
Its independence lies in its criteria and not in its content. In Calhoun's
words, "Christian thought . . . [is] a viable, growing spiritual movement
that has received much from its social contexts and has also criticized,
resisted, and helped change the latter by virtue of an enduring genius of
its own."[52] Nevertheless, he thought that ignoring creeds and confessions
would be no less disastrous for understanding the history of Christianity
than erasing the Declaration of Independence and such other foundational documents as the Constitution would be for understanding that of
the United States.

Moreover, returning to Calhoun's point that "theological doctrines
. . . have their primary locus in religious devotion," scholarly neglect of
what was important to believers in favor of external factors of which,
however influential they may have been, the believers may not have even
been aware is a failure to which those who are not personally engaged in
what they are studying are especially prone. Personal engagement may

---

49. Calhoun, "Role of Historical Theology," 446–47.

50. I am at this point identifying Calhoun's reference to "the sociological level" with
the sociology of knowledge. It was only through the influence of Karl Mannheim's
*Ideology and Utopia* (1936) that the latter had come into existence as a distinct sociological subdiscipline by 1941 (when the above article was written), but it soon became widely
influential. Calhoun was never as dismissive of the sociology of knowledge as he was of
such other empirically causal approaches to religion as Marxist dialectics, Durkheimian
anthropology and sociology, and Freudian psychoanalysis. Calhoun, *LHCD* (1948),
23–24.

51. See below chapter 1, page 18.

52. Calhoun, "Role of Historical Theology," 447. See also the remarks of Hans Frei
cited above at length.

or may not involve agreement, but it is an indispensable precondition for empathy. This understanding was perhaps more of a commonplace in Calhoun's day than it is now. Anthropologists in particular stressed that without fieldwork in an alien culture, no one is qualified to describe that culture. Calhoun reported that Margaret Mead, whose works were reputedly more widely read than those of any other anthropologist of her generation, once explained in his hearing that she was "in no good position to talk about the nature and meaning of religious commitment" because she had "never said a prayer in her life and never expected to."[53] Students who thought of themselves as religionless as Margaret Mead (as did much of the Yale faculty and student body) occasionally enrolled in the history of doctrine course.[54] They had studied the history of philosophy with Calhoun and, deeply impressed (as were most people), they had become curious about the *what* and *why* of his religious convictions. His lectures on doctrine did tell them something about what they presumed these convictions were, but he remained as silent as ever regarding his reasons for believing whatever it was that he did believe.

Partly compensating for this reticence were the after-class discussions in which the evenhandedness of Calhoun's methodological agnosticism became especially vivid. Both the liberal-minded followers of Schleiermacher, who agreed with Hume that the objective reality of Jesus' resurrection was historically impossible, and their diametrical opposites, the occasional rationalistic believers for whom it was an article of faith that history could prove the possibility of that event,[55] found themselves agreeing against their wills that the possibility of the objective event could be neither historically disproved (as the theological liberals had supposed) nor historically proved (as the theological rationalists had maintained). What both began unhappily to suspect was that Calhoun had demonstrated that insofar as anything is historically demonstrable, first, it was *belief* in the transcendent origin of the resurrection appear-

53. See below, chapter 1, page 14.

54. I came to know or hear of only a few who professed as total a lack of religious background as Margaret Mead, and my generalizations about them may not be representative.

55. Neither Richard Swinburne of Oxford (1934–) nor Wolfhart Pannenberg of Munich (1928–) can be called naïve; but both, especially Swinburne, come close to holding the kind of position I have in mind although they differ from each other in their reasons. For Pannenberg, see "History and the Reality of the Resurrection," 64. For Swinburne, see *Resurrection of God Incarnate*.

ances, whatever they were, that was the historically identifiable cause of a "transformation" in the lives of Jesus' hopeless and frightened followers "so amazing as to be almost inconceivable,"[56] and second, that the truth or falsity of what those followers believed regarding realities outside space and time could not be decided by historians. This approach assured most students of their teacher's lack of bias but it did not satisfy the few who regarded themselves as irreligious.

For them, Calhoun's agnosticism *qua* historian was excessive—evidence for rather than against his partisanship. They were willing to grant that science by its very nature cannot rigorously demonstrate the impossibility of miracles, but in the absence of any scientifically testable evidence of the existence of nature-transcending realities, so the argument went, their possibility must be regarded as minuscule. A purely theoretical agnosticism about their impossibility was perhaps legitimate, but viewing this position as of the slightest practical importance was deserving of ridicule from all unprejudiced and decently educated people. These sentiments were often heard, as I recall, while Bertrand Russell was a visiting professor during the 1940s. As he put it when asked whether he was certain of God's nonexistence: "No . . . I think it is on exactly the same level as the Olympic gods, or the Norwegian gods. . . . I think they [too] are a bare possibility."[57] It presumably didn't take long for those who had studied philosophy with Calhoun to abandon their suspicions. They would soon come to realize that as an historian of philosophy he had been no less evenhanded than as an historian of Christian doctrine for reasons independent of his theological neutrality or agnosticism, though not for altogether the same reasons. More needs to be said about the mostly unarticulated principles that grounded his practice of methodological agnosticism before returning to how this agnosticism affected his interactions with the irreligious.

For Calhoun, as we have already begun to see, the first or foundational level of historical inquiry consists of seeking to understand the past in its own terms rather than ours, from within rather than from without. As there is even now no specific name for this not uncommon practice of interpreting and describing the past from within, let us borrow a neologism used only by anthropologists in Calhoun's day and call it

---

56. See below, chapter 2, page 28.

57. Russell, *Bertrand Russell Speaks His Mind*, 24–25.

an emic approach. Such aspects of this approach from within as empathy and participation have already been mentioned in citations from his article on the role of historical theology, and the following quotation from the same source amplifies these features:

> [T]he historian's ideal ... is accurate, illuminating, unbiased description or reconstruction of modes of life and thought as they have actually existed, perhaps still exist. Such work calls [one] ... to put aside one's own preferences; to examine with hospitality and insight the available records of life and thought different from one's own and from one another; and to use imagination judiciously under the control of a strong sense of responsibility for giving a just picture as well as a vivid one.... [T]he habit of seeing what lies before one's eyes, not too much discolored by wishes, preconceptions, or fears that lie behind them, is indispensable to even the most elementary historical work.[58]

Interpretation from within was given a technically more precise description some decades later by Louis Mink (1921–1982), a philosopher trained at Yale who taught at Wesleyan University and remained in touch with Calhoun until his death:

> [I]n the age of anthropology ... it has become a rule of historical inquiry that the significance of past actions [including speech] must in the first instance be understood in terms of their agents' own beliefs ... not in terms of our possibly very different ones; we must at least understand their own action-descriptions before we venture our own redescriptions.[59]

58. Calhoun, "Role of Historical Theology," 446–47.

59. Mink, *Historical Understanding*, 194. This excerpt is taken from the reprint of an article, "Narrative Form as a Cognitive Instrument," 129–49. Seven years before Mink published this article, he wrote that the only places "where an extended discussion of narrative as a *cognitive* instrument has been going on have been among theologians." Mink, "Art without Artists," 81–82. Hans Frei was the theologian Mink chiefly had in mind in making this comment, as I can testify on the basis of having participated in their exchanges on this and other topics during the last fifteen years or so of his life. All three of us belonged to a discussion group of which he and Frei were leading members, which met in two-day sessions twice each year. Calhoun was not infrequently mentioned in our discussions, and although I don't recall his ever being numbered among those who held that narrative is a cognitive instrument, he at times treated it as if it were—as we shall see—and he may have been one of the theologians beside Frei whom Mink had in mind in the above remark. Mink had also heard in these discussions about the role of narrative in Niebuhr's *Meaning of Revelation* and in the work of Karl Barth as interpreted by Frei. Calhoun's indirect contributions to Frei's and Mink's understandings of narra-

Whether Mink ever discussed this formulation with Calhoun is unknown, but it both reflects and helps clarify the principles underlying the latter's practice. One instance of this improvement is the replacement of the vague exhortation to understand past actions "from within" by the recommendation to understand them first of all "in terms of their agents' own beliefs ... [i.e.,] action-descriptions."

It is even more helpful, however, that Mink calls attention to "our own rediscriptions" of the original agents' descriptions. Rediscription by definition follows description, but that does not make it any less an integral part of historical inquiry nor diminish its importance in determining how history is done. In a consistently emic approach, the evaluative and explanatory criteria and beliefs employed in present-day redescriptions are absent but not incomprehensible on the descriptive level; or to make the same point differently, care is taken that the modern standards that are redescriptively utilized are compatible rather than incompatible (or, even worse, incommensurable) with the descriptive context of beliefs in terms of which past actions and communications must in the first instance be understood. In contrast to this, non-emic or inconsistently emic approaches are free to ignore first-level descriptive understandings whenever such a practice is convenient. Historians now have the resources to be much better informed (as well as misinformed) about numberless factors ranging from concretely scientific to abstractly philosophical ones that unbeknownst to the ancients helped shape their being and thinking. These resources encourage the outlook that we in our day know the ancients better than they knew themselves, and that redescribing them ought in many cases to replace rather than build upon the initial describing.

When this urge to project our world onto past worlds becomes predominant, the results can be disastrous. Calhoun observed, for example, that it led in biblical scholarship before World War I to "the tendency prevalent at the turn of the century to find in the gospels the story of a modern-minded religious leader." It was not until Albert Schweitzer's *Quest of the Historical Jesus* (1910) that this long-dominant trend to redescribe Jesus as a contemporary was decisively discredited, at least during Calhoun's career: "[N]obody now tries to present Jesus as a modern

---

tive as cognitive were, however, *sui generis*, a product of his own distinctive practice of interpreting history.

man."[60] Schweitzer's historical approach was only partially emic, however, and for that reason only partially successful from Calhoun's perspective. In Schweitzer's redescription of the death and resurrection of Jesus in particular, he did not even try to make emical sense of the descriptions of the gospel writers but flatly contradicted them. If in redescribing, he had supplemented, corrected, and where puzzled, been agnostic without contradicting their descriptions, his second level of historical inquiry would have remained emic. Instead of doing that, however, Schweitzer based himself on liberal Protestant criteria of credibility and concluded—though with a truly moving rhetorical flourish—that Jesus died as a failed messiah who now rises spiritually in his followers as a supreme example of moral power. Calhoun's comment in this volume is that "[t]he result is a brilliant *tour de force* made unconvincing by logical, exegetical, psychological and chronological shortcomings. But [the *Quest's*] main concern is accomplished."[61] His critical comments, it should be noted, are directed entirely at Schweitzer's weaknesses as an historian, and not at all to philosophical or theological problems with his work. Calhoun's emic methodology, one might say, enabled him to be selectively agnostic in such a way that understandably admiring devotees of Schweitzer, of whom there were not a few in those days, were not in the least offended.

An emic version of the second redescriptive level of historical inquiry presupposes an emic understanding of the first descriptive level; and it was precisely this emphasis on understanding Jesus in terms of the gospel writers' beliefs rather than modern ones that demolished the previously prevalent redescriptions. On the second level, however, where Schweitzer ventures his own redescriptions of Jesus' significance, he failed to distinguish between the emic and non-emic, the inside and outside, between on the one hand, the internal coherence and comprehensive sweep of the narrative that can be inferred from the synoptic accounts by the use of criteria that both we and the original authors and audience could understand, and on the other hand, liberal Protestant criteria of credibility. Thus when assessing what the gospel writers meant, Schweitzer did not stick to the historian's task as charitably and accurately as possible; and so it is not surprising that he confusingly mingled his theological preferences with his historical evaluation; and only then rendered his

60. See below, chapter 2, page 21.
61. See below, ibid.

necessarily theological rather than historical interpretive judgment on the meaning of all this for us today.

This emic approach, to repeat, is the first precondition of the methodological neutrality (or, as I have termed it, agnosticism) that seemed excessively skeptical about science to the irreligious among Calhoun's students when applied to such a doctrine as that of the resurrection. It was in reference to the second, evaluative phase of historical work that he was exceptional, for here also he proceeded from within, judging the success or failure of the thinkers with whom he dealt by the standards internal to the perspectives and traditions within which they worked. Individual beliefs were in consequence evaluated primarily in terms of how well they fitted into the immense network of beliefs that was possible by their own internal standards. Such an approach is not uncommon among historians, but internalizing the evaluative phase of historical work as Calhoun did is less frequent: that is, evaluating different positions by standards that are internal yet also common to each. For example, one of the two foundations that are "equally necessary" for both philosophies and theologies is "the principle of relevance or coherence which is basic to all rational living." The other foundation or criterion for testing adequacy that Calhoun mentioned from time to time was comprehensiveness in covering all the available pertinent data.

In addition, there may be external standards of universal applicability by which the adequacy of all positions can be evaluated. Because there is no agreement to speak of as to what these standards are, Calhoun as a historian simply bracketed these disagreements rather than making his own choices or developing his own position. His business as he saw it was not to become a systematic theologian or philosopher but simply to report on the history of his subject. Last, Calhoun's work leads to the conclusion not that truth is relative to fundamentally different positions but rather that the validity of beliefs in terms of each candidate for adequate coherence and comprehensiveness can be tested and reported by historians. Whether the beliefs are true is not for the historian to debate unless he changes his role.

Although there was much more opportunity to deal with religion versus irreligion in after-class discussions in the Divinity School than there had been in Yale College, the irreligious found that here also they were confronted by Calhoun's methodologically agnostic practice of withholding his own views. Now, however, the agnosticism was of a kind more closely associated with philosophical than theological history. Like Socrates in the Platonic dialogues, he shifted attention from his opinions to the views of others. Fortunately for his interlocutors, however, he was more consistently charitable in his interpretations of what others thought than Plato's Socrates had been. He regularly refused to evaluate their outlooks by means of alien standards but rather employed internal criteria of clarity, coherence, and comprehensiveness of thought and practice.

Calhoun's agnosticism, it will be observed, did not extend to the use of common standards internal to such a tradition as Platonism or Aristotelianism by means of which the relative worth of the various versions of the tradition could be compared; his writings abound with internal critiques of this kind. What he was agnostic about *qua* historian of philosophy was the existence of common external standards commensurable with both traditions by which they could be differentially evaluated—though he was persuaded to make an exception in the rare instance of present-day unanimity on the existence of an external commensurable standard applicable to the "natural philosophies" of both these traditions.[62] One reason for the rareness of commensurability is that each person, as Calhoun put it, "sees the world in a perspective no one else can have." Yet the individual both can and does learn from the perspectives of others, for "his [*sic*] power of generalization enables him to conceive and acknowledge the validity of other points of view" even when unsure of their truth.[63]

The crucial word in this last sentence is *validity*. When applied to the example earlier cited, one can say that the belief that the sun orbits around the earth was valid (or, as is now usually said, justified) though never true in pre-Copernican times, but is now neither true nor valid. Conversely, beliefs that are invalid because based on false information may coincidentally be true. Moreover, everyone normally develops by habit and acculturation an immense and distinctive web of beliefs whose validity is indubitable in the sense that they cannot all be doubted at once

62. The example that Christian had in mind in his comments on Calhoun was that of comparing the "natural philosophies" of Plato and Aristotle (to Plato's advantage) by standards consistent with modern science, for example Whitehead's. Cf. Christian, "In Memory," 11.

63. These two sentences are plucked out of context from an instructive, though by Calhoun's later standards, outdated sketch of nonreligious and religious perspectives. Calhoun, *What is Man?*, 57–58.

without destroying the possibility of coherent thought and action.[64] It follows from this and other considerations that Enlightenment evidentialism is epistemologically faulty. If human beings are not entitled to believe much of that for which they have no evidence, as those claiming to be enlightened supposed, life as we know it would be impossible. To put it in religious terms, faith is warranted provided that no good arguments against it are available.[65] On the other hand, it will be recalled, a warranted or validated belief is not necessarily true: many beliefs that were scientifically well validated in a three-dimensional Newtonian universe, for example, are not valid in an Einsteinian four-dimensional one. Validity, in other words, is clearly relative to context whereas truth has commonly been spoken of as unchanging. The belief expressed in the formula $2 + 2 = 4$ remains true, for example, even if everyone were to revert to Roman rather than Arabic numerals—or as far that goes, to counting on their fingers—with the result that the expression "$2 + 2 = 4$" would become incomprehensible. Reflecting this unchangingness is the practice of referring to the negligible differences between Newtonian and Einsteinian measurements in space/time as ordinarily experienced not as changes in the *true* distance but rather as asymptotic approximations to the *truth*—whatever that eventually is discovered (or not discovered) to be.[66]

Calhoun did not systematically articulate the outlook just summarized, but it was an integral part of his teaching, especially in the history of philosophy. What was most impressive to the irreligious in his doctrine course, however, were the extracurricular exchanges with him on the validity of the views they held and that he considered false. He put into actual practice the distinction between validity and truth by his manifest respect for what they thought; and the most vivid evidence of this respect was his labors on behalf of better validating their beliefs even while not in the least reneging on his own belief in their falsity. It was this same distinction, it should be added, that enabled him to take for granted

64. My memory is that Calhoun was acquainted with this last point from the work of C.S. Peirce (1839–1914) who, if I am not mistaken, was the first to articulate it fully.

65. A notable discussion of this point is in Wolterstorff, "Can Belief in God Be Rational?," 135–86.

66. For a highly condensed but useful account of recent discussions of the invariant or nonrelative character of the truth of especially moral beliefs in contrast to their justification, see Stout, *Democracy and Tradition*, 231–40.

the compatibility of intellectual virtue with what Roman Catholics call invincible ignorance.

While it was Mr. Calhoun's charitable yet not uncritical understanding of their beliefs that led the invincibly irreligious to greater knowledge and appreciation of at least some religion than they would otherwise have had, it would be a mistake to exaggerate the importance of these effects. No one as untouched by religion as Margaret Mead was ever reported to have become religious through taking Calhoun's course on Christian doctrine. Calhoun's agnostic methods in philosophical and doctrinal history may have opened minds to matters before undreamt of, but this agnosticism was not by itself a heart-transforming force.

## Scripture, Narrative, Theological Loci, and Doctrinal Development

Neutrality regarding the truth or falsity of theological claims has become common in histories of doctrine in the last half century, but the same is not true of other aspects of Mr. Calhoun's methodology. The most notable example of this neutrality is in the late Jaroslav Pelikan's five-volume *The Christian Tradition* (1971–1989), widely and rightly acclaimed the greatest history of doctrine since Adolf von Harnack's even larger *History of Dogma*, first published in German in its entirety more than a century earlier in 1885. Calhoun's comments on Pelikan's *magnum opus* are confined to a review of the first volume,[67] and for the most part join in the general praise of its strengths. He did, however, have two major "difficulties [that] stem directly from the author's chosen method," and the first of these bears directly on the relation of biblical studies to historical theology.

> To begin the account [of the history of the doctrine] at the start of the second century [as Pelikan did] suggests inevitably that the New Testament itself is not an embodiment of diverse and developing tradition. It is legitimate, of course, to urge that biblical study is a field for specialists, and that a historian of doctrine cannot be an expert in their field. . . . But to speak of the Bible as simply "the Word of God" and to treat it as a fixed point of reference for later thought, rather than to read the New Testament as our best source of insight into the birth, the stressful growth, and the many-sided thought of the newborn Christian community is to bypass generally accessible findings of biblical scholarship. From the beginning, not merely from 100 A.D., the Christian

67. Calhoun, "Robert Calhoun Reviews," 1–4.

community displayed in its beliefs, teachings, and confessions the same sort of consensus-in-disagreement, and the same sort of un-even development, that the author rightly traces in later stages. He does, of course, recognize that the New Testament was accorded status as scripture gradually (pp. 114–15), and that it is not all of one piece. But the main concern is the church's doctrine about the New Testament as a touchstone for proof of later tenets, rather than the doctrines embodied in it; and his numerous citations and quotations of it are almost all proof-texts used by patristic writers. One unfortunate result is to convey an impoverished and in some respects a distorted picture of the rich legacy left to those writers by the founding fathers.[68]

In this quotation, "to speak of the Bible as *simply* [italics added] 'the Word of God'" (as if it were not, first of all, a witness to that Word) was the basic error to result from beginning the history of doctrine with the second rather than the first century. This tardiness left undiscussed the obvious distinction between the authors and readers of the early Christian writings that later became the New Testament. "The proper subject matter for theology is the Word of God, not the Bible taken literally and infallibly, but rather the Word of God which comes in and with and through the words of human beings that [now] constitute the biblical text. The true Word of God is Jesus Christ."[69] The absence of that understanding in turn "inevitably suggests," as the above quotation puts it, "that the New Testament is not itself an embodiment of diverse and developing tradition." To be sure, Calhoun acknowledged that the deficiencies (more numerous than we have cited) resulting from this omission of the opening episode were largely repaired in Pelikan's descriptions of later doctrinal developments, yet he also held that these belated corrections did not entirely eliminate the damage done by a methodologically mistaken starting place.

As can be seen from this critique, it was Mr. Calhoun's own principles that mandated his excurses into the biblical domain in the second chapter of the present volume in the sections dealing with "Jesus and His Teaching" and "The Faith and Preaching of the Primitive Church." As the earlier remarks on his treatment of the resurrection made evident, he

68. Ibid., 2.

69. The quoted words are from Calhoun's characterization of the Barthian view of this distinction (see below, chapter 1, page 5), a view with which he agreed despite his disagreement with what he, like almost everyone else at the time, took to be Barth's re-striction of God's revelatory Word to the scriptural witness.

was methodologically agnostic in what was for him a strictly historical fashion: his fairness struck almost everyone as exemplary, even including dogmatically committed secularists, liberals, and conservatives. While the lectures in this chapter, as Calhoun would be the first to say, were not unusual from the perspective of much of the biblical scholarship of the 1950s, those in the third chapter on Johannine theology were independent of the work of others. He reworked them after his retirement into the form they have in this volume. While lacking the extemporaneous *élan* of his oral delivery, this chapter is the best example of Calhoun's application to Scripture of his theologically neutral history-of-ideas approach. Most remarkably, thirty to forty years after receiving its final touches, the chapter reads for the most part as an arguably important and still fresh contribution to contemporary Johannine scholarship.[70] More relevant to our present inquiry, its autonomy as a work of conceptual analysis helped free it both from traditionalistic opposition to historical criticism on the one hand, and from the cultural captivity to which theologically liberal scriptural scholarship was prone on the other.

Two of the three references to liberalism in this volume concern the shattering of the Bible's unity. Calhoun appealed with characteristic modesty to the historical work of a New Testament scholar rather than to his own insights in correcting the greater of these two errors. This error was in part characterized by "the tendency prevalent at the turn of the century to find in the gospels the story of a modern-minded religious leader." As was mentioned earlier in the context of Calhoun's preference for an emic approach to historical redescription, the first major scholarly setback to this modernization of Jesus and related liberal tendencies was Albert Schweitzer's *Quest of the Historical Jesus*. Calhoun was by no means uncritical of Schweitzer's historical work and was theologically alien to his liberalism, but like virtually everyone, he regarded the *Quest* as the beginning of a new era in New Testament scholarship. This is the way he put it: "When we speak of the teaching of Jesus, we must think of one brought up in a Jewish community, steeped in its traditions, its

---

70. While I have given my own spin to the opinions expressed in this sentence, I am very much indebted for them to New Testament scholars who have done much work on Johannine materials and were kind enough to read the Calhoun chapter. The two from whom I requested letters deserve special thanks for their carefully composed and helpful replies: they are Wayne Meeks, who taught in Yale's Department of Religious Studies until his retirement; and the current dean of Yale Divinity School, Harold Attridge.

thought and its ways, and conceiving his own role to be proclaiming and reinterpreting what was fundamental in the Jewish religion."[71]

In this passage the Old Testament is presupposed as a necessary source of the Bible's unity. From it comes "what was fundamental in the Jewish religion" and also in "the religion of Jesus." It was also indispensable in the formation of "the religion about Jesus" that developed after his death.[72] This approach was in marked contrast to the nineteenth-century liberalism in which Calhoun had been reared. For the latter, both the teachings of Jesus and the teachings about him that developed after his death were fundamentally independent of Jewish faith and Scriptures. The absence of this Old Testament glue, so one might say, not only produced the primary rupture in the Bible's unity—that between the two Testaments—but it also so widened the difference between the religion "of" and "about" Jesus as to turn it into a rift within the New Testament itself. It was the minimizing of the Judaism common to both Jesus and the first generations of his disciples that made possible the liberal disparagement of the early church's theology and dogma as contrary to what Jesus taught:

> To place Jesus in his [Jewish] historical setting, however, changes but does not eliminate the once fashionable distinction between "the religion of Jesus" and "the religion about Jesus." This distinction was commonly emphasized by scholars and liberal theologians who were concerned to affirm and exalt the validity of the former and disparage in some measure the claims of the latter. It is not necessary to accept that disparagement of the Church's theology and dogma, but it is necessary in the interest of clear understanding of specifically Christian doctrine, to keep the initial difference clear. The kind of thought about God and man that was possible for Jesus' followers after his death and resurrection was different from what his could have been before his death. He thought of himself as pointing towards the new age. His followers thought of themselves as already living in it by reason of his saving power.[73]

Needless to say, theologically liberal biblical interpretation continued after the trauma of World War I; however, it changed its character.

71. See below, chapter 2, page 22.
72. See below, ibid.
73. See below, chapter 2, page 21–22.

The old optimism was absent from the work of the reputedly greatest New Testament scholar of the period, Rudolf Bultmann (1884–1976). For a time he was considered a dialectical theologian in close alliance with Karl Barth. Calhoun perceived, however, that although Bultmann gave an existentialist twist to dialectical theology, he stood nonetheless in the tradition of Albrecht Ritschl (1822–1889) and ultimately of Schleiermacher rather than of Barth.[74] Bultmann's work had New Testament as well as Heideggerian roots and was regarded by others as biblically normed.[75] His reputation as a post-liberal dialectical thinker arose from his repudiation of the complacent culture-bound religiosity characteristic of pre-World War I liberalism. Bultmann possessed what was thought of as a full measure of biblical realism about human sinfulness, God as judge as well as redeemer, and the desperate need of all human beings for salvation. Calhoun could have noted, however, that the German scholar's postwar existentialism fragmented the Bible by de-Judaizing it much as had been done by prewar liberalism. On the other hand, Calhoun also saw that Bultmann's stand against the Nazis[76] made it important to guard against saying anything that could be misinterpreted as suggesting this friend of his was anti-Semitic. What Calhoun did make clear by implication, however, was that he regarded as historically ludicrous the attempts of professedly critical biblical scholars to take the Jew out of Jesus in particular and of the New Testament in general.

It should not be supposed that Calhoun never publicly expressed his theological convictions about the Bible's unity. These expressions happened in church gatherings, not in his role as academic historian. The most important of these occasions was his plenary presentation in 1957

74. See below, chapter 1, page 5.

75. Paul Schubert, at one time Buckingham Professor of New Testament, often retold in his later years the story of Bultmann's first encounter with Calhoun. While alone in the Schuberts' house during a brief visit to New Haven in the 1950s, Bultmann opened the door to admit an "egg man," as he put it, clad in overalls who inquired whether the German visitor was indeed Professor Bultmann. He then hesitatingly asked a question about a point of Bultmann's Greek exegesis, which led to a brief and erudite exchange. Bultmann's astonishment at the level of education of the American working class was later replaced by surprise at the neighborliness of the American professoriate, when he learned from his host that the egg man was a learned polymath and holder of a Sterling chair who sold and delivered eggs laid by his own chickens to faculty colleagues.

76. See, for example, Bultmann's introductory remarks at the beginning of a new semester on May 2, 1933, shortly after the Nazis had consolidated their power. Bultmann, "Task of Theology in the Present Situation," 158–65.

at what was in some respects the most notable purely North American ecumenical conference ever held. He started with a substantively traditional insistence on the normativity of the Bible taken as a whole; and then, in the last two sentences, strongly emphasized the need for what can be conveniently called methodological liberalism.

> Perhaps the simplest way to identify the God in whom we believe is the most familiar. He is the living God known in the history of Israel, especially in the discerning eyes of the prophets and seers, by his mighty acts of judgment and mercy; decisively revealed in Jesus Christ; and thus recognizable by faith as unceasingly and all-powerfully active in the life of the Church and of the entire world. To begin thus is to affirm once for all that the Bible—the whole Bible and not some fraction of it—is indispensable as a guide to Christian faith. Probing critical study that tries incessantly to press closer to what the biblical writers really say and mean, and candid, responsible use of the results of such study are presupposed. Otherwise we should find ourselves guided not by acquaintance with the Bible as it is, but by notions of our own as to what it ought to be.[77]

Fresh though the wording of this passage was in some respects, there was nothing in its doctrinal content that would have surprised his audience. The view of the Bible it represented had been growing strongly in scholarly circles since World War I, and had become dominant in mainline ecumenism by the 1940s. In accordance with historic doctrine, Calhoun affirmed the hermeneutical authority of "the whole Bible" against the liberals, classically exemplified by Schleiermacher and Harnack, for whom only "some fraction of it," namely parts of the New Testament, was "a guide to Christian faith."

On the other hand, however, he also agreed with the liberal Enlightenment emphasis on "[p]robing critical study" of "what the biblical writers really say and mean." He held that this critical study is necessary, for "[o]therwise we should find ourselves guided not by acquaintance with the Bible as it is, but by notions of our own as to what it ought to be." The "notions of our own" that would come immediately to mind in an ecumenical gathering of that period were the divisive interpretations of Scripture, supported by proof-texting, that fill the annals of historically separated churches. It was a commonplace in the

77. Calhoun, "Christ and the Church," 52–78.

early days of ecumenism (as it still is among the knowledgeable) that without the historical-critical uncovering of the original meanings of misused proof texts, the ecumenism of the twentieth century would have been impossible. Historical criticism was an essential condition for the beginnings of the movement among Protestants, and it was its later use by Catholics that made possible the approval of ecumenism by the Roman Catholic Church at Vatican II a few years after Calhoun's address. As Calhoun and other ecumenists saw the situation, openness to the unifying guidance of Scripture required the correctives supplied by modern critical scholarship just as much as it needed the historic theological emphasis on the oneness of Scripture and the interpretation of every part in relation to other parts and to the whole.

This observation brings us to Frei's climactic claim in his *in memoriam* remarks that "[w]hat is so clear in retrospect is the distinctive harmony of liberalism and Christian traditionalism, without detriment to either, in Professor Calhoun's thinking." One way of understanding this claim is that Calhoun's methodologically agnostic evenhandedness seemed hyperliberal, and that it was the combination of this characteristic with other liberal features of modern historical theology that fortuitously led him to the unexpected retrieval of tradition. It was this unintended and thus empirically accidental conjunction of liberalism and traditionalism that insured their harmony in his work. Each remained independent, for it was uninfluenced by the other, and thus they were conjoined "without detriment to either." Other considerations also support Frei's claim, as we shall see, but this one seems to me the most important.

As for what made modern historical theology seem liberal, Calhoun identified this feature when he commented on Ferdinand Christian Baur (1792–1860), whom he regarded as its first practitioner:

> [In Baur,] we begin to see an effort not simply to describe changes which have come about [such as Paolo Sarpi gave of the Council of Trent], but to account for them—to give a genetic and not simply descriptive account of such changes. That seems to me the proper task of historical theology—to show both the continuity and discontinuity in the Church's teaching, to give a basis for understanding why some views have been lastingly approved within the Church and why some views have been promptly or at length disapproved.[78]

78. See below, chapter 1, page 17.

In our day, it is helpful to substitute *narrative* for *genetic* in identifying the accounts of change that were for Calhoun "the proper task of [modern] historical theology." To be sure, many genetic analyses do not take a narrative form, but there was no alternative to narrative in such histories as his, in which the connections between origins and later developments are constituted by sequences of interrelated events occurring in space and time. Critical use of sources is another general feature of modern history but not exclusively so; as Calhoun admiringly pointed out, it can also characterize such descriptive history as that of Father Sarpi (1552–1623) on the Council of Trent. Furthermore, to state the obvious, narrative does not exclude description: Calhoun sometimes brilliantly exemplified this combination by his use of something like a Melanchthonian categorical scheme in describing the diverse subject matters treated by theologians, alien though that pattern was to many of them with their often confusing classificatory habits. Nevertheless, to use technical terms, the configurational comprehension appropriate to narrative was, as it should be, his strong suit in historical work; and the categorical comprehension appropriate to description, though by no means unimportant, was secondary.[79]

Methodological agnosticism, however, was only for historians to practice when dealing with biblical material. Biblical scholars were disqualified because it was contrary to their disciplinary duties to stop, as he could *qua* historian, with the historically identifiable character and effects of the beliefs prompted by the resurrection appearances. Biblical scholars were duty bound also to address negatively or positively questions regarding the validity of historically undecidable truth claims about, for example, God's role in the resurrection and Jesus' present status as the ascended yet ever present Lord. This position does not mean that biblical scholars had to develop their own theological or philosophical views regarding these metahistorical issues; but they were obligated by their scholarly discipline to be candid about the allegiances or preferences that influenced their interpretation of scriptural data. For Calhoun, their scholarly field exceeded that of historical theologians in both importance

79. Mink, *Historical Understanding*. See "Comprehension" in the index for the page references to Mink's extensive discussions of the two modes of comprehension described above. Mink had had Calhoun as one of his teachers while completing his PhD in philosophy at Yale, and he was in frequent conversation with Frei until his death at Wesleyan University in 1982. It was to Frei that Mink was chiefly referring when he complained in a 1968 talk that it was only among theologians and not philosophers that "deepening discussion of narrative as a *cognitive* instrument has been going on." Ibid., 17.

and difficulty. Its practitioners had to bear the double burden, as was suggested earlier, of engaging in a hybrid historical-theological discipline that required binocular expertise in studying Christianity's foundational text. Only when acting as an historian who took no stand on theological or philosophical questions did he consider himself competent to enter the biblical domain.

Emphasizing the importance of the Enlightenment and of the modern critical thinking that developed from it was by no means a liberal monopoly in that day and age either for Calhoun or for others. He referred to notable counter-examples to theological liberalism in a history of doctrine lecture in 1947 that was cited earlier:

> Toward the end of the 18th century, a new theological method and temper came into being. To it Kant affixed the label *critical,* and that term continues to serve better than any other to identify the essential difference between newer and older theologies, whether affirming or dissenting from traditional norms. . . . [T]hinkers as diverse as Schleiermacher and Ritschl, on the one hand, Kierkegaard and Barth, on the other, display the characteristic effects [whether in assent or dissent] of Kant's fresh analysis of the grounds and limits of human knowledge. . . . [L]iberalism, romantic or moralistic, and dialectical "neo-orthodoxy" are modes of thought essentially different from both patristic, scholastic, or confessional theologies, and from the pre-Kantian rationalisms of all kinds.[80]

The fact that Calhoun was able to assume that his audience knew his counter-examples well enough to clinch his argument says much about the postwar theological situation. Students may have heard no more than the names of Søren Kierkegaard and Karl Barth when they entered divinity school, but by the time they took the course in the history of doctrine they would have been flooded with reports about these luminaries. They would not only have heard that Kierkegaard was the nineteenth-century precursor to neo-orthodoxy, but that he was even more famous in the world at large as the inaugurator of the philosophical existentialism that was becoming *à la mode* in both chic and serious intellectual circles on both sides of the Atlantic to a degree that is now scarcely imaginable. The atheist Sartre and the agnostic Heidegger, beginning to be acclaimed in Europe as the supremely important philosophers of the age, were regarded

80. Calhoun, *LHCD* (1948), 525.

as having been deeply influenced by the Danish virtuoso, and there were times and places in which his non-Christian and anti-Christian admirers greatly outnumbered his Christian followers.[81] As for Karl Barth, his work, unlike Kierkegaard's, was not studied in philosophy seminars, but his name was familiar to the educated whether religious or irreligious, and there were many in Europe, including some Communists, who considered him among the most interesting and important thinkers of the age. Nor were these the only theological celebrities of an eminence that now seems unthinkable. Reinhold Niebuhr was beginning to be heralded by not a few secularists as the most able and influential public intellectual in America, and Paul Tillich's fame as a thinker was greater in this country than was Karl Barth's.

Let us stick, however, with Calhoun's two examples. Kierkegaard and Barth were the most widely known and doctrinally orthodox practitioners of innovative theologizing, and their credentials as masterful deployers and inventors of new modes of critical inquiry into the human condition were widely celebrated even by secularists for whom religion was a dispensable adiaphoron. All this was familiar to advanced divinity students, not to mention those working for higher degrees. They may never have thought of Kierkegaard and Barth as sharing in and perhaps surpassing the methodological liberalism of Schleiermacher and Ritschl, but they knew enough to recognize the aptness of Calhoun's description. Largely because of neo-orthodoxy, they were far more open to the reconcilability of methodological liberalism and substantive traditionalism than a similar audience would have been a few decades earlier.

On the other hand, the students' openness to Calhoun's traditionalism was limited. When he spoke of traditional norms as in the above quotation, those influenced by neo-orthodoxy generally tended in typical Protestant fashion to think only of Scripture. Their interest in retrieving the foundations of the faith did not extend to postbiblical developments except to the extent that these, as happened during the Reformation, were interpreted as maintaining biblical truth. Much of later Protestantism, however, came to understand *sola Scriptura* narrowly. Not only liberals but also many of the neo-orthodox (though not Karl Barth) together with virtually all anti-liberals of Pietistic and revivalistic provenance were wary of even such catholic creeds as those of Nicaea and Chalcedon.

---

81. This was my impression when I studied in Paris between 1949 and 1951.

Calhoun, in contrast, saw these creeds as crucial for coherent construals of Scripture when it is treated as a unified whole. On this point, his historical work favored Barth's view that traditional dogmas, especially the historic Trinitarian and christological formulations, should continue to be regarded as criteriologically though not conceptually normative for mainstream Christianity.[82] As a consequence, so his work suggested, it was the common guidance given by these affirmations of the ancient church to the exceedingly diverse communal readings of the Bible that provided the best historical explanation of the otherwise unintelligible persistence down to the present of a Christian mainstream that has not ceased to be identifiably one despite its fissiparous appearance. As we have seen Frei emphasize, Calhoun's traditionalism was ecumenically expansive to a degree that was beyond the ability of his audience to comprehend.

## The Development of Calhoun's Thought

The closest thing to an explanation that Calhoun left behind of this tension in his teaching among liberalism, traditionalism, and neo-orthodoxy is in an article he never mentioned to students and of which I, for one, did not become aware until long after I had become his junior colleague. In it he tells of what "amounts to a Copernican change in my orientation" that took place between his thirty-third and forty-third years—that is, between 1929 and 1939.[83] His "personal theology" at the beginning of this period was modern "liberalism of a familiar sort," but after "years of continuous hammering by the more 'dialectical' members of a theological discussion group" to which he belonged,[84] he had become "some obsti-

82. The most massive examples of criteriological but not conceptual agreement with historic doctrines are provided by the so-called creedless evangelical and Pentecostal churches, in which preaching and worship are in practice compatible with the Trinitarian and christological standards of the Nicene and Chalcedonian creeds, of which the members of these bodies either know nothing or else reject as conceptually unintelligible or unscriptural.

83. Calhoun, "Liberal Bandaged But Unbowed," 701–4.

84. Ibid., 702–4. The "more dialectical members" whom Calhoun listed in the article were "Richard and Reinhold Niebuhr, William Pauck, John Mackay, and later Paul Tillich and Emil Brunner" (703). It is also of interest that Calhoun gave seminars not only on Schleiermacher and Plato throughout his career but also on Frederick Tennant (1866–1957), whom he regarded as the best of the theologically liberal philosophers of religion. While his own personal preference was for seminars on such mainstream theological figures as Augustine and Calvin, he always deferred to colleagues who wished to teach them; or in the case of those who were very much his junior, urged them to take his

nate sort of liberal . . . bandaged but unbowed." Before considering what
made him a bandaged liberal at forty-three, however, we need to look at
his description of where he had been ten years earlier:

> My thinking ranged between the romantic immanentism of
> Schleiermacher, at one extreme, and the science-minded, sharp-
> edged theism of [Frederick Robert] Tennant, on the other. Kant
> was presupposed in both. . . . Platonism [nevertheless] became a
> growing enthusiasm and "rational theology" a kind of passion.
> . . . I scarcely distinguished [philosophy and theology] except as
> regards their scope. Theology seemed to me essentially a more
> specialized kind of religious philosophy. . . . For years I tried to
> resolve . . . the Bible, the creeds, theological tradition, and the
> Christian church . . . into illustrations of familiar logical formu-
> las, while overlooking or apologizing for their more refractory
> aspects.[85]

Calhoun had been asked to write about how his mind had changed theologically, and his sole remark about philosophy is that he moved "from a
primarily philosophic toward a more definitely theological orientation."[86]
This gap needs to be filled, however, for it seems that it was his philosophical enthusiasm for Plato that first disabused him of liberal prejudices
against premodern thought. He had already abandoned the Kantian-
influenced critical idealism that undergirded liberal experientialism (as
it still often does, unbeknownst to its practitioners) when he wrote "Plato
as Religious Realist" in 1931.[87] It was replaced with what Frei identified
as an epistemological critical realism—a term to which he did not object,
although he never adopted that name for his own use.[88] For a critical
realist, theology, if there is such a thing, must be based on revelation; that
is, on disclosures of the ultimately good and real coming from without
rather than, as for the liberal experientialists, from within. In his essay on

---

place—for the sake of our own development, as we very well knew. My first experience
of this generosity was when he asked me to teach an Augustine seminar although, to the
delight of prospective students, I was unable to do so on that occasion.

85. Calhoun, "Liberal Bandaged But Unbowed," 701–4.

86. Ibid., 703.

87. See n. 4 above.

88. He would have considered it pretentious to place himself in the same group of
notable professional philosophers as A. K. Rodgers, J. B. Pratt, A. O. Lovejoy, George
Santayana and, by a stretch, Roy Wood Sellars (1880–1973) and his son Wilfrid Sellars
(1912–1989).

Plato he never used the word *revealed* in reference to Plato's insights, but he later became aware that his view of the origins of Plato's "clearly stated confidence in the sovereignty and the goodness of a living God"[89] was compatible with the early Christian Logos theology and with what came to be known in later Protestantism as the general revelation that impinges on all human beings, not only convicting them of sin (as in Rom 1:20–21) but also making possible the goodness and wisdom that exists even apart from scripturally witnessed special revelations. In Calhoun's form of realism, furthermore, general revelation even apart from special revelation may on occasion evoke a response of faith—a basic confidence that may not be explicitly religious but holds that life is worth living and the cosmos is meaningful despite its seeming meaninglessness. He himself had had an experience of this sort at some point between 1926 and 1929.[90] But, given his commitment to maintaining disciplinary boundaries, he never mentioned in his history of doctrine either his personal or philosophical reasons for favoring revelation over religious experience as the basis for theology. Similarly—that is, conversely—his fullest philosophical treatment of the notion of revelation, the Dudleian lecture that he delivered at Harvard in 1957, is bereft of explicit references to theological implications even when analyzing "the revealing word of God."[91] That lecture can be read as if it were a modernized and improved version of his description more than a quarter century earlier of what for Plato was the source of knowledge of God; only in the last sentences are there hints that his theme had a bearing on specifically Christian considerations.

Calhoun didn't approve of everything he learned from Plato. In his "Bandaged but Unbowed" article he specifically retracted his youthful efforts to turn theology into a "more specialized form of religious philosophy" by treating the "more refractory aspects" of Christian doctrine

89. Calhoun, "Plato as Religious Realist," 216.

90. Calhoun, "Liberal Bandaged but Unbowed," 701.

91. Calhoun, "Reason and Revelation in Religious Knowledge." A printed copy of this lecture but with no publisher indicated is available in the Yale library system. The following excerpts from 42–43 give the barebones gist of its central thesis: "The revealing word of God, however it may come to a given person, is always incarnate in a particular event or series of events that actually happen, a person that actually lives or has lived. . . . [Faith] grows . . . in response to impacts of actualities beyond the self. . . . [It] is a disposition that arises, if at all, in the active interrelation between a person and the actual entities that confront him. . . . [Contrary to what liberal experientialists think, it] is not an *a priori* category like causality or oughtness, for some lose it and some apparently never have it."

as metaphors for philosophical themes much as Plato had done with the Greek myths.[92] It was the hammering of dialectical theologians that liberated him from this philosophic straitjacket without, however, removing all his liberal (and at the same time traditional) reservations about neo-orthodoxy:

> I have been driven, willy-nilly to recognize that theology cannot get on without special revelations, either. Indeed, I have been convinced that it must start from such revelations, above all from those that center around Jesus Christ, and the faith which they evoke. This amounts to a Copernican change in my orientation. With it has come a new sense of the special significance—long obvious enough to others, but to me unsuspected—of the Bible, the creeds, theological tradition, and the Christian church. ... Now, with the sort of relief that comes when one moves from thin ice onto solid ground, I found myself taking them still more simply as concrete instances of living give-and-take among men, and between God and man, which both demand and resist logical inquiry. That they resist it is no reason to adjourn the effort to get them into rational perspectives. On the other hand, in their presence our logic seems clearly to have neither the first nor the last word. ... *Fides quaerens intellectum* would more nearly describe my thinking today than at any prior time.[93]

Given the traditionalism of this view, why was Calhoun often labeled a liberal both by himself and by others? Hans Frei, it will be recalled, suggested that it was his difference from the neo-orthodox that made him seem liberal. Their problem from his perspective was that "special revelations—the only kind recognized by this sort of theology—have always needed to be checked by some more general frame of reference." This framework is supplied by general revelation, by God speaking through the "cool" and "historical" study of "the written Scriptures ... the tradition and common experience of the church" and, more broadly, through "history, philosophy and common sense." In their at times undiscriminating opposition to modern liberalism combined with their post-Reformation

---

92. Calhoun's adoption of this Platonic approach to theology is easier to understand if we remember that his teaching was exclusively in philosophy before he joined the Divinity School faculty and was assigned by Dean Luther Weigle to change an already existing course on the history of religious education into one on the history of doctrine—a task for which he was totally unprepared.

93. Calhoun, "Liberal Bandaged But Unabowed," 703–4.

Protestant tendency to bypass ancient creedal and theological traditions when appealing to the Bible, many of the neo-orthodox narrowed the role of reason and the scope of theology by in effect denying that God also utilizes this whole range of human activities (including what was traditionally named natural theology and natural law) as revelatory means for safeguarding the faith against the "vagaries to which intensely sincere minds are sometimes . . . liable."[94]

Liberals, in contrast, sought to understand the relation of a similarly broad range of phenomena to religious experience with the result that the scope, though not the functions, of reason and theology in their outlooks overlapped extensively with general revelation (which, to be sure, they did not think of as revelation). Calhoun's article also suggests a strong and a weak overlapping among the members of his discussion group at two additional points: first, "mutual understanding and respect" among those who agreed in principle on the starting point of theology even though they disagreed in detail; and second, "the principle of coherence or relevance." The "more 'dialectical' members" of the discussion group tried to abide by the first of these two emphases (for without the common courtesy it required, there would be no discussion). That was enough, from Calhoun's perspective, to include them in the broad "*liberal* tradition" [emphasis added] going back to "the beginning of Christianity."

The case was rather different, however, in reference to "the principle of coherence or [logical] relevance,"[95] which tended to be underrated by the neo-orthodox not only because of the narrow scope of their theology but also because of what Calhoun viewed as their dialectical tendency to ignore nuance and think too readily in terms of either/or alternatives. In his concern for coherence as well as in the expansiveness that general revelation brought to his outlook, he was closer both to tradition and to liberalism at their respective bests than he was to neo-orthodoxy. Given the prevailing prejudices against tradition, however, it was his apparent liberalism that was chiefly noticed; and thus it was as a liberal that he stood unbowed under neo-orthodox hammering.

94. Ibid., 703–4.
95. Ibid., 704.

## The Enduring Value of the Lectures

The book as it now stands covers that half of Calhoun's history of Christian doctrine on which he had done the most work, and extends from the New Testament to the end of the patristic period, or if you prefer, from Jesus Christ to the beginning of the Middle Ages. The last Western figure to be treated is the seventh-century Pope Gregory the Great, while in the East, it is the eighth-century theologian John of Damascus. In Calhoun's version of history, all later developments of Christian doctrine depend positively or negatively on these seven hundred years, and the question to which we shall now turn is whether his account should be published a half century or more after it was first conceived.

There are here three possibilities. First, if the book is historically unreliable, it should not be published. Second, if it is reliable in what it includes but inadequate because of what it leaves out, then it may be publishable but not worth publishing. In the third place, however, it not only can but should be published to the extent it makes abidingly distinctive and helpful contributions to the understanding of early Christian doctrinal development.

On the first point, I shall simply assert rather than argue: the Calhoun volume is basically reliable in what it says. The few factual points at which it is contradicted by the present-day scholarly consensus are noted in footnotes and do not mar the larger picture. Even on Gnosticism, Calhoun read extensively in the new Greek (though not Coptic) materials that became available after his retirement and thus was able to correct misrepresentations, dating back in some cases to Irenaeus, which were unchallenged at midcentury and therefore also present in the 1948 transcript of his lectures.

At the very end of his life, Calhoun began expressing doubts regarding traditional ways of picturing the relation of orthodoxy to heresy in general, and not simply to Gnosticism. Instead of the heresies being off-shoots of an orthodox mainstream going back, let us say, to Pentecost, one can think of a relatively unified mainstream gradually coalescing in the course of the second century out of an initial multiplicity of often-competing groups claiming to be not only Christian but also, in the most significant cases, apostolic and catholic. This developing mainstream is what scholars now generally call the Great Church, and it grew in the course of the third century to embrace the vast majority of Christians.

Naturally it defined orthodoxy for subsequent generations. It viewed its understanding of the faith as in continuity with that of the apostles and treated those who disagreed (that is, heretics) as innovators who had distorted the faith once for all delivered to the saints. These seeming innovators, however, can sometimes be plausibly represented as survivors or conservers, marginalized heirs of versions of Christianity no less ancient than those to which the majority appealed. If they can be so understood, then doctrinal development is a matter of constructing orthodoxy rather than of developing (as Catholics since Newman have held) or distorting (as such liberal Protestants as von Harnack have maintained) the original deposit or experience of faith.

Calhoun was wary of talking in terms of either organic growth or degeneration, and consequently his account is rather easily reconcilable with the constructionist picture that he seemed increasingly to entertain in his last year. He had in any case no inclination to adopt the anti-Roman (yet ironically romanocentric) explanations of a Walter Bauer for the construction and triumph of the Great Church; nor is it likely that he would have been impressed by any of the other *cui bono* theories inspired by various forms of the hermeneutics of suspicion that have become increasingly popular since his retirement. The communities that developed in the "orthodox" Great Church had no political, cultural, social, or economic advantages; indeed, they seem to have been the most persecuted of the professedly Christian groups. Their victory can be plausibly—perhaps most plausibly—explained as a function of their success in constructing unity-and-community-constituting polities, canonical scriptures, liturgies, and rules of faith. Such a view would not require Calhoun to change the fundamental story line of doctrinal development of which we shall shortly speak. He might have wanted to alter some of the details, but it would be sheer speculation as to what those alterations might have been.

There are also other respects in which Calhoun would no doubt now consider his account inadequate. These faults, however, are of omission rather than commission. Let me list some of the omissions noted by others or in some cases by myself. There are, for example, only passing references to Gregory of Nyssa and Maximus the Confessor, although these Eastern theologians are now widely regarded as comparable to Augustine of Hippo in theological stature. Moreover, Calhoun shortchanged aspects of Trinitarian doctrine, especially pneumatology, and he apparently never read such treatises as Gregory the Great's *Moralia*, which a professional patrologist (which Calhoun was not) would be expected to have perused. More seriously, he neglected the importance of patristic exegesis to the history of doctrine even though there were such authors as Henri de Lubac and Jean Daniélou who were already beginning to mine its riches by the 1950s. Finally, social, cultural, and liturgical studies related to theological developments were relatively undeveloped; and our present concerns regarding patristic attitudes to women and to Judaism had not yet even begun to attain their present prominence. It is the failure to deal with topics that were unnoticed fifty years ago but are now at the center of research which is the main reason for asking whether Calhoun's manuscript, although publishable, is worth publishing. It can be plausibly maintained that it does not make what would at present be regarded as distinctive or significant contributions to the advancement of historical understanding; and, so Calhoun would be the first to say, it certainly should not be used as a primary text or textbook for the study of the history of Christian doctrine.

The counter-argument is that current views of what is historically valuable are themselves deficient. They often emphasize understanding doctrine in terms of external (or etic) theories—which in our day are generally hermeneutical but no less alien to the self-understanding of the participants in doctrinal developments than the progressive or evolutionary schemes that prevailed in the nineteenth and first part of the twentieth centuries. These theories often do not even try to make sense from the inside (that is, emically) of the ideas that were of central importance from the participants' perspective. The emic approach, however, as I have tried to show, is Calhoun's forte. Much of this volume is better than any other book known to me in presenting a readable and at the same time reliable running narrative of the conceptualities employed by the shapers of Christian doctrine in the first seven hundred years. This opinion does not mean that it competes with Turner or the first volume of Pelikan, which are in their particular ways the best recent surveys we have. However, these authors deal with doctrines one by one (which was also true of von Harnack). Calhoun, in contrast, provides us with a comprehensive overview of the entire thought of each major author he treats, viz., Irenaeus, Tertullian, Origen, Athanasius, Augustine, Gregory the Great, and John of Damascus, and then integrates these accounts into a continuous story of doctrinal development. This type of treatment is what enables readers to think that they are getting an insider's view. Good full-scale studies of individual authors can of course draw us into their doctrinal worlds far better than can rapid sketches, but among historically reliable surveys of comparably extended scope, Calhoun's is arguably the best at drawing theologically and ideologically diverse readers into the ongoing tale.

What then is the overall story line, the basic theological and historical plot, of this book? The plot is in part traditional: it centers, as any treatment of doctrine in this period must, on the articulation of the classic Trinitarian and christological creeds. Three considerations, at first unarticulated, controlled that development. First, Jesus Christ is genuinely human; second, salvation is through him; and third, "God alone and no created being, even the highest of creatures, can save from sin and death." The logic whereby the interaction of these three principles taken together produced the creeds of Nicaea and Chalcedon is laid out by Calhoun with exemplary clarity, but at the same time with attentiveness to the historical complexities and contingencies that made the outcome anything but a foregone conclusion. It was this ability to give order to a confusing picture without sacrificing either interest or detail that makes him persuasive; and it is this persuasiveness combined with the centrality of God in Christ for the Christian present no less than the past that gives his work its enduring value for those who want to understand the development of the mainstream doctrinal heritage common to Eastern Orthodoxy, Roman Catholicism, and Reformation Protestantism.

## PREPARATION FOR PUBLICATION [96]

Preparation for this publication started in 1947 and 1948 when a group of students recorded and transcribed the approximately ninety tightly packed lectures Calhoun delivered that year in his biennial course in the history of doctrine. The result was a five- to six-hundred-page single-spaced manuscript that he corrected and approved "for private circulation only." Many hundreds and perhaps thousands of multilithed copies of this copyrighted transcript were made over the years. In the early 1950s, Calhoun signed a contract with and received an advance from Harper & Row to prepare his lectures for publication. He worked sporadically

---

96. The material in this section in particular is treated in greater detail in my presentation on "Robert Lowry Calhoun as Historian of Doctrine," the Day Mission Library Lecture for 1998, and there are also borrowings from the same source in the other sections of this introduction.

on this preparation both before and after his retirement, but he was a perfectionist. He would expand ten pages into forty, realize the expansion was far too long, and then instead of compressing it, return to ground zero and reread the sources in their original languages in an effort to find another approach that would be more satisfactory.

His failures wore on him. He was a Congregationalist of Presbyterian stock from Minnesota, where his father, one-time mayor of St. Cloud, had been a struggling lawyer notable for *pro bono* work; and he had a conscience for which a signed contract was an unbreakable bond. Finally, a year or so before Calhoun's death, Hans Frei, who also is now departed, proposed that he and I should take over the project. Calhoun consented and, no longer weighed down by the responsibility of deciding what was publishable and what was not, proceeded to make great progress in his last months with the help of a graduate student, David Dawson, who is now himself a scholar of distinction.

Calhoun's perfectionism, however, was undiminished although no longer paralyzing. He kept going back to the original sources whenever he had any doubts; and that, because of a back problem, meant reading while lying flat with his head propped up and a light shining down on the book he would hold on his chest. His wife Ella, a medical doctor, told Hans Frei that she thought his eighty-six-year-old body had not been able to stand the strain of that final year. Yet it was worth it even if it killed him, she said: it had been the happiest year since his retirement.

Frei and I promised the Calhouns that we would complete the task, but it went slowly after Calhoun's death and even more slowly in the more than twenty years since Frei died in 1988. Progress has been sporadic and indeed would have been impossible without the help, encouragement, and counsel of many friends. Procedures have remained unchanged: they are the ones agreed upon and put into operation the year that all three of us—Calhoun, Frei, and I—were working together. The first and basic phase of the task as we then envisioned it is now completed for all of Calhoun's lectures while the second and, it is hoped, final phase is also finished for the present volume, which is approximately half the total.

In the first phase of the work, the 1948 transcript has been collated with three other types of material authored by Calhoun. The first type consists of fragmentary and uncorrected student transcripts of post-1948 lectures that need to be checked to see whether they contain improvements over the 1948 material. In second place, there are those post-1948 fragments that were reworked by Calhoun into possible replacements of or additions to sections of the 1948 transcript. Third, there are other possible replacements that he worked up *de novo*. These additions and replacements were simply possibilities in the first phase of the work because Calhoun had with few exceptions not made up his mind which to choose and how to use them and left such decisions up to the editors. The basic work of collating these materials, a fair amount of footnoting of Calhoun's sources, and the job of entering two to three thousand pages of double-spaced text into a computer was done by graduate students and has been completed, as I have already said, for the entirety of the *History*.

As for the second phase of preparing the text for publication, completed only for this volume, it consisted of deciding what should be left out and what retained in the final draft, and how to weave the various sources together. These are editorial tasks that cannot very well be delegated, and the guidelines are those with which Calhoun agreed. When confronted by alternative versions of the same material, we (or, in recent years, I) have chosen the version that seems best to combine readability and scholarship and that also, whenever possible, was *not* part of the 1948 transcript. There is, it seems clear, no point in duplicating material already widely circulated in private copies. When the 1948 versions are the best available, however, we have naturally used them, and they constitute the whole of at least a third of the chapters in this volume. Whatever the version, Calhoun's own words have been retained. To be sure, such changes as the insertion of transitional material have sometimes been necessary, but these alterations are always enclosed in brackets. The only unbracketed changes are corrections of factual errors or of verbal infelicities. Among the latter is Calhoun's insistent use of generic masculine language, especially in his earlier years. When the referents are human beings rather than God, these usages are replaced by inclusive language to the extent that this change can be made without syntactical or grammatical clumsiness. Interpretive material clearly outdated or discredited by recent scholarly developments has not been replaced or rewritten, but has either been retained with a footnote indicating what scholars would now more or less unanimously regard as erroneous, or has been omitted where the omission can be done without substantial loss of coverage. In other words, there has been no attempt to speculate about how Calhoun might have revised his lectures if he had lived longer, as he certainly would have done at least in reference to the transitional material that the editors have here supplied in brackets. Rather, the effort has simply been to present whatever he had already done and would have regarded as reasonably accurate—or, as he would have put it, "not wholly inaccurate"—during that last year of his work on the project. To the extent this effort has succeeded, there is nothing here Calhoun would have been unwilling to have published under his name. This book has a single author, Robert Lowry Calhoun: all the substance and almost all the words are his.[97]

---

97. Just as Professor Lindbeck considered it important to inform readers of the editorial process preceding the publication of the *Lectures in the History of Christian Doctrine*, so too a brief description of the preparation and editing of the introduction seems necessary. Professor Lindbeck had written several different versions of his introduction at intervals between 2006 and 2009; a perfectionist like his mentor, he continued to work on the various drafts prior to falling ill in the summer of 2009. As none of the drafts were complete—or had been completely satisfactory to him—the task of collating a much-revised electronic file and several older hard-copy versions of the introduction fell to his wife, Vi Lindbeck; his daughter Kris Lindbeck; and Rebecca Frey, a former graduate student who had written her dissertation under Professor Lindbeck. The introduction as it now stands is an edited version of the electronic file with some material added from the earlier hard-copy printouts to clarify some of the points made only briefly in the electronic file. But to echo the author's words about his own work on Calhoun's lectures, the introduction has a single author, George Arthur Lindbeck: "all the substance and almost all the words are his" [ed.].

## Bibliography

Bainton, Roland. "Tribute to Robert Calhoun." *Yale Divinity News* 62 (1965) n.p.

Berger, Peter. *The Sacred Canopy: Elements of a Sociological Theory of Religion.* New York: Doubleday, 1967.

Bultmann, Rudolf. "The Task of Theology in the Present Situation." In *Existence and Faith: Shorter Writings of Rudolf Bultmann,* translated by Schubert M. Ogden, 158–65. New York: Meridian, 1960.

Calhoun, Robert L. "Christ and the Church." In *The Nature of the Unity We Seek: Official Report of the North American Conference on Faith and Order, September 3–10, 1957, Oberlin, Ohio,* 52–78. St. Louis: Bethany, 1958.

———. "The Dilemma of Humanitarian Modernism." In *The Christian Understanding of Man,* by T. E. Jessop, R. L. Calhoun, N. Alexeiev, et al., 57–95. Chicago: Willett, Clark, 1938.

———. *Lectures in Systematic Theology.* Mimeographed notes recorded by Robert H. Smith. Privately circulated manuscript, Yale Divinity School, 1954.

———. *Lectures on the History of Christian Doctrine (LHCD).* Privately circulated manuscript, Yale Divinity School, 1948.

———. *Lectures on the History of Philosophy (LHP).* Privately circulated manuscript, Yale Divinity School, 1958.

———. "A Liberal Bandaged but Unbowed." *Christian Century* 56 (1939) 701–4.

———. "Plato as Religious Realist." In *Religious Realism,* edited by Douglas Clyde Macintosh, 195–251. New York: Macmillan, 1931.

———. "Reason and Revelation in Religious Knowledge." Dudleian Lecture, Harvard University, 1957. Cambridge, MA: n.p., 1958.

———. Review of *The Nature and Destiny of Man,* by Reinhold Niebuhr. *Journal of Religion* 24 (1944) 59–64.

———. "Robert Calhoun Reviews Jaroslav Pelikan's *The Christian Tradition.*" *Reflection* 70 (1972) 1–4.

———. "The Role of Historical Theology." *Journal of Religion* 21 (1941) 444–54.

———. *What Is Man?* New York: Association, 1939.

Christian, William, and Hans Frei. "In Memory of Robert L. Calhoun, 1896–1983." *Reflection* 82 (1984) 8–11.

Corwin, Virginia. "To Recall in Gratitude Robert Lowry Calhoun." In *The Heritage of Christian Thought: Essays in Honor of Robert Lowry Calhoun,* edited by Robert E. Cushman and Egil Grislis, 1–7. New York: Harper & Row, 1965.

Cushman, Robert E. "Introduction." In *The Heritage of Christian Thought: Essays in Honor of Robert Lowry Calhoun,* edited by Robert E. Cushman and Egil Grislis, vii–viii. New York: Harper & Row, 1965.

DeHart, Paul J. *The Trial of the Witnesses: The Rise and Decline of Postliberal Theology.* Challenges in Contemporary Theology. Oxford: Blackwell, 2006.

Frei, Hans W. "Barth and Schleiermacher: Divergence and Convergence." In *Theology and Narrative: Selected Essays,* edited by George Hunsinger and William C. Placher, 177–99. Oxford: Oxford University Press, 1993.

———. *The Eclipse of Biblical Narrative: A Study in Eighteenth- and Nineteenth-century Hermeneutics.* New Haven, CT: Yale University Press, 1974.

———. "Niebuhr's Theological Background." In *Faith and Ethics: The Theology of H. Richard Niebuhr,* 9–64. New York: Harper, 1957.

———. "The Theology of H. Richard Niebuhr." In *Faith and Ethics: The Theology of H. Richard Niebuhr,* 65–116. New York: Harper, 1957.

Harnack, Adolf von. *History of Dogma.* 7 vols. Translated by Neil Buchanan. London: Williams & Norgate, 1896–99.

———. *What Is Christianity?* Translated by Thomas Bailey Saunders. New York: Harper, 1957.

Hunsinger, George. "Afterword: Hans Frei as Theologian." In *Theology and Narrative*, 256–69. Oxford: Oxford University Press, 1993.

Kerr, Fergus. *Twentieth-Century Catholic Theologians: From Neoscholasticism to Nuptial Mysticism.* Malden, MA: Blackwell, 2007.

Leith, John H. *Crisis in the Church: The Plight of Theological Education.* Louisville: Westminster John Knox, 1997.

"Liberalism, Theological." In *Encyclopedia Britannica*, 14th ed., edited by William Benton, 13:1020ff. Chicago: University of Chicago Press, 1973.

Lindbeck, George A. *The Nature of Doctrine: Religion and Theology in a Postliberal Age.* Louisville: Westminster John Knox, 1984.

———. "Robert Lowry Calhoun as Historian of Doctrine." Day Mission Library Lecture, 1998.

Lonergan, Bernard. *The Subject.* Milwaukee: Marquette University Press, 1968.

Lovejoy, Arthur O. *The Great Chain of Being: A Study of the History of an Idea.* Cambridge, MA: Harvard University Press, 1936.

Mannheim, Karl. *Ideology and Utopia: An Introduction to the Sociology of Knowledge.* New York: Harcourt Brace, 1936.

Mink, Louis O. "Art without Artists." In *Liberations: New Essays on the Humanities in Revolution*, 70–87. Middletown, CT: Wesleyan University Press, 1971.

———. *Historical Understanding.* Ithaca, NY: Cornell University Press, 1987.

———. "Narrative Form as a Cognitive Instrument." In *The Writing of History: Literary Form and Historical Understanding*, 129–49. Madison: University of Wisconsin Press, 1978.

Niebuhr, H. Richard. *The Meaning of Revelation.* Louisville: Westminster John Knox, 2006.

Otto, Rudolf. *Das Heilige—Über das Irrationale in der Idee des Göttlichen und sein Verhältnis zum Rationalen.* 1917. Reprinted, Munich: C. H. Beck, 1963.

Pannenberg, Wolfhart. "History and the Reality of the Resurrection." In *Resurrection Reconsidered*, 62–72. Oxford: Oneworld, 1996.

Pelikan, Jaroslav, *The Christian Tradition.* 5 vols. Chicago: University of Chicago Press, 1971–1989.

Russell, Bertrand. *Bertrand Russell Speaks His Mind.* Cleveland: World, 1960.

Schleiermacher, Friedrich. *The Christian Faith.* Translated by H. R. Mackintosh and J. S. Stewart. Edinburgh: T. & T. Clark, 1928.

Schweitzer, Albert. *The Quest of the Historical Jesus; A Critical Study of Its Progress from Reimarus to Wrede.* Translated by W. Montgomery. 1910. Reprinted, Mineola, NY: Dover, 2005.

Stout, Jeffrey. *Democracy and Tradition.* Princeton, NJ: Princeton University Press, 2004.

Swinburne, Richard. *The Resurrection of God Incarnate.* New York: Oxford University Press, 2003.

Thelen, Mary Frances. *Man as Sinner in Contemporary American Realistic Theology.* New York: King's Crown, 1946.

Wolterstorff, Nicholas. "Can Belief in God Be Rational If It Has No Foundations?" In *Faith and Rationality: Reason and Belief in God*, 135–86. Notre Dame, IN: University of Notre Dame Press, 1983.

# CHAPTER 1

# Revelation, Religion, Theology, and Dogma[1]

IT SEEMS WELL TO begin this survey of the development of Christian doctrine by examining three primary terms: religion, theology, and dogma. Our concern will be centrally with the rise, elaboration, and criticism of dogma, but we shall need to keep the surrounding context of theological reflection and religious experience always in view. In a sense,

---

1. Professor Calhoun, gifted with an extraordinary memory and extemporizing talent, outlined his lectures in his head and delivered them without notes. Inevitably they changed considerably from year to year, and the alterations increased after the circulation for private use, beginning in 1948, of multilithed copies of his 1947–48 *Lectures on the History of Christian Doctrine* (1948 LHCD). Once this authorized transcript was available, he deliberately tried to refrain from repeating himself and made alterations that at times (though by no means always, as he himself said) improved on the 1948 LHCD. As a result, although the 1948 transcript provides the framework and much of the content of the sections in this volume that he did not himself rework—of which this chapter is one—the text that follows is interwoven with selections taken primarily from student records of lectures delivered in later years. These selections are unmarked; however, footnotes indicating the sources are added when the borrowing is from Calhoun's own publications or lectures that were not part of the history of doctrine course. Responsibility for the decisions as to what to borrow rests exclusively with the editor. I have, however, tried to follow Calhoun's preferences as I remember them from the discussions with him and with Hans Frei, starting in 1982 and continuing until their deaths in 1983 and 1988 respectively. Given the incompleteness of the discussions and of the written record, my choices may not always be the same as those that Calhoun or Frei would have made. Nevertheless, with the exception of bracketed material and editorial corrections that have no influence on content, all the words and ideas are those of Calhoun himself even when they are pieced together from a variety of places.

While this compilation is not a critical edition of Calhoun on the history of Christian doctrine, the data for checking its adequacy are available in the surviving multilithed copies of the 1948 transcript and more fully in the editorial archives deposited in the Yale Divinity School Library. Unless otherwise indicated, the footnotes, except for editorial corrections and updating, originate from Calhoun [ed.].

dogma continually crystallizes out of a wider and more fluid body of Christian experience and reflective thought, and it can hardly be understood apart from this setting. Before entering into detail on religion, types of theology, and the nature of dogma, it will be well to remind ourselves of different ways of envisioning the theological enterprise in relation to God's revelatory activity, on the one hand, and human religious experience, on the other.

## REVELATION

Three main conceptions of the task of theology have been familiar in the life of the Western church. The traditional conception was that the theologian was concerned to expound and interpret the revelation of God to man. Revelation, in its simplest sense, means disclosure or unveiling, and in the context of religion and theology, it means the self-disclosure of God to those who have eyes to see and ears to hear. We can use the word properly enough with respect to the communication of one human being with another. We disclose ourselves to one another in part through speech, through action, and through the employment of various media, and this self-disclosure involves initiative on the part of the one who is seeking to make himself known, together with sensitive apprehension on the part of the one to whom the message is supposed to go. In the religious context, revelation maintains that primary sense—initiative from God's side and apprehension from the human side—but the primary stress in the traditional view is laid upon the content of what God discloses of himself.

This divine self-disclosure occurs in various ways. It is seen primarily in the life, death, and resurrection of Jesus Christ. More generally, it is to be found in the Bible as a record of the experiences of the Hebrew people and of the words which God spoke to their lawgivers and prophets; of the events of Jesus' earthly career and the teaching in which he undertook to make the nature and will of God clear to his hearers; and of the growth of the Christian community after his death. Then, with a shift of meaning, revelation is discerned in the propositions, the words spoken or written by witnesses, and quite particularly in the written accounts which were gathered together along with the Old Testament to compose the Scriptures of the new community, revelation in and through the Bible as itself the word of God to human beings. Still more generally, it has been held that God makes himself known through the whole realm of nature ("the heavens declare the glory of God and the firma-ment shows his handiwork"), and the whole course of history, as well as in exceptional experiences of illumination and vision which help to make plain the meaning of everyday life and of the human struggle in which all persons share. Whatever the mode of revelation, however, the primary stress in this traditional view is upon the initiative of God, and the task of the theologian is understood to be that of observing correctly, describing carefully, and interpreting clearly the truth which is thus given to human beings by the God who speaks.

In the medieval period and at the beginning of the modern period of the church's life, I think it is fair to say that revelation was sought mainly in the words of Scripture, in the sacraments which were central to the worship of the church, and in what came to be known as unwritten tradi-tion—tradition that went back to the apostles and was preserved within the life of the church. Revelation came to be understood as consisting largely of sets of propositions, the truth of which were guaranteed by the power and truth of God himself.

Then there came increasingly in the seventeenth and eighteenth centuries a reaction against what was called revealed religion. The claim that the Bible is the infallible Word of God was attacked by those who were at pains to find conflicts between the Scriptural text and what the growing knowledge of nature was bringing to light, between one part of Scripture and another part, and between the moral presuppositions of what we now regard as relatively primitive strains and relatively advanced strains of insight in the growing life of humankind. The result at length was to call into question the validity of the very concept of divine self-disclosure or revelation. If then theology was to have a task, it must be sought elsewhere.

An alternative view was first explicitly defined by Schleiermacher at the beginning of the nineteenth century. Confronted by widespread skepticism concerning the authority of Christian teaching and by what seemed to him a fundamental misunderstanding of the very nature of religion, Schleiermacher undertook to defend the validity of theology upon a new ground by urging that its task is the systematic elaboration of the content of religious experience. The emphasis now is not upon an objective act of God but upon the personal experience of human beings. Schleiermacher had no intention at any time of denying the presence and activity of God; that was an indispensable presupposition. But it seemed to him that all that one could know of God, and all that one could intelligently talk about as a theologian was what happened in God's presence and in response to God's action. It seemed to him that religion, as the rationalists of the eighteenth century had understood and attacked it, was misconceived. They had tried to identify it with a particular set of doctrines, or with a particular set of morals, pronouncements of the intellect or guidelines for the will. But religion for Schleiermacher is a fundamental way of apprehending reality, more profound than either thought or action. In it one is aware of the basic unity of all things, and of one's own ultimate and unconditional dependence upon the Ground of that unity.

But now what distinguishes Christianity from other religions? The Christian also shares in the religiousness common to all human beings. Like them, he also feels creatureliness. His existence is not of his own making. He cannot maintain his own being from one moment to the next. He is sustained perpetually by a greater power. The Christian, however, knows two further moments: he is not only creature but is also sinner. He is one alienated by his own failure; he is one for whom the world is broken asunder into fragments which he is unable to hold together. He is separated from the world and struggles vainly to find a stable selfhood. Yet he is not only a sinner, he is also aware of salvation through Jesus Christ. He doesn't know himself as a sinner until he has been saved. Then rescued effectively, he can see that even when he was not aware of sinfulness in himself, it was there. Now Jesus Christ becomes for him redeemer because he, first and alone of humankind, had perfect God-consciousness. That is to say, he was one who at every moment of his life knew and acknowledged God as the ground of both being and good for him. Through Jesus, this insight is made accessible to those who associate themselves with him in faith as a community. The Holy Spirit is nothing other than this spirit of Jesus Christ perpetuated in the life of the community of which he is the historical center. The job of the theologian, then, is to examine this deep-going experience of the human self, to set its components in order, to make plain its implications for human existence. And so theology is concerned in the first instance not with revelation, but rather with religion. The content with which it is concerned is nothing other than the immediately observable content of human experience of dependence upon God. This view has come to be associated with liberal Protestant thought, and in the mid-twentieth century has come in turn to be the target of vigorous attack.

Out of this reaction beginning after the First World War against the effort to redefine theology as an exposition and interpretation of religious experience has grown a third understanding of the relation of theology to revelation and religion. Religion is declared to be of man's making: it is human, all too human. It is necessary therefore to return, as Karl Barth in particular insists, to the Reformers' clear insight that the theologian has nothing to talk about except what God has disclosed. So we have here the dialectical theology with its insistence that the proper subject matter for theology is the Word of God; not the Bible taken literally and infallibly, but rather the Word of God which comes in and with and through the words of human beings that constitute the biblical text. The true Word of God is Jesus Christ. He is the true Word of God witnessed to in the Scripture and affirmed in genuine preaching—which in turn depends on what God grants preachers and hearers. The Word of God is God's Word—not mine, not yours, not that of the biblical writers, nor of preachers, nor of great churchmen—but the Word of God. And the theologian's job is once more to make plain the meaning and the import of what God has said.

But there still persists alongside that dialectical position a kind of successor to the mood of Schleiermacher and the liberals. If Barth is the spokesman for the dialectical theology, I suppose Bultmann would be regarded in many circles as a typical spokesman for a theology which is sometimes willing to be called existentialist. The task of the theologian is still the task of making plain the significance of Jesus Christ in me, not as an objective event on the Judaean hillside, but as a perpetually repeated event in the depth life of persons. This seems to me clearly in the lineage of Ritschlian theology, which arose out of the transformation which Schleiermacher had brought about. Ritschl insisted that judgments of facts are always dubious; it is judgments of value which must be regarded as having primary significance for Christian thinkers. The reality of the life of Jesus Christ for me is that Jesus Christ enables me to deal with the powers of darkness which I confront, to find life in the world which is perpetually pressing upon me the threat of death.

I myself am inclined to welcome especially the reaction of those who say revelation is the chief concern of the theologian: God, but God speaking to man, God as he is known to human beings in his presence, judgment, and mercy. It seems to me that the primary emphasis must be placed where the traditional view placed it: upon the impact of God on man. At the same time Schleiermacher's insights simply cannot be brushed aside. Barth also has defended Schleiermacher against quite one-sided attacks from Brunner, who has indicated that Schleiermacher is the arch-heretic who has substituted human for divine truth. Barth says that is not what Schleiermacher is really doing; he was one-sided, but not completely off the track.[2] While the primary emphasis must be placed where the traditional view placed it, upon the impact of God on man, the human response to that impact, the response familiarly called religious experience, is inseparable from the account of God's self-revelation. Theology is concerned with the nature of this response as well as with the significance of the primary reality that confronts human beings.

Finally, there may be yet another way that is today being increasingly pursued. It is to be hoped that it will not be burdened with "muddle-headed" liberalism nor be a victim of the weaknesses of Neo-orthodoxy. It is a sort of ecumenical theology, not of a particular church . . . [but] a theology which tries to find itself at home in all of Christian thinking. Thus far its outlines are not clear, but the forward steps are stimulating. To this trend with its incalculable promise for the church on earth, historical theology should be able to contribute substantially.[3]

To evaluate these reactions is not now possible. We have only begun to see them take shape. One thing is clear: new light is breaking into a world which we have barely begun to understand, and the one certain way of folly is to suppose that now we know substantially all that can be known. This lesson the history of Christian thought teaches as surely as another lesson more fundamental still: that truth already has been grant-

2. Student notes on Calhoun's lectures dating from the early 1950s are the source of these approving remarks on Karl Barth's criticism of Emil Brunner's view of Schleiermacher. Calhoun may have known of this criticism through personal encounters with Barth in ecumenical contexts or from the German original, first published in the 1930s, of the treatment of Schleiermacher in Barth's *Protestant Thought: From Rousseau to Ritschl*, trans. Brian Cozens (New York: Harper, 1959) 306–54. For a discussion of Barth's relation to Schleiermacher that makes use of Barth's later writings, see Hans Frei, "Barth and Schleiermacher: Divergence and Convergence," a 1986 lecture now reprinted in *Theology and Narrative: Selected Essays*, eds. G. Hunsinger and W. Placher (Oxford: Oxford University Press, 1993) 177–99 [ed].

3. Except for the last sentence, this paragraph is taken from notes on Calhoun's 1954 *Lectures in Systematic Theology* (LST, p 7E) as recorded, condensed, and mimeographed by R. H. Smith, with Calhoun's permission but without his reading or corrections. Copies are available in the Yale Divinity School library. The last sentence comes from R. L. Calhoun, "The Role of Historical Theology," *Journal of Religion* (1941) 453 [ed].

ed which human beings try in vain to escape, and which they neglect at their peril.

## Religion

Turning now to religion understood as human response to God as revealed, it is hardly possible not to suppose that there are ranges of his being which are not thus disclosed, and with them neither religion nor theology can be concerned in any detailed way until further revelation comes about. Theology deals with God as he becomes manifest through nature, history, personal experience, and for Christians, centrally through Jesus Christ, the focal point of revelation. For Christian faith, it is through Jesus Christ that the meaning of all the other media of God's confrontation of man must be understood. And such understanding comes most directly in and through religious response.

### *The Religious Life of Human Communities*[4]

Religious experience is individual as well as communal, but as it is the religious community that determines and shapes theology and gives content to theological language, we shall first comment on the communal aspect. To be sure, the community is related to the individual, not as an additive or simply collective body of individuals, but rather as the context in which individuals themselves come to full self-realization. The attempt, therefore, to talk of individuals in isolation or to talk of communities as though they were individual entities seems to me always to land in confusion. Communities are made up of individual believers, and individual believers are such in the context of a living, growing, responsive community. Three forms of religious social expression deserve especial notice: cultus, propaganda, and polity.

*Cultus* is an organized provision for repeated experiences of worship. To that end, the community employs ritual, which is a patterned social ordering of words and acts that in the long course of time develop out of the spontaneous impulses of worship into settled forms. Ritual embodies the attempt of the community to confront and to enthrall the members of the community again and again with the long history, the life story, of

---

4. The individual aspect of religion is treated before the communal in the LHCD of 1948, but the order was reversed in later years. It was also reversed in the much more extended discussion in 9–19 of LST (see note 3 above)[ed].

this group of worshippers in order to provide a setting in which renewal of the living insight may be hoped for, though it cannot be compelled.

The central place of sacraments in ritual need not detain us here. The church from a very early time regarded the sacraments as means of communication between the believers and God. The initiative comes primarily from God's side. The sacrament is truly *mysterion, sacramentum*, only as God makes it so. I can perform a ritual act, but whether or not it will be filled with living content depends not upon the doing of the act, but on the presence and grace of the one whom I address in this active way.

Besides corporate worship as represented by ritual and sacraments, there is what I hesitate to call *propaganda*, but find unhappily no other word inclusive or precise enough to say what seems to me needed here. In its simplest and most direct form, propaganda is proclamation, *kerygma*, announcement of what God has done. The word of the prophets, the word of the apostolic witness, the word of the one who is able to say, "That which our eyes have seen and our hands have handled concerning the Word of Life, that we declare unto you"—that is propaganda in its primary sense. In a second phase, it is evangelism addressed still to members of the group and seeking to kindle in them again and again the primary convictions to which they have professed allegiance. In still another phase it is addressed to outsiders, as a missionary effort to make known to them in persuasive terms the principle of life which the group has found commanding. Such propaganda includes preaching or proclamation and enunciation of the kind of life which has become authoritative for the community. In all three phases, there comes very soon the need for interpretation. The meaning of this *kerygma*, this announcement, may be clear enough to the one who is offering it, but it may be anything but clear to his listeners. And if he is really to reach and help them it is necessary for him or for someone to engage in the long task of puzzling out what the impact of this new insight upon the whole range of human existence may be. And this interpretation is various forms and modes of theology—discourse about God, yes, but also an effort to make plain the structure and relationships of human response to God.

*Polity* as an expression of religion along with cult and propaganda also needs to be mentioned. Polity is the organization of the members and the life of a religious community to provide for suitable division of labor, continuity of function, and authoritative discipline. Three main types of such organization are familiar. One is the organization of a whole social community into a religious community. This is the pattern of folk religions in general. Of the advanced religions, Judaism is the one that originally represented this type in a form most familiar to Christians. Puritan New England once provided smaller examples. In a theocracy, to be a member of the social community is by that very fact to be a member also of a religious community. A second main type is the church (*ecclesia*). Whether "established" or not—that is, whether or not officially recognized and supported by the government of a secular society—an *ecclesia* is likely to include in its membership representatives of the various modes of living characteristic of the community at large. Its membership is not coextensive with the community as a whole. One may seek to become a member of the church and be accepted or rejected, and one's citizenship need not be affected thereby. At the same time, the ways of life accepted in the community at large are likely to be reflected in the standards and behavior of the membership of the church. The third main type is the sect, which represents a somewhat sharp reaction against the inclusiveness and secular acceptability of the church. Membership in the sect is normally selected on more rigorous grounds than the membership of a more inclusive church. Sects are indeed not infrequently minority groups which have asserted their independence of a church which seems to them too comfortably established in the world. Membership in a sect requires commitment to standards of conduct and sometimes standards of belief more stringent than those required of the members of an inclusive church. The sect is likely to take as its model the form of membership suggested by such a phrase as "the communion of saints." It may seek a historical pattern in an earlier and purer stage in the life of the church from which it has broken away. Or it may find its model nowhere in history but rather in an ideal state not yet actually achieved. With its more homogeneous pattern of membership and its more stringent discipline, the sect is often able to mount an effective protest against compromise and to bring about important reforms within the life of a larger religious group. Much of the history of Christian theology as well as life is concerned with the tensions and interrelations between communities of these major types.

*Religious Response of the Individual Person*

The nature of religious response can most readily be indicated briefly by two descriptive terms: worship and devout work. In the concrete course of human life, each leads to the other and the two become goals of a continuously alternating movement. While both terms have communal as well as individual application, it is in reference to the personal lives of religious people that their distinctive features and their interplay are most clearly manifest.

Worship is a highly complex response called forth by the presence of a Being that seems overwhelmingly great and good. One who finds himself confronted by such reality is constrained to acknowledge its presence by that profound reverence we call religious awe. I would suggest that reverence is, in the first instance, genuine acknowledgment of an other as other, as superior to oneself. We can use that word too in respect to human relationships; we can speak of reverence for life, as Schweitzer does, or reverence for the personal being of a child on the part of an adult. We know at least roughly what we mean. We mean the adult's apprehension that the child is not an instrument for the adult's satisfaction or self-fulfillment. The child is an independent center of being who has claims upon the adult because in a certain sense the child is not merely other than but greater than, better than, the adult; he will live through struggles and insights of which I will know nothing. As I decrease, he will increase, God willing. If I see him as one who is other than I, and as one who is in his own way superior to me, I am maintaining towards him an attitude of reverence.

Now if this reverence becomes overpowering, so that the Being that confronts me is radically Other, supremely great, terrifyingly good, so that in the presence of this Other I find myself shrinking with the sense of unworthiness which is not merely fear—dread goes deeper than fear—my being is threatened. It is not that I am in peril of pain or loss, but the validity of my self is threatened. In the presence of such a Being I find myself driven into deep-going revolt like that of the Gerasene maniac: "What have I to do with thee, Jesus, thou Son of the Most High God?" That is the normal response of a person compelled perhaps for the first time in his life really to acknowledge the triviality, cheapness, and falsity of the self he has thus far claimed to be. That is awe; that is acknowledgment of One in whose presence all that I can do to be confident would shrink into nothingness.

Yet as Rudolph Otto has made plain, religious awe combines in a profound and intricate way responses of deep revulsion and dread with even deeper responses of fascination and acknowledgment. My dread is transmuted and overcome, but not by anything I can do, or think, or aspire to. Reconciliation is effected from the side of the Other; the One whom I now acknowledge as my judge proves to be also my Savior, so that I am enabled to live in the presence of God as one accepted, not by reason of merit on my side, but by reason of the infinite understanding and mercy of God; so that I can say not merely, "God be merciful to me a sinner," but "the Lord is my light and my salvation." The God who appears at first as enemy turns out to be one's Savior. One can now say, "He in his infinite mercy has made of me other than I could have come to be through my own power."

And the result of such reconciliation is, on my part, not identification with God—he is still God; he is in heaven and I am on earth. Face to face with his perfection, we can never again be content. An experience far more profound than simple contentment has become possible—the experience of yielding up life and soul and for the first time finding myself. I discover that what hitherto I have thought of as my life and have clung to desperately in the face of the threatening presence of God was after all not truly my life. It was a warped, self-centered, anxious travesty of human existence. In making it impossible for me any longer to claim virtue and importance in my own right, God has opened the way for me to enter on a new mode of living, oriented toward a truth and reality that is forever other than mine, yet forever the condition of my fulfillment. His thoughts are not my thoughts, and his ways are not my ways. But his thoughts and his ways have awakened in me commitment which now becomes the most crucial thing in the life that has for the first time become possible for me, a life which the Christian religion has described by the term *faith*.

Faith is more than belief or intellectual assent. It is more than trust in a human friend or in a cherished cause. Religious faith transcends all of these familiar but limited and conditional commitments. However great my reverence for and trust in a human friend, I cannot commit my life unreservedly to his keeping. However deep my loyalty to country or class or people, I cannot without self-destruction abdicate my responsibility to judge the very object of my loyalty, and in the name of good conscience to refuse at some point obedience to its demands. In the presence of God I find myself face to face with the very principle that demands of me such reservation with respect to all finite loyalties. My trust in God is neither a particular act nor a specific agreement. It is a fundamental and complete reorientation of my whole being. The springs of thought and feeling and action are drawn without reservation into the new way. Criticisms are called for with respect to them all. I believe in God and trust him, not because such trust seems to me advantageous but because such trust has welled up in me. Whereas I was anxiously intent upon values and goals of my own, now I find myself possessed by a new understanding of values and goals and a new craving for goals hitherto unsought. Such inclusive faith is not achieved by human intelligence and good will. It is called forth by the transforming presence of God.

This raises the question whether faith is a kind of reflex or involuntary response. I think not, and I would want to find a suitable way to avoid the concept of faith as an attainment without resort to this other extreme. One reason I dislike quite acutely—perhaps more acutely than I should—the phrase "the leap of faith" is that it seems to me to lay far too much stress on an active effort on the part of the believer. Faith is then an athletic accomplishment. It seems to me that this is precisely wrong, for faith is awakened if at all by the presence of One in whose presence one can do no other than believe. Yet at the same time, it is not in any sense to be regarded as a mechanical imposition. It is not as though my arm were twisted until at length the response is called forth. Rather, in this sort of response, as has already been said, I am fulfilling myself. I am finding a new set of dimensions for being myself as in love and loyalty I learn how to be other than the self that self-centered existence produces. The response of faith is voluntary, but voluntary not as the outcome of a cool choice. Rather it is a reorientation of my whole being so that my choices henceforth are differently grounded and conditioned and directed. It is a change that involves my will; it is not a change that is produced by my will. It is not the outcome of a chain of reasoning, but chains of reasoning become relevant when I find myself thus redirected. Faith is this reorientation of the self, and it is the heart of the experience of worship.

Worship, in turn, naturally seeks outlets in devout work. Without such active expression, the vision of God would not involve an authentic transformation of personal existence, and so would not be genuine worship but a sentimental substitute. Faith without works is not faith. At the same time, not every sort of work is an appropriate expression of genuine vision. When we speak of devout work, we mean an actual effort to transform the actual world, including oneself, into closer accord with what we take to be the will of God. This does not mean that the faithful workman is constantly conscious of himself as a religious person, nor that he is continually reminding himself to remember that what he does is done to the glory of God. This sort of perpetual distraction of attention from the requirements of the task in hand is not likely to improve one's service to either God or man. The surgeon must keep his eye and his mind on the thin line of his moving blade. The woodsman must fell his tree, the steelworker must set his beam in place, with full attention to the demands of the masses moving under his hand. What makes work devout is not an oscillating or divided mind, but the whole context and temper in which the work is done. A devout servant of God will demand from himself, whatever tasks he finds to occupy his resources, a clear integrity of purpose and a pervasive love for the things and people who are concerned in what he is trying to do. Such work is not worship. The old aphorism *laborare est orare* cannot be taken quite literally. But honest and devoted work in service of needy living creatures is, at the same time, genuine service to God. It belongs alongside worship as an integral part of religious living.

## THEOLOGY AS REFLECTIVE PRESENTATION OF THE REVEALING WORD OF GOD

When we talk of theology in its broadest sense, I would suggest, we are talking of the reflective development of faith. This is a controversial statement. There are those who would want to regard theology as essentially and always proclamation; it is a statement of what God has revealed, and anything beyond that is a sin. But there is another opposing view which regards theology as simply a theoretic science, essentially dispassionate and uncommunicative, which is related to faith much as art criticism is related to the concrete work of the artist. This view would, in effect, identify theology with phenomenology of religion, which describes the way in which believers behave as an outside observer can see it; or with psychology of religion, which gives dispassionate explanatory accounts of it.

Both of these definitions of theology are unhappy ones. In the first instance, response in faith is not self-conscious, self-analytical, self-interpretative; it is spontaneous and unreflective. But as soon as the believer begins to raise with himself, as St. Paul found it necessary to raise within himself, the question, "What does the vision on the Damascus road mean?" Then he does not cease to be a believer; he becomes a reflective believer. He begins to engage now in inquiry concerning the nature and import of what has transformed his life, but at the same time not as the cool observation and interpretation of one who—as I once heard Margaret Mead say of herself—never said a prayer in her life and never expected to. Such a one, she implied, is in no good position to talk about the nature and meaning of religious commitment. Theology is not then an uncommitted, detached, theoretical science, and not simply proclamation, but rather the effort by believers to understand in conversation with fellowbelievers, and in conversation also with neighbors who are unbelievers the meaning and structure, the long-term significance, of what they take to be revelation and of their response thereto.

Within this general area, we may still distinguish a number of modes of theological effort. Most fundamental is *dogmatic theology*, often called *confessional theology*, whose primary concern is to give a clear, articulate exposition of what is believed to be true respecting God and man. The exposition thus set forth may be quite simple or very complex. It may be couched in the language of concrete appeal and command, or in the language of calm analysis and construction. In any event, it purports to set forth what the theologian himself genuinely does believe. At the same time, it professes to be a fair expression of what the religious community of which he is a member believes. No individual experience can cover more than a small fraction of what a long-lived community can learn through years, generations, centuries of time. Confessional or dogmatic theology professes to be a faithful though partial transcript of what the community thus learns and what the individual member of the community should know.

Alongside this dogmatic and confessional theology, there is what has long been called *systematic theology*—a readiness to inquire about the adequacy of dogmatic definitions already agreed upon. Within Roman Catholic theological disciplines, systematic theology still abides by the rule that although dogma can develop, it can never be rescinded or replaced. Yet development is taken as an obvious and important fact. So the dogmatic theologian and the systematic theologian here are seen to stay within the bounds of what has been proclaimed so that neither of them will pronounce false what the church has declared to be true. Yet the systematic theologian is ready to inquire what this now means in a new time, what further insights have become accessible. In Protestant tradition, a very considerably greater amount of free play has been characteristic. One is open to the possibility that some of the dogmas which the church has promulgated are mistaken and need to be not merely developed but replaced. Any and all dogmas as decisions of the church as contrasted with the Word of God must be regarded as susceptible of this kind of historical conditioning and need to be continually examined and at times superseded. Systematic theology then operates within this wider framework. Dogmas are there but not necessarily final; they too are to be subjected to critical examination and appraisal.

The third mode of theology is what is ordinarily called *apologetics.* This is the effort on the part of believers to defend against misunderstanding, against attack usually from outside the community, on what they and their fellow believers take to be true. As a matter of fact, the first effort of the early church to engage in something like extensive theological inquiry was prompted by an apologetic concern to make the pagan world more clearly aware of what the Christians were affirming and what they were not affirming, what their life did and did not entail. The early Christian presupposition was that among pagans there were presumably men of intelligence and good will to whom one could, as a spokesman on behalf of the church, appeal on the basis of common presuppositions from which one could then go on to derive consequences that the outsider of intelligence and good will had not recognized. Perhaps, for example, the unbeliever professes to be a completely impartial observer and interpreter of the world, but upon what conditions can this effort be maintained? Presumably only if there is a stable order in the world which is accessible to human inquiry. But what ground for such order can be specified? Is there anything in the physical world of things and events which guarantees the kind of order which this sort of exploration requires? And the Christian apologist will say, "No, it is the Word of God, the Logos, the uncreated declaration of God's mind which provides the base upon which you philosophically-minded pagans are undertaking to carry on with your task as philosophers. You have not recognized it as yet, but this is in fact what you are tacitly presupposing, and it is time you did come to recognize it and also the consequences."

Apologetic theology is then the effort to appeal to the outsider, making clearer to him the meaning and accessibility of that view of God and humanity which the believing community has thus far worked out. What has often been called *natural theology* or *philosophical theology* has its most appropriate place in this third area of theological effort. Sometimes it has been offered as a substitute for confessional theology, but always with considerable losses to both. The function of natural reason is not to take the place of the response of faith to revelation, but rather to work out the lines of connection that bind significant revelation and the universal needs and insights of humanity.

An additional mode of theology which concerns us here is *historical theology*, which, as I understand it, differs both from a simple chronicle of what theologians have thought and from a tendentious effort to prove one's party line correct as over against competing party lines. Historical theology has emerged very late in the life of the church. In the earliest days there was no adequate subject matter with which a theologically-minded historian could deal; the events had not yet come to pass. When in the course, let us say, of the Arian controversy, Athanasius undertakes to write a *History of the Arians* or a treatise on the decrees of Nicaea, or on the synod of Sardica, he is starting in the direction of an historical account of what has been held and what opponents have maintained. But he is writing as a partisan, not as one who is concerned first of all to give each spokesman his full and unslanted right. When we come into the fifth century and the beginning of the Christological controversies, we find another kind of quasi-historical work emerging. Theodoret probably started it: a *catena* ("chain") or anthology of quotations from the Fathers in support of a certain theological view. Photius in the Greek Church and Abelard in the Latin Church turned such collections of apt quotations from an approved ancient past into a kind of textbook for theological instruction. Abelard's *Sic et Non* is of that sort, recording questions posed and answered by some of the recognized spokesmen for the Church in the affirmative, and by certain others in the negative, creating an interesting dialectical situation with which the alert theological mind will hasten to engage. But this still is not historical theology.

Perhaps the first genuinely historical work was Father Paul Sarpi's history of the sessions of the Council of Trent, a perfectly amazing *tour de force* on the part of one who himself was not a participant. Sarpi gives a balanced picture, full of detail but not smothered in it, of the discussion and debates over points of doctrine which went on there session after session. What he wrote is recognizably an historical work in the modern historian's understanding of that term. But even so, putting on one side really partisan sketches of the development of doctrine such as Petavius' Jesuit history of doctrine from the point of view of post-Tridentine Roman Catholic thought, or Thomasius' similar account from the point of view of dogmatic Lutheranism, it seems to me that not until the nineteenth century do we discover clear efforts to do something more deep-going than Father Sarpi undertook. He was giving an impartial account of what happened, but he was not concerned primarily with the sources out of which the discussion had stemmed and the decisions reached.

It is in the post-Hegelian Tübingen school, of which F. C. Baur is the first great shining light, that we begin to see an effort not simply to describe changes which have come about, but to account for them— to give a genetic rather than a merely descriptive account of such changes. That seems to me the proper task of historical theology—to show both the continuity and discontinuity in the church's thinking, to give a basis for understanding why some views have been lastingly approved within the church and why some views have been promptly or at length disapproved.

## DOGMA AS NORMATIVE THEOLOGY

If we understood the task of historical theology in some such fashion as this, we come to the point at which we have to make a decision concerning its proper relation to what we have already termed dogmatic or confessional theology. Originally *dogma* simply meant teaching; it was the Greek equivalent of the Latin *doctrina*, that which is taught to members of the community. But then speedily it came to mean specifically authorized teaching. Fundamental to this development was the second century, when divisions within the community over questions of right and wrong belief became dangerous to the life of the Church. We are assured, for example, that when Marcion came to Rome about 140, he was so persuasive that he carried away about one-half of the membership of that congregation in Rome; and that Valentinus, who was teaching in Rome at about the same time, really hoped that he might become the next bishop of the Roman congregation by reason, Tertullian says, "of his eloquence and his acuteness of intellect." The church had to make up its mind about the essentially anti-historical line that the great Gnostics were proposing and about the place of the Old Testament, which Marcion insisted must be rejected for the sake of a right understanding of the novelty of the Gospel. The church had to make up its mind whether the Marcionite or the Gnostic understanding of Christianity was tolerable at all or whether it was in effect destructive of the very meaning of the Gospel. It was necessary to decide what is *orthodoxa*, right belief, as over against *heterodoxa*, deviant belief.

Deviant belief came to be known fairly early by a term which originally had quite a different signification. *Hairesis* means in the first instance choice, a choice by a human being rather than the sort of decision one can get for example by the lot, that is, by a sign of God's decision. *Hairesis* means a way that I have chosen for myself; it comes to mean those who follow the way which they have chosen for themselves, the school or party which they constitute. In the book of Acts, Pharisees and Sadducees and Christians are called heresies; they are simply component parts of a larger body. But by transfer of meaning, *heresy* comes to mean that which the defenders of the original divine revelation must reject.

Dogma then stands over against heresy. Dogma is not simply doctrine, but is approved and required doctrine. Normally it will be formulated by official representatives of the community, preferably meeting in a regional or at length a universal council, a synod which represents the churches of Palestine, the church of Syria, Asia Minor, and eventually the churches of the entire Constantinian world, a council which decides in cases of bitter controversy what is henceforth to be regarded as approved teaching. Dogma is then a core of communally mandated doctrines surrounded by theology, theology both approved and disapproved, surrounded still further by the totality of religious response and surrounded at length by the entire secular environment of nature and of history, of thoughts, actions and developments both religious and nonreligious. The interrelationships of dogma and theology and of dogma and religion constitute, in effect, the subject matter with which the historian of theology is primarily concerned. It is to the beginnings of Christian theological reflection that we shall next turn.

# CHAPTER 2

# Jesus and the Faith of the Primitive Church[1]

**CC**THE BEGINNING OF THE gospel of Jesus Christ." So Mark starts his account of the man from Nazareth who "came into Galilee" proclaiming the gospel of God, and saying, "The time is fulfilled and the Kingdom of God is at hand; repent and believe in the good news." Less than a year later that man died on a Roman cross, accused of sedition. And the world began to undergo a tidal change that, with many ebbs and flows and shifting currents, is still going on.

Christian doctrine results from the centuries-long effort to grasp and to articulate more clearly, consistently, and truly the meaning of that gospel. The effort began in the astonishment and joy of men and women who felt themselves in the presence of a life that was stronger than death. The master and friend who had been taken from them was now restored in new glory by an act of God. The mystery that had puzzled them in his earthly presence—the aura of power and of limitless compassion for human weakness—was now made plain.

Our earliest clue to the impact Jesus made on his time is Paul's summary of what had been conveyed to him as church tradition: "That Christ died for our sins according to the Scriptures, and that he was buried, and that he rose on the third day according to the Scriptures, and that he appeared to (*ophthe*, was seen by) Cephas, then to the twelve; then he appeared to more than five hundred brethren at once, most of whom are still living, but some are fallen asleep; then he appeared to James, then to all the apostles," to which Paul added: "Last of all, as to one untimely

---

1. The first six paragraphs of this chapter are from a manuscript that Professor Calhoun left uncompleted at his death in 1983. The remainder combines portions of the 1948 LHCD with material from student copies of lectures delivered in later years [ed.].

born, he appeared also to me" (1 Cor 15:3–8). Paul wrote those words perhaps twenty-five years after the crucifixion. The "tradition" he had received from his church (perhaps Damascus) when he became a Christian (about 32 CE) was that of Greek-speaking congregations, but it obviously was based on still earlier Aramaic testimony of eye-witnesses. The primary stress on the saving death and attested resurrection of Jesus now proclaimed Messiah and risen Lord is underscored by all four canonical gospels. The one segment of his brief recorded career which they all cover despite their wide divergence in viewpoint and in detail is the final week that changed their world; and it was this, not surprisingly, which was the center of early Christian preaching and witness as recounted in the book of Acts (2:14–36; 3:12–26; 4:8–12; 8:30–35; 10:34–43; 13:16–41).

For Paul, who may have seen Jesus in Jerusalem and who surely was acquainted with his life and teachings (Gal 1:18–19), it was finally enough to know that Jesus both died and was raised by the will of God as recorded in the scriptures. But for other Christians—in Palestine, in Syria, in Rome—it was different. Memories of his "mighty works" and of his startling words stayed with them or were reported to them as they waited for his coming in glory. These memories were retained through repetition; entered into their preaching and their common life; were collected, interpreted and reinterpreted; were puzzled over, modified, expanded, shortened; written down as episodes and sayings, as narratives, parables, discourses, eventually as a multitude of varying records called "gospels" or "acts," claiming as authors Thomas, Philip, Bartholomew, and Peter—not to mention the writers of the four accounts which were finally canonized.

How much, then, out of this hoard of documents can we learn about Jesus of Nazareth: what he did, what he said, let alone what he believed about God, the world, humankind, himself? In a sense, a century and quarter of efforts to answer that question was brought up short and forced to a fresh start in 1900 by Albert Schweitzer's magisterial survey of earlier research, translated and published in England as *The Quest of the Historical Jesus* (1910). Instead of the tendency prevalent at the turn of the century to find in the gospels the story of a modern-minded religious leader, Schweitzer proposed to describe a "thoroughgoing eschatology" in which, under God, John the Baptizer and Jesus were the moving forces. Both proclaimed that the reign of God, once foretold by prophets and more recently by apocalyptists, was about to break in on a world long bedeviled by powers of evil. John expected the speedy coming of Elijah the forerunner (Mal 3:1—4:5). Jesus named John as that forerunner, and secretly knew himself destined to appear as "the Davidic Son-of-Man Messiah," the great central presence of "the Daniel-Enoch apocalyptic" (*Quest*, 369) ennobled by prophetic moral vision. Jesus "in the knowledge that He is the coming Son of Man lays hold of the wheel of the world to set it moving on that last revolution which is to bring all ordinary history to an end. It refuses to turn, and he throws Himself upon it. Then it does turn and crushes him. Instead of bringing in the eschatological conditions, he has destroyed them. The wheel rolls onward, and the mangled body of the one immeasurably great Man, who was strong enough to think of Himself as the spiritual ruler of mankind and to bend history to his purpose, is hanging upon it still" (*Quest*, 270ff.). That is his triumph and his reign.

That obviously is magnificent drama, backed by critiques of some seventy preceding views and by resourceful, detailed use of all four canonical gospels, with no apparent effort to distinguish between early tradition and later elaboration. The result is a brilliant *tour de force* made unconvincing by logical, exegetical, psychological, and chronological shortcomings. But its main concern is accomplished: nobody now tries to present Jesus as a modern man. He was indeed steeped in the prophetic tradition of his people and shared the eschatological hope that the preaching of John had rekindled.

## JESUS AND HIS TEACHING

To place Jesus in his historical setting, however, changes but does not eliminate the once fashionable distinction between "the religion of Jesus" and "the religion about Jesus." This distinction was commonly emphasized by scholars and liberal theologians who were concerned to affirm and exalt the validity of the former and to disparage in some measure the claims of the latter. It is not necessary to accept that disparagement of the church's theology and dogma; but it is necessary, in the interest of clear understanding of specifically Christian doctrine, to keep the initial difference clear. The kind of thought about God and man that was possible for Jesus' followers after his death and resurrection was different from what his could have been before his death. He thought of himself as pointing toward the new age. His followers thought of themselves as already living in it by reason of his saving power.

When we speak of the religious teaching of Jesus, we must think of one brought up in a Jewish community, steeped in its traditions, its thought and its ways, and conceiving his own role to be proclaiming and reinterpreting what was fundamental in the Jewish religion. We cannot tell exactly when Jesus came to think of himself as having a special mission. Perhaps it began with his hearing John the Baptizer. The oldest synoptic narrative, in the Gospel according to Mark, strongly suggests that this is the case. But the lack of all trustworthy information concerning the details of Jesus' early life makes it impossible to do more than to recognize that his contact with John affected decisively the beginning of his public ministry. Moreover, it is futile to attempt to sketch precisely the course of development in his thought. The gospel narratives and the records of his teaching have so plainly been worked over by the evangelists in the interest of their varying conceptions of his life and mission that we must be content if the major features of his life and thought can be made out.

The simplest way to understand the main current of his teaching, as it seems to me, is to recognize the soundness of that contemporary judgment that saw in him one who continues the prophetic tradition. He was indeed a prophet in the great succession of Hebrew prophets. This was true not only with respect to the manner of his teaching but also with respect to its major content. Not only did he speak "as one having authority, and not as the scholars." Not only did he display the intense urgency and the startling independence of one whose word came straight from God even when it arose directly out of the tradition of his people. He spoke also as one whose primary conceptions of the sovereignty and saviorhood of God and the duty and destiny of man were conceptions in the direct line of familiar prophetic teaching.

### God as Sovereign and Father

The presupposition and center of all his religious thinking is the overarching majesty and saving power of God. Here his conception is, at nearly all points, identical with the conceptions of his great prophetic predecessors. The God of Jesus Christ is the Creator, Sustainer, and Judge of the universe. His power, his knowledge, and his care extend to the humblest creatures and the smallest details of his world, to the sparrows, the roadside flowers, the very hairs of human heads. He rules with calm impartiality, sending his sun and his rain on the evil and on the good. But his patience is not indifference. He is a righteous and terrible Judge as well as Creator and sustainer of his world. He will let the weeds grow up along with the grain until the day of harvest, but then the tares will be separated out and burned. Neither lazy servant nor predatory husbandman can hope to escape his wrath when the day comes. He is one to be feared far more than those who can kill the body and after that have no more that they can do. He is a God terrible in his power and judgment.

At the same time, he is an infinitely merciful Father. If people know how to give good gifts to their children, far more God. As Hosea had affirmed long before, he is ready and eager to forgive when men and women turn to him penitently. We find in the Old Testament and in the rabbinical interpretations repeated references to God as Father; a familiar phrase with which Jewish prayers opened was "Our Father." For Jesus, God is ever ready to seek his children out as a shepherd searches for a lost sheep or a father who goes to meet a recreant son. Whether or not in these last touches Jesus has gone beyond previous teaching as to the fatherly mercy of God, it may perhaps be affirmed at least that in the vividness and persistence of his apprehension of God's fatherly presence, he broadened and deepened the traditional view. The difference was not in a new definition of God. It was in a new embodiment of the significance of the familiar definition of God as Father. The impression conveyed by the gospel accounts is that Jesus lived perpetually with a sense of God's sustaining presence. Everything he said and thought and did was set in that context. It has been noticed that when Jesus on the cross repeats the psalmist's cry, "My God, my God, why hast thou forsaken me?" it is as though he were shocked to find the familiar presence taken away.

The concrete focus of his confidence in God takes shape in his conviction respecting the nearness and moral import of the Kingdom of God. The primary fact about the Kingdom is its existence. God reigns perpetually in the heavens so that his kingdom is now and always present. On the other hand, this abiding reality is about to be made visible on the earth. Already the coming day is casting beams of light into the darkness. Both physical and moral evils are being overpowered with good. The belligerent Lord of Darkness who has long ruled this present age is beginning to feel the force of a power greater than his own. "The time is fulfilled, and the Kingdom of God is at hand: repent ye, and believe in the good news." "Repent, and believe." To Jesus, as to each of the great prophets, the imminence of the Kingdom of God involved searching ethical demands. The specific demand upon man was a demand for filial response to God as Father. Participation in the new order is for those who become as little children. Faithful servants will enter into the joy of their Lord; unfaithful ones will be thrown into utter darkness. The time is short, the need for speedy repentance acute, and the requirements for life in the Kingdom high enough to discourage all but those who are ready to put their full trust in God.

## The Ethics of the Kingdom of God

In his ethical teaching no less than in his affirmation concerning the sovereignty and the fatherhood of God, Jesus is portrayed as displaying the authentic spirit of the great prophets. In the continual controversy between those who regarded God's will as prescribing first of all a formal system of worship and sacrifice, and those who insisted that what God requires first of all is justice and mercy on the part of humankind, Jesus takes sides uncompromisingly. For him, as for the great prophets, the primary stress is laid upon repentance and trust, not upon ritual and sacrificial offering. There seems to be no evidence that he went as far as Amos and Jeremiah had gone in condemning the cultus itself, but as between the imposing ritual and costly sacrifices of the temple in Jerusalem and the simpler assembly for prayer and the study of God's word in synagogues, he is pictured as preferring the synagogue where he seems to have worshipped regularly. The commercialism and ostentation that defaced the worship in the temple, he condemned unsparingly. His insistence on the primacy of moral over ceremonial requirements is unhesitating and unmistakable. He comments with scorn or with amusement upon those who are careful about tithing garden herbs and neglect the weightier matters of the law, of those who make a public show of piety with broad phylacteries and long prayers. Ceremonial washings have nothing to do with the essential cleanliness of a person's heart. Not contact with things taboo but conduct that violates the moral law makes one unclean. Moreover, the whole elaborate system of distinction and restriction, dear to the heart of the scholarly scribes and the Pharisees, hinders people rather than helping them to obey what is fundamental. The requirements of God are simple and uncompromising: utter devotion to God and wholehearted love for one's neighbor.

This emphasis in the texts we have on the moral, as contrasted with the ceremonial, side of Judaism is worked out consistently in a primary stress on inward disposition rather than outward acts. Jesus' teaching at this point can be compared with the teaching of Jeremiah 31 concerning the time when the law of Yahweh is to be written in the inward parts, on the hearts of men. To avoid the overt acts of murder and adultery is not enough. The law is broken if one cherishes resentments and lustful intentions from which such overt acts proceed. What God requires is not that spoken oaths shall be kept, but rather that persons shall maintain the inward integrity that requires no oath to make it good. God takes no joy in lives like cups or platters shining on the outside and sticky inside with crusted remnants, or like whitened graves clean and fair outwardly but full of corruption. Public alms are no substitute for love of one's fellows. Great reputation does not count with God as much as the humble penitence of one who knows himself a sinner and asks only forgiveness. Indeed, harlots and publicans are more likely to find the way than self-satisfied enjoyers of wealth and prestige. For such little ones, having no grounds for self-satisfaction and touched now and again with genuine impulses of love, are more likely to become aware of their infirmity and to acknowledge their utter dependence upon God. Only such as become like little children can hope to be admitted into the new life.

Underlying the whole of Jesus' moral teaching there seems to be a principle more radical even than any that the prophets before him had enunciated. To be sure, it is implied by the essential message of the prophets and by Jesus' singling out of the two great commandments as embodying the whole law. Moreover, the startling sayings about the Sabbath day and the laws of divorce can hardly be understood except in its light. This principle seems to be that the primary requirement of God and the end of the whole law is a personal relationship between human beings and God: a relationship of filial dependence and trust that works itself out into lives of devoted sonship and brotherhood. In as far as the law subserves this fundamental relationship, the law is to be observed, both in its great and in its lesser demands. If at any point the law conflicts with this relationship, then the law itself must give way. "The Sabbath was made for man, not man for the Sabbath." This great saying, in its context of service to a needy but by no means desperate fellowman, is inseparable from the companion saying: "It is lawful to do good on the Sabbath day." One can scarcely avoid the judgment that Jesus is deliberately appealing from the law of the Sabbath, which is admittedly a divine commandment, to a more fundamental divine imperative. The same judgment applies to the sayings about grounds for divorce, especially in the more uncompromising form reported in the Gospel according to Mark. If Jesus is here correctly reported, he seems to be saying not that a more stringent or a more liberal set of requirements for divorcing a woman represents more correctly the will of God. He is saying rather that the will of God demands a personal relationship between husband and wife of such a sort that the question of divorce simply does not arise. Any provision society may make for the dissolution of marriage must be regarded as a compromise made necessary by human imperfection, not as the embodiment of God's perfect will.

To put the matter in another way, it may be said that the authority of the whole law and the prophetic teaching derives from the fundamental commandments of devotion to God and of concern for one's neighbor. The authority of these primary demands is overriding. Whatever conduct subserves the maintenance of these relationships of filial and neighborly love is lawful. Whatever damages or impedes these relationships arises from human fault, not from divine decree.

This is an ethic of uncompromising demand for perfection. The Sermon on the Mount, with its staggering sequence of calls for thoroughgoing integrity and unlimited generosity, summed up in the principle of human imitation of God, makes this demand for perfection explicit. The injunctions, "Be ye perfect," or, "Be ye merciful as your Father in heaven is merciful," are the logical culmination of Jesus' entire ethical teaching.

Since all of this is inseparably bound up with his vivid sense of the sovereign presence of God and the impending end of the present age, it clearly is necessary to ask how this theological context affects the content and meaning of the gospel ethic. Schweitzer's answer to this is widely known. To him, it seems clear that the ethic is essentially determined by the expectation of a speedy end of the age. It is, in fact, an "interim ethic" applicable only to the brief interval until the visible coming of the Kingdom of God. Its perfectionist rigor is quite inappropriate to the ordinary relationships of human beings in history, but entirely suited to the tense and short time of waiting for the end. Martin Dibelius and other influential scholars hold a somewhat different view. They regard the Sermon on the Mount in particular as defining the kind of life that is to be lived when the Kingdom has come. By contrast with the prosaic moralism attributed to John the Baptizer, we have in the Sermon on the Mount an ethic of exalted vision whose proper setting is the transformed society of the coming age.

This latter view seems to me the more persuasive, but I think that its implications call for a little further analysis. Perhaps one may say that an ethic which sets forth the requirements for life in the Kingdom of God is an ethic that sets forth uncompromisingly a vision of fundamental divine imperatives. Such imperatives are valid not only in a new age but in every age. The fact that men and women cannot perfectly fulfill these requirements does not mean that they are at any time free from the obligation to be guided by them and to test their lives by them. All history and all human society stand under the judgment in the light of that perfect order that will be more fully manifested in the new age. The divine sovereignty that is eternally real in the heavens, and that is at any moment to be manifested on earth, broods in its perfection over the whole imperfect life of man. The ultimate standards by which human life is judged are set not by what is customary or even by what is possible in history, but by the perfection of God that confronts man at every turn.

The shortness of time remaining, in Jesus' view, before the bursting-in of the divine perfection upon the earthly life of men and nations does not alter, it seems to me, the essential nature of the divine commands. In especial, it is scarcely conceivable that the fact that the time remaining is short can be thought to make easier human obedience to the demands for perfection. If the injunctions to give away one's coat, to go the second mile, to lend without stint, to turn the other cheek, were regarded simply as social rules—specifications for particular overt acts—then one could make a case for the view that such conduct might be feasible and appropriate in a situation in which all responsibility for long-range maintenance of institutional society was abolished. But if these and similar injunctions be taken, as I think they must, as illustrations of the one underlying and overruling principle of wholehearted integrity and love, then however long or however short the time remaining to imperfect human beings, the fulfillment of this underlying demand is in plain fact not possible. The shortness of time remaining seems to me to have quite another sort of significance for Jesus' teaching. It neither determines the content nor affects the feasibility of the primary demand, but it heightens to the point of desperate urgency the mood in which the demand for repentance is made. Once the end has come, it will be too late for repentance. The foolish virgins will be shut outside the door. The wicked husbandmen will be overtaken in the midst of their wickedness. The tares will go into the fire. Now is the time to repent and turn toward God, and the time is short. Not even the Son of God himself can say when the end will come. The one thing clear is that the end is not far off. While time still remains, repentance is still possible. The son who refused to go into the vineyard at his father's bidding may still change his mind and go. Laborers who begin work even at the eleventh hour will receive the same reward as those who have worked all day. But once the door is closed, there is no more hope. To the religious and moral insight of the prophets, Jesus adds the fierce urgency of the apocalyptical teachers.

[This is not the place to explore the much-debated topic of Jesus' self-understanding. What proved decisive for later Christian history is what his disciples came to believe about him after the resurrection appearances. It is to their thought, the thought of the primitive church, that we now turn.][2]

## THE FAITH AND PREACHING OF THE PRIMITIVE CHURCH

Christian theology, properly so called, begins after Jesus' death. It begins, moreover, not as a system of thought but as a spontaneous, enthusiastic, and irrepressible proclamation on the part of his followers, after a transformation in their lives so amazing as to be almost inconceivable. If we follow St. Paul's account, and what seems to me the more probable of the two main lines of tradition in the synoptic records, we are told that to Peter and to James, to all twelve of the apostles and to a great company of disciples gathered in one place, Jesus appeared—as he did later to St. Paul himself, with startling force. The word went around among those who had believed in him, "The Lord is risen." Death had not been strong enough to hold him. Indeed, the power with which his once despairing friends now found themselves filled and uplifted was actually greater than any they had experienced while he was alive in the flesh. Far from being

---

2. This bracketed transitional paragraph is an editorial addition replacing the discussion in the 1948 LHCD (I:30–31) of the "Messianic consciousness" of Jesus that Calhoun found unsatisfactory in his later years, but for which no replacement has been found in his own writings or in student notes [ed.].

a prisoner of the grave, he had turned death itself into an instrument for greater life.

## The God Who Has Raised Up Jesus Christ

In this situation, the early Christian community had its beginning. The humble folk who had left Jerusalem in despair now reappeared as preachers of a new gospel. Its primary affirmation is not a new tenet but a familiar one, the declaration of the sovereignty and fatherhood of God that Jesus himself had shared with the prophets and sages of Israel. Yet even this ancient and familiar tenet is set in a new perspective. The God of Abraham, Isaac, and Jacob is now in a special sense the God and Father of Jesus the Messiah, the God who has raised him from the dead and publicly vindicated him: "That which I have received from the beginning I have transmitted to you, that Christ died for our sins according to the Scriptures, that he was buried, and that the third day he was raised according to the Scriptures, and that he appeared first to Peter, then to the twelve, then to more than five hundred and finally as to one born out of due time also to me" (1 Cor 15:3–8, abbreviated and paraphrased). In Christian preaching, traditional Hebrew monotheism has all its accustomed elevation and force, and in addition a new immediacy of contact with the contemporary scene. Its indispensable core was that God had acted in a way comparable to the way he had acted through the centuries, but now decisively and in a new manner. He had acted in one who has a different role, a different status, from all those who have come before. To call this a herald's announcement is to use the most appropriate sort of description; it is *kerygma* which can be expanded and which can become eventually the core of a lengthy and elaborate confession of faith, but for the moment it is so brief that it can be written on a small scrap of papyrus.

## Jesus as Messiah, Lord, and Son of God

The second major affirmation of early Christian preaching, which distinguished it crucially from its neighbors, was a gradually developing doctrine of the nature of Jesus called Messiah. Not only for the little Galilean band that had accompanied Jesus to Jerusalem and suffered disappointment there, but for all first-generation Christians, the most grievous problem for Christian faith was the death on the cross. It was bad enough that one who thought of himself as the Messiah and who was being presented by his followers in that role should have been forced to suffer and die at the hands of men. But it was worse that his death had been the most shameful and humiliating known to the ancient world. Not only was public crucifixion reserved by the Romans for those whom they regarded as the most depraved criminals, but of all the forms of capital punishment, it had the unhappy distinction of doing the greatest violence to human dignity. The naked victim hung up to die by slow exhaustion, with no concealment for the agonizing demands of his tortured body and no protection from the stares and jeers of bystanders, was made, as far as human power could make him, a grotesque and obscene figure. This was the death to which Jesus had been subjected. How then could his followers proclaim him with any conviction to be the Anointed One of God?

It was the faith of the early church that God himself had supplied the answer. By raising Jesus from the dead, permitting him to rejoin his disciples on earth, and receiving him then into the heavens, God had put the unmistakable stamp of divine approval upon the life and message of one who was thus plainly shown to be indeed his anointed. In the simple affirmation that Jesus was Messiah (*Christos,* anointed one), the early preachers offered their first and most obvious appraisal of the life of their master.

To speak of him as Christ or Messiah, however, was to use a title significant primarily for Jewish hearers. In preaching to Gentiles another sort of interpretative concept was required. To such hearers it was more meaningful to declare that Jesus was *Kyrios,* Lord. If we may judge from its occurrence in the second chapter of Paul's letter to the Philippians, commonly regarded as an ancient liturgical passage, the confession, "Jesus Christ is Lord," may have served very early as a kind of touchstone of Christian affirmation. To Gentile listeners accustomed to the language and beliefs of the mystery religions, such an affirmation would most naturally mean that Jesus is, for members of the Christian cult, the Lord of life in whom his followers find assurance against the power of death. In this guise, many cult deities had been presented to the peoples of the Mediterranean world, and had been accepted without any serious misgivings about their multiplicity. But when Christian preachers used the title *Kyrios,* they were using a term that in Jewish tradition had been applied almost always to the one God of all the earth. In the Septuagint and other Greek translations of the Old Testament, *Kyrios* was the Greek equivalent of the Hebrew *Adonai*, a title almost never used for anyone except God himself. There is one notable exception, a passage used again and again in the New Testament and in the writings of the early Christian Fathers to establish the title of Lordship for Jesus Christ. In the first verse of Psalm 110, a Maccabean psalm, we read: "The Lord said unto my Lord, sit thou at my right hand, until I make thine enemies thy footstool." Here it seems plain that the term *Kyrios* was used both for God himself and for his anointed one, and attribution of the passage to the person of Jesus Christ is put by each of the evangelists into the mouth of Jesus himself. It appears again in the speech of Peter in the book of Acts, in Paul's first letter to the Corinthians, and in the letter to the Hebrews, so that although in this single passage, the term *Lord* clearly refers to the Messiah as one who is other than God, the usual significance of the term could scarcely be escaped, and it seems necessary to regard its use as a prime factor in the development of "high Christology."

At the same time, another title for Jesus Christ came very early into use: the Son of God. Like the familiar messianic name, Son of Man, this title *Son of God* could be understood in two quite different ways. *Son of Man* might mean generically any human being, or specifically the celestial messianic figure of the books of Daniel and of Enoch. The phrase *Son of God* likewise might mean generically a faithful Israelite or an angelic being. But in the New Testament it means, first of all and uniquely, Jesus Christ and then Christian believers who through him are enabled to become sons of the Most High. As applied to Jesus, the title left room for quite diverse conceptions. It was held by some early Christians that he became Son of God by adoption, after first living as a man obedient and pleasing to God. The Gospel of Mark, lacking any story of miraculous birth or of preexistent life, appears to retain traces of the view that Jesus became Son of God by divine decree, whether at the time of the transfiguration or at the time of his baptism at the hands of John. In the discourse in the thirteenth chapter of Acts (which the author attributes to Paul), the crucial point seems to be the resurrection. God was fulfilling the promises that had been made to the fathers in raising Jesus from the dead, and as also it is written in the second psalm, "Thou art my Son, this day I have begotten thee." (Here the resurrection is the beginning of his Sonship. It is that which constitutes him Son of God, just as in the early discourses in Acts he is constituted Lord and Christ by his being raised from the dead.) The birth stories of Matthew and Luke, in contrast, place the beginning of his life as Son of God at the very moment of his conception. But the view which became normative in the church made a still more drastic affirmation: that he was Son of God even before the beginning of his earthly life.

One of the earliest versions of this doctrine of preexistence seized upon the concept of Wisdom in the book of Proverbs and in various later Jewish works, affirming bluntly that Jesus Christ was the Wisdom of God, who had been present at the creation of the world and who took part in both the work of creation and the enlightenment of rational creatures. This view was developed with many variations, as Rendel Harris has shown, in the very early books of *Testimonies against the Jews*. These were compilations of passages from the Old Testament that could serve Christian preachers in controversy with Jewish opponents who sought to discredit messianic claims on behalf of Jesus, and the whole gospel which was preached in his name. There is good evidence that such collections of proof-texts or testimonies were in existence before the books of our New Testament were written down. Some of this ancient material is to be found, along with a good deal that is later, in the three books of *Testimonies* edited by Cyprian of Carthage in the third century and now published with his works. Here we find Jesus referred to as the Firstborn, the Wisdom of God, the Word of God, the Hand and the Arm of God, the Stone that should fill the whole earth, the Son of Man, the Son of God. The easy bracketing of Wisdom and Word (*Sophia* and *Logos*) indicates that in this early Christology no single approved terminology had been fixed. And even after the title *Logos*, or Word, had come to be the preferred mode of expression, the Church continued to speak of the preexistent and risen Lord as the Wisdom of God.

Obviously we have raised the question whether these represent successive steps in a kind of crescendo of Christological affirmation. It seems to me very doubtful that is the case. Rather, these various cycles and the modes of thought that go with them in all likelihood grew up side by side, so that some among the early Christians found one, some found another of these titles, or ways of thinking about him more congenial. If the second chapter of Philippians goes back into a pre-Pauline age of the church's preaching, preexistence is pretty plainly implied, and the title *Kyrios* was current from as far back as we can trace any title at all. Similarly, in the testimony chosen to support the church's preaching, we first do not find passages chosen to support the view that he is the Messiah, then passages chosen to support the view that he is Servant, and so on. The passages chosen prove all of these things at once through that transvaluation of the meanings of each of these terms to which we have referred.

The Christology of the earliest preaching, then, is complex, is addressed both to Jewish and Gentile hearers, and is even from a very early time rather frighteningly daring. Despite perplexing genetic relationships, the logical culmination of these Christological affirmations is the statement that Jesus Christ is God. Whether that affirmation was characteristic of the thought of the early Christian communities, I do not know. In early second-century writings, it has become explicit and unmistakable, but I question whether it goes back to the beginning. Rather, it seems likely that the extreme difficulty for Jewish Christians of reconciling monotheism and the affirmation that Jesus Christ is divine would have delayed the appearance of the final Christological assertion. At all events, when the church does make this affirmation, a central theological problem is posed. To Jewish hearers in particular, even to call Jesus *Kyrios* is to risk breaking the first commandment, and of course one of the arguments with which the earliest Jewish Christians had to contend constantly is that they are at this point heretics. In a certain sense, I suppose, distinctive Christian theology begins to take shape around precisely this issue: how can we affirm that God is one and at the same time that Jesus Christ is Lord? Solutions of this problem were not worked out to the satisfaction of the best-trained Christian thinkers until near the end of the fourth century.

## The Gifts of the Spirit and the New Israel

No less distinctive than its new concern with the Christological problem was the concern of the early Christian community to interpret adequately the new age and its own place therein. Whereas Jewish Messianic hope had always looked forward to a future transformation of society, the early Christian believers were now confronted with the problem of interpreting convincingly the actual presence of the new order. What was the evidence that the Messianic age had come, and what were its primary characteristics and demands?

A first main theme in the thought of the early church centered about the outpouring of the Spirit of God. The vivid prediction of the prophet Joel that in the last days the spirit of prophecy would be spread abroad so that young and old, masters and servants alike should prophesy, was thought to have found its fulfillment in the day of Pentecost. For the company of believers gathered in the upper room, the Spirit had indeed descended with power. When in the height of their excitement they looked at one another and saw flickering tongues of fire, and heard strange voices issuing from one another's lips, they were persuaded that the promise had most literally been fulfilled. We need not suppose, with the prosaic narrator of the second chapter of Acts, that the sounds that filled the room were in fact the sounds of unlettered Galileans speaking a dozen different Near Eastern languages. We are to think rather of a devoted company of believers carried away upon a rising tide of emotional exaltation so powerful that it could find no articulate expression in the language of everyday life. Such enthusiasm can find voice only in the half-articulate sounds that lie perhaps at the base of all languages, and in which it may well be that bystanders of a dozen nationalities might, if they were sympathetic, discern syllables vaguely familiar to their ears. It seems pretty clear that the gifts of the Spirit were thought of for the most part in kerygmatic quasi-physical fashion. The safest guide we have to the nature of the "gift of tongues" is the fourteenth chapter of St. Paul's first letter to the Church in Corinth, where this practice was, it seemed to him, too highly prized. "Speaking with tongues" is indeed a gift of the Spirit, as the eighth chapter of Romans further testifies, but it is not the decisive gift nor by any means the most important. St. Paul would have agreed with the reported reply of St. Peter to the cynical onlookers at Pentecost who said, "They are filled with new wine." Such enthusiasm he also had experienced and prized, and he recognized the substantial values of the strange powers which it conferred: not only ecstatic utterance, but flashes of penetrating insight that mark the prophet, and extraordinary control over bodily ailments. The first dozen chapters of the book of Acts are eloquent with respect to the high valuation that the simple folk of the early Christian communities placed upon these "gifts" or "powers." To minds less discriminating than St. Paul's, they were the most convincing evidence that the Spirit of power and prophecy had now come and the new age had in fact dawned.

In this time of transition to the full realization of God's Kingdom on earth, the growing community of believers held a place marked off clearly from the surrounding world. It had become the "new Israel" [a term, to be sure, which is never actually used in the New Testament], the true heir to the promises which God had made to Abraham and his descendants long ago. A foretaste of the full glory to come was already granted to those upon whom the Spirit had come. The heightened imagination and insight, the power to speak with more than ordinary force and persuasiveness, the courage to defy ecclesiastical and political authority, the experience of mastery over physical weakness—all these gifts clearly set apart their possessors and the community in which they had membership. It was natural that in such a mood of exaltation and expectancy the unity of the Christian group should have been strongly affirmed in word and action. The holding of goods as a common pool, the special provision for the poor and unfortunate in the community, baptism, above all the elevation of the common meal to a central place in the life of the fellowship were appropriate expressions of the conviction and hope that made them one.

The precise relationship between baptism and the gift of the Spirit is hopelessly vague in the New Testament record as we find it. In the book of Acts, for example, there are passages in which baptism is administered and then the Spirit comes at a later time not closely associated with the rite; and then there are instances in which the Spirit is given before baptism has been performed, as in the case of the household of Cornelius, which Peter found to have been granted the gift of the Spirit and so presumably to be eligible for baptism. The familiar formula for baptism—"in the name of the Father and of the Son and of the Holy Spirit"—is to be found only in the last verses of Matthew. Elsewhere, in the book of Acts, baptism in the name of Jesus or in the name of Christ Jesus was the usual formula. And whether baptism was universally required for membership in the new community—even that is not made plain. At all events, that it was commonly the sign of inclusion in the new fellowship is fairly evident.

As for the common meal, again I do not know what can be said with very much confidence about a uniform practice throughout the little companies of Christian believers who assembled here and there and yonder. Still, it seems clear that in the early church the common meal had two phases closely linked together. On the one hand, Christians came together, rich and poor, bringing food to be spread on a common table and shared as by members of a single family. These common meals were given the picturesque name of *agapai*, "love feasts." They were apparently introduced by a ritual blessing of wine and broken bread after the pattern of the Last Supper, in a formal observance called *eucharistia*, "thanksgiving." We are simply left at a loss to determine from the

New Testament record whether the *agape* was itself the sacramental rite or whether it preceded or followed that rite. Chrysostom in the fourth century was inclined to think that the sharing of food was simply one aspect of the sharing of goods in common: if the rich members of the community brought more food with them than their poorer associates could afford, they were to share.

Besides the stress upon unity in the group that was common to both phases of the communion of food and drink, the Eucharist was explicitly regarded as an expression of gratitude for God's favor already granted and of eager and confident expectation of the glory to come. Christians gathered around the common table felt themselves pilgrims alert and ready for their Lord to come again and lead them into the promised land. There is no warrant for referring the prayer in the *Didache* of the second century at the breaking of bread to the earliest generation of the Christian community, but the spirit voiced in that prayer with extraordinary grace and simplicity may perhaps be thought to have characterized the primitive Eucharist at its best. "We thank Thee, Our Father, for the life and knowledge which Thou madest known to us through Jesus Thy Servant; to Thee be the glory forever. Even as this broken bread was scattered over the hills, and was gathered together and became one, so let Thy Church be gathered together from the ends of the earth into Thy Kingdom."

One of the words which is associated with the last meal exemplifies the Christological thought of the early community—the conception namely that the death of the Lord is a saving death, a sacrificial gift on behalf of others. In Mark 10:45, when Jesus tells his disciples that the one who seeks to be great among them shall be their slave (*doulos*), we find the words "the Son of Man came not to be ministered to, but to minister and to give his life a ransom for many." We never find this particular phrasing in Paul; rather it is characteristic of a more archaic and more Hebraic tradition. Here is a substitutionary concept of a sort which goes back to the familiar theology of sacrifice in the temple cult. Paul, in contrast, invariably speaks of Christ giving his life "on our account," "for our sake," never of paying a ransom or price "instead of us." In any case, such phrases remind us of the early Christian sense of shortcoming and need for forgiveness.

Human frailty no doubt kept expressions of common life from being always at their best, as the story of Ananias and Sapphira and the admonitions of St. Paul to those who disrupted the fellowship of the Lord's Table make evident. Even when the second coming of the Lord was expected at any day or at any hour, the actual church was not simply a communion of saints. Emotional fervor has never been enough to guarantee saintliness. But there can be little doubt that the earliest Christians felt themselves a unified company set apart from the world, standing at the threshold of a tremendous consummation of their best hopes.

## *The Gospel as Law*

At the same time the New Testament supplies ample evidence that the responsible leaders of the early community were alert to the dangers of undisciplined enthusiasm and did what they could to counteract them by steady stress on the moral demands of the Christian life. Thus the Gospel is itself frequently regarded as a new law; it is a code to guide behavior of those who desire to be members of this community of salvation. There is little point in trying to document or elaborate this point: it is very familiar. The letter attributed to James in the New Testament is a classic voicing of this understanding—those who hear the Word, then do nothing about it, cannot expect to be saved, but those who fulfill the requirements are the genuine members of the new community. Similarly, the twenty-fifth chapter of Matthew puts words into Jesus' mouth with respect to the separation of the sheep and the goats: it is those who have acted in love toward their neighbor, not those who have said the right words who are going to be accepted into the Kingdom.

# CHAPTER 3

# Johannine Theology[1]

O UT OF THE MULTIPLICITY of professedly Christian writings that survive from the late first and early second centuries, only some were gathered into what we know as the New Testament. Of these, those which reflect Pauline and Johannine thought are most significant for Christian dogmatic development. St. Paul has perhaps been most influential in the

1. This survey of Johannine thought is the only one of Professor Calhoun's treatments of New Testament theologies that he considered publishable at the time of his death in 1983. While it originated in his lectures, he reworked it during his retirement into a scholarly monograph seemingly unsuited for a volume of originally oral presentations. It was Hans Frei, I believe, who reassured him on this point, and his reasons for wanting the essay in the book were shared by all of us who were helping with the editing that final year. First, the essay illustrates better than any other item in this collection the astonishing memory and scholarship undergirding Calhoun's lectures. What students came to expect from him in question periods and in discussions with him outside of class was the kind of detail found in the following pages, often including extemporaneous and yet exact references to the sources he was citing.

Second, and more important, is the intrinsic worth of this essay. Even now, there appears to be nothing in the Johannine secondary literature that is equally helpful to those who want to study the history of Christian doctrine in the way Calhoun practiced it. He undertook to describe the origins and organization of Johannine concepts in abstraction both from studies of the particular historical settings in which the Johannine literature was composed (such as those of Raymond Brown and J. Louis Martyn) and from translations into contemporary conceptual idioms (of which Bultmann's is probably still the best-known instance), and he did this concisely and thoroughly in almost entire reliance on primary rather than secondary sources (about which, to be sure, he knew a great deal, as questioners soon discovered). Moreover, his version of a history-of-ideas approach does not ignore the literary and practical uses of the concepts he examines. The result, it can be argued, is maximally helpful for understanding Johannine influence on later doctrinal development, i.e., on the intellectual continuities and discontinuities in Christian theological inquiry, particularly in the centuries with which this volume is concerned [ed].

long run, but St. John was crucial for the formation of Trinitarian and Christological doctrine in the first centuries. [If one chooses just one of the New Testament theologies for consideration, as we shall do, his is the most important for understanding the earliest and decisive phase of post-biblical doctrinal history.]

In contrast to the letters of Paul, the Gospel of John is the work of a contemplative thinker: a daring but carefully ordered meditation on the Christian message as disclosure of eternal truth. The book is plainly the work of a subtle and disciplined man of letters, well acquainted alike with Judaism and Hellenism, aglow with his own fervent Christian faith, and intent on persuading those of intelligence and good will to share his vision of the Truth. His language and thought-forms often suggest those of the sober, non-ecstatic "mystical" piety familiar in the Platonic tradition. The ruling temper of his gospel, however, is not intellective contemplation but love, not pure *theoria* alone but *agape* that gives contemplation the substance of power and life.

Among the Jewish writings of the Old Testament and Apocrypha, he has closest affinities with the Wisdom literature. More frequently and fully than Paul, he shares the fascination of Ben Sirach, the Wisdom of Solomon, and Philo of Alexandria with the great principle of creative intelligence and moral order—Wisdom, Logos—that sustains and illumines the world. But like Paul, the Johannine author is centrally concerned not with cosmology, nor even with theoretic convictions about God, but with human salvation through Jesus Christ. At the same time, he indicates, sketchily and suggestively but more explicitly than Paul, a doctrine of creation and the nature of the world.

## GOD AND THE WORLD

Johannine thought about God is dominated throughout the gospel by the novel and venturesome portrayal of the Most High in relation to Jesus Christ, with whom he is said, in many contexts and in diverse ways, to be one. Of this characteristic and crucial insight more will be said in the next section. Here we notice first the grand vista in which John's version of the Gospel is set.

"In the beginning" (*en arche*)—the very words that opened the creation story in Genesis are the first words of this Gospel. Mark had begun with the preaching of John, Matthew and Luke with traditions about Jesus' birth. John begins with God before the world was made, and "the Word" that was with him "in the beginning." The Word, too, "was God (*Theos*). He was in the beginning with God (*pros ton Theon*—literally, "turned toward God"); and all things came to be through him, and without him came to be not one thing that has come to be" (John 1:1c–3).

The phrase is careful and precise. On the one hand, something like Philo's distinction between the Supreme God (*ho Theos*) and the Logos that is divine (*Theos*) but not supreme[2] may be intended in verses 1–2 (although in verse 18, and often in Philo's writings, God is called merely *Theos*). At any rate, it is clear that "the Father" and he who is "in the bosom (*eis ton kolpon*—again "turned") of the Father" (v. 18) are not simply identical. On the other hand, there is no suggestion that the Word was "created" or "came to be." On the contrary, "not one thing" (*oude hen*) that has come to be" has its being otherwise than through the Word. The author seems intent on ruling out, by his emphatic double assertion (v. 3), the inference easily drawn from the oft-quoted *testimonium* in Prov 8:22 (LXX), where Wisdom is made to say: "The Lord created me (*ektisen me*) the beginning (*archen*) of his ways, unto his works," or from the similar passage in Sirach 24:9: "He created me from the beginning, before the world." The Word in the Johannine prologue is Creator, not creature. He can properly be spoken of as "begotten" (cf. Prov 8:24, 25), as like "an only child from a father" (*monegenous para patros*—v. 14), as *monogenes Theos* (v. 18, best reading). But creature he is not.

It had long been familiar doctrine that the work of creation was achieved and the world governed by God's commands, by his Word, by the wisdom that belongs to him alone (Ps 104:24; cf. Jer 10:12). The distinctive form of the doctrine in the Wisdom literature—especially Proverbs, Sirach, Ecclesiasticus, and Wisdom of Solomon—personifies Wisdom, at first perhaps merely as a vivid literary device (e.g., Prov 1:20ff; 4:1–9; 8:1–21; 9:1–6) But even in the earliest, least Hellenized of these writings, metaphor slips over into metaphysics, and Wisdom appears as God's companion at the creation of the world—as builder (or as child) closely joined to him (more clearly in the Hebrew than in the Greek text), yet distinguishable in activity, and apparently in being. (Prov 8:22–31). This distinctness is more strongly marked in Sirach, in which Wisdom is, in our present text, expressly identified with the Torah as God's first creation

2. Philo, *Somn.* 1, 229–30.

(Sir 24:1–39, especially vv. 9 and 23; and cf. v. 20 with Ps 19:10; Ps 119:103; Sir 1:1–10, 14–20, 26–28; etc.). Here also much of the language suggests a cosmic ordering power more than a detailed legal system. The Torah (literally, "instruction") as Wisdom is itself an agent of divine world government. Finally, in the Wisdom of Solomon, the most strongly Hellenistic of the three, Wisdom emerges fully as both a power "who effects all things" (Wis 8:5) and a conscious subject who "knows" and "understands" (Wis 8:8; 9:9–11; 7:21—8:8). At the same time, her closeness to God is eloquently maintained: "For she is a breath of the power of God, and a pure emanation of the glory of the Almighty; . . . For she is a reflection (*apaugasma*) of eternal light, a spotless mirror of the active being (*energeias*) of God, and an image of his goodness" (Wis 7:25–6).

The Spirit in her is "alone in kind (*monogenes*)," "all-powerful," all-pervading. She is superior to the sunlight, for that is overtaken by the night, whereas "evil does not overpower wisdom" (Wis 7:22, 29–30). She is a patient savior of the righteous in all times (Wis 10:1–20): "In every generation she passes into pious souls and makes them friends of God and prophets" (Wis 7:27, 14; cf. 8:8; Sir 24:23).

Here plainly we are surrounded by words and ideas that fill the Johannine prologue. "In him was life, and the life was the light of men. The light shines in the darkness, and the darkness has not overcome it. . . . He was the true light (*to phos to alethinon*—not mere visible sunlight) that enlightens every man who comes into the world" (John 1:4–5, 9). It is tempting, then, to see in these statements about the Logos a simple reassertion of what had been said generations earlier about Wisdom. This is in fact very near the truth. It is all the more plausible since the older writers themselves had sometimes made similar statements about the Word of God (e.g., Ps 33:6; cf. 104:24, 119:89ff., Sir 34:17; 43:26; cf. Wis 18:15–16), at times seem to identify Wisdom and Word (e.g., Sir 24:3; Wis 9:1–2), and often connect one or both with Spirit—a major theme in the Gospel (cf. Wis 1:6–7; 7:7, 22; 9:17).

Scarcely less tempting is the precedent in Philo's elaborate doctrine of the Logos as second God (*Alleg. Interp.* 2, 86), in which both Wisdom and Spirit are intricately involved. We have already noticed the precise verbal parallel in John 1:1 with Philo's distinction: *ho Theos* as the Supreme Being (*ho on, ho ontos on*), or more often the neuter impersonal *to on, to ontos on*) and *Theos* as a characterization of the Logos. Moreover, the functions ascribed by Philo to the Logos, bearer of life and light, as agent in creation, world government, and revelation and instruction to human beings, have close parallels in John, as in the earlier Wisdom books. But with all similarities there is a fundamental difference between Philonic and Johannine thought about God and the Logos. Philo's thought continually shows an uneasy effort to think of the Highest as at once personal Ruler to be trusted and loved, and impersonal Absolute (*to on*), pure Being, whose existence (*hoti estin, hyparxis*) indeed can be known by a few but whose character (*hoti hoios estin*) cannot be known at all, except negatively and in ecstasy.[3] Philo's Logos, likewise, is impersonal[4] and "not unoriginate like *ho Theos*."[5] John never suggests this sort of impersonal absoluteness in God, nor a comparable impersonality of the Logos as ideal world order, archetypal plan, cosmic structure. His affinity is only with that side of Philo's thought that follows more closely the concrete, personal traditions of biblical and Wisdom theology.

Indeed, John alone among biblical writers ventures to define concretely and succinctly *what* God is—not merely to affirm *that* he is or what he does. "God is Spirit" (John 4:24), not bound by place or by local custom, not visible nor calculable, but living and life-giving, purposeful, and rational (cf. John 4:20–24; 5:26; 6:63; 3:5–8; 15:26; etc.). "God is light" (1 John 1:5). Not only is the Logos "the true light." God himself is light, the very principle of "truth" against all untruth. Above all, "God is Love" (1 John 4:8, 16; cf. vv. 7–19; John 3:16, 35 etc.). In Philo's thought, love is a duty toward God, a duty whose fulfillment is human well-being (*eudaimonia*), and a reciprocal benevolence of God toward those who love him. But for John, it is hardly too much to say that the essential being of God is love, even toward those who do not love him. "We love, because he first loved us." "In this is love, not that we loved God, but that he loved us and sent his Son (1 John 4:19, 10; cf. John 3:16). Here John and Paul are of one mind. God is before all else the merciful Father, and not—even in metaphysical perspectives—an impersonal Principle.

To ask whether this God is triune has as little relevance for John as for Paul. Certainly he speaks freely of the Father, the Word or Son, and the Holy Spirit or Spirit of Truth; and ventures a bit closer than Paul to defining the relations of Word and of Spirit to the Father (John 1:1,18;

3. Cf. Philo, *Deus.* 55, 62.

4. It is God's world-planning thought, like that of a city planner—Philo, *Opif.* 24, cf. 17–20—or the world plan itself (*Opif.* 25)—not a "Counselor" (*Opif.* 23; cf. 42:21).

5. Philo, *Her.* 206.

15:26; cf. 5:19–36; 10:30; 14:26). But like Paul, he leaves it an open question whether Logos and Holy Spirit may not be different names for the same divine being, performing like functions indifferent contexts (e.g., John 5:22, 26–27; 6:63; 16:7–11; 8:31; 12:49; 16:13; 20:22–23; 1 John 2:1; 5:7, etc.). His thought can readily be adapted for Trinitarian belief; whether by conscious intent or by sound instinct, he avoids the trouble-making forms of thought that plague the Church during the succeeding centuries. For this trailbreaker, the technical dogmatic problems of a later time simply have not arisen.

## The Human Plight

As in much ancient thought, the good God confronts a major antagonist, "the Devil," the "ruler (*archon*) of this world," "the father of lies," "the evil one" (John 8:44; 12:31; 13:27; 14:30; 16:7–11: 17:15; 1 John 3:8, 10, 12; 5:18, 19). Nothing is said of his origin, but he is subject to God's power (John 14:30; 10:29) and presumably a creature, albeit a perverted one (cf. Wis 1:12–14; 2:24). At any rate, he is the chief purveyor of falsehood, a deceiver and destroyer who flourishes in darkness, the antithesis of truth and light.

In Johannine language, "truth" (*aletheia*) and "true" (*alethinos*) mean more than correctness of judgment. They mean genuineness, reality, what is basic and abiding, as against appearance and falsehood. "Light" is truth, veridical being, knowledge, life, love; "darkness" is deceptive appearance, ignorance, destructive error, death, hatred. Both are in the created world, and human beings align themselves with one or the other. The Light is present to everyone (John 1:9), but some believe in him while many—perhaps most—do not.

In the Wisdom literature, there was earnest discussion concerning one's freedom to choose. Sirach declared emphatically that every person has the choice of life or death, and everyone who knows the law can keep it (Sir 15:11–20). The Wisdom of Solomon at first implies similar freedom of choice (Wis 1:12–16), but later describes the Canaanites as innately bad, "an accursed stock who would never change from the beginning" (Wis 12:10–11), and describes with some hesitation the Egyptians and similar idolaters who, though "foolish by nature," are rightly blamed for misusing noble powers (Wis 13:1–9). The Qumran *Manual of Discipline* and *War Scroll* are a good deal less subtle. For them, people simply are "sons of light" or "sons of darkness," or "the lot of God" or "the lot of Belial" (1QS 1; 1QM 1, 4, 12, 14).[6] They are beset in this life by two contrary created powers, "the spirits of truth and of error," "of light and of darkness," operating "in equal measure until the last period," which God has ordained "for the ruin of error" (1QS 2; cf. 1 John 4:6). Nothing is said in the texts at hand concerning a person's ultimate freedom to choose. In point of fact one shows by one's conduct—as faithful covenanter, as backslider, or as open enemy—to which camp one belongs. In God's mysterious providence, even "the sons of righteousness" in this life are plagued by "the angel of darkness" and "the spirits of his lot," but at the end, God will purify his own, and grant them "knowledge" and wisdom. "For God has chosen them for an eternal covenant, and theirs is all the glory of man."(*Gos. Truth*; 1QS 2).

John uses language that superficially is like that of the Qumran texts. For him, too, human beings are "children of God" or "children of the Devil (1 John 3:10; John 8:38–47; cf. 1 John 3:12). But for him the division is based neither on race nor on legal righteousness. The criterion is acceptance or rejection of the Light—"believing" or not believing, recognizing or not recognizing, loving or hating, the truth (John 1:9–13—*before* the Incarnation; 3:16–21; 12:44–50; and *passim*). It is a nice question whether decision determines one's status, or vice versa. Sometimes it seems clearly implied that "believing" is the basis for becoming "children of God" (John 1:12; cf. 9:38–41; 12:36); sometimes the reverse may be implied (John 6:44, 65). In any event, the vivid language used (as in 8:41–47) could easily be taken as warrant for the kind of genetic determinism that appeared later among the Valentinian Gnostics, who preferred John's gospel to the synoptic gospels.

Those who reject the Light suffer entanglement in "the world" of seductive but deceptive appearance, (e.g., John 4:13; 5:26–33; 7:24; 11:9–10; 15:18–19), and enslavement to sin (John 8:31–8, 13:30; 15:22–5) and to "the father of lies" (John 8:44), whose "lusts" rule the wills of his vassals. They "walk in darkness"; and "he who walks in the darkness does not know where he goes" (John 8:12; 12:35; 13:30—cf. Judas; cf. Psalm 82.5; 1 John 1:5; 2:9–11). Their plight can most simply be characterized as alienation from truth (i.e. reality): disorientation, ignorance, "lawless-

6. Calhoun seems to have used Millar Burrows, *The Dead Sea Scrolls* (New York: Viking, 1955) as his basic text for Qumran material [ed.].

ness," falsity. The only cure is to "be born anew" (*anothen*), which means also to "be born from above" (John 3:3, 7), to be born "of the Spirit" that no man controls (3:6, 8), which again is to be "born of God" (1:13). God must act if man is to be saved.

## GOD'S SAVING ACT

The decisive and irreducible divergence in thought between John and his closest non-Christian predecessors—the Wisdom writers, Philo, the Alexandrian Platonists who produced the perhaps somewhat later Hermetic writings—is uncompromisingly affirmed in the Gospel prologue and maintained as the basic theme of all that follows. "And the Word became flesh (*kai ho logos sarx egeneto*) and dwelt for a time (*eskenosen*—"tented") among us, full of grace and of truth. . . . For out of his fullness (*ek tou pleromatos autou*) we all have received, grace upon grace; for the Law was given through Moses, grace and truth came through Jesus Christ" (John 1:14, 16–17). Except in the letter to the Hebrews, this bluntly stated, daring theme and its Johannine development have no real parallel in either Jewish or Hellenistic writings before John. The Wisdom of God as dwelling with the righteous and making them "friends of God and prophets"; the Philonic Logos in which rational and righteous men can participate; the Hermetic Word and Reason (*Nous*) from which man as rational being derives, and with which by suitable discipline he may be united—none of these is ever said to "become flesh," to assume human status as a creature on earth.

The Synoptic Gospels, of course, despite one or two echoes of the Wisdom motif (Matt 11:27 = Luke 10:22; Matt 3:24–26 = Luke 11:49; Matt 23:37–39 = Luke 13:34–35), have no such doctrine of the incarnation. Neither does Paul. Whatever the origin of the Christological passage in Phil 2:5–11, it gives no hint that "Christ Jesus" is the incarnation of creative, cosmic Reason, Wisdom, Word, or that the details of his earthly life are an essential disclosure rather than a temporary veiling of divine reality. The author of Colossians, whether Paul or an early Paulinist, comes measurably closer to John's perspective, and the powerful Letter to the Hebrews comes much closer. But when all this is said, it remains true that John's most central insight is not shared: the detailed reinterpretation of the Logos that is made possible and mandatory by the earthly life of Jesus, son of Joseph. The author of Hebrews, though plainly holding an incarnation doctrine closely akin to John's, is so preoccupied with Jesus' role as high priest and the supplanting of the old covenant by the new, that Jesus as witness to the Truth as Lord on earth is scarcely noticed (cf. Heb 2:3—4:9; 8:1). Once again his death, resurrection, and session in heaven focus and almost fill the whole scene. Prophet and king are virtually absorbed into the priest who, like Melchizedek, towers over Moses, Aaron, and Abraham.

But for John it is the whole life and ministry, as well as the death and resurrection of the Logos *in the flesh* that composes the substance of the Gospel and becomes an insistent theme in the letters (1 John 2:22–23; 4:2–3; 5:6; 2 John 7). To understand the towering significance of "Jesus of Nazareth, the son of Joseph," one must recognize in him, with the insight of enlightened belief, the very Logos who was in the beginning, through whom the world was made. But conversely, it is just as true that to understand the essential nature of that Logos, it is necessary to watch and listen as a believer, while he acts and speaks, lives from month to month and dies, suffers and conquers, in first-century Palestine. This reciprocal unifying of divine and human in Jesus of Nazareth and what it means for mankind is once more the basic theme of the Gospel. Every episode, conversation, and discourse must be seen in this double perspective, or it is not clearly and fully seen.

### 1) Jesus as Messiah, Son of Man, Son of God

In working out his Christology, John uses of course both terms and ideas that were current among his predecessors. The most obvious claim for Jesus, against Jewish refusal, is Messiahship. He is "the one of whom Moses in the Law and also the prophets wrote" (John 1:45). It was around this title that much of the reported popular debate and official hostility centered (John 4:29; 7:25–52; 9:22, 24–34; 10:22–24; 12:13–19; 18:33—19:22). Moreover, unlike the Synoptists, John represents Jesus as affirming that he is in fact the Messiah (John 4:26; 5:46; 10:24–25). At the same time, the traditional expectations that the Messiah would come of David's stock from Bethlehem (7:40–42; cf. 1:4b), or else mysteriously from some unknown place (7:27), are brushed aside. Finally, the traditional concept of the Messiah as temporal ruler is explicitly rejected, and kingship redefined (18:33–38), in line with the author's distinction between "this world" and "the truth."

A second title used often, especially in the first twelve chapters before the Passion story, is "Son of man" (John 1:51; 3:13, 31–35; 5:27; 6:27, 53, 62; 8:23, 28; 9:35; 12:34; 13:31). At first sight, this looks like the familiar figure—human victim or apocalyptic judge—of the Synoptic accounts. But the phrase from John's pen, though it connotes both victim and judge, ascribes both these roles to one who differs radically from any figure in either Mark or Q. Unlike the apocalyptic Assessor, John's "Son of man" is already present and judging now, though his primary task is not to condemn but to save; and to that end he himself must "be lifted up" in suffering (John 3:17–21; 5:19–30; 8:15–16, 23–29; 12:31–36, 47). On the other hand, unlike Mark's suffering Son of man, he is expressly described as one "from above," "he who descended from heaven" (John 8:23; 3:13; cf. 6:33–38, 41, 62).

The Johannine "Son of man" is at the same time uniquely "the Son of God" (*ho huios tou Theou*), as John the Baptizer testifies at the start (John 1:34). His uniqueness has been reaffirmed in the prologue and is taken for granted throughout the Gospel. To call him "only son" (*monogenes huios*—John 1:14; cf.1:18; 3:16, 18) is to declare that he is "alone in kind," *sui generis*—a term sometimes applied in secular literature to an only child, and with especial significance to Wisdom as the matchless image and radiance of God (Wis 7:22, 26). Again, for John the order of insight is not from a general principle to a recognizable instance, but from the concrete life of Jesus to the inward meaning of Sonship. At the same time, it is this meaning that illuminates the other titles, Messiah and Son of man, with which "Son of God" is often joined or used alternatively (e.g., John 1:49–51; 5:25–27; 11:27; cf. 8:28–29; 12:34–36), while "the Son" implies always "of God" (e.g., John 3:35–36; 5:19–26; 6:40; 8:36).

Sonship means obedience, dependence, mutual understanding, shared power, reciprocal indwelling in love: in a word, filial piety undergirded by paternal vindication and support. Jesus never wearies of declaring his dependence on the Father who has "sent" him to save "the world," whenever he can win some to "believe" in him as witness and so in the Father whose works he does (John 4:34; 5:23–24, 30, 36–38; 6:38–40, 44–47, 57; 7:16–18, 28–29; 8:18, 26, 28–29, 42; 9:4; 10:36–38; 11:42; and so repeatedly to the end, 20:21). For the evangelist, this is a kind of motto for the whole Gospel (3:16–17, 34–36). For Jesus, it involves a perpetual denial of independence or variance from the Father: ". . . the Son can do nothing by himself, but only what he sees the Father doing; for whatever he does, the Son does likewise" (5:19). His power and authority are all from the Father (5:17, 20–30, 36; 6:32–40, 45, 57, 65; 7: 16–18; 8:54; 9:3–4; 11:41–42; epitomized in 12:44–50 and 14:28). He "knows" the Father, as "the world" does not, and the Father knows him, bears witness to him by sharing with him divine power and authority, and "glorifies" him as his own Name (John 5:19–38; 6:46; 7:28; 8:17–19, 38, 54–55; 10:15; 11:41–42; 12:27–30; 13:31–32; 14:6–7; 16:3; 17:1–15, 25).

It is worth notice that the evangelist goes out of his way to affirm that in knowledge and power the Son is more than a prophet. John the Baptizer too was "sent," and God gave him special knowledge concerning the One who was to be made known (John 1:6, 30–34; 3:27–28; cf. 5:33–36; 10:41). But the evangelist's comments and the speeches ascribed to the Baptist declare expressly (as the Synoptists, even Matthew, did not) that Jesus—not some apocalyptic Winnower (Matt 3:11–12; Luke 3:16–17)—is the "mightier." He is one who "baptizes with the Holy Spirit" and who is in fact "the Son of God" (1:6–8, 15, 29–34).

Most basic and crucial of the marks of sonship is mutual love between Son and Father. It would be hard to exaggerate the vital priority that John ascribes to this motif in working out his Christology. In a sense, this is the key to the whole Johannine theology, and the point of closest kinship to Paul and to the Synoptic portrait of Jesus. John goes further than either in developing the substantive significance of this motif, but in his choice of a theological center he is at one with both.

The development of this motif swells to a great climax in the five chapters recounting the scene of the Last Supper, with Jesus' concluding words before going to the cross (John 13–17). Here the theme is varied to bring the disciples fully into the circle for the first time, and to spell out in subtle reiteration the ultimate meaning of love between Father and Son, and between God and man. The groundwork had been laid in the earlier chapters. If God's love for the world has led him to send his Son (3:16–17), his love for the Son illuminates their sharing of power and knowledge (John 3:35; 5:20ff; 10:17). On his part, Jesus says: "My food is to do the will of him who sent me, and to carry out his work: (4:34; cf. 5:17). For the rest, he proves his love for God in action rather than talking about it, until at last he spells out his guiding principle during the final evening with his friends. Then, face to face with death and the gloating "ruler of this world," he says of the Evil One: "On me he has no hold at all;

but in order that the world may know that I love the Father, as the Father has bidden me so I do" (14:30–31).

The theme of devoted love (*agape*) as unfolded in the farewell scene, moreover, helps make clear the startling words about Son and Father in earlier chapters that had enraged "the Jews" and left Jesus' close companions baffled. This is true all the more since the disciples are now woven into the powerful counterpoint, and it is made evident that *agape* is used with a meaning directly applicable to human experience, not in some esoteric and unnatural sense. Jesus in this gospel had never said, "I am God," any more than he said, "I am Man." But in brief glimpses he had unveiled an understanding of the oneness of Father and Son that could scandalize Jewish orthodoxy and that differed radically from Hellenistic mysticism. "You know neither me nor my Father; if you knew me, you would know my Father also" (8:19). "I and the Father are one. . . . The Father is in me and I am in the Father" (10:30, 38). "And he who sees me sees him who sent me" (12:45). The first impression given by these sayings may be Greek, but their root is in Hebrew piety, given now a fresh and daring turn. In prophetic usage, the person who "knows" God is one who seeks faithfully to do his will. At the same time, it was the familiar doctrine that "like is known by like," so that human reason can know the true world of eternal Forms and the divine Principles that undergird it because mind is akin to Mind, and can become one with it. For John the key to both knowledge and union is love—not primarily vision (*theoria*, onlooking) but consonance of will and deed. To the Jews' charge of blasphemy, "Because you, being a man, make yourself God" (10:33), Jesus replies: "If I am not doing the works of my Father, then do not believe me; but if I do them, then even if you do not believe me, believe the works, that you may know and understand that the Father is in me and I in the Father" (vv. 37–38).

Love is active devotion—God's devotion to "the world" and to the Son, the Son's devotion to the Father and so to "the world"—and in this living reality Father and Son are one. Further, as the farewell discourse makes clear, this reality is one in which all who love the Son and Father and one another can be one (John 14:12, 21, 23; 15:9–10; 17:11, 20–26). It would be rash to attempt here a detailed analysis of the metaphysical issues involved in such a view, and still more to conjecture how many of these issues John had consciously in mind. Three comments may be in place. The first has already been hinted; John's doctrine of love as the living marrow of unity, whether in God, among human beings, or between human beings and God, combines Hebraic and Hellenistic insights in a new way. The concrete, dynamic, poignantly moral and personal understanding of love is Hebraic. The concept and vocabulary of union (*henosis*), participation (*methexis*), presence (*parousia*), inherence (*enuparchein*), immanence or permanent in dwelling (*emmenein*), had been most carefully elaborated in the Greek schools, though the radical experience of solidarity in a kindred group and the constitutive force of a binding covenant were familiar in Hebrew life from ancient times. All these traditional factors are brought to a fresh and vital focus when John declares that love is the bond, perhaps the actual reality, of such union as God and humans can realize without loss of concrete, diverse being.

Second, it is noteworthy that John never makes Jesus say: "The Father and I are the same" (*autos*) or "a unit" (*monas*). Almost always his words are some variant on the form: "The Father is in me and I am in the Father" (John 10:38; 14:11–20; 17:21). The single dictum, "I and the Father are one" (*henesmen*)—verb plural, not singular) in 10:30 is immediately interpreted by the words of 10:37–38: "in me . . . in the Father." The center and determinant is love. "God is love, and he who abides in love abides in God, and God abides in him" (1 John 4:16).

Third, it is vital to notice that love is here neither subjective feeling nor abstract relationship. It is concrete will in act—the very stuff of personal existence. It is "to do the will" of the Father, "to carry out his work." (John 4:34; 5:19–20; 10:37–38). It is to "keep the commandments" of the beloved One (John 14:15, 21, 23, 31; 15:10; 1 John 2:3–6; 5:2–3; cf. 2 John 6). It is to lay down one's life if need be (John 10:11, 15, 17–18; 4:31; 5:13). To say, "God is love," is not to say that God is a warm glow of affection, or a kind of togetherness. It is to say: God is devoted will in action, the most concrete Being we know. Such is "the active being" (*energeia*) of God, whose "spotless mirror" is Wisdom; the divine "goodness" of which Wisdom is the true image (Wis 7:26). But this, says John, is love, in whose life and light both the Father and the Son, God and Man, can be one in concrete reality.

## 2) Jesus as Savior, Word, and God

Thus far we have been examining roles that John has Jesus affirm as his own: Messiah, Son of man, Son of God. At least three more are ascribed to him by others: the evangelist or participants in the story. It is thus that he is called Savior, Word, and God.

Like the Synoptists and Paul, John of course regards Jesus as one who works salvation for those who "believe in" him. This is made plain from the start, when John the Baptizer first sees Jesus and says at once: "Behold the Lamb of God, who bears (*airon*) the sin of the world" (1:29, 36). The same point is made in the various passages that say the Son of man must be "lifted up" (John 3:14; 8:28; 12:32–34; cf. 12:23–36), that he lays down his life for others, (John 10:11, 15; 15:13–14), that his flesh and blood are a medium of eternal life ( John 6:47–63) and so throughout the Gospel, almost always in oblique rather than direct statements. The word "savior" (*soter*) was by no means unknown in the Septuagint, usually applied to God, and rarely (e.g., Judg 3:9; 2 Kgs 13:5) to a military leader, but not to a spiritual redeemer other than the Most High—not even to the Messiah. Neither Matthew nor Mark applies it to Jesus. In Luke-Acts, it is used once of God and thrice of Jesus (Luke 1:47; 2:11; Acts 5:31; 13:23). It is almost wholly absent from the Pauline letters (cf. Eph 5:23; Phil 3:20), increasingly frequent only in the Pastoral Letters and 2 Peter.[7] The fact is that *soter* as a title was more familiar in pagan cults than in Messianic tradition, Jewish or Christian. John expands it into a title of his own: "the Savior of the world" (John 4:42; 1 John 4:14), with nice dramatic tact put first on the lips of Samaritan converts, and ironically hinted, in a warped perspective, by the hostile Caiaphas (John 11:49–50). The words of the high priest are immediately tagged as an unwitting intimation that Jesus' role is like that of the suffering servant, "to gather into one the children of God who are scattered abroad" (John 11:51–52; cf. Isa 49:6–7, 12; 53:6, 10–12; John 10:14–17; 12:31; 17:2–21). Again the evangelist's eye is not on "the nation" only but also on "the world" (cf. 1 John 2:2).

This wide perspective is of course integral with his understanding of Jesus as incarnate Word, the universal Wisdom of God. Little more needs to be said here of the meaning of Logos for John. But one characteristic and startling set of overtones in his usage must be noted. In the Old

---

7. Of God, in 1 Tim 1:1; 2:3; 4:10; Titus 1:3; 2:10; 3:4; of Jesus Christ, in 2 Tim 1:10; Titus 1:4; 2:13; 3:6; and several times in 2 Peter.

Testament, the active presence of God was very often indicated by one or both of two terms so familiar that they became stereotypes in Hebrew thought about God: the Name of God, and his glory. Like the name of any great sovereign, "the Name of Yahweh" (Ps 138:2) was a vehicle of power—if not indeed, by a slight shift of perspective, the divine Power itself. Similarly, the Name of the Son is identified again and again as a vehicle of power (John 1:12; 2:23; 3:18; 14:13–14; 15:16; 16:23–26), while at the same time it is God's Name that he has "made known" (17:6, 26), and God's Word (*logos*) that he has proclaimed (17:14–17). Perhaps the most startling link in this chain, noticed by many critics, is the repeated ascription to Jesus of the word, strange at the end of a clause or sentence: "that I am" (*hoti ego eimi*; 8:24, 28; 13:19—obscured in the translation "I am he"). At the end of a heated controversy with "the Jews" who rely on their descent from Abraham, John has Jesus say: "It is my Father who glorifies me. . . . Truly, truly I say to you, before Abraham was, I am" (*ego eimi*—a signal for stoning (8:58–59), like the other scandalous word: "I and the Father are one" (10:30–31). It is hard to avoid judging that John means to present Jesus as one who shares the Name, I AM (Exod 3:14).

Obviously, this leaves little that could be added to make plain the evangelist's thesis that in Jesus Christ human beings are face to face with God. Still, if any of his readers did need an assertion more succinct than any of these elaborate ones, that too is provided at the beginning in the prologue and at the end after the resurrection. We have noticed the opening declaration: "And the Word was God" (1:1). It is balanced in the last verse of the prologue by a scarcely translatable statement that leads straight into the Gospel narratives: "No one has ever seen God (*Theon*); the divine being alone in kind (*monogenes Theos*)[8] who is in the bosom of the Father, he has interpreted him" (1:18). Only God can interpret (*exegein*) God. Then follows the account of the ministry of Jesus, his voluntary death, and his resurrection, through which the meaning of 1:18 is set forth in careful detail without totally calling Jesus *Theos*—though in various ways his identity as God-man is intimated. Finally at the very end, eight days after the resurrection, Thomas the doubter is constrained to say, "My Lord and my God" (*ho Theos mou*, 20:2—and the Gospel ends [if, as is widely held, John 21 is a later addition].

---

8. This is Calhoun's version. It differs from the RSV but is in basic agreement with the NRSV[ed.].

## 3) *The Way of Salvation*

This distinctive Christology overshadows and supports the Johannine account of the way of salvation for human beings. Their primary fault, once more, is lack of "truth." Too many of them, despite the presence of life-giving Light—always present and now for a time incarnate—are still in the dark of worldliness (John 7:24; 8:15; 1 John 2:15), falsehood (John 8:43–45; 1 John 1:6–10; 2:4), and hate (John 15:18–25; 17:14; 1 John 2:8–11; 3:13–15). All this can be summarized, again, as not knowing God, personally and effectively (John 8:19–20, 55), and so not knowing one's own destiny: "He who walks in the darkness does not know where he goes" (12:35; cf. 11:9–10). Jesus has come as the way out of this deadly fog (14:6), the door to safety (10:7–9), like Jacob's ladder between earth and heaven (1:51).

As witness to the truth—while being himself the truth and the light (John 3:11–13, 31–36; 8:26–28, 38, 40; 12:49–50; 18:37; cf. Luke 10:22)—he is also, as it were in spite of himself, the judge of those whom he has no desire to condemn. John's treatment of this theme is full of paradox and acute perception. On the one hand, God's love for the world is the reason for Jesus' coming. "For God sent the Son into the world, not to condemn the world, but that the world might be saved through him" (3:17). So too the Son does not "judge" (8:15, 12:47) by any legal code. On the other hand, his very coming in love brings inevitable judgment. "And this is the judgment, that the light has come into the world, and men loved darkness rather than light" (3:19; cf. 15:22–24). Hence the Son does "judge" by his very presence and veracity, not arbitrarily or externally but by evoking response that makes for life and death (John 5:19–30; 8:16, 24–26, 42–43).

This "crisis," moreover, is both present and future. "Now is the judgment of this world" (12:31; so 3:18); but also, "the word (*logos*) that I have spoken will be his judge on the last day" (John 12:48; 5:28–29; cf. 16:8–11).

The obverse of condemnation, without which it has no meaning, is the gift of life in freedom from sin, and John conjoins this gift in the closest way with judgment through the Son (John 3:16–21; 5:21–29; 8:16–38; 12:35–36, 46–50). "For as the Father has life in himself" (5:26)—the life that is "the light" (1:4) both judges truly and gives power to "become sons of light," "children of God" (12:36; 1:12).

For John as for Paul, both judgment and the giving of life center in the cross (12:37–36). This is the decisive disclosure of the Son's identity and mission (John 8:28; 12:23; 13:31–32; 14:20), the first irrevocable step in his return from the world to his Father (John 7:33; 13:1; 14:12, 28; 16:10, 17, 28). It is his willing and ultimate demonstration of obedience and devoted love (John 10:11, 17–18; 12:27–28; 13:1; 15:13); he who is "the Lamb of God, bearing the world's sin" (1:29), who in death will "draw all men" to himself (12:32). His flesh and blood thus offered are "the living bread" that gives life "forever" (6:51ff.)—not "flesh" as the world understands it but "the spirit" of devoted love (6:52, 63). Like Paul, John declares consistently that this sacrifice is made for the sake of (*hyper*), not in substitution for (*anti*), those who are saved.[9] And even more consistently than Paul (because his distinctive Christology and his interweaving of time and eternity pervade and underlie every verse of the Gospel), John assumes that in the cross, resurrection and ascension are implicit. He does not even hint that the cross can be a scandal (cf. 1 Cor 1:18–25), because to him it appears always in the light of eternity.

In this same context, too, he views the giving of the Spirit to believers. The definite inspiration of the apostles is for John not at Pentecost, after Jesus had disappeared into heaven (cf. Acts 1:9; 2:1–4), but on the evening of the resurrection day, as a direct act of Jesus in person (John 20:19–22). In a word, for John there is no lapse of time between Jesus' presence on earth and the coming of the Spirit, but rather explicit continuity and implicit coalescence. It could hardly be otherwise with respect to "the Spirit of truth" and the Son who himself is "the truth" (John 16:13–15; 14:6; 8:31–32; cf. 1 John 5:7). The task of the Spirit is in effect to continue the work of the Son as teacher and witness (John 14:26; 15:26; 16:13ff.), as judge (16:8–11), as life-giver (3:5–8; 6:63). The Spirit is "Advocate" (*parakletos*—Paraclete) for believers (John 14:16–17, 26, etc.) and so too is the Son (1 John 2:1). The Spirit "goes forth (*ekporeutai*) from the Father" (15:26); so too does the Son (John 8:42—*exelthon*; so also in 16:27–28, etc.). The Father "will send" the Spirit (14:26; 16); but also the Son "will send" the Spirit (15:26; 16:7) to continue his work and the Father's (16:14–15).

---

9. John 6:51; 10:11,15; 11:50–52; 15:13; 17:19; similarly I John 2:2; 4:10 (*peri*).

ETERNAL LIFE

For those who "believe," the outcome is "eternal life."[10] The familiar ambivalence of present and future, temporal and supra-temporal, is evident
here again. On the one hand, the ubiquitous phrase sometimes refers
explicitly to endless life after bodily death, or to the Jewish hope for resurrection "at the last day." (John 6:39–40, 44, 51, 58; 10:28; 14:2–3; 1 John
3:2; 4:17). But this is not its basic meaning. When Jesus talks with Martha
after Lazarus' death, John affirms once again the supplanting of traditional Judaism by the new Truth.

Jesus said to her, "Your brother will rise again." Martha said to him,
"I know that he will rise again in the resurrection at the last day." Jesus
said to her, "I am the resurrection and the life; he who believes in me (*ho
pisteuouon eis eme*), though he die, yet shall he live, and whoever lives
and believes in me shall never die. Do you believe this?" (11:23–26; cf.
5:39–40).

For John, eternal life is not only the future; it is also present—present
first of all in the Son whom the Father enables "to have life in himself"
(5:26; 1:4; etc.). True life now and life hereafter are one and the same reality in two perspectives.

With characteristic skill, John makes his point at first in tantalizing
figures of speech—new birth (3:3–7), living water (4:10, 14), true bread
(6:27, 32). Yet this figurative language gives way to plain speech concerning "eternal life" as the evangelist dwells with ever increasing particularity
on "believing" and "knowing," and on union with the Son and Father in
devoted love. "And this is eternal life, that they know (*ginoskosein*) thee
the only true God, and Jesus Christ whom thou hast sent" (John 17:3; cf.
Wis 15:3). These words near the climax of the last evening together illuminate much that has been said earlier. We have seen that to know God is
first of all to do his will devotedly, and so to become acquainted with "the
truth." "My teaching" (*didache*) is not mine, but his who sent me; if any
man wills to do his will, he shall know (*gnostetai*) whether the teaching is
from God or whether I speak on my own initiative (*ap' emautou*) alone"
(7:16–17). But once again, "This is the work of God, that you believe in
(*hina pisteutete eis*) him whom he has sent" (6:29). Evidently the key to

10. John 3:15–16, 36; 4:14, 36; 6:40, 47, 54, 68; 10:28; 12: 25, 50; 17:2–3; 1 John 1:2;
2:25; 5:11, 13, 20. Cf. John 5:39; 6:39–40, 51, 58; 10:28; 11:24–25; 12:25; 14:2–3; 1 John
3:2, 4–17.

"believing" and "knowing" is commitment in active devotion. Whether in fact these three terms all mean substantially the same sort of personal response is easier to ask than to answer.

Unlike Paul, for whom *to know* has almost always its ordinary secular meaning, who is suspicious of human knowledge as a dim, fragmentary, and deceptive thing (1 Cor 8:1–2, 4, 7, 11; 13:8–12) whereas true knowledge belongs only to God (Rom 8:26–29; 11:34; 1 Cor 2:11, 16; 8:3; 2 Cor 12:2–3; etc.), John puts knowing and believing side by side. Sometimes for John "to know" (*ginoskein*) is used in its most ordinary sense, to mean intellectual cognizance or certitude—often with "that" (*hoti*) expressed or implied.[11] But far more significant though less frequent are passages that speak of knowing" (*ginoskein, eidenai*) the Father, the Son, the Spirit, the truth, in a way that recalls, with all its dynamic sense of moral commitment, the other phrase, "to believe in" divine reality (John 3:11; 4:22; 7:28–29; 8:19, 31, 55; 10:14–15; 14:7, 17; 15:21; 16:3; 17:3, 25–26).

The full weight of John's use of knowing in this last sense is clearer when it is understood as inseparable from vision and from devoted love, the one more familiar in Hellenistic, the other in Judaistic tradition, and now joined in a new way. "No one has ever seen (*heoraken*) God" (1:18): that is an unmistakeable Hebraic axiom. "He that has seen me has seen (*heoraken*) the Father" (14:9): that is a culmination that is thinkable for a Jew only if he is steeped in Hellenistic piety and thought. For John, the bridge over an otherwise impassable chasm is not mystic ecstasy but incarnation evoking personal commitment. Thus Jesus to Nicodemus: "We speak of what we know (*oidamen*—a verb that itself suggests vision), and testify to that we have seen" (*heorakamen*—3:11). The Son "sees" (*blepe*) the Father at work, whom strict but imperceptive Jews have neither heard nor seen—because they "have not the love of God" within them (5:19, 39, 42). The Son and he alone "has seen (*heoraken*) the Father" (6:46). Thus the way is drawn straight to the last evening's plain declarations: "If you had known (*egnokeite*) me, you would have known (*edeite*—have known by seeing) my Father also; henceforth you know (*ginoskete*) him and have seen (*heorakete*) him. . . . Do you not believe that I am in the Father, and the Father in me?" (14:7, 10). To know (*ginoskein*) this one true God is eternal life (17:3).

---

11. E.g., John 1:25; 1:31; 2:9; 3:8; 4:42, 53; 5:6, 13, 42; 6:6, 61, 69—"we have believed and known." John 7:26–27; 9:20–25; 17:7–8—"know . . . have believed"; etc.

In the discourse on the last evening also are gathered up with conclusive power the recurrent intimations that thus to know God is possible only in love. In love, the immediacy of vision is matched with dynamic power that vision alone would lack. Those who "have not the love of God" in them lack both faith and knowledge: they have no vision of God, they disbelieve John the Baptist and they do not even understand Moses and the Scriptures (5:33–47). The positive side of this insight is developed almost exclusively in the account of the last evening, that begins with Jesus' symbolic act of devotion to the companions whom he "loved . . . to the end" (13:1–20), and concludes with the final words of his parting prayer: "I made known to them thy name, and I will make it known, that the love with which thou hast loved me may be in them, and I in them (17:26). This is the vertebral theme of the whole farewell discourse, developed and varied in a close-knit fabric, too subtly interwoven to be taken apart without damage and too familiar to need quotation. In these chapters the full force of believing and knowing, of seeing and testifying, of truth and life is brought to clear focus in the love that comes from and returns to God.

A final stage of insight, already intimated in the discussion of the relation between love unreservedly is to "be one" with Son and Father (17:20–23). True to his habit, John uses in the Gospel no abstract noun for such union: "faith" (*pistis*), "knowledge" (*gnosis*), and "unity" (*henosis*), are alike foreign to his way of speaking. He prefers to talk, now in vivid kinesthetic figures, now in the plain terms of personal devotion and action. The living vine—deep-rooted in the life and tradition of the Hebrew people, often used by prophets and psalmists as a symbol for Israel, planted by Yahweh himself[12]—and the branches whose life is the life of the vine, the love that unites the Father, Son, and friends (John 15:1–17); the water of life that quenches all thirst (4:10–15); the "true bread from heaven" whose participant "abides in me, and I in him" (6:27–35, 47–58): these are poets' language for a living and permanent union. So is the symbolic washing of the disciples' feet, an act of love which cannot be rejected without forfeiting one's "part" in the Lord (13:8), and which leads up to the "new commandment . . . ; even as I have loved you, that you also love one another" (13:1–20, 34–35).

---

12. E.g., Ps 80:8–18; Isa 5:1–7; Jer 2:21, 6:9; Ezek 17:1–10; Hos 10:1, 14:7; cf. 2 Esd 5:23; Sir 23:12–17.

There are other writings in the New Testament in which theological affirmations of greater or less interest are to be found, but except for those of Paul, none were as influential as the Johannine corpus. The Letter to the Hebrews stands in a subsidiary strain of thinking. This is true also of the metaphysical passages in such writings as the Letter to the Colossians, and the Letter to the Ephesians, which may well be a companion letter written about the same time. But in spite of the predominance of St. Paul and St. John, we have in the New Testament a considerable variety of modes of thinking about the person of Jesus Christ, his relation to the Father, the manner in which he brings human salvation, the relation in which the believer stands to him and to the Father, and the character of the Law and its importance in the new life of freedom. So if when we move outside the realm of the New Testament we find a diversity of view even greater, it should not surprise us.

# CHAPTER 4

# Apostolic Fathers and Second-Century Apologists[1]

O UT OF THE MULTIPLICITY of professedly Christian writings that survive from the late first and early second centuries, some were eventually canonized, others were rejected by the later church not merely as unauthoritative but as aberrant in various ways and degrees, and still others were preserved as edifying but not canonical.

Some of those attributed to the so-called apostolic fathers—1 Clement, Barnabas, the *Didache*, the Shepherd—barely missed being included in the New Testament; and all in this group were regarded (with varying degrees of plausibility) as the work of apostles or of their hearers, associates, or close successors. Most of them are theologically unpretentious, more interested in good conduct than in reflective understanding. But they are invaluable clues to the emerging internal disputes that forced the church to attempt more precise doctrinal definitions. [The same can be said of the so-called apologists; they also need to be looked at briefly for the light they shed on the context within which developments took place.]

## JEWISH-CHRISTIAN WRITINGS

Two small treatises in the group considered apostolic may be called Jewish-Christian, not in the sense that they are sectarian but because

---

1. After his retirement and at dates that are uncertain, Professor Calhoun wrote for publication two treatments of the Apostolic Fathers of very unequal length. The longer version contains much of interest that is omitted from the shorter, but its length is excessive for this volume; moreover, it is incomplete. The briefer text has therefore been chosen, though not without regret. As for the section on the Apologists, the main source is 1948 LCHD; however, parts of this have been omitted and other parts added from student transcripts of later lectures [ed].

their primary concerns, their literary forms, and their moral and religious outlook strongly suggest that they are the work of converts from Judaism whose understanding of Christianity is determined primarily by their reactions, negative and positive, to Jewish tradition.

## Barnabas

One is an anonymous letter very early attributed to Barnabas, Paul's colleague, quoted as though it were Scripture by Clement of Alexandria, written with engaging earnestness, singleness of purpose, and naïveté in both style and thought. Its preoccupation with Scripture refers almost if not entirely to the Old Testament and to early apocryphal and pseudepigraphal literature. It shows no concern with heresy, even the sorts noticed in the New Testament, but is intensely anti-Judaic. It enjoins community of goods and expects a speedy end of "the present evil time." Its style and mode of argument are rabbinic, not peculiar to any place or date. Its theology is far more primitive than Paul's or John's, or that of the Letter to the Hebrews (which it parodies in part). Its simple, single-minded effort to discredit the orthodox Jewish reading of the Old Testament—supporting Paul's insistence on freedom from the old law, without remotely approaching his new insights—could indeed plausibly be ascribed to a former Levite filled with the enthusiasm of a true convert but without theological subtlety. At all events, a date under Vespasian (69–79 CE), Domitian (81–96), or Nerva (96–98) seems more appropriate than Harnack's dating of around 131.[2]

The teaching of Part I can be summarized under three heads: the true meaning of the Law and Temple, the crucial significance of Jesus Christ, and the pattern of world history.[3]

MEANING OF LAW AND TEMPLE. First of all, the Law and the Temple cult were never meant to be taken literally. The great prophets tried to make this plain. True sacrifices are obedient and penitent hearts, not burnt animals (*Barn.* 2:4–10). Acceptable fasting is generous kindliness to the needy (*Barn.* 3:1–5). Genuine circumcision is the opening of ears and

2. Adolf von Harnack, *Geschichte der altchristlichen Literatur* II, 1 (Leipzig: Hinrichs, 1897) 427. Harnack's late dating remains common [ed].

3. For the Greek text with English translation, the reader is referred to *The Apostolic Fathers* (I), ed. Kirsopp Lake, Loeb Classical Library (Cambridge, MA: Harvard University Press, 1975).

hearts to "the word of the Lord" (*Barn.* 9:1–9). The food laws require of us not "abstinence from eating," but separation from persons who are swinish, predatory, mud-dwelling, sexually perverse. To eat the flesh of cattle that are ruminant and two-toed means to seek the company of those who meditate inwardly on "the requirement of the word which they have received," each one of whom both "walks in this world and awaits the holy age" to come (*Barn.* 10:1–11). Only in that new time, moreover, can the Sabbath really be kept holy (*Barn.* 15:1–8). In a word, the true covenant "of Jesus the Beloved" (*Barn.* 4:8) has never belonged to imperceptive legalists, but always to "the people who followed," who although later in time are "the first and the heirs of the covenant" (*Barn.* 13:5, 6). Witness of this is Moses' breaking the tablets that bore the first covenant, meant for Israel but violated even before it was received by the people (*Barn.* 4:7–8; 14:2–4); and the preferment of the younger of Joseph's sons to the elder (*Barn.* 13:1–7). The old law is superseded by "the new law of our Lord Jesus," and the old Israel by the new "people whom he [God] prepared in his Beloved" (*Barn.* 2:6; 3:6).

Similarly, God's temple is not a building made with hands, but obedient human hearts. It was almost a pagan misconception when people "directed their hope to the building, and not to their God who made them the real house of God" (*Barn.* 16:1, 2). His enemies "destroyed" it, made it "a house of demons by doing whatever was contrary to God" (*Barn.* 16:4, 7). But by God's saving power, "we have become new, created again from the beginning," and "God truly dwells in us" through faith and obedience, "himself prophesying in us," so that we are enabled to make him known to others. Thus is "a spiritual temple built for the Lord," and it can be said that "even those subordinated to the enemies (*hoi ton echthron hypertai*) will build it up again (*Barn.* 16:4).

SIGNIFICANCE OF JESUS CHRIST. This saving work of God is focused on Jesus Christ. It presupposes the hostile power of an "evil ruler," Satan, "the Black One," in this world, and the entrapment of humankind, including most of Israel, by his deceits (see for example *Barn.* 18 and *Barn.* 20).

Chapters 5–9 and 11–12 are an almost unbroken sequence of *testimonia* and typological *aperçus* drawn mainly from the Old Testament, partly from detailed accounts of Jewish ritual. Along with some familiar themes—the suffering servant, the cornerstone, the word in Gen 1:26, the agonized appeals in Psalm 22, the outstretched arms of Moses, the brazen serpent—the writer finds prefigurations of Jesus, baptism, and the cross in some unaccustomed places. Not only are streams prefigurations of Christian baptism, but Jesus himself is "the good land" of milk and honey promised to Abraham's heirs (*Barn.* 6:8–18). The scapegoat, scarlet wool, gall and vinegar, and a bramble: the heifer slain as a burnt offering, scarlet wool bound on sticks with thorny hyssop, and a ceremonial sprinkling of ashes for cleansing from sin—these provide in surprising ways "the type of Jesus," "of Jesus who was to suffer," "of Jesus placed in the Church," and "the type of the cross" (*Barn.* 7:7, 10, 11; 8:1). More astonishing still, circumcision—the very watchword of old Israel and of Judaizing Christians—when rightly understood signifies not Judaism but the Gospel. "For it says, 'And Abraham circumcised from his household eighteen and three hundred men.'" But eighteen is indicated by the Greek *Iota Eta* (for ten and eight), while three hundred is *Tau.* Hence, *IH* and *T*—Jesus and the Cross.

PATTERN OF WORLD HISTORY. The author is clear that the end is close. The present is an evil time, and it may be that worse rigors are ahead (see for example *Barn.* 2:1; 8:6). But beyond all such trials is the true Sabbath rest. Six days in God's time are six thousand years, in which "everything will be completed." Then, "when his Son comes he will destroy the time of the Lawless One, and will judge the impious, and will change the sun and the moon and the stars, and then he will truly rest." Then we too, for the first time, can "keep holy the day which God has made holy"—as no one can keep it now. And that millennium of rest God "will make the beginning of an eighth day"; that is, the beginning of another world (*allou kosmou*) (*Barn.* 15:8). For on the eighth day, Jesus rose from the dead and ascended into heaven.

In a general sense, this is chiliastic doctrine, expecting a millennium of rest after the return of the Son to "judge the godless." But there are no pictorial details. The author's thought seems closer to that of Heb 4:1–10 than to Revelation, to Enoch and other apocalypses, or to the exuberant fancies of Papias and Irenaeus.

All this comes in one main section of the letter. The second main section is moral rather than speculative, and is based upon a Jewish document which is often referred to as "The Two Ways." There is the way of darkness and death and the way of life and light. Stipulations for recognizing the vices of the one and the virtues of the other are put forward in quite full detail.

## The Didache

If *Barnabas* thus gives expression to one form of relatively uncomplicated Jewish Christian thought using rabbinic methods to discredit traditional Judaism, the Teaching of the Twelve Apostles (the *Didache*) represents it in another stage and perspective. In another stage, because the *Didache* apparently draws upon *Barnabas'* moral section as well as various other sources; it quotes copiously from New Testament writings (especially Matthew) and relatively little from the Old Testament; and in form and style it is a concise manual rather than a loose-jointed midrash; and in another perspective, because it is concerned with the proper ordering of catechetical instruction and church life rather than with the errors of Judaism. As a matter of fact, though it is probably later in date, it retains much more of the spirit of Jewish piety.

The compendium begins with six chapters of moral instruction—the "two Ways, one of Life and one of Death" (*Did.* 1:1). *Barnabas'* angels have disappeared. The two Great Commandments again provide the theme; but this time the exposition begins in the mood, and partly in the terms, of the Sermon on the Mount (*Did.* 1:2–5a). It continues in general accord with *Barnabas*, including his injunctions not to be "double-minded nor double-tongued," to "share all things" in common, and to shun favoritism (*Did.* 2:4; 4:4, 8, 10). Its mood is disarmingly unfanatical.

> If indeed you can bear the whole yoke of the Lord, you will be perfect; but if you cannot, do what you can. And concerning food, bear what you can; but guard strictly against what is offered to idols, for it is the worship of dead gods. (*Did.* 6:2–3)

On this practical note, reminiscent of the decision at Jerusalem, the moral teaching ends.

There follow instructions for true baptism, which in various details are said to have rabbinic parallels. The Lord's Prayer in a form nearly as in Matthew, expanded to include a brief doxology—"For thine is the power and the glory forever"—is to be offered three times a day (*Did.* 8:2–3). Most interesting are three beautiful Eucharistic prayers—before the cup, before the broken bread, and after the communion—full of explicit and implicit reminiscences of Jewish ritual (the Kiddush, the synagogue

Benedictions, the prayers for the regathering of Israel), and ending with the ancient Christian invocation: "Maranatha, Amen" (*Did.* 10:6). Unlike *Barnabas*, the *Didache* does not say that the end is near—only that you do not know the hour in which our Lord comes," so be ready (*Did.* 16:1ff).

Both early date and close affiliation with Jewish tradition are all but guaranteed by the Eucharistic prayers, full of Hebraic imagery and doxologic formulae. There is thanks "for the holy Vine of David thy servant, which thou didst make known to us through Jesus thy servant" (*Did.* 9:2). There is thanks "for thy Holy Name which thou didst make to encamp in our hearts" (*Did.* 10:2). There is the reiterated ascription: "To thee be glory forever," or "the glory and the power forever" (*Did.* 9:2, 3, 4; 10:2, 4, 5). There is, finally, "Hosannah to the God of David. . . . Maranatha, Amen" (*Did.* 10:6). By no possibility can these prayers have come from any other tradition than Judaism, and that at no far remove. Moreover, if the "broken bread . . . scattered upon the mountains," and the possible scarcity of water (*Did.* 9:4; 7:3) be taken at face value, Palestine or Syria (as many scholars have urged) seems the most likely place of origin. Thus in conclusion, no other early Christian writings outside the New Testament but fully accepted by the church display so vividly the undistorted Jewish Christian mind.

## ASIAN THEOLOGY

A second group of writings originated in Syria and Asia Minor. Of these, only the seven letters of Ignatius have much theological content, and it is on these, together with some comments on Papias, that we shall focus. There are characteristic features in which most of these writings differ from *Barnabas* and the *Didache*. For one thing, the personal reality of Jesus Christ is for them far more concrete, central, and powerfully felt, and expressly stated against doctrinal disparagement. For another, along with their insistence on righteous living they make much of grace as God-given energy and of Spirit as living, saving, present power, and not simply as the source of prophetic clairvoyance. Third, in various ways they give a major place to intimate involvement of the believer with the active being of Jesus Christ and of God. Using the language sometimes of imitation (*mimesis*), that is, active personal identification rather than copying or duplication, sometimes of participation: (*metechin*), and most often the Pauline-Johannine language of being "in Christ," or of "union" (*henosis*) or "unanimity" (*homonoia*) with Christ and his Father, they deepen a moralism not unlike that of *Barnabas* and the *Didache* with a more strongly mystical piety.

## *Ignatius (d. c. 107)*[4]

The seven accepted letters of the second bishop of Antioch, metropolis of the important Roman province of Syria, on his way to martyrdom in Rome, display all these characteristics vividly. Despite the comparatively sober policy of Trajan (98–117 CE) respecting members of the Christian congregations, the emperor's reply to an inquiry from Pliny the Younger, governor of Bithynia about 110, declared Christian membership *ipso facto* illegal,[5] liable even to capital punishment. Probably after this decree, Ignatius and perhaps others from Antioch were sent to death in the Roman arena. The bishop, a passionate and humble man, both desired and dreaded the coming ordeal, mistrusting his own constancy, though in fact he proved steadfast at the end.

Like the writers of *Barnabas* and the *Didache*, he is concerned most of all for genuine Christian living. Unlike them, however, he is worried about heresy and schism, urging vehemently the need for sound doctrine and well-knit church order in service of the unity that is Life, of which God is the Ground and Giver.

His understanding of the life of a true believer is defined not by lists of precepts but by the marks of a basic disposition. He shares the traditional view that "two things are set before us, death and life" (Ign. *Magn.* 5:6) but the two alternatives are, quite simply, willingness through Christ to suffer and die "into his suffering," or refusal, so that "his life is not in us" (Ign. *Magn.* 5:2). The primary disposition that bears "the imprint (*charaktera*) of God the Father" is marked by faith and love, integrity, conformity to God, life-giving unification.

Genuineness is a fairly obvious mandate for believers. "It is meet, therefore, not only to be called Christians, but to be such." (Ign. *Magn.* 4:1). Ignatius makes the point in a characteristic and striking way. "It is better to be silent and to be, than to talk and not to be" (Ign. *Eph.* 15:1).

---

4. For the writings of Ignatius, see the *Apostolic Fathers* (I), ed. Kirsopp Lake, Loeb Classical Library (Cambridge, MA: Harvard University Press, 1975).

5. For this exchange of correspondence, see Pliny, *Letters and Panegyrics* (II), ed. Betty Radice, Loeb Classical Library (Cambridge, MA: Harvard University Press, 1969).

This contrast of being and seeming, typified sometimes by silence versus empty talk, sometimes by valid utterance versus spurious or meaningless noise (Ign. *Rom.* 2:1), pervades the whole of Ignatius'—as of John's— theology. It colors strongly his understanding of God, of Jesus Christ, and of the gospel, as well as of the Christian life.

This interconnection of motifs can be seen once more in a third moral perspective. Genuine Christians are "imitators of God"(*mimetai ontes Theou*—Ign. *Eph.*1:1; Ign. *Trall.* 1:2) and of Jesus Christ (Ign. *Rom.* 6:3; Ign. *Eph.*10:3; Ign. *Phld.* 7:2), who was himself an "imitator" of his Father (Ign. *Phld.* 7:2). This last dictum, embedded in a proclamation ascribed to "the Spirit" himself, makes doubly clear what is clear enough on other grounds. *Mimesis* is not external duplication of a model but active personal identification with a source of power and meaning. In these letters it has virtually the same sense as life "according to God" (*kata Theon*— Ign. *Eph.* 8:1; Ign. *Phld.* 4:1), or to Jesus Christ (Ign. *Pol.* 5:2), or in Jesus Christ (Ign. *Eph.* 3:1, 8:2, 10:3; Ign. *Magn.* 6:2; Ign. *Trall.* 1:1, 9:2; and many other places). At the same time such active identification (*mimesis*) is not simply identity. It is participatory striving toward a fulfillment not yet attained: toward God, toward Jesus Christ, toward true discipleship (Ign. *Eph.* 1:1–2, 3:1; Ign. *Rom.* 5:3). For Ignatius it is above all willingness to suffer, "to be a participant (*mimetes*) in the suffering of my God," the crucifixion of "craving" (*eros*) for "the pleasures of this life" (Ign. *Rom.* 6:3, 7:2). Martyrdom in faith and love is preeminently the way to fulfillment.

If a single word be sought to identify that fulfillment, participable here but completed hereafter, it is active union (*henosis*): of flesh and spirit, of faith and love, of silence and speech, of word and deed, of individual and communal life, of laity and clergy, believer and Lord, Son and Father, man and God.

Such union, once more, does not make human beings Christ or God. It does make them participants in both. They become "bearers of God (*Theophoroi*) of the temple, of Christ, of holiness" (Ign. *Eph.* 9:2), "members" of Christ, without whom Christ himself could not come to birth as head (Ign. *Trall.* 11:2). In union, they can "always partake of God" (*Theoupantate metechete*), even "be full of God" (*Theou gemete*—Ign. *Eph.* 4:2; Ign. *Magn.* 14). Ignatius' favored term (*henosis*) does not occur in the New Testament. His teaching is the daring Johannine doctrine of the climactic discourse and prayer: "That they all may be one (*hen osin*); even as thou, Father, art in me, and I in thee, that they also may be in us" (John

17:21). The ground of Christian life thus powerfully conceived is God, made known in Jesus Christ, bestowing his grace on those who in love believe in him.

Like the biblical writers, Ignatius speaks of "the one God" without argument and without attempt at detailed characterization. Indeed, in common with many of his contemporaries, he regards God as strictly indescribable. Not merely is God too great for human thought and speech, his being is in principle veiled in mystery, unknowable until he makes himself known. He is precisely *Deus absconditus*, God hidden, until by his own act he becomes God self-disclosed, *Deus revelatus*.

The decisive act is "the coming of the Savior, our Lord Jesus Christ, his passion, and the resurrection," to whom the patriarchs and prophets of Israel looked forward (Ign. *Phld.* 9:1–2). In an eloquent passage, often quoted in full, Ignatius speaks of "three mysteries of a cry" (*krauges*), which were wrought in the stillness of God (*en hesychia Theou*): "The virginity of Mary, and her giving birth, and likewise the death of the Lord" (Ign. *Eph.* 19:1). These mysteries are "hidden from the Prince of this age" (*aionos*), until "that which had been fully prepared by God" is "disclosed to the ages" (*tois aiosin*) and to sun, moon, and stars, "by divine dispensation" (*kat' oikonomian Theou* —Ign. *Eph.* 18:2). Both thought and language recall irresistibly "the dispensation (*oikonomia*) of the mystery hidden for ages (literally, from the ages—*apo ton ainon*) in God," and now made known "to the principalities and powers in heavenly places," the mystery of God's will set forth in Christ "as a dispensation (*oikonomia*) for the fullness of time, to sum up all things in Christ" (Eph 1:10; 3:9–11).

But even less than the Johannine author, whom he most closely resembles, is Ignatius concerned to spell out a well-defined doctrine of the Godhead. For example, John's care to distinguish without dividing "the Word" from "God" (*ho Theos*) on the one hand and from "Jesus of Nazareth, the son of Joseph" on the other has no real counterpart in these letters. They use freely the traditional language: "God the Father," "the Father of Jesus Christ," even (once) "the Son and the Father and the Spirit" (Ign. *Magn.* 13:1). But there is no hint of concern, still less of uneasiness, over problems of interrelationships within the Godhead. In fact, discussion of such problems might well have seemed to the desperately earnest bishop inappropriate (like nice definitions in angelology) because irrelevant for salvation. "For many things are lacking to us, that we may not lack God."[6] Enough to know that God is one, that he "has willed all things that are," has revealed himself in Jesus Christ, is patient with human beings, knows their secrets, and gives them grace.[7]

The real center of Ignatius' theology is Jesus Christ. Both his positive affirmations and his warnings against error converge here, in a boldly stated paradox that brushes aside arguments and explanation. His Christology, in common with his doctrine of God of which it is the heart, is confessional rather than systematic.

The paradox is God-manhood: "God being humanly manifested" (*Theou anthropinos phaneroumenou*—Ign. *Eph.*19:3). Ignatius drives home both sides of this affirmation with unprecedented vigor. On the one hand, Jesus Christ is God—called *Theos* and *ho Theos* almost indiscriminately (e.g., Ign. *Eph.* inscr., 18:2). The historical person himself is "the Word coming forward from Silence," "the undeceptive mouth by which the Father has spoken truly," "who was with the Father before the ages (*pro aionon para patri*) and at length was manifested" (Ign. *Magn.* 8:2; Ign. *Rom.* 8:2; Ign. *Magn.* 6:1; Ign. *Eph.* 3:2). He himself is "the will of the Father"; he raised from the dead both the prophets and himself (whom the Father also is said to have raised). Before, during, and after his incarnate life, he has the distinctive characteristics of deity: he is "unbegotten (or unborn—*agennetos*) . . . impassible" (*apathes*), "supratemporal" (*hyper kairon*), timeless, invisible, impassible" (Ign. *Smyr.* 2; Ign. *Magn.* 9:2; Ign. *Eph.* 7:2; Ign. *Pol.* 3:2). His full deity, as authentic as that of the Father, is fundamental to Ignatius' piety and understanding.

At the same time, in many of these passages and elsewhere in the letters, his real humanity is avowed with even greater vehemence. He is a man of flesh and blood, who "was of the family of David, and of Mary, who was truly born, both ate and drank, was truly indicted under Pontius Pilate, was truly crucified and died (Ign. *Trall.* 9:1).

This unwavering assertion of God-manhood leads to some startling expressions: "the blood of God"; "the passion of my God" (Ign. *Eph.* 1:1; Ign. *Rom.* 6:3). It leads also to a number of confessional passages in which deity and humanity are paralleled in emphatic counterpoint: "one Physician, both carnal and spiritual, begotten (or born) and unbegotten (or unborn), God in man, true life in death, both of Mary and of God,

---

6. Calhoun's manuscript lacks the reference to this citation [ed.].

7. Cf. Ign. *Rom.* inscr. (creation, grace); Ign. *Eph.* 17:2; Ign. *Magn.* 8:2 (revelation); Ign. *Pol.* 6:2 (patience); Ign. *Magn.* 3:2 (knowledge of secrets).

first passible and then impassible, Jesus Christ our Lord" (Ign. *Eph.* 7:2). These brief letters had no room for a detailed portrayal of "the new man Jesus Christ, in his faith and his love, in his passion and resurrection," which Ignatius hoped to send the Ephesians in a "second booklet" (Ign. *Eph.* 20:1). Short of such a *vita Christi*, it is hard to see how his genuine humanity could have been more strongly if sketchily affirmed.

By comparison with these robust convictions about Jesus Christ as God-man, Ignatius' doctrine of his saving work is mostly intimated rather than defined. Much of it is implicit in his account of the Christian life and of God's self-disclosure in Jesus Christ. Through his coming, the ancient forces of evil are broken and "the abolition of death put in train" (Ign. *Eph.* 19:3). He brings knowledge of God (Ign. *Eph.* 17:2). He suffers, dies, and rises again "for our sake (*hyper hemon* or *di' hemas*), so that we may be raised likewise" (Ign. *Rom.* 6:1; Ign. *Smyrn.* 7:1) Above all, he is at one with the Father and "did nothing without him" (Ign. *Magn.* 7:1), becomes "our inseparable life," makes us his "members," and brings us into union with God (Ign. *Eph.* 3:2, 4:2–3).

The primary stress in all these glimpses of atonement doctrine is our salvation from death to life rather than from sin to righteousness: life which, as in the kindred Johannine account, is at once present and yet to be. But this life (again as in Johannine theology) is morally conditioned and structured through and through. It calls for repentance (Ign. *Eph.* 10:1), humility (Cf. Ign. *Eph.* 10:1–3), and that "concurrence with the will of God" (Ign *Eph* 3:2) that consists in faith and love. Fulfillment of these demands results both from divine ordination and grace, and from human obedience. The questions of priority and compatibility of grace and freedom are not noticed as problems, though it is affirmed as a matter of course that God "has willed all things that are" (Ign. *Rom.* inscr.), and has opened the way of life for man.

Far more than any New Testament writer, Ignatius identifies the life of "union" (*henosis*) here and now with strictly ordered life in the church. As in his crucial treatment of Christology, his omnipresent concern with church order and discipline bespeaks both his positive understanding of oneness as the very substance of Christian life and his acute awareness of heresy and schism as clear and present dangers. His letters take for granted, in his home church at Antioch and in the Asian churches to which he writes, a clear distinction between clergy and laity, and a regular hierarchy in the clergy: bishop, presbyters, and deacons. The informal fluidity of leadership by itinerant prophets and teachers is replaced by the stability of a regularly ordained clergy, though the prophetic Spirit may indeed speak through a bishop, as on occasion through Ignatius himself (Ign. *Phld.* 7:1–2). The three clerical ranks are always treated as having a definite sequence of subordination, as types of divinely established order: the bishop typifying God the Father or Jesus Christ, the presbyters usually the Apostles. But though the primacy of the bishop is urged strongly and repeatedly, even the deacons also, "entrusted with the service (*diakonian*) of Jesus Christ," "servants (*diakonous*) of the mysteries of Jesus Christ . . . not of food or drink," are to be "revered as Jesus Christ" (Ign. *Magn.* 6:1; Ign. *Trall.* 2:3).

The true function of the whole clergy, in due order, is to serve as a rallying point and safeguard of that unity without which there is no Church (Ign. *Trall.* 3:1). The congregation must be "blended" (*eakekra-menous*) with the bishop "as the Church with Jesus Christ, and as Jesus Christ with the Father" (Ign. *Eph.* 5:1).

In practice, this means harmonious sharing of worship centered in the Eucharist, and of good works. Common worship is salutary not only for the joy it affords believers but also as a concrete way of conquering evil (Ign. *Eph.* 13:1). Ignatius has little to say of baptism, which he takes for granted as an essential sacrament requiring approval by the bishop, authorized by the Lord's own example, and providing in some sort a shield against the enemy (Cf. Ign. *Smyrn.* 8:2; Ign. *Eph.* 8:2; Ign. *Pol.* 6:2). The Eucharist plainly is more central to his thought. But its meaning for him is by no means simple and obvious, combining charismatic realism with moral and religious imperatives in highly poetic language. Thus in the context of the congregational assembly "in shared (*koine*) grace, in one faith, and in Jesus Christ," in obedience to bishop and presbytery, he speaks of "breaking one bread, which is the medicine (*pharmadkon*) of immortality, an antidote (*antidotos*) that we die not, but live in Jesus Christ forever" (Ign. *Eph.* 20:2). Docetists "abstain from Eucharist and prayer because they do not agree that the Eucharist is the flesh of our savior Jesus Christ, which suffered for our sins, which the Father raised up" (Ign. *Smyrn.* 7:1). Like baptism, "a dependable Eucharist" requires authorization of the bishop; and there is but "one Eucharist, for there is one flesh of our Lord Jesus Christ, and one cup for union in his blood (*eis henosin tou haimatos autou*) . . . one altar (*thysiasterion*) as there is one bishop," and so on (Ign. *Phld.* 4). All this sounds as if the bread on the altar were literally "the flesh," the physical actuality of the crucified and risen Lord, having in itself, when properly offered, supernatural power to ward off death. If this were the whole story, it would seem to conflict with Ignatius' insistence on the uncompromised humanity of Jesus Christ. But in fact his understanding of the Eucharist has another side, strongly reminiscent of the Johannine gospel. To the Philadelphians, immediately after the words on the "one Eucharist," he writes of himself as "taking refuge in the gospel as the flesh of Jesus"; and to the Romans, concerning his eagerness for martyrdom, "I desire the bread of God, which is the flesh of Jesus Christ, . . . and for drink I desire his blood, which is deathless love" (Ign. *Phld.* 5.1; Ign. *Rom.* 7:3). Elsewhere "the bread of God" seems to be public prayer, and "the altar" (*thysiasteriou*) the worshipping congregation (Ign. *Phld.* 5.2). Even the strong condemnation of the Docetists for refusing to join in the celebration "because they do not agree that the Eucharist is the flesh of our savior Jesus Christ" concludes: "It behooves them to love (*agapan*), that they also may rise again (Ign. *Smyrn.* 7:1). Love, then, concretely manifested in Eucharistic worship, is the true safeguard against death. In a word, Ignatius' doctrine of the sacrament, like the Christology with which it is closely bound up, is highly paradoxical and poetic. Here as everywhere in the letters, flesh and spirit are inseparably bound together: "Faith, which is the flesh of the Lord, and . . . love, which is the blood of Jesus Christ" (Ign. *Trall.* 8:1). A final manifestation of unity in the Church should be a sharing of right belief and rejection of doctrinal errors. Interestingly enough, Ignatius has various pungent terms for error—"heresy," "bad doctrine," "heterodoxy," "null doctrine" (Ign. *Eph.* 6:1, 9:1; Ign. *Magn.* 8:1)—but none for orthodox belief. His closest approach to such a term is: "You all live in accordance with truth (*kata aletheian*), and no heresy (*hairesis*) at all dwells among you" (Ign. *Eph.* 6:2); but even this phrase is an elaboration of "good discipline" or "orderly behavior" (*eutaxia*) rather than a specific name for sound doctrine.

But with or without a distinctive label, Ignatius manifests anxiety to underscore the necessity of sound doctrine in the numerous Christological summaries already noted, some reiterating the substance of the traditional *kerygma*, some expanded into brief personal credos (Ign. *Trall.* 9:1; Ign. *Smyrn.* 1:1–2; Ign. *Eph.* 18:2). He obviously is confident that they accord with "the teachings (*dogmasin*) of the Lord and the Apostles," whose authority he holds in deep regard (Ign. *Magn.* 13:1). The literary form of these summaries is his own, without close parallels in other second-century writings. Most of their ideas are drawn from the tradition embodied at length in the New Testament, and many of them naturally reappear in church creeds later on. But there is no good ground to suppose that they are taken from creeds in public use, nor even that such formulae existed in his time.

Two final words may be added concerning his overall concept of the Church. First, it is God's work, "the temple of the Father," which even in its local embodiments can be addressed as "predestined before the ages (*pro aionon*) to exist forever to enduring, immutable glory, united and chosen . . . by the will of the Father and of Jesus Christ our God" (Ign. *Eph.* inscr.). Second, its earthly history is near an end. "These are the last times." Hence, "let us either fear the wrath to come, or love the grace that is here—one of the two; only let us be found in Christ Jesus unto the true life" (Ign. *Eph.* 11:1–2).

### Papias of Hierapolis (fl. late first and early second centuries.)

[Omitting discussion of the Bishop of Smyrna, Polycarp (69/82–155/168)], we turn briefly to another spokesman for this second-generation Asian Christianity.][8] Papias of Hierapolis in Asia is said to be a man who delighted in collecting anecdotes. Of his work we have only fragments quoted by others.[9] He was not as much interested in what had already been written down as he was in the stories that were passed around from mouth to mouth in the Christian community—stories about the Lord and stories about the Apostles. In collecting these he felt that he was doing an important service for the community. Apart from some interesting and important but enigmatic information about the literary methods of "Mark, Peter's interpreter" and Matthew, his taste seems to have run to wonder tales and apocalyptical fantasies. Eusebius, a sophisticated Origenist, hostile to literal-minded millennialism as a crude misunderstanding of figurative gospel teachings, writes him down as "of very small wit" (*sphodra gar toi mikros on ton noun*).[10]

---

8. Professor Calhoun discussed Polycarp only in the longer and incomplete version of this material (see n. 21 above), and then only the account of his martyrdom, which, Calhoun says, "gives voice to theological insights more impressive than anything" he wrote" [ed].

9. For fragments of Papias' writings, the reader is referred to *ANF* 1 [ed.].

10. Eusebius, *Hist. eccl.* III:39:13; for an English translation, see *NPNF2* 1.

His compatriot Irenaeus, on the contrary, welcomes a vivid picture of the coming earthly renovation, which Papias in his fourth book had ascribed to the Lord on the testimony of certain elders who had it from "John, the Lord's disciple." This supposed logion describes the promised growth in the new age of gargantuan vines, each bearing 100,000,000,000,000,000,000 grapes, each grape giving roughly 250 gallons of wine. Similar fruitfulness of wheat field, orchard, and meadow will restore the peaceful conditions of Paradise for animals and human beings.[11]

Without knowing more of what Papias wrote, it is impossible to know how far he may have been aware of the threat of Gnostic or Marcionite disparagement of God's world. To Irenaeus, this danger is deadly plain, and his exuberant pictures of the coming Paradise are expressly meant to set against disparagement the concrete bounty of the Creator of heaven and earth. "For God is rich in all things, and all things are his."[12]

This robust yea-saying with respect to fleshly life, earthly history, literal reading of Scripture, grace as wonder-working power, and salvation as total renewal is characteristic of the Syrian and Asian theologians in this group, and of many more to follow. Both orthodoxy and heresy, whose roots are set in the subsoil of this part of the Christian world, display in various ways an earthy realism much like that of Biblical Judaism, and on the intellectual side more like Stoicism (itself originated among thinkers, very possibly of Semitic stock, from this region) than like Platonism, the other school that stood highest in early Christian favor. When Origen introduced a powerful stream of Christian Platonism into Palestine, whence it spread into Syria and Asia Minor, it was recognized as alien and for a long time fiercely resisted by Christians of the older native tradition. Loofs's well-known phrase, "Asia Minor theology," should not be taken in too narrow a geographic sense, but it points to a readily recognizable tendency of very great importance.

## ROMAN THEOLOGY

Of the remaining documents that belong among the Apostolic Fathers, two are definitely assignable to Rome. In literary genre they differ widely: an elaborate, rhetorical, somewhat stilted letter to Corinth, and a ram-

11. *ANF* I: 153–54.
12. *ANF* I: 563. [= *Haer.* V:33].

bling apocalypse or prophetic visionary treatise. Both are moralistic, and are preoccupied with the Church and offer distinctive theories about its nature. Neither shows any such anxiety about heresy as Ignatius displays, although Marcionite and Gnostic teachers were active in Rome when one of them presumably was written. Together they suggest that theology in the Roman church during the first half of the second century was hospitable to very diverse views.

### First Clement

The earliest and soberest of the two is the first letter of Clement, bishop of the Roman Church in the last decade of the first century.[13] It is a letter written to that turbulent congregation in Corinth that had given Paul so much trouble. Apparently the same old story was being reenacted there in factionalism and strife and bickerings and schisms within the church. What Clement does, writing not as an individual but on behalf of the brethren in Rome, is to urge upon the people of Corinth the need for decency and order, for due subordination of members of the church to their constituted officials, and for the maintenance of peace and tranquility in God's great world. The argument is carried out in rather prosaic but to my mind, very persuasive fashion by a man whose strong point is not intellectual brilliance so much as a sober kind of good sense and fineness of temper.

He urges upon the folk in Corinth the examples of humility on the part of the patriarchs and heroes of the Old Testament, of the prophets, of Jesus himself, and of the apostles. All of them displayed the spirit of submission and self-devotion rather than the spirit of contention. He urges on the congregation the example of the world of nature in which God provides an example of harmony which ought to be observed and followed by his people. This is rather a favorite passage of mine. It is so unusual in the writing of the early Christian period that it is quite striking—full of authentic feeling for nature and its spiritual significance.

13. See *Apostolic Fathers* I, ed. Loeb Classical Library (Cambridge, MA: Harvard University Press, 1975 rpt.). A second letter has also long been attributed to Clement, but it was written decades later by an unknown author in an uncertain location (which, to be sure, may have been Rome) and can for our purposes be omitted from consideration. As in the case of Polycarp earlier referred to, Professor Calhoun also dealt with this second letter in the longer of his two post-retirement reworkings of his material on the Apostolic Fathers; but the longer version, it will be recalled, is not the one we are following. See n. 20 above. [ed.]

Therefore, having so many great and glorious examples set before us, let us turn again to the practice of that peace which from the beginning is the mark set before us; and let us look steadfastly to the Father and Creator of the universe and cleave to his mighty and surpassingly great gifts and benefactions of peace. The heavens revolving under his government are subject to him in peace. Day and night run the course appointed by him, in no wise hindering each other. The sun and moon and company of stars roll on in harmony according to his command within their prescribed limits and without any deviation. The fruitful earth, according to his will, brings forth fruit in abundance in the proper seasons for man and beast and all the living things upon it, never hesitating or changing any of the ordinances which he has fixed. The unsearchable places of the desert and the indescribable arrangements of the lower world are restrained by the same laws. The vast unmeasurable sea, gathered together by his working into various places, never passes beyond the bounds placed around it, but does as he has commanded. The ocean, impassable to man, and the worlds beyond it are regulated by the same enactments of the Lord. The seasons—spring, summer, autumn, and winter—peacefully give place to one another. The winds in their several quarters fulfill at the proper time their service without hindrance. The ever-flowing fountains, formed both for enjoyment and health, furnish without fail their breasts for the life of man. The very smallest of living beings meet together in peace and concord. All these the great Creator and Lord of all has appointed to exist in peace and harmony, while he does good to all; but most abundantly to us who have fled for refuge to his compassion through Jesus Christ our Lord, to whom be glory and majesty forever and ever. Amen.

The temper of the whole letter is that of one who is moved to wonder and love by the display of due subordination and co-working in God's world, and among his best servants, and who desires to see in the church the same sort of harmony and tranquility reestablished. If one were speaking of the Roman temper at its best, one would find an excellent illustration of it here.

## Hermas: The Shepherd

Another writing that comes from the church of Rome is the work, not of a bishop, but of a prophet—one of those specially gifted individuals in the congregation to whom, from time to time, new insights come. His name is Hermas, and he is described as the brother of one who was bishop in Rome at some time in the second century.[14] The question whether the work should be dated early or late in the century turns on extremely tenuous evidence. Its content is set forth in terms of five visions, twelve commandments, and ten similitudes or parables. The central figure of the writing, called simply the Shepherd, is a heavenly guide who appears to Hermas when he is in trouble and interprets for him the meaning of the vision that he has seen or the meaning of the commandment over which he is pondering. The Shepherd is an angelic figure who is the organ of revelation to Hermas, the prophet.

Without attempting any systematization of material, let us pick out two or three characteristic sections. First of all, there is a body of material related to a question that was warmly debated in the church respecting the forgivability of sins committed by Christians after baptism. Shall post-baptismal sins be regarded as debarring the sinner from membership in the church, or shall he be permitted to continue as a church member even though he has fallen into more or less frequent wrongdoing after baptism? Baptism of course washed clean the life of the one baptized to that moment, but what he did thereafter could not be cleansed by a second baptism because no such thing was permissible. Regarding post-baptismal sin, we find that the fairly widespread practice in the church was to distinguish three types. On the lowest level there were such trivial sins as losing one's temper, telling small lies, and falling into the sort of unchristian behavior into which even Christians fall from time to time. The notion was that sins of that sort did not require exclusion from the church, or any recompense other than daily repetition of the Lord's Prayer with its petition that we be forgiven our transgressions as we forgive those who sin against us. In addition to these trivial faults, there were certain grave faults which could not be so easily passed over. Among the graver sins again, two classes were recognized. Some were forgivable upon condition of the doing of a somewhat painful and protracted penance. Finally, some were unforgivable, and these called for permanent exclusion of the sinner from membership in the church. These unforgivable sins were of the three sorts which the Old Testament law had punished with death. They were labeled technically: murder, which included homicide of all

14. *Apostolic Fathers*, II, ed. Loeb Classical Library (Cambridge, MA: Harvard University Press, 1976 rpt.).

sorts; adultery, which included sexual wrongdoing of all sorts; and idolatry, which meant for Christians in the Roman Empire most especially apostasy—burning the required pinch of incense before the emperor's statue, and thus renouncing the sole deity of the God of Jesus Christ.

Now Hermas centers his examination upon the relation between post-baptismal sins which are forgivable and those which are unforgivable. Here is an example. One of his visions is of the building of a great tower upon a mighty rock. The work is under the direction of six archangels, who are having stones brought to them from various parts of the surrounding landscape. These stones must be shining and white and square, and they are set into the tower as it goes up. As Hermas watches, he sees that some of the stones that are brought in are stubbornly rounded boulders. If those are put into the wall they wobble and make other stones wobble, and they just will not do. Some are shattered so that they would crumble under weight, and some are so dirty that they would deface the wall if they were built into it. He watches to see what will be done with stones of those sorts, and he sees that some of them are thrown in a heap nearby, whereas others are thrown a long way off. Then he sees some of the angelic workmen go to the stones in a nearby pile and scrub them and hew them square and make them fit to be put into the wall of the tower which is going up.

Now the Shepherd tells him what all this means. The tower is the church eternal and the stones that are being built into it are the souls of believers. Some of the souls are ready to be put into the structure, but some have been spoiled; they are stubborn, they are obdurate in their sins, they have been treacherous, they have failed in more or less grievous ways. Of these some are curable and are the ones which, under suitable penance, can be made into useful church members again. But some are hopeless, and they are the stones which are thrown at a distance.

The same pattern of thought occurs in another of these vivid pictures which Hermas gives us. This time the stones are being brought from twelve mountains and the twelve mountains have different characters, so that the stones that come from them are recognizable as people of various moral types. Once again the notion is that some of them can be used as they are brought in. Others, having been put into the wall, turn black or crumble and have to be taken out of the wall and either cleaned or thrown away. Eventually, when the overseer, who is none other than the Lord himself, comes to see what the angels are doing, he approves their work, which is the work of building a church tower that will have none but the finest materials in it.

Next the Shepherd throws additional light upon the meaning of the moral presuppositions of the story. He does so in part in connection with another story of a master who owned a vineyard and who, when he was going on a journey, instructed his slave to train up the vines in the vineyard. The slave not only did that but finding that he had some more time on his hands, weeded and dug around all the vines, and when the master came home he found the vineyard in apple-pie order. He was so pleased that he called his son and said, "Look what our servant has done here. What would be a proper reward for him?" The proper reward must take into account the fact that he not only has been obedient, but he has also gone beyond that which was required of him. That is the point of the story. He has done more than he was required to do, and that excess of virtue clearly requires something more than a reward which a faithful servant would normally expect. "So," says the master, "What we shall do is to adopt him into sonship and make him a co-heir in this household." Later this sort of notion is called a theory of supererogation. Hermas never heard that expression, but he did have clearly in view the idea that if you do everything that the law requires of you, it is possible for you to go still further and do more works of perfection in addition to the required works of the law. For such excess of virtue you may properly expect a very special recognition.

Besides this moral lesson, the parable has also an allegorical interpretation, offered with Hermas' usual unconcern for everyday precision. "The slave is the Son of God," who fenced about God's people with guardian angels, and then "himself cleansed their sins, performing many labors and exhausting himself with much toil. For no vineyard can be dug without toil or hardship. When therefore he had cleansed the sins of the people, he showed them the paths of life, giving them the law which he received from his Father."[15]

This is all that Hermas has to say about redemption. It consists, apparently, in laborious redirection of the people by the Son as preexistent Wisdom-Torah. He is "the Holy Spirit that preexists, that created all creation."[16] The reference to "Wisdom, the artificer of all things," seems

---

15. *Herm. Sim.* V:6:1–6.

16. Ibid.

unmistakable. "For in her there is a Spirit intelligent, holy (*hagion*), alone in kind (*monogenes*)," (Wis 7:22) and so on through the familiar majestic lines. For Hermas, Wisdom is the Son of God, at once slave and master, "with great power and Lordship."[17]

But there is a further complication:

> The Holy Spirit that pre-exists, that created all creation, God made to dwell in the flesh which he chose. This flesh, therefore, in which the Holy Spirit dwelt, served the Spirit well . . . and did not at all defile the Spirit. So when it had lived well and purely, and had toiled with the Spirit purely and not lagged in any deed but acted strongly and bravely, he chose it as participant (*koinonon*) with the Holy Spirit. . . . For all flesh in which the Holy Spirit had dwelt shall receive a reward, if it be found undefiled and spotless. And another moral: "Keep this flesh of yours pure and undefiled, that the spirit that dwells in it may bear witness to it, and your flesh may be justified." Reject every hint of libertinism.[18]

Thus abruptly, in three sentences that point an oddly far-fetched moral, Hermas offers his sketchy avowal of incarnation. It is "the flesh" of the indwelling "Holy Spirit" that now is the slave promoted to sonship. But "the flesh" has no name. We are confronted here with allegorical and moralistic abstractions, not with the concrete stuff of salvation history.

Thus in both these writings from Rome, Clement and the Shepherd, the stress on the need for disciplined harmony, uprightness, and timely repentance quite overshadows the occasional glimpse of Pauline trust in grace alone, or Johannine confidence in union with God through love. There is little or no anxiety about "false teaching" save as it encourages bad conduct. The dominant motif, to be sure, is not simply legalistic but has a Judaic aspect: Repent, for God is merciful. But "repent," when the Shepherd of Hermas was translated into Latin, became "penance": *Agite enim paenitentium utilem nobis.*[19] And, as the lengthy revelation ends, "Do good works, therefore . . . lest while you delay, the building of the tower be finished.[20]

17. Ibid., *Herm. Sim.* V:6:1.

18. Ibid.

19. *Herm. Sim.* IX:32:5. The last few pages of the *Shepherd* are extant only in the Latin Vulgate version.

20 *Herm. Sim.* X:4:4.

## THE SECOND-CENTURY APOLOGISTS

The subapostolic second-generation spokesmen for Christianity whom we have considered were simple men who were very practical and very earnest, but who were not for the most part either learned or intellectually brilliant. Now we turn to the way in which more instructed Christians undertook to defend Christianity against the accusation that it was a religion for the unlearned. This is the group commonly spoken of as the Apologists of the second century. (In the courts of the Roman Empire, an *apologia* is a defense—not an indication of regret but a vindication.) The work of the Apologists is directed primarily to the Gentiles, and specifically to educated persons in the Gentile world who, in the view of the Apologists, were sufficiently open-minded, perhaps sufficiently sympathetic, to understand or even to be persuaded by an adequate defense of the Christian faith. These men, without exception as far as I can see, had some training in the Greek schools, and the common motif that runs through all of them is that Christianity is a new philosophy. It is a revealed religious philosophy, and they undertake to make it acceptable, therefore, to disciplined reason.

As in the case of the so-called Apostolic Fathers, it is well to remember that when one comes upon references to the theology of the Apologists or the Christology of the Apologists, there simply is no such thing. They differ so widely in their presuppositions, in their intellectual temper, in their use of Scripture, and in their theological findings, that one can class them together under a single head only for convenience. "Apologist" is not a scientific term; it is an opportunistic label.

The second-century writings thus classified are by Athenagoras of Athens (or Athenagoras the Philosopher), Melito of Sardis, Theophilus of Antioch, Justin Martyr, and an anonymous *Letter to Diognetus*. Without attempting to be comprehensive, we shall glance at the anonymous *Letter to Diognetus*, then turn to the best-known of the Apologists, Justin Martyr.

### Letter to Diognetus

We know nothing about the identity of Diognetus, except that he was clearly an educated and friendly Gentile.[21] The letter cannot be dated with

---

21. *Apostolic Fathers,* II, ed. Loeb Classical Library (Cambridge, MA: Harvard University Press, 1976 rpt. of 1913 ed.).

much confidence. It may have been written in the first half of the second century, perhaps about 130. It is a little gem of both argument and literary composition. In a most friendly temper, conciliatingly, reasonably, and persuasively, it calls attention to the fact that the rejection of idolatry by the Christians is matched by the rejection of idolatry by the best-informed pagans; and to the way in which the word of wisdom—the Logos, the philosophical Word—has been scorned by the less well-informed folk in Gentile society, and yet has been extensively regarded as illuminating by the best-trained minds in the pagan world. As regards the relationship of the Christian church to the world, the writer insists that Christians are a third race yet not localized geographically or ethnically; they are found in all lands. Nor are they isolated occupationally; they take part in ordinary callings. What makes them different is that it is they who hold the world together. The writer uses the very suggestive figure of the relation of the soul to the body. The Christians are in the world as the soul is in the body. As the body wars against the soul, represses it, and frustrates it, so the world does with the Christian community. Yet the soul loves and serves and sustains the body; it pervades it gently and is the basis of its life and health. So the Christians undertake to be the regenerative force in a world which does not understand them or accept them, but which, nevertheless, profits by their presence. What is happening to the Christians now has happened to the disciples of the Logos in past time; and yet the Logos continues persistently, quietly, peaceably ("For," says the writer, "there is no violence in the nature of God") to persuade a refractory world to accept the teachings of the light which is the way of life.

## Justin Martyr

The apologist of the second century whose works we have at full length is Justin Martyr, a native of Samaria.[22] He was born early in the second century, lived for a time at Ephesus, and then went to Rome. We do not know how long he was in Rome, but so far as the tradition enables us to judge, he was martyred there under Marcus Aurelius between 163 and 167. A great many writings are attributed to him, but only three are regarded as authentic. The best-known is an apology addressed to the emperor Antoninus Pius, the father of Marcus Aurelius. There is also an appendix which is commonly listed now as a second apology. There is nothing to

22. *ANF* I.

indicate that it was an independent work, and it appears rather to have been an addendum to the first Apology. Finally there is a dialogue with a certain Trypho, a Jew, who may or may not have been an historical figure. Besides these three works, another on the Resurrection and various other smaller works are commonly regarded as spurious. At least they are so doubtful, and so unimportant for Justin's views, that there is no point in bringing them in.

To understand the content of the Apology, it is necessary to have in mind a sort of stereotyped procession of indictments which were brought against the Christians by popular or learned pagan critics. The roster of charges was so mechanically set that if a new apologist were discovered we could expect to find him dealing with the very same charges. These include, first of all, a declaration that the Christians are atheists. That means on the face of it that they refused to worship the gods recognized by the imperial government, and centrally, the divine genius of the emperor. On public festivals they, along with the Jews, refused to offer incense before the emperor's statues. The force of the specific charge of atheism here is like the force of the charge of impiety which was a capital offence in the old Greek cities. It is in essence treason. Fundamentally, it is a rejection of responsibility as one concerned for the well-being of the commonwealth. The Jews had had to face this charge. They were willing to pray for the health and prosperity of the emperor, but they were quite unwilling to acknowledge his divinity. Now the Christians are on essentially the same ground and have to meet the charge all over again.

Second, they are charged with being bad citizens in respect to particular civil duties. They evade taxes; they evade military service; they refuse to take an active part in the political life of the community. In short, they leave the burden to be carried by others while they receive the advantages which come from residence in settled society.

Third, they are grossly immoral people. The worst charges that are brought against them are charges of infanticide, cannibalism, and incestuous orgies which are given a pseudo-sacred character. Infanticide and cannibalism are charged against them, with lurid details, on the score that the common meal which they ate together involved the slaughter of an infant whose body had been covered with flour and then was divided up and actually consumed as the material element of the Eucharist. Then, after that savage feast, it is charged that the torches were all knocked out and there ensued an orgy of incestuous sexual indulgence. These charges arose out of the fact that the Christians met secretly—no one on the outside knew what went on at their secret meetings—and to pagan minds of a not especially discerning kind, the use of the term *agape*, love feast, seemed to suggest that here was a Dionysian orgy of the old savage sort. It was known that religion had at one time taken these lines, and the Christians were regarded as primitives who were reviving the kind of abominations that civilized folk had long since put aside.

Finally, they were accused of being proletarian. Their membership was drawn from the riffraff, the outcasts, the lower strata of the Roman world.

Obviously these were primarily social and ethical indictments. Alongside of them there is a second kind of accusation: pagan intellectuals charged that Christians could not stand the test of literate analysis of the foolish message they were bringing. Christianity was for slaves, not for gentlefolk. Christianity is intellectually beneath contempt. It is full of the sort of contradictions and absurdities that no disciplined mind could accept. It is for that reason that the Christian preachers avoid the trial of the critical analysis of what they have to say at the hands of people who are genuinely well trained.

In his *Apology*, addressed to the emperor, Justin undertakes to meet these charges one after another right down the line. The first three of the ethical and social accusations he denies flatly and in fact retorts them upon the folk who make them; or else, somewhat unsportingly, declares that not the true Christian church but the fringe of heretical groups is guilty of some of the offensive particular charges. When he comes to the accusation of proletarianism he avows it and makes a virtue of it. "Why yes," says he, "the membership of the christian Church is made up in large part of the poor of the earth, but then God has always found his better servants among the poor. The wise and the powerful and the prosperous have always tended to be self-complacent and arrogant, and God has found pure hearts and devoted wills rather among the disinherited."

As for atheism, the Christians worship the only true God. As far bad citizenship, they go beyond their neighbors in seeking to maintain social order. As for the immoralities which are charged upon them, these are either sheer fiction or else they involve cases of mistaken identity. So, on the social and ethical side Justin is prepared to give the Christian church a clean bill of health.

But now he must confront the charge that Christianity is intellectually absurd, self-contradictory, and lacking in any sort of rational appeal. Justin's recourse at this point, as in the other points raised by the general indictment, is a scheme of defense which takes account of the fact that the Jews had already had to meet every one of these accusations, and that learned Jews like the historian Josephus and the philosopher Philo of Alexandria had actually argued the case on behalf of the Jewish community. Justin takes over several of the arguments that these men had already employed. When he comes to the question of intellectual inadequacy he does much the same thing, as we shall later see, but he gives a curious new twist to the defense which seems to him to be possible there. Those who state that Christianity is incapable of appealing to a philosophically disciplined mind must be made to recognize that Christianity is the truth which all of the philosophers have been seeking. Like the truth in Judaism, it is revealed truth. Sages of the Greek world were continually groping after light, and light came to them, but in fragments and glimpses. It came to them through the gift of the Logos of God; yet it was always piecemeal and incomplete. In Judaism, God revealed to the prophets and sages of the Hebrew people more of the truth than any of the Greek sages had been able to puzzle out. As a matter of fact, since Moses was more ancient than Plato, it was necessary to say that the Jewish wisdom had the real advantage of antiquity. It may even be that the Greek wise men borrowed important parts of their views from the Hebrew Scripture. Josephus and Philo had said that, and Justin was prepared to agree with them. But in comparison to Judaism, Christianity has the further advantage that, whereas even the prophets were given specific words on specific occasions, Christianity can point to the incarnation of the full Logos. The truth has now come in complete and final form. It was made known in the past to Heraclitus and to Socrates and to Plato who were genuine servants of Logos, of Reason in the world; but now Reason has actually come and dwelt among human beings, and what the Christian preachers are proclaiming is that ultimate and final truth.

That plainly requires that Justin undertake to say what the content of the truth is, and this he was glad to do. He speaks as one who, having gone through the philosophical schools one after another without finding satisfaction in any of them, has finally found what he was seeking at the hands of Christian teachers, and who has become himself a Christian teacher who still wears the long-sleeved gown of the philosopher. He likes to be accounted a Christian philosopher.

The truth which he is prepared to offer refers first of all to the one true God, whom he conceives in a way influenced by the Middle Platonism of his day, but after the fashion of Philo and the Hellenistic Jewish philosophers. God is the Absolute, the utterly incomprehensible, the One who is so completely transcendent that he is neither in time nor characterized by time. Neither is he contained in space although, curiously, Justin thinks he has a specific place for his throne. He is not characterized by number nor by any of the Aristotelian categories by which we describe whatever can be described—quantity or quality or relation or state. None of these descriptive categories apply to God. He is the utterly transcendent, absolute being.

His relation to the world is mediated through his Word. And here again, as Professor Goodenough has shown, Philonic treatment is clearly discernible. The Logos of God is declared by Justin, using Philo's language, to be "the second God" (*ho deuteros Theos*). The relation of the Logos to God the Father is described for the most part in metaphors. To speak of the Logos as the Son of God suggests immediately the metaphor of begetting. The Father begets the Logos as his only Son. Yet it seems to Justin that that way of putting the matter may be misunderstood, because human begetting involves separation and essential difference of father and son. Therefore he uses another metaphor: the metaphor of emanation taken from the shining of the sun and the spreading of its rays. Its light and its warmth come out in a continuous stream. According to ancient scientific thought, moreover, it was thought that the sun never diminished in brightness and in heat; it loses no energy; it is a perpetually active spring of light and of warmth. The Logos, then, is the emanation of the eternal being of the Father. But that has a tendency to fall too far in the other direction and to diminish too much the distinctions between the Father and the Son. So finally Justin resorts to another metaphor. When one fire is kindled from another fire, in essential character they are alike. In respect of numerical identity, they are two and "not one." Hence, it can be said the Logos is *deuteros*, the second in number, but not different in kind. So far Philo has been Justin's guide.

Now he finds references in the Christian literature to the Paraclete, the Spirit of truth, the Holy Spirit; but Philo had not done very much with the conception of the Holy Spirit. He had used it, but for him it was the spirit of the prophets, the spirit of power and of wisdom; and he tended usually to make it another title for the Logos, although at other times he treated it as the spouse of the Logos, or somehow a companion or a special manifestation of the Logos. Justin is just about as vague as Philo at this point. He refers to the Holy Spirit, but he never examines in anything like full detail its intrinsic character or its relation to the other beings that can be called God.

In most of this, he is on Philonic ground with relatively little modification. But now his major and specifically Christian affirmation is that the Logos becomes incarnate. That, Philo had never said. In Jesus Christ the Logos takes individual human form for the salvation of human beings. The fate which befell Jesus Christ is the fate, Justin urges along with the other Apologists, which has always befallen the true servants of Wisdom. These people have always been persecuted by misunderstanding and malicious neighbors right down through the centuries; and it is not surprising that when the Logos comes in the fullest, most authentic form, rejection and persecution is carried to the extreme. As incarnate Word, Jesus undertakes to save first of all through his teaching. He is one who shows people the true nature of God, the way of life. On the other hand, he brings to them a new basis of community. He is one through relation to whom believers become a new Israel. The old Israel had had an opportunity beyond any granted to the world, but it had rejected and thus missed the special privilege accorded to it. It is the followers of the new embodiment of the Logos who become the recipients of what had been promised to Israel in olden times.

Now when Justin gets into this specifically Christian area of thought, it is curious to see how the detail and originality of his affirmations thin out. While he is on the ground Philo had already covered, he speaks with confidence and fullness and with large-scale suggestiveness, but when he comes into the territory in which philosophic wisdom is not the most appropriate basis for insight and interpretation, he begins to falter. What he can say about salvation is said primarily in terms of enlightenment. His understanding of the thing that happens to Christian believers is that it is like what has happened to himself. He had gone seeking wisdom at the hands of the philosophic schools. But it was only when he came to the Christian teachers that he really had the feeling that he was in the presence of the truth. Just such enlightenment of the mind is his conception of the essential regeneration that differentiates Christian believers from those who have not found the way and the truth as he found it. Of any suggestion of St. Paul's tragic understanding of the inner conflicts of man, which are resolved through the divine grace that brings reconciliation, there is not a glimmer in the writings of Justin. An indication of the Johannine conception of the entrance of eternal life as a dynamic principle of existence is perhaps adumbrated but by no means apprehended. This is much too simply a "liberal" version of the early Christian teachings. Justin is humane, heroic, morally devoted, but his religious insight is just not profound.

What has just been said with regard to his understanding of the life of salvation is in some respects also true of his understanding of the nature of the Church. It is the Ark of salvation into which human beings come through acceptance of the truth taught by Jesus Christ, and in the Ark where they have been enlightened they will be saved from the final destruction when the judgment of God descends on the disobedient world at the Last Day. The imagery of the Body of Christ, the organic unity in which individuals find fulfillment, is lacking. Justin thinks rather in terms of the schoolroom and he never gets very far beyond those concepts in his theology.

Yet it is when he is talking about the new community that his language really catches fire. Here now is a company of folk who can be thought of as one, one people, one assembly, a totality of members of a single body. He refers to words of the prophets, words of the apostles, which seem to him to point to this kind of unity in a collective or corporate whole. There is no suggestion of—how shall we say?—a corporate inheritance of sinfulness; that is not in accordance with his whole perspective. But there is stress on the corporate character of salvation: to be a member of the community that now is redeemed, that is to be saved, to be saved against that day when the Lord will return in glory, and when, says Justin, although some of our people (*genus*) disagree with me, I believe there will begin a thousand year reign of the Lord on earth, before the day when all the dead shall be raised and the final separation between righteous and unrighteous will be carried through.

When Justin was called upon to confront the Roman court and say whether or not he was prepared to die for his Christian faith, there was no ambiguity, no superficiality. The truth which has enlightened his mind was the truth for which he was prepared to give his life, and he did so. One is confronted by the difficult task of seeking to play fair on the one hand with the utter genuineness and heroism of Justin's understanding of Christianity, and on the other hand with the rather meager interpretative terms in which he found it possible to articulate that understanding. This in general is true of the Apologists as a whole.

# CHAPTER 5

# Heresies: Irregular Versions of the Gospel[1]

THE NEXT CHRISTIAN THINKERS with whom we shall deal are of a different order. They advocated aberrant forms of the Christian message.[2] Eventually they were labeled *heretics*—a word which originally had an innocent meaning, but came in the course of the second and third centuries to refer to those who regarded themselves as Christians but were judged by the church as a whole to have deviated widely enough from Christian teaching not to deserve the name. There were two major sources for such deviations. One is the tendency of views which had been accepted to persist after they had become no longer appropriate expressions for what the growing community considered its essential faith. This was true, for example, of modalistic Monarchianism, of Adoptionism of the Jewish-Christian type, and of Montanism. Each of these ways of

1. This chapter is compiled from materials that Professor Calhoun had begun to rework in preparation for publication but to which he had not added footnotes and other features of scholarly apparatus. A few sentences here and there from the 1948 multilithed lectures have been retained by Calhoun or the compilers [ed.].

2. Professor Calhoun in this paragraph as in his whole presentation, gives his own version of the traditional view, now widely disputed, that what developed into "orthodoxy" was more deeply rooted in "original Christianity" than were what he calls in the title of this chapter "irregular versions of the gospel." He was aware of the challenge to this outlook (raised most influentially by Walter Bauer, *Orthodoxy and Heresy in Earliest Christianity*, English translation and supplement by R. Kraft and G. Krodel from the second German edition and supplement by G. Strecker [Philadelphia: Fortress, 1971; orig. Germ. 1934, 1964]), according to which "orthodoxy" was simply that form of early Christianity that happened to win. None of his writings, however, refer to this view, much less argue against it explicitly. Yet Calhoun's version of the traditional view is sufficiently devoid of the defects that have rendered the latter vulnerable to such critiques as that of Bauer as to make proposed alternatives seem superfluous and hence unpersuasive. For more on this theme, the reader is referred to the Introduction to this volume [ed.].

thinking stressed a factor which from the earliest days of the church had had a legitimate place; but by giving exclusive or one-sided or exaggerated stress to it, and making it the core of the faith, each of these groups came under condemnation. [Of them, the discussion of the Monarchians will be partially, and of Montanists entirely, postponed to following chapters.] A second major source, and presumably the more familiar and more fertile source, was the introduction into Christian belief by converts from a wide variety of religious and cultural backgrounds of the motifs which they had known in their earlier careers, but which are regarded as in one way or another incompatible with the Christian *kerygma* and with the developing interpretation of the *kerygma* as Christian theology becomes more elaborated and sophisticated.

Our information about early deviations comes in large part from the biased accounts of their opponents, but we also have a body of primary texts which has in the last century greatly expanded. Indeed, there is an embarrassment of riches at present. Only the specialists (which I am not) have access to much of the new material, and only the specialists have the kind of background knowledge which makes it possible for them to interpret it with some degree of confidence.

In a way, that does not greatly matter, however; for our concern is with the heretical groups which had the most significance for the development of Christian doctrine. In the second century, there are two names that are outstanding, Marcion and Valentinus. Those are the men who appealed most dangerously to members of Christian churches. Together with Valentinus, we can place the names of Ptolemy and Heracleon who followed him as leaders of Valentinianism in the West. Happily we have much information about Marcion (thanks to Tertullian's five books quoting from Marcion's Antitheses in order to refute his views). We also have a sizable amount of information about Valentinian thought, including now the *Gospel of Truth*, which may be a primary work of Valentinus, the founder. Before dealing with Marcion, however, it will be well to say a word about the Judaizing tendencies to which his work may in part have been a reaction; and after discussing Valentinian Gnosticism, I shall append some comments on a fourth type of irregular teaching, Monarchianism.

## JEWISH-CHRISTIAN GROUPS

We can begin, I think, by looking first at certain Jewish-Christian groups, some of whom were creating difficulties when the Church first established itself as a distinctive community. In Paul's letters, particularly the first two chapters of Galatians, and in the book of Acts, we have reference to Judaic legalists who when they were converted to Christianity brought their legalism along with them—not at all a surprising thing to do. The essential difference between a Jewish legalist and a Jewish-Christian legalist was that the convert was ready to say "Jesus is Messiah; he has already come"; whereas the Jewish legalist, looking for the Messiah of Old Testament prophecy or rabbinical teaching, declared that the Messiah is still to be awaited. But many of those who crossed the line and became recognizably converts to Christianity nevertheless declared that essential portions of the Jewish law were requisite either for all Christians or at least for converts from Judaism. The more moderate position as described in the fifteenth chapter of Acts was taken by James and Peter in the Council of Jerusalem. Even after that Council's decision, however, there were still Jewish rigorists who continued to make trouble by turning up in the mission communities outside Palestine, insisting that the Jewish law is requisite for all Christians without exception. According to Acts, Peter wavered, as you remember, in his understanding of the meaning of that original decision; and when some were come from James to Antioch, Peter gave up his insistence that it was allowable that there be one table for both Jewish and Gentile converts to sit down and eat together.

Now when we ask what sort of Judaizing Christians we can recognize toward the end of the first century and on into later periods, we find ourselves at first confronted by textbook accounts which try to distinguish quite neatly Nazarenes, who are declared to be moderates (following roughly the line that James and Peter took at the Jerusalem Council); Ebionites, who are rigorists; and then certain Elkesaites, who represent a curious combination of legalism and Gnostic speculation; or perhaps it would be more accurate to say, astrological and theurgical interests; and lastly a vague group from among whom the *Pseudo-Clementine Homilies* and *Recognitions* emerged. Let me urge that you just wipe out that neat classification; it seems to me that it has become quite meaningless by reason of the fact that we know a good deal more than we once knew about the character of Judaism at the time of the emergence of the church. We know that within the tradition of rabbinical Judaism there were already those writing apocalypses, revelations of one kind and another, containing speculations about the beginning and about the end. The great rabbis warned against the dangers of this kind of speculation, but it was going on. Some of them ventured so far from the Old Testament tradition as interpreted by the rabbis that they were flatly called *apostates*, heretics in the disapproving sense of the term. Moreover, the listing that I gave you a moment ago is the listing which Epithanius uses, and Epithanius is one of those people who just incorrigibly categorize whether there is good ground for it or not.

Let us then say something like this. There is good evidence that there continued in the early church for a period that cannot be specified converts from Judaism, some of whom were moderate, some of whom were extreme in their demands for recognition of the Law as incumbent upon all Christians. Justin Martyr in his *Dialogue with Trypho* says there are some who regard the Law as obligatory for themselves but do not try to impose it upon their neighbors, and those he regards as fellow Christians. There are others, however, who insist that the Law is mandatory for everyone as the source and way of salvation, so that unless one fulfills the requirements of the Law one cannot be saved, one cannot be a Christian. There are some, says he, among our Christian brothers who reject both groups, but his own tolerant attitude towards the first group may well have been representative of the Christian attitude generally. There is little later evidence of the survival of this first group, while the second rigorist group which in Paul's time insisted on imposing the Law upon everybody had a long lived group of successors in the sect that we know as the Ebionites (a term which comes presumably from the description of themselves as *ebionim*, the poor who are inheritors in the Kingdom of Heaven). We have various descriptions of them; and the most plausible ones represent them as insisting on the Law for everybody (circumcision, food laws, Sabbath observance), and as regarding Jesus indeed as Messiah but as the son of Joseph and Mary, one who is born as—using a phrase of Justin's which he applies to folk of this sort—"a man of human ancestry." He was the Messiah, but he was chosen as Messiah by reason of his obedience to the Law. It was precisely his faithfulness to the Law (and it is this which justifies) that made him *Christos*, so that if we had been equally successful in fulfilling the requirements of the Law, we also would be *christoi*. Now this makes a perfectly straightforward and consistent picture. Not unnaturally, if the picture given of the Ebionites is accurate, these folk rejected Paul; they put him among the apostates from the Law.

Now we find that same term applied to a very different group, a speculative group, and we find Epiphanius giving us what I think is a sort of clue to the double way in which the terms come to be used. He wants to distinguish sharply between two periods in the development of Ebionitism: the first period started way back in the days of Peter and Paul, and the Ebionites in those days were simply the rigoristic Judaic party; this was true until the moving of the Jerusalem church across the Jordan just before the conquest under Titus in 70 CE. But then, says Epiphanius, a certain Ebion (by common consent, no such person ever existed, although the name had already appeared in Tertullian) began to introduce speculative lines of thought into what hitherto had been a straightforward form of rigorist Jewish legalism. Some of the lines of thought can also be found among the Elkesaites (given to their leader in an angelic revelation, Epiphanius says), some parallel the Pseudo-Clementine writings, and some are very much like certain strains we find in the Qumran documents (in the *Manual of Discipline* and the *War Scroll*). Thus Epiphanius understands this later stage of Ebionite development to be a kind of catchall for a whole spectrum of Judaizing Christians, speculative as well as legalistic and rigoristic. The chief significance of the name for later Christian doctrine arises from its insistence that Jesus was a mere man. Wherever you have that view, you are likely to find its adherents described as Ebionite. Adoptionism, if you will, can be associated with this Christology. The primary point about what came to be rejected as Ebionitism, in other words, is neither its adoptionism nor its legalism but the assertion that Jesus is wholly human and not God.

In addition to legalists, there are Judaizing Gnostic views which appeared in the early church. Cerinthus is perhaps the earliest of these folk that we know. He tried to combine Jewish legalism with speculative thought about the beginning and the end; and in common with various other Gnostics, denied the creatorhood of the God of the Old Testament: the world is made by an inferior being. He also denied the genuine messiahship of Jesus Christ, declaring that *Christos* was a being from heaven who descended at the baptism upon the man Jesus and left him before the crucifixion.

There was also, as we have already mentioned in passing, the Elkesaite group or tendency which had astrological and theurgical rather than strictly theological interests; and finally there is the so-called Clementine literature, the works called the *Homilies* and *Recognitions* of Clement. In point of fact these have nothing to do with Clement, the first-century bishop of Rome, save that he is made the central figure in a narrative romance that pulls together a good many earlier sources and becomes itself the basis for both of these works.

## Ultra-Pauline Radicalism: Marcion

For all these Judaistic Christian groups, varied though they were, the Old Testament held inspired revelations of the one true God; some version of the Mosaic Law was binding on all Christians; and Jesus was the Anointed One foretold by the prophets—i.e. the Old Testament writers. Paul was in disfavor, and the gospel was conceived as a completion of the Law rightly understood.

The Apostolic Fathers and the Apologists [i.e., those recognized as orthodox by the later Christian mainstream] also agreed that the Old Testament was inspired Scripture for Christians, but claimed to understand better than their Jewish-Christian adversaries the continuities and discontinuities between the old dispensation and the new; between the subtly-worded prophesies and the actual coming of the Messiah; between the universally valid core of the Law and the new freedom from ceremonial requirements no longer needed. To be sure, in their strikingly diverse but exalted views of Jesus Christ, they differed from their Judaizing fellow Christians even more than from one another. All of them in some fashion, if they discussed the question at all, regarded him as preexistent Son of God (Logos, Wisdom, Holy Spirit, Other God) who came to earth, was virgin-born, and suffered death and resurrection for man's sake. But all this they found predicted and foreshadowed in the Old Testament, if interpreted with requisite ingenuity. This basic conviction of continuity as well as contrast between Hebrew faith in God and the Christian proclamation they shared with Paul, and some of them quoted approvingly from his letters and counted him a true apostle. But none of them understood his passionate vision of Christian liberty through faith and the costly reconciliation of wayward, helpless men and women by the grace of God in Christ, "apart from law."

It was the man whom Polycarp called "the first-born of Satan," and whom various spokesmen for the second-century church regarded as the most dangerous of all the heretics, Marcion of Sinope, who did understand this side of Paul's thought, and he declared it to be the whole gospel. From his home in Pontus on the Black Sea, Marcion came by way of Asia Minor to Rome about 139; and though he seems to have scandalized both his home church and various other communities by his explosive convictions, he was received in Rome as a fellow Christian. But not for long. In 144 he was formally arraigned before a local synod, adjudged a heretic, and excommunicated, taking with him, according to Tertullian, half the Roman Church's membership. Whether or not this is an exaggeration there is no way of knowing, but at all events it testifies to the very great depth of the impact that Marcion's reform movement made upon many who wanted to regard themselves as genuine Christians.

During the rest of his life—perhaps ten or fifteen years—he continued single-mindedly to proclaim the simplified gospel as he understood it, and Marcionite churches came into existence in all regions from Italy to Persia. Harnack insists on the radical novelty of Marcion's thought. It is true that five centuries earlier, Sinope had been the birthplace of Diogenes the Cynic, a trenchant critic of elaborate speculation and comfortable living; and that Tertullian and Hippolytus think they find Stoic and Cynic components in Marcionite doctrine. More important, certainly, was the existence of an active Jewish community in and near Sinope. Thence had come "a Jew named Aquila, a native of Pontus," who with his wife Priscilla had become a close associate of Paul and a tutor of Apollos (Acts 18:1–3, 24–26). In Marcion's own lifetime and apparently in Sinope, another Aquila was at work, a Jewish proselyte and scholar who made a literal translation of the Hebrew Old Testament into Greek, following the Hebrew text far more closely than the Septuagint had done, or even the Septuagint as corrected by Theodotion, another Jewish proselyte translator in Asia. Aquila's version was preferred to any other in rabbinic circles partly because its more exact rendering of passages like Isa 7:14 ("young woman," instead of the LXX "virgin") deprived the Christians of some of their most cherished proof-texts. Despite the lack of all explicit information, it is tempting to suppose that Marcion knew his Jewish neighbor's strict translation. That he shared Aquila's conviction that the Hebrew Old Testament should be precisely and literally interpreted is beyond doubt. He rejected as improper and unnecessary the all but universal Christian (and Gnostic) practice of allegorizing ancient texts to make them support new teachings.

Implicit in this rejection was a startling insight that no one before Marcion had avowed: the Gospel is utterly new, unprepared by anything in prior history, and antithetic to the whole tradition of Judaic faith and practice. This insight and its emotional impact on Marcion are dramatically indicated in a sentence (preserved now in an anti-Marcionite tract of unknown authorship) that may have opened his Antitheses: "O marvel beyond marvel, ravishment, power, and wonder it is, that one can say just nothing about the gospel, nor think about it, nor liken it to anything at all." The Lord's word about new wine and old bottles must be taken seriously. The Gospel cannot be reconciled with the Law and the prophets. There is only one covenant—the covenant of grace, not new in the sense that it was preceded by an old covenant, but unprecedented—so alien to our natural modes of thought that it can be neither understood nor discussed but only believed.

Marcion held that most Christians have not seen this radical novelty of the Gospel. Even the Twelve who were chosen to be the immediate companions of the Lord did not see it; they all fell back into Jewish error, and that was why Paul had to be selected as a new apostle and the only one who really understood the newness and power of the Gospel. Since the life of Jesus was originally presented in oral discourse and not in writing, we just have to brush aside the Gospels which have been attributed to Matthew and to John. So far as regards the accessible words of Marcion, we have no reference to Mark, but presumably Mark also was rejected. Now that Gospel to which Paul refers always in the singular—he never knew anything about four gospels, but one Gospel—presumably that Gospel is the one assignable to his friend and companion, Luke the physician. Yet even Paul's letters have been interlarded with quotations from the Old Testament that have no business there at all. But you can take ten letters of Paul, and by a very careful use of the scalpel you can get rid of these Judaizing interpolations, and you will then have an *apostolikon* which deserves to be treated by the Church as Scripture. In reference to the one Gospel to which Paul continually refers, well, you can at least make an attempt to recover that by a similar expurgation of the Gospel of Luke. Plainly enough the birth story and the genealogy, the baptism, and the temptation have to come out, as these all presuppose a Hebraic background.

Now since Marcion has decided that the Old Testament as a whole has to be excluded, that entails some drastic theological consequences. Relegating "the Law and the prophets" to Judaism entailed disavowing also the Demiurge, the craftsman-god, the Maker whom the Jewish Scriptures described as framing and governing the present world with its human denizens, and as imposing the Law upon them and punishing them when they broke it. The Demiurge was not malicious, but he was inept, inflexible, and so (like the "unsound tree" in the Lord's sermon) a source of evil to human beings—as he himself expressly declared (Isa 45:7, Jer 18:11). To make a world he needed raw material: "some sort of underlying matter, unborn, unmade, coequal with God," and to matter Marcion assigns evil, likewise, "unborn . . . unmade . . . eternal." The resulting world, then, is definitely bad: "an evil nature produced from evil matter and a 'righteous' Maker." It is defaced with useless trivialities: "snakes, scorpions, crocodiles, and fleas and bugs, and gnats"; and worse, with the filth of fleshly life and death: of carnal union producing bodies "stuffed with dung," of bloodshed at birth, circumcision, animal slaughter, sacrifice, warfare, and death. The Maker himself is not "evil." He is stupidly "legal and laborious," entangled in the ills that he himself has brought about, finding grim satisfaction in bloodshed, making favorites of killers like Moses and Joshua: in short, an ignorant despot who knows nothing higher than his own contemptible sovereignty. His kingdom is wholly of this world. His Law (like himself not simply bad, since it warns against seeking evil, as well as enjoining much nonsense and worse) is relevant with its earthly rewards and punishments only to life on earth. His Messiah—still vainly awaited—is an earth-born warrior, incapable of bringing eternal salvation. The verdict on the Maker, Lawgiver, and Judge must be: not wholly bad, but not really good.

The Gospel is good news of quite another God, not merely "just" (*dikaios* in a narrow legal sense) but "good" (*agathos*, gracious, merciful), not tangled up in earth-bound law. This God, "pure kindliness," dwelling far above the Demiurge, unknown to him and all his creatures until "the fifteenth year of Tiberius Caesar," is permanently "alien" (*xenos*) to the earth-maker, a "strange God" not of brute power and stiff, punitive "justice," but of unearned pity and gracious redeeming love. He too requires "what is right" (*dikaios*), in terms of faith and love toward God, love of neighbor, and purity of life. But his gratuitous disposition to help at his own cost the human creature-victims of the Demiurge entails antagoniz-ing the despot on his own ground.

Hence the beginning of the Gospel story: "In the fifteenth year . . . Jesus came down," i.e., "appeared," to set human beings free from the old Law and prophecy, from the world of birth and death, and from the power of the Demiurge. This redemptive act—preaching the truth, enduring the cross for man's sake—is the sole "work" that can be ascribed to the good God; and only in such an act—not in any display of world-making or wonder-working power—can disinterested love be revealed. In fact it was no subordinate being but "that better God" himself who for man "took the trouble (*laboravit*) to descend from the third heaven," and even was crucified for us "in this hovel (*cellula*) of the Creator." God "was revealed, in Christ Jesus, by himself alone" (*per semetipsum*). This is Tertullian's re-port. A later anti-Marcionite spokesman (Adamantius, ca. 300) adds: "The death of the Good (*ton agathon*) became men's salvation." The evidence is fairly slim, but Harnack is convinced that Marcion identified Jesus Christ as "the good God" in everything but name. If this be true, it was simply *God* who "came down" and "appeared" on earth to save.

It is much more strongly attested that the Savior was not born, did not assume a genuine body of flesh, and was not really man. Marcion seems to have compared his sudden appearance on earth to the famil-iar appearances of the angels to Abraham and Lot. They seemed solid enough: "They really talked and ate and did what had been commanded them," yet their fleshly seeming was all "illusive" and "suppositious." So Christ ate and drank, was weary, suffered and died "in the likeness of man"—yet he was not really a human being, born of a human mother, emergent in the Creator's world of growing things. It is hard to tell how subtle Marcion's thought may have been: whether he saw the good God really entering—spiritually, not physically—into the hapless human expe-rience of suffering and death, or whether as his critics all declared, he saw the Passion as an unreal dramatic show by a God who could not suffer. He used such words as *phantasia* (seeming, likeness), and "putative" often enough to make any Christian realist suspicious; yet the very point of his insistence that in Christ the very God of gracious, unmerited love made himself known is lost unless he did think of the cross as really redemptive self-sacrifice. On the one hand, his God is "tranquil," "impassible." On the other, he lets himself be crucified "in the likeness of man" by the jealous, violent Demiurge, giving his life as a ransom-price for humans. It seems impossible to clarify this harsh paradox from the sources that are still accessible, and perhaps it was actually as far as Marcion himself had gone at the center of his gospel.

The crucial response of those who would be saved is faith—not fear, not "legalistic" obedience, and not esoteric "knowledge" (*gnosis*). Among those who heard Jesus preach the true God of forgiving love on earth, as has already been mentioned, believers were not numerous. But in the underworld prison where multitudes of pre-Christian sinners and pagans were being punished by the despot Demiurge, the new word of forgiveness would be welcomed *en masse*—except by Abraham, Moses, and the other "righteous" servants of the "righteous" Ruler. Since their trust was still in him and his earthly promises, they would be deaf to the new word that Jesus, "the Good," brought into the prison house after rising by his own power from the dead. But the vast disillusioned majority believed with joy and were set free in spirit for the "eternal life" that the Demiurge could not in any case bestow.

The end of the despot's rule is now near. When it comes, this world and its Maker will dissolve, along with those who still trust in him. That will be in a sense a day of judgment by the Good God—but only in the sense that He and those who trust Him will survive, and all that is incompatible with his goodness will disappear. "The God who is better judges evil simply (*plane*) by not willing it, and condemns it by holding it in check" (*prohibendo*).

Meanwhile, those whose faith is in the Christ-God must live as the true church of the redeemed, with bishops and presbyters, baptism (with water and oil), and Eucharist (with bread and water), a simple liturgy and a stern ethic. Not only the cruder sorts of self-indulgence were forbidden but also marriage, bloodshed, and the eating of meat—concessions to the Demiurge and his doomed world. Secrecy and evasion were scorned, and even their opponents bear witness to the noteworthy number of Marcionite martyrs. Apelles, a more moderate follower of Marcion, who held that the Good God was himself the "one source" (*arche*) of existence and that the Old Testament, having been falsified by interpolations, was to be partly but not wholly discarded, summed up very simply the Marcionite faith as he understood it: "Those would be saved who have set their hope on the Crucified, if only they were found doing good works."

This is not Gnosticism, despite Marcion's contempt for this world and its Maker. It is exaggerated, one-sided Paulinism, without Paul's sense of history, of the meaning of sin, of man's need to be reconciled to himself and his Maker, of the patient agony of "the whole created world" awaiting release from futility, or of the many-sided saving act of God in Christ and the profound transformation signified by the word *faith*. If the church was wrong in its failure to appreciate what Marcion saw with vivid intensity and preached with fierce honesty—the newness of the Gospel and the radical meaning of grace—it was right in judging that his insistence on isolating the church from its Jewish ancestry, his scorn for the natural world as a witness to Jesus Christ, and his refusal to allow that the Redeemer was truly man, made it impossible to regard his teaching as Christian.

## GENTILE GNOSTICISM

After this consideration of Judaic and anti-Judaic heretical tendencies in the early church, we come to Gentile Gnosticism, which is in itself a whole universe. This is an enormous and incompletely mapped territory in which we are still waiting, among other things, for a scholarly consensus on how to understand the Nag Hammadi materials.[3] One reason for the inadequacy of our sources is that the early Gnostic conventicles, unlike the Marcionites, were secretive about their teachings, cults, and writing, so that even second-, third-, and fourth-century orthodox opponents were largely dependent on limited personal contacts, on hearsay, and on documentation that was often not easy to identify and evaluate. Such opponents usually laid great stress on the plurality and diversity of the Gnostic sects, with lengthy checklists of leaders (or supposed leaders) and groups, with or without thumbnail refutations. Their concern was not to provide dispassionate expositions of Gnosticism, but to contrast the discordant multiplicity and frequent bizarreries of the sects with the declared unanimity and sober antiquity of the "catholic" Church. They were seeking to discredit rather than simply to understand rivals, some of whom were clearly dangerous.

Modern scholars, not surprisingly, have been more interested in seeking common patterns of thought and tracing lines of common ances-

---

3. These were discovered in Egypt in 1945 and are available in translation in James Robinson, ed., *The Nag Hammadi Library in English: Revised Edition* (San Francisco: Harper One, 2004). Calhoun read much of this material before it was translated and after his retirement, wrote the present account as an unfinished and undocumented draft of what he hoped to publish [ed.].

try to make the rise of Gnosticism more understandable. This obviously necessary quest has made real headway in identifying some major lines of affiliation, especially among the Valentinian groups treated by Irenaeus and Hippolytus, and in tracing some second-century Gnostic motifs to earlier sources known or presumed.

The Gnostic leaders and groups noticed by Irenaeus and Hippolytus include some that were born in paganism and either remained pagan or assumed a Christian veneer. Some, on the other hand, originated within the loose confines of the Christian community, presenting a serious speculative reinterpretation of the Gospel rather than a mere overlaying of pagan piety with Christian motifs. The end products of these two opposite processes often came to be very much alike, and there seems to have been a good deal of intergroup borrowing of mythological names and themes, and of both titles and texts of sectarian scriptures. But in their beginnings, pagan and Christian Gnostics differed in basic temper. Pagan Gnostics began with an experience of salvation from worldly powers, which they held to be effected by supracosmic Beings and mediated through various superhuman agents, of whom Jesus might or might not be one. Christian Gnostics began with salvation through Jesus Christ, for whom then a place was found in some divine hierarchy. Our concern here is chiefly with the latter group, of whom Valentinus and his immediate successors are the ones now most clearly identifiable. But some comment is needed respecting the kaleidoscopic context in which they worked.

It has long been held, and the new documents confirm the judgment, that Gnostic thought was largely preoccupied with four problems: the nature of God; the origin and nature of the world and humankind in relation to God; the origin of evil; and the way of salvation, including the final disposition of the world and of human life.

The Gnostic writings known to us often agree in ascribing to God a most exalted nature, stressing his inaccessibility to all ordinary ways of knowing. We have already seen in Philo and some of the Apologists an ambivalent doctrine of God: declaring on the one hand his transcendence of all descriptive categories and on the other his concrete, active self-manifestation as Maker and Ruler of this world and Savior of those who do his will. The Gnostics show a similar ambivalence, but on a different level. They emphasize especially the first moment in such a doctrine: the radical otherness of God from all finite existence. He is incomprehensible, ineffable, indescribable—all the familiar negations that forbid placing him within the scope of human thought. Hippolytus explains at length how Basilides goes even beyond Philo, his earlier Alexandrine compatriot, by speaking habitually of "God Who is Not (*ouk on Theos*), surpassing Being itself; not Being (*ouk ousia*), not devoid of Being (*ouk anousion*), not simple, not composite . . . not at all any of the things that are called by name or perceived or thought." This particular way of spelling out the mystic *via negativa* may have been peculiar to Basilides (ca. 133), but his meaning—that God cannot be classed with things that "exist" as the world exists—is common doctrine. On the other hand, all the great Gnostics speak of God as Father, the ultimate Source of all that is. Some even call him "the First Man," or ascribe to him "love"—not desire or need but pure benevolence, untroubled and unmoved. But they are at pains to insist that even as Father or as primal Love he can be known only by initiates through secret revelations.

He cannot be known through the world as his handiwork, for he is neither the maker nor the ruler of this world. Always this world is scornfully regarded as the work either of underlings—often a company of seven "angels," headed by "the god of the Jews"—or of a single hostile and deceptive power. Likewise it is ruled—ignorantly, clumsily, and jealously—by these angel-Archons, and perhaps by multitudes of their henchmen; or else by the one power that is hostile to God. Unlike the pure tranquility of the Godhead, worldly existence is vitiated by the matter from which it is molded and the ineptitude of its makers. It is subject therefore to the slavery of time and change, passions and fatalities, under the oppressive rule of jealous astral powers. It is a world that groans and travails—but of itself is without hope. God neither made it nor rules it, nor indeed has any direct contact with it at all.

But this account needs further elaboration. On the one hand there are gradations within the Godhead. Much as a light source produces light or a mind produces thought, so the "Father" somehow gives rise to "sons" or other offspring, some very near him, others farther away, but all in some sense divine. On the other hand this plural Godhead is related to the world through some sort of intermediary being, so that light strikes down even into the ignoble realm of what otherwise would be chaos—"the waters," "the shadows." Sometimes this mediation was stated bluntly to involve three primary "principles" (*archai*): Light (the Divine, the Real or True, the Fullness or *Pleroma*), Darkness (Chaos, Matter, the Void), and between them Spirit (perhaps Holy Spirit or Wisdom, Sophia,

*Prounikos*—"burden bearer"), not divine but capable of aspiring toward the divine and of conveying aid to the world below. Sometimes this intermediary was not a primary principle but a product of emanation —and perhaps of deviation—from the Godhead. At all events, by the agency of Holy Spirit, Sophia, or Soul, or perhaps of Son-Word-Serpent (as the Ophite Gnostics put it), living contact is maintained between the Godhead and the world.

This contact is especially important with respect to the origin of man. Like the rest of the world, human beings are produced by ignorant or inferior powers. But without the awareness of these quarrelsome bunglers, "seeds" of divine capacity for knowledge and life were conveyed into the first earth-man and into some—not all—of his descendants. This outwitting of the jealous, self-important world rulers was most often ascribed to the feminine Mother-principle (Sophia or Holy Spirit), sometimes to a Son perhaps aided by the Holy Spirit, and ultimately, of course, to the ineffable Father acting through intermediaries. Not all can be freed from entanglement in this sorry world and from its shabby rulers (often portrayed in the patterns of astrological fatalism). A favorite Gnostic device was to adapt the formula of "three races" or genera of people—pagans, Jews, Christians, found in the ancient *Preaching of Peter* and in Aristides' *Apology*—so as to divide humankind into "material" (*hylekoi*) or "earthy" (*xokoi*), "psychical" (*psychikoi* in the Pauline sense of 1 Cor 2:14), and "spiritual" (*pneumatikoi*) segments. The first were by nature incapable of enlightenment, and so of immortality; the third, also by nature, were sure of it. The fate of psychical persons, when they were recognized as a distinct class, is less clear. Sometimes, at least, they seem to have been destined for an intermediate sphere of existence. Sometimes this class was subdivided—still by nature—into good and bad psychical persons, the former destined to "rest in the intermediate place," the latter to perish. In any event, only spiritual beings can enter the presence of the Godhead and live.

From these conceptions of God, the world, and man, the Gnostic concept of salvation follows inevitably. Human beings are enslaved through ignorance to ignorant world rulers. Some of them cannot be freed. For those who can, the way of salvation must be enlightenment: the reception of "knowledge" (*gnosis*) from above—neither scientific information nor philosophic insight but an occult, vivifying *gnosis* that awakens in "spiritual" persons a saving apprehension of divine reality. Such *gnosis* obviously cannot be got by study of this world, the work of sub-divine powers and itself pervaded by material distortions. It must come as supernatural revelation. So far all the Gnostic sects were agreed. In naming the agent of revelation, who was properly to be called Savior (*soter*)—a familiar term in pagan syncretism and in Gnostic literature—there was less unanimity. Those we have called pagan Gnostics named various saviors (sometimes declaring that several names were merely variant titles for one being), and usually included among them Jesus or Christ or both as a salute to the new gospel. A favorite device was to represent the secret revelations as words transmitted privately to a group of disciples by the risen Christ while he sojourned on earth during months or years before his final ascension. The Christian Gnostics put salvation through Christ at the center, though even they felt compelled to disparage or to deny the human reality of Jesus; and some of them, distinguishing between "Jesus" and "Christ," assigned the former a permanently subordinate role. None of them could overcome a profound disesteem for the world of space, time, and flesh.

Salvation, then, must be escape from this world, not redemption or transformation of it. The "spiritual" persons to whom liberating *gnosis* is granted must show in their lives on earth a real *contemptus mundi*. Usually this would take the form of stringent asceticism: no marriage, no meat, no wine. In rare instances (the Simonians, Nicolaitians, Cainites, and Carpocratians were most frequently named) it seems to have taken the opposite form, libertinism, still by way of declaring contempt for this world and the laws laid down by its overlords, sometimes adding that the spiritual person must "pass through lower things."

In principle, the end result sought is the return of all the "seeds" of divine spirit, now scattered among mankind in a muddy world, to their proper place in the realm of true being. In detail this return is variously conceived, and rather more vaguely described than the original dispersal. Often it involves perilous journeys of the enlightened soul (or its spiritual part) through the heavens, whether seven or three hundred and sixty-five, ruled by hostile Archons. But whether at the end material bodies simply dissolve into persisting chaos, or whether the whole material world is annihilated and only spirit remains, salvation means not the renewal of God's cherished creation but the annulment of a huge and mischievous digression.

The particular Gnostic group that spokesmen for the early church found most dangerous (and fascinating) was the Valentinians. Tertullian, writing between AD 190 and 215, tells us that Valentinus had been so outstanding in the church at Rome about the same time Marcion was excommunicated that he had good reason to hope that he might be chosen the next bishop. Yet the major polemical counterattacks which we have, those of Irenaeus and his disciple Hippolytus, were written fifty or more years later. Thus an elaborate mythology which they attribute to the Valentinians may largely be the work of the second or third generation. Indeed, Irenaeus specifically names, in connection with a good many of the ideas he sets out, the school of Ptolemy who, along with Heracleon and a certain Mark-the-Magician, seem to have been the successors of Valentinus in the West.

According to Irenaeus, the Valentinians taught that in the beginning there was *Bythos* (Depth, called also *Proarche* and *Propater*—Beginning and Forefather). "At invisible and nameless heights a perfect *Aeon*, uncontainable and invisible, eternal and ingenerate, has been (*gegenonai*) during infinite ages of time in silence and absolute rest (*remia nolle*). Bythos' only companion was his own Thought, *Ennoia* (also called *Charis*, grace or mercy, and *Sige*, silence). At some point, he decided to send forth from himself a new being, and so implanted as it were seed in his companion, Thought or Silence, and there came into being *Nous* and *Aletheia* (Mind and Truth). *Nous* was called also *Monogenes* (Unique One), who alone could fully comprehend the greatness of his sire. He was called also *Pater*, as father of all those who were to follow and make up the divine *Pleroma*, the complement of divine beings. *Nous*, "similar and equal to his progenitor," with *Aletheia* as an inseparable participant, produced *Logos* and *Zoe* (Word and Life); and they in turn *Anthropos* and *Ekklesia* (Man and the Church). *Logos* and *Zoe* then produced ten more aeons, also in pairs of male and female, all named for mental and moral virtues; and *Anthropos* and *Ekklesia* produced another twelve, the youngest of whom was *Sophia*.

So far all is well. The thirty aeons (an ogdoad, a decad, and a dodecad), symbolized by the thirty years of the Savior's age when he began his public ministry, and by the sum of the hours in the parable of the workers in the vineyard (one, three, six, nine, and eleven) make up a total godhead.

But *Sophia*, straining to comprehend the greatness of *Bythos* (a mystery reserved for *Monogenes* alone—so John 1:18), achieved only a false birth named *Achamoth*—a caricature of Wisdom, mingling with unformed spiritual grief, fear, and bewilderment. This unhappy offspring of *Enthymesis* (Anxiety) had to be shut out of the *Pleroma* by a new boundary called *Horos*, Limit (also called *Stauros*, a cross, and other names), while *Sophia* herself, repentant, was kept inside. *Nous/Monogenes* thoughtfully produced a new "yoked pair" (*syzygy*), Christ and the Holy Spirit, to fortify the aeons against similar folly, and so "restore" (*katartithenai*) the *Pleroma*. As a code to its renewed harmony, each aeon contributed what was best in himself/herself to form a new composite being, "supremely beautiful, even the star of the *Pleroma*, the perfect fruit Jesus," also called Savior, *Paraclete*, "the second Christ," and *Logos*. "In him dwelt the whole *pleroma* of deity" (Col 1:19; 2:9).

Meanwhile, *Achamoth* (cf. *chokhma* = Wisdom, in Hebrew) began sorting out the confused mass with which she had been left in the void, the *Kenoma* outside. The spirit that she had from her mother, *Sophia*, though it was imperfect, yearned to return to the *Pleroma* and its tranquil fellowship; and at the same time, it prompted her to give such order as she could to the unruly stuffs that burdened her: material stuff from her mother's unlawful passion and psychical stuff from her repentance. To make *Achamoth's* project possible, Christ in pity extended to her his power through the cross and gave a measure of form to her wayward spirit, giving her "mind" (*phrenoma*) but not "knowledge" (*gnosis*).

When Christ returned to the *Pleroma*, *Achamoth*—still lacking knowledge despite her partly spiritual nature—struggled in lonely frustration with her grief, terror, and bemusement, longing for Christ to return. But instead of coming a second time, he sent to her "the second Christ," the *Paraklete*, Jesus the Savior, who came with a retinue of shining angels, at last granted her *gnosis*, and segregated her passions so that they were no longer out of control but were transmuted "into incorporeal matter" (*eis asomaton ten hylen*), suitable for compacting into bodies. *Achamoth*, now free, is enraptured by the beauty of Jesus' attendant angels, and conceives within herself a new race of spiritual beings "according to the image" of the Savior's entourage.

Next comes the task of shaping up the stuffs now on hand: material, psychical, and spiritual. She can give no new form to the spiritual stuff, "because it is the same in essential being as herself" (*homoousion hyparchan auto*). First she forms out of psychic stuff the Demiurge, a craftsman alive but unintelligent, to give shape to all psychic and material things under prompting from his mother. So this world comes into being, produced by the power of *Achamoth* working through the Demiurge, who ignorantly supposes that he had made the world which he rules: the heavens, man, the earth, and all its inhabitants. Knowing none of these, he imagines that he is all: "I am God; beside me there is not one." But from his mother's grief, which is spiritual, he makes unknowingly the devil, *Cosmokrator* (World-ruler), and demons and wicked angels. And he made the earthy frame of man, and breathed into it the power to live (*ton psychikon*). But unknown to the unintelligent Demiurge, his mother *Achamoth* by his agency slipped into some humans the spiritual substance she had conceived when she saw the angels with the Savior. Perhaps because of the ambiguities of language, the *psyche* (*anima*), the breath of life breathed into man's body by the Demiurge, is treated as though it were *pneuma* (*spiritus*), originating in "a spiritual outpouring" (*ek pneumatikos apporrhoias*) so that the instillation of *pneuma* (spirit, mind) into *all* human beings seems implied.

On this reading, what follows is surprising. There are three basic kinds of human beings: material, psychic or animal, and spiritual. The first are doomed to ultimate destruction. The third are assured of immortality: they are the earthly *Ekklesia*, mirroring the yoke-mate of *Anthropos* (man) in the *Pleroma*. But for the second kind, the *psychikoi*, who unlike the others have freedom to choose an upward or downward path, the Savior (Jesus, the *Paraklete*) comes again to offer them salvation. As a spiritual being, he is clothed by the Demiurge with a psychic body shaped "with indescribable skill" (*arreto techne*), so as to be visible and tangible and capable of suffering, though without any tincture of matter (*hyle*). Under the Savior's instruction, the middle group, such *psychikoi* as ordinary Christians, may win a relative salvation by faith and good works, and ultimately a place in the intermediate home between this world and its *Pleroma* where *Achamoth* lives. When all the *pneumatikoi*, the spiritual folk in this world, have reached mature knowledge of the Kingdom of God, their spirits, stripped of psychic and earthly nature, will pass into the *Pleroma* to become espoused to the angels who first brought spirits to seminal existence in *Achamoth*. She herself will accompany them and become the bride of Jesus, the Savior. The Demiurge will move with her into her former intermediate state together with the souls of the righteous.

Matter and material people, and those *psychikoi* who have turned away from faith and good works, will be destroyed.

It may be difficult in our day to glimpse from this account the attractiveness of Valentinianism for many early Christians. Happily, however, we now have what may be a work of Valentinus himself, the so called *Gospel of Truth* which Irenaeus mentions (but whether he had actually seen it there is no way of knowing).

Once this work was published,[4] I could begin for the first time in my life to see why Valentinianism could have made an appeal to intellectuals of the second-century church. What it presents are not the endless genealogies of those theogonic and cosmogonic mythical systems that Irenaeus and Hippolytus describe. Rather we are given an existential account of man's plight and man's release. It starts from the tradition of the Fourth Gospel, which was the favorite gospel among the Valentinians, carrying further certain of the motifs which are found there.

As the text now stands, it begins in this fashion:

> The Gospel of Truth is joy for those who have received the grace of the truth from the Father, to know whom through the power of the Logos who has come from the Pleroma, that is, in the thoughts and the mind of the Father, who is the one whom one calls the redeemer [*soter*] because this is the name of the work which he must do for the redemption of those who did not know the Father, because the name of the Gospel is the revelation of hope, because it is discovery for those who seek him. For the all, the universe, has sought him, from whom it has come. And the All is within him, the incomprehensible, the unthinkable, who transcends every thought.

The document goes on to explain that uncertainty concerning the Father has produced anxiety and dread, and the anxiety has thickened itself like a mist so that no one could see. Therefore error has received power, has produced its own matter in emptiness, without knowing truth. It has shaped this world of ours as phenomena in the midst of emptiness, standing over against the *Pleroma*, the Father, who is the Father of truth and reality.

In the midst of these shadows in which anxiety has thickened like a mist, human beings are of different sorts though they are all having

---

4. In 1956. An English translation appeared in 1960, but whether Calhoun consulted it is not known [ed.].

a common experience. Some have a form and a name which has been derived on their behalf from the Father, but in this place of shadows even these have forgotten from whom they have come. Then there seem to be—I'm not sure of the text at this point—also some who never have been real and who consequently never can become real. They do not have a name. In contrast, the names of those who are eventually to be enlightened are written in a book which is closed, but their names are there. Meanwhile they wander in this world as though in a nightmare (the picture is extremely vivid and detailed), trying to pursue what perpetually eludes them or trying to escape what perpetually pursues them, finding themselves engaged in a battle of blows against they know not what or being struck by they know not whom. This is man's present plight; human beings mistake shadows for substance and see no way out.

The only way out must come from God; and God sends the savior in the guise of a mortal inhabitant of this globe, but he is none other than the name and Word of the Father. He comes to make the Father's name known to those who have forgotten, and so to enable them again to know their own names which are in the book which he alone is permitted to open. He is set upon and nailed to the cross—again, presumably in seeming, because he is not real flesh but rather in the likeness or guise of flesh—and his resurrection is a manifestation of the Father's approval of what he has done. Now the way of truth is open to those who are capable of recognizing it. There are those who are not capable of recognizing it because they never have been real, but the others fundamentally belong to the *Pleroma* even though for a time their eyes are closed and their minds are clouded.

This, then, is the "Gospel." It is not a narrative account of the life and teachings of the Savior, but rather a speculative meditation on the problem of salvation from the grip of terror. It ends in a hymn of thanksgiving and joy.

With this before us, I can see why Valentinus would have attracted those who liked to think of themselves as more intellectual, more sophisticated, than their fellow Christians. The presentation is relatively simple. Aeons are mentioned, but there is no indication of a gradation among them. They all issue from the Father, and they are emanations which can return. But the elaborate dramatic structure that Irenaeus talks about is absent. Here is the Father; here is error over against him; here are the members of the human race; and here is the Savior. And the way of salvation is the way of reminder, so that human beings are enabled once again to remember who and whence they are.

Yet even in this sober rendition, Gnosticism is anti-historical mysticism and mythmaking, not *kerygma*, and not a Gospel that seeks to illuminate history. Its attractiveness, especially in its less pretentious forms, and its positive contribution to the Church's thought about God have become more evident through the newly discovered Valentinian sources. At the same time, it has become no less evident that, like Marcion, Gnosticism's most discerning spokesmen appear as advocates of an alien mode of thought, incompatible with the proclamation of God as Maker of the world and Lord of history, truly made known in Jesus of Nazareth.

## MONARCHIANISM

A fourth group of these irregular theologies differed from the rest in that it stays closer to Christian orthodoxy than any of those that we have just mentioned. It stems, as a matter of fact, from a kind of special zeal for monotheism. It is the view which we know, chiefly from the accounts of its opponents, as Monarchianism. The term is taken from the key word in the view of these Christians: the *monarchia*, the sole sovereignty of God. That God is but one—that is their primary and normative affirmation. Tertullian indicates that their appeal is first of all to "the simple—who always make the majority of believers." To them a Monarchian teacher can say "Brother, do we believe in one God or more?," and the answer of course would be, "One God." "Ah, then you are with us. These others 'are preachers of two gods and three gods,' but we Monarchians are truly worshippers of the One God."

In effect, two types of Monarchian thought are recognizable.[5] The one, less subtle than the other, is ordinarily spoken of as dynamistic Monarchianism. The reason for that name is that those who held this view thought to safeguard the unity of God even while they affirmed the divinity of Jesus Christ by saying that in Jesus Christ, a man, there was resident an impersonal Power, *dynamis*, emanating from God. God's unity remains uncompromised because the *dynamis* ("Christ" or "the Spirit") which he put forth, and which indwelt in and empowered the man Jesus,

5. Harnack, although he himself uses this distinction, points out that "the name of Monarchian was not applied in the ancient Church" to the first but only to the second of these two types. Harnack, *History of Dogma*, III: 10n1.

was not a second individual being at all. There is but one individual being in the Godhead, and that is God the Father. This is one major type of Unitarian thought, subordinationist and adoptionist in its Christology. Among the people who held this view were Theodotus of Byzantium, a well-educated and respected tanner, and his disciples Theodotus the Younger, a money changer, and Asclepiodotus, both of whom studied with him in Rome. After being excommunicated by Pope Zephyrinus shortly after the year 200, he tried without much success to establish a schismatic Theodotian sect. A generation later, Artemas or Artemon tried again to revive the ancient adoptionist Christology, but by this time the prevailing sentiment in Rome was strongly against it. By far the ablest of those commonly accounted dynamistic Monarchians was the powerful third-century bishop of Antioch, Paul of Samosata, who developed the view with such originality and subtlety that only after two regional councils had failed to find grounds for condemning his teaching was he finally declared a heretic by a third synod at Antioch about 268. We shall have more to say of him and his opponents later. He stands as the best representative of dynamistic Monarchian doctrine in its most mature form.

The other type of Monarchianism, far more widely influential, is called variously modalistic Monarchianism or simply modalism, Patripassianism, or Sabellianism. Like the dynamistic Monarchian thinkers, the modalists affirm that God is but one individual Being. Father, Son, and—in the views of later thinkers like Sabellius—Holy Spirit are taken as names for modes or aspects of that one individual God. But unlike the older thinkers, these Monarchians hold that this God, the Father himself, became manifest in Jesus Christ, so that the Father is born, suffers, and dies, in or with his earthly Son. Hence Patripassianism—the doctrine that the Father is passible and suffers. Father and Son are essentially identical, though the names stand for distinguishable phases of the full reality. This also is a Unitarian doctrine, though obviously different from the older form in both intellectual and religious implications. Among its leaders, adherents, and patrons, we have the names of Noetus of Smyrna, who arrived in Rome from Asia Minor around 200 and was perhaps the earliest modalist of appreciable influence; Praxeas, also from Asia Minor; at least two popes, Zephyrinus and Callixtus; and, most distinctively, the Libyan Sabellius, by whose name the whole movement was known in the East. The early defenders of the Nicene Creed, as we shall see, were freely denounced by their opponents as Sabellian. One of them, the veteran bishop Marcellus of Ancyra, and his successor Photinus were modalists in fact, and others of the Nicene leaders closely approached modalism in their view of Father and Son in the Godhead. The greatest of the Latin Fathers, St. Augustine, whose work *On the Trinity* became a guidebook for both Scholastic and Protestant theologians, is regarded by Harnack and Loofs as for practical purposes a modalist, and it would be hard to deny that some passages in that book could be thus construed.

As a matter of fact, Monarchian thought in both its major forms was obstinately trying to safeguard an essential strain of Christian thought about God. The movement seems to have arisen first of all in Asia Minor as a protest against Gnosticism, with its multitude of intermediaries between the All-Father and the world of men, and its strong tendency to polytheism. The Monarchian leaders went on to oppose also the Logos theology that had its chief base in Alexandria, and that developed the subordinationist conception of the Logos that culminated in Arianism. The Monarchians kept firm hold of one immensely important truth: that God cannot exist in several grades of perfection: when we say God, we must mean one Being, not two or more beings of different ranks. They were not able for the most part to formulate that stubborn conviction in ways that would avoid lumping together divine roles that their opponents thought needed to be kept distinct. If Sabellius, for example, used seriously the analogy of the sun, as his always crabbed critic Epiphanius reports, declaring that the one God is (adjectivally) Father, Son, and Spirit as the sun is round, bright, and hot, it is not hard to see why his view was rejected. If it be true as Epiphanius further seems to say, that Sabellius regarded these three modes or properties of God's Being as successive rather than eternal characters of the Godhead, the ground for dissatisfaction is all the more plain. Marcellus of Ancyra did hold some such view, whether or not he learned it from Sabellius. Monarchian thought is best to be regarded in the main as the persistence within the church of archaic and crude but very vital statements of monotheistic conviction. Its chief fault lay not in radical divergence from Christian faith but in clumsy thought and expression. The outstanding exception was Paul of Samosata. His chief fault, as we shall later see, was of a different kind.

CHAPTER 6

# The Formation of the Apostles' Creed[1]

WE HAVE HAD OCCASION to recognize that certain teachers in the church, even early in the second century, were worried about what they called heterodoxy or henodoxy or heresy, and we have had a look at some of the deviant views which particularly frightened them, most especially those of Marcion and of Valentinus and of his successors. These worries raised the question of what the church can do to combat deviations and mark out a path for legitimate Christian thinking.

## SAFEGUARDS OF ORTHODOXY

The appeal which we have already noted in relatively early writers like Ignatius was to the tradition which stemmed from the apostles and which, so far as it could be recognized, was a safe guide. Now this tradition was in part transmitted by word of mouth, but it was also to be found in certain writings, some of them by the apostles themselves (like Paul's letters), and some of them in writings by those who knew the apostles and their teaching well enough to give a trustworthy account of it. Tradition could then be either written or unwritten. In the first couple of hundred years in the church's life, there seems to have been no question raised as to whether unwritten tradition should be regarded as an alternative to written tradition. Following the lead of Marcion, written renditions of tradition were eventually chosen, collected, and called Scripture; but Scripture tended

---

1. This chapter's first section, "Safeguards of Orthodoxy," comes from Professor Calhoun's post-1948 lectures, but as he never repeated in later years the detailed analyses in the second section, "Development of the Roman Symbol into the Apostles' Creed," that section is drawn entirely from the 1948 LHCD [ed.].

113

to be viewed initially as one version and unwritten tradition as another version of one and the same body of apostolic teaching.

A second protective measure was to tighten discipline within the church's body. We have seen how free-wheeling some of the thinkers in Rome were during the earlier part of the second century, and that seems to have continued right on into the third century as well, so that even bishops like Zephyrinus and Callixtus were regarded later as having trod on very dangerous ground. A tightening of the discipline of the church would mean in the first instance being careful about admitting as fellow Christians people who came without suitable warrants from their own home congregations. The need for this could be illustrated by Marcion, who came to Rome about 139 and was accepted as a Christian even though he had been in trouble in his home church in Sinope, and had also gotten into difficulty in places in Asia Minor which he had visited on his way to Rome. Now if we insist on having letters of admission for those who profess to be Christians in good standing, that will help to exclude people who, though calling themselves Christian, do not deserve the name. It means also, of course, clamping down on the charismatic teaching of prophets, those who declare themselves to be moved by the Spirit and who cry out in the moment of ecstasy teachings which may or may not accord with what the church has taught in the past. Ignatius himself speaks of an occasion in Philadelphia when he found himself prompted by the Spirit to cry out in a loud voice, the very voice of God, to the people who were listening to him. And what did he say to them? "Pay attention to the bishop." It was a curious kind of spiritual revelation, because it pointed in the direction of more stress on institutional authority and less value given to the free promptings of momentary and individual inspiration. Thus tightening of church organization and discipline is another means by which heresy can be brought under better control.

Yet a further guide was needed. How is the tradition to be understood and how is the genuine church to be recognized? From a very early time we find references to what is called sometimes a rule of faith, sometimes a rule of truth. We have these phrases in both Greek (*kanon tes pistos* and *kanon tes aletheias*: the measuring stick by which faith and truth can be clearly recognized) and in Latin (*regula fidei* and *regula veritatis*). Sometimes also it is called the ecclesiastical canon or apostolic canon. At first, pretty plainly, this was not a written formulation of any kind but was rather an intuitive consensus within the church as to what the true teaching of the Apostles had been and what it meant. An unwritten rule, obviously, was a feasible measuring stick only when there was agreement about it. But when a congregation split right down the middle as to whether, for example, Marcion with his ultra-radical Paulinism or the more conventional teachers are really teaching the tradition, then the consensus itself needs to be guided. So what we find happening apparently in the latter part of the second century is the shaping of formal creeds, brief confessions of faith, which could be used as a check on various judgments as to what the tradition was, and as to where the Catholic church (that is, the orthodox church as over against the conventicles of the sectaries) is to be found.

The earliest such credo that was widely circulated and used in the church is the one which traditionally has been called the Apostles' Creed. It has of course nothing directly to do with the Apostles save that it seeks to define more closely the substance of their teaching. The received text of the Apostles' Creed goes back apparently to the eighth century in Rome. We have both a Latin and a Greek form which is ascribed to a certain Pope Gregory, almost certainly not Gregory I (who was pope from 596 to 604), but rather to Gregory II or Gregory III, that is to say to a time somewhere between 715 and 741). And here we have both in Latin and Greek a text virtually identical to our Apostles' Creed:

> I believe in God, the Father Almighty, Creator of Heaven and earth; and in Jesus Christ, his only Son our Lord, who was conceived of the Holy Spirit, born of the Virgin Mary, suffered under Pontius Pilate, was crucified, dead, and buried; he descended into the lower regions (*ad inferna*); on the third day he arose from the dead, ascended into the heavens, sitteth at the right hand of God the Father Almighty; thence he will come to judge living and dead. I believe in Holy Spirit, holy catholic Church, communion of saints, remission of sins, resurrection of flesh, life eternal. Amen.

This is in all essentials the creed now used in Western churches, but it did not appear in this final form until the eighth century.

If we try to trace this creed back further, we find that what we confront is not this final form but rather simplified versions. One simplified version can be derived from Rufinus, who wrote what he calls a commentary on the Apostles' Creed around 400. He specifies that the creed on which he is commenting is the one in use in the Church of Aquileia in North Italy, and notes that it has certain clauses in it which are not to be found in a very closely similar creed used then in the Church of Rome. We can therefore, by omitting those clauses from the Aquileian Creed, get a text which Rufinus says was the baptismal creed Rome was then employing as a test for admission into the church. We go back then to about 336, and find that a prelate in Asia Minor, Marcellus of Ancyra, who was under accusation of Sabellianism, had been deposed from his own see and had come to Rome to seek the approval of Pope Julius. He offered in testimony to his own orthodoxy a creed which was in all likelihood the creed that Julius and the Roman Church were accustomed to use. How else would Marcellus assure them of his orthodoxy? Here we have a Greek text which parallels so closely the Latin of Rufinus that there can be very little doubt that they are one and the same creed.

Now we come to Rome itself. In the *Apostolic Tradition* of Hippolytus, written about 215, we have much the same language and substance of the later Apostles' Creed in interrogatory form, a form which is to be used at the baptism of a new convert: "Do you believe in God, the Father Almighty? Do you believe in Christ Jesus, his Son, our Lord?" and so on. Hippolytus was a fanatical defender of antiquity who presented himself as the guardian of the truth from which the previous and the upcoming bishop in Rome were turning aside. Consequently the text which he offers may be regarded with a good deal of confidence as one that antedates very considerably the time when he wrote it down. It apparently carries us back into the second century. If we try to go further back still, we have the writings of Tertullian in Carthage. In his *Prescription against Heretics*, in *Against Praxeas*, and in *On the Veiling of Virgins*, he has formulations of a "rule of faith" which tallies very closely with the interrogatory creed which we know from Hippolytus.

Irenaeus, writing slightly earlier around 185, most notably in the first book of his five books *Against Heresy*, seems to have a similar statement in view: the word order is different and the order of ideas is different, but the substance is much the same.

Now, however, if we go back of Irenaeus to Justin Martyr, we suddenly find no hint that any such formula existed. When in the sixty-first chapter of his *Apology*, Justin describes Christian baptism, he says simply, "Baptize in the name of the maker and master of the universe, and of Jesus Christ, crucified under Pontius Pilate, and of the Holy Spirit." That is all: no creed. In still earlier apologists, there is something that looks like a creed in Aristides, but this is derived from what was probably a late first-century missionary tract, the *Preaching of Peter*, and is best understood as a statement to guide preachers to the Gentiles. In Ignatius, there is a whole series of creed-like statements, but all differ from one another and from the later formulations we have been considering.

The upshot seems to be that the origins of the Apostles' Creed are to be found in Rome in the second half of the second century, and quite possibly in the third quarter of the second century; that is to say, before Irenaeus wrote. If we try to reconstruct a text for that place and that time, we come up with a form which has been called the core of the Old Roman Symbol (which frequently is indicated simply by the letter *R*). The Old Roman Symbol is somewhat more extensive than the core text which can conjecturally be regarded as still earlier, a text which follows Hippolytus and Tertullian rather than the later writers, Marcellus and Rufinus. If we follow this line, as McGiffert does, we get this result:

> I believe in God, the all-sovereign Father. And in Christ Jesus his Son, The One born of Mary the Virgin, The One crucified under Pontius Pilate, and buried; the third day risen from the dead, ascended into the heavens, seated at the right hand of the Father, whence he comes to judge the living and dead. And in Holy Spirit, resurrection of flesh.[2]

Next the question has to be raised, clearly enough, what is the intent that this formula subserved? The traditional view has been, of course, that it is simply a summary of Christian preaching for the guidance of Christian missionaries and the propagation of the Gospel. Here is a convenient brief résumé of what they are supposed to teach, and what their converts are supposed to believe. I find McGiffert's argument basically convincing—that this creed, like all the important later creeds that we know, is not merely expository but polemical.[3] The purpose of the

2. See A.C. McGiffert, *The Apostles' Creed: Its Origin, Its Purpose, and Its Historical Interpretation,* a lecture with critical notes (New York: Scribners, 1902). For the text of the Apostles' Creed and other early creeds, see *The Creeds of Christendom,* ed. Philip Schaff (New York: Harper, 1877; reissued and expanded 1931). This collection of creeds has now been superseded by *Creeds and Confessions of Faith in the Christian Tradition,* eds. Jaroslav Pelikan and Valerie Hotchkiss (New Haven: Yale University Press, 2003). See especially vol. 1 [ed.].

3. Professor Calhoun was unusual but is not unique among scholars in the degree to which he followed McGiffert's stress on the "polemical" aspect of the Creed. Justo L. Gonzalez takes a similar line in his recent and widely used *A History of Christian Thought,* rev. ed. (Nashville: Abingdon, 1987) 1: 151–55 [ed.].

formulation was not merely to provide a convenient brief summary of Christian teaching. In fact it does not do that. Too much that is fundamental in Christian teaching was omitted. There is no reference here to the moral obligation under which human beings stand in reference to God nor to the sin into which they have fallen and from which they need to be redeemed. There is no reference here to redemptive work which is accomplished "as a ransom for many" by Jesus as Savior, nor to the life of faith. If this reconstruction of the original text be accepted, there is even no reference here to the Christian community. Less drastic analysis of the material would leave the phrase "Holy Church" in the concluding article as a part of the original text, and it may have been so. It appears in Marcellus' version and other early texts, but in none earlier than Cyprian, about 250. Hence I am inclined to think that McGiffert's reasons for omitting it from his version of the second-century creed are persuasive. The argument about the phrase "Holy Church" and its meaning was a third-century, not a second-century argument. If the omission of so many basic Christian doctrines from any mention in the creed be taken as establishing its polemical purpose, then one would expect to find other phrases put in as other controversies came to the fore. On the whole I think that this is the right view of the matter.

On the other hand, see what is included: a declaration in relatively novel terms that the God in whom Christians believe is the creator and sovereign of this world; a declaration that Jesus Christ is his Son (not the son of some other and better God); and a stress on the historicity of Jesus' life (he was born and he died in a time that can be pinpointed: he will come to judge, and there will be a resurrection of flesh). Now the thesis which McGiffert develops and which still seems to me to have withstood well later criticisms is that this is the Roman Church's answer to Marcionite and Valentinian doctrine in the second half of the second century. It presents the apostolic tradition, interpreted in opposition to these teachers who profess to have that tradition in a purer form. It focuses on those points which exclude their theosophic and dualistic aberrations. If one thinks in these terms, the creed falls into a clear and convincing pattern both in what it omits and what it affirms.

If we ask how this creed was used in the life of the church, Canon Kelly has a persuasive answer.[4] It was used in conjunction with baptism,

---

4. See J. N. D. Kelly, *Early Christian Creeds,* 3rd ed. (New York: McKay, 1972).

and probably in an interrogatory form such as Hippolytus supplies. In the declarative form, Kelly suggests, it was employed as a guide to the teacher of the catechetical class preparing candidates for baptism. That makes excellent sense. We have, for example, the catechetical lectures of Cyril of Jerusalem in the fourth century, in which he describes in detail to those who have been baptized the meaning of the creed of the Church of Jerusalem, and we have Rufinus' statement that the creed on which he was commenting was used for the admission of catechumens in the church of Aquileia.

## DEVELOPMENT OF THE ROMAN SYMBOL INTO THE APOSTLES' CREED

Now suppose that the Roman Church had the formula we have described somewhere about 160 or 170. Why should that formula have been altered and expanded into our familiar creed? The answer is perfectly clear in the light of what Rufinus tells us about the way the Roman creed was used in his own Church at Aquileia. In that Church, a pressing doctrinal problem had been to stave off modalistic Monarchian thought, often spoken of as Patripassianism—that mode of thought which declares that it is the Father who suffers on the cross. So, as Rufinus goes out of his way to mention, a little phrase was inserted at the end of that first article: "I believe in God, the all-governing Father." He was using, of course, a Latin text in which "all-governing" (*pantokrator*) becomes "almighty" (*omnipotens*): *Credo in Deo Patre omnipotente*. Then these words were added: *invisibili et impassibili*. Why those words? Because in Aquileia, Patripassianism was a heresy that had to be excluded. Rufinus notes that these words were not in the creed as it was used in Rome, but they were inserted in this north Italian town; and he adds that changes were made "in other places" than Rome, where heretics appeared—changes through which it was believed the sense of the novel doctrine was excluded.

In the text of the creed which apparently was known to Cyprian in the third century, we find inserted after the phrase "Holy Spirit," another phrase, "Holy Church." As we know from Cyprian and Novatian and Hippolytus, an acute issue in controversy in the third century was what should be understood by calling the church "holy." Roughly there were three main views on that point. The first, and the most primitive, was held by the Novatianists. Their view was that the phrase "Holy Church" means a communion of morally blameless members. Holiness is moral righteousness and only that church can be called holy all of whose individual members are saints. That is, of course, the sectarian view of the church which has been reaffirmed again and again by groups dissatisfied with what has seemed to them the moral ambiguity of the inclusive institutional *ecclesia*.

A second view, held by Cyprian himself, was that the phrase "Holy Church" can be used only of a church whose bishops are morally blameless and endowed with the Holy Spirit. This view arose in the course of one of those difficult situations presented by an outbreak of persecution in which respected members of a church community lapsed because they lacked the stamina, the particular sort of heroism which is called for when the issue is either yielding to the demand of the state or suffering martyrdom. Many good people in the Church of Carthage yielded to the demand that they should sacrifice to the emperor's statue. Many others did not yield and were subjected to mutilation, torture, and some of them to death. Now the question arose whether those who had lapsed during the persecution should be readmitted into good standing as church members. Many of the confessors who had stood out against the persecution and had taken the consequences supported strongly the view that their neighbors should be readmitted—that they should be readmitted, moreover, at the behest of the confessors. Now Cyprian was prepared to agree that they should be brought back into the church again after doing suitable penance; but, he said, the people to decide which of the lapsed shall be readmitted must not be simply their heroic fellow-laymen, but rather the duly constituted authorities in the church. Cyprian's own position in reference to the confessors was a delicate one, because during the persecution he had gone underground. He had kept out of sight because it seemed to him important that the direction of the life of the church should continue and he was responsible for that direction. Now, when the persecution is over, the confessors point to him and say, "Is it for you to decide whether or not people who acted as you yourself acted shall be brought back into the Church again?" And to that Cyprian's answer was perfectly clear and unwavering: "It is the office of the bishop to determine matters of this kind, for the college of bishops constitute the basis of the unity and authority of the Church." He used this phrase again and again. *Collegium episcoporum*, the company of bishops, is the church *par excellence*, and that by reason of the endowment of the bishops with the Holy Spirit at the time of their due and proper ordination to the episcopal office.

The third view that was maintained during this time, specifically by Bishop Stephen of Rome, was that the phrase "Holy Church" is not really a phrase that has reference to ethical matters at all. It is a sacramental phrase, and a holy church is a church whose sacraments are divinely ordained as effectual means of grace. The moral character either of the lay membership or of the clergy is not really in question. The sacraments must be regarded as valid, as having their due and proper effect, as vehicles of saving power whether they are administered by priests who personally are righteous or not. If those priests have been duly constituted custodians of the power which God makes available through the sacrament, then the requirements are met for defining the church which they serve as a holy church.

In the middle of the third century, the reason for including in the creed a phrase of this sort, then, is much more clearly evident than it would have been in the middle of the second century, when the particular question posed by persecution and the response of Christians to persecution, and the resulting argument over the meaning of the church had not yet become widespread. I am inclined, therefore, to McGiffert's conjecture—though once again regarding it as nothing much stronger than that—that this phrase "Holy Church" goes into the third article of the creed probably in the third century. At a still later date, there is added in the middle of this phrase the additional controversial term, "Catholic." The question whether holiness in the church consists in moral or in sacramental attributes is paralleled by the question in what sense the church can be called universal. That is a question which was agitating the minds of Christians in the lifetime of St. Augustine. The Donatists of North Africa, who professed to be the spiritual descendants of Cyprian, had split the North African church. The issue had been posed by the varying reaction of the clergy to the order of the emperor Diocletian to hand over their mass books and Scriptures for destruction. The emperor presumably hoped that this would eliminate the possibility of holding public services of worship and consequently would destroy, without real violence, the organized life of the Christian community. Now the Donatists held that any bishop who knuckled under when the imperial agents came and demanded the books of his church for destruction was not fit to be regarded any longer as a bishop in the holy church. The holy church is to be found only where the bishops have behaved with proper heroism. Their adversaries, among whom Augustine comes to be the most effective, laid stress upon the judgment that the church in which Christians believe and find salvation is not merely a church describable as holy, but also a church that is describable as universal. Now in what sense can the Catholic church be called universal? In the sense, says Augustine, that it includes people from all parts of the civilized world, and that it includes in each of those areas people from all walks of life. It is inclusive, not in the sense that all people are members of the Church, but that it includes "all sorts and conditions of men" in all of the areas of the Roman world. So the addition of the term "Catholic" to the term "Holy" is a balancing of ideas respecting the church as the company of the faithful.

Along with this clause on the church, there is added, presumably in the third century, another clause which takes its point from the same controversy: "forgiveness of sins." Once again we remember the way in which the question, "What shall be done about Christians who have fallen into grave sins after baptism?" had agitated the church in the second century and had called forth such answers as that that we find in the Shepherd of Hermas. For grave post-baptismal sins it is necessary to distinguish between some which are unforgivable by the church, though God may forgive them, and some which the church is at liberty to forgive once. The unforgivable sins, you remember, are murder, adultery, idolatry—and idolatry at this stage of the church's life means, quite concretely, burning incense on festival days before the statue of the emperor. Now the question about these lapses in Cyprian's time is precisely a question whether that which had traditionally been treated as unforgivable can after all be forgiven, whether the *lapsi* can be restored to the status of genuine believers. And the answer which is now affirmed is, "Yes, they can—upon the proper performance of penance duly assigned by the bishop or by an assembly of bishops." This hitherto unforgivable transgression can be forgiven once. But if a believer lapses a second time there is no remedy. Just as there is but one baptism, cleansing life up to that moment, so there is but one further cleansing possible for these really grave transgressions.

The question about forgiveness of sins had already been raised with respect to homicide and sexual misconduct by certain decrees of the Roman bishop Callixtus of the early third century, about 217. Callixtus had had a very strenuous and checkered personal career. He had been condemned as an embezzler and sent to the mines of Sardinia for a time, and then had been permitted to return to Rome, working his way up in the church until he succeeded Zephyrinus as bishop of the Roman Church. Perhaps by reason of his own personal experience, he had a realistic sympathy with folk who found the rigorist pattern of life too difficult for them, an attitude which scandalized certain of the rigorists, among whom Hippolytus was his most unrelenting opponent. Callixtus appears to have been the first who readmitted, after penance duly performed, church members who had been guilty of what was called adultery. That is to say, they had fallen into some sort of sexual wrongdoing which was regarded as so serious that it came under the head of the traditionally unforgivable sin. Now Callixtus took the initiative in saying, "These people have done what is gravely wrong and yet they should be forgiven and reinstated." He justified his position by appealing to the teaching of forgiveness which comes from the Lord himself; to the parables which recognize that tares are permitted to grow up along with the wheat until God finally makes the decision between them; to the judgment that the church is the Ark of Salvation and the clear record that the ark contained both clean and unclean beasts. On the basis, in short, of numerous scriptural authorizations, Callixtus was prepared to say that the church should regard itself as a school for the Christian mind, and as having room in its membership for those whose Christian living is as yet very far from perfect. Even those guilty of homicide might in certain cases be restored to church membership after doing penance.

When we come to this pattern of thinking, none of the unforgivable sins is any longer to be regarded as really unforgivable by the church. On Callixtus' view of the matter no sins are to be regarded as unforgivable, provided it is clear that the person concerned is genuinely repentant. He must prove his repentance by undergoing a very arduous period of exclusion from the membership of the church, perhaps wearing garments of mourning—sackcloth and ashes, appearing on the steps of the church and begging for the prayers and forgiveness of his fellow Christians, and so on. Tertullian describes in these terms the practice of repentance at Carthage. Anyone who will go through that sort of public humiliation for ten years, for twenty years, for forty years, perhaps for the rest of his life, receiving ultimate forgiveness only on his deathbed, is regarded as sincerely repentant. Callixtus' affirmation now is that such a one is fit to be accepted once again into church membership even if he had committed adultery or murder. The church has room for the worst of sinners provided they are genuinely repentant sinners. Hence the force of the addition of the clause, "forgiveness of sins." The church, once that clause had been inserted, declares: We regard it as a fundamental tenet of the Christian faith that sins can be forgiven, and the holiness of the church is not thereby compromised.

Two other familiar phrases which got into the Creed at one time or another include that mysterious one which in the text of the Creed as used at Rome appears first in a Latin version of the eighth century. After a reference to the crucifixion and burial comes then the statement, "He descended to the lower regions" (*descendit ad inferna*). That appears to have been an addition made first in the churches of Gaul, apparently before 500, and precisely what it is intended to convey doctrinally is not so easy to define. What it conveyed presumably to the minds of ordinary Christians who repeated the Creed, is, I think, not mysterious at all. One of the favorite representations in medieval religious drama was the pageant which portrayed what was technically and universally known as the Harrowing of Hell. The Harrowing of Hell was in a way the dramatic climax in a drama which portrayed, first the Creation of the world and of man, and then the steady deterioration of man under the growing strength of the Devil. The Devil was winning—again, again, and again against God. And when God sent his Son to save the world, the Devil won even over him, for the Devil brought it about that he was put to a shameful death. Then comes the tremendous shock and glory of the revelation that the lowest point of the divine defeat was paradoxically the very moment and means of the Devil's undoing. For with the coming of the Lord of Glory down into the places of darkness, light was brought into the darkness and the darkness overcame it not. Origen put the matter in precisely that fashion. The descent into the realm of the demons is in and of itself a conquest of the demons because truth and falsehood, light and darkness, cannot exist side by side. The descent into the lower region would be then, for the popular mind, the conquest of the Devil. It is supposed to have its Scriptural basis in that very obscure reference in 1 Pet 3:19 to the preaching "to the spirits in prison." Now the phrase is itself, as you see, sufficiently ambiguous. What prison? What spirits? If it be the prison house of the lower world, then the preaching to spirits there would be a part of the whole drama of redemption, and presumably the inclusion of the phrase in the Creed is intended to convey that message. There may be other peripheral senses of the word also. To my own mind, by all odds the most profound, although I think not historically the most literally correct interpretation, is that of Calvin, who sees in this clause of the Creed the final testimony to the perfect obedience of the Son to the will of the Father. The Son has taken upon himself on behalf of human sinners the utmost length of humiliation and defeat. Now his humiliation is not a good thing in itself. It is simply testimony to his complete devotion to the will of the Father and to the salvation of humankind. So this phrase has for Calvin, and in a different way for the simple folk of the Middle Ages, a kind of climactic value.

We now have before us most of the doctrinally important materials which have got into the Apostles' Creed, beginning with its core, the Old Roman Symbol, in the rather drastic reconstruction that McGiffert suggests. We noted certain additions made to the Creed during the third and early fourth centuries, and just by way of review, there may be some point in running over the text which we find in the confession of Marcellus of Ancyra. He came to Rome, we remember, about 336 and by way of proving his orthodoxy, repeated for Bishop Julius of Rome the creed which had been in use in the Roman Church. The text as we find it in Epiphanius' account of Marcellus runs as follows. "I believe in God the all-sovereign." Curiously the term *Father* is not included here. Whether it was actually lacking in the old Roman creed is debatable; but I think that since the word appears in both Irenaeus and Rufinus, and since agreement is general that the creed was based on the baptismal formula—Father, Son, and Holy Spirit—the greater likelihood is that the term *Father* was in the creed used by Marcellus but has been dropped out perhaps by Epiphanius, perhaps by a copyist. "I believe in God the all-sovereign; and in Christ Jesus, his only Son, our Lord, the one born of the Holy Spirit and Mary the Virgin." The phrase "of the Holy Spirit" has been added to the original text of *R*. "The one under Pontius Pilate crucified and buried and the third day risen from the dead, ascended into the heavens and seated at the right hand of the Father, whence he cometh to judge living and dead. And in the Holy Spirit, Holy Church, forgiveness of sins, resurrection of flesh, life everlasting." Once again, the phrase "life everlasting" appears to have been an addition to the original creed. There are various other small words and phrases that were added, but I think there is no point in dwelling on each of these.

But there is one additional phrase which appeared sometime during the fifth century in the concluding article of the creed: the one that began with affirmation of belief in the Holy Spirit and in resurrection of the flesh; but which by the time of Marcellus includes belief also in "Holy Church, forgiveness of sins." Then comes in many Latin versions of the creed beginning in the fifth century, *communionem sanctorum*, the communion of saints; so we translate it ordinarily and in all likelihood correctly. Certain commentators have noted that there is an ambiguity here because in Latin the term *sanctorum* could be either masculine or neuter, referring either to persons or to things. If the latter alternative were the correct one, the term would mean sacraments, so that "partaking of holy things" or "participation in sacraments" could stand for the dominant Roman conception of the nature of the church. But this is not the usual way of referring to the sacraments. I am inclined to think we do well to leave the issue open, but to recognize that while the evidence is inconclusive, the preponderance of likelihood seems in favor of the more familiar reading.

We have then, by some time in the seventh century, a creed which is substantially our so-called Apostles' Creed. It has grown during some 500 years with additions at specific places and at specific times for the most part, we may suppose, in response to particular doctrinal needs. In general that conception of the creed seems to fit in so perfectly with the knowledge that we have about the development of later creeds that I am inclined to regard it as probably a correct understanding.

One more comment with regard to this creed may be in place in relation to the later ones. The very fact that this formula was developed to meet the crude and simple heresies of the second and third centuries meant that when new and more sophisticated errors had to be faced, new creedal formulae were indispensable. We shall find that the heretics of the fourth century were able to affirm everything that is said in this old Roman confession without any difficulty at all. So when Marcellus undertakes to prove his orthodoxy by repeating the old creed, he is showing a certain naïveté which, as we shall see in due course, actually does mark his whole theological outlook. New creeds were required, and new creeds were forthcoming to meet new doctrinal issues.

# CHAPTER 7

Irenaeus of Lyons[1]

N OW WE TURN FROM the church in general back to particular individual church leaders, and first of all to Irenaeus of Lyons—to my
mind one of the most engaging and profound of early Christian thinkers.
In some respects, I should be inclined to go further than that, and to say
that he is one who in his conception of essential doctrine appears to have
laid hold of certain fundamental principles which even in our own day
we have not as clearly and fully grasped. Irenaeus was born probably in
Asia Minor and tells us that in his early youth he saw and heard Polycarp,
Bishop of Smyrna. Polycarp was one of the friends of Ignatius of Antioch,
and was himself accustomed to talk "of his intercourse with John and
with the others who had seen the Lord."[2] The claim of a direct line from
"the eyewitnesses" through Polycarp to Irenaeus, who is himself a link between East and West, is unmatched in the record as we know it. Irenaeus
lays great stress on the continuity of tradition, written and oral, from "the
Apostles"; and more than any predecessor, he provides the elements for a
comprehensive Christian theology.

Polycarp had sent as a missioner from the church of Smyrna to
Marseilles (Massillia), in the south of Gaul, his pupil and friend Pothinus,
who went from Marseilles to Lyons (Lugdunum) and there established
a Christian missionary church. Irenaeus joined him and became a
presbyter in the church. In 177, when fierce persecution broke out un-

1. Professor Calhoun rewrote this chapter and added footnotes after his retirement
in preparation for its publication. Some of the material is from pre-retirement lectures,
but the bulk is fresh. It has been left unaltered except for minor editorial changes and the
insertion of a few transitional sentences from the 1948 multilithed transcript [ed.].

2. Letter from Irenaeus to his one-time friend Florinus, in Eusebius, *Hist. eccl.* V:20:6,
*NPNF2* 1.

der Marcus Aurelius, particularly in Lyons and the neighboring city of Vienne, Irenaeus was sent to Rome with a letter to the pope to protest against the encroachment of various heretical views, but it was mostly in Rome that he encountered the heresies with which his surviving writings are chiefly concerned. While he was gone, Pothinus died as a result of the persecution. Irenaeus succeeded him as bishop of Lyons on his return and continued in that office until his death in 202.

## Opposition to Montanism

When Irenaeus arrived in the capital city, he found that Montanism, the extravagant Phrygian movement, had won the favor of Pope Eleutherus himself. As one who had himself been a resident of Asia Minor, Irenaeus knew about Montanism, The movement had arisen in the first instance as a protest against the secularization of both the life and the faith of the church. The Phrygian Montanus, converted about 150–60 CE, was very much impressed by the record of the driving power of first-century Christianity. It appeared to him that the wonder-working which was taken as the work of the Spirit as well as the eager expectation of the coming end of the age were essential parts of the Christian outlook. But both had been lost. Now the Christians do their day's work like their non-Christian neighbors. They have no urgent consciousness that the end is coming speedily. They still look forward to it, but only in some indefinite and distant future time. As for the works of the Spirit, they are no longer to be found anywhere. Christians live pretty much as non-Christians live, save that they go through certain rituals and they affirm certain doctrinal beliefs, but the fierce spiritual energy which once had marked them indelibly is now missing.

In Montanus' own day, the power of the Spirit seemed to him clearly to be manifest once more; and he and certain of his followers, notably two devoted women, Priscilla and Maximilla, began to preach a fresh interpretation of the timetable of the Christian dispensation. There are three ages of the world. The first was the age of the Father, which lasted from creation until the Incarnation. The second was the age of the Son, stretching from the Incarnation until the present. The third is the age of the Paraclete, which begins in the lifetime of Montanus and will last until the end of the age—again affirmed to be not far away. Montanus is himself the instrument of the Paraclete. "Behold," says the Spirit speaking through him, "man is like a lyre, and I sweep across it like a plectrum."[3] The Christian life preached by the Montanists is the familiar life of the enthusiastic saint: a life marked by a rigorous asceticism, a discipline associated with ecstatic visions, a sense of exceptional power and spiritual freedom, and a disregard for the ordinary ties of economic, political, and domestic life. With Montanus there came a newly intense conviction that the Kingdom of God was at hand, the end very near.

For a time he was regarded as genuinely a restorer of the authentic life and teaching of the church. In Phrygia and throughout the eastern Mediterranean world, this movement spread rapidly with the approval of local church authorities. It got a hearing also in Rome, where even the pope was impressed by what appeared to be the authentic and powerful Christianity that these men and women represented. A time came, however, when it became apparent that what these new prophets were proclaiming was a kind of irresponsibility of both thought and action that simply was out of place in a church that had to become organized on a fairly large scale. In the first century, when the church consisted of scattered, loosely associated companies of individual believers, the prophet was a very much more appropriate member of the Christian economy. But now, when a prophet's life and teaching cuts across the hard-earned, growing stability of the church and urges the loosening of all its social ties, he becomes a source of peril.

When he meets Montanist thought in Rome, Irenaeus is not unsympathetic with the aims these folk have in view. As we shall see, he himself has much of the temper of millenialism in his thinking, and he knows something of the emotional warmth and devotion which characterizes the Phrygian type of Christianity. These things he knows, but he recognizes also the peril involved in a flat disregard of the authorized ways of a community which must hold together if it is to survive in a world that is becoming increasingly and officially hostile.

This was a growing problem. The Roman government at first had maintained the attitude of a more or less benevolent tyrant looking upon the lives of Christians as no great threat to the order of the empire. Persecutions in the early days came chiefly from disquieted neighbors of the Christians rather than from the authorities. Flare-ups under Nero and

---

3. Epiphanius, as quoted in the *Realencyklopädie für protestantische Theologie und Kirche*, 13:420, 39–40.

Domitian were exceptions. From the early years of the second century we have the testimony of Pliny's letters to Trajan seeking light on the policy to be followed with respect to Christians.[4] The emperor answers: There is to be no hunting out of Christians. If individual Christians are denounced to the authorities, then of course they must be punished. Henceforth, it is illegal just to be a Christian, a member of a new religious community which, like the Jewish community, rejects the demand for worship of the emperor, but unlike Judaism, is not legally recognized. So if Christians persist in refusing to obey the law, the law must do what is required. No more than that: individual executions if need be, but no witch-hunts.

But now as the second century runs its dreary course, the peril to the empire becomes increasingly evident. The peril is associated partly with the decline of the solid middle and upper-middle classes in Roman society through the impoverishment of the old senatorial landowners, partly with growing pressure of restless tribes around the margin, partly as always with internal rivalries and factionalism. The familiar urge to look for scapegoats naturally increased at the Christians' expense, and the government itself became the persecutor. Irenaeus saw clearly that the Church must try to achieve a common front against that increasing threat, and so must resist sources of divisiveness within its very diverse body. His own efforts in this direction were as an interpreter of "Asiatic" (namely Johannine) theology to the Roman clergy during his stay in Rome and afterwards to his flock in Gaul, and as an opponent to those strains in either Eastern or Western thought that seemed to him most threatening to essential Christianity.

## Opposition to Valentinian Gnosticism

The title of Irenaeus' chief work, *A Refutation and Overthrow of Falsely Named Gnosis* (or more briefly *Against Heresies*), focuses on Valentinian and several other Gnostic systems with a brief glance at Marcion. It is an able polemic, one of the earliest and most trustworthy. But more than half—the more impressive half—of the five books sets out the author's understanding of Christian truth. We have the work, written in Greek about 185, in a virtually contemporary and seemingly accurate Latin translation. Tertullian, writing not far from 200, uses the Latin text, and sizeable segments of the Greek text preserved by Hippolytus in Rome

---

4. Eusebius, *Hist. eccl.* III:33 (Following Tertullian, *Apol.* 2.).

and by Epiphanius in Cyprus provide a basis for judging the accuracy of the Latin.[5] There is also a much smaller work called "A Demonstration of the Apostolic Preaching," preserved in various Oriental versions of less assured veracity. Excerpts from letters and from various lost writings are quoted by Eusebius and others.

The polemic in *Against Heresies* focuses on the Valentinian and several other Gnostic systems together with a brief glance at Marcion. It makes use of obvious and all-purpose charges: novelty and conflicting multiplicity. Before Valentinus, there were no Valentinians; before Marcion, no Marcionites. Yet the true Christian tradition reached back more than a century to Jesus Christ. Moreover, the heretics show a fantastic array of inconsistencies among their views, each of which professes to be the authentic version of Christianity. When a medley of incompatible voices each proclaims itself the sole expression of the truth, not all can be right, and all may well be wrong. The church, by contrast, speaks with one voice guaranteed, Irenaeus promises to show, by self-consistent, unbroken tradition.

Marcionite doctrine gets short shrift. In trying to teach two gods, it ends up with none. If the Creator and Lawgiver called "just" does not recognize and espouse what is good, he is not just, and without goodness and justice there is no God. If the Redeemer called "good" is not just, he is not wise, and so no God. But by their own account neither is he "good" in the Marcionite sense, as being indiscriminately merciful, for he does not save all people but only some. By separating justice and goodness, Marcion negates both. Plato does better than this.[6]

Valentinianism, a more complex doctrine, requires a more complex refutation. Let us begin with Ptolemy's conception of God, an intricate system of thirty aeons, all somehow dependent on *Bythos*, the Forefather. Are they or are they not all "of the same essential being" (*ex eadem substantia* or *homoousioi*) with him? If they are, then all should be immutable and impassible. Since *Nous/Monogenes* is able to comprehend fully the being of his progenitor, it would seem that *Nous* is indeed of the same essential being. But all the rest are excluded from such knowledge, and

---

5. Critical editions of *Adversus Haereses* (*Haer.*): W. W. Harvey, *Sancti Irenaei ep. Lugdunensis libros quinque adversus haereses*, 2 vols. (Cambridge, 1857); Adelin Rousseau et al., *Irénée de Lyon, Contre les hérésies*, SC 1965–. English translation by Alexander Roberts and W. H. Rambaut, available in *ANF* 1.

6. Irenaeus, *Haer.* III:25.

*Sophia* transgresses, falls away, and suffers. This godhead then is composite, partly self-identical and partly diverse in its essential being.

But if some other *substantia* is present in the lesser aeons, whence comes it? From *Bythos*? Then the very source of godhead is divided. From some other source? Then is that other source coeval with the Forefather, so that deity is plural rather than unitary? Further, whence and of what nature is the *kenoma*—the void into which *Achamoth* was somehow pushed out? Does it exist alongside the *Pleroma* all the time? If so, the void is ultimately just as real as the fullness. Why then call one divine and the other not? But if the *kenoma* is produced and so not coeval with the *Pleroma*, by whom is it produced? And of what is it made? Is it produced by the All-Father? Then presumably it is "of his essential being" (*eiusdem substantiae*), unless there be some other stuff waiting to be shaped into an empty space—a receptacle, Plato calls it in the *Timaeus*. Once again, we discover a situation which is logically contradictory; the Valentinians are trying to hold together ideas which, closely examined, prove to be incompatible.

Or consider another and somewhat less fundamental point. The Valentinians talk about Silence as continuing even after Logos (speech) has come upon the scene. But how can this be? Ignatius had spoken of "the Word issuing from silence,"[7] but silence in that case had given place to speech. But these Gnostics want to have it both ways, contending that Silence persists even in the presence of utterance. Once again, they are presenting a logical contradiction. Irenaeus resumes this argument at various points, in what from one point of view is verbal fencing, but from a more penetrating view, radical criticism. The Valentinians must draw a line between creator and creation somewhere, but they draw it at the wrong points; they draw it within the Godhead—between *Nous* and the rest, or between *Sophia/Achamoth* and the rest of the aeons. Irenaeus is going to insist on drawing a sharp line too, but at a different place. The Marcionites also drew sharp lines, but again at the wrong places: they draw one between the old covenant and the new, not seeing the continuity between them, and another between the creator God and the redeemer God, not seeing that they must be one and the same. So Marcionites and Valentinians alike are trying to teach a version of the Gospel which logically falls apart.

---

7. Ign. *Magn.* 8:2.

Throughout their writings, the heretics grossly misuse the Scriptures. They tear texts out of their proper context and interpret them in frivolous ways.[8] And they construct for their own purposes works which they profess to regard as scriptures, but which actually have no authentication at all.[9] Irenaeus affirms that there are just four Gospels, neither more nor fewer. The sectaries would like to add some gospels, like the Gospel of Truth produced by the Valentinians, or to subtract some. The Ebionites use only the Gospel of Matthew; the Valentinians prefer the Gospel of John; and the Marcionites, having ruled out Matthew, John, and presumably Mark, use only an expurgated Gospel of Luke. But the church has precisely four Gospels from the apostles, which secure for it the sort of solid foundation established by the four corners of heaven, the four primary winds, and the four pillars of the earth. And the church will not let the sectaries deprive it of the testimony of any of these primary documents.

One of the things Irenaeus is especially urging here is the scriptural character of the Gospel of John. The three Synoptics had found easier acceptance. The Fourth Gospel, so different from the others, but an essential part of Irenaeus' heritage, found the going considerably more difficult. On this issue, Irenaeus is perfectly confident that the author was one of the original twelve. The church also possesses the letters of Paul, and once again, as in his handling of the Johannine literature, Irenaeus reads Paul with deeper insight than had his predecessors. He genuinely understands in substantial part what Paul was driving at, and he urges that respecting the essential gospel, Peter and Paul agree.

The apostles know only one God, the God of the Old Testament, who is also the God and Father of our Lord Jesus Christ. They know only one Jesus Christ, not an inferior Jesus and a celestial Christ separate from him, who descends upon him at his baptism and leaves him on the cross. Rightly understood, these apostolic writings provide a solid safeguard against the errors of the various heretical schools. Of course, rightly understanding the Scriptures demands adherence to the rule of truth which churches everywhere acknowledge, and which they regard as a touchstone for true apostolic tradition. But Irenaeus proposes an even surer way of testing the apostolic tradition. The best safeguard of such tradition

8. E.g., Irenaeus, *Haer.* I:9.
9. Irenaeus, *Haer.* III:11:9.

is an unbroken succession of authorized teachers within the Church, and specifically within certain of the leading churches: in the East, there are Jerusalem and Antioch, Ephesus and Alexandria; in the West, preeminently there is Rome. The Church in Rome had the advantage of a double apostolic foundation because both Peter and Paul had played important roles in the initial building of the community there. Moreover, the Church in Rome has had further advantages. An unbroken succession of bishops from the apostolic times to the present is known by a listing of names, each one succeeding his predecessor in unbroken line right back to both Peter and Paul. Consequently, the direct, personal transmission of the authentic account of the Christian Gospel is safeguarded by this known continuity, this apostolic succession. If, as the Gnostics hold, the apostles had possessed any secret teachings to purvey, surely they would have transmitted these teachings to the men they themselves had chosen to be their successors. But what we find is not concealed esoteric knowledge, as the Gnostics claim, but a perfectly open set of teachings in an unbroken line of succession. This is primarily a succession in transmitting and safeguarding the truth of the tradition, not a basis for exercising autocratic power. It is a succession neither of charismatic gifts nor of transmitted jurisdiction, but rather a succession of witnesses, an unbroken line of testimony. If we want to know then what the apostles taught, let us turn to those churches that were founded by the apostles and ask the men who are the leaders in those churches, the present successors and representatives of the original teachers.

Moreover, Rome has a further advantage because it is the imperial city of the Mediterranean world and to it Christians come from all quarters of the world, so that if errors crop out in Rome, they can be corrected speedily by representatives of other parts of the church.[10] The consensus can therefore be found in Rome as in no other part of the Christian world. Over against the heretics with their diversity, we can appeal to the essential unity of the genuine Christian teaching. Moreover, we can appeal to its continuity. It is the same from the time of the eyewitnesses themselves. Unity of life and belief instead of chaotic diversity; authenticity of origin guaranteed by unbroken succession of oral and written

10. Irenaeus, *Haer.* III:3:2: a once hotly-debated passage which seems most naturally to convey the sense indicated.

testimony; these are the marks of Christian teaching which can stand against the heretics.

## DOCTRINE OF GOD: FATHER, WORD, AND WISDOM

Now what is the truth that is thus safeguarded by the rule of truth, the continuous tradition, the apostolic writings? Consider first Irenaeus' understanding of the bases and limitations of religious knowledge as against the Gnostic claim to possess secret insight granted as a special favor. There are two bases for knowledge of God: on the one hand, what lies before our eyes in the created world; and on the other hand, the plain meaning of Scripture, stripped of all allegorical and fanciful interpretation, consisting of the words as they stand there on the page, understood according to what they do plainly say. There are, however, limitations to knowledge derived from both of these sources. On the one hand, there are many things in nature which we do not understand: what makes the Nile annually rise and overflow, the migration of birds, the ebb and flow of the tide, the source of lightning or the properties of stones and metals, and so on through a whole catalog of aspects of the natural world that still remain hidden. Inquiry here is both legitimate and desirable; but let us not fool ourselves into thinking that we have a special source of insight that will enable us to bypass the gradual acquisition of further understanding of these contents of the natural world.[11] A similar comment applies regarding Scripture. God has set down in Scripture what it is needful for us to know, but there are many things which are not to be found there, and we shall be very unwise if we try by speculation to provide them. For example, the being of God is not spelled out there; Scripture bears witness to the one true God, but it does not explicate in detail the nature of his inner being. And if we try to replace with our own imagination what God has seen fit to tell us, then we shall go off down one or another misleading trail. We must then accept limitations; there are things which God knows but which he has not seen for man to know—at least not yet.[12] At the same time, we embrace our right to explore both nature and Scripture to see whether or not we can extend the range of legitimate understanding. Forsaking legitimate understanding of Scripture, Gnostics have torn verses out of context, giving them

11. Irenaeus, *Haer.* II:28:3–4.
12. Irenaeus, *Haer.* II:28:1–2.

fanciful meanings. The result is a little like what one would get by taking single lines from different places in Homer's poems and putting them together so that they describe an episode that Homer never heard of.[13] Or it is like taking the jewels out of a portrait of a king and rearranging them so that they make the figure of a fox. Would the fox then be the king? Would the episode be what Homer taught? To read the Scripture correctly is to read it with common sense—to read it with a concern for the plain and literal meaning—and not to read it in such fashion that one takes thirty years of Jesus' public ministry as a numerical symbol for the thirty aeons in the *Pleroma*, or the twelve years during which the woman with an issue of blood had suffered as a figurative type of *Sophia*, the twelfth and youngest in the group of aeons in her generation.[14]

We have then sound bases for knowledge of God even though we cannot know everything about either God or the world. God is first of all the Father who is Creator and Lawgiver. He has made both the matter and form of this world; he has brought it into being out of nothing. (Irenaeus is the first Christian thinker to my knowledge who has said this in so many words, underscored it, and paraphrased it often enough so that there is no chance for mistaking his meaning.) Creatures cannot make things except by shaping a material that exists, but God has not only shaped a world—he has *made* the material as well. We do not know how. There is much that we do not know even about the observable aspects of the world, let alone how it has been brought into being. But one thing we know, if we read Scripture correctly: it has not been made by intermediaries, angels, or aeons, or any other lesser agents. God himself is its Creator. His hand spans the heavens, and the earth with its vast depths is for him a mere handful.[15]

His hands "with Him always are Word and Wisdom, Son and Spirit, through whom and in whom he made all things, freely and without help" (*sponte*).[16] For the Son and the Spirit are not assistants, subordinate as the Gnostics say. Nor does God's Word, like any human word, have a beginning in time. Both Word and Wisdom coexist with God always. Nay more: the Word is in essential being none other than the Father himself.

13. Irenaeus, *Haer.* I:9:4.

14. Irenaeus, *Haer.* II:22–23. Irenaeus himself is misled by a legend current perhaps in the Johannine community around Ephesus into a bizarre interpretation of John 8:57.

15. Irenaeus, *Haer.* IV:19:2–3.

16. Irenaeus, *Haer.* IV:20:1.

"But God being all Mind and all Logos "(*totus exsistens Mens et totus exsistens Logos*), speaks what He thinks and thinks what He speaks. For His thought is Logos, and Logos is Mind, and Mind comprehending all things, Himself is the Father" (*ipse est Pater*).[17] I find it hard to see how an expression can be more emphatic than that one. Here we have the Johannine tradition which verges strongly in the direction of Monarchian thought as over against the Philonic (and Valentinian) tendency to subordinate the Logos, keeping the Father in the position of the utterly remote Absolute. This is the tradition which tends to identify the Father and the Logos, so the deity that can be affirmed of the one can also be affirmed of the other.

> He, therefore, who speaks of the mind of God, and ascribes to it a special origin of its own (*prolationem propriam*), declares Him a compound Being, as if God were one thing, and the original Mind another. So, again with respect to Logos, when one attributes to him the third place of production from the Father; on which supposition he is ignorant of His greatness; and thus has separated Logos far from God. As for the prophet, he declares respecting Him, "Who shall describe his generation?" But you, divining His generation from the Father, and transferring the production of the word of men by means of a tongue to the Word of God, plainly (*iuste*) show yourselves that you know neither things human nor things divine.[18]

Granting the eternity of the Logos, it is necessary to say God is the Logos and the Logos is God, and there is no succession involved in their being. This suggests in the first instance, of course, that Irenaeus is approaching a triune understanding of the being of God. God, his Word, and his Wisdom are coeternal in their compresence. Now Irenaeus does not take the further step of saying they are coequal, still less that they are one and the same. The Word which is mind (*nous* or *logos*) and which is also thought (*ennoia*) is the Father himself. Yet Irenaeus distinguishes also between the Father and his two hands with which he engages in the work of giving existence to everything that exists other than himself.

---

17. Irenaeus, *Haer.* II:28:5.

18. Irenaeus, *Haer.* II:28:5. [*ANF* translation, modified and corrected.]

### The World and Human Nature

Consider next what Irenaeus understands to be the only proper Christian account of the world. Created as regards both its form and its matter so that in every respect it is dependent upon God for its being, the world does not include any competing or independent substance upon which God has to work. The whole world as we know it, whether visible or invisible, is created. And it is above this world that Irenaeus draws the critical line between God and the created order. The primary distinction is that the creator is himself unchanging, perpetually active, ever giving existence and character to what he creates, whereas the creature is perpetually receiving and becoming. God is unchanging, but it is of the essence of creaturely being to change and to grow.[19]

Creation is not the act of an instant which immediately comes to an end but a perpetual shaping and reshaping at the hands of God; only as creatures grow do they display their creaturely being. In the midst of the world which is thus perpetually being created, the human being has a crucial place. Scripture says: "And God made man: according to the image of God (*kat' eikona theou*) he made him; male and female he made them" (Gen 1:27 LXX). Here is a concept to which Irenaeus refers over and over again. That which is distinctive of human beings, by comparison with stones and trees and birds and four-footed creatures, is that they are able to manifest divine character at the end of their growth to maturity. The human person is not itself the image of God, for the image of God is the Word, the Son. But human beings are created "according to" that image, and the meaning of their existence is to be found in growth toward fuller and fuller manifestation of it.

This likeness to the image of God is discernible in three respects: (1) Human beings are free and responsible creatures. (2) They are created and capable of immortality. (Mark the precise way in which that notion is phrased. Men and women are not created as immortal creatures, but as those upon whom the grant of immortality can be conferred, and it is God's intent to make them immortal.)[20] (3) There is implanted in them the law of nature. This last is conceived by Irenaeus in two perspectives: it is the law of love to God and neighbor, the two great commandments, and it is the Decalogue. The law of the old dispensation and the law of

---

19. Irenaeus, *Haer.* IV:11:2.
20. Irenaeus, *Haer.* IV:13:4.

the new dispensation are essentially one and the same Law, which is ingrained in the very make of human nature.[21]

Man as created is an infant (*nepios, infans*); he is a child. Although he has no knowledge of good or of evil, he is made capable of free action toward maturation so that he can become a responsible self in the presence of God. He is not created immortal, but he is created capable of either living or dying. If he had continued to follow the will of God, he need not have died. On the other hand, since he was capable of free choice, he was able to disobey the plan that God had for him and so to lose, temporarily or permanently, the reward that God had in view when he brought him into being. For God had created mankind "so that he might have (someone) on whom to bestow his benefactions."[22]

Written on our innermost being is the command to love God with all our heart and to love our neighbor as ourselves. This is what we require to become fully human,[23] and such was God's desire and intent for us. But now that we have turned away from God, we are stunting our own growth, failing to develop our capacities fully. Having rebelled against God and lost our childhood innocence, we have lost the chance to develop the maturity of those who will display the lineaments of the image of God according to which we were created.

Twice God renews the law. Having broken the initial covenant, humanity grows in wickedness until God sends the flood to wash the earth clean, saving only Noah and his household; and with Noah he makes a second covenant, intrinsic like the first. But people break it again. So God at length spells out the covenant now in an external law, the Decalogue, which is nothing other than the first law expanded and made visible. Moses brings this version of the covenant to guide humanity. But they break it once more, and they keep on breaking it. Now the Decalogue is not to be regarded as something radically different from the great commandments. Because its essence is innate in us, its requirements can be called natural precepts (*naturalia praecepta*) or the natural components of law (*naturalia legis*).[24] It is supplemented now by a whole array of additional injunctions, including many directions for ritual detail. This

---

21. Irenaeus, *Haer.* IV:15:1.
22. Irenaeus, *Haer.* IV:14:1.
23. Irenaeus, *Haer.* IV:12:3–5.
24. Irenaeus, *Haer.* IV:13:1, 4.

ceremonial law is meant to be both a burden and a reminder of our having condemned ourselves to unnecessary death. [25]

Irenaeus' conception of the punishment of sin also points to God's long-term plan for human beings. Remember that in his view God is both just and merciful. Now as just, it is impossible for him to treat human beings as though they had been obedient all the while. They must be punished. But physical death, the punishment which is inflicted on them, is at the same time an indication of God's mercy, for it involves putting a limit on human capacity to sin.[26] Suppose that human beings were given immortality in their capacity as sinners. Then they would risk slipping down into a bottomless well. They could sin and sin and keep on sinning without any limitations at all. As a safeguard against this, God ordained death for human beings after a limited number of years, a merciful provision on God's part against their making their plight completely hopeless.

Irenaeus thinks he can see some indications, too, of a kind of residual human repentance and of divine mercy in the story about the clothing of Adam and Eve in the Garden of Eden. When Adam knows that he has done wrong and becomes shamefully aware for the first time of his nakedness, he covers himself with fig leaves. Irenaeus wonders: Now, why fig leaves? There are plenty of other leaves that would have been far more comfortable to wear, for fig leaves are sticky and prickly. So when Adam picked out fig leaves to cover himself, that is a sort of indication that he wanted to do penance for the wrong he had committed. And he shows his remorse also by his embarrassment in God's presence. Human beings thus become repentant almost as soon as they are lawbreakers.[27] And God recognizes that Adam and Eve sinned because they were tempted into sin. So God lays a curse not upon them but upon the serpent and upon the ground which will no longer bring forth fruit without human toil. Meanwhile, God specifies clothing made of skins, which will be softer and warmer—much more comfortable for men and women to wear. So even though human beings have for a while impeded God's plans as well as ruining their own prospects, God has their welfare (and his own purpose) still at heart. He is a God whose original plan for humanity cannot ultimately be defeated. These are still beings created according to

25. Irenaeus, *Haer.* IV:15–16.

26. Irenaeus, *Haer.* III:23:6.

27. Irenaeus, *Haer.* III:23:5.

the pattern which is the Word of God, and God will bring it about that their maturing will still come to pass. His mercy is shown as regnant even in his justice, "goodness coming first" (*praecedente bonitate*).[28] But human beings plunge themselves into a succession of generations of wrongdoing during which they sink deeper and deeper. And God lets them sink until a point is reached at which they become thoroughly convinced of their own inability to get out. That was necessary, because otherwise they would have thought of themselves as having achieved their own release and would not have recognized their ultimate dependence upon God.

## SALVATION THROUGH *RECAPITULATIO*

The heart of Irenaeus' theology is the fulfillment of God's creative purpose through Jesus Christ. That purpose was to bring into being a world inhabited at the center by a race of mortals who would grow to full stature as responsible persons, and receive at God's hands the gift of immortal life and perpetual fellowship with him. The natural law ingrained in humanity modeled in likeness to the eternal Son, the law of love to God and neighbor, was meant to be a guide to freedom and fullness of life. When, tempted by the Devil (himself a recreant creature, a ruined angel), mankind broke the law again and again, the original law remained in force; and through Moses, other requirements were added to serve at once as burdensome punishment and, more basically, as gracious ceremonial reminders of and signposts toward the way of righteousness.[29] Yet mankind persisted in the way of self-destruction, mercifully limited by God's imposition of death. But to leave the project of creation at that point would be to accept defeat—which for God is unthinkable. Hence the crucial intervention in and through Jesus Christ. A man—not an angel, not a divine stranger—a true member of humanity, born of woman, must fulfill the law and defeat the Devil. But only God, entering into the conditions of mortal existence, has the requisite power. Only one who is both truly God and truly human can do what needs to be done.

Here then there now finally comes God's redemptive intervention. The fullness of time begins with Jesus Christ. He who came is the Word of God the Father, who had been made a Son of man; "the Son who is in

---

28. Irenaeus, *Haer.* III:25:3.
29. Irenaeus, *Haer.* IV:26–28, etc.

the Father, and has the Father in himself."[30] He is also truly born a man, of a virgin mother; he hungered, grew weary, wept for a friend, "sweated great drops of blood," experienced the weakness of human life.[31] But the Septuagint was right in reading Isa 7:14 as "a virgin (*parthenos*) shall conceive." The Judaizers Theodotion and Aquila, who (correctly) translate *almah* as "a young woman" (*neanis*) are presumptuous and wrong.[32] In Jesus Christ, God and man are united.

The work of Jesus Christ on man's behalf has both a negative and a positive aspect. He has first of all to break the power of evil and specifically the power of the Devil over man, the enemy who had led man astray and had cracked a whip over him ever since. In the desert, the Son of God confronts the Devil at close range, meets his blandishments, and defeats, for the first time in human history, the work of sabotage that the Serpent had been carrying on all down the centuries. Now mankind stands before God with a representative in whom perfect obedience to God has been achieved; and once that has been done, the hold of the Devil—not merely upon the man Jesus Christ, but upon mankind at large—is in principle broken. In the crucifixion, the Devil has done his utmost to bring about the ruin of God's work to salvage men and make them eligible once again for the eternal life for which they were destined. When that supreme effort fails and the Lord is raised again from the dead, the power of the Law and the power of the Devil over man are at one and the same time annulled.[33] The basic law is still enforced; love for God and neighbor is still required. But it has been fulfilled through perfect obedience on the part of the crucified Lord. So the law is no longer a threat to man, but instead becomes what it was always meant to be: a way of fulfillment.[34]

The positive salvation which Jesus Christ accomplishes is crucially what Irenaeus calls "summing up" (*recapitulatio, anakephalaiosis*), a crucial act of God which is many-layered and heavy with meaning. Irenaeus has borrowed the form presumably from Eph 1:10, i.e., from the Pauline or deutero-Pauline discourse on God's mighty plan for human history, in which all barriers are broken down, hostilities abolished, "until we attain

30. Irenaeus, *Haer.* III:18:6; 6:2.

31. Irenaeus, *Haer.* III:22:2.

32. Irenaeus, *Haer.* III:21:1; cf. 3.

33. Irenaeus, *Haer.* V:21; 23.

34. Ireneaus, *Haer.* IV:13–15.

... to mature manhood, to the measure of the stature of the fullness of Christ" (Eph 4:13). At the time of the Incarnation, the Word of God, who is at one with the Father, becomes man. Beginning with infancy, he passes through all the stages of human life—boyhood, youth, full manhood. Irenaeus expressly adopts here a Johannine tradition (derived from John 8:57) that Jesus was fifty years old or thereabouts when he was crucified. For our sakes, the Word of God subjected himself to the conditions of all the stages of human life and fulfilled completely the possibilities of every stage on his way up to full maturity, not shirking even death, "but sanctifying every age through that likeness which was present at that particular time" (*per illam quae ad ipsum erat similitudinem*).[35] Or again: "assimilating himself to man, and man to himself, that through that likeness to the Son" (*per eam quae est ad Filium similitudinem*) man might be made precious to the Father."[36] In Jesus Christ the full stature of human life is perfectly achieved. This is *recapitulatio*—a summing up of all that has gone before, a bringing to a climax what hitherto has been unfinished, a pulling together into unity a humankind that since Adam has been broken and scattered and estranged. As the genealogy in Luke has shown, after the passing of seventy-two generations, it is Jesus "who has summed up in himself all nations dispersed from Adam onward, all languages, and the generation of mankind with Adam himself."[37] A Syriac version is said to indicate, appropriately enough, that Jesus Christ "commenced afresh" the history of humankind.[38] The Old Latin holds to the more familiar expression: "he summed up in himself (*in se ipso recapitavit*) the long array of human existence . . . so that what we have lost in Adam, that is, to be according to the image and likeness of God, this we may recover in Christ Jesus."[39] The second Adam thus becomes the epitome of the whole race. And not only does he sum up in himself all that is essential in humanity, but since man is the center of the whole created world, he sums up in himself all that God has intended for all created beings. He is therefore the epitome of God's entire creation, which now receives its fulfillment (remember the eighth chapter of Romans) in "the glorious liberty of the

35. Irenaeus, *Haer.* II:22:4.
36. Irenaeus, *Haer.* V:16:2.
37. Irenaeus, *Haer.* III:22:3.
38. Irenaeus, *Haer.* III:18:1 ; and n. 1 (*ANF*); cf. III:10:2 ; III:22:4.
39. Irenaeus, *Haer.* III:18:1 ; cf. 22:3.

children of God." Since Jesus Christ fulfills perfectly the status of created life, humankind—and indeed the whole created world—enters a new era. "All things became new" (*nova aderant*).[40]

Some Gnostics, we recall, had taught that Jesus Christ was a phantasmal being, a theophany who was not genuinely human and who therefore did not genuinely suffer. At most, the man Jesus suffered, but the divine Christ left him and flew away to heaven. For Irenaeus, priest and bishop of a congregation that had seen its members tortured with red-hot metal plates and roasted in an iron chair,[41] that was a blasphemous travesty of the gospel. Instead,

> He who was acknowledged by Peter as Christ ... said that He must Himself suffer many things, and be crucified ... "If any one wishes to follow, let him deny himself, and take up his cross, and follow me".... Plainly Christ said these words, he the Savior of those who because of their confession would be handed over to death, and would lose their lives.... If, however, He was Himself not to suffer, but should fly away from Jesus, why did He exhort his disciples to take up the cross and follow Him ... ?
>
> For the Word of God, who said to us, "Love your enemies, and pray for those who hate you," Himself did this upon the cross; loving the human race so much that He even prayed for those who were putting him to death. If, however, any one, going upon the supposition that there are two beings, forms a judgment in regard to them, that one shall be found much the better, and more patient, and the truly good one, who, in the midst of His own wounds and stripes, and the other [cruelties] inflicted upon Him, was beneficent, and unmindful of the wrongs perpetrated upon Him, than he who flew away, and sustained neither injury nor insult.[42]

That, I submit, is an extraordinary sort of Christology. And an extraordinary sort of theology, befitting a spokesman for an age of martyrs. For what Irenaeus is saying in effect is that God proves not only his love, but also, so to say, his goodness, his deity, by genuinely suffering on behalf of men and women. It seems to me in the most radical way a rejection of the two-world theology of the Marcionites or of the Gnostics, in which the real world is the world into which no pain and no change can enter,

---

40. Irenaeus, *Haer.* III:10:2.
41. Letter of the churches of Vienne and Lyons, in Eusebius, *Hist. eccl.* V:1.
42. Irenaeus, *Haer.* III:18:4, 5. [*ANF* translation, modified.]

whereas the world of history is unreal. On the contrary, Irenaeus is insisting that the reality of God is to be seen most visibly manifested precisely where God submits himself to the uncertainty, the suffering, the struggle of history.

He comes, to repeat, as a man born of woman, and lives through every stage of human life, including death. Thus was made plain once more what for so long had been lost through human sin: that human beings really were "made according to the image of God" (*kat' eikona Theou*). The lost likeness (*similitudo, homoiosis*) is restored; and since the Son is one God with the Father, the incarnate Son has "assimilated man to the invisible Father."[43]

This does not mean, of course, that humanity ceases to be a creature. A human being cannot become God. Rather, it means that through Jesus Christ, humanity is given once more, as at the beginning, a chance to be freed from the tendency of all creatures to lapse into nonbeing. It means being able again, like the "righteous fathers" of old—Enoch, Noah, Abraham—to share as "friends of God" a companionship of clear vision and of devoted love, freed from the burden the Law lays upon men and women while they are slaves and from the constraint of death.

> To follow the Savior is to participate in salvation: to follow the light is to participate in the light. Those who are in the light do not themselves illuminate the light, but are illuminated and made manifest by it. . . . So too serving God adds nothing to God . . . but to those who follow and serve Him He grants life, and incorruption, and eternal glory. . . . For this is the glory of man: to persist and to abide in the service of God.[44]

Thus both God and man are disclosed in new perspectives. In revealing man for the first time as fully grown, Jesus, given the conditions of perverted history, has perforce revealed God for the first time as one who at his own grievous cost makes possible such full human growth. As he presents man to God in new dimensions, so he reveals God to man in a new perspective. God, who has always been Creator, now (the very same God) makes himself known as Redeemer. It remains true that God's greatness is still, and will be always, beyond human comprehension, but

---

43. *loc. cit.* A fragment of the Greek text here is preserved by John of Damascus: "assimilating" is *synexomoiosas* in Greek, *consimilem faciens* in Latin.

44. Irenaeus, *Haer.* IV:14:1.

Jesus Christ makes his love truly known. "One God, therefore, who by Word and Wisdom made and ordered all things . . . who as regards His greatness is One unknown to all His creatures . . . but as regards His love He is known always through him by whom He made everything."[45]

But equally important and inseparable from this new revelation of God is the revelation of man to himself and to God. Now, for the first time, human beings can see what human beings are. Man is set before God in a new light because Jesus Christ has introduced into human existence an instance of perfect fulfillment, so that humanity now occupies a new level. Man is enabled to approach God because God has first approached man, so that the end is made to be what the beginning was intended to be. The *imago* according to which man was made now has come to fulfillment in the sphere of human existence, and the last things which are still to be awaited will be a manifest realization of what in principle has already been brought to pass. Jesus Christ is thus doubly the Revealer, and he can be so precisely and only because in him the full nature of humanity and the full nature of Godhead are combined.

> Therefore, as I have already said, He caused man [human nature] to cleave to and to become united with God . . . And unless man had been joined to God, he could never have become a partaker of incorruptibility. For it was incumbent upon the Mediator between God and men, by His intimacy (*oikeiotetos*) with both, to bring both to friendship and concord, and present man to God, while He reveals God to men. For, in what way could we be partakers of the adoption of sons, unless we had received from Him through the Son that communion which is His, unless His Word, having been made flesh, had entered into communion with us? Wherefore also he passed through every stage of life, restoring that communion which is with God.[46]

Irenaeus, in a word, envisages a divine act which is in principle an act that lifts humanity to the level which God had intended from the beginning men and women should reach. And that is the work of the mediator, who has to be man, because it was necessary that the mediator be himself a full-fledged member of the erring group. On the other hand, it was not less necessary that in him human nature should be genuinely

45. Irenaeus, *Haer.* IV:20:4; cf. *Haer.* IV:20:1.

46. Irenaeus, *Haer.* III:18:7. [*ANF* translation, modified.] Theodoret has preserved the Greek text of a part of this passage.

united with divine, immortal nature; apart from that there would have been no elevation of the race. So this is a view which in some respects anticipates Anselm's account of the necessity for God to become man to bring about the salvation of humankind. The stress here is not laid on the propitiation of God. From beginning to end, God is gracious even to sinful humanity.[47] And in due course, it is he who takes upon himself the full burden of human life and death.

Upon that basis human beings are saved through faith like that of Abraham,[48] which issues in repentance, obedience, and righteousness. The primal law of love to God and neighbor which man has broken is still in force. Indeed, it is sharpened and clarified. But it is not in force any longer as a condemnation for those who now enter into the sort of relationship with Jesus Christ which makes them heirs to the gift which he has brought. The primary demand of love to God and love of neighbor, written on the heart of man at his creation, renewed after the cleansing flood, externalized and elaborated in the Decalogue, has been brought back finally in the person of Jesus Christ. Consequently, persons who are united to him in obedient faith are members of a humanity whose obligation to the law is in principle fulfilled. Jeremiah had said that in latter days the law would be written on tablets of human hearts and not any longer on tablets of stone (Jer 31:33). Irenaeus in effect says that this has now been accomplished. The law is an inward law, and obedience must be an inward obedience: the achievement of that disposition of love towards God and the love towards man which is, for the whole Johannine tradition, the very sum and substance of what God requires. Faith and love—these are for Irenaeus, as for the Johannine writer, the poles around which the saved life must necessarily be focused.

One characteristic emphasis in Irenaeus' theology is the demand that the whole person shall be saved—not simply one's spirit, but one's body, one's flesh. As he says very emphatically, the Lord became "an actual man, consisting of flesh, and nerves, and bones."[49] It is not true that God disparages the physical creation. On the contrary, God enters into physical creation. The summing-up includes not simply a *Pleroma* of spirits and eternal beings but the historical reality of earthly life. As

---

47. Irenaeus, *Haer.* IV:17:2.

48. Irenaeus, *Haer.* IV:5:4; 7:2; 21:1.

49. Irenaeus, *Haer.* V:2:3. [*ANF* translation.]

for those Marcionites and Gnostics who seek to denigrate the incarnate, true humanity of Jesus Christ, they are undercutting the very possibility of redemption; in defending a redeemer who is radically other than the Creator, they are unwittingly talking of one who cannot bring redemption to actual humanity at all. In contrast to this rejection of the created order, and as an active affirmation of the salvation of the whole man, the sacraments as physical rites are included in the life of the Church and are to be used by believers. Baptism and the Eucharist employ physical media to lay stress upon the use that God makes of the physical body to reveal himself and to effect the salvation of believers. Thus the bread and wine of the Eucharist, standing for the body and blood of the Lord, are actually for the believer the body and blood of the Lord. They are the food and the drink which nourished that body. They are the food and drink which now nourish this body. At the same time, they are the vehicle of the recreating presence of the Word which, once operating through the body of the man Jesus of Nazareth, operates now through the physical elements and through the body of the participants who enter into communion with God in this very literal and realistic way.[50]

That same stress on the importance of physical salvation carries over into Irenaeus' doctrine of last things. His eschatology is as vivid and uncompromisingly realistic as any that we find in Christian literature.[51] He is the one who preserves and comments with approval on the fragment that we noticed in Papias' account of the coming Kingdom, with the miraculous vine and the miraculous wheat fields. So far as Irenaeus is concerned, Papias really offers an important insight. The end will be achieved in the body, *this* body, made incorruptible "not by its own nature, but by the action of God,[52] not apart from it. Those Gnostics and Marcionites who were inclined to degrade the world of the body are dishonoring God who created the body and its life. Concerning the story about the wheat fields, Irenaeus comments that plainly enough the grain in these fields is the grain whose straw the lions will eat in the last days when they lie down in peace with the lambs, and if the straw is fit food for lions, "of what a quality must the wheat itself be?"[53] The coming Kingdom, in a

---

50. Irenaeus, *Haer.* IV:18:4–6; V:2:1–3.

51. Irenaeus, *Haer.* V:2–14.

52. Irenaeus, *Haer.* V:13:3.

53. Irenaeus, *Haer.* V:33:4

word, is going to be a kingdom which you and I will enter with a full sense of at-homeness. We shall find there the familiar foods and the familiar drinks that have gladdened the hearts of human beings since the days of the Judges [i.e., after the manna of the wilderness]. We shall find there a landscape in which we can settle down and be fully at home. And to Irenaeus' mind that is what we need. Meanwhile, there is the Church, the Church of those who are in the process of growing—and I wish I knew how to keep that motif sounding alongside all these other aspects of Irenaeus' thought—always growing, as an obedient creature; and in growing, manifesting more and more fully God's purpose and the pattern which he implanted in man in the beginning and which in Jesus Christ is given perfect embodiment.

## SUMMARY

What we find here in the thought of Irenaeus is a quite extraordinary combination of profound religious insight and intellectual naïveté.[54] He is a man who has hold of certain basic affirmations with a tenacity that is never shaken loose. Harnack says that the two ideas on which he had that kind of firm grip were the unity of God and the God-manhood of Jesus Christ.[55] That is, of course, a conventional thing to say about any Christian thinker. But Irenaeus had hold of these ideas in his own peculiar individual manner: the unity of God in which God is all Mind, all Word, all Wisdom, fully just and above all merciful, and the God-Manhood of Jesus Christ in whom is epitomized the whole creation, so that in him and by him and unto him all things are oriented. Certainly Irenaeus did not formulate these basic insights with precision or with neatness. The affirmations come in sporadic and disjointed fashion, intermingled with attacks on Gnosticism or Marcionitism or on some other aberration. There is no straightforward cumulative argument to be found anywhere in Irenaeus' books *Against Heresy*. Rather, we have what are to my mind deeply moving conceptions of the nature of God and the nature of man, and the relationship which God has effected between them. They are

---

54. Having ridiculed the numerology and other fanciful readings of Scripture by Gnostic teachers, he himself is fascinated by the calculations of the number of the Antichrist (666) in Rev 13:18 (Irenaeus, *Haer.* V:29–30).

55. Adolf von Harnack, *Lehrbuch der Dogmengeschichte*, 4th ed., I:556–57 pp.

present like precious metal in a great mass of ore, and the ore at times is unfortunately like clay.

One feature that helps to make Irenaeus distinctive and impressive is that he lays so immense a stress upon the unity of physical and spiritual nature and the need for the redemption of the whole of God's creation. Normally, I suppose, one would expect a Greek-speaking thinker to maintain a sharper dualism of flesh and spirit, of mind and matter. A partial explanation is that Irenaeus is not a Greek from a thoroughly Hellenized center of culture like Alexandria or Athens. He comes from Asia Minor, where Hellenism was superimposed upon a far more deeply rooted indigenous mode of thought in which immanence, emotional intensity, and the accessibility of God, rather than the remote transcendence of God and the mediation of his transcendent Being through intermediaries, have been the customary emphases. We have noticed similar emphases in Ignatius, and we shall find numerous other representatives of this Greek-speaking Orient maintaining positions which are more or less like that of Irenaeus. But besides all that, I suspect that his experience of the tortured martyrdom of his fellow Christians in the Gallic churches was crucial to his conceptions of God, of Jesus Christ, and of salvation.

# CHAPTER 8

# Tertullian of Carthage[1]

ERTULLIAN IS A MAN of very different temper than Irenaeus. His
background is different; his personality is different. He thinks and
writes mostly in Latin rather than in Greek, and his manner and habits
of thought clearly were shaped in part by his experience as a practicing
lawyer. At the same time, he knew, admired, and used Irenaeus' language
against the Gnostics,[2] and is like him in urging the merits of the human
body and the physical world. Jerome speaks of him as "a man of a sharp
and vehement temper," and of his writings as "packed with meaning," but
"rugged and uncouth" in style.[3] We know of Tertullian's personal life only
what we can find in his own writings, which do not include information
about the time of his birth. We may conjecture that he was born somewhere around 150 and lived until about 220, or perhaps later. Jerome
reports that he flourished (meaning "was about forty years old and therefore in the prime of activity") under the Emperor Severus and Caracalla
his son, i.e. between 193 and 216.[4] Those dates are fairly well assured,
and we also know the date of one of his main writings, the first book
*Against Marcion*, which he clearly implies was written in the fifteenth year
of Severus (ca. 207).[5] But the remaining four books *Against Marcion* were
written at various intervals which are impossible to determine, and only

1. Professor Calhoun was at the time of his death in the process of rereading Tertullian
(in Latin) in order to complete the footnoting of this chapter in preparation for publication. The work was almost complete, and the note about editorial procedures at the
beginning of the last chapter (on Irenaeus) applies here also [ed.].

2. *Adv. Valent.* V. *et seq.*

3. Jerome, *Ep.* LVIII in *NPNF2* 6.

4. Jerome, *De Viris Illustribus*, LIII in *NPNF2* 3.

5. *Adv. Marc.* I.xv.

by careful inspection of cross references among the various writings can one obtain relative dates.

By his own description, his youth had been devoted to self-indulgent pleasure rather than to hard study. Nevertheless, he appears to have acquired a very competent working knowledge of Roman law. He practiced as an advocate, perhaps in Rome, before he became a Christian, and he carried over his forensic habit of systematic analysis and precise formulation, and a tightly knit, but sometimes not particularly profound, mode of argument into his contribution to Christian theology. About 190, at the age of forty or so, he became a Christian, and five years later a priest, in Rome or in Carthage. That he lived out the latter part of his life in Carthage seems to be fairly certain.

A very important turning point in Tertullian's career came somewhere about 200 when he was converted to Montanism. Jerome somewhat dubiously says the occasion was "envy and abuse" by the Roman clergy.[6] As time goes on he begins to write with bitter disappointment of the ordinary churchgoing Christians, who as it seems to him, were lamentably lukewarm, unimaginative, and unheroic in their understanding of Christianity. With its stress on the new age of the Paraclete in which the charismata of the early days of the church—the Spirit's gifts of tongues, of prophecy, and of healing—are once more being renewed, Montanism tallies precisely with Tertullian's own fiery make-up and his temperamental demand for a dangerous kind of Christian living, and henceforward he speaks, not simply as a Christian, but as a Montanist Christian. He begins to condemn not only heretics like Marcion and the Gnostics but also the people whom he calls "psychics", that is to say, his former fellow Christians in the ordinary churches of the Mediterranean world. As we shall see, his new allegiance has an essential bearing upon his major contribution to later Christian theology. It is, no doubt, somewhat ironical that a man who read himself out of the church should nevertheless have been one of the most conspicuously vigorous defenders of what he understood to be the Gospel against Marcionites, Valentinians, and other heretics, and the contributor of certain formulae with respect to the being of God and the person of Jesus Christ which ultimately supplied terminology for the creeds which the church adopted to determine right belief. The fact is that Montanism, reaffirming a powerful emotional

---

6. Jerome, *De Viribus Illustribus*, LIII in *NPNF2* 3.

dimension of primitive Christianity, enriched and expanded his theological thinking. Montanism infused into a keen legal mind results in something very different from simple Phrygian enthusiasm.

## APOLOGETIC AND POLEMICAL WRITINGS

The range of his writing is quite extraordinary.[7] We know him on the one hand as an apologist for Christianity in works addressed to the pagan world. His *Apology* is the longest, the most vehement, and the most reckless of all the Christian apologies that have come down to us, in the sense that he not merely seeks to meet and turn aside the indictments against Christianity but retorts those charges violently upon the pagans who make them. He undertakes to show that the evils of which the Christians have been falsely accused are to be found instead in pagan culture. He writes upon the Roman theater, upon the career of the soldier, upon the nature of conscience, upon various subsidiary practices within and without the church—the veiling of virgins, the allotment of laurel wreaths to victors in the games, and what not. His apologetic writing undertakes to set Christianity in the sharpest contrast to the life of the pagan world. The one pagan achievement he approves is Stoicism.

He writes also as an opponent of heresy. His most general work here is called *On Prescription Against Heretics*. This is a kind of introduction to five big books *Against Marcion*, from which we get most of our information about what Marcion and his follower, Apelles, appear to have taught. Tertullian quotes them in order to answer them, and his quotations provide the chief body of material which Harnack has organized into a provisional reconstruction of Marcion's *Antitheses*.[8] We have, in addition, other anti-heretical writings. One is against a certain Hermogenes, a Carthaginian artist, who appears to have been a Platonist with a tendency to stress the existence of a preexistent, independent, unformed matter upon which the Creator had to work. Perhaps most important for the development of later thought is his work against Praxeas, a modalist Monarchian of the second century. He was not a man of Tertullian's generation but one who had come to

7. Crit. ed. *Q.S.Fl. Tertulliani Opera, CCSL* I-II; English trans. by various hands, *ANF* 3–4.

8. Adolf von Harnack, *Marcion: Das Evangelium vom fremden Gott, eine Monographie zur Geschichte der Grundlegung der Katholischen Kirche* (Leipzig: Hinrichs, 1921). See also Harnack, *Neue Studien zu Marcion* (Leipzig: Hinrichs, 1923).

Carthage from Rome considerably earlier, whose thought, however, was well-known in North Africa, and appeared to Tertullian an extremely dangerous deviation from Christian truth.[9]

The general principles upon which he writes against heresy are worked out in the *Prescription*. Tertullian lays down the dictum that there is an irreconcilable contrast between reason and faith. Athens has nothing to do with Jerusalem. Philosophy is of the Devil, and Christian belief must not be entangled in the philosophical speculation or argument that characterizes all heretics. No doubt it is written, "Seek and ye shall find," but when you have found, stop seeking. What Christians possess is the truth for which philosophers have been questing in vain. Now that we have the truth, briefly summarized in the Rule of Faith, nothing should tempt us to move away from the treasure that is ours. Moreover, there is nothing to be gained in trying to appeal to reason by way of defense of of Christian truth. Rather, let the basic appeal be simply to authoritative creed and tradition.[10]

In these passages a sharp difference of temper between Irenaeus and Tertullian is plain. Both affirm as a necessary guide for Christian thought "the rule of faith," "of truth." But Irenaeus, acknowledging that human comprehension of both nature and scripture is limited, urges the need to seek fuller understanding of both. Tertullian says "stop." He is a fideist, who can write "It is all the more credible because it is absurd," "it is certain because it is impossible" (*magis credibile est, quia ineptieme est; certum est, quia impossibile est.*[11] These statements concern the crucified and risen Lord—the traditional paradox that to the well-trained Greek philosophic mind always seemed ridiculous. Faith in such teachings is to be affirmed not because it is reasonable, but all the more if it appears to be unreasonable. Within the limits prescribed by the rule of faith, we may think as actively and as acutely as we are able. But the point is we must not rove outside the bounds marked out by the norm that determines for us what is truth, nor seek to subject the norm itself to rational tests.[12]

I am inclined to think that Tertullian is displaying in his celebration of absurdity a habit that he displays elsewhere, of making a point vividly

---

9. Harnack, *s.v. Monarchianismus* in P.B.E. XIII. 329–33.

10. *Praescr.* vii–xii.

11. *De carne Christi*, V.4.

12. *Praescr.* xiv.

by overmaking it. He deliberately uses extravagant and offensive language to lay hold of the minds of his listeners. An advocate in the courtroom will do the same thing. He will undertake to make sure that his point is grasped by putting it in words that are shocking. Tertullian is doing that here. On occasion he himself is quite prepared to engage in logical analysis and argument, as we shall see when come to his work against Marcion.[13] At all events, the primary basis for meeting heresy is an affirmation of faith, not a speculative argument.

Having repudiated the heretics' philosophizing, Tertullian undertakes in good lawyer-like fashion to rule out any chance that heretics should be permitted to resort to Scripture as a way of establishing their own positions. Never argue with a heretic over Scripture, says Tertullian; it will serve merely to turn your head or your stomach. The Scripture belongs to those who from the beginning have followed the rule of faith or the rule of truth (*regula fidei*, or *regula veritatis* or simply *regula* appears again and again in his writings). Moreover, the "rule" (literally a measuring rod) has for him a far more precise, detailed content than any similar guideline in Irenaeus, for whom it is still a largely intuitive Christian consensus rather than an explicit conceptual form of belief. Tertullian as lawyer likes specifications.[14]

This legal bent is especially clear in the treatise *de praescriptionibus*, the title of which comes straight from familiar practices of the Roman law courts. Suppose that some one lays claim to a piece of real estate which has been in the hands of the present occupant for a considerable time. The newcomer now professes to be the original owner, or to represent the original owner, and he wants to take title to the property. He will seek from the *praetor*, a jurist, a legal expert, to have a *scriptio* setting forth the plaintiff's claim and the pertinent law. But the defendant may claim to offset the profession of the plaintiff, seeking from the *praetor* a *praescriptio* as a pre-emptive measure. He is permitted to say: "I have been in undisturbed possession of this property for so and so many years." If the property were away out in the provinces, the length of time required would be twenty, thirty, forty years; if nearer the capital, it would be a shorter time (for there presumably the question could have been raised

13. Cf. e.g., Marc. I. xxiii.

14. Cf. Tertullian, *De praescr.* xiii; *adv. Praxean* ii; esp. *De velandis virginibus*; *impossibile* Irenaeus, *Adv. Haer.* I.ix.4; III.i.2; xxxiii.7. [Nota bene: RLC's handwriting not legible with certainty in reference to this footnote.]

more simply and quickly). At all events, he will enter a claim of "length of possession" and ask for a *praescriptio longi temporis* (or *longae possessionis*): "I have been the acknowledged owner of this property for a long enough time now so that there has been ample opportunity for a claim to be posed. This present claim is made so late in the day that it should be ruled out on grounds of the passage of a sufficient period of time during which my claim has not been challenged."[15]

Tertullian is in effect utilizing this legal concept for theology, entering a counter-claim which declares that the plaintiffs (in this case, the heretics) should be ruled out of court because of prior conditions which make it impossible for them to expect judgment in their favor. In this instance, the question is, "To whom does the Scripture properly belong?" And the answer is, "It belongs to those who for so many years have been acknowledged to be its proper possessors; it belongs to those who have maintained from the beginning the rule of faith.[16] Four queries are to be put and answered in order to determine who properly possesses the rule, and hence the Scriptures that are to be interpreted by the rule: from whom, through whom, when, and to whom has the property in question been transmitted?[17] The answer to the first question is, "From Jesus Christ." It is he who first transmitted the truth of the Gospel through his apostles in his lifetime, and that which has been thus transmitted is itself nothing other than the Gospel rightly understood. And it has been transmitted to the apostolic churches.

Here Tertullian is reasoning much as Irenaeus had also done, but from a somewhat different perspective. Certain churches are known to have been founded by apostles, and in those churches we can trace a continuity of approved later men. Now through the apostles the truth which came from Jesus Christ has been transmitted to their successors in these apostolic Churches. But how do we now recognize and define apostolic Churches? Not merely by saying, as Irenaeus seems to do, that "this Church in Ephesus was founded by the apostle Paul, this Church in Alexandria was founded by Mark, Peter's companion; this Church in Rome was founded by Peter himself." Rather we say that all those churches, old or new, which agree in their teaching with the churches

15. Justinian: *Corpus juris civilis*: Codex VII. xxxiii-xxxix.

16. *Praescr.* xv–xviii.

17. *Praescr.* xix.

of apostolic foundation in which the line of continuity can be traced are properly to be regarded as apostolic churches. Agreement upon a common faith is ultimately the decisive test. We apply, of course, the test of antiquity against novelty, but that is after all a preliminary check; the final test is whether or not there is agreement now with the substance of what has thus been transmitted from Jesus Christ through the apostles to those who succeeded them.[18]

Now the heretics may attempt to discredit this sort of verification of the truth. Obviously they cannot say the Gospel came from some one other than Jesus Christ, for all agree on that point; but they can argue that perhaps he did not tell all of the truth to the apostles, or, if he did, they did not understand it all; or he did not teach everything publicly and openly but taught some things secretly, so that these secrets could be transmitted "sub rosa." Tertullian goes to some length to refute all of these possibilities and to prove that the apostles all say essentially the same thing. What was taught to one was taught to all the rest. Moreover it was taught out in the open, and there is no hint that there was an esoteric teaching which was kept somehow from public view. As a matter of fact, Jesus himself is continually talking about a lamp placed on a lampstand so that it will be seen by every one in the house, about a city set on a hill which cannot be hid, about how everything that is taught secretly will be declared openly, and so on. All the way through the gospel account, the stress is upon openness and candor. There is no reason to suppose that the apostles did not have everything that Jesus thought it important to teach them.[19]

Now if one should suppose that the apostles had misunderstood, one would expect the teaching in these apostolic churches to be mutually contradictory. But that is not the case. One finds instead unanimity with regard to the content of the normative rule. And that is sufficient to discredit a final suggestion: that those to whom the apostles transmitted the teaching have falsified it. Falsification by diverse spokesmen does not lead to ultimate unanimity; it would naturally lead to ever more diversity. So it is necessary to say the rule of faith is to be found where this sort of unanimity exists, unanimity which can be traced back to the beginning, and, therefore, before any of the heretical sects were started at all. It is only where this sort of teaching is found that the Scriptures can be

---

18. *Praescr.* xx–xxi.
19. *Praescr.* xxv–xxviii.

rightly understood. In the unified teaching of the apostolic churches, the present-day church has a touchstone to which true teaching must conform.[20] But now having laid down the principle that one is not to argue over Scripture with heretics, Tertullian proceeds on occasion to argue over Scripture with heretics. He will argue Scripture with Marcion, lest, he says, the Marcionites get the idea that the Christians are incompetent or afraid.[21] He will argue Scripture against Praxeas and the Monarchians lest it be thought that Christians mistrust the applicability of their rule;[22] and the points on which he will do so include those on which the heretics seemed to go most sadly astray: in the first place, their understanding of God and God's relation to the world, and, in the next place, their understanding of Jesus Christ and his relation to man and man's need. But as a working principle, argument with heretics over the interpretation of Scripture is best avoided.

## THE UNITY OF GOD

Whether misled by vain philosophy or by wrongheaded exegesis, the heretics have gone astray primarily and most fundamentally in their efforts to think rightly about God. Here the errors extended in two opposing directions. There are the Marcionites, on the one hand, for whom the creator of this world and the redeemer of mankind are two beings and not one.[23] There are the modalistic Monarchians, on the other hand, who have so completely identified the Father and the Son and the Holy Spirit that they leave no proper room for distinction within the Godhead. The Marcionites split the Godhead apart; the modalistic Monarchians fuse it completely together.[24] It is necessary, Tertullian thinks, to avoid both of these sources of error.

Against the Marcionites and, in subsidiary fashion, against the Valentinians and any other Gnostics who multiply beings in the Godhead, he argues on both logical and empirical grounds for the unity of God. His argument begins with a logical analysis of the meaning of the term "God." What is it that we have in mind when we speak of deity? What we have in

---

20. *Praescr.* xxvii–xxviii, xxxv–xxxvi.

21. *Marc.* I.i; xxii.

22. *Prax.* ii.

23. *Marc.* I–V.

24. *Prax.* I–xxxi

mind is the Supreme Being. God is *Summum Magnum*, and no other being can properly be called God. But there can be but one Supreme Being,
for if there two or more, they would be either equal or unequal in rank.
But if they are equal in rank, then as far as regards status they become
indistinguishable. In as far as we are focusing simply upon the essential
nature of supremacy, their essential status must be identical and there
must be, therefore, but one genuinely Supreme Being.[25]

On the other hand, there is an empirical argument that reaches the
same conclusion. Apart from Scripture, our knowledge of God must
come through experience of a world.[26] As far as our knowledge goes,
there is one world and only one. And if we say that the Creator of that
world—the world that lies all around us—is not God, and therefore that
God is not discernible from the sensible world at all, then we find ourselves constrained to say we have no experiential basis upon which we
can get knowledge of God.[27]

Now the Marcionites, of course, say that there is a hidden God, dwelling in another world, who has made himself known here through a special
revelation. Fair enough, says Tertullian, but that special revelation itself
must come to us within the world of space and time.[28] Indeed, only upon
the basis of what happens in this world are we able to judge even that there
may be another world, different from this. We have to say, then, that the
unity which we find in the only world we know argues to the unity of the
Ground of the existence of that world and of its ordering. There is then
one God who is Creator and Ruler of the one world which alone we can
experience, and the harmony which we discover within that world is additional and specific evidence of the ordered operations of the Creator and
Ruler. Moreover, if we agree that this universe belongs to the Creator-God,
there is no place in it for that Redeemer-God who is not the Creator. The
Marcionites say that the third heaven is such a place, but how can they know
anything about the third heaven except as an extrapolation from what they
see in the inhabited world?[29] They are inclined to disparage the beauty and
the goodness of this world, but, says Tertullian, I challenge them to decry

25. *Marc.* I. iii–vii.
26. *Marc.* I. xviii.
27. *Marc.* I.viii–xi.
28. *Marc.* I. xiv.
29. *Marc.* I. xv.

the beauty of a world that has flowers (little flowerets from a hedge-row, let alone the carpets of flowers in the meadows); that has an ordinary sea-shell (let alone the beauties that you can find in the Red Sea); that has a stray feather from a common bird to say nothing of a peacock. A world that has graciousness and symmetry of this sort is a world of which no Creator need be ashamed.[30] What have the Marcionites to show by way of comparison with these manifestations of the power and the order properly to be ascribed to the Creator of this world? Tertullian's Stoic perspective is clearly visible here and elsewhere. He fully shares the Stoic conception of the pervasive Logos[31] which orders the world and also the conviction that all substantial reality, even spirit, is corporeal. "For who will deny that God is a body, although 'God is a Spirit'? For Spirit has a bodily substance of its own kind, in its own form."[32]

On the other hand, Christians have Scripture as a second way of access to God. "For we hold that God is to be known first by nature, and then by instruction; by nature, from deeds, by instruction, from proclamations" (*natura ex operibus, doctrina ex praedicationibus*).[33] But where in the Scripture can Marcionites find a God other than He who made heaven and earth? Whether Old Testament or New Testament writings, all witness to one and the same God. There simply is not anything in nature or in Scripture that points to a God other than the one God whom Christians acknowledge and worship.[34]

Like Irenaeus (and no doubt every other critic of Marcion) but much more systematically, Tertullian insists that God must be both just and good, and that Marcion's concepts of justice and goodness are grossly defective. Divine goodness being inherent in divine nature must be perpetual, but the "goodness" of Marcion's new god did not manifest itself when sin and death first appeared. And how shall we say a god is good if, being able to save hapless men, he fails to do it? That is not goodness, but malignity.[35] Moreover, such "goodness" when it does manifest itself is irrational and unjust; for it involves invading the alien domain of

---

30. *Marc.* I.xiii, xix, xxi.
31. Note approving citations of Zeno and Cleanthes in *Apol.* xxi.
32. *Prax.* VII.
33. *Marc.* I.xviii.
34. *Marc.* I.x; esp. IV. *passim.*
35. *Marc.* I.xxii.

the Demiurge, to which the new god has no proper claim.[36] Further, it is restricted in range, saving a few and abandoning many.[37] The fact is that by oversimplifying both goodness and justice, Marcion vitiates both, and makes both unworthy of God.

God's true goodness is shown precisely in creation: most notably the creation of man by his Word, according to his image, alone worthy "to receive the law from God; so that as a rational, free, living being capable of understanding and knowledge, he should be restrained by that very rational freedom (*ipsa quoque libertate rationali contineretur*), and subject to him who made all things subject to him."[38] This gift of responsible freedom, not mindless amiability, is the hallmark of genuine goodness— the goodness of God who is is the Creator of all human beings, the God whom Tertullian extolled against pagans, Gnostics, reductionists[39]—the one God of Christian faith.

## THE TRINITY

Against the Marcionites, then, is to be affirmed on both logical and empirical grounds that God is one. But that is precisely what the modalists have been doing. Simple and conservative brethren, they have been saying that God is indeed one and that his unity must be so conceived that there is no chance of separating Father from Son. Among these Monarchians, who were carrying over into a newer stage of Christian thought a very archaic insight, we know the names of Noetus of Smyrna, a certain Cleonomes who taught in Rome, and Praxeas. Praxeas was the particular modalist attacked by Tertullian (now a Montanist), who characteristically opened his tract *Against Praxeas* by saying that the Monarchian had done two works for the Devil in Rome at the same time. He had driven out prophecy and brought in heresy. He had put to flight the Holy Ghost, and crucified the Father.[40] His heresy was Patripassianism, which affirmed the sole individual being of a God in whom Father and Son are identical, and in which the Holy Spirit has no place. These modalistic Monarchians teach that if we truly believe in one God alone, we must say that this

36. *Marc.* I.xxiii.
37. *Marc.* I.xxv.
38. *Marc.* II.iv.
39. *Apol.* xvii–xviii; *Adv. Valentin.* ii–iii; *Adv. Hermog.* xvii–xxii; xxix–xxxiv.
40. *Prax.* i.

God, although called sometimes Father, sometimes Son, and sometimes Holy Spirit, is in all essential respects one and the same; he is a single, individual being, and Fatherhood, Sonship, and Spirithood are aspects or modes of his being. Epiphanius reports (how reliably is quite unsure) that Sabellius, a representative of this tradition of the following century, used the analogy of the sun, saying it is at once round, hot, and bright; likewise God may be called Father, Son, and Spirit, but these are merely facets or modes of the being of one single individual entity. So too body, soul, and spirit are aspects of one individual human being. Whoever speaks of Father and Son as being in some important way different from one another is in effect abandoning monotheism and teaching ditheism. If one brings in the Spirit, one then becomes a tritheist. And there is no reason to stop at two or three, for if one intends to be a polytheist at all, one may as well be a whole-hearted polytheist! Such is the outcome feared by these simple folk who staunchly defend the unity of the Godhead.[41]

These heretics are obviously of a sort quite different from the speculative thinkers who draw upon extra-Christian sources, elaborating into a syncretistic scheme both Christian and non-Christian tenets. Such Monarchians start from an essentially Christian truth but stubbornly hold on to it in a naive and uncritical way, not recognizing that the form they give to this belief conflicts with plain Scripture. Against this modalistic misconception of God, Tertullian holds that in some proper sense God is three. Obviously it will not do to think like a Marcionite or a Valentinian and end up with three gods. There is but one God. Therefore the threeness within the Godhead must be so construed that it will not interfere with the primary affirmation of God's unity. But it is perfectly possible to have sovereignty (*monarchia*) that is shared. Actually in Tertullian's own lifetime, the Emperor Severus, his son Caracalla, and his younger son Geta all held the title of Augustus. Did that mean that there was more than one sovereignty in the empire? It did not; there was one sovereignty, shared and executed by more than one holder. Now, says Tertullian, can we recognize something of this sort in thinking of God?

His answer is stated in terms that prove to be not only convenient but strategically important for the development of the later Christian doctrine of the Trinity. When we speak of God as One we are speaking of his

---

41. *Prax.* iii.

supremacy (*monarchia*), and this supremacy, as already noticed,[42] is what makes God what he is. It is his *substantia*. In the Roman courts of law, *substantia* is that in virtue of which a person's status in the community is determined. (We still say "a person of substance," meaning a person whose position in the community is established.) In the case of God we must say that the *substantia* is one. It is precisely God's absolute supremacy in the whole range of being.[43] When we say that God is three we have reference to another conception, to divine activity or *oeconomia*—"administration" or "creative and redemptive operation." It is the pattern of active divine government that Tertullian here has in view.[44]

In respect to supremacy God is one; but in respect to administrative action we distinguish three beings within the Godhead which we may call *personae*. Like *substantia*, *persona* is a legal term. In the Roman law courts it meant a party to a legal action—for instance, one of the parties to a contract, whether it be an individual or a partnership or a corporation, or an estate or a unit of government. For the purposes of the contract, each party is considered an individual being and can be called, therefore, *persona*. (In our law courts, the word *person* is still used in that manner. Yale University or the State of Connecticut can appear in legal documents as a person.) The term means primarily a functioning unity. The same general sense is familiar in the Roman theater, where *dramatis personae* are the roles to be performed. Sometimes one actor will play one role throughout the drama; sometimes he will play two or more roles, and then there are a number of *personae*, though only one actor, and the parts will be identified by masks which also may be called *personae*.[45] Tertullian gets this term—or at least a warrant to use it—from Prov 8:30 LXX, in which Wisdom is speaking of herself as in the presence (*en prosopo*) of God.[46] Now *prosopon* for the Greeks is what one sees when looking at something; it is the outward and visible sign of the presence of a real being, and in the case of a human being, the *prosopon* especially is one's face by which one is quickly recognized. But for Tertullian the term has initially another sort of meaning, functional rather than ontological.

42. *Marc.* I.iii *sqq.*
43. *Prax.* iv.
44. *Prax.* iii. etc.
45. *Spect.* xxiii. Not a usage favored by our author.
46. *Herm.* xviii: *in persona ejus.*

In the Godhead, however, function cannot be denied substantive status (*aliquam substantiam*).[47] In the Godhead there are three of these functioning *personae*: to them we refer the names Father, Son, and Holy Spirit. It must be emphasized that the threeness is not a difference of kind or of essential being (*substantiae*). The Father, Son, and Holy Spirit share in the status of supremacy. Just as a king may share his throne with his son, so that each may exercise sovereignty without being divided or diminished, so Tertullian thinks it is in the divine economy. The Father, the Son, and the Holy Spirit share the divine supremacy in creation, redemption, and sanctification. Each occupies such a position that we must ascribe *monarchia* to each and to all. The unity of the divine *substantia* is unbroken. Yet they are distinguished in a manner much more radical than that in which the modalistic Monarchians are accustomed to distinguish them. For they held that the Father, Son, and Holy Spirit (if they recognize the Holy Spirit) are all aspects of one individual being—facets or properties but not functioning realities. Apparently Tertullian is groping for a form of statement that will enable him to say that the whole Godhead is Father, the whole Godhead is Son, the whole Godhead is Holy Spirit, without confusing one of these primary active roles with another. It is not enough to speak of God as though he had three adjectival properties that can be distinguished one from the other, but which are mere aspects of the same active identity. Rather we must say that each of these roles has a distinctive active identity (*persona*) in a God who in primary status (*substantia*) is nevertheless indivisibly one.

In the *Apology*, an early work, it is oneness that is stressed: the ray is no doubt "a portion of the whole, but the sun will be in the ray"(*portio ex summa, sed sol erit in radio*).[48] In the tract against Praxeas the Monarchian, the stress is altered, though the basic insight persists. Now "the three"— Father, Son, and Holy Spirit—"are one reality but not one individual (*tres unum sint, non unus*).[49] Now "an administrative disposition" (*oikomonia*) must be recognized, "the unity disposed into Trinity . . . three however not in essential being (*statu*)[50] but in stage (*gradu*), not in substance but in mold (*forma*), not in power but in form; and yet of one substance and

---

47. *Prax.* vii.

48. *Apol.* xxi. Cf. *Prax.* xviii: *quasi non et radius in sole deputetur.*

49. *Prax.* xxv.

50. In *Fug.* iv, *status* is used repeatedly to mean reality as opposed to perception.

of one essential being and of one power, because God is one, from whom those stages and molds and forms are accounted as Father and Son and Holy Spirit."[51] The familiar Stoic (and Eastern Christian) distinction between inner and outer word (*logos endiathetos* and *logos prophorikos*, word thought and word uttered) is used again here.[52] "Before all things God was alone." It is over-simplification to say merely: "The Word (*Sermo*, spoken word) was with God, in the beginning." Better to say: Reason, older than the Word, was within God, for God always is rational. Yet in a sense the Word (*logos*, which to the Greeks means thought, while to us Latins it means utterance) is present as "thought" before it is uttered.[53] As Wisdom, the Word is present as a kind of other (*secundus*). So one can say: "Before the establishment of the universe God was not alone, since he had Reason in himself and in Reason the Word, which he made a second from himself (*secundus a se*) by setting it in motion within himself.[54] And when God said: "Let there be light!" then the Word was born to his full identity as Son, "first-born, before all created things, and sole-born (*filius factus Primogenitus . . . unigenitus . . .*), since he alone has his being directly from the heart of the Father who thus made the Son equal to himself (*parem sibi faciens*), a second established by God to make two, Father and Son, sharing alike in the very *substantia* of the Godhead."[55] And never was the Son separated from the Father, or of another nature (*alius*) from the Father, because "I and the Father are one (*unum sumus*)."[56] And with them the Paraclete clearly constitutes "a third stage (*tertium gradum*)" in a triune Godhead.[57]

When Tertullian tries to distinguish between these several *personae*, he begins by using material analogies. He likens them to a root of a tree, the trunk, and the fruit; to a spring, a stream, and the mouth of the

51. *Prax.* ii.

52. Zeller, *Die Philosophie der Griechen*, IV, p.67, n.1, identifies the technical phrase in a writing of Heraklitos, a first century Stoic, and the idea as far back as Plato's Eleatic stranger's identification of "the soul's soundless conversation (*dialogos*) with itself," at *Sophist* 263E. The technical expression was used by the second-century Christian apologist and commentator Theophilus of Antioch (*ad Autolycus*, II.xxii).

53. *Prax.* ii.

54. *Prax.* v.

55. *Prax.* vii.

56. *Prax.* viii.

57. *Prax.* ix ; cf. iv: *quia spiritum non aliunde puto, quam a patre per filium.*

stream. The tree and the stream are each one, yet each has three indis-pensable constituents.[58] Obviously such analogies cannot be taken too seriously. The parts of any physical body are separable and divisible, whereas Tertullian insists on the indivisibility of God. He is searching for a suitable form of speech to give expression to a subtle insight, but some of the similies that he chose are much too crude for the purpose. He chose them partly because he thought of God as corporeal. The basic *substantia* in the Godhead is spirit. For the Stoics *pneuma* is a very much rarefied but nonetheless space-filling corporeal unity. And Tertullian says that of course God has a body, because that is the nature of spirit.[59] But this leads to such unhappy expressions as that the Father is the whole substance (*tota substantia*), the Son indeed a derivative portion of the whole (*derivatio totus et portio*).[60]

A more suitable analogy is a human self, made in the image and likeness of God. Consider the way in which you think within yourself and, in a sense, carry on a conversation with yourself; you confront yourself as other. And this confrontation is constitutive of your being the one that you are. In a certain sense, word is a manifestation of the mind or thought. But in another sense, word is what generates thought, or produces mind; so there is reciprocal productive activity.[61] So it is, we may suppose, in a far more exalted way with God. God could not think if he did not think articulately, and one can say that the shaping of his thought, which is word, is another than he. He confronts himself within himself. Being alone supreme, God is at the same time one who thinks, in thinking (inwardly) speaks, and in (overtly) speaking may be said to give rise to a Son. The Word is in some sense the offspring of the mind, but at the same time the mind is constituted by the Word, so that we must say the Son is *unius substantiae* (of one undivided substance with the Father.[62] There is no doubling of God here, though his unity is such that it is self-differentiating, such that the Father and the Son "differ in mode

58. *Prax.* viii.
59. *Apol.* xxi.
60. *Prax.* ix.
61. *Prax.* v.
62. Ibid.

from one another (*modula alius ab alio*)." The Son and the Father are really two, two beings (*res*), or, if you prefer, two *personae*.[63]

But the question is raised whether the Son thus understood is a real being at all or merely an attribute of the Father. And, by way of arguing that he is to be thought of as a real being, Tertullian insists that what issues from the Father who is, of course, Being in its fullness cannot be other than Being. If you ask whether we are talking about an extension of deity (*prolatio, probole*)—yes, we are. But we are not talking of the same sort of emanation that the Gnostics talk about, because they divide the one *Pleroma* into a multiplicity of greater and lesser Aeons.[64] And of course Marcion sets asunder the creator and the redeemer. We do not do that, but instead are talking about a basic *substantia* or reality which remains undivided; there is distribution and distinction, but there is no separation or division.[65] Tertullian is still wrestling with thoughts that he has not yet succeeded in getting clear.

For if we speak of the Reason of God as eternally present in and with him, we cannot say the same about the Word as uttered, and still less about the Word as Son. The word-as-uttered begins to be only when God speaks the first command at the time of the beginning of creation. When God says "let there be light," then the thought and inward word which had been the plan upon which the created order is to be established becomes in fact an uttered word. And one can call the Word the Son only from this moment. Before creation, the Word one is contemplating is hard to distinguish from God himself; after the creative utterance, one is contemplating a being that can be regarded as second to the Father, next in order of being. Tertullian is even willing to say "there was a time when ... the Son was not,"[66] which, when we come to fourth-century orthodoxy, will be condemned explicitly as a heretical view.

Are we then to say the Son also is *Deus*? Of course. But it is best to use that expression only when we are speaking of the Son by himself. I readily speak of a ray of the sun as "sunshine," unless I am speaking of it in relation to its source; then I will keep the term *sun* to refer to the

---

63. *Prax.* ix.

64. *Prax.* viii.

65. E.g., *Prax.* xiii: *unius et indivisae substantiae.*

66. *Herm.* iii: *Fuit autem tempus cum . . . filius non.* Cf. *Prax.* xii: *nondum filio apparente.*

source, and speak of the ray as derived from the source.[67] So, if I speak of the Son by himself, I will call him God (*Deus*); if I speak of the Son in relation to the Father, I will reserve the term *Deus* for the Father and speak of the Son as Lord (*Dominus*). At the same time, there is never any doubt that the Son shares the essential Being (*substantia*) of the Godhead, and so is himself a substantive Being, with the characteristics proper to deity. "And the name of the Father: God Almighty; Most High; Lord of hosts (*virtutum*), King of Israel, He who Is . . . We say these are suitable also to the Son."[68]

As for the Spirit, it seems to me that though Tertullian declares more definitely than his predecessors that there is a distinct place for the Paraclete in the Godhead, he doesn't go much further than earlier thinkers in defining just what distinctive role that Spirit has. On the one hand, following the Stoic tradition, he speaks of spirit generally as the *substantia* of the Godhead, that is to say, of the Father and also of the Son. He even goes so far at one point as to say, "Whatever be (*Quaecumque fuit*) the *substantia* of the Word, that I call *persona*,[69] and that, so to speak, spirit is the body of the Word (*et ut ita dixerim sermonis corpus est spiritus*)[70] —which are very puzzling statements indeed unless one recognizes that here Tertullian conceives of spirit in a generic rather than a specific sense. But when he talks about the Holy Spirit or the Paraclete as the third member of the Godhead alongside Father and Son, the spiritual substance which is common to them all now assumes a third embodiment or individuation.

All this reflection leads Tertullian to use a formula which on the face of it seems to be as clear as anyone could wish: *una substantia, tres personae*[71]—*qui tres unum sunt, non unus.*[72] But in light of our examination of the ideas that have entered into the making of that formula, we find that the clarity is superficial rather than essential. Nevertheless, this is a formula which the Western Church developed, and which the Eastern Churches began to take seriously beginning from the fourth

67. *Prax.* xiii ; but cf. *Apol.* xxi.

68. *Prax.* xxii.

69. *Prax.* vii.

70. *Prax.* viii.

71. *Prax.* xii.

72. *Prax.* xxv.

century onward. It underlies the doctrine of the Godhead which was adopted at the Council of Nicaea. The Council's debt to Tertullian begins with an ontological meaning for *prosopon* to go along with the meaning that it can have in a legal action or in a dramatic presentation. At one point, incidentally, he speaks of the Father as assigning *in personam filii* (to the *persona* of the Son) a role to be performed in the course of the creation and administration of the universe. Therefore, although starting with a functional meaning, *persona* takes on a meaning comparable to the Greek *hypostasis*, i.e., being individuated or made concrete. *Substantia*, which is the precise Latin counterpart to *hypostasis* (that which stands beneath the perceptible character or properties or relations of a thing) is used by Tertullian again in a sense which starts with the law courts and moves from there into metaphysics. That which makes God what he is is sovereignty, supremacy—that is his *substantia*. But the moment one speaks of supremacy in being, one is speaking no longer merely of sociology or jurisprudence but ontology. With respect to the Godhead then, Tertullian's formula has its roots in his familiarity with legal concepts, but these concepts, transferred from a forensic to a metaphysical context, become genuinely metaphysical concepts. Thus we discover in Tertullian terminology which is translated almost literally into the language of *homoousia*. He says that the Son is *unius substantiae* with the Father—of the same *substantia*, having the same fundamental or essential status.[73] I do not believe that he uses the precise Latin equivalent for *homoousion* (i.e. *consubstantivum* or *consubstantialem*), but he says enough to show that what he has in mind is the assertion that in God we have but one essential being, and that is the heart and core of the Nicene decision.

## Person of Jesus Christ and the Christian Life

Another crucial point at which Tertullian thought the heretics had gone astray was in their views of the person of Jesus Christ. Tertullian devotes the last few sections of the work *Against Praxeas* to this question and also the entire treatise, *On the Flesh of Christ*. Without going into too much detail, we may note that his formula for describing the work of Jesus Christ is a kind of inversion of his formula for describing the Godhead. In Christ we have one *persona* and two natures (*una persona, duae naturae*), while in God there is one nature (*substantia*) but three *personae*. Christ

---

73. *Prax.* xii.

has fully divine and human nature. One essential point that he insisted on here is that the divine nature cannot undergo change. Although for all created beings, becoming something other involves ceasing to be what one was before, in the case of God that is not true. God is able to become what he was not without ceasing to be what he was. Consequently, we say that deity in Jesus Christ becomes incarnate without ceasing to be the deity that it always has been. At the incarnation, therefore, divine nature is not to be thought of as "transformed into flesh." Neither are the two natures fused into a third. Tertullian refers to the way in which gold and silver can be melted together to form electrum, a new kind of metal. We must not think of humanity and divinity as thus fused in Jesus Christ so that the resulting person is neither divine nor human but some third sort of being—*tertium quid*. The two natures, Spirit and flesh, retain their own properties.[74] On the other hand, we must not separate them into a human Jesus and a divine Christ. The Monarchians had done this, declaring that "Christ" was the Father himself, the divine being dwelling in the man Jesus and separable from him. Tertullian points out quite rightly that "Christos" is a descriptive adjective predicated of Jesus—Jesus the Anointed One—and is not the proper or substantive name of a divine being. The truth is that the Word "assumed flesh," without any essential change in his own divine nature, and the union of the two natures or two substances (he uses both of these terms) constitutes one, concrete, active individual, one *persona*.

In the Godhead then we have three *personae* and one *substantia*. In Jesus Christ we have two *substantiae* and one *persona*—a beautifully neat schema for formulating a doctrine which, on the one hand, seeks to conserve the unity of God without obliterating distinctions, and which, on the other hand, seeks to conserve in a correlative way the unity of Jesus Christ without obliterating distinctions. In Jesus Christ the deity works the miracles, and enables him to rise from the dead, whereas it is the humanity that hungers, suffers, and dies. Tertullian is trying to be very sharp and clear in this sort of formulation, but hasn't yet really seen where the cutting edge of the problem is to be found. His Stoic presuppositions of the corporeality of both God and the human soul seem to make it a little easier for him to accept these formulae of his own without uneasiness. But it is when the post-Origenistic thinkers have declared that God is

74. *Prax.* xxvii.

utterly incorporeal and have declared, at Nicaea, that the Son is fully and truly God that the question how God the Son could be fully one with the man Jesus becomes particularly disturbing.

Even so, Tertullian's thought foreshadows a position later to be declared authoritative. The Council of Chalcedon in 451 adopted a western formula provided by Pope Leo the Great which appears to have been based upon the earlier formula of Tertullian. This Carthaginian lawyer was building much better than he or his contemporaries could know. Although as an adherent of Montanism he could scarcely be cited in the Councils as an authority, he helped to shape the accepted Western thought about the Trinity and the person of Jesus Christ.

We noted earlier that Tertullian was a determined defender of the idea of the freedom of the individual. Each person is free to obey or to disobey the law of God, and sin is to be regarded not as something natural and inherent, but rather as willful misdeed. On the other hand, Tertullian's Stoic inclinations led him to believe that the individual is acting always in accordance with a pattern of law which is ingrained, and under powerful influences that are at work both in the universe and in his own make-up. Consequently, the dilemma of the Stoics between affirming both human freedom and the complete control of the events of the physical world by the Logos is also present in Tertullian. At the creation of each new soul, especially among the heathen, the Devil is at hand to contaminate it with evil inclination that becomes "another nature." Man thus stands condemned as one disobedient to the law, and Jesus Christ takes upon himself the burden of fulfilling the law on man's behalf. When the sinner is regenerated and becomes a believer, sharing in the salvation which the Church offers, he undergoes baptism. Normally, this is indispensable to salvation. Tertullian held that it should be postponed until maturity, to minimize the risk of losing the benefits of baptismal cleansing through irresponsible behavior. The baptismal water is energized by the Holy Spirit at the time of the pronouncing of the words of institution, and comes to be the physical medium for the cleansing, reinvigoration and new inspiration of the delivered person. The Holy Spirit is present, brooding over the water, so that it becomes not only a symbol but a vehicle through which the power of God comes into the reordered life of the one who has been baptized. If such a one falls into grave sin after baptism, then as a plank is thrown to a shipwrecked mariner, one chance for repentance is offered him, and the penance which the bishop may prescribe. In this way a soul may be reclaimed which otherwise would be lost. Thus, "satisfaction" is made to God, and the penitent sinner is relieved of the condemnation which otherwise would be his. (This term *satisfactio* becomes of great importance in the medieval idea of penance, and as far as I know, Tertullian is the first to use the term and the idea.) The only other recourse, open also to unbaptized persons, is the "second baptism" of blood—martyr's death.

As far as I can see, Tertullian's thought from beginning to end is shaped by his training as a lawyer. We recall that many of the terms he uses in his doctrine of God he finds first in the literature of jurisprudence even though he then endows them with a metaphysical or ontological significance for purposes of theological thinking. [Little of this transformation is evident, however,] in his forensic assessment of man's duty and of Christ's redemptive work, with its prospect of reward and punishment. Legal categories provide the framework for understanding how those who associate themselves with Jesus Christ will achieve the life of immortality—a life, to be sure, which is in principle written into the soul of man by God in virtue of the fact that it is God's own breath that constitutes the source of the souls of all human beings. [It is on the doctrine of God that Tertullian has been a teacher of the church as a whole; but in reference to the Christian life, this North African's way of thinking has remained foreign to the East, and in the West, though influential, has also been resisted.]

# CHAPTER 9

# Alexandrine Theology: Clement and Origen[1]

M OVING OVER A THOUSAND miles eastward along the North African coast to Alexandria, we find in Clement, Tertullian's contemporary, and in his successor, Origen, a widely different set of presuppositions and a very different mode of thought. First a word or two about the situation of the Christian community in Alexandria, which appears to have been quite unusual at the beginning of the third century, for it had grown up alongside a very remarkable center of Hellenistic learning. Alexandria was the great intellectual capital of the Mediterranean world at the beginning of the Christian era. Although the Platonic Academy continued at Athens some nine hundred years after its founder's death, it was Alexandria rather than Athens which had become the great cultural meeting place for scholars, students, and representatives of various religious movements. The *Museon* (or university dedicated to the Muses) had endowed professorships and scholarships that brought promising students from various parts of the Greco-Roman world. At the time it was destroyed by Muslim invaders near the beginning of the seventh century, it had a library of about seven-hundred thousand volumes. There are said to have been four hundred theaters in and about the great city, in which the plays of the Greek dramatists were produced for people who regarded this as a natural part of the life of the civilized world.

Three major ethnic groups in the population of Alexandria lived side by side. Alexander's Macedonian version of Hellenism had superimposed Greek modes of thought and of action upon the original Egyptian

---

1. This chapter combines Professor Calhoun's treatments of Clement and Origen. It is taken mostly from the 1948 LHCD, but with some omissions and with insertions from later lectures [ed.].

population. More recently the Romans, after they had become masters of that part of the Mediterranean world, sent the official ruling class into the city, while still keeping a place for those who had been there before. Then there was the large Alexandrine Jewish community, which had its own dynastic rulers, its own literature, and its own mode of worship; the Alexandrine Judaism of which Philo is our best representative continued to have a distinctive and on the whole recognized and accepted place.

The foundation of the church in Alexandria traditionally was ascribed to Mark as Peter's personal amanuensis and representative; and the church, thus claiming what was in effect apostolic foundation, emerged for a time as the most important of all of the churches in the eastern part of the empire. As Alexandria was the great cultural center, the church of Antioch itself came to be overshadowed, and only when Constantinople became the eastern political capital did Alexandria face a really major ecclesiastical rival.

Partly by reason of the cultural environment which the Alexandrian church confronted, a distinctively Christian school seems to have developed. We find it referred to as the Catechetical School of Alexandria, and its character is very uncertain. Usually the term *catechesis* applied simply to the common course of instruction given to the catechumens or candidates for church membership in preparation for baptism. It usually was given at the outset by one of the minor clergy and in the concluding stages by the bishop, but without any formally organized curriculum of study. The Catechetical School in Alexandria seems to have offered more than the relatively informal teaching for church membership which took place elsewhere. It appears to have provided side by side with the pagan schools a Christian education for members of the Christian community and also for interested non-Christians that would move through the stages of introductory and intermediary study to instruction on a higher level.

## Clement

During the later years of the second century its head was a certain Pantaenus, whom we know of chiefly through reports from Clement. After he had tried various other teachers, Clement came to Alexandria and found Pantaenus, "that true Sicilian bee" who had gathered honey from fields of human knowledge, and settled down to become himself a member of the catechetical organization.

Whether Clement was born a Greek (there is some indication that he was born in Athens) or whether he was a native of one of the outlying districts of Hellenistic culture is not clear; but his reading in Greek literature appears to have been very wide, very diverse, and very eclectic. When Pantaenus died about 183, Clement succeeded him as head of the catechetical school and continued in that position until 203. In that year a persecution which hit Alexandria especially hard led to the proscription of the foremost church leaders, and Clement fled the city. We hear of him again about 216 in Syria, and then no more. But for twenty years he was the head of an Alexandrine Christian school which was concerned not only with the teachings about the scriptures and Christian morality, but with aspects of higher learning.

Three major works of Clement remain to us, and their titles and themes are highly suggestive.[2] The first is called *Protreptikos*, a term which cannot satisfactorily be translated into a single English word. It means, as Clement uses it, one who urges upon non-Christians the need to leave their pagan ways of life and come into the Church; one who meets them with urgent exhortation to abandon error and follow truth. The second of these works he called *Paidagogos*, again a word for which the close English equivalent is not very illuminating. If we say *pedagogue*, we must remember that in Hellenistic society the pedagogue was the elderly slave who led the child to school and who saw that he got safely home again. He was not the teacher but the one who introduced the student into the atmosphere of learning. Apparently the third of these works would have been called *Didaskalos*, the teacher. But for reasons which remain obscure, Clement never published a work by that title. Instead he published a work titled *Stromateis* or miscellanies—literally, a carpet bag, holding all sorts and varieties of material. E. de Faye[3] has suggested ingeniously that Clement chose both the form and the title because he expected what he had to say to arouse opposition, and he wanted to disarm the opposition in advance by suggesting that this was not to be taken as a serious work, but rather as random reflections by one who intended to be whimsical about it all rather than combative. We may note that these three works correspond to three stages in the normal life of a Christian. First he is converted from paganism. Then he is taught the elements of Christian living, and

2. Critical edition, Otto Stählin, CGS, 4 vols English translation in *ANF* 2.

3. E. de Faye, *Clément d'Alexandrie: étude sur les rapports du Christianisme et de la philosophie grecque au IIè siècle*, 2nd ed. (Paris: Leroux, 1906).

specifically of Christian manners and morality. Finally he is introduced into what Clement conceives as the deeper aspects of Christian truth: the theological and the philosophical insights which are not for the beginner. The teacher throughout is one and the same, the Logos of God. In a sense he is the hero of all three of these works, and the conception of the Logos is a conception which dominates and shapes Clement's conception of Christian truth and Christian life.

## Theological Method

Two major areas of Clement's thought demand our attention. The first is his conception of theological method and the second is the content of his Christian theology. The question of method in Christian theology was whether pagan philosophy may be regarded as in any way legitimate as a subject of study and as a procedure for Christian thinkers. The attitude which Clement confronted included, first, violent rejection of philosophy at the hands of a group in Alexandria to whom he referred rather playfully as the "Orthodoxasts," and more generally, of such men as Justin Martyr's disciple Tatian and Tertullian who declare that Athens has no place in the life of Jerusalem. These men hold that the content of philosophy is the work of devils; for them, the teaching of philosophy was the result of the fall of the angels who offered it as a gift to their human brides, and had succeeded thereby in making trouble ever since.

Over against such a position, Clement urges that there is need to rule out pseudo-philosophy of the sort which is indeed taught in too many of the pagan schools. He likened the schools of rhetoric to nests full of birds which make a great deal of chattering noise, but offer little in the way of enlightenment; to rivers of words with only now and then a drop of sense; to old shoes of which everything but the tongues are worn out. Similarly, the dialectic disputation of the Sophists must be rejected. The same is true of the materialistic naturalism of the Epicureans and similar Greek schools. The opponents of philosophy are right to disparage all philosophies of this sort. But on the other hand, it is necessary to recognize that some of the Greek thinkers found in philosophy what the Hebrews found in the Law: an introduction to Christian truth. To those of the Greeks who have approached it with a sincere recognition of God's nature and of God's will, it has been a *paidagogos*. This comment would apply most especially to the Platonic and Stoic schools, for here Clement thinks the preparation for the Gospel was most clearly recognizable.

But he is willing to go even further than that and say that in certain philosophical insights there is not only a preparation for truth but also a vision of truth. No doubt, says he, a great many philosophical thinkers have plagiarized from Moses. It is well known that the Mosaic books are older than Plato, so that if we find Plato saying something that we can also recognize in the Old Testament, we say that Plato has borrowed it. True enough, one may say *stolen* rather than *borrowed*, but when that which is stolen is gold, one should recognize it as gold even when he finds it in the wallets of thieves. So one must be ready to recognize truth even when one finds it in unexpected places. The river of truth, says Clement, is one and streams flow into it on this side and on that. When one finds a pagan philosopher dealing properly with the good, the beautiful, the right, there one may say that one sees the work of the one Logos. This truth has been torn into fragments and presented piecemeal by the pagan thinkers. What the Christian must do is bring these insights together once again into a coherent and unified statement about God.

Philosophy, however, cannot be a substitute for the Gospel. The sound philosophical reason for this is that first principles cannot be arrived at by a process of reasoning. Logical inference requires presuppositions which are not themselves derivable but which must be simply apprehended and accepted. And what is true in the region of pure formal dialectics is true likewise in any field of human inquiry. Further, the processes of inference are the same whether one's premises are true or false. Christianity's advantage over the pagan philosophies lies in the truth of its first principles, and these principles are to be accepted on a basis which may be described either as vision or as faith. Clement means by faith a sort of confidence, a firm judgment with regard to what is so. This is obviously neither the Pauline nor Johannine understanding of faith, but rather a conception of faith that is primarily cognitive and intellective. Even so, involved in such a faith is the orientation of the will. To be able to recognize what is fundamentally so demands that one's outlook shall be in a condition of health; and that means, to Clement's mind, a condition of moral health. Only the one who is willing to follow the good when he sees it is ever likely to see the good and to have the chance to follow it.

The first principles from which the Christian sets out in this venture must be consistent with the rule of faith. We have noted more than once that recourse to this was common in the early church as protection against the aberrations of heresy. One will use philosophy, not to establish the rule of faith, but as a sauce for the solid meat of Christian teaching and as a bulwark against attack on Christian truth.

On that basis it seems to Clement that one's delight in philosophy can be given pretty free play. Those who say that philosophy was invented by the devils cannot have read very carefully the story of the Temptation in which the Devil plays a very unphilosophic role. Anyone, says Clement, who can be deceived by a simply amphiboly, as the Devil was in that story, obviously is not very much of a philosopher. He does not specify the amphiboly, but perhaps it comes in Jesus' use of *live* to refer to a full and significant life. Man shall not live in that sense by bread alone. Since the Devil did not notice how he was being tricked, he pretty obviously was not a very skillful dialectician. One may use philosophy, then, without fear of winding up on the side of the darker power, provided one uses it with the clear recognition that it is subsidiary to, and not a substitute for, fundamental Christian truth.

### Doctrine of the Godhead

But what is fundamental Christian truth? Here we are constrained to extract from the *Miscellanies* ideas which another thinker than Clement might have put together systematically, yet the pattern of theological thought which emerges is not difficult to recognize. In general terms, Clement represents well the kind of Alexandrine Platonism which, having taken the concept of the Good developed in both the *Republic* and in the *Philebus* proceeds to abstract the transcendence of the Good so much that it became necessary to think of intermediary beings intervening between the Good and the things of this world. Plato, in contrast, regarded the things of this world as participating directly, though in varying degree, in *to agathon*: there was no need for any intermediary. But the people of a Platonic cast of mind who succeeded him moved more and more in the direction which eventually is systematized by Plotinus and the Neoplatonists, for whom the Good or the One is, as Plato had said, beyond being and beyond thought but so extremely that it is necessary to have a graduated series of stages between that far-off

One and the place where mortals live. This Absolute is so completely removed from all the details of the world of space and time and sensory perception, from the content of human feelings and emotion, and even from the basic forms of human thought that one can say of God that he can best be spoken of only in negatives. None of the ten Aristotelian categories is applicable to him—neither substance nor place nor time, nor quality nor quantity nor relation, nor any of the others. But these are the terms in which we have to think; and if none of these terms is applicable to God, then clearly he is by his very nature incomprehensible to us. One can say of him most truly that he is pure unity (*Monas*). Yet one must not take that to mean that God is numerically one, for that would mean that he is one among a group that can be numbered. One uses this word with respect to God, not because it is correct but because any other word would be more certainly misleading.

God is knowable only by reason of his Logos. The background common to Philo and Clement is emerging here. The Logos of God is the Mind of God, in which the Being of God is projected or objectified. God's Being remains inaccessible to human beings. But in the Mind of God that Being is presented as if it were unity in plurality. In itself it is sheer unity, but the projection of it in the Logos presents it as in a mirror. The Logos is the perfect mirror of God's Being. The Son is the unalterable image of the Father in which the Father's true being is set forth. There is a point-for-point relationship between the Logos and the hidden being of God, so that those who know the Logos are, to use again a Platonic phrase, in the antechamber of the Good. The Logos is coeternal with the Father, so that there is no time when the Logos was not. It is this Logos, the very Mind of God, that has inspired the philosophers, the prophets, the poets, and that provides the perfect archetype for the life and thought of all. But the Logos is not to be regarded as identical with the high God, but rather as Truth made articulate; and Truth made articulate is the norm after which all human thought must be modeled, and according to which all right human conduct must be guided.

In Clement's thought, the Holy Spirit appears only in a rather ambiguous way. It is an energy which, like the Logos, is active in the lives of the prophets and of the thinkers. He says that as magnetic attraction holds together iron rings, so the Spirit holds together the whole universe of rational beings. The Father, the Son, and the minds of believers are all pervaded by this unifying force. The relation of the Holy Spirit to the

Father and to the Son is nowhere clearly defined in Clement's writings. He is one of those early Christian thinkers for whom God is essentially dipolar, and the reference to the Holy Spirit is an acceptance of a traditional affirmation without any clear-cut intellectual rationale.

### Human Nature as Fallen and Redeemed

Consider next the nature of man, sin, and salvation. The essential thing that differentiates human beings from the other animals is the capacity to know God. This is what makes them rational. At the same time that we say they are rational, we must say they are free. They are capable of responding to God in the manner of those who can recognize the non-coercive call of truth and justice. They are also free to reject the promptings of these divine realities. At this point Clement is genuinely a child of Greek thought, uncompromised by any kind of fatalism. When human beings are understood in these terms, they are understood in a way that is radically opposed, for example, to the Gnostic ways of thinking. The Valentinians regarded human beings as grouped in three categories: there are those who are merely hylic or fleshly, those who are psychical or animal, those who are spiritual in the metaphysical sense. Only the third are sure of being saved, though some of the second group will be saved by companionship with their good angels. Over against determinism of that sort, Clement is arguing his libertarian conception of rational, responsible freedom. A human being is not to be thought of as a Trojan horse full of irrational impulses which are his enemies. He is primarily a mind capable of recognizing truth and affirming or denying it. In so far as man denies truth and rejects the will of God, he falls into sin, which is described in the familiar Greek term as *hamartia,* a defect, or missing of the target at which one is shooting, not as disease or corruption. The idea of sin as pervading and distorting man's nature is wholly lacking in Clement. Sin lies on the surface. It is wrong choice. One is always free to make a choice which is better. Those who fall into sin therefore require primarily to be instructed and put right, and be prompted and inspired to follow that which is good rather than to turn away from it. So the redemptive work that needs to be performed is appropriately enough the work of the Logos in the role of Teacher, as the embodiment of truth and the illuminator of rational being.

This Logos becomes incarnate; but in Clement's thought, he becomes incarnate in a very ambiguous way. He takes human form but he is not in the full sense a human individual. He eats and drinks and rests, but simply to avoid comment by the folk around him. He chooses to behave as if he were a fully human being, but in reality he is the divine Logos and consequently cannot be thought of as suffering any real deficiency. As thus incarnate, he achieves a work of redemption which centers around two functions: revelation and enlightenment, and paying a ransom on man's behalf. In Clement's mind the former is what is really essential. The latter is introduced almost entirely in the *Paedagogos* as a factor in the more elementary level of Christian teaching. What man really needs for salvation is to have the truth presented to him in so vivid and moving a form that he will be led to accept it and to live by it.

The Christian life as Clement understands it is lived at two levels. One is the level of simple belief (*pistis*). This is the way—and a good way—of those members of the Church who accept and follow the lead of the Master without seeing deeply into the reasons why this life is better than any other. They employ the sacraments and accept the disciplines of the church. They accept the teachings of the Bible. They are in all respects good, sober, trustworthy Christians. But they have no systematic understanding of the life they are attempting to live. On the other hand, there are Christians who are "true Gnostics." Their virtuousness is not a bit less clear and steady than that of the believers, but they have clear intellectual insight in addition to their moral excellence. Theirs is the life of knowledge and love, for that is the goal of faith. This represents a genuinely higher level of Christian living. One recalls the distinction made in some of the heretical sects between the simple followers and the initiates who are perfect, or are called by some other equally eulogistic name. Clement believes that the Christian life is thus graduated, and that the duty of the teacher is to produce as many as possible who are candidates for the upper level. For help in expounding the latter conception, he appeals to the Platonic picture of the philosopher and to the Stoic conception of the sage—the one who is genuinely wise and whose life displays both the perfection of virtue and the insight which gives virtue its rationale and meaning. But the true Gnostic is to be found nowhere save in the church of Christ.

It is characteristic of Clement's whole outlook that his conception of the future life of the Christian is stated primarily in spiritual terms.

There is to be a resurrection of the body, but it will be a purely spiritual or ethereal body. References to reward and punishment must be interpreted in terms of spiritual states. There is no such thing as an earthly paradise. There is no such thing as bodily torment, but rather all that goes on in the future will concern the mind and soul of the individual.

In short, his whole outlook is given a distinctive bent by his reading of Greek philosophy and especially his enthusiasm for Platonism. There is some question whether he got his knowledge of Greek philosophy from anthologies, or whether he studied these philosophers independently. The evidence seems to favor a middle view. He quotes at times from known anthologies. On the other hand, his references to the Platonic dialogues are sufficiently specific and extended to seem to indicate that he had read them at some length. Surely the qualities of his mind, with its breadth and humane outlook, its delight in discovering truth, its contempt for those who suspect reason without recognizing that reason is itself a gift of the divine Logos—all these are marks of a man of genuinely Platonic temper. He was the sort of thinker who is more interesting and impressive for the basic temper of his mind than for his intellectual grasp and architectonic competence: he wanted to make room for truth from any quarter.

## ORIGEN

The man who succeeds Clement as head of the Catechetical School in Alexandria is of very different temper, and of perfectly extraordinary influence on the development of Christian thought. Indeed, he is the individual thinker who did more than any other to shape the development of Christian doctrine for the next one-hundred and fifty years. This was Origen, the son of Christian parents in Alexandria. He was born about 185, near the time when Clement became head of the Christian School. His father, Leonides, a member of the Alexandrine Christian church, trained him in Greek literature and appears to have regarded him from an early age as a child of quite exceptional promise. In the same persecution under Septimius Severus that led to the removal of Clement from Alexandria in 203, Origen's father, with other prominent Christians, was arrested and put to death. Origen was a boy of seventeen at the time, and he endeavored to join his father and the other martyrs of the Church, but his mother succeeded in keeping him home by a simple stratagem. She is said to have hidden all his clothes. The boy survived the persecution, but since his father's property was confiscated, his mother and his younger brothers and sisters were left without any adequate support, and he himself undertook to support the family by becoming a teacher in the secular schools of Alexandria. He offered himself as a grammarian and apparently did a very acceptable job, winning pupils and gaining a reputation, so much so that he is described by the somewhat censorious Neoplatonist Porphyry as having illegitimately trespassed upon territory that rightly belonged to other people. Demetrius, the energetic bishop of Alexandria, heard of the boy's exceptional talent, and in spite of the fact that he was not a cleric, appointed him to head the Catechetical School in succession to Clement. Origen, then a lad of eighteen, set to work to master a new range of subjects. He began to study Hebrew in order that he might understand the Scriptures more effectively. He attended the lectures of Ammonius Sakkas, who had been a Christian, but who was diverted from Christianity and became the teacher of Plotinus as well as other less eminent pagan thinkers. Origen quite possibly was a fellow student of Plotinus, who later moved to Rome and became the founder and systematizer of what we know as Neoplatonism. (The names are always troublesome because we know of more than one Origen; whether it was our Origen or another who was in this particular student group, it is not possible to be quite sure, but it looks very much as though Origen himself had that kind of training.) In the course of his career as head of the Catechetical School, Origen increased tremendously the reputation which he had begun to acquire not only as a vigorous mind and an accurate scholar but also as a teacher of genius.

Two people as vigorous as Origen and Demetrius are very likely to come into collision at some point, and the first serious collision between them involved a trip that Origen made in 216 to Palestine to help with certain doctrinal problems. While he was there, Alexander, the bishop of Jerusalem, and Theoctistus, the bishop of Caesarea, invited him to preach in a Christian assembly in which they themselves were present, and which included other bishops. Now Origen was still a layman. As a matter of fact, there existed in his case a disability which later came to be adjudged a canonical hindrance to ordination to the priesthood. In the course of a career of quite extraordinary austerity and enthusiasm, he had taken literally the word about those who voluntarily make themselves eunuchs for the sake of the Kingdom of God; and a council later decreed that one who had thus mutilated himself in a manner condemned by the Mosaic law and characteristic especially of the priests of various pagan cults, was not to be eligible for the priesthood of the Christian church. When Demetrius heard that Origen had actually preached at the invitation of the Palestinian bishops, he was furious; he said nothing of this sort had ever been heard of before—a layman teaching bishops how to understand the Bible! He demanded that Origen should return to Alexandria at once and reprimanded him severely. Later, in 228, Origen was invited to visit the churches in Greece to help them out of some sort of difficulty. On the way, he once again visited Alexander and Theoctistus, who this time did the very injudicious thing of having him ordained, perhaps to avoid the difficulty into which they had once got him by asking him to preach to his ecclesiastical superiors without ordination. Now this was, if anything, still worse than what they had done before, because Origen was still under the jurisdiction of the bishop of Alexandria. And Demetrius maintained that the Palestinian bishops consequently had no authority to raise this man to clerical rank. When Demetrius heard what they had done this time, he called a synod to sit on the question whether Origen was any longer a fit person to be a member of the Alexandrian Christian community. In 230 Demetrius stripped Origen of his new dignity as a presbyter, and the next year a synod consisting only of bishops under the leadership of Demetrius, excommunicated him from the Alexandrian Church. He was compelled therefore to leave the place where his early reputation had been made, and he removed to Caesarea in Palestine. There he taught for the remainder of his life, following up the lines which he had developed earlier in his Alexandrian career and establishing a school centering around himself which both Christian and pagan students attended. We know of a certain Cappadocian named Gregory, later known as Gregory the Wonder-Worker (*Thaumaturgos*), who became bishop of Neocaesarea in Pontus. He and his brother had come to Caesarea in earlier days to study law but stayed to study theology because Origen had made such an impression on them. When the persecution under Decius broke out in 250, Origen was one of the men who was bound to attract the attention of the authorities, and he was arrested and put into prison and subjected to torture over a period of years. He survived the experience and was ultimately released from prison, but his health had been completely broken and he died in 254. He had become a confessor, and in pretty clear fashion, a martyr.

The work that Origen did during his life is perfectly stupendous. Epiphanius, who was an expert on the literature of the first three centuries, said that Origen was the author of six-thousand separate works. Of course that means not only major works, but the short one-page papers which he must have turned out from time to time. But six thousand titles, as Epiphanius said, was more than any individual could read. During his Alexandrian career, Origen attracted the attention of a wealthy man named Ambrose who supplied him with seven expert secretaries, together with assisting copyists. They were able to multiply many times the amount of physical labor that Origen could have done with his own hands, and the works that issued from his mind and were published and put into circulation totaled a really staggering quantity.[4]

## Biblical Criticism and Exegesis

Origen was primarily a Biblical scholar. I think it necessary to stress that fact because his reputation in the church has been that of a systematic theologian and Christian philosopher with heretical leanings. Actually he conceived himself to be first and last a student of the Scriptures. It was for that reason that he had learned Hebrew, so that he could read the Old Testament more intelligently and more accurately than if he had depended wholly upon the Greek translations. His greatest single work was a critical text of the Old Testament, which we know as the Hexapla; that is to say, a six-column text (only fragments are extant). The first column contains the Masoretic Hebrew text, the one regarded by the rabbis as authoritative; the second column contains the Hebrew text transliterated into the Greek alphabet, for the benefit of those who knew no Hebrew but who might be able to get some idea of the Hebrew text if it appeared in their own alphabet; and four Greek versions: the Septuagint, a revised version of the Septuagint to bring it more into line with the Hebrew, and two translations directly from the Hebrew. Origen introduced into this huge corpus certain diacritical signs that scholars still use: the obelus ($\div$) to mark additions (where something has crept into the text from a marginal note or something of the sort) and the asterisk to signal lacunae, among other things. It was a serious and expert effort on his part to make sure that when he set about the task of Biblical theology, it was the Bible that he had in front of him. By comparing these several Greek versions

4. *Origenes Werke*, ed. Paul Koetschau, et al., 13 vols, (Leipzig: Hinrichs, 1899–1955).

one with another and with the Hebrew original, he thought it possible to detect addition or deviation; and to recover, as nearly as it could then be done, the true text of an Old Testament passage. He worked on this job for a period of some twenty-eight years, and when it was eventually set down by his copyists, it filled some fifty volumes.

Having labored to establish a true text of the Scripture, Origen makes that text, in theory, the basis of all his theological thought. The Scripture, he says, is inspired, it is genuinely the word of God. The best evidence is that the Law of Moses on the one hand and the teaching of Jesus on the other hand have become acceptable to people of many nations. There is no other lawgiver than Moses whose laws have been accepted and followed by members of any community other than that in which the legislation originated. There have been no philosophers other than Jesus whose teachings, similarly, have found acceptance outside their own cultures. The indication is that here we have a genuinely universal and not merely a local Word.

Yet the Scripture demands interpretation because it has obscure places in it. Indeed, it has material which, to one trained in the Greek schools, appears to be not only absurd but offensive. Origen also notes that certain heretics, because they have only a literal understanding, have declared that the Old Testament refers to a *demiourgos* and not to the God and Father of Jesus Christ. (He obviously has the Marcionites in view.) They are put off by references to human imperfections in the God of the Old Testament or by references to morally repellent commands (e.g. to massacre a population of captives). To meet such objections, Origen undertook to interpret the Old Testament according to the Platonic principle, "Nothing is to be believed which is unworthy of God."

Accepting that principle and following a precedent which had already been set by Stoic interpreters of Homeric and Hesiodic tales of gods, by men like Philo and Josephus, by apologists for the Hebrew Old Testament, and by earlier Christian thinkers—St. Paul himself and the author of the letter attributed to Barnabas—it seemed proper to regard the Old Testament as displaying a number of levels of meaning. The first, simplest, most obvious level is the physical or somatic—the literal meaning of the text. Most of the Old Testament and the New Testament, by and large, Origen thinks will give perfectly good sense intepreted at this level. The historical portions give a straightforward account and may be accepted as the record of events that took place in time and space. But secondly there is a moral level. The record of events will carry with it ethical implications, and these the careful interpreter will try to make clear. Third, there is a spiritual or allegorical level, and sometimes one will find a text which is interpretable only in this third way. There are texts which, taken literally, would be either absurd or repulsive, but if one interprets them with an eye to discovering the figurative sense which is hidden under the shell of an apparently ridiculous or offensive story or a tedious genealogy or what have you, one can discover the truths that are worthy of God. Who, for example, are the enemies to be annihilated? Not people, but sins. One must look for the inner mystery, the mystery which was kept secret through many ages and finally made known through the prophets and through Jesus Christ.

The commentator who is trying to get at not only the true texts but also the true meaning must be concerned with all three levels of interpretation. Upon this basis Origen writes, in the first place, many *scholia*, brief interpretative notes on various verses or phrases in Scripture. On some books he writes full-length commentaries, volumes of interpretative analysis. Then he wrote and preached something like two hundred exegetical sermons in which he felt free to suggest, not merely the way in which a Scripture text may be defended against the attacks which have been made upon it, but also the way in which fresh and unsuspected truths can be derived from it by suitable interpretation. Taking this entire body of commentary into account along with the body of textual analysis, one can realize that as a biblical scholar, Origen was an extraordinarily busy man. The result, as it appears to him, is an understanding of the Word of God upon which one can build with confidence.

## Opposition to Celsus

In addition to his work as a biblical interpreter, Origen undertook an elaborate defense of Christianity against the attacks of the acute pagan scholar and critic Celsus, a second-century critic who was commonly called an Epicurean, but is now identified as more probably a Platonist. His references to the eternal matter which the Creator shapes sounds more like the *Timaeus* than like any of the Epicurean writings. In any event, Celsus, living perhaps during the reign of Marcus Aurelius, about 160 to 170, had written a very detailed and determined attack on Christianity in a work called *A True Discourse*. His effort was to show up the absurdities, the inconsistencies, and the moral defects in Christianity; and he did a very sturdy job indeed. He attacked not only the behavior and the intellectual non-respectability of Christians in his own day but also the life, the person, the teachings, the death and the resurrection of Jesus Christ. Origen undertook to defend Christianity against this careful and able opponent in a way that should be so thorough as to be conclusive. As a matter of fact, we recover the text of Celsus' writings because Origen quotes passage after passage as a basis for the detailed refutation which he offers. *Contra Celsum* is a model of painstaking, scrupulously fair, if repetitious and somewhat tedious apologetic.

In addition to biblical and apologetic writings, he undertakes what nobody before him had attempted. Quite early in his life he publishes a work which he called *On First Principles*[5]—a title that might have come straight out of one of the Greek philosophical schools. This is intended to be a Christian philosophy of the universe. He looked upon it later as a youthful work with somewhat regrettable looseness and speculative ventures which were none too happy, but the position which is developed in it is discoverable also in his later work against Celsus.[6] The text of this early work usually bears the Latinized title *De principiis* because we have it at full length only in a Latin translation by Rufinus, the man who commented on the Apostles' Creed about 400.[7] He was a warm admirer and defender of Origen, and he prepared the translation on the very benevolent and innocent principle that nothing was to be included in it which was unworthy of Origen. Consequently, when he came upon passages which had been the cause of misunderstanding, he said that he recognized that Origen's work had been manhandled by unfriendly critics, and so he had smoothed out these places until they would not give offense or lead to misapprehension on the part of Christian believers. Occasionally he found that Origen had dealt obscurely with something or other, and he had simply expanded the passage, always drawing, he says, on other of Origen's work and never adding anything of his own, but giving to Origen in the text of the *De principiis* material which Origen

---

5. Greek: *Peri Archon.*

6. Standard English translation by Henry Chadwick, trans. and ed. *Origen Contra Celsus* (Cambridge: Cambridge University Press, 1953).

7. Standard English translation by G. W. Butterworth, trans. and ed. *Origen on First Principles: Being Koetschau's Text of the 'De Principiis' Translated into English with an Introduction and Notes* (London: SPCK, 1936).

had set down elsewhere. Of course, material taken from one context and put down into another would undergo some strange transformations of meaning. Therefore Rufinus' friendly effort to give us the text of Origen's work has had an unhappy result. We have the Greek text of certain considerable portions with which Rufinus' translation can be compared, and the results are not at all reassuring. What one has to do in trying to interpret the *Peri Archon* is to compare it with the work *Contra Celsum* and with certain of the commentaries, of which the commentaries on the Gospel of Matthew and the Gospel of John are extant at full length.[8] In that way one can see the fashion in which Rufinus has sandpapered off some of the rough edges and filled in some of the cracks and crevices in Origen's thought so as to make his intellectual portrait more acceptable. In addition to his work *On First Principles* he, like Clement, published a work called *Miscellanies*. This work remains only in fragments. So we are dependent on *De principiis* and *Contra Celsum* in the main, with the exegetical homilies and the commentaries which are extant, for our understanding of Origen's conception of God and the world.

## Doctrine of God

We turn now to the content of his thought, which viewed from one angle is Christian philosophy, and from another angle is dogmatic theology. He thinks that he is grounding everything that he affirms about God, the world, and human nature and salvation upon the Scriptures. Surely he had a better right to make that claim than any of his predecessors, who were less laboriously and devotedly grounded in Biblical learning. His conception of God, which emerges from his study both of philosophy and of the Scriptures, he reaches by three philosophical methods that Celsus had distinguished and employed, and another which to Origen's mind is more fundamental than any of the other three. Celsus had said that when we try to think about God we are constrained to use first the method of analysis. Perhaps we might more accurately say the method of negation. We seek to reach a true understanding of God by denying of Him any predicates which are clearly inapplicable to the Supreme Being. We deny that he has spatial extent; we deny that he is limited to the operation of physical senses; and so on. Negating, one after another, the partial or deficient characters that we can properly ascribe only to created being,

---

8. English translations of portions of these commentaries in *ANF* 10.

we reach a conception of God which is free from inappropriate affirmations. Clement, we remember, had taken much the same line that Celsus recommends, speaking of God as one who is utterly beyond all categories of thought and all possibility of human speech, except that one may say "God is one (*monas*)." Second, we can follow the converse method of synthesis. In this we ascribe to God in an infinite and perfect degree all those predicates which stand for positive perfection. In the first instance we deny of God any imperfection, in the second instance we affirm of him all perfection. Third, we may employ the method of analogy. We can argue on the basis of similarity between the workman and his works. *Analogia* among the mathematicians says 2 is to 4 as 4 is to 8 as 8 is to 16; if this kind of proportional relationship obtains between creator and creature, between the infinite and finite, then one can discover certain traits in created and finite beings which can be said not to characterize the creator but to stand in such a relation to their origin in the creator that they point one's mind in the right direction. If we say God is just, we must not mean he is just in the manner of the police-court magistrate; we must mean rather that our idea of justice is derived from a character in God of such sort that it would be a worse mistake to say he is unjust. Origen regards all three of these methods—negation, perfection, and proportionality—as intellectually appropriate, but all of them must be guided and validated by another which is made possible by the fact of revelation. Properly speaking, revelation is not a method, but dependence upon revelation is a safeguard against the inappropriate use of any of these purely speculative procedures. On the basis of the Word of God, we employ our reason in the ways which the philosophical schools have defined and developed.

If then we attempt to describe the character that Christians will ascribe to God, we find that the primary affirmation we desire to make about God the Father is that he is perfect. This is radically different from asserting that he is absolute, wholly aloof, so that none of the affirmations of human reason can apply to his being at all. To Origen's mind this is unduly misleading and abstract. So we say not that God is absolute, but that he is perfect. Now that will involve the use of the method of abstraction or negation. We say of him that he is incorporeal, devoid of bodily character; he is immutable, not subject to the changes that take place in time; he is incomprehensible by reason of the limitations of the human mind; he is impassible, not subject to violent changes of feeling. So by the method of negation or analysis we clarify our conception of God along these various lines.

But on the other hand, we immediately employ the positive method of affirming perfection of him. We say that he is incorporeal because he is pure Spirit. We say that he is impassible, but not because he is wholly devoid of sensitivity, for he is pure love. He is indeed free from those violent and irrational movements of emotion which characterize creatures, but as one who is pure love his impassibility is not impassivity. We say that he is incomprehensible, but not because there is any irrationality in him; he is pure light, the very essence of truth; his incomprehensibility does not arise from some contradictoriness in his nature, but only from the narrow range of our understanding. We say of God, still speaking of God the Father, that he is perfect in the sense that his being displays complete inner harmony. Perfection means determinateness, for the indefinite (*to apeiron*) cannot be the perfect. Perfect being is being in utter harmony with itself. This is a harmony of such a sort that each of his attributes limits and defines every other. Note how far this is from the characteristic Alexandrine ascription to the Absolute of the complete absence or specifiable characters or attributes. God's power is restricted and defined by his justice, his justice is restricted and defined by his mercy, and so on. The perfection which we ascribe to God is a concrete perfection; it is not the absence of all attributable character. It is the unity of perfect concord, not the unity of absence of all diversity. It is not an abstract but a concrete unity. All this we affirm of God the Father.

Then alongside God the Father, on the basis of the revelation which guides us, we affirm the reality of God's Son, who is the Logos and among whose attributes we can distinguish some that are essential and some that are accidental. His essential attributes are four: he is Wisdom, Word, Light, and Truth. These are intrinsic to his being, and he is eternally characterizable by these conceptions. On the other hand, his accidental attributes, those which are contingent rather than necessary, are bound up with his earthly career. We say of him that he contingently becomes the God-man. His incarnation is not an eternal and necessary character of his Being as God. It is rather the assumption of a character which was contingent upon a historical situation that called for this action on his part. We say that he is Sacrifice, Propitiation, Physician, and so on. In such words we specify characteristics which refer to his incarnate being. These are characteristics that are historical and contingent, rather than eternal and necessary to the Being of the Word of God.

If we try to characterize the Logos further, we say on the one hand that the Logos is coeternal with the Father. This is the part of Origen's thought which was picked up and stressed in the later controversies by what we shall call the right-wing Origenists. They are the ones who stress those affirmations in his thought which treated the Logos as equal to the Father rather than as subordinated. The Logos is coeternal in the sense that the Father is always Father. That implies that there is always a Son. The Logos is perpetually the expression of the Father's Being; and only upon that ground can one correctly understand the significance of the Logos in the Godhead. One must say that the Logos is coequal with the Father in goodness. He is the perfect image, the perfect mirror of the Father's Being; and if there were any lack of goodness in the Logos, that would mar the perfection with which the Logos represents the being of the Father.

On the other hand, Origen said—and here is where the left-wing Origenists pick up the story—that the Logos is subordinate to the Father in derivation of being. It is the Father who is the original, and it is the Logos who is the image—the perfect mirror no doubt, but still the mirror. Consequently, there is an asymmetrical relation between the Father and the Son. The Son is always there with the Father, and yet the Son depends upon the Father for his being in a manner different from that in which the Father depends upon the Son for his expression. The Father could not be the Father if the Logos were not there, but the Logos could not be at all if the Father were not continually expressing himself through the Logos. However, that divine self-utterance is not to be construed as like the spoken word of man, as though the Father could have been silent and then arbitrarily uttered speech. Rather, the relationship is to be compared to the relation of a ray to a torch. You cannot have a lamp save as it gives light, and the light that it gives is an expression of the light-giving power of the torch. Such is the Son's relation to the Father. The emanationist pattern of thought which is characteristic of Neoplatonism is perfectly apparent in the things that Origen is saying here. So we have these two strains in Origen's thought. On the one hand there is something like the Johannine affirmation that the Logos and the Father are one. On the other hand there is something like the characteristic Alexandrine subordinationist affirmation that the Logos is the second God. Origen does not use that phrase, but he does find place for that sort of thought.

The Holy Spirit has a distinctive place with the Father and the Son in Origen's thought. In the first place, the Spirit described in the Old Testament is the same as the Holy Spirit described in the New Testament; there is no such thing as a beginning for the Spirit in a point in time. The Spirit that moved then on the face of the waters at the creation is the same Spirit poured out in the latter days. And if this be true, then the Spirit as well as the Son has a role in creation as well as in later human history. Although very much less specific attention is given to the being of the Holy Spirit, a special sphere of influence is defined for each of the three. The Father is the source of all existence who brings the world into existence through the Son. There is not a sharp distinction between the Father and the Son at this point, but the Father is the Ground of all that is. The Son is especially the principle of rationality. Once again that does not mean that the Son has no concern with existence. He is in fact the Creator, in the sense of the one through whom the world is brought into being and sustained in being. But the distinct factor which his particular and peculiar mode of being involves is order, truth, reason. He is therefore in a peculiar way the source of rationality in those particular existents that have mind. Among such rational beings, at any given time some but not all can be called holy. It is the Holy Spirit who is responsible for regeneration and sanctity among rational creatures who have this particular character. And it is possible to talk of the Spirit being withdrawn from some who possessed it—not the Spirit in its generic role as creative power, but the Spirit in its sanctifying role as the giver of grace. So the Father and the Son and the Holy Spirit, acting always together, act nevertheless in ways that are distinguishable. Origen thinks the distinction can be made clear by assigning to each a function that is not separable from the functions of the other, but that involves a further specification in each case. With the exception of Tertullian, Origen comes closer than any of the Christian thinkers before him to making the Holy Spirit a being having a status coordinate with that of the Father and the Son. But we must not forget that this statement is itself not free from ambiguity as regards the relation between Son and Father, and the status of the Holy Spirit is similarly ambiguous.

*Trinity in the Godhead*

Now that so much has been said about the individual members of the Godhead, it is possible to make a summary statement about the Trinity in which these three members are regarded as essentially one. If we consider first the nature of their unity, we can specify three ways in which Origen regards them as in some sense identically God. First, they are alike in respect of mind and will. The Father does not will one thing and the Son another and the Spirit something else, but there is complete unanimity in their actions. In his work *Against Celsus*, he says the Father and the Son are two considered as *hypostases* (a term which usually means individual existence and about which we shall say more later), but "one in mental unity, in agreement and in identity of will."[9] Second, they are one in respect of derivation of being. There is no other principle involved in the being of the Spirit and in the being of the Son than simply and solely the being of the Father, so that the concept *begetting* denotes the unique and sufficient grounding of the existence of the whole Godhead in the existence of the Father. Third, we have a statement which might be so interpreted as to contradict what was said in *Contra Celsum* and elsewhere about two hypostases. The statement occurs in the *Apology* of Pamphilus, a defense of Origen, of which the first book is extant in Rufinus' Latin translation, with some Greek words interspersed. Pamphilus professes to quote from Origen's now-lost commentary on the Letter to the Hebrews a passage in which Origen finds in the statement (Heb 1:3) that the Son is "the outpouring of the glory" of the Father, ground for affirming "unity of substance" (*communionem substantiae*) of Father and Son. For an "outpouring"(*aporrhoea*) appears *homoousios*, that is, "of one substance" (*unius substantiae*) with that body of which it is the effluence, as for example, light from a torch or from the sun.[10] Whether Origen really used the highly controversial and finally normative term *homoousios* of the Son and the Father is debatable, especially in view of the non-appearance of the term in any other of his extant works and the very shaky character of the one passage in which it does occur. In any event, it is clear that he rejects any view that the Son is of any other essential being than that of the Father.

---

9. Origen, *Cels.* VIII:12.

10. Pamphilus, *Apology*, I:4, in C. H. E. Lommatzsch, *Origenis Opera* V:24, *regenitorum. Pars III: S. Pamphili martyrus apologia pro Origene* (Berolini: Symtibus Haude et Spener, 1846) 359: *Aporrhoea enim* [Gk. *homoousios*] *videtur, id est, unius substantiae cum illo corpore, ex quo est vel aporrhoea, vel vapor.*

At the same time, it is just as important to insist upon the distinctions between Father and Son. In Origen's own day, the primary reason for insisting on such distinctions was the prevalence of the Monarchian thought of those who, like Noetus and Sabellius, want to assert that the Father and the Son are identically the same individual, which Origen expressly and repeatedly rejects. For example, in his commentary on the Gospel of John, he notes that there are some who seek to prove by such a text as John 2:19[11] that the Son does not differ in number from the Father, but that both are one not only in *ousia* but also in status as subject (*hypokeimenon*), that the Father and Son differ in certain predicates (*epinoias*) but not in fundamental existence (*hypostasin*).[12] On the contrary, says Origen, the language of the New Testament makes it impossible not to recognize that "the Son is another along with the Father, and that it is necessary that the Son be Son of a Father, and the Father be Father of a Son."[13] This rejection of Monarchianism is made even more emphatic in the late work *On Prayer*. In a discussion of the Lord's Prayer as addressed solely to the Father by the Logos himself, Origen says, "For if, as is shown elsewhere, the Son is another than the Father in essential and substantial being (*kat' ousian kai hypokeimenon*), then certain consequences follow for the life of prayer."[14] This does not mean that in Origen's mind the unity of the Godhead is given up. What it seems to mean is that the terminology for defining unity and distinction in the Godhead is still in a fluid and inchoate stage. When he is arguing against Sabellianism, Origen is prepared to stress the difference between the Father and the Son in respect of number, of individuation, and even of essential or substantial being. But when he is arguing against Marcionites, Gnostics, or pagan polytheists, he strongly urges the inseparable unity of the one true God. We have then a Godhead which is a closer approach, it seems to me, to the later doctrine of God as triune than we have found in any preceding

11. John 2:19: "Jesus answered them, 'Destroy this temple, and in three days I will raise it up.'"

12. Origen, *Comm. Jo.* X:37:21 in A. E. Brooke, ed., *The Commentary of Origin on S. John's Gospel: The Text Revised with a Critical Introduction and Notes.* 2 vols. (Cambridge: Cambridge University Press, 1896), 1:231.

13. Ibid.

14. Origen, *Or.* XV:1. English translation by Eric George Jay, *Origen's Treatise on Prayer: Translation and Notes with an Account of the Practice and Doctrine of Prayer from New Testament Times to Origen* (London: SPCK, 1954). For a recent translation, see Rowan A. Greer, *Origen* (New York: Paulist, 1979).

figure. The essential thing that makes Origen's thought here superior to the others is his insistence on the eternal concrescence of Father and Son and Spirit.

We shall examine soon the way in which Origen's followers failed to understand the tension which he tried to maintain in his thinking about God, and exaggerated one side or the other of his affirmations. It is such breaking asunder of the complex affirmations that Origen was trying to work out that leads directly into the essential issues of the Arian-Nicene controversy. If one stresses the subordination of the Son to the Father, then one is on the edge of declaring that the Son is a created being. And this is what the Arians eventually do. Meanwhile, we simply recognize that these two not easily reconcilable tendencies are both clearly present in Origen's own thought.

### The World and Redemption

At the beginning of the letter to the Hebrews, Origen finds what seems to him justification for affirming that this world is not the first created world. God "in these latter days has spoken to us in a Son whom he has appointed heir of all things, through whom also he made the worlds" (*aionos*) (Heb 1:2). There is then a plurality of worlds. And that seems to him right, for just as it is necessary to think of God as eternally Father, it is also necessary to think of him as eternally Creator. This is one of the doctrines of Origen that gets him into difficulties later on. That God is always Creator must mean that there has always been a created world. This world did indeed have a beginning in a moment of time, but it was preceded by earlier, and to Origen's mind, nobler worlds than this. Moreover, St. Paul indicates (Eph 2:7) that a plurality of ages will follow this one. It seems to Origen likely that the first creation was peopled by spiritual and rational beings in celestial bodies. There were a definite number of them, and all were free and responsive to the presence of God. Such are the sun, moon and stars, and the angelic hosts. God who is Father, Son, and Holy Spirit is confronted perpetually by a society of created, rational, and free spirits. They are other than God. As the schoolmen later would say, their being is contingent being. They are dependent at every point on the creative activity of God, who alone can exist wholly without body, which is the basis of change. Origen lays very great stress on that point against the

Stoic conception of God as spirit in the sense of a finely but nonetheless corporeally-extended mass.

If one asks why did God create a world other than himself, the answer is because being good, he desired these to whom his goodness could be shown. (This is a good Platonic answer; if you remember the *Timaeus*, precisely the same thing is said there about the maker and father of all things; he created the world because he is good and because he desired that there shall be a world as nearly like him as may be possible.) Created beings are capable of turning toward God as the principle of light and of love and finding in him their full satisfaction. But they are capable also of turning away from and seeking their satisfaction in themselves. Now Origen thinks that some such deviation on the part of rational spirits in some earlier phase of the creation must be posited. Some did not turn away, and those are the spirits that we still think of as angels. Even among them one can recognize differences of grades: witness the plurality of terms that Paul uses for the hosts of the spiritual order— thrones, dominions, principalities, and powers. These are the beings that have remained nearest to the state in which they were created. Then in an intermediate rank are souls. Origen finds a certain satisfaction, with one may hope at least a twinge of humor, in that fanciful etymology which associates *psyche*, soul, with *psycho*, to blow, and so with *psychetai*, grow cool. The pure fire of the spirits as they were created has dwindled, and in this intermediate level which we ourselves occupy, one finds the results of a turning away from God which still does not reach the lower depths inhabited by the fallen angels, who now are demons and devils. Here then are three levels: the angelic hosts, the souls of human beings, and the hosts of spiritual wickedness.

Originally every one of these beings stood on the same plane. All of them were God's creatures; all of them originally were near the throne; all of them once found satisfaction in the principle of good; and all of them have reached their present levels through their own freely chosen constancy or falling away. Origen defends this conception of freedom on the part of created beings almost through the whole of Book Three of *On First Principles*. It seems to him indispensable for vindicating the justice of God. How could we regard God as just if initially he had made beings so different in nature that for some it would be impossible to approach him, and for some it would be impossible to fall away from him? It is necessary to say that a just God has given all an equal chance. Now if we seek to understand what is involved in this declaration of creaturely freedom, Origen suggests we begin by distinguishing between beings capable of self-movement and beings that are not so capable. Sticks and stones have to be pushed or pulled by forces outside themselves, but living plants and animals and human beings and spirits higher on the scale are capable of moving themselves. They therefore have the principle of animation; they are *enpsychoi*.

But now further: although plants and animals are capable of self-movement, they are not capable of holding before themselves alternatives and preferring one to the other. The being of man is such that it includes *to logistokon* as well as *to epithumetikon*. The latter is impulse, an impulse to move, toward food, away from danger. But *to logistokon* is the capacity to form images; or more precisely, to apprehend images when they arise. And freedom means the capacity to compare one image with another and to choose one and reject the other. So it is possible for a being genuinely free to envisage two modes of conduct and to choose one rather than the other. There are plenty of passages in Scripture, says Origen, which make plain that this is in fact the essence of human nature: "Behold, I set before you the way of life and the way of death," and commandments to choose righteousness rather than wickedness.

There are, however, other passages which have seemed to a good many people to refute this affirmation that human beings are free. Think of the passages about the hardening of Pharaoh's heart and the apostle's affirmation that "he has shown mercy to whom he will show mercy, and them that he chooses he hardens (Rom 9:17–18). Well now, if this be the way God acts toward us, it looks very much as though what we do is not genuinely free but is controlled ultimately by God's will. Or consider Ezekiel's words about the substitution of a new heart of flesh for a heart of stone. Now how can one who is made with a heart of stone choose to obey rather than disobey? Origen says these passages all require very careful attention and accurate interpretation.

With respect to Pharaoh, there are certain Gnostic teachers who are all too glad to say there are some earthy natures incapable of salvation, as well as some spiritual natures incapable of perdition. Now let us ask these Gnostics whether Pharaoh is initially one of the earthy or not. If so, then plainly there was no need for God to harden his heart; it was already hard. And to say God hardened Pharaoh's heart would make sense only on the supposition that initially Pharaoh's nature was of such a sort that he could have chosen to set Israel free if he had willed to do so. Taking the other alternative, suppose that Pharaoh was not of the earthy sort but rather of those who were susceptible of salvation. If God then deliberately makes him incapable of salvation, God is surely no longer a just God. We can't have it both ways. God would be unjust if he made some incapable of being saved, and God would be unjust if he deliberately altered the character of those who of themselves were capable of being saved until God intervened to destroy them. Now as a matter of fact, there is a passage in which Pharaoh is represented as softening under the pressure which God brings to bear upon him, and saying "Yes, I'll let the Israelites go but only for a three-day journey; they mustn't go too far," and so on. And so actually what we confront is a picture of Pharaoh as one who in the familiar manner is neither stone nor air; he is one who is capable of turning either toward or away from fulfillment of God's commandment. Moreover, we have to ask what is meant by God's hardening of Pharaoh. In point of fact, we find other passages that throw light upon this one. The rain falls equally upon cultivated ground and uncultivated ground, and where the ground is well tended, then good fruits are produced; and where the ground is neglected, there thorns grow up. Well now, shall we blame the rain for making the thorns grow where the ground is neglected? It's the same rain, and the ground as such has the same nature; it's capable of absorbing the rain and making things grow, but what is made to grow depends upon the care with which the ground has been treated. So also in human life: the same fundamental nature is in all, and not merely in human beings but also in other rational beings (whether higher or lower on the ontological scale); and the hardening comes about not by reason of a deliberate attempt on God's part to exclude some but rather because of a bad response on the part of some who could have responded otherwise. Therefore it is not true, as the Gnostics would hold, that the creation is a bungled job and that created beings are fated by the blundering of one or more creators to lots which have no correspondence at all to their own worth. Rather, the state that each created spirit now occupies is an outward and visible reflection of its own history. It is a kind of doctrine of karma. In the far stages of creation, before this age began, each spirit was determining the place that it would have in the present age of the world. Now since all of us, with the angels above us and the devils below us, have come to occupy the places that we do occupy, it is quite clear that if the will of God is to be carried out through his creatures, it is necessary that the consequences of our own pre-terrestrial wrongdoing must somehow be put right.

It is perfectly clear that the redemption of the created world can be wrought only by God, and for that reason the Logos of God who is eternally Wisdom and Word and Life and Truth, becomes contingently a God-man, a Ransom, a Physician, and a Sacrifice for the redemption of fallen spirits.

Origen's conception of the manner of the incarnation is significantly different from that of Clement. In Clement's thought the incarnation is verbally described as a real assumption of human life; but the human life thus assumed by the Logos lacks the defects and wants and weaknesses that mark our ordinary human experience. Clement verges on a Docetist Christology. Not so with Origen. But if we ask how it is possible for God who is utterly incorporeal to take on body, we must look for some mediating factor. And this Origen finds in one of the created intelligences which never turned away from God. As he describes them in the work *On First Principles* and in certain commentaries, the sources of turning away are especially inertia and pride (*neglentia*, a cooling off, a weariness; and *superbia*, a preference of self to God—and there are passages in which he says that *superbia* is the worst of all the sins). But there is one created intelligence which has never slipped into either neglect or self-assertive pride, but rather has found satisfaction in steady, unremitting love of God. And through such unswerving love—"in a union inseparable and indissoluble"—that soul has come at length, according to the words of St. Paul, to become one spirit with God—this created intelligence then becomes the first choice to be anointed with the Holy Spirit and so to become *Christos*.[15] Once again, Origen never makes the mistake of calling God *Christos*, the anointed One; God is the one who anoints, but it is this created being that is chosen and anointed with the oil of gladness above his fellows. What that means is that whereas the prophets were granted partial participation in the gift of the Spirit, this intelligence is granted the gift of radical partaking. Now this created being is capable of becoming incarnate because it is a creature; it already has a body, presumably, although the text is ambiguous on this point, whereas God could not directly take on an earthly body. But at the same time, this created being is an intelligent being; he is capable of such participation in God as a body

---

15. Origen, *Princ.* II:3.

would not of itself be capable. Here then is a mediator between God and body. With that soul the Logos comes down, undergoes birth, and enters into a fully rounded human life. In the face of this mystery, says Origen, "We must pursue our contemplations with all fear and reverence."[16]

How one can think of the eternal Word of God as a wailing infant or as a suffering man simply cannot be expressed in the language of the philosophical schools. Origen is inclined to suggest that what one sees here is the Word shining through the limitations of space and time and human weakness, somewhat as one can see the nature of fire being assumed by iron which is heated to incandescence. The iron is iron, and yet it is so fully assimilated to the fire that all the properties of fire are characteristic now of heated iron. If one tries to distinguish between the cold, opaque mass that was there before and the blazing, melting heat of the flame, one finds it impossible any longer to distinguish one from the other, they have become so completely unified. So with the human nature and the Logos in the incarnate Word.

The work which is performed by the Redeemer who thus comes into this present age for our sakes is in the first instance a work of revelation and instruction. How, asks Origen, could infinite God most readily have made himself intelligible to finite minds? Presumably by putting before them a miniature of his own being. Suppose, he says, a statue so immense that the human eye could not take it all in at one look. What would be the best way of conveying the lineaments of that statue? The answer is obviously to set forth a small copy of it in which all the features would be represented on a smaller scale. That is something like what has happened in the incarnation. The lineaments of God have been manifested, but within the limits of a finite individual life, so that one can say, this is what God is like within the bounds of finiteness. This is the genuine image of God. It is not something second-best, but the real image scaled down in such a way that the revelation is at once authentic and at the same time apprehensible. We remember, in Origen's doctrine of God, that God is said to be incomprehensible not because of any contradictions within himself but because of the small scope of our thought. Here is the answer. God the incomprehensible becomes comprehensible now by his own act of self-revelation. And this revelation of God, once again, is the revelation of one who is perfect in justice and perfect in mercy. Now our

16. Origen, *Princ.* II:2.

human minds which had been clouded by our own turning away from God and focusing upon ourselves—our interests, our imperfection—are illuminated with a fresh and vivid awareness of what God really is. This is the first part of the Savior's task.

The second and equally indispensable part is that he offers his soul, his finite spirit, as a ransom for the souls of those who are held under the sway of the demonic powers. He gives himself in order that they may be set free. The way in which Origen dramatizes this conception has a powerful emotional impact. The Savior who had been crucified goes down into the place of the devils themselves, and when he who is essential light appears in the place of darkness, the power of darkness even in its own stronghold is broken. It is broken not by violence; it is not that he has used the methods of the Devil against the Devil, but rather that he has brought into the place where they are trying to maintain their hold by violence the sheer inexorable light of truth and of love, and in so doing he breaks the power of the devils. It is not merely their power over those who have died in sin and who are now held in prison that has been destroyed, but even the obstinacy of the power of wrong in the hearts of the demons themselves. His conquest is not merely a conquest on behalf of human beings over the power of evil. It is that. But it goes deeper than that. It is the conquest of evil in the hearts of the fallen spirits, so that they themselves are now turned back towards God in varying degrees. The light has come and found them where they had fallen. Redemption is offered for the whole of creation and not merely for a part.

Then third, redemption involves the participation of believers in the life through which is the true light. It is not simply that a new vision has been set before them. It is that a new motive has been quickened within, so that the light of the Logos becomes their life. That is where the Holy Spirit takes up the work of the Logos and becomes the principle of light in individual believers and in the Christian community. In a certain sense the whole drama of creation and fall has now reached its climax and turned back once more in the direction of God. Origen conceives the life of the redeemed within the church in much the same way that life was conceived by Clement: there is the life of the simple believer who follows the precepts of Christian morality and who lives with faith in Jesus Christ as Logos; but there is also the more enlightened life of the Christian gnostics into whom the truth has made its way, not simply in terms of obedience but in terms of rational insight. In the church one recognizes that both these groups of Christians are on the way back. The believers will come to have in time (if not in this life, then in some later time) the sort of understanding of God that is the only basis of full return to him.

According to Origen's doctrine of things to come, the Christian life in the present age looks forward to a succession of ages after this one. There is Hades, into which the spirits of unrepentant sinners will pass, to be held there until the end of the present cycle. There is Paradise, which is likewise an intermediary stage, into which the souls of believers will pass, to wait also until the end of the present era. Eventually the age will come to an end, and a new age will begin. Then both repentant and unrepentant souls will go forward, learning through punishment and through regeneration. Origen thinks of regeneration not as an instantaneous changeover from a state of being in sin to a state of being fully saved, but rather as a process of learning and of growth. Hereafter we look forward to a long-continued schooling at the hands of God, whose punishments, Origen thinks, must all be regarded as educational rather than as vindictive. One brilliant if somewhat one-sided interpreter of Origen's thought, Hal Koch, has titled his work on Origen *Pronoia und Paideusis* (Providence and Nurture).[17] Origen conceives God as concerned for human beings primarily in the way of an all-embracing providential order, and in the way of a progressive illumination. These two factors define, as far as definition is possible, the long slope of the future. But although the end will be like the beginning, it will not be precisely the same as the beginning. In the beginning, human beings were created according to the image of God, but there is another word alongside image, namely *likeness*: "Let us make man according to our image" means according to the Logos in whom human beings and all other created beings are made. But likeness to God must be attained through *mimesis*, for if we are endowed with the power to return to God, the return must be through our own choice. And if and insofar as we do return, we attain not only the status of being created according to his image, but the status of being assimilated to him and so displaying his likeness. The end will be reached, Origen says, according to the apostle's word, when the work of the Savior is com-

---

17. Hal Koch, *Pronoia und Paideusis: Studien über Origenes und sein Verhältnis zum Platonismus* (Berlin: de Gruyter, 1932).

pleted, and when he hands over his kingdom to the Father and God will be all in all.

This Origen refers to sometimes as the eternal Gospel—the Gospel that looks not only to this present age of history but to all succeeding ages and to the ultimate outcome in which the succession of time will be swallowed up. Does it mean that all individuals are swallowed up into a single, unitary whole? No; what it means rather, says Origen, is that each individual will be so purged of everything that is not according to the image and likeness of God that God becomes in each individual the ruling and absorbing principle. Then God will be all, we may say, "in each," and collectively "in all." This includes all human beings and all demons—even the Prince of the Devils.

Whether this will actually come to pass, it is impossible to assert dogmatically, because on Origen's own principles created spirits retain their freedom: if they continue to be free, they have the option of turning away again. But I think Origen's hope is indicated in what he says about that soul which has never deserted God; that soul remains free, yet by perpetual love of God the freedom to turn away is practically excluded by the gradual formation of the character which becomes, as it were, a new nature. The nature which God has given is still there, but the nature which is superimposed upon that original nature, resulting from the choices of the one who has been given the power to say yes or to say no can be regarded as steady and henceforth indestructible. I suspect that something of the sort is in Origen's mind when he looks toward the remote future.

## Summary

The thought of Origen is on the one hand a Christian philosophy and on the other hand a philosophical theology. To say that he presents Platonism in the language of the Old and New Testaments is to say what up to a point is plainly true. But it is not simply Platonism that grounds his ideas. Celsus, Origen says, accuses the Christians of teaching what is inferior to the teaching of Plato. Origen's reply is that

> ... our prophets, and Jesus and his apostles, were careful to use a method of teaching which not only contains the truth but is also able to win over the multitude. After conversion and entrance into the Church each individual according to his capacity can ascend

to the hidden truths in the words which seem to have a mean style. If I may venture to say so, the beautiful and refined style of Plato and those who write similarly benefits but a few, if indeed it benefits anybody; whereas that of teachers and writers with a meaner style which was practical and exactly suited to the multitude has benefited many.[18]

The preference for a Gospel that is for the many and not simply for the few must be put on the other pan of the balance when we think of Origen as one who regards some, including himself, as having been granted by the Holy Spirit superior powers of interpretation, of analysis, of theoretical construction; and yet the root of the matter is available for the humbler brethren as well.

Origen insists that he finds justification for all these affirmations in the Scriptures, and that upon the Scriptures and the rule of faith the legitimacy of this whole structure must depend. Yet he was able to find things in the Scriptures through allegorical interpretation that one who is restricted to a literal or historical reading of the text would find difficult to recognize. It is clear that in the impressive sweep of his thought, there are certain affirmations which are most awkwardly out of line with the Christian tradition by and large. In the first place, there is the declaration that the world is created eternally. It is created, but it has always been— that is a Greek, not a Hebraic conception. In the second place, there is the doctrine that human souls have been preexistent; they have had a long existence before they appear in these bodies. In fact, these bodies are a rather unfortunate manifestation of the distance the souls have fallen. But to say that we have existed from all eternity as individuals is to say what the church before Origen had never been accustomed to say. In the third place, to regard the salvation of the created world as extending to all human beings and even to demons is a departure from the general drift of traditional thought. In the fourth place, to regard the future as a continuation of spiritual exercise and growth, in which the body falls more and more into an unhappy past and the outcome is the restoration of the community of pure spirits in celestial bodies has a Gnostic flavor, which the church, committed to the declaration of the resurrection of the flesh, inevitably found difficult to accept. On these four grounds, primarily, Origen's thought aroused bitter criticism, partly among his contempo-

---

18. Origen, *Cels.* VI:2.

raries but still more among certain of his successors, so that eventually, at the Fifth Ecumenical Council (II Constantinople, 553 CE), he was explicitly condemned as a heretic. Fifteen anathemas were adopted denouncing him for doctrines some of which he never held.

Yet unjust though this condemnation was, it must be granted that Origen held views which are hard to square with the simple proclamation of the act of God in Jesus Christ; and that more generally, he is inclined to be too cursory in his evaluation of history. His Gospel is a Gospel for eternity, and earthly history constitutes a single episode in the whole drama from the beginning to the distant end. The one time when it seems to me he really senses the vital significance of historical affirmations is when he talks about the incarnation, but for the most part, he presents what we do here on earth as only preparation for a later and happier time.

# CHAPTER 10

# Efforts to Define the Christian Doctrine of God[1]

I F ONE WERE TRYING to describe inclusively and consecutively the development of doctrine during the latter half of the third century and the first decade of the fourth, one would have to shuttle back and forth between the East and the West, and would have to refer to a great many detailed events and figures. Rather I shall take one strain of development, the Christian doctrine of God, and concentrate on the East. From the time of Origen's death in 254, our information about theological developments in the church through the rest of the third century nearly blacks out. Yet we do gain glimpses here and there. In general, Origen's thought had become very widely influential, with its insistence upon the rather sharp distinction between the Father and the Son and the Holy Spirit within the Godhead, and its equally emphatic insistence that the Father and the Son are coeternal in their being. Now among Origen's followers, who had come to occupy numerous bishoprics in Egypt, Palestine, and Asia Minor, the tendency was to simplify by disproportionate emphasis upon one or another particular aspect of the transmitted thought. The aspect to be thus emphasized was determined primarily by local and temporary conditions. Whenever an Origenistic thinker is confronted by Sabellianism or some other form of Monarchian thought, he is likely to stress the subordinationist emphasis in Origen's theology. On the other hand, an Origenist confronted by a too-radical emphasis on distinctions in the Godhead is likely to stress the closeness of relation between the Son and the Father. So within the complicated pattern of Origenistic thought, we have a chance for quite different schools to develop by reason of

1. The bulk of this chapter is taken from the 1948 LHCD, but with some omissions from that source and insertions from lectures delivered in later years [ed.].

emphasis upon one side or the other in response to the requirements of local controversy.

## GREGORY THE WONDER-WORKER

One may illustrate the way in which a first-generation Origenist understood the master's thinking by referring to the personal confession of Gregory Thaumaturgos (the Wonder-Worker), whom we have already met as one of the early pupils of Origen after he had moved to Caesarea about 230. He penned a rather extravagant panegyric on Origen as man and as teacher, containing a confession of faith which, according to Caspari, is probably authentic.[2]

> One God, Father of a living Word, of a substantial Wisdom and Power and eternal Image; perfect Genitor of a perfect (offspring), Father of an only Son.
>
> One Lord, alone from the Alone, God from God, Image and Likeness of Deity, active Logos, Wisdom containing the structure of the universe and Power formative of the whole creation, true Son of true Father, Invisible from Invisible, and Incorruptible from Incorruptible, and Immortal from Immortal and Eternal from Eternal.
>
> And one Holy Spirit, having its being from God and made manifest through the Son; Image of the Son, Perfect from Perfect, Life the Source of Living, Sanctity the Master of Sanctification, in whom is made manifest God the Father who is over all and in all, and God the Son who is through all.

Then comes the part which is sometimes taken to be of later date (though not by Caspari):

> A perfect Trinity, in glory and eternity and sovereignty neither divided nor alienated. For there is neither creature nor servant in the Trinity, nor anything brought in from outside so that what was not hitherto, has come in after; for the Son has never been lacking to the Father, nor the Spirit to the Son, but the same Trinity unchanged (*atreptos*) and immutable (*analloiotos*) forever.

---

2. Caspari, *Alte und neue Quellen*, 10. English translation in *ANF* 6.

I think Harnack's comment on this confession of Gregory's is very just. It is extraordinarily devoid of Biblical terms and Biblical ideas.[3] The terminology is the speculative terminology of the schools. It is a creed that reflects the temper of a man who, unlike his teacher, conceives theology as theoretic rather than experiential, a product of inference rather than a response to revelation. And that temper, rather than anything that is said about Father or Son in the creed, is what I think is of importance for the further development within the Origenistic groups toward what is eventually to emerge in full bloom as Arian rationalism. We do not have Arianism here. We do not even have a stress upon the subordinationist side of Origen here. What we do have is the tendency to prefer speculative concepts and speculative terms and to encourage therefore a theology which seeks to be primarily rationalistic rather than affirmatory and confessional.

## Dionysius of Alexandria

In the same generation with Gregory the Wonder-Worker, another Origenist was bishop of Alexandria—Dionysius, who came to be known on various grounds as Dionysius the Great. We now have only fragments of his writings, most of them because Eusebius quoted them in his work *On the Preparation of the Gospel*.[4] But the fragments are enough to show that Dionysius was a Biblical scholar of quite unusual fineness of temper and balance of judgment. We have, for example, a discussion which he prepared regarding the Johannine authorship of the Fourth Gospel, the First Epistle of John, and the book of Revelation. He distinguishes between the Apocalypse and the other two writings on grounds of differences in style and mode of thought. He is not prepared to say that the book of Revelation should not be treated as authoritative. He thinks that it is the work of a man to whom extraordinary insights have come, although he confesses that he cannot understand most of what the book is talking about. It may even be the work of a man called John, but that it is the work of the author of the Gospel and 1 John must be denied, he

---

3. Harnack, *History of Dogma*, III: 103. Harnack finds in Gregory "the danger . . . of passing wholly over to the domain of abstract philosophy, and of relaxing the union of speculation with exegesis of Holy Scripture."

4. Charles Lett Feltoe, ed. *Dionysiou leipsana*, Cambridge Patristic Texts (Cambridge: Cambridge University Press, 1904). English translations of some works, Feltoe, *St. Dionysius of Alexandria*; also *ANF* 6: 81–120.

thinks, on both stylistic and doctrinal grounds. His comment as far as we can judge is a nice job of critical examination and appraisal, the work of one who has clearly fallen heir to Origen's insistence on the need for accurate Biblical scholarship.

We have still other fragments which arise out of a controversy with the people of his own parish. He was bothered by the influence of Sabellian thought in the region around Alexandria, according to which God is a single, individual being. Now in his work against Sabellius, Dionysius says that the Son of God is no longer preached in the churches, and he undertakes to reemphasize the distinct existence of the Son. In his efforts to do so he uses illustrations—homiletical metaphors which certainly lack something of caution and precision. In the chapter on the vine and the husbandman, God is the husbandman, and Jesus Christ is the plant which he trains up. Or he refers to the shipbuilder who makes a ship and then launches it forth; thus does the Logos come from the Father. Now some of his hearers were very much bothered by what seemed to them a rather crude affirmation that the Son is a creature. They decided to write to Dionysius, the bishop of Rome, who was a good friend of their Dionysius, to tell him that their bishop was teaching that the Son is a created being and that he is not of the same ousia (homoousios) with the Father.[5] Thereupon Dionysius of Rome wrote a very friendly but very firm letter to Dionysius of Alexandria, saying in effect: "It sounds as though you are surely using dangerous language. Now I doubt that you mean all that this language implies, but if this is not what you mean, you had better make yourself clear."[6] The response of Dionysius of Alexandria was the most immediate, friendly, and conciliatory reply conceivable, which might be paraphrased in some such fashion as this: "Yes," he said, "I certainly have been using unfortunate language. I have been doing it because I wanted to stress the distinct and concrete existence of the Son, not permitting him to be absorbed into the Father's being. I probably spoke incautiously about the plant; however, if I had spoken of the plant and the seed, or the

5. For the documents concerning the two Dionysii, see Feltoe, *Dionysiou leipsana,* 165–98.

6. Dionysius of Rome responded to charges against his Alexandrian namesake by writing two letters: a public letter to the Alexandrian Church concerning Sabellianism and a private letter to the bishop himself. An extract from the former may be found in Feltoe, *Dionysiou leipsana,* 177ff.

relation of plant to root, the question about their difference of essential being (*ousia*) would not have been raised, and I am quite willing to say that that is what I mean. As a matter of fact, in other sermons I have used other metaphors which it seems to me now were better chosen. I have spoken of the spring and the river which flows from it—the two are not one, and yet they certainly are of the same essential being. But I do not find this term *homoousios* anywhere in the Scriptures, and I myself prefer Scriptural language, though the idea is one I am concerned to maintain."[7]

We recall, perhaps, that *homoousios* is a term which the Gnostics had used most freely and frequently; the Valentinians or the Ophites were likely to assert that the spiritual is *homoousion* with the *Pleroma* and that the material is *homoousion* with the lower creator. It is not altogether surprising that as a noted biblical scholar, Dionysius should have preferred not to use non-scriptural language unless there was no other way to avoid the sort of misunderstanding which apparently had arisen.

Plainly, this is a situation in which theological terminology was so completely in flux that a man of enthusiasm and good will could use language which, judged by the dogmatic norms of the later generation, is misleading in a very high degree. Once his attention is called to its unhappy consequences, Dionysius is ready to admit that he was incautious.

## Paul of Samosata

Consider a third illustration of the way in which Origenism was working out in the middle of the third century. Just as Dionysius of Alexandria was confronted by Sabellian Monarchianism and tried to counter it by stressing the distinctive existence of the Son as compared with the Father, so Eastern Origenists were confronting the other brand of Monarchianism, which we earlier spoke of as dynamistic and which played a considerable part in Syrian Christianity. The man in whom this Eastern Monarchianism had its most influential presentation was Paul of Samosata, who had become bishop of Antioch somewhere around 260 and who continued in that office until he was finally deposed by Emperor Aurelian in 272. We know about him chiefly because he got into trouble with a group of Origenist

---

7. Dionysius of Alexandria's response, a treatise called *Refutation and Defense* (*Elengchos kai apologia*); a fragment in Feltoe, *op. cit.*, 170ff; English translation of some extracts in Feltoe, *St. Dionysius*, 103ff.; *ANF* 6: 92–94.

neighbors who called a series of synods to decide whether or not he was a proper person to be bishop. For a long time they could not trip him up on any crucial issue; but eventually in 267 or thereabouts, a decision was reached with the aid of a certain Malchion, head of the Greek philosophical school in Antioch and a member of the church who was ready to help with his professional philosophical training to detect the precise location of the error in Paul's thought. The synod of 267 or 268 decided that he was clearly a heretic, and the bishops who took part in the discussion wrote an account to Dionysius of Rome, which has in part been preserved by Eusebius.[8] This letter takes the interesting line that if Paul had not been a heretic, it would have been necessary to accuse him of grave moral improprieties. The authors were prepared to pass over his arrogance in the conduct of episcopal affairs, his greediness, his readiness to profit from the revenues of his diocese, his preference for the pomp of a political official—which led him to wear his robes of office as a representative of Queen Zenobia rather than the plainer garb of a clergyman, and to have a political tribunal like any high magistrate in which he heard cases and put himself on public display. They would pass over his secularity of manner, the way he had developed the arts of the rhetorician and made impassioned speeches from the tribunal, tramped up and down waiting for the plaudits of the auditors and berated them if they did not applaud. He often paused for handkerchief-waving on the part of his congregation, occasionally signaling for applause by slapping his thigh and making it plain that this was the point now at which the listeners ought to express approval. He played favorites among his congregation, seeing that those he favored had the opportunity to get rich. He overlooked misconduct on their part, perhaps because he himself was guilty of similar misconduct. He was much too fond of having beautiful women in his ecclesiastical company. However, all these things could be overlooked because he was a heretic and could be rejected on that ground.

As we have noticed, the precise form of his heresy was so subtle that it took a number of synods to find out exactly where it was that he went wrong. Furthermore, the evidence for Paul's heresy is fragmentary, and there seems to have been also some confusion of identity: things are said about Paul or about a follower of his which really apply to someone else. To try therefore to get something like a sober notion of what Paul thought means sifting a good deal of chaff for a very small amount of

8. Eusebius, *Hist.eccl.* VII:30.

grain. Gustave Bardy[9] is the scholar who has conducted one of the most plausible and minute inspections of this material,[10] and one of the fragments which he regards as authentic comes from the sixth-century writings of Severus of Antioch.[11]

Paul apparently endorsed the Monarchian party line: the Word is a power or an aspect of the being of the Father, and Jesus Christ becomes Christ through a special endowment, not by reason of the fact that the preexistent Word actually takes human shape in him. Thus Paul's Christology is Adoptionist. It is less crude than the old Ebionism, which thought of Jesus simply as a prophet and teacher adopted by God at his baptism in response to his human perfection. Rather, for Paul there is present in him from the beginning, not a personal or substantive Logos, but the impersonal power and wisdom which comes from God and is named alternatively *Logos* or *Sophia*. This was also at work in Moses and the prophets, but less perfectly. Jesus is the one whose will is always in complete accord with the will of God. He grows in favor with God and man; and in course of this progress, he reaches a level at which he himself is assimilated with the divine. At his baptism, the Holy Spirit came upon him, and by this anointing, he became Christ.

It was hard to discredit Paul for these views, since he came from an area where they had long been accepted in principle. Paul is not the only representative of dynamistic Monarchianism whose name has come down to us. We know, for example, of a certain Theodotus the cobbler, a leather merchant of Byzantium who came to Rome in the last years of the second century; and we hear of another Theodotus who became his disciple while in Rome—Theodotus the banker, or the money-changer; and we have the name of Artemon (or Artemas) and also of a certain Acliptiodotus. A man somewhat closer to him in place and time was a third-century bishop of Bostra in the province of Arabia, Beryll (or Beryllus), who sometime about 240 to 244 became the object of some criticism by his neighbors. Origen, apparently then teaching at Caesarea, was called in as a kind of expert consultant to try to persuade Beryllus

---

9. Gustave Bardy, *Paul de Samosate: étude historique* (Louvain: Bureaux, 1923).

10. Fragments are available in the following collections: Martin Joseph Routh, *Reliquiae Sacrae*, 2nd ed. (Oxford: E Typographeo Academico, 1846–1848) 3:287–367; Lawlor, "The Sayings of Paul of Samosata," *JThST* 19 (1917/18) 20–45; 115–120.

11. Professor Calhoun did not further identify the location of the fragment he here had in mind [ed.].

to acknowledge his error in teaching that the Word was a power of God but not really a member of a substantial Godhead. Apparently Origen succeeded in convincing him to change his view, and he was accepted back into fellowship. [Paul of Samosata, in short, had predecessors; and his special significance for later developments does not lie in what little we know of his own opinions but in the opposition evoked by the Monarchian tendencies he represented.]

The fullest statement of this opposition is in a letter signed by six of the bishops who planned to be at a second synod of Antioch somewhere about 269.[12] Its authenticity has been debated, but it does represent the kind of theology that his opponents at that council would have represented, and it is interesting enough to warrant our spending a little time with it. They are careful to insist that the view they hold is one which has come down to them through tradition, and this is their faith.

They begin by affirming "that God is unbegotten." This is a fateful declaration. They are saying not merely that he has not come into being—everyone would affirm that of him—but that it is essential as a matter of definition to speak of him as unbegotten. It is at such points that difficulties arise when the Arians later seize upon such terms of the left-wing Origenists as this and begin to insist upon them as indispensable. If it is necessary to think of God as in his very essence unbegotten, then to speak of the Son as begotten and at the same time as God will pretty obviously involve a contradiction.

> That God is unbegotten, one, without beginning, invisible, immutable, whom no man has seen or can see; to know and to interpret whose glory and greatness in a manner worthy of the truth is unattainable to human nature and to apprehend however modest a conception of whom is by revelation through his beloved Son. This the Son the only-begotten, being the image of the invisible God, first-born of every creature.

That phrase from Col 1:15—*prototokos pases ktiseos*—was a perilous phrase because it obviously is in some manner ambiguous. The first-born of creation—does that mean he himself was included in creation? The first-born of every creature—was he himself then a creature, the first of

---

12. The text of this letter from which Calhoun translated the following excerpts has not been located [ed.].

all? The Arians are going to make great capital of that phrase as good Scriptural language.

> Wisdom and Word and Power of God before the ages, divine not by foreknowledge, but in *ousia* and *hypostasis.*

That is to say, against Paul of Samosata, there is never a time when the Son of God awaits adoption to divine status, as the outcome of providential grace, but from the very beginning and throughout eternity, the Son is Son side by side with the Father. Here we find the phraseology which later comes to be normative: *ousia* and *hypostasis.* We remember those phrases from Origen's use of them, and once again we shall find them central in the debates of the fourth century.

> The Son of God known in the Old and New Testament, him we confess and proclaim. Whoever shall say on the contrary that the Son of God is not God before the creation of the world, saying that it is to believe and confess two gods if the Son of God is declared to be God, this we consider to be out of line with the ecclesiastical canon, and all the Catholic churches agree with us.

Proof-texts follow to support this judgment.

> This one we believe being with the Father eternally, has fulfilled the Father's will for the creation of the universe. . . . Thus also as truly existing and acting, as Logos and as God, through whom the Father has created all things, not as through an instrument, not as through abstract knowledge (*di'epistemes anhypostaton*), but, the Son begotten of the Father as living energy and as concrete in his existence (*enhypostaton*),

*Anhypostaton* and *enhypostaton* are among the terms which have led critics to question whether this sort of language would have been used as early as the third century, because these are terms which appeared especially in the Christological controversy of the fifth century. But the fact that they become prominent at this or that time is to my mind not evidence that they could not have been used before then; it seems to me that they are precisely evidence for the kind of question which is being debated between Paul and these Origenistic opponents of his.

> . . . working all things in all, not simply as though the Son were watching or present, but as acting to effect the framing (*demiourgion*) of the universe. This one it is, we say, who fulfilling

his Father's will, [note the reference to the will of the Father as controlling what the Son does—again a theme which the Arians will emphasize] appeared to the patriarchs and spoke to them in general and summary terms first as an angel and then as Lord, and then as evident God. We confess and declare that the Son was with the Father as God and Lord of all things that are begotten, was sent by the Father [another subordinationist phrase] from the heavens, and was made flesh and became man. He also received a body from the Virgin, setting forth the whole fullness of the Godhead in bodily form, and he was united to the Godhead immutable and deified.

The point which here is of primary interest is the indication that in the Incarnation, the Logos, who has been declared to be a substantial agent alongside the Father, enters into a physical frame and becomes man. Note that Origen's suggestion that the Logos first is united to a human soul has simply dropped out. Pretty clearly the reason is that for Origen the human soul was preexistent, so that the Logos assumed the soul before coming down to earth and appearing in the flesh. Now with Origen's preexistence theory abandoned because it could not be squared very easily with the Christian tradition, it is no longer easy to think of the Logos as assuming a human soul, so that what is said here is simply that the Logos assumes human flesh—a body from the Virgin. These Origenists do not say that the Logos assumes a human personality from the Virgin or takes on an individual human life. They say rather, "The fullness of Godhead is set forth in bodily form." The Christology involved is one that sees the Logos indwelling in a human body, rather than one which says that God was in a man.

This sort of Christology is on the way toward Arianism. Those who promote it are not Arians; they are left-wing Origenists representing a Hellenistic tradition which reflects the thought patterns of Alexandrine Platonism. But I think that the studies of scholars like Gwatkin, Loofs, and Bardy have shown that the line of Arian theology is most readily derivable from this left-wing tradition in Origenistic thought, and not from the dynamistic Monarchianism that Alexander of Alexandria and very many later interpreters have declared to be its starting point. These two views were rivals, not allies.

## PERSECUTIONS UNDER DIOCLETIAN AND HIS SUCCESSORS: THE DONATIST SCHISM

We come now to the opening years of the fourth century, which was more trying to the church, by and large, than any preceding period had been. It was more trying in part because of the straits to which the Roman world had been driven, and the desperate efforts that were made by the last of the pre-Christian emperors to stave off the threat of collapse. By all odds the most capable of these later emperors was Diocletian, who undertook through what have been described as totalitarian methods to draw the economic and social as well as the political affairs of the empire into imperial control. At first he did not go out of his way to persecute the Christians as Christians so long as they were quiet and did not make trouble. Christianity was by now a legally tolerated religion which had become a sizable component in the life of the empire. But toward the end of his reign, Christian officials and servants of the royal household were accused of involvement in a plot to murder his much more brutal colleague Galerius, who had been urging general persecution. Then Diocletian, apparently with great reluctance but eventually with ruthless energy, set out to bring any such subversive activity under control. He struck first not primarily at individual Christians but at the life of the Christian community. The method that he employed as his first line of attack was to remove Christians from public office and from positions as household servants, reducing the latter to slavery. He ordered also the destruction of church buildings and of Scriptures from the churches, hoping to make it impossible for the Christian community to carry on systematic public worship and normal life. It would appear that in most places, it was possible to hide enough copies of the Scriptures to make the imperial censorship only partly successful. Some churchmen refused utterly to hand over anything which was in their trust.

This opposition happened most notably in North Africa, where the followers of a certain Donatus regarded themselves as the spiritual successors of Cyprian, who had insisted that the bishops must be beyond any shadow of blame in their personal and professional lives. The Donatists held that any clergyman who had yielded to the imperial demands should be deprived of his office; and since a good many of their fellow clerics did precisely that, the Donatists withdrew from communion with the Catholic church in the provinces of Northern Africa.

They were a schismatic group but not a heretical one. In belief they held practically the same convictions as the church from which they were now withdrawn. Their dissent was over a point of ecclesiastical discipline; and they divided the Church, maintaining that anyone who wanted to come into the Donatist churches from the Catholic church must submit to rebaptism, for they no longer regarded Catholic baptism as valid. Any Catholic cleric, moreover, who wanted to transfer to the Donatist Church had to be reordained, for Catholic ordination had likewise lost its effectiveness. Ordination performed by cowards and traitors could not be regarded as valid ordination. The Donatists became a hard core of resistance to the increasingly secular organization of the churches. They had influence only in North Africa—nowhere else.

As we have seen, the first measures employed by Diocletian were only partially successful, but the temper in which they were applied led to a sense of peril within the church more widespread than in any previous time. When riots broke out in two places, a second edict of general imprisonment of church officers was announced, and eventually the death penalty was restored. This was not a local persecution but a policy of general repression. When Diocletian retired, the tempo and cruelty of persecution was stepped up under his successors Galerius, Maximian, and most especially Maximinus. Christian leaders and laymen were sought out and tortured and compelled, if possible, to recant. Many died first, under the rods, the sword, or the fire. A number of Christians whose names are known to us as persons of importance were put to death under Maximian; one of them was the warm admirer of Origen named Pamphilus, who began to compose a life of Origen and edit a collection from his writing—a project carried on after Pamphilus' death by the church historian Eusebius of Caesarea. After forty years of toleration and tranquillity, the church had become acutely aware once more of its insecurity in the midst of a political rule that was itself feeling extremely insecure.

## LUCIAN OF ANTIOCH

One of the men who were martyred in that period was a teacher in the classical school of Antioch, Lucian by name. He appears to have carried on in Antioch teaching which reminds one in many respects of the teachings of Origen—the sort of philosophical theology which stems from

Alexandrine Platonic presuppositions. Like him, Lucian was a Biblical scholar of unusual competence. Apparently, his chief contribution to the life of the church was the preparation of a new critical text of the Bible, based upon Origen's work but undertaking to correct errors that had crept in even since Origen's day. Moreover, it omitted the elaborate apparatus of critical scholarly marks which Origen had used to indicate variants in the text. It was a simple, faithful version of the Scriptures which ordinary clergymen could use. Apparently this Lucianic text was very widespread in the churches of the Eastern world.

At the same time, Lucian's thought appears to have been close to that of the left-wing Origenists to which we have referred more than once. He seems to have had a tremendous following, so that just as Origen had numerous pupils of his placed in important posts in the Eastern churches, much the same thing happened to pupils of Lucian. When the Arian controversy breaks out, we find these men referring to one another as co-Lucianists (*sulloukianoi*), or fellow Lucianists. Among them we find such prominent men as Eusebius of Nicomedia; Theognis, bishop of Nicaea; Maris, bishop of Chalcedon; Arius,[13] who was a priest of Alexandria, and very many more. These all had studied with Lucian and counted themselves members of a fellowship and defenders of a common point of view. When one of them gets into trouble, the others rally to his support. Lucian was put to death in January of 312, and his relics became the center of a martyr cult on which the Arians and their supporters capitalized in the years of controversy that lay ahead.

Harnack, together with many other scholars going back as far as the fourth century, has identified this martyr Lucian with a successor of Paul of Samosata of the same name, and has held, therefore, that the line of proto-Arian thought runs straight through the dynamistic Monarchianism and Adoptionism of Paul into the subordinationism of Arius and his supporters. [It is now generally agreed, however, that they misinterpreted a cursory remark][14] in a letter by Alexander of Alexandria

13. Professor Calhoun followed the scholarly consensus of his time in including Arius among Lucian's pupils, but according to what appears to be the most thorough study of Arius to date, the evidence for this is slim. See Rowan Williams, *Arius: Heresy and Tradition* (London: Darton, Longman, and Todd, 1987) 30–31. In any case, Calhoun and other historians agree that whether or not Arius studied with Lucian, his views, though not without affinities to those of the Lucianists, were also distinctly different. For a recent discussion of what little is known about Lucian, see ibid., 162–67 [ed.].

14. The bracketed material in the text replaces a detailed argument for this point by Professor Calhoun [ed.].

himself to his namesake and colleague Alexander of Byzantium, describing the outbreak of the Arian trouble.[15] Moreover, what we know of Lucian's own theology appears to stand in antithesis to the thought of Paul of Samosata. Paul, as we have noted, was a Monarchian who stressed the unity [non-distinctness] of the Father and Son in the Godhead, who denied the subordination of a concretely existing, individual Logos to the Father. He was an Adoptionist in his Christology, but as regards the Godhead he was Monarchian. But now Lucian of Antioch teaches, as even Harnack recognizes, a Logos theology which is rather clearly subordinationist in its tendency. In other words, this Lucianic theology is more like the theology of those left-wing Origenists who attack and condemn Paul of Samosata than it is like the theology of Paul himself.

The conclusion is that we have in the teaching and the school of Lucian a further development of left-wing Origenism, so that the line from Paul of Samosata in Antioch runs not to Arius but to a continuation of that relatively archaic kind of Syrian thought in which the Son and Father are closely identified. On the other hand, the Logos Christology, if we may use a generic phrase in a specific sense, running through Clement and Origen and then through Origen's left-wing disciples, and thence through Lucian, eventuates finally in Eusebius of Nicomedia and the other Lucianists as well as Arius; these are at the other extreme from the Monarchian views which the Nicene defenders are charged with holding. Paul of Samosata's views, in contrast, are continued rather in the doctrine of Eustathius of Antioch, one of the chief opponents of the Arians, and in Marcellus of Ancyra and his successor Photinus, though these last two men are modalistic rather than dynamistic in their Monarchianism.

The Nicene thinkers attempt to find the proper path between subordinationism which separates the Father and the Son in more and more emphatic terms, and Monarchianism that tends to blur the distinctions between Father and Son and Holy Spirit. But this middle road is a way that is easily identified with Monarchianism by the extremer subordinationists. Sabellianism is the standard charge brought against the defenders of the Nicene theology. We are suggesting, then, that this Lucian who was the teacher of many of the Arian leaders, [even if not

15. Opitz (3) I, 19–29 (*Urkunde*, 14). English translations of Alexander's epistle in *ANF* 6:291–96, and recently also in the convenient anthology of Rusch, trans. and ed., *The Trinitarian Controversy* (Philadelphia: Fortress, 1980) 33–44. It is now generally agreed that the Alexander to whom the letter was sent was bishop of Thessalonica [ed.].

of Arius himself], has a rather clearly identifiable place in an unbroken succession of Hellenistic Logos theologians who tend to be more and more strongly subordinationist as they become more and more concerned about precise definitions and logical consistency. For if one is going to stress the distinction of the Logos from the Father, one will be insisting that the Logos is of another sort of being than the Father. That is in line with the major emphasis in the late-Platonic Alexandrine tendency. It defined God as the utterly incomprehensible Absolute, aloof from all created things, needing therefore to be mediated to the created world by one or more such beings as the Philonic Logos. That is the pattern of thought that we have in this succession.

To describe Lucian's thought in this fashion clearly requires some sort of documentation, and the best evidence available is to be found in a creed adopted and published by a council at Antioch in 341.[16] At the dedication of a new church there under imperial patronage, a council attended chiefly by Arianizing leaders adopted no fewer than four creeds. The second of these is the one that is important for our purpose because it was offered as representing the thought of Lucian, to whom by this time the Arianizers all looked back as their revered teacher. And as Bardy has shown by very ingenious and detailed comparison of the phraseology of this second creed of Antioch of 341 with certain passages in Eusebius of Caesarea's suggested modifications of the creed of his own church which he promoted at Nicaea, the likelihood is that Lucian's thought does form the basis of this second "Dedication" creed. I am inclined myself to think that the first two-thirds or three-quarters of the text probably contain Lucian's thought and quite probably Lucian's words, while the last quarter or so is an addition. There is no point in going in through the whole of it, but a little of it here and there may prove of value.

> We believe, following the evangelical and apostolic tradition, in one God, all-governing Father, the Maker of the universe, and its Creator, and its Planner. And in one Lord Jesus Christ, his only Son, God, through whom are all things; the one begotten before the ages by the Father, God from God, Whole from Whole, Alone from Alone, Perfect from Perfect, King from King, Lord from Lord, Living Word, Living Wisdom, True Light, Way, Truth,

16. Extant fragments of Lucian in Routh, *Reliquiae Sacrae*, 4:1–17. For the text of the second creed, see Gustave Bardy, *Recherches sur saint Lucien d'Antioche* (Paris: Beauchesne, 1936) 92–94.

Resurrection, Shepherd, Door, unchanged and immutable, the exact Image of the Godhead, of the essential being and will and power and glory of the Father, Firstborn of all creatures, being in the beginning with God as it is said in the Gospels.

Now the phrase, "the exact image of the Godhead," which appears in Heb 1:3, becomes a kind of trademark of this brand of Origenist thought, and saves it from Arianism. For Origen, the mirror image of the Father is in every specifiable character the same as the Father, not only exact in all detail, but undeviating and unchanging; it never began to be and never ceases to be this exact counterpart and manifestation of the Father's being. On the other hand, the words which come shortly after, "Firstborn of all creatures," is a phrase the Arians constantly use. Lucian, if it be he who actually is here represented, is wavering in the familiar, fluid manner between the right wing and the left wing in the Origenist position. On the one hand, the Son is himself unalterable, and at that point Lucian is denying Arian doctrine; on the other hand, the Son is the firstborn among all of the created beings—a Pauline phrase, but one which it was easy for the Arianists to turn to their own advantage. It marks Lucian's mode of thought as left-wing Origenist; the right-wing Origenist would have been hesitant to say that because it suggests a beginning for the Son; moreover, it can be taken as implying that the Son is himself a creature. Yet immediately is added, "Being in the beginning with God," which is a swing back to the right-wing side. Then, concluding the section which interests us, inferences are drawn from the baptismal formula. "In the name of the Father and of the Son and of the Holy Spirit," and then it is added: "Plainly the name Father is here used of one who is truly Father, and Son of one who is truly Son, and Holy Spirit of one who is truly Holy Spirit." (These are not three aspects or modes, but three clearly distinguishable individual beings.) "For the names are not used simply or idly as words, but as signs clearly indicating the distinctive character of each, naming the substantial being (*hypostasin*) and the order and the glory; for they are three in *hypostasei* but in concord (or harmony) one."

The temper and character of that statement is quite unmistakable. It is Origenism which still has something of the complexity and ambiguity of original Origenist thought; and yet the emphasis is laid, particularly in these concluding clauses, rather upon the distinctions between the persons in the Godhead and the implied subordination of one to another than upon the unity. The unity is declared to be a unity of concord or harmony, but it is said that there are three beings in respect to *hypostasis* or substantial being.

Lucian the Martyr was not an Arian. Neither was he a dynamistic Monarchian. If the evidence now available be taken as trustworthy, he was a transitional thinker in the school of Origen from whom the Arian leaders were able to learn much, but some of whose phrases become hallmarks of orthodoxy.

# CHAPTER 11

# Theology in the Nicene Age[1]

D URING THE PERIOD OF which we have been speaking, the face of the church was being turned toward happier times by the rise of Constantine, son of the Caesar Constantius, a man who in his dealings with the Christians had been tolerant, fair, and humane. In 323, Constantine succeeded as the sole Augustus of the Empire, and the Christians found themselves not merely tolerated, but favored and given a preferred place among religious groups at the hands of an emperor who, no less than Diocletian, was intent upon the unity of his world. Constantine conceived that the favor of the Christian God had been with him, and he had his name put on the roll of catechumens as a candidate for membership in the church.

Moreover, he became concerned over religious unity in the whole of the territory over which he had become the ruler. He had tried to settle the Donatist controversy on his way toward achievement of imperial power. In 314 a synod was held at Arles in the south of Gaul, at which a vain effort was made to deal with the schism, but the Donatists held to their position and continued to compete in North Africa for membership and church property against the Catholic churches and clergy.

## THE RISE OF ARIANISM

But a much more dangerous threat to the unity of the church and the Empire had broken out in Alexandria in 319. Alexander was the bishop. He was a moderate Origenist who was bothered by Sabellianism but at

---

1. The first sections of this chapter, "The Rise of Arianism" through "Qualified Acceptance of the Creed," are a slightly modified version of chapter 16 of the 1948 LHCD, while the last two sections, are greatly reduced versions of chapters 17 and 18. [ed.].

the same time was cautious about any such subordinationist language as Dionysius of Alexandria had used against it and then retracted. Now Arius, one of the priests of Alexandria, had been a pupil of Lucian.[2] He had studied at Antioch and prided himself on his theological and philosophical training. Moreover, he was a man of great energy, [a presbyter of the most important church in Alexandria, and a popular preacher]. Physically he was an impressive person—tall and eagle-faced and handsome—a man noted for ascetic habits of life. [Later writers report that he] regarded himself as a suitable candidate for the bishopric of Alexandria. Apparently he had been a priest in the church at least a year before Alexander's election as bishop in 313, and he is said to have regarded Alexander as an inferior choice for the position.[3] In particular, he was on the lookout for theological ineptitude in the public pronouncements of the bishop, and it would seem that he criticized him increasingly. Arius was perfectly correct in thinking that Alexander was not too sharp as a theologian. We have a lengthy letter from Alexander to his namesake in Byzantium [Thessalonica][4] which may be well meaning, but without very clean-cut distinction of ideas and of terms. At first, Arius voiced his criticisms in small groups, but then he made them more and more publicly and declared that Alexander was giving away Christian truth to the Sabellians. Alexander put up with this insubordination for a considerable time, but at length the situation developed to such a point that it seemed to him necessary to have Arius disciplined, and he called a synod in 321 which deposed and excommunicated Arius, together with bishops and priests in Alexandria and in the surrounding communities who were inclined to agree with him.

Forthwith Arius began to write letters to his "fellow Lucianists,"[5] some of whom were in positions of very real influence. Among them the one who was most strategically placed was Eusebius, who had been bishop of Beretus (modern Beirut in Lebanon), but had got himself transferred to the much more important city of Nicomedia, the summer residence of

2. See n. 13 in chapter 10.

3. As Arius's contemporaries, including his opponents, make no mention of these reports, they are now generally regarded as later fabrications; yet as Rowan Williams observes, "It is not clear that we can be absolutely certain that all this is pure legend." Williams, *Arius*, 40 [ed.].

4. See n. 15 in chapter 10.

5. See n. 13 in chapter 10.

the imperial household. To him Arius protested the treatment which he had received at the hands of the theologically blundering Alexander, and insisted that the issue which had been raised was the issue of theological clarity and consistency—the demand for a rational theology, as over against the vagueness and inconsistency which theological incompetence had kept alive too long in the church.[6] [Nontheological motives were of course also operative on both sides of the issue and the dissension became, among other things, a major ecclesiastical power struggle.] When word of the controversy came to Constantine, it seemed to him that the chief issue was the reestablishment of harmony and tranquility in the empire; and to that end, of tranquility and unity in the church. Naturally the theological niceties involved were not transparent to the mind of a man who had been a masterful soldier and was now engaged primarily in the extremely difficult administrative tasks of reorganizing a political empire. He sent Hosius of Cordova, who had accompanied him on his journeys in the West as a trusted theological advisor, to Alexandria to talk to both parties to see if they might not get back together again. But by now the rift had become so large that Hosius reported that there was no chance of effecting a reconciliation. The upshot was that the emperor resorted to a very appropriate device, the calling of a synod which was to be representative not merely of the churches of a particular area but of the churches over the entire empire. The first ecumenical council met in the summer of 325 in Nicaea, near the new Byzantine capital.

## THE DOCTRINE OF ARIUS

The position which Arius took was apparently stated in deliberately extreme terms. The creeds adopted by the Arian sympathizers[7] during the later years of the controversy never go as far as the incautious phrasing to which we find Arius committing himself at the beginning, before the Nicene Council had pronounced on the issue. He does this in the let-

---

6. Opitz (3) I, 1–3 (*Urkunde* 1). English translation in *NPNF2* 3:41.

7. Judging by the absence of references to or quotations from Arius in the writings of those their opponents called Arians, these latter should not be thought of as followers or disciples of the heresiarch. In Calhoun's perspective, it will be noticed, they were not directly influenced by Arius but were left-wing Origenists who endorsed neither the Arians nor the Nicene positions and were traditionally called "semi-Arians" or sometimes "Arians" for the most part [ed.].

ter which he wrote in 321 to his old chief Alexander from his refuge in Nicomedia:[8]

> Our faith, which is the faith of our ancestors, and also that which we have learned from you, our dear father, is this: We know one God, alone unbegotten, alone eternal, alone without beginning, alone true, alone having immortality, alone wise, alone good, alone powerful, judge, maker, and ruler of all things, inconvertible and immutable, just and good, God of the law and the prophets and the New Testament; who begat an only Son before the ages of time,

This is a technical Arian phrase, which is deliberately ambiguous. The Logos is created and begotten before time, and yet he is not coeternal with the Father. There was when he was not, and before he was begotten he was not. Not that there was a time before he was begotten; but by using the language of his preexistence before time, the Arians seem to be saying what in fact they do not intend to say—namely that he shared in the eternity of the Godhead. At least one English translation,[9] it should be observed, says "There was a *time* when he was not," which the Arians did not say.

> . . . through whom also he had made the ages and the universe; who begat him not in seeming but in truth; who gave him substance by his own will, inconvertible and immutable, a perfect creature of God but not as one of the created beings.

These phrases become a key in the whole controversy: "inconvertible and immutable" (*atrepton kai analloioton*) and therefore "a perfect creature"; but remember that the inconvertibility and immutability of the Word results from the will of God and not from its own nature. A created being is by nature mutable; and since the Word is described as a creature, it must be mutable by its nature, but by the will of God it acquires immutability. "A perfect creature of God," then, "but not as one of the created beings" (that is to say, the Logos is created in a unique way and all other created beings are subordinated to the Logos.)

---

8. Opitz (3) I, 12–13 (Urkunde 6). Preserved in Athanasius, *De Synodis* 16; English in *NPNF2* 4:458. [Unable to verify source (ed.).]

9. The English translation could not be verified.

... an offspring but not as one of the things begotten; not as Valentinus teaches that the offspring is an emanation from the Father; not as Manichaeus declares that the offspring is a consubstantial part (*meros homoousion*) of the Father; not as Sabellius holds that God is a monad, a being who is at once Father and Son (*huiopater*); not as Hieracas teaches, a fire from a fire or a lamp divided in two; nor yet as one who previously existing is later begotten or recreated as a Son; as you also, my dear father, in the midst of the church and in the assembly very often have condemned those who teach these things; but, as we say, by the will of God created before time and before ages and receiving life and being from the Father, and having his glories established along with him by the Father. For the Father in giving to him the heirship of all things did not divest himself of what he unbegottenly had in himself, for he is the source of all things, so that there are three hypostases [the same sort of phrase that we find in Lucian]. And God, being the cause of all things, is most uniquely without beginning, but the Son, begotten not temporally by the Father, and created and established before the ages was not before he was begotten, but non-temporally begotten before all things, he is given substance only by the Father.

There is the crucial issue between the Arians and the Nicene defenders. The Son is declared by both of them to be a preexistent being as Son—not simply as Logos but as Son; but that preexistence, declared by one group to be eternal, is declared by the other group to be of such sort as to have a beginning. The Father alone is without beginning, the Father alone is eternal. But the Son has his beginning uniquely from the Father and is at all points dependent upon the Father.

For he is not eternal nor co-eternal nor co-ungenerate with the Father, nor does he have his being with the Father, as some say, relationally,

That is, in calling the Father Father, the right-wing Origenists held, one has already implied that he has a Son, so that the being of the Son is just as eternal as the being of the Father. If God is properly called Father, the implication of that name is that the Son is already there "relationally."

... introducing two unbegotten principles; but God as Monad and Principle of all things is before all. So he is before the Son, as indeed we have learned from you preaching in the midst of the

Church. But the Son has his being from God and his glories and his life, and since all things have been transmitted to him, God is his Source. For he is over him, as his God, since he is before him. But if any should take the words "of him," or "from the womb," or "I came from the Father and I am come," as meaning a consubstantial part (*meros homoousion*) of the Father, or an emanation (*probole*), or as some hold, they make the Father composite, and mutable and changeable, and a body, and as far as their views are held, the incorporeal God would have the properties of body.

As far as we can judge from this statement, the Arians represent an extreme form of that subordinationist strain in Hellenistic, and specifically Origenistic, thought which urges the absolute uniqueness of the absolute God (the Father) and declares that all other beings, even the Logos, must be put in another category as having not the essential being of deity but the essential status of creature. In one of his attacks on the Arian position, Athanasius includes a kind of convenient [though polemically slanted] summary of the views these men held.[10] They held, in line with the old Alexandrine position, that God is the utterly remote absolute Unity (the Monad) who is alone to be called unbegotten or ingenerate as well as uncreated; who is wholly aloof from all created things so that no created being can be like God in any important way. There is alongside God, who is properly to be called Father as well as Creator, a demiurgic power, the Logos of God, called also by the Arians Only Son (*monogenes huios*), who is not only begotten but also created. He is one of the creatures, though his creation is not like the creation of other beings since it is the work of the Father alone. Other beings come into existence through him; he is the agent in the creation of the world. Nevertheless, he is to be accounted as one who himself had a beginning—not a beginning in time but a beginning of such sort that it can properly be said of him that once he was not; there was when he was not (*en hote ouk en*). It can be said of him also that he had his beginning from what is not; he is to be spoken of as "of what is not" (*ex ouk onton*). He is a creature, therefore, as well as Son, although the first-born of all creatures and the one through whom all other creatures came to be. He is a "second God" (*deuteros theos*"—Philo's term), and may properly be worshipped because we are his crea-

10. See Athanasius' first oration against the Arians. Critical edition by William Bight, *The Orations of St. Athanasius against the Arians According to the Benedictine Text* (Oxford: Clarendon, 1873). English: *NPNF2* 4.

tures, even though from the standpoint of the absolute deity of the Father, the Son must be regarded as not in the full and true sense deity. He is on a lower level even though he stands in the position of mediating between the absolute God and the created world. When he becomes incarnate, he takes a human body—not a human spirit—and his work as Redeemer is carried out, therefore, as the work of one who is neither fully God nor fully man. He is not fully God because the Logos is God only relatively and derivatively. He is not fully man because there is no human mind and spirit but only a human body in his makeup.

These Arian tenets are stated not only in the confessional formula just examined but still more extravagantly in certain popular verses Arius wrote to make his views more widely accessible. Here is the account that Athanasius gives of the *Thalia*, these curious theological jingles, including the text of some of them, in his relatively late work *On the Synods of Ariminum and Seleucia*.[11]

> God himself then is in his own nature ineffable (unknowable) to all men. Equal or like (*homoion*) himself or the same in glory he alone has none. Ingenerate (*agenneton*) we call him because of him who is generate (*genneton*) by nature. We praise him as without beginning, because of him who has a beginning. And adore him who is everlasting, because of him who in time (*en chrono*) has come to be.

I doubt that Arius customarily said that. He prided himself on carefully avoiding the cruder expressions of those who think that there is here a chronological priority rather than one of being.

> The Unbegun made the Son the beginning of things originated [that alludes directly to the Arians' favorite proof text, Proverbs 8:22, which we shall examine later] and brought him to be his own Son by adoption. He has nothing proper to God in his own substantial being (*kath' hypostasin*), for he is not equal, no, nor one in essence with him (*homoousios auto*). Wise is God for he is the teacher of wisdom. There is full proof that God is invisible to all being; both to things which are through the Son and to the Son himself he is invisible. Now I say expressly: How is the invisible seen by the Son? By that power by which the Father sees, the Son

---

11. Athanasius, *Epistula de synodis Arimini in Italia et Seleuciae in Isauria* in Opitz (2) I, 231–78. English translation in *NPNF2* 4: 448–80. Critical edition of the *Thalia* by Gustave Bardy, "La Thalie d'Arius," *Revue de Philologie* 53 (1927) 211–33.

in his own measure is permitted (*hypomenei*) to see the Father, as far as is right. Thus there is a Triad, not in equal glory; their substances (*hypostaseis*) are not intermingled with one another; one is infinitely more glorious in glory than another. Alien to the Son in essence (*xenas kat ousian*) is the Father, for he is without beginning. Know that the Monad was, but the Dyad was not, before it existed. It follows at once that though the Son was not, the Father was God. Hence the Son, who was not (for he existed at the will of the Father), is God Only-begotten (*monogenes theos*), and he is other than either [the Father or his will].

This is a very characteristic Arian statement. Wisdom is the subordinate being. God was wise even before he produced wisdom, and consequently his wisdom is superior to the wisdom which he produces. Relatively, the Son is granted some knowledge of God, but by his own nature he has no direct access to God. The Father is different in nature from the Son as well as from all lesser creatures. God always was, but in unity; and the duality which involves Father and Son was a secondary and subsequent rather than an original and essential characteristic of God. Summing up, the Son is brought into being by the Father's will, and so would not have been begotten if the Father had willed otherwise. Athanasius, on the contrary, insists that the Son is begotten of the Father's essential being, and so is just as inextricable and essential a member of the Godhead as the Father himself.

The passage that Athanasius quotes from the *Thalia* goes on in this strain to a further length about equal to that of the section just cited. The doctrine is unmistakable, and the manner in which it is set forth is deliberately provocative. Arius is challenging Alexander, his bishop, who seems to him a vague and clumsy thinker, supported only by "unlearned" and more or less heretical colleagues. Arius is concerned to develop a theology that will appeal to the mind of a fully trained modern man. He considers himself a spokesman for the Christian doctrine that can meet the tests of students and not merely appeal to the ignorant.

The favorite Scripture to which the Arians appealed as a support for their doctrine was a part of the speech of Wisdom, at Prov 8:22, which in the Septuagint reads: "The Lord created me (*ektisen me*) the beginning of his ways, unto his works." (The Hebrew verb could bear this meaning, or it might mean simply *possessed*.) The passage continues: "Before the world (*pro tou aionos*) he established me. In the beginning (*en arche*) before the earth was made, before the abysses were made, before the springs of waters issued forth, before the mountains were produced, and before all hills he begat me (*gennaei me*). . . ." (Prov 8:23–25). The whole speech of Wisdom had, of course, long been accepted as a basis for affirming the existence of the divine Logos, and this the Arians affirm. But they focus attention upon v. 22 and insist on the literal sense of the LXX phrase, "He created me." It was, in fact, an awkward phrase for those who defended the anti-Arian position. About all that Athanasius can do in rebuttal is to insist with stubbornness on the other phrase in v. 25, "He begat me," and to urge that this, not the earlier expression, gives the true meaning of the passage. Wisdom is begotten indeed, but not created.

The Arians continued in the interval between the synod in Alexandria in 321 that deposed Arius and his Libyan adherents and the general council of Nicaea in 325 to exchange letters and to work out an agreed common position. Eusebius of Nicomedia was the recognized leader of the party. Arius was steadfastly supported by his two Libyan friends, Theonas and Secundus, who to the end refused scornfully to compromise or to recant. Theognis of Nicaea and Marius of Chalcedon were likewise in an inner core of Arian leadership; and a dozen others—Eastern churchmen, some of them pupils of Lucian, all of them strenuously opposed to Sabellianism—rounded out the Arian faction at Nicaea.

## The Council of Nicaea

The great council, the first assembly representing the entire Church, convened in May and adjourned in August 325. It was called by the Emperor Constantine, who offered transportation and food at public expense to churchmen from all parts of the Roman world. Accounts of the number who came vary from "more than 250" to 318—the last, a figure of mystical significance (we recall the 318 men of Abraham's household, and the interpretation of that number in the *Letter of Barnabas*) to be viewed with some suspicion. Roughly, 300 churchmen may have assembled as delegates, besides many companions not seated in the council. Among the number were confessors widely known as heroic victims of the persecutions under Diocletian and Maximian. Some, like the church historian Eusebius of Caesarea, a warm admirer of Origen though not one of his pupils, were learned men; and others, like Eustathius of Antioch, were competent theologians. The great majority were practical churchmen, not well equipped for intricate theological debate. Very few came from the West. Pope Sylvester of Rome, too aged to risk the journey, was represented by two presbyters. Caecilian of Carthage was present. But the outstanding Western cleric was Hosius of Cordova, the emperor's confidant and counselor, and a most influential participant in the work of the assembly.

In the makeup of the council, those who supported Arius, as already noted, seem to have numbered seventeen. Those who supported Alexander numbered about thirty, if we include the score of signers of the Alexandrine decree of 321 deposing Arius. Obviously the two parties together made up only a small fraction of the council. The overwhelming majority occupied a middle position, which was conservative chiefly in the sense that the emperor himself was conservative: they were concerned with the tranquility of the status quo. Most were Origenists of one sort or another, practical churchmen who had not given too much attention to theological niceties, and were not quite sure precisely what the issue was that had so disturbed Alexander and his supporters.

The leader of the Arian group was Eusebius of Nicomedia. He was leader partly because of his superior ecclesiastical position; but partly because of the acumen and vigor of his mind and his extraordinary diplomatic resourcefulness, which comes out in the years after the council had judged his position to be wrong. By a kind of polite understanding Alexander of Alexandria was recognized as the leader of the opposite group; but actually by reason of sheer intellectual abililty and aggressiveness the leader was Eustathius of Antioch, a biblical scholar who held a doctrinal position close to that of the Monarchians—if he was not in fact himself one of them—with Hosius of Cordova holding about equal rank. The leader of the middle party was the cautious Origenist Eusebius of Caesarea. Others among the defenders of Alexander were Marcellus of Ancyra, Macarius of Jerusalem, and Alexander's secretary, the young Alexandrian deacon Athanasius. Athanasius was present with both eyes open and all his senses alert, but he was as yet without prestige in the Church.

We have only Athanasius' eyewitness account of what went on in the council, so that it is a little precarious to try to reconstruct in detail the sequence of events.[12] What appears to have happened is something like

---

12. Athanasius, *Epistula de decretis Nicaenae Synod* in Opitz (2) I, 1–5. Also in a separate edition, Hans-Georg Opitz, *Athanasius: über die Entscheidungen des Konzils von*

this. The council assembles, and praise to the emperor is the first order of the day. The church feels itself secure for the first time in its three centuries of history. The emperor himself, though he is only a catechumen, is invited to sit as a member of the council with Hosius, no doubt, at his elbow. The first major item of business brought before the council is the debate between the Alexandrine followers of Alexander and the followers of Arius. After some preliminary alignment of parties, the Arians are confronted with various biblical texts that seem to affirm the full deity of the Son. The Arians are quite ready to accept all the traditional affirmations. They can interpret all the biblical phrases in their own sense without the least difficulty. The anti-Arians quoted various texts against them: "Christ is the wisdom and the power of God." But, says Athanasius, you could see the members of the Arian party raising their eyebrows and winking at one another, signaling, "Yes, we can accept that; after all, the book of Job speaks of locusts and caterpillars as a great power of God." "Lo, I am with you always"—ah, yes, but it is said that we who believe shall be always. "The Son is from God"—but then all things are from God, and so on right down the list. There isn't a single text of Scripture that the Arians are not able to interpret in their own manner and so to accept in a sense which the majority of those present regarded as unacceptable.

Now they are called upon to make a statement of their own, and Eusebius of Nicomedia presents an Arian creed. The word that we have is that it so incensed the members of the assembly that they snatched it out of Eusebius' hands and tore it to pieces. So historians unfortunately do not have the text of that statement examined earlier in this chapter. In any case, once the Arian view is made plain and explicit, it is evident that even the majority party wanted nothing to do with it. Then a further attempt is made to find some basis upon which to condemn the position of those who have now clearly shown themselves to be out of accord with the understanding of Christianity held by the majority. But test after test is proposed without the slightest wavering in the readiness of the Arian group to accept everything. The second-century creeds such as the Old Roman Symbol are of no use here.

Now Eusebius of Caesarea, who was much more eminent as a churchman and scholar than he was as a theologian, offers a compro-

---

*Nicaea. De decretis Nicaenae Synodi.* Sonderdruck für Seminarübungen. (Berlin, 1935). English translation in *NPNF2* 4:150–72.

mise. There is, he says, an ancient creed of the church of Caesarea which was used when he himself was baptized long years before, and which has everywhere been regarded as a most orthodox statement of faith; and he asks permission to read this creed as a basis upon which perhaps the whole assembly can agree. He then proceeds to read the creed of Caesarea and to add to it certain interpretative phrases of his own. This creed [or a creed of the same type] was presented to the council as a basis for compromise, but was referred instead to a group of theologians for revision into the Nicene Creed that made compromise impossible. We have the Caesarean creed preserved both by Athanasius in his work *de Decretis* and by Theodoret in his *Church History*, and so we are on fairly secure ground when we present it as they record it.[13]

> We believe in one God, all-governing Father, maker of all things without exception (*ton hapanton*), visible and invisible. And in one Lord Jesus Christ the Logos of God, God from God, Light from Light, Life from Life, only-begotten Son, firstborn of all creatures, who before all ages was begotten of the Father, through whom also all things (*ta panta*) came to be; one who for our salvation was made flesh and dwelt among men; suffered, rose the third day, ascended to the Father, whence he shall come again in glory to judge living and dead. We believe also in one Holy Spirit.

To the text of this creed Eusebius appears to have added certain explanatory remarks. Whether they were in the original creed is impossible to say, but the probability seems against that.

> Each of these we believe to be and to exist, the Father truly as Father, and the Son truly as Son, and the Holy Spirit truly as Holy Spirit, as the Lord himself has shown us in the commission to his disciples: "Go and make disciples of all peoples, baptizing them in the name of the Father and of the Son and of the Holy Ghost."

Now this text, says Eusebius, was at once recognized by all as most orthodox; and in fact, so it was. There is nothing in any part of the statement which could offend a good Christian. Everyone said, "That

---

13. Caesarean creed preserved by Athanasius, *Decr.* (See previous note) PG 20, 1537; English translation in *NPNF2* 4:74–6; Socrates, *Hist. eccl.* 1, 8 (PG, 67, 68); Theodoret, *Hist. eccl.* 1, 12. (Eusebius' claim that what he presented to the council was the baptismal creed of his own Caesarean diocese is now discredited. The most that can be determined is that it was a "local baptismal creed of Syro-Palestinian provenance." Jaroslav Pelikan, *The Christian Tradition* (Chicago: University of Chicago Press, 1971) 1:201 [ed.].)

is wonderful; that is what we all believe"—including Arius and all his friends. You can see how easy it would be to interpret in an Arianizing sense everything which is here said.

"We believe in one God, Father all-governing." Yes. One God who is alone unbegotten and absolute. "Creator of all things without exception." The peculiar terminology here (*ton ton hapanton . . . poieton*) plays straight into the hands of the Arian group. He is the Creator of "all" things, and they could say to themselves in parenthesis, "including the Son." "And in one Lord Jesus Christ, the Logos of God." Yes. This was their customary way of speaking of him, leaving open, you see, the possibility of saying that the Logos precedes in existence his becoming Son; *Son* can be regarded in this total pattern as a not merely subordinate but subsequent title. "God from God"—God in a secondary sense from God in a primary sense, i.e., God viewed from our standpoint, but not necessarily God viewed from God's standpoint. The same consideration applies to "Light from Light, Life from Life"—perfectly good Johannine phraseology all the way through—nobody can quarrel with it! "Only Son (*monogenes huios*) was a phrase which they themselves were willing to use, construing the term *unique* as meaning that the Son is unlike all other created beings. He is alone derived directly from the Father, and then all other things are derived through him. "Firstborn of every creature" was a particularly happy phrase. As the firstborn of created beings, he was numbered among the created beings, which was just what they wanted to affirm. Once again, good Pauline language is used; who can reject it? "Begotten of the Father before all worlds." Yes. He was preexistent, begotten not in time, but before time. But once again in a little mental parenthesis, "nevertheless not coeternal with the Father." They had rejected that side of Origen's thought and were insisting on the subordinationist side of it, which we've been calling, following a lengthy precedent, the left wing of Origenist theology. "Through whom all things came to be." The world was created through him, but he himself was created by the Father. "Who for our salvation was made flesh." It is not said "was made man," but "was made flesh." He assumed the body that is characteristic of human life, but not the spirit of a true man. "He dwelt among men." This is a useful phrase. "He dwelt among men"; not being a man, but living as a companion of men. He suffered and rose and ascended "to the Father," who was the one from whom he had come and to whom he now returned. This was a creed perfectly adapted to acceptance by everybody from the extreme right to the extreme left. It was a reproduction of that body of confessional material which in the form of the Old Roman Symbol or in other forms (such as the creed of Jerusalem on which Cyril's catechetical lectures are based in the middle of the fourth century) had been very widespread among the churches.

This creed, so Eusebius says, was affirmed by the most gracious emperor himself to be obviously most orthodox. The emperor was not yet a member of the church, and it is not hard to guess his probable expertness in these matters. Of course, what Eusebius meant is that the emperor welcomed what looked like a chance to get everybody to agree. That was what he wanted. He was not concerned about the theological issue, which he did not understand. What he was concerned about was that the controversy should be quieted down and that the church be brought once again into something like full unity.

## THE NICENE CREED

Precisely because the Arians could accept this creed so easily, the defenders of the position of Alexander were determined that it should not be made the definition of faith by this council. It repeated all of the familiar traditional and theologically acceptable affirmations, but in such a way that the Arians could pretty well do with it what they did with the Scriptural text; they could understand it in their own way. Eusebius remarks that after the emperor had affirmed that this is a most orthodox and excellent statement of faith, he suggested one little modification. He thought that it would be well if the term *homoousion* could somehow be included in that creed. Now *homoousios* was the term which Arius, in both of the statements which we have examined, declared to be unacceptable. In his regular confession of faith he affirms that the term *homoousion* is a Manichean term. It suggests division of a material substratum. In the *Thalia* he says, "We are not prepared to affirm that the Son is of the same essence with the Father" (*homoousios autoi*).[14] So, in suggesting that *homoousion* be put in the creed, the most gracious emperor is suggesting nothing less than that the acceptability of the creed to everybody shall be torpedoed.

Why Constantine should have thought of that addition is an interesting question. The most plausible suggestion that I know is Harnack's—

14. Arius, *Thalia*, in Athanasius, *Syn.* 15 (see n. 11).

that Hosius of Cordova "whispered" it to him. Hosius was from the West, where Tertullian's work against Praxeas had long before emphatically described the Trinity as "of one substance (*unius autem substantiae*) and of one status and power." We recall that in the third-century exchange of letters between Dionysius of Rome and Dionysius of Alexandria, the Alexandrine bishop was skidding a little in the direction of subordinationism. He used unfortunate metaphors in combating Sabellianism and declined to speak of Father and Son as *homoousios*. Dionysius of Rome, in contrast, employed this term without hesitation as corresponding to the Tertullianic *unius substantiae*. Apparently Hosius had been brought up in that way of thinking about God. And if he suggested to the emperor the desirability of putting in *homoousion*, he was suggesting the addition of a term which had, in a sense, been familiar in his part of the church for a long time.[15]

If Hosius suggested putting *homoousion* into this statement, he was pretty clearly intending that the statement be thoroughly revised, so as to avoid the glaring contradiction of saying, "of the same substance with the Father" in the midst of a statement which otherwise suggested subordinationist views. The revision was carried out, and a creed was reported back for consideration and action by the council. In it the inclusion of the term *homoousion* led to a number of other very eloquent revisions. The result of that process of revision was more or less like this:[16]

> We believe in one God, all-sovereign Father . . .

That is far too ancient and long-accepted a phrase to be dispensed with; but instead of saying now "the maker of everything without exception," which too easily could be understood to include the Son, we say simply,

---

15. Professor Calhoun is here following A. Harnack's (and before him, T. Zahn's) theory of the Western origin of the Nicene use of *homoousios*, but this has been discredited in the most thorough study to date of the terminological background of the Nicene Creed, Christopher Stead's *Divine Substance* (Oxford: Clarendon, 1977), especially 251–56. Stead persuasively argues that Hosius' role was minimal, and that *homoousios* was not employed at Nicaea in the sense of Tertullian's *unius substantiae*. With the second point, Calhoun obviously agrees, given what he says about Tertullian. The main difference between the two is that what Calhoun takes to be the intention of the Council, Stead describes as a consequence: "Theologians have been rightly convinced that the ultimate effect of Nicaea has been to assert, not merely the equality, but also the essential unity, of the three Persons" (251) [ed.].

16. Text of Nicene Creed in Athanasius, *Decr.* (see n. 13).

> Maker of all things (*panton*) visible and invisible. And in one Lord
> Jesus Christ, the Son of God . . .

The phrase "Logos of God" had been used by most of the subordinationists, so this more familiar Biblical phrase was substituted for it. Now if
we are going to carry on the connotation of that word *Son*, we had better
get the statement about his being begotten brought from its position later
in the creed and placed in direct conjunction with the word *Son*. So we
continue:

> Begotten of the Father uniquely, that is, of the essential being (*ek
> tes ousios*) of the Father . . .

This is what it means when we say that he is begotten uniquely. He is begotten in a different way from all the finite sons of God who are adopted.
He is begotten uniquely because he alone is "of the *ousia*" of the Father.
Next we drop out all reference to "the firstborn of all creatures." To keep
that phrase would be to ask for trouble.

> God from God, Light from Light . . .

Now instead of the ambiguous "Life from Life," which can mean all things
to all people, we say something which really hits the target:

> True God from True God . . .

not relative or derivative, or secondary, or verbally affirmed, but full
intrinsic Deity; and while we're about it, let's make a distinction which
hitherto has not sharply and finally been made, between begetting and
creating:

> Begotten, not made, of one substance (*homoousion*) with the
> Father, through whom also all things came to be . . .

Now just by way of making doubly sure that we are giving the Son such a
place that no one will suppose that he is in some sense to be less honored
than the Father, let's expand this a little bit and say:

> Those things that are in the heaven and those things that are on
> earth . . .

So far, you see, we've been talking about the Godhead, for it was about
the Godhead that this dispute had primarily arisen. Now we talk about
the Incarnation, and we make a change from the Caesarean statement—a

change which doesn't really alter the theological sense, but which does alter the temper and spirit.

> Who for us men and for our salvation came down, [implying that he had already been above with God] and was made flesh, and was made man (*enanthropopesanta*) . . .

That is the essential Christological addition in the creed. We recall perhaps the corresponding term in that Origenistic synod of Antioch in 269 which had condemned Paul of Samosata, and which used the term *enanthropopesanta* ("he became man"). Origen insisted that the Incarnation involved first the assumption of a rational soul and then the assumption of a human body, and any suggestion that there is an assumption only of the human body is to be rejected.

> Suffered, rose the third day, ascended into the heaven, [rather than "to the Father," which might carry a faint suggestion of subordinationism] whence he will come again in glory to judge living and dead. We believe also in one Holy Spirit.

Then after the Arian position was convincingly excluded, we find the council adding at the end of its creed some anathemas by way of making doubly certain that there is no misunderstanding of what they had intended to do:

> And those who say, "There was when he was not," and "Before he was begotten he was not," and that "He came to be of what is not," or that the Son of God is "of another substance or essence" (*ex heteras hypostaseos e ousias*) . . .

(*Hypostaseos* and *ousias* are used, you see, in synonomous fashion: the one and the other both refer to fundamental being in the Godhead.)

> Or that he is "a creature" or that he is "changeable" or "alterable," the Catholic Church anathematizes them.

Plainly enough the supporters of Arius were put in an extremely difficult position. They faced now three crucial statements which are genuinely new: *gennethenta ou poiethenta* ("begotten, not made," distinguishing between begetting and coming to be); *ek tes ousias tou patros* ("of the essential being of the Father"); and then of course *homoousion toi patri*. Theologically these are touchstones of this new formula. The older formulas couldn't deal with the kinds of questions that the Arians were raising—the far subtler sort of deviation from traditional teaching that the Arians represented. And when I say *deviation*, I have in mind the fact that as soon as their position was explicitly stated, it was rejected right straight across the board; even the conservatives in the middle said that this was not what they believed. The question was whether the Arians would subscribe to this revised creed or whether they would refuse. In the upshot, all but three members of the council subscribed. The weight of the emperor's prestige as the first imperial ruler who had tolerated and favored the church was a kind of pressure hard to resist. Arius, who as only a priest was not expected to sign, and his two Libyan friends, Theonas and Secundus, who stayed with him through thick and thin, refused. Eusebius of Nicomedia, Theognis of Nicaea, and Maris of Chalcedon signed the creed but not the anathemas. Everyone else signed both, including Eusebius of Caesarea and the whole great middle party, who regarded him as their best spokesman. Those who refused to sign were by the act of the council anathematized, and that meant deposed and excommunicated.

Then Constantine takes a hand again. By way of sustaining and extending the action by the ecclesiastical council, he adds the political penalty of banishment, which is something completely new. Hitherto the Christians had been at odds with the empire, and now suddenly the power of the empire is declared to be ready to add its own sanctions to the spiritual sanctions of the Christian community. So it would appear that the Arian position has been definitely crushed. And the council goes on to other affairs. Yet within five years, we shall find the Arian leaders back from banishment, engaged in counterattacks upon Eustathius of Antioch and upon Athanasius, who in 328 succeeded Alexander as bishop of Alexandria, and winning support for a long period of years. That is one of the most interesting of the problems in the development of early Christian thought.

## QUALIFIED ACCEPTANCE OF THE CREED

After the adoption of the creed, Eusebius of Caesarea found himself seriously embarrassed by the action in which he had taken a leading though an increasingly reluctant part. Consequently, he felt it necessary to write a long letter to the people of the church of Caesarea explaining what he had done and why.[17] He assured them that before he had signed, he had been at great pains to understand the meanings of the new and unfamiliar phrases which had been added, such as "of the essential being of the Father," "of one substance with the Father," "begotten, not made," as well as the phrases in the anathemas.

"We were assured," he said in substance,

> that the phrase "of the essential being of the Father" did not mean that the Son is a part of the Father's substance, but merely that while he is "of the Father" this is not in the same sense that other created beings are "of the Father." As regards the statement "begotten, not made," we were assured that this was simply to call attention to the fact that the Son stands in a different relation to the Father from that in which the created world stands. As to the phrase "identical in essential being" (*homoousion*), careful inquiry convinced us that this does not mean that there is a material substratum which is divided between the Father and the Son, but merely that this is one more way of insisting that the Son is closer to the Father than are other created beings. Now regarding the anathemas, to state that it is false doctrine to say that the Son comes to be "of what is not" is an affirmation with which we agree. For after all, we are agreed that in the strict sense nothing comes from what is not, but all things are of God, including the Son. To say that the Son is not "of any *ousia* or *hypostasis*" but that of the Father is to say what we all believe. He is "of the Father." To affirm that it is false doctrine to say that "there was when he was not," or that "before he was begotten he was not," is understood to refer to his existence before his human birth, and we all agree he existed before that birth.

"Furthermore," said Eusebius, "the emperor himself pointed out that before Christ existed he existed virtually (*dynamei*) in the mind of the Father. Consequently, with all these assurances we signed the statement and believe that we were right in so doing."

This was an extremely melancholy performance. It is difficult to suppose that Eusebius did not realize how slippery and uncandid this statement of his would appear to those members of the council who knew what they were talking about. Those historians who have tried to play fair with him have suggested that his own thinking was just muddled. He was a left-wing Origenist who was most afraid of anything that suggested

17. In Athanasius, *Decr.* (see n. 12).

Sabellianism. His people were accustomed to the same sort of thought, and what he is chiefly inclined to do is to assure them that he has not sold them down the river into a forthright affirmation of Sabellian thought. Beyond that, the more friendly critics suggest that he did not understand the significance of the issues involved. I find myself inclined to be more severe than that. Granted that Eusebius was not primarily a theologian, it seems to me quite inescapable that the particular verbal dodges which he employs in this letter must have appeared to him to be dodges, and that he signed as a matter of expediency and not of conviction.

However, this letter of his is important not primarily because it reveals the uneasiness of a single mind, but because it represents a point of view which turned out to be quite common after the council adjourned. In the atmosphere of Nicaea, confronted with the naked statement of Arian principles which had been revolting to them, in the presence of the emperor and faced by the steady and effective presentation of the case for the creed that the leaders of Nicaea had kept before them, these bishops and priests had thought that signing the creed was the right thing to do. Now they scatter to their homes and take up again the habits of an anti-Monarchian theology. At home, more and more of them begin to wonder whether they had been hypnotized and led to say something that they did not really mean at all. Here as in certain later councils, a thing has happened which was bound to make trouble for the church: a brand-new confessional statement was produced which nowhere had existed before and which included terminology that is not to be found in the Scriptures, that certain admired teachers of the past like Dionysius of Alexandria had found dangerous, and that was associated (as in the case of *homoousion*) with Valentinian Gnostics, Manicheans, and Sabellians.

## Increasing Arian Influence

It is certain that the new creed contains some very dangerous language indeed. It is clear that it contains language more acceptable to right-wing Origenists and Monarchians than to the left-wing Origenists who made up the majority of Eastern churchmen. It was a statement which a clear-headed, able, and devoted minority group, aided by the backlash against the bold statement of Arian views by Eusebius of Nicomedia, had succeeded [with the Emperor's help] in making acceptable to a majority who did not really believe in it. Now that majority is back on home grounds and badly worried over what had been done. The result is a steady swing away from the decisions of Nicaea, so that for a period of approximately thirty years there is a rising tide of Arian sentiment throughout the Near East. Aided by sympathetic emperors, the Arian tide reached its climax in 357 at the Second Council of Sirmium with a new and at times forthright statement of anti-Nicene doctrine.[18]

This second creed of Sirmium, which we have only in a Latin version, is in part a skillfully evasive document, but the passage which comes just in the middle is unambiguous and crucial.

> For that indeed some—nay, many—are concerned about the term *substantia* which in Greek is called *ousia*, that is, as one may say more expressly *homoousion*, or what is called *homoiousion*.

That is, "same" or, less expressly, "like" in essential being to the Father. The full-scale Nicene defenders stuck to the first term, while some more moderate right-wingers preferred the second.

> Of these terms absolutely no mention ought to be made (*nullam omnino fieri oportere mentionem*), nor should any one preach of these matters; for this reason, that they are not contained in Holy Scriptures, and that the matter is above human knowledge, nor is any one able to tell concerning the birth of the Son, of whom it is written "Who shall tell of his generation?".... there is no ambiguity, the Father is greater; no one can be in doubt that the Father in honor and dignity, in glory and majesty, and in his very name of Father is greater than the Son, who himself bears witness "he who sent me is greater than I"—and this no Catholic will fail to recognize, that there are two persons of Father and Son, the greater the Father, the Son subject with all those things which the Father has made subject to him. The Father has no beginning; he is invisible; he is immortal; he is impassible; but the Son is begotten of the Father, God from God, Light from Light [very God from very God?—not a bit of it], the generation of whom as Son, as has already been said, no one knows except the Father himself.

Now there is a statement which nobody could possibly misunderstand. The language used at Nicaea is to be prohibited.[19] To make mat-

---

18. The 1948 LHCD, unlike the records of lectures from other years, contains a lengthy account (in vol. 1:152–55) of the events leading up to 357. This account is here omitted [ed.].

19. August Hahn, *Bibliothek der Symbole und Glaubensregehen der Alten Kirche*, 3rd

ters worse, the emperor at that time, Constantius II, had summoned the aged Hosius from Spain to Sirmium, where he was detained for a year. According to Athanasius and the church historian Socrates, the veteran Nicene leader, now a hundred years old, was beaten and tortured until he was broken and compelled to sign the blatant Arian creed. (Hilary of Poitiers, who joins with another Gallic bishop, Phoebadius of Agenum, in calling it the "Blasphemy of Sirmium," regards Hosius as one of its authors, but Athanasius' and Socrates' account is the more plausible.) The Nicene cause for the first time seemed hopelessly lost.

## Defeat of Arianism

The beginnings of a reversal of fortunes came, however, with extraordinary promptitude. Regional synods opposed in various degrees to Sirmium began meeting almost immediately; and the death in 360 of Constantius, an imperial supporter of the Arians, was followed by the accession of Julian who, while not siding against them, leveled the playing field to their disadvantage.

Julian came to be known as the Apostate—a sufficiently dishonorable name for one whose action, judged in its own context, is understandable and even admirable. He had been reared in an atmosphere in which the continual bickering between factions in the Christian church had seemed to him to contrast in a most deplorable way with the tranquility, the reasonableness, the humanity of what he learned in Neoplatonism. He had been tutored in Neoplatonic philosophy; he had written works in which Neoplatonism was set forth; and when he came to the throne in 361, he undertook a very exalted type of thinking in an empire which, as it seemed to him, the church, or at least the churchmen, was leading toward ruin. The first step in a rather devious campaign toward that end was to recall from banishment representatives both of Nicene orthodoxy— including Athanasius—and of extreme Arianism. Apparently his notion was that if he maintained a completely judicial calm in the presence of the fighting groups, they would kill one another off and ruin the church, so that the way would be open for the restoration of pagan wisdom. Julian's accidental death in 363 ended that dream.

Meanwhile in 362, Athanasius, who had thus been recalled from exile, headed a council in Alexandria which took a very far-sighted and

---

ed. (repr. Hildesheim: Olms, 1962) §161, 199–201.

portentous step. He and his companions recognized legitimate diversity among those who did not find it possible to agree fully with their own position. This was part of a reshuffling of party lines which contributed to the defeat of Arianism and the reaffirmation of Nicaea. The original lineup of Arians, left-wing Origenists (the great majority), and the old defenders of Nicaea was replaced under the pressure of tactical maneuvering by groups to which may be applied three ancient and one modern label: Anomoian, Homoian, Homoiousian, and Neo-Nicene.

Anomoians were extreme and consistent Arian thinkers who declared quite frankly that the Son is essentially unlike the Father (*anomoios kat' ousian*). Since he is a creature and since the Father is the Creator, the Son, in his essential being, must be affirmed to be unlike the Father. They go farther and say, unlike not only in essential being but in goodness. The Son is fallible and changeable. The early Arians had said that, but these extreme Arians stress it and make it central. The Son is capable of sin [not that He in fact ever did sin]. He is unlike the Father, not only in essential being, but "in all respects" (*kata ta panta*). The men who take that position include Aetius of Antioch and his pupil Eunomius of Cyzicus. They stand out in the later controversy as honorable men, in the sense that they are entirely candid and consistent in affirming what appears to be necessitated by the theological premises with which they start. They are not shifty. They are steadily and frankly committed to a view which seems to them inescapable.

Secondly, there are the so-called Homoians. Here we have the names of men like the three bishops who were especially active in the Council of Sirmium in 357, Ursacius, Valens, together with Germinius, Eudoxius (who started as bishop of Germanicia and then became bishop of Constantinople), and Acacius of Antioch (a pupil and successor of Eusebius of Caesarea), and a great many more. What these men say is that the Son is "like the Father" (*homoios to patri*). Sometimes they add, like the Father "according to the Scriptures." Now that phraseology is deliberately slippery and evasive. They are trying to avoid putting themselves in the out-and-out position of the consistent Anomoians. They want to keep the good will of the conservatives, that Origenistic majority in the East, who had always been theologically vague and can perhaps be taken in by language that is not too blunt. The difficulty with Eusebius of Nicomedia's statement in the Nicene Council was that it called a spade a spade. It said exactly what the Arians affirmed and what they denied;

and we remember what happened to the statement. These Homoians are unwilling to risk that kind of rejection. They prefer to use language that will seem to be conciliatory and cautious, staying within the bounds of what the traditional view would approve. And the phrase "according to the Scriptures" is one of the most characteristic and ignoble of the devices that these men employ.

I suppose that we should distinguish within this Arian group the so-called political Arians, who are men without clear and honest convictions but follow the lead of the emperor. Under Constantius, compromising Arian views are the acceptable views and these political Arians trim their sails according to the opinions of the sovereign. It has been pointed out (Professor Bainton first called my attention to this point) that some of these men were in a peculiarly exposed position in the empire. Their sees were in the Pannonian province up the Danube, and the barbarians were staring at them across the river continuously. They were on the exposed outskirts of the Roman world; and if they were to be sustained there, they had to have political support. Consequently, the temptation to conform to the views of the emperor at the moment was especially strong for them. But they did their conforming with a degree of bellicose enthusiasm which is a little disturbing for one concerned about devotion to truth rather than to the dictates of opportunism. Ursacius and Valens are the typical Homoians of this sort. Acacius, a disciple of Eusebius of Caesarea, is judged by some good critics to have been even more unprincipled than these border bishops with less excuse. In any case, Athanasius' scathing indictment of Acacius and Eudoxius portrays them as beneath contempt.

Next we recognize the group often spoken of as semi-Arians, the Homoiousians, of whom the best instance is Basil of Ancyra. He was the leader of that party of conservatives who in 358, having been shocked by the action taken by the Homoian leaders at Sirmium in 357, rejected the action that was there taken and sought to affirm a relationship between the Son and the Father which is, as it appeared to them, in line with the ancient tradition. They were still afraid of the term *homoousion* because it seemed to them to be a straightforward affirmation of Sabellian doctrine, but they also rejected no less strenuously the declarations of the Arians. They preferred to say, "The Son is like the Father in essential being" (*homoion kat' ousian*), or "in all respects like the Father" (*homoion kata ta panta*), which is the same form of expression as that used by the

Anomoians but in the reverse sense. They use the old Lucianic phrase (really an Origenist phrase, and uncritical Origenism is the position these men represent), "an exact image (*aparallaktos eikon*) of the Father," which suggests both precision and unchangingness. They are even ready to use a term explicitly condemned in the Sirmian statement: "like in essential being (*homoiousion*) to the Father," but they do not affirm identity of essential being (*homoousion*), for that appears to them to be saying that there is only one individual being in the Godhead. On the other hand, they are prepared to use that other phrase out of the Nicene statement, *ek tes ousias tes patros*, ("of the essential being of the Father"), which is one of the phrases the Arians steadily refused. This is a crucial addition, because to say simply that the Son is "like the Father in essence" was not enough. Those who are afraid to say that the Son is of the substance of the Father are always in danger of slipping over the edge into the Arian or Arianizing affirmations. But if you are willing to interpret "of the essential being of the Father" quite literally, then you have indicated that while you are timid about using the Nicene language, you are at least on the side of the teaching which the Nicene Creed sought to formulate.

To call this group semi-Arian, as most of the textbooks do, seems to me to be sadly misleading. They were not semi-Arians in the sense that they were teetering halfway between the Arian position and the Nicene position. They were in the status, rather, of right-wing Origenists who, when they are faced with a showdown, choose the Nicene rather than the Arian alternative.

This is the group, then, that Athanasius, as leader of the council in Alexandria in 362, said must be treated as brothers. They "must not be treated as enemies . . . but we discuss the matter with them as brothers with brothers, who mean what we mean, and dispute only about the word."[20] In short, if they are afraid of the term *homoousion* for reasons which we can understand, let us try to get them to see that what they have affirmed leads naturally and logically to the further affirmation from which, so far, they have shrunk.

Here then at Alexandria is taken the step which begins the reconciliation of groups in the Eastern Church that hitherto had been suspicious of one another. They are driven together by the action taken by the thoroughgoing Arians at Sirmium. Once again, I think it is not unfair

---

20. Athanasius, *Syn.* 41 (See n. 11).

to compare what happened there to what had happened in the council of Nicaea, where the positive statement of Arian beliefs led right-wing and even left-wing Origenists, who were present in overwhelming majority, to say, "That is something we cannot accept." From this time forth we have Athanasius and his Old Nicene group working in closer and closer harmony with the right-wing Origenists of the East, who hitherto had been standoffish and a little inclined to think that the Arians were the safer group to support. This is Athanasius' final and decisive contribution to the triumph of Nicene doctrine which took place in 381.

Athanasius was the last of the Old Nicene leaders. After his death in 373, there emerged a new group of younger leaders—call them Neo-Nicene leaders if you like. Three Cappadocian Origenists, Basil of Caesarea and his younger brother Gregory of Nyssa, and their friend Gregory of Nazianzus reinterpreted the Nicene formula in such fashion as to guard even verbally against any hint of Sabellian doctrine. The line they insisted on is defined by the conjoint use of the two phrases "of the same substance with the Father" (*homoousios toi patri*) and "of the substance of the Father" (*ek tes ousias tou patros*). The use of the second phrase is supposed to guard against the Sabellian understanding of the first. To say that the Son and the Father are identical in *ousia* need not be taken as Sabellian if it be affirmed in the next breath that the Son is "of the Father." A distinction from Sabellianism is clearly indicated. And if it be affirmed that the Son is "of the essential being" of the Father, the distinction is made in a way that safeguards it from falling at the opposite extreme into Arianism or some other kind of subordinationism. Moreover, the Cappadocians distinguished between *ousia* on the one hand and *hypostasis* on the other hand. The two terms had been treated as synonyms in the anathemas of the original Nicene Creed as well as by Athanasius himself. Now, however, the Cappadocians suggest that *ousia* be used for the essential being that is unitary in the Godhead, and *hypostasis* for the individuations of that being, which are three in the Godhead. Thus a differentiation was made in Greek corresponding to the one in Latin between *substantia* and *persona*; and Eastern Christians acquired linguistic resources comparable to those the West had possessed since Tertullian [to affirm God's oneness without lapsing into either modalism or subordinationism].

That, then, is the way that the parties and issues lined up on the eve of the decisions of 381 which, after more than half a century, marked the final and, for most Christians, definitive triumph of Nicaea. That triumph presupposed the fresh Neo-Nicene analysis of terminology we have just reviewed, but it also depended on individual leaders whose theologies were not in all respects the same. Some of the defenders of the Nicene position in the East and in the West will next be considered in conjunction with the reaffirmation of Nicaea in 381.

## APPENDIX: NOTES ON TERMINOLOGY[21]

At the conclusion of this survey of Nicene controversies, it may be well to summarize what would appear to be the meanings of some of the technical terms which were bandied about by the disputants.

Let us note first of all, that as far as the Latin terminology used by Western participants is concerned, Tertullian's formula had been normative for a long while. One recognizes in God one *substantia*, which is supremacy or sovereignty; and one recognizes in God three *personae* in which that one essential deity is alike present. The Father and the Son and the Holy Spirit are not then three Gods. There is only one Supreme Being, but there are three participants in the one status of sovereignty. That was the terminology that Hosius of Cordova undoubtedly had in mind. It is the terminology which lies back of the work *On the Trinity* of Hilary of Poitiers. And as far back as we know, it was by and large characteristic of Western thinking. Even those Westerners who were accustomed to use Greek as the language of scholarship nevertheless always had this Tertullianic usage in mind for the interpretation of the Greek terms employed.

In the Eastern Church, on the other hand, there were no fewer than three terms corresponding to that single Tertullianic term *substantia*. In the first place there was the common Platonic and Aristotelian term *ousia*. We can translate that "essential being." It is that which makes a thing what it is, and not anything else, says Aristotle. Or as Plato used the term, it is that fundamental and unchanging basic character which is present in all instances of a specified kind; it is the character which defines all

---

21. These notes were delivered as an integral part of the lectures recorded in the 1948 LHCD, but with the reordering of the material in the present work, they have been placed in an appendix to the present chapter. Apart from points indicated in the following two footnotes, Calhoun's analysis is different from and yet also consistent, as far as the editor can judge, with recent scholarship, including Stead's exhaustive study (for the latter, see n. 15 above) [ed.].

members of a certain class. We had better examine Aristotle's treatment of that term after a little while by way of cluttering up the picture a bit further, and thereby making the whole thing much more exciting than it would be without complications. Next there was the term *hypostasis*. This was used freely as a synonym for *ousia*, but conveyed a little more definitely the sense of "individual being," yet not so definitely as to exclude "essential being." *Ousia*, unhappily, can mean both those things too. Then there is a third term which is characteristic chiefly of the Stoics' language, although Aristotle recognizes it primarily for the sake of rejecting it as a synonym for *ousia*: *hypokeimenon*. *Hypostasis* is that which stands beneath a given set of properties. It is the precise terminological equivalent of *substantia*—that which is the underpinning of an observable set of characters, that which is the subject of characters, that which is the subject of predicates. *Hypokeimenon* has almost that same meaning. It is that which "underlies" a set of properties. In its most usual sense it is "substratum," but it can also mean "individual being," and therefore can be a precise equivalent for *hypostasis,* which the Stoics also used; while *ousia* belongs more to Platonist and Aristotelian tradition. Stoic terminology, however, is predominantly tinctured with materialism, or with corporeal connotations. For Stoic thought, all reality is corporeal reality. It varies in degree of refinement. When we speak of spirit (*pneuma*) we are speaking of a highly refined body; when we speak of flesh (*sarx*) we are speaking of a cruder, less highly refined body.

Thus the Latins using their one term *substantia*, were confronted by Greeks who were accustomed to at least three ways of saying the same thing. Now suppose that a Latin should come upon a Greek who was affirming that in the Godhead there are three *hypostaseis*. Origen said that in some passages. Such a statement could readily seem to a Latin to mean that there are three *substantiae* in the Godhead. That is not what Origen meant. He meant that there are three individual centers in the Godhead, in which the common being of deity is present. And if he used the term *homoousion* to describe the relation of the Son to the Father, as Pamphilus said he did, that would be asserting in the most explicit way that the *ousia* of the Godhead is identical in Father and in Son.

Suppose, on the other hand, that a Greek who has been trained to affirm that there are three *hypostaseis* in the Godhead as a safeguard against Sabellianism comes upon a Latin who insists that there is but one *substantia*. The Greek is likely to fear that his Latin-speaking brother is talking modalistic Monarchianism. And until that confusion of terminology could be straightened out, the chance for misunderstanding on both sides was perfectly evident. (Now there is another term which in effect has this same range of meaning, namely *physis* or nature. *Physis* can mean "a concrete particular"; *physis* can also mean "essential nature." And again the possibility of misunderstanding an opponent who uses *physis* is perfectly obvious. He may be using the term in the sense of essential nature, but if one understands him to mean a concrete individual, one is going to think he is saying what he doesn't intend to say, and vice versa.)

Misunderstanding was made the more easily possible in the period we are speaking of through the lack in the Greek terminology of any precise correlate for the Latin term *persona*. Later in the fourth century, a term which did correspond to *persona* came to be used. The term was *prosopon*, which can be translated roughly "individual appearance." *Prosopon* is what you see when you look at an individual. It is what presents itself to your gaze as identifying this individual and distinguishing him or it from all others. It came to mean more specifically not the appearance of the whole human body, but the face, the most readily usable mark of individual identity. It means also the mask that an actor wears to identify that part that he plays on the stage. In short, it corresponded at point after point to the Latin term *persona*. In any case, *prosopon* was not used in the theological debates of the first half of the fourth century. It came into the picture chiefly with the rise of Christological debate, when first Apollinaris and then Nestorius undertake to use this word as a way of describing, not one of the beings in the Godhead, but rather the unitary, phenomenal personality of Jesus Christ.

So the Greeks, in trying to say what the Latins said by using the term *persona*, were almost driven to employ one of the terms which could also mean *substantia*. *Hypostasis* can be used, and is used by Athanasius and in the anathematism of the Nicene Creed, as a synonym for *ousia*. Eventually *hypostasis* does come to be used, largely under the influence of the group we refer to as Neo-Nicene thinkers—Basil the Great of Caesarea, Gregory of Nyssa, and Gregory of Nazianzus—as a synonym for the Latin *persona*. Its metaphysical connotation was somewhat different, but still it was distinguished clearly from *ousia*.

Now let us confuse that picture a bit further by noting the diversity of ways in which the term *ousia* itself could be employed. In the *Metaphysics*, Aristotle raises the question of what can properly be meant by *ousia*. The question is raised partly in conjunction with Aristotle's table of descriptive predicates—the categories—by which you can describe completely anything you know. The first of the categories is precisely the name of the thing. When I give the thing its name, I specify its essential being. Then I can go on and describe its size and location, present state and relation to other things, etc. There are nine subsidiary categories, all of which refer to that which is named by the first category, which Aristotle labeled *ousia*. But he notes forthwith that *ousia* has two senses which must be sharply distinguished. The first and primary sense is the sense of *this*, this thing. It is a particular individual existent. So I speak of a "substance" as being a real thing. I say that the desk is a substance. It is not desk in general, but *this* desk. On the other hand, *ousia* means secondarily the whatness of a thing; not the thing itself, but its character (the Schoolmen later say the *quidditas*)—that which is the first specification, underlying all other specifications, that tell what a thing is. Now *ousia* in this sense can be predicated. *Ousia* in the first sense cannot be predicated. I cannot predicate this desk of anything else in the world, not even of itself. For this desk is not a predicable character; it is a subject to which all predicates which are applicable must refer. Only in the secondary sense of *ousia* can I use it as a predicate.

Thus one can see how impossibly difficult it is going to be, without elaborate discussion and qualification in each situation in which the term *ousia* is employed, to make clear whether the term is being employed to mean individual being (namely, *this*) or essential being (namely, *what* this is). So we have confusion running right straight down through these three terms (*ousia, hypostasis, hypokeimenon*), and there is no way to avoid it, except by an arbitrary agreement to use one of the words in the one sense and another word in the other, and not to use them in any other way.

Now what exactly does *ousia* mean in its secondary, predicable sense? For Plato, *ousia* means being without becoming. And in that sense *ousia* is what is intelligible, what can be clearly defined and grasped as though distinct from the perceptible (*ta doxasta*), that which is perpetually in flux. In the *Euthyphro*, for example, Socrates says there must be *eidos* or *ousia* that is common to all of the persons and acts that we call pious. Piety should be defined by specifying the intelligible *what*—meaning, character, whatever—that can be found in all of the instances to which the predicate *hagios* applies. It is an essential character in which individual occasions, things, or events can participate; by that participation in it, by that exemplification of it, they are what they are.

Usually we translate *eidos* as form, and Aristotle has a considerable polemic against his former companions in the Academy concerning the status of form, and the theory that things are understandable best if we recognize that they are what they are through participation in form. Forms, he says, must be either particulars or universals; if they are particulars, they constitute a duplicate order of particulars and don't help us at all to understand the things we are trying to understand. If, on the other hand, they are universals, then they have no independent being at all, and once again can't help us. It seems to me that Plato never speaks about form as either simply particular or simply universal. For him, form has its own sort of status, the status of meaning or validity; one can't place it in space and time, and one can't evaporate it into a mere abstraction. Aristotle uses the concept of abstracting from a group of particulars that which they have in common, which is the residue after you have removed all of their individual differences. But that will not do as an interpretation of Plato, because for Plato, the form is not in the things at all; consequently, one cannot find it by stripping away a whole series of components which are present in them; they exemplify the form, they do not contain it; they participate in it, but they are not identical with it. Plato therefore is using the term *ousia* in a way of his own which bypasses the familiar and useful but in this case irrelevant distinction between particular and universal. The form is neither the one nor the other; it is something of a different order.

Aristotle insists, as does Plato, that the proper use of the term *ousia* is to indicate what the thing is not merely at a particular time, not at a moment, but always. *Ousia* is what makes the thing that it is, and not any other thing. But it is not a generic or universal character. That which makes a desk *this* desk is predicable of the desk as a certain kind of thing, and yet it is predicable peculiarly of this particular desk. But Aristotle's use of the term *ousia* deviates from Plato's use of the term *eidos* (which Plato equates with *ousia*) in the direction of declaring that essential being is in some inexplicable sense individual being. It is not individuality as such (generic character), but that which makes an individual the individual that it is.[22]

22. Calhoun here pronounces "inexplicable" Aristotle's understanding of *ousia* (substance or essential being) as "that which makes an individual the individual that it is" for reasons that he explains more fully, but too technically to be discussed here, in his

Now it is in some such sense as that that the term *ousia* gets into this theological controversy.[23] When the question is raised whether the Son is identical with the Father in *ousia*, the question is not simply whether they are two beings of the same kind. The question cuts deeper than that. It is the question whether they share an identical being which is at once descriptive character and concrete exemplification of that character. If I speak of the *ousia* of God, I am speaking not of a character which God shares with other members of a class. There are no other members of the class. I am speaking of that which is uniquely to be found in God. Now if I affirm that the same *ousia* is in the Father and the Son, I am affirming, not that they are two beings alike in kind; I am affirming that they are two participants in one identical state of being, which is the unique being of supreme existence. *Ousia* common to the Father and the Son is then essential being which tends to be understood concretely, rather than abstractly. There is the source of all the trouble. If it were simply a question whether the Logos is *Theos*, the answer, of course, would be "Yes" by both parties. The Logos is *Theos*, and so shares a predicate with the Father. But suppose the question is put: Is the Logos inseparable, both in fact and in thought, from the Father? Then the Nicenes will answer "Yes," and the Arians will answer "No."

---

*Lectures on the History of Philosophy*, [1958 LHP] 91. He there suggests that Aristotle's confusions led to the later Aristotelian view (which Aristotle himself never clearly affirmed) that materiality is the principle of individuation; and that other candidates for this principle such as Duns Scotus' *haecceitas* are more consistent with Aristotelian principles. Jonathan Lear has proposed that the difficulties of understanding Aristotle on *ousia* are increased by the common practice, shared by Calhoun, of translating *tode ti* as "an individual" or "a particular" instead of using the more literal but admittedly artificial-sounding "this something" [*Aristotle: The Desire to Understand* (Cambridge: Cambridge University Press, 1988) 270ff. *et passim*]. Another and more crucial mistake contributing to these difficulties (not, I think, attributable to Calhoun but characteristic of most modern as well as premodern interpreters), is the failure to recognize "that Aristotle changed his mind about what counts as primary substance" (Ibid., 272). Whether Lear's interpretations solve Calhoun's problems with Aristotle on *ousia*, I am not prepared to judge, but it does need to be noted that these problems are a major source of Calhoun's acknowledged preference for Plato's theory of forms—which, to be sure, he interpreted in carefully nuanced ways [ed.].

23. This paragraph better describes later understandings of the Nicene *ousia* than it does those of the Council fathers. They did not have the benefit of modern research into changes and developments of Aristotle's thought such as have been intensively pursued since Werner Jaeger's work (1912), and were therefore even more likely than we are to be confused about what they and their predecessors meant by the term [ed.].

# CHAPTER 12

# Defenders of Nicaea and the Niceno-Constantinopolitan Creed[1]

THE PREEMINENT DEFENDER OF Nicaea in the East was of course Athanasius; and in the West, of about the same age, but of a later generation of Christian thought, Hilary of Poitiers. We shall treat of them and of the Neo-Nicene Cappadocians before discussing the creed formulated in 381, and conclude this chapter with some comments on St. Augustine's trinitarianism and the *Quicumquevult*, which became normative for the understanding of Nicaea in the Western Church.

## ATHANASIUS

It will be recalled that Athanasius, at that time a young deacon in the church of Alexandria, was present at the first Council of Nicaea. He was there presumably as a secretary and assistant to Bishop Alexander. When Alexander died in 328, Athanasius succeeded him. He was about thirty at that time, and he lived through a very stormy career until 373. His efforts, far more than those of any other individual, account for the success of the Nicene cause.

The two works of Athanasius which represent his early theological position are the *Incarnation of the Word of God* and the work called *Contra gentes*, "Against the Heathen."[2] In these two early and more or less

---

1. The first section in this chapter, on Athanasius, closely follows the 1948 LHCD (I:165–70), but the remaining four sections omit some of that source and include substantial insertions from later lectures [ed.].

2. Athanasius, *C. Gent.* (PG 25:3–96); *Inc.* (PG 25:95–198). F. L. Cross, *Athanasius De incarnatione: An Edition of the Greek Text*, SPCK Texts for Students 39 (London: SPCK, 1939). English translation in *NPNF2* 4, *C. Gent.* 1–30; *Inc.* 31–67.

systematic theological treatises, we see the mind of the man presented more concisely than in the long series of controversial works which embody his chief contributions to the later debates. It has been said more than once that Athanasius' strength is not as a systematic, and especially not as a speculative, thinker, but rather as one who has a tenacious grip on three vital insights and a logical skill that enables him to sort out the ambiguities, the evasions, and the deviations in the positions of his opponents that obscure or vitiate these primary tenets of faith.

The first of these affirmations, and the one which is the center of his theology from beginning to end, is that our salvation is from God. When Christians say that their redemption comes through Jesus Christ, it is to say that in Jesus Christ it is God himself who is redeeming human beings. The central and fatal error of the Arian position is to say that our salvation comes through a creature. On that affirmation Athanasius never wavers; and given that point of view, the opposition between his faith and that of the Arians is inescapable.

The second affirmation has to do with the nature of the God who is thus said to be our redeemer. Whereas the Arians are thinking of God as that utterly remote being who can have no proper contact with created reality, Athanasius holds a view which strongly suggests the position of Origen, whose right-wing strain, as a matter of fact, Athanasius follows. Origen had said that the way to think about God was not as the aloof Absolute but rather as the Perfect Being. Now if one thinks of God as Perfect Being, it is not impossible to think of him as having contact with created beings and to think of the world which he has made as of such nature that God can maintain perpetual contact with it. "The world is capable of bearing the hand of the Father." That was a statement from which Athanasius never turned aside. God then is to be thought of in such fashion that there is no need of an intervening layer of reality; rather, God is to be thought of as directly in contact with the created order.

The third main point of Athanasius' theology has reference to the nature and destiny of man. Here he follows lines which strongly suggest the theology of Irenaeus. Man is created in such fashion that he is capable of receiving the gift of immortality from God's hand. He is not immortal by nature, but he is destined for immortality, and salvation is primarily the restoration to human beings of that destiny which they through their own misdeeds have lost. When Athanasius speaks of God as our Redeemer, he is not thinking primarily of a forensic vindication or acquittal but rather of a change in human nature. That change of nature is a creative act, and the moral change which will be connected with it is subsidiary to that fundamental change which is "existential," if you want to use a contemporary epithet. Given these three foci of concern, it is not too difficult to see how the main line of Athanasius' theology works itself out.

Let us begin with his conception of God. God he declares to be at once immanent in the created world and transcendent beyond it. He is immanent in it precisely because he is its Creator, and that not at some time in the past, but as Athanasius says, "Now and ever." Creation, in other words, is continuous. God is perpetually creating—that is to say, sustaining in being—the world, the nature of which is to slip into nonbeing. God who is thus perpetually creating the world performs this act directly; there is no need for an intervening nature of any sort. That Logos that the Arians were talking about, which is neither fully God nor a creature like the rest of the creatures, simply has no place in a scheme in which the world as God makes it is good, and from which therefore there is no need to exclude the presence of God himself. Athanasius here rejects all the pessimism which had characterized the Gnostic systems and the Marcionite dualism. Moreover, he rejects that negative theology which had characterized so much of Alexandrine thought: a theology which stressed primarily the total otherness of God from the world. As God makes it, the world has no evil in it; evil results from the deviation of finite will. And since the world originally has no evil in it, there is no reason why God cannot act upon it directly and continuously, as in fact Athanasius believes him to do. However, at the same time that God is thus present in the world as its continuous Creator, he transcends every created being in such fashion that he remains unknown to the mind of fallen human beings. If they had not fallen from their initial state of transparent innocence, they would be able to recognize God in the world order. But precisely because God is transcendent in such fashion that his nature is not completely containable in the created world which is all that we in our fallen state can know, we are unable, so to say, to read between the lines of creation and to see that creation points beyond itself to its Creator. Therefore, since God is unknowable to us in our fallen state, it is necessary that he should reveal himself. The incarnation is the only way in which such self-manifestation can be effected. God is thus declared to be both immanent in the created world and transcendent beyond all created things, and in the latter aspect is inaccessible to the sinful mind.

Since God, however, has made himself known it is possible for the Christian to say something further about the nature of God. What is to be said is that God is, unlike every created being, "unoriginate" (*agenetos*). The notion involved here is the difference between things which come to be (*gignomai*) and things which do not come to be. Becoming is process, and things which come to be do not have an original and intrinsic reality of their own. By contrast with all that, God is unoriginated, unbegun, "unbecoming." In his very nature, he is essentially real. At the same time, one will say that the Father in the Godhead is unbegotten (*agennetos*), which is a quite different conception; and one will say that the Son who, like the Father, is quite unoriginated (*agenetos*) is, nevertheless, in his relation with the Father, begotten (*gennetos*). The Arians tried to identify these two terms. It was not too difficult because the terms sound almost exactly alike, and on paper they look enough alike to make the slip from one to the other very easy. Therefore, when the Arians said that God is "not begotten," it was very easy for them to say that the Son who is begotten is not God. What Athanasius is insisting upon is the distinction between the conception of what comes to be and what stands in a relationship to the ultimate principle of Being, which, metaphorically, can be described as being "begotten." The Son is then begotten, not made, *gennethenta, ou poiethenta*. The clause in the creed is decisive on that issue. Moreover, the Son is begotten, not of the Father's will, but of the Father's nature (*ousia*); and here again the phrase in the creed, *ek tes ousias tou patros*, is decisive. The Arians insisted that the Son is begotten by an act of the Father's will. Athanasius says that in that case the Son would indeed be a product, a thing made (*ktiston*). But a son, truly speaking, springs from the nature of his parents. The nature of the son does not result from a plan of his father. It results, rather, from the nature of the father himself. And so it is, Athanasius insists, with the Godhead. We cannot speak of the divine Son as split off from the divine Father as a human son is from his human parents, but we can say that the relationship indicated by the term *gennetos* is a relationship that is grounded directly in *ousia*, not produced by an act of will. The Son is begotten eternally and essentially, and the term *begetting* does not refer to origination but simply to a relationship in the eternal being of the Godhead. So far Athanasius is quite unambiguous.

Now with regard to the Holy Spirit in the Godhead, his doctrine remains undeveloped. We tend to think of the Church's doctrine of God as Trinitarian, but as a matter of fact, no doctrine of the Trinity was affirmed in Nicaea. The doctrine which was affirmed was primarily the essential identity of Father and Son, but belief in the Holy Spirit was merely affirmed without any sort of elaboration at all. The question whether the Holy Spirit then is likewise identical in essential being with Father and Son was left open at Nicaea. It was only toward the latter part of the fourth century that the question was so much as raised explicitly at all, and then it was by one of the *homoiousion* group, the old conservative Origenists of whom Basil of Ancyra was for a time a leader. Macedonius of Constantinople was one who said we affirm that Son and Father are indeed *homoousioi*, identical in essential being, but we do not affirm that the Holy Spirit belongs in this same level of being. We recall that the Homoiousians were worried about affirming identity of *ousia* at all with respect to the Godhead for fear of Sabellian implications. So this was a real concession on the part of one of this group. But immediately he excluded expressly the Holy Spirit from *homoousia*. Once that view had been stated, Athanasius was ready to reject it and to say that the Holy Spirit as well as the Son is *homoousion toi patri*. Although the relationship of the Holy Spirit to the Father and the Son is rather vague in his thought, it is not the relationship of genesis. It may perhaps be described as "procession" (*probole*) from the Father to the Son, but he is not willing to try to be very specific on the matter, perhaps because he has not given the question nearly as close attention as he has given the relation of the Father and the Son. Like the Nicene Creed itself, Athanasius is doing his thinking about the Godhead in reference to two rather than three coordinate terms. It is perfectly clear to him that Father and Son must be put on precisely the same footing, save as regards their relational difference. The Holy Spirit is, in general, likewise to be called God [just as they are God].

Consider next Athanasius' conception of the creation of the world and humankind, and the need for and the manner of the redemption of the world. As we have seen, the world is created directly and continuously, and that creation, says Athanasius, is itself to be regarded as an act of grace. God does not make the world in a quite impersonal and neutral manner, but rather the world as it is made is good, and its creation is the result of the outflowing love of God. Now all created beings have as their nature the "tendency to perish" (*phthora*)—the term that Aristotle had used to balance *genesis*: *genesis* is "coming into being," *phthora* is "passing away." It is the nature of all things that come to be that they tend to lapse once again into nothingness. It is not that their nature itself is the principle of unreality; it is that their nature is such that if left to itself it tends to slide toward nonbeing.

Like all other creatures, humankind has this precarious status as its nature. But in addition to the fundamental tendency to nonbeing, we have the distinction that we have been made according to the image of God, and the image of God is the promise of immortality, or incorruption, or invulnerability of being. The image of God is never totally losable; no matter what human beings do, they cannot cease to be human. At the same time, the image of God is not in itself the status of being immortal. *Aphtharsia*, indestructibility, which is the antithesis of *phthora*, or *athanasia*, which is simply deathlessness, the antithesis of mortality, is not given to us at the outset but is promised to us. It is our destiny; we are made for eternal life, and the image of God in us is an indication that we are destined for a different future from that of all other created beings. Now this destiny is conditional, as it was with Irenaeus. It is conditioned upon human beings living in accordance with the vision of God. But since human beings are rational and free, they are capable of following either that road which leads to immortality or a road that deviates from the right one; and any other road which they follow will diminish the effectiveness of the divine image and will emphasize their mortality, their tendency towards nonbeing. For when we turn aside from God, we are turning aside from the principle of our own being, and by so much are lessening our own hold upon that which gives our being its distinctive and promising status.

That is precisely what we do in sin, and the change which is brought is at once a moral change and a metaphysical change, for the reason just indicated. In sinning, human beings violate the laws of God and pile up upon themselves demerits. At the same time, by so doing they altered their own existence for the worse, so that the change which they have effected for their own hurt can be reversed only by a redemptive act which is at once ethical and metaphysical—an act which can be performed on their behalf by the Creator himself. (This anticipates a main line in Augustine's thought, which says that human beings had lost status in the realm of being and require a fresh creative act on the part of God to put them right. Athanasius is thinking on lines not wholly unlike those.) We require then to be saved from the results of our own self-corruption, and the salvation which can come to us comes through the incarnation of the Word of God.

At this point, we come again to a vague area in Athanasius' thinking. Like other Nicene leaders, he was concentrating so hard upon the problem of the Godhead that the problem of Christology—that is, the problem of the manner in which the divine and human are united in Jesus Christ—was left for later consideration. The result is that the answer to the Christological problems on the part of many Nicene leaders is far from satisfactory. That unsatisfactoriness manifests itself in Athanasius in a tendency to waver between two sets of terms. On the one hand, he speaks of the Incarnation as the assumption on the part of the divine Logos of manhood (*anthropos*). That is a direct refusal of the Arian assertion that the Logos merely assumed flesh, or a human body, rather than full human nature. Athanasius is prepared to use upon occasion a very awkward and almost barbarous phrase, *kyriakos anthropos*, sometimes translated in the impossible manner, "the Lordly man." It is clearly intended to mean "the Lord's manhood." (Compare it with other phrases such as *kyriakon deipnon*, the Lord's Supper; *hemera kyriake*, the Lord's day.) "The Lord's manhood," then, indicates the incarnation of the Logos in a full human life. But over against that, and in nearby passages, Athanasius is prepared to speak of the Logos as assuming a body (*soma, sarx*) like a garment (*himation*), a priestly vesture (*estheta*) which like Aaron's can be put on and off. Clearly that is Christology of a very different sort. (Whether it goes appropriately with Athanasius' frequent references to Mary as *theotokos*, Mother of God, is a question which will be considered later.) It is a Christology which, in the course of the later and bitter arguments over the person of Jesus Christ, worked out into Monophysite doctrines—that is to say, that the only personal being in the Lord was the divine Logos, and that all the rest was an impersonal façade which veiled the true divine reality. Athanasius' Christology, therefore, is inchoate rather than fully worked out. At the same time it must be said that in opposition to the Arian kind of thought, the first emphasis on "the Lord's manhood" comes closer to affirming what Athanasius wants to say. Moreover, when Apollinarian Christology takes shape later, he opposes it steadily. At the same time, even when he speaks in these terms, he is saying that the center of personal thought and will and activity in Jesus Christ is the Logos; there is no question of a human individuality or subjecthood in addition to the Logos. The Logos assumes, if you will, the full stature of a human being, but there is not alongside the Logos in the incarnation a human person or personal existence with a human will at its center.

Athanasius thinks of the incarnation as, in a sense, the culmination and climax of God's creative work. It had been foreshadowed already by the granting of insight to Israel's lawgivers and the prophets. In them the Logos was at work. But in Jesus Christ, the Logos not only acts but is fully present. And the incarnation, which becomes a climactic point for the whole work of creation and illumination becomes at the same time the central point for sacred history, for it is continued, in a sense, in the working of the Holy Spirit in the Christian community. For Athanasius, therefore, there is a continuous line from the beginning of the world's existence through the incarnation and crucifixion and resurrection and on into the life of the Christian community. He is speaking here not of continuity between God and world, but of continuity of the work of God within the world. There is no opposition between the coming of Christ and what God has been doing in history up to that moment. Rather, this is a fulfillment, a climactic and effective focusing, of what God had been doing up to this time.

The redemption which is brought about by the Lord has a many-sided effect for Athanasius. He makes use of the conception of the conquest of evil on our behalf and the fulfillment of the law so that we are no longer debtors under the law. But the key point on which he lays his primary stress is the coming of divine life into human existence so that human existence is thereby transformed. This transformation is not simply a restoration of human beings to the level from which they had fallen; rather, it is a restoration which carries them beyond that point, so that the promise of immortality which was granted to them at the outset has now begun to be realized. Through Jesus Christ, immortality becomes actual within the limits of human existence. Now for the first time, we realize God's intent for all human beings. And in that sense the Redeemer is himself the firstfruits of God's intent. He becomes the representative for the whole body of believers in the actualization of eternal life within this finite frame.

Athanasius is ready to use for this process the dramatic term *deification, theopoiesis.* Irenaeus had used it sparingly; Athanasius uses it habitually. What has happened is that human beings have been made partakers in that sort of life which is distinctively the life of God. It is not that they have become God. They have, however, become the heirs of divine life, and the life which is now granted to them is granted in fulfillment of God's initial intent in spite of their deviation from the line that would have brought them directly to this fulfillment. It is at this point that Athanasius uses a conception of predestination: not that God chooses in detail particular people to be saved and particular people to be lost, but rather that the eternal intent of God has been that those who associate themselves with God as believers shall enter upon this higher level of life. Predestination is for good, and it is in principle for all, though not all will take advantage of it. Those who hold viciously wrong conceptions of God, as the Arians do, and of humanity and redemption, are cutting themselves off from the chance that is given. For believers, eternal life is the outcome.

According to Athanasius, that outcome can be experienced now within the Christian community, with its moral discipline and its sacramental ordinances. In the use of the traditional sacraments, one can make an affirmation of his membership in a community in which the new life can already be lived. The essential effect of the sacraments is what we should speak of, probably, as a spiritual effect. Here it is spiritual not in the sense that it represents a remote ideal, or even the aspiration toward such an ideal, but in the sense that it represents a present status of being. Those who use the sacraments rightly can do so because they stand in a relation to God which is the relationship in which the principle of light is triumphing over the principle of nonbeing, so that the moral fruits of the Christian life are symptoms of the inner health of the Christian being.

Such in general is Athanasius' conception of the Christian teaching which has, he holds, been sadly misunderstood and misrepresented by the Arians.

On the basis of this position, his refutation of the Arians is incisive and ruthless. In the first instance, he accuses them of being grossly illogical even though they pride themselves on being defenders of logical consistency. They have set out to clear away the ambiguities and confusions in the traditional Christian outlook, and in so doing have fallen into even more glaring confusions themselves. For example, they set out to defend the uniqueness and aloneness of God, and they end with a kind of polytheism; they have a second God alongside the one and true God. They set out to keep God clear of any contact with created being, and then they declare that the Mediator, the Logos himself, is a created being, and God is after all the creator of a creature. And if contact between God and this created mediator must be avoided, they must interpose another mediator and still another and still another, and so they get into that hopeless *absurdum* of all rational people, the infinite regress. In trying to save the aloofness of God, they land in the utter confusion of chaotic thought.

Yet although their system is silly from the standpoint of logic, a far more serious defect is that religiously it is empty and vicious. They declare that our redemption comes through one who is himself a created being; who is, therefore, by the nature of created being, changeable. They grant that he did not in fact deviate from complete obedience to God, yet he could have done so. Our redemption therefore according to the Arian theory is made to rest upon a happy accident, rather than the fundamental nature of God. It is entirely possible that the created Logos might have turned aside from the good. (Indeed, the Anomoeans later affirm that he did, if Socrates the church historian is accurate.) If he had done so, there would have been for us no salvation, so that our salvation rests upon wholly insecure ground. Moreover, what these men do in urging that God alone is to be worshipped because he is high and lifted up above all created beings is to end by recommending that we are to worship one who is himself a created being. Viewed from our side, they say, the Logos is our Maker, and we may therefore properly worship him as divine though not as the high God. So that Arianism in trying to be ultra-pure in its monotheism lands in paganism.

As the controversy unfolds with new statements of Arian doctrine, with fresh creedal formulae, with fresh distinctions of terms upon which they insist, at each stage Athanasius tracks down with complete ruthlessness and inescapability the essential defect which seems to him to lie at the very center of the Arian conception. The fundamental error, once again, is that our salvation comes from a created being, not directly from God. Once that error is clearly recognized, then no evasion and no ambiguity can escape detection.

## HILARY OF POITIERS

The other of these middle-of-the-century defenders of the Nicene position referred to above is Hilary of Poitiers, bishop of a not very important church in Gaul, who wrote for the most part after 350. We know almost nothing about his early life. He was born perhaps about 300. It seems clear that he was converted to Christianity as an adult after years of study of Greek letters and especially of Neoplatonic philosophy. He had no part in the early stages of the controversy around the Nicene Creed.

It would seem that it was in 353 or 355 that there came to his attention the issues that interested him in such an Eastern thinker as Athanasius. Two Western synods were held at Arles in 353 and at Milan in 355 to pass judgment on Athanasius at the behest of Constantius. In the West, as we have often remarked, the position which Tertullian had sketched out so rapidly and with such apparent simplicity was prevalent. Hilary lined up with those who took the words that Tertullian had bequeathed to his Latin-speaking, Latin-writing successors as a good definition of the Godhead: *una substantia, tres personae*. Constantius, however, had thrown his power on the side of uncompromising Arianism; and at the two synods named, the position of Athanasius was specifically denounced. Hilary became aware that the position condemned was the one which, without associating it with the name of Athanasius, he had believed to be right. He published a vigorous attack on those who had condemned it. Shortly thereafter he was singled out for condemnation and driven into exile. So in 356 he went to Asia Minor and spent a number of years there as a wanderer in communication with men in the East who seemed to him to be spiritual brethren, especially the Cappadocian Origenists of the Neo-Nicene group who were busily engaged in an effort to rethink in Origenistic terms the meaning of the Creed of Nicaea.

The position which Hilary worked out is set forth most systematically in a treatise which is known as *De Trinitate*.[3] The original part of the treatise is a purely polemical, detailed analysis of the letter of Arius to Eusebius of Nicomedia rather than a detailed and systematic statement of a positive position. Yet the lines taken associate Hilary very closely with the lines being taken by Athanasius at the same time. We should note that Hilary is described as a student of Origen. It is a curious thing that a man who is a Westerner and who looks upon Cyprian and Tertullian as his great predecessors in Western thought nevertheless finds his most illuminating insights in Eastern theologians.

A distinctive feature of the position he defends is assertion of the reciprocal interpenetration of the three persons within the Godhead. He uses the term *circumincessio*, and we find Greek thinkers using a precisely

---

3. Hilary, *De Trin.*, CCSL 62, 62A. English translation in *NPNF2* 9.

parallel term, *perichoresis*. If we try to think, he says, of two beings, Father and Son, each of whom is, as the Gospel has it, present in the other so that each reciprocally has his being in the other (e.g., "I am in the Father and the Father in me"), we find it impossible to give a clear analytic definition of that sort of relationship. How can one being be contained in and still be the container of another being? Yet this is what we must affirm with respect to Father and Son. There is a certain indwelling of each in the other. That doesn't mean they are simply identical, but it does mean that they are so related that everything that can be affirmed of the one can also be affirmed of the other as regards their deity. With respect to Fatherhood and Sonship, they are reciprocally related. But as regards their Godhead, they are one and the same; each finds his status as God only through this paradoxical and unique relationship of reciprocal indwelling. The stress is primarily upon the active or dynamic character of the Godhead and of each member of it, so that the Father and the Son and the Spirit are thought of not simply in the way of derivation but in the way of active interpenetration. The status of each is defined by its active coincidence with each of the others, and that interpenetration is Hilary's way of giving a concrete meaning to the conception of unity. Unity is not merely numerical unity, nor yet static, substantial unity, but unity of coincident activity. That position is taken by the Cappadocians when they attempt to redefine the Nicene terminology.

## THE CAPPADOCIAN ORIGENISTS[4]

The Cappadocians followed through the implications of right-wing Origenism of the sort represented by Basil of Ancyra into a fresh definition of the terms of the Nicene formula, which helped measurably to get it accepted into the Eastern churches. We may label this group with some such *ad hoc* phrase as Neo-Nicene. We have here a more precise interpretation of the Nicene terminology, which is worked out in correspondence by three Cappadocians: Basil of Caesarea, often called Basil the Great; his contemporary and friend, Gregory of Nazianzus; and Basil's younger brother, Gregory of Nyssa. Basil and his friend Gregory Nazianzen had studied for some years in Athens in the Platonic Academy. So they brought

4. As Westerners have come to recognize far better than in Calhoun's day, the Cappadocians are of much greater importance for Trinitarian thought, as well as for a wide range of other theological themes, than one would guess from this brief and unoriginal section. It is retained, however, because of its linkage to the next section [ed.].

to consideration of the issues posed by the Nicene formula minds well trained in that philosophy which underlay Origenism as its most important metaphysical factor.

Of the various charges brought against the defenders of Nicaea, that of Sabellianism was the most damaging. The charge of materialism was pretty obviously trumped up; the Niceneans were not Manichaeans, and they had no intention of going that way. The charge that they used unscriptural language, Athanasius could meet effectively by showing that the Arians did the same. All of them used terms borrowed from the philosophical schools because the scriptural language was susceptible to more than one interpretation, and in order to specify the meaning that was intended, it was simply indispensable to bring in another vocabulary. Both sides did it. But on the charge of Sabellianism there was real color to the Arian declaration, not least because some of the defenders of Nicaea—particularly Marcellus of Ancyra, Photinus, and in another manner and a different degree, Eusthathius of Antioch—held modalistic views.

As we have already remarked, the Cappadocians distinguished between the term *ousia* and the term *hypostasis*. They argued that the meaning of the Nicene formula is that in the Godhead there is one *ousia*, but that it may properly be said (although the creed does not expressly say so) that there are three *hypostases*, Father, Son, and Holy Spirit, sharing without dividing the one essential character of being of deity. There are not three deities, there is one; but that one is to be found equally and identically in Father, Son, and Holy Spirit, so that these three concrete, individual centers may be spoken of as three *prosopa* (although these men prefer the term *hypostases*) in the deity, the Godhead.

Thus interpreted—*mia ousia, tres hypostases*—the formula is a virtually exact parallel of Tertullian's anti-Monarchian *una substantia, tres personae*. The simplicity and clarity that seemed thus to be achieved appealed rather strongly to Eastern thinkers who had been worried about Arian attacks on Nicene thought but who were worried only a little less by the possibility that, after all, Nicene thought did mean Sabellian thought. In the latter years of his life, apparently from 370 on, Athanasius was in correspondence with Basil; and just as eight years earlier he had approved the line taken by Basil of Ancyra, so now he indicates sympathy with the efforts of this younger generation to clarify, without too obvious modification, the creed which to Athanasius' mind had become the all-essential mark of orthodoxy.

Whether they were defending the creed in its original sense, or defending a different interpretation which was really a new kind of subordinationism, is a controverted question. J. F. Bethune-Baker is one of those who have discussed this issue.[5] He examines the position taken by Harnack and by other historians of dogma, that what the Cappadocians did was to water down the doctrine affirmed in the Nicene Creed so that instead of meaning what it had for Athanasius, the term *homoousion* had come to mean only abstract unity. As a matter of fact, some of the illustrations the Cappadocians use lend themselves quite uncomfortably to that judgment. Gregory of Nyssa says: Consider Peter, James, and John. You say they are three men; but no, there is in the three only one "man," one *ousia*, one common humanity.[6] So Father, Son, and Holy Spirit share one Godhood as these three share one manhood. Obviously, that would sound persuasive only to somebody so steeped in Platonic realism that for him the form of *ousia* was the fundamental reality and the individuation a kind of derivative and secondary manifestation of that ultimate reality. For an extreme Platonic realist, this way of putting the matter could seem to be significant and even perhaps conclusive. To most of the folk to whom the Nicene Creed is presented, however, that would seem to be giving the case away, even though that illustration is accompanied—as it was—by the warning that when we think of God, we must not think of three individuals who are members of one genus. That would be the case with three men, but the members of the Godhead do not belong to a genus or kind at all. So *ousia* in the Godhead has a more concrete meaning than *ousia* used in respect to particular beings.

They also offer other interpretations of their basic formula: one *ousia*, three *hypostases*. Basil of Caesarea said that *ousia* refers to that which is identical in the Godhead, *hypostasis* refers to the differentia of each of the three persons. Thus *ousia* refers to the deity (*theiotes*) which is the same for all, but Father refers to the peculiarity or differentia of Fatherhood (unbegottenness); Son refers to the differentia of Sonship (begottenness); and Holy Spirit to the differentia of the being of the Holy Spirit

---

5. J. Armitage Robinson, ed., *The Meaning of* Homoousios *in the "Constantinopolitan"* *Creed*. Texts and Studies 7 (Cambridge: Cambridge University Press, 1901).

6. The force of this argument in its original Greek becomes more evident if one substitutes *human*, as in "human nature," for *man*. Then, as Pelikan explains, "It was, strictly speaking, inaccurate even to speak of Peter, James, and John as 'three humans,' since 'human' was a term for the nature they had in common." Pelikan, *op. cit.,* 221 [ed.].

(procession). Gregory of Nyssa offered another suggestion. He said that the three hypostases refer to three modes of being: the Father is the First Cause; the Son is of the Cause directly; the Holy Spirit is of the Cause indirectly through the Son. That, however, suggests subordination. Other terms used—*energeia* or "activity" for the unitary *ousia*, *perichoresis* or "interpenetration" of the three hypostases—help to lessen this suggestion. Yet it is hard to avoid the impression that these men, striving so hard to make the Creed acceptable to their Eastern brethren, are using the language of a particular school which does not look dangerous to them but would be less than satisfying to folk of Athanasius' cast of mind. They seem to be letting go something of the concreteness, of the unique and unitary being in the Godhead, in order to make more clear the distinction among the three "persons."[7]

At any rate, under the leadership of these men and with the turn of events which brought to the throne a new emperor, Theodosius, who was favorable to the Nicene rather than to the Arianizing parties, a second ecumenical council was called to meet in Constantinople in 381. At that council, the leaders of the defense of the Nicene formula represented this Cappadocian point of view, but no new formula was adopted there. The Nicene formula was declared to be officially, authoritatively, and definitively a boundary within which further inquiry concerning the nature of God can properly go on, but outside of which any affirmation about the nature of God must be regarded as unchristian.

## THE NICENO-CONSTANTINOPOLITAN CREED

It may be wise to glance at the Niceno-Constantinopolitan Creed at this point, even though it comes into the picture at a later date, and has no direct relation with this council at Constantinople.[8] Actually the Creed called by this misleading name [seems to have been derived from] a fourth-century creed influenced by the Nicene Creed[9], so we may say

---

7. This view, once standard in Western circles, has been largely abandoned in recent scholarship. See for example Ayers, *op. cit.*, and Behr, *op. cit* [ed.].

8. It is now considered probable that the Council did issue the Creed [ed.].

9. Professor Calhoun later lost the confidence he expressed in the 1948 LHCD (I:174) regarding Hort's theory of the origin of the Niceno-Constantinopolitan formula in a creed brought to the council in Constantinople by Cyril of Jerusalem. See Hort, *Two Dissertations*. I. *On* [Gk.:] *"monogenos theos" in Scripture and Tradition*. II. *On the "Constantinopolitan" Creed and Other Eastern Creeds of the Fourth Century* (Cambridge: Macmillan, 1876) [ed.].

that the Niceno-Constantinopolitan formulation is based on the Nicene Creed at second hand. In any case, this formulation was referred to at Chalcedon in 451 as if it were the Nicene Creed, and to this day that custom continues. Now let us look at the text:

> We believe in one God, all-sovereign Father, Maker of heaven and earth, and of all things visible and invisible. And in one Lord Jesus Christ the only Son of God, the one begotten of the Father before all ages ...

We remember that this phraseology was specifically omitted from the Nicene formula because it was too readily accepted and interpreted by those of the Arian and Arianizing groups.

> Light of Light, true God of true God, begotten, not made, *homoousion* with the Father, through whom all things came to be.

The most significant change here is the omission of the phrase *ek tes ousias tou patros*—"of the substance of the Father"—which had been inserted parenthetically into the Creed of Nicaea. This omission has led to the question on the part of Harnack and others as to whether this creed was not framed by the Cappadocians, and whether the omission is not a watering down of the meaning of *homoousion* by deliberately leaving out "of the substance of the Father." Against that position of Harnack, the argument of Bethune-Baker seems to me persuasive. Once the danger of Sabellian interpretation is past, not least because of the Cappadocian distinction between *ousia* and *hypostasis*, the omitted phrase was no longer needed.

> The one who for us men and for our salvation came down from heaven and was incarnate of the Holy Spirit and of Mary the Virgin and became man, was crucified for us under Pontius Pilate and suffered and was buried, and rose the third day according to the Scriptures, and ascended into heaven and sitteth at the right hand of the Father, and will come again with glory to judge living and dead; of whose kingdom there will be no end. [Now comes another major change.] And in the Holy Spirit, the Lord, the Life-giver, the One who cometh forth from the Father, the One who with the Father and the Son is venerated and glorified, the One who spoke in the prophets. And in one holy catholic and apostolic Church. We confess one baptism for the remission of

sins, we await the resurrection of the dead, and life through the ages to come. Amen.

Here is a creed which, with the Nicene faith as its basis, has brought in significantly different language to express that faith. The clause on the Holy Spirit, as was noted in discussing Athanasius earlier in this chapter, was pretty clearly inserted because of the rise of a curious party led by Macedonius, bishop of Constantinople about 340, who tried to compromise with the Nicenes by saying, "We recognize that the Son is *homoousion* with the Father, but we deny that the Holy Spirit is so." The question of the Holy Spirit was thus injected into the controversy, and the subordination of the Holy Spirit affirmed. Athanasius, it will be recalled, immediately reacted against that, saying that the Holy Spirit must be regarded as *homoousion* with the Father, just as the Son. That is the position taken by the creed just quoted; the Holy Spirit is to be glorified along with the Father and the Son. It is not expressly said that the Holy Spirit is *homoousion* with the Father, but that is pretty clearly intended, since the issue whether one could properly worship a being essentially lower in rank than God had been settled in the negative. To worship a Logos who is only relatively divine is to worship a creature, and that is idolatry. So the effect of this statement is to place the Holy Spirit, so to say, on the upper side of the line which, in this whole controversy, has come to divide God from all created beings. Both the defenders of Nicaea and the Arians agreed in that division. God alone is of necessary and eternal being. The Arians wanted to say that the Father belongs up there, and the Son and the Holy Spirit belong down here among the creatures. Against that view, it has now been affirmed that the Father, Son, and Holy Spirit belong together on the upper side of the line, and the created world with angels, human beings, and all other creatures belong in a class that is of another *ousia*.

## AUGUSTINE

Finally we note the winding up of the discussion of these issues by a thinker whose definitions become normative for most of the Western—that is, the Latin-speaking Church—throughout the Middle Ages. That thinker is Augustine, who was converted to Christianity five years after the decision at Constantinople. He was born in 354 in the midst of the Nicene struggle, became a Christian in 386, being baptized at the hands of Ambrose in Milan at the age of 32. At that time, the action of Constantinople was still new and still in debate. There were Arians who continued to teach in the West. Ambrose's own predecessor in the church at Milan was Auxentius, who had been a determined propagandist for Arianism. After he had become a recognized Christian thinker, Augustine spent many years of his life working on a treatise which he called *De Trinitate*.[10] It was finally published somewhat prematurely because someone got hold of a preliminary draft and published it before Augustine was ready, and he was forced to hurry up a revision of the text so that it could appear in something like a form he could approve. It appears to have been a work of at least fifteen years.

The fifteen books of the treatise undertake two primary tasks. First comes an examination of the Scriptures to see whether the faith set forth by the church is inconsistent with what the Scriptures say. There are some passages of Scripture that seem to imply subordination of the Son or of the Holy Spirit to the Father. Numerous passages, for example, speak of the Son as "sent" by the Father. Augustine interprets all those passages as referring to the difference between the eternal being of God and the temporal and spatial manifestation of the incarnate Son. In that sense, he said, it could equally well have been declared that the Son sent himself, for *send* is a metaphorical term that has reference to appearance in the temporal order. So one may say that these statements do not refer to subordination within the Godhead; they refer to the subordination of a creature to the Creator in whom the Son is an essential member. In the same way, the references to the theophanies in the Old Testament mean simply that the Logos temporarily and for a particular purpose projects a phenomenal manifestation of himself upon the earth without altering in the slightest degree his eternal status in the Godhead. The upshot of the examination of Scripture is that there is no case here for the affirmation of the subordinationist views.

The second half of the work deals with the question whether it is possible to find analogies in experience which throw some light upon the meaning of the church's creed. Starting with new insights that come with our experience of created being, we may discover analogies to point our minds in the direction of the being of God who remains, by

---

10. Augustine, *Trin.* (PL 43). Critical edition CCSL 50–50A; English translation in *NPNF1* 3.

common consent, always beyond our grasp. These analogies can never be regarded as literal description; they are rather signposts which point us toward one way of thinking about God rather than another. The affirmations of the creed are not called into question. So far as Augustine is concerned, the church has settled the content of right beliefs. We are not to inquire whether what is set forth is demonstrable to reason, but we may properly inquire whether it is in accord with reason and whether, in particular, there are empirical data which, reasonably interpreted, suggest something of what the church has here affirmed. Augustine was a little concerned about the formula the Greeks were using—one *ousia*, three *hypostases*—because to him three *hypostases* sounds as though it might mean three *substantiae*, and to say that would be all wrong. But he acknowledges that his understanding of Greek is not strong and that the men who used the term would probably know what they mean by it; but he says that he would prefer to say simply "one," "three," without saying one and three "what." If you say that God is one and three, you are affirming what the faith of the church demands. Anything beyond that is likely to make for trouble.

At all events, if you ask whether *one* and *three* are predicates which can be meaningfully ascribed to one and the same being, and if you seek to get an answer to that question within the range of human experience, it seems to him clear that the place to look is not to groups of three individual creatures, like three men, but rather to something more unitary. He examines a whole array of analogies, some of which he declares to be wholly inapplicable, some of which he thinks a little closer to the mark. I think there is no need to go through the entire list. The method is not difficult to grasp, though the results are very diversely appraised.

First then, the very incomprehensibility of God stops us at the outset from affirming he is triune when we look at him directly, until we find God spoken of in Scripture as love. Now love implies a kind of triadic inner structure, for when we use the word *love*, we use a word which implies one who loves, one who is loved, and love—love that is so to say a bipolar bond between the lover and the beloved. If God then is love, we have to raise the question whether love can be thought of as *substantia*, and Augustine affirms unhesitatingly and emphatically, "Yes, love is precisely essential being of that sort which we know in persons and we do not know anywhere else." We do, then, get a glimpse of a triune character in the nature of love, but we cannot get beyond that point. So we back off and start now with ourselves who are declared in Scripture to be made according to the image of God. Therefore, one may be able to trace in the structure of the individual something, shall we say, of the structure of the Godhead.

First consider an instance of sense perception. Three factors enter in each case of vision: the eye, the visible object, and the fire which passes back and forth between the eye and the object seen. If any one of these is missing, there is no act of vision, and yet the act of vision is one even though these three indispensable constituents enter into it. (This comes out of Plotinus' examination of the nature of sense perception in his *Enneads* dealing with the nature of souls.) Since the act of sense involves corporeal organs and corporeal media, however, it can apply in no direct way to God. Consider then a purely mental act, the act of remembering. In an act of remembering, again, three factors are involved. One is memory (*memoria*), considered as a storehouse of previous impressions; another is a particular image called up out of that storehouse and presented to the mind as a present object; and the third is the will that draws the chosen image out of the whole mass of images stored in the memory. Again, if any one of these three were missing, no act of remembering would take place. This analogy breaks down most obviously when we think of its transiency. An act of memory comes and goes and is no more. But the permanent structure of the mind may throw more light on what is meant when we say that man is made in the image of God. In the structure of the mind Augustine thinks that the primary factors are memory, understanding, and will; and these three factors together make up the one mind. The mind consists permanently of these constituents. Yet one must recognize that each of these is not a part of the mind, it is the whole mind functioning in a certain manner. The memory is the mind remembering, the understanding is the mind thinking, the will is the mind acting. So each of these three is the whole mind, and the mind at the same time consists of these several faculties.

Now Augustine turns to another sort of situation. He thinks that he is getting closer all the time to an analogy which may be suggestive of the divine being. Consider an instance of a self-conscious mind; not just the mind which has these capacities or functions, but a mind which is exercising these capacities upon itself. We say that in self-consciousness there is a subject and object which are the same; it is myself of which I am conscious. There is also the knowledge or thought by which I am conscious of myself. This last is neither distinguishable from the subject (ego) which is thinking nor from the object (me) which is thought; for the self of which I am conscious, I am conscious of as conscious. The unity of the person is not to be thought of as being a sum of these three terms, but rather the unity of the person is to be identified in turn with each of them. Each of them is the full person. Their sole difference is one of relation. No matter how you shift these names around, the object is always related to the subject in a way that is different from the way in which the subject is related to the object. Likewise, the consciousness by which the subject is aware of the object is related to each of them in a unique manner. Yet descriptively each is indistinguishable from each other. What is more, each of them is indistinguishable from the whole, for the whole is nothing more than each of them standing in a special relationship to each of the others. The self-conscious mind suggests this sort of idea of the being of God, essentially one, relationally differentiated. If we substitute for self-consciousness self-esteem or self-love, precisely the same thing is still to be said. The self acting with respect to itself in any manner is affirming triplicity in unity. And the unity is identical with each of the three which enters into it although at the same time it is identical with all of them.

Finally, Augustine suggests an analogy which appears to be comprehensible only with respect to a mystical experience. When I am aware of myself, I am aware of a temporal being. But suppose we consider an instance in which I say that I love God, or I am conscious of God. Am I to say that here I have a closer analogy to what God in his own thought does? Augustine thinks so. For now the object to which I am giving my attention is an eternal Being and not a temporal or transient one. He does not work out in detail what right I have to say here, as I have said before, that the subject and the object are one. But I suggest that if one use the familiar language of mysticism, one can see here a sense in which this could be affirmed. In a sense, God is the Ground of my true being; I know myself most truly when I know myself in God. Or, to put it as Karl Barth and some of his followers have done more recently, in human apprehension of the Word of God, God is not object but Subject.[11] It is the Holy Spirit at work within the human mind that alone is able to apprehend the Word of God that is presented to the human mind. Indeed, even to say

11. While this is a fair enough statement of Barth's position in the *Römerbrief*, it is wrong as far as the *Dogmatics* is concerned. Throughout this work Calhoun's references to Barth reflect the common Anglo-American perceptions just after World War II [ed.].

"presented to the human mind" is dangerous because that suggests that God after all is given as object. What these men want to affirm is that God is never given as object, but that God is the energy through the action of which alone apprehension of divine truth can be effected. If one use some notion as that with respect to Augustine's final analogy, it appears to me that a part of his meaning may be discernible. At any rate, this is the point at which he thinks we fall least far short in seeing meaning in the dogma of the Trinity. If one never has this sort of experience, then the dogma must be accepted on authority without even the measure of insight that may be humanly attainable in optimum circumstances. It seems to me that what Augustine is trying to suggest is not a way to close the gap between man and God; not a way to make revelation unnecessary; but a way to see how revelation striking in from God's side can be apprehended from man's side in a way that will narrow the chasm and enable man to say not merely "I believe" but "In this way I understand."

In what way does the triune being of God differ from the manifold trinities—and I merely hinted at the multitude of them: each of these acts is itself triune in character, and all of them taken together constitute a sort of contrapuntal structure that characterizes the mind *qua* mind. Now how can I suppose the being of God differs from the being of this multitudinously trinitarian being of my own mind? The answer is: God is utterly simple whereas I am composite. Hence in myself, the very structured acts are susceptible of the kind of distinction between subject and property to which we have referred over and over again. I say a mind is capable of thinking—it has the power to think, and thinking is a property of that which is other than itself. But with respect to God, I cannot permit myself to use that language; in God, thinking is being; in God, loving is being; and the very being of God is indistinguishable from what we call divine powers and divine acts. Augustine is inclined to take wisdom as a sort of touchstone here. If we say God is the Father of wisdom, does that mean the Father first becomes wise when wisdom is eternally begotten? By no means. Rather we say wisdom is begotten by wisdom which is already there in the Father's being. We say the Holy Spirit as God is through and through wisdom just as Father and Son are through and through wisdom. And we must say once again, no one of these is less than the whole being of God. And we must not say any two of these are greater than the third. We must say rather we are dealing with a being in whom this triadic structure is so reduced to another unity in respect of essential being that each is the whole and the whole is each. And any two are identical in their deity with the third, and any two are identical in their deity with all three.

Now here we have a doctrine of the triune being of God. And it works itself out in what is sometimes called an ecumenical creed. In point of fact it is not that, but it is the so-called Athanasian Creed which has nothing really to do with Athanasius, but rather was influenced by Augustine. It is called also *Quicumquevult*—"whoever wishes" to be saved must affirm the being of God in the terms which we have just been looking at.[12] So far as the West is concerned, this Augustinian view became normative: this is the right way of thinking about God; this is the way in which the Nicene decision should be interpreted.[13]

12. Critical edition by Turner, "A critical text of the *Quicumquevult*," *JTh* 11 (1910) 401–11.

13. Calhoun here avoids siding either for or against the once widespread view that Augustine emphasized the oneness at the expense of the threeness of the triune God, with the result that "the tendency toward a Modalistic or Sabellian interpretation has always been common in the West (Arthur Cushman McGiffert, *A History of Christian Thought* [New York, 1932] I:270). For the most persuasive counter-argument of which I know, see Lewis Ayers, *Nicaea and Its Legacy: An Approach to Fourth-Century Trinitarian Theology* (Oxford: Oxford University Press, 2006) 364–83 [ed].

# CHAPTER 13

# Christological Controversies before and after Chalcedon[1]

SETTLEMENT OF THE DISPUTES with respect to the church's doctrine of the Godhead forced into the foreground another prime issue for Christian thought: the problem of the relation of the man Jesus of Nazareth to the fully divine principle, the eternal Son of God. More than once when we were discussing the Arian controversy, we noted that although Christological issues entered into it on both sides, they were not central. Both those who affirm and those who deny the Arian position concentrate their attention upon the nature of God himself and not upon the relation between God and man in the incarnate God-man. We recall that in the Nicene Formula there was a Christological passage, but it was secondary to the dispute concerning the nature of the eternal Word. But now that it has been settled at Nicaea and reaffirmed at Constantinople that the Logos, the Son, is in the full sense God—not a created being but an eternal principle—the problem of the relation of that second person in the Godhead to Jesus of Nazareth becomes very acute.

## APOLLINARIS AND HIS EARLIER CRITICS

The man who seems first to have realized how acute this problem is for Nicene theology was one of the foremost of the defenders of Nicaea— Athanasius' friend Apollinaris, Bishop of Laodicea in Syria, not far from Antioch. Without any hesitation or ambiguity, this younger churchman put himself on the side of those who declared that the Nicene formula sets forth the only acceptable position regarding the being of God. We have two creedal formulae in which his position is recognizable. One is

---

1. Most of chapter 20 of the 1948 transcript (II:180–199) is incorporated into the present chapter, but nearly half is drawn from later lectures [ed.].

taken from a work of his own, and is without any real doubt a statement of his own personal faith. The other, curiously enough, is to be found in a creed attributed to Athanasius and regarded as his work as early as the fifth century. Yet the text is such that it is incredible that Athanasius should have written it. I believe the most likely conjecture is that it was either by Apollinaris himself or by a member of the Apollinarian group.

But before we examine either of these two formulae, I shall sketch his position as this has been generally understood. His father had come from Alexandria, and both father and son were skilled in the rhetoric and logic of the Greek schools. Like his father, the younger Apollinaris had been a teacher before he became a bishop. For him the problem of Christology was to make intelligible the statement that a nature which is eternal, immutable, infinite, and perfect, should be present in time without alteration. Human nature is temporal, created, transient; it is not eternal. It is corruptible, not unchangeable. It is finite and imperfect. In all these respects, it is opposite to God's nature. In fact, that is what the Nicene controversy had been about—not the difference between God and man in particular but the difference between God and created being. Now, how could the full divine nature and the entire creaturely nature be conceived as existing together in one unitary being? It seems to Apollinaris that there is no way in which that can be affirmed on sound philosophical principles. A perfect or complete nature cannot be present along with a contrary perfect or complete nature in one single, undivided being. He thought that the only consistent view would be to affirm that either the divine nature or the human nature was complete and perfect in the God-man and that the other is present in some incomplete way. Now to say that the divine nature is imperfect or incomplete is to speak contradictorily, for the divine nature must be there fully or not at all. The only alternative is to say that the human nature is present in an incomplete way. The divine nature is fully present; the human nature present only in part.

But what part? Here Apollinaris was understood as appealing to a familiar conception of the human self as tripartite, consisting of flesh or body, the animating and sensitive soul which is the vital principle of that body, and the rational principle of mind which distinguishes man from other earthly beings. His suggestion was that in Jesus Christ we have what corresponds to these three factors: we have in him human flesh and a human animating and sensitive soul, but in place of the human rational principle or mind, we have in him the divine Logos. The center of personality is, of course, the rational principle. So in Jesus Christ, the center of personality is the divine Word which is fully personal, incarnate in a truncated or abbreviated human nature consisting of a body animated with its vital principle.

This conception not only avoided the logical difficulty of trying to combine infinity with finiteness, eternity with temporality, immutability with change, but also guaranteed our salvation according to the principle which Athanasius had laid down in opposing the Arians. You remember that in saying that the Word of God is a created being, the Arians had said he was therefore subject to change. But Athanasius countered that if salvation results from what is a happy accident rather than from an eternal necessity, then our salvation is not really guaranteed; if the divine Word could conceivably have gone astray, then the fact that we have been saved rests not upon a basic and inescapable principle but upon a contingent historical event. Apollinaris put forward a way of getting around that difficulty; if in Jesus Christ the highest principle is divine, then he could not conceivably go wrong. In all good faith he offered this solution for those who believed that the Godhead must be construed in Nicene terms; and that the incarnation must be declared not simply an assumption of the flesh, as the Arians had said, but in some more adequate sense the assumption of full humanness.

Now turn for a moment to the confession which is included in Apppolinaris' work which bears the interesting title, "The Faith in Detail" (*he kata meros pistis*).[2]

> We confess, therefore, one true God, one Source [or principle, *arche*] and one Son, true God from true God, having by nature the Father's deity, that is, *homoousion* with the Father; and one Holy Spirit, in nature and in truth Sanctifier and Deifier of all, being of the *ousia* of God. And those who say that the Son or the Holy Spirit is a creature we anathematize. We confess that all things made and subordinate [literally, creatures—*poiemata*—and slaves—*doula*] are made by God through the Son and sanctified in the Holy Spirit.

---

2. Critical edition in Lietzmann, *Apollinaris von Laodicea und seine Schule*; *Texte und Untersuchungen* I (Tübingen: Mohr, 1904) 167–85; Hahn, *Bibliothek*, §204.18, 278–80.

So far we are obviously dealing with a statement of Nicene doctrine in which Apollinaris follows the pattern which now has come to be regarded as obligatory; but then he continues:

> We confess that the Son of God became Son of man, not in name but in truth, taking flesh from Mary the Virgin; and that perfect [or complete, *teleion*] is this Son of God and son of man, one person [*hen prosopon*], and one the worship [*proskunesis*—adorableness, worshipability, or divinity construed in terms of the function of human worship] of the Logos and of the flesh which he assumed; and we anathematize those who declare that there are two beings here worthy to be worshipped; one divine and one human, and who worship the man (born) of Mary as another than the God of God.

What he is urging, you see, is unification of the person of Jesus Christ. He goes on to say:

> For God incarnate in human flesh keeps pure his own active energy, Mind being untouched by animal and bodily passions, and guiding the body and its movements divinely and sinlessly; not only unconquered by death but destroying death. And he is true God, the incorporeal, appearing in flesh, perfect in true and divine perfection, not two persons [*prosopa*] nor two natures [*duo physeis*].

Here is the key phrase in the whole statement. Neither two persons nor two natures, but rather one and two-thirds natures, comprises the full combination of one divine-human person.

> For we do not say that there are four to be worshipped—God, the Son of God, and a man, and the Holy Spirit. We therefore anathematize those who are thus impious, and those who make a man share in the divine glory.

In this sort of statement, Apollinaris is making plain a number of the concerns of Alexandrine Christologists. They want to regard the being of God as utterly untouched by historical or human accidents. At the same time, they want to be able to say that it is the incarnate word, God himself, who has effected the deification of human nature—the raising of human beings into a status of such union with God that the disabilities of human nature have been overcome.

The other statement, a creed attributed to Athanasius within two generations after his death, but far more probably Apollinarian, is important for the part it plays in the development of the theology of Cyril of Alexandria.[3] This is a fairly long creed, but I believe that we should get the opening of it into the record here.

> We confess the Son of God, the one who is begotten of the Father eternally before the ages, who in these latter times for our salvation was born according to the flesh of Mary the Virgin, as the divine apostle teaches saying, "When the fullness of time had come God set his son to be born of a woman." And that he is the Son of God and God according to the Spirit, but son of man according to the flesh. Not two natures [*ou duo physeis,* the same phrase that we had in the other writing of Apollinaris] (in) the one Son, one worshipped [*proskuneten,* divine] and one not worshipped; but one nature of the divine Word made flesh [*mia physin tou theou logou sesarkmenen*] and adored with his flesh in one adoration.

This phrase, "one nature of the divine Word become flesh," is a phrase that in the course of Christological debate in the fifth century becomes a sort of touchstone of the Alexandrine view, which develops straight into Monophysite doctrine. Its ascription to Athanasius strongly encouraged some of his successors in Alexandria in their opposition to Antiochene Christology, which tended to stress both human and divine as distinguishable principles. Apollinaris expressly directs his arguments against that sort of Christology.

We have then in Apollinaris an effort to find a Christological view which would be compatible with the Nicene decisions. He has stated the problem more clearly than anyone before him. For his pains he was attacked in all quarters and all schools by representatives of every theological view. Although Athanasius admired Apollinaris for his defense of the Nicene position, he nevertheless rejected his Christological formula insofar as this implied that the incarnate Logos is incompletely human. Athanasius himself, as you will recall, was ready to use quite loose phrases, declaring on the one hand that the Logos had assumed manhood (*anthropos*), but declaring on the other hand that the flesh was a garment which the Logos puts on and puts off. In any case, Athanasius' fundamental instincts begin

---

3. Lietzmann, *op. cit.,* 250–53; Hahn, *Bibliothek,* §195.10, 266–69.

to protest when he confronts Apollinaris' formula; whatever may be the right formula, this is not it.

The Cappadocian theologians who also were trained in this Platonic-Origenistic tradition likewise were strenuously opposed to Apollinaris' suggestion. Gregory Nazianzen puts his finger squarely upon the crucial point.[4] That in human human beings, he says, which most needs to be redeemed is precisely their rational minds and wills. It is neither their flesh that is in need of salvation nor even their animal souls; it is their rational, personal self that has gone most disastrously astray. According to Apollinaris' view, as Gregory understood it, it is precisely this rational self which is omitted from the God-man. And, says Gregory, "That which is not assumed is not healed"—a principle that poses the central issue and phrases it as sharply as possible.

Gregory of Nyssa offers a proposal for an alternative view which has its own defects. In a way it suggests Origen's view of the iron heated to incandescence in the fire until the character of the fire comes to pervade completely the iron which is thus heated. Gregory of Nyssa comes close to an illustration of that sort, but it seems to me his illustration misses the precision of Origen's. Gregory suggests that a drop of wine or vinegar in the ocean would become dispersed throughout the ocean without losing its authentic nature as wine or vinegar. Now suppose that the divine nature has a drop of humanity immersed in it. Although it will be genuine humanity, it will be so completely absorbed into the infinite deity that it will be as undetectable as would be the drop of vinegar or wine spread through the sea. That seems to be a particularly unfortunate kind of suggestion. It may save the complete humanity for logic, but for all practical purposes that humanity simply vanishes into a compound which is in no sense able to function as a human being.

---

4. In contrast to such past accounts as those of Calhoun (or Pelikan) of the Christological differences between Apollinaris and the Cappadocians, present-day scholars place the emphasis on an aspect neglected by their predecessors. In what is now the fullest treatment of the contrast and in partial dependence on Brian E. Daley, Rowan Greer, and K. M. Sproel, John Behr writes that the problem for the Cappadocians is that Apollinaris shifted "[t]he crux of Christ's work and of understanding his identity from his Passion to the new being and mode of life that he, as heavenly redeemer, has brought into the world ... an invincible divine mind ... who remains unmoved by the flesh ... and whose flesh imparts to us a new point of origin." *The Formation of Christian Theology*, vol. 2, *The Nicene Faith*, Part 2 (Crestwood, NY: St. Vladimir's Seminary Press, 2004) 401 [ed.].

## The Antiochene Christology

Still another group of theologians found Apollinaris' position quite un-acceptable. There was Diodore, bishop of Tarsus, who had received his training in Antioch and whom Apollinaris attacked. Only fragments remain of Diodore's own teaching, but we have a good deal more of the writing of his pupil and follower Theodore, who became bishop of the relatively unimportant town of Mopsuestia somewhat to the northwest of Antioch, between Antioch and Tarsus. Theodore was an extremely able Biblical exegete—indeed, the most noted Biblical scholar of his day—and a very sharp theological thinker.[5] There was in this same group a younger man, Ibas, who became bishop of Edessa, where the chief Syrian school of the later patristic and the medieval age was located. There was the church historian Theodoret, bishop of Cyros, and there were others. These men were all committed to a conception of the person of Christ which grew out of their uniform concern for careful, detailed study of the Scriptural record and its interpretation, as far as possible, in literal and historical terms. They did not make use of the allegorical method of interpretation by which such Alexandrine thinkers as Origen and his successors had moved easily away from the facts set down on the page into a realm of ideas of which those recorded facts were mere symbols. The school of Antioch held rather that the best way to get close to the initial spirit of the Gospels is to steep oneself with patience, care, and precision in the record of what Jesus said and did in his years on earth. They were impressed by the concrete detail the Scriptures afford of the human life of Jesus Christ; and it appeared to them indispensable that one should hold a view which did full justice to that historical detail. What emerges from that sort of study of the Gospel record is a vivid, concrete, intense picture of the man Jesus of Nazareth, and any Christology which substitutes some divine principle or other for that concrete human figure is rejected as simply not in accord with the teaching of the Scriptures.

The Christology that is characteristic of this Antioch group has rather obvious affinities with what seems to have been that of Paul of Samosata. We suggested that if he inclined to be Monarchian in his concept of God

5. Fragments of Diodore are collected in Abramowski, "Der Theologische Nachlass des Diodor von Tarsus," *ZNW* 42 (1949) 19–69. The best critical editions of Theodore's extant writings are often editions of separate works and may be found in Quasten's *Patrology*, vol. 3. For an English translation, see Mingana, *Woodbrooke Studies* 5 (1932) and 6 (1933).

the Father, he tended to be Adoptionist in his view of the relation of Jesus of Nazareth and the divine Logos. He declared that the unity of human and divine in Jesus Christ is a unity of will. This is the point which these Antiochene thinkers picked up and developed. It is an idea of perfect moral harmony, not a unity of *ousia*; it is that sort of unity which is to be described not first of all ontologically, but morally and personally. It is a unity not of nature (*kata physin*) but of grace (*kata charin*).

This indwelling (*enoikesis*) of God as moral unity is affirmed by all the Antiochene Christological theorists, and they speak of this moral unity very frequently in the rather cryptic phrase *henosis schetike*—a term for which I find no very satisfactory English equivalent. We can see what it means by a contrast with the alternative phrase, which we have already noted that the Antiochenes expressly reject. The unity is not natural unity or unity of nature (*henosis physike*); it is rather a unity of state or condition, harmony. What presumably underlies the adjective here is *schema*, which means pattern or structure or arrangement or order; and *schesis*, in the sense of habit or attitude or acquired disposition. The union of the divine and human in Jesus Christ, then, is the kind of union for which *harmony* is as good a word as I know.

This understanding of the relation of the divine and human in Christ has consequences for what is most essential in thinking about human salvation. The emphasis falls on moral regeneration rather than ontological change. Such change is also involved, to be sure, but fundamentally salvation demands a change of will and of action. Consequently, the Christology of the Antiochenes sets out from the concept of the image of God according to which human beings have been created and from which Adam has fallen away. And they understood the image of God as obedience to God's will; this is the sense in which we are made in some fashion corresponding to his divine author. And it is this image that Adam through disobedience lost. If the image of God is to be restored, the restoration must be fundamentally in terms of will and action, and this is precisely what the life of Jesus Christ effected. He wills and does at every moment precisely what God wills, and therein consists the restoration of the image of God. He completely filled out for the first time God's will for humankind as one capable of free and responsible initiative. And in so doing, he unites divinity and humanity by conjunction (*synathea*).

Yet there is not in the Antiochenes' view a duality of person in Christ. They do not say that there is a divine person and alongside the personal

Logos a human person; there are not two *prosopa*. There are not two sons, one divine and one human. There is one *prosopon* in which two natures are united, but they are not united in such fashion that they fuse together into one metaphysical compound. (That is what Apollinaris seemed to be suggesting.) They are present in such fashion that each remains distinguishable from the other, so that what Jesus does as hungering, tiring, suffering man is distinguishable from what he does as wonder-working, redeeming God. Once again, that does not mean that there are two halves of a dual personality here, one of which ceases to function when the other takes over. Rather, what is to be affirmed is that the power of God works in and through this man in such fashion that at no point is it possible to say: "*Here* is nothing of the human, whereas *here* there is nothing of the divine," nor yet to say: "*Here* the distinction between the human and the divine disappears."

Thus moral will and moral action effect an ontological conjunction, but it is a *conjunction*, rather than what the Alexandrines wanted to say, a *blending*. If the Antiochenes used most frequently the term *synathea*, the Alexandrines used perhaps most frequently and characteristically the term *krasis*, the term which comes from the mingling of water and wine in the mixing bowl, the *krater*, so that deity and humanity are fused together. They were willing to say similarly *synkrasis*; and they insist that the unity which they are talking about is *physike* or *kath' hypostasin*, which is to say a unity which goes to the very ontological center of the person of Jesus Christ. If we keep in mind the divergent concerns of these two sets of thinkers, we can see more clearly the reasons why each was inclined to regard the position of the other as unacceptable. The Alexandrines are urging the necessity that humanity be transformed into the state of incorruptibility—assimilated to God in such fashion that God's incorruptibility is made available for human beings. And this they think can come about only if the union of divine and human in Jesus Christ is, as they say, a "natural union," or union as regards basic nature. However, the Antiochenes, thinking that what is needed primarily is moral restoration which carries with it a change of character, but not in such fashion that the creature can ever become so assimilated to the Creator that we can properly talk of man as deified, want to describe the human in Christ [in relation to the divine] in terms which will suggest that it is *consonance*, or perfect harmony. And for that purpose they use characteristically terms drawn from personal life and personal action, for this is the area in which such a union is effected.

This is rather a subtle kind of Christology which tries to maintain within the conception of a single person the affirmation that true divinity and true humanity are both fully present—that is to say, without qualification or defect. [For Alexandria, however, this Antiochene conception failed to preserve the unity of Christ's person, just as for Antioch, the Alexandrine approach did not do justice to Christ's full humanity.]

## NESTORIUS AND CYRIL: ANTIOCH VS. ALEXANDRIA

Apollinaris, then, had started a discussion in which his own contribution was condemned on all sides—condemned in part by people who have not themselves worked out very satisfactory alternatives. The issue comes to light again in a peculiarly acute form in 428, about seventy five years after Apollinaris had first proposed his solution and had it rejected. In April 428, the year in which Theodore of Mopsuestia died, an Antioch man, Nestorius, who had been trained in the school of Theodore and held the views that had been taught there, became bishop of Constantinople. He took with him certain clergy from Antioch who had been trained in the same way of thinking in which he had been reared, and one of them began to urge the impropriety of talking of Mary as *theotokos*, that is to say, as one who has given birth to God. Now this formula had been for a long while liturgically entrenched; it carried with it emotional response of a deep-going kind. And to say to the congregation in the cathedral at Constantinople who were accustomed to give Mary this rank of honor: "You are talking nonsense; it is impossible for a created being to precede, as a parent must, the God who created her"—that was bound to stir up all sorts of hostile responses.

Nestorius came to the defense of his Antiochene priest, preaching a series of Advent sermons on the term *theotokos*. Those sermons exist now in fragmentary form, but we have very considerable portions of some of them, and they are extremely interesting.[6] Used by Origen, Eusebius, and Athanasius, the term *theotokos* is usually translated with poetic if not with

6. Loofs, *Nestoriana: die Fragmenta des Nestorius* (Halle, 1905) 225–31; new ed., 230–42 ; Nau, *Le Livre d'Héraclide de Damas, traduit en français, suivi du texte grec des trois homélies de Nestorius sur les tentations de Notre-Seigneur et de trois appendices* (Paris, 1910) 335–58; Baur, "Drei unedierte Festpredigten aus der Zeit der nestorianischen Streitigkeiten," *Traditio* 9 (1953) 101–26.

literal correctness as "Mother of God." I suppose a more literal rendering is "God-bearing," but the word means God-bearing as a mother bears a child, not as a believer bears the Holy Spirit. The more colorless translation *God-bearing* simply evades the issue. The issue is whether or not it is proper to speak of Mary, even in a poetic way, as the one whose child is by nature divine. Nestorius says no. Mary is the mother of the man Jesus, not of the divine Logos. Call her *Christotokos* if you like, for she was in literal fact *anthropotokos*, mother of the man who was assumed at the incarnation by the divine Word, but *theotokos* is out except in the carefully guarded sense that she can be called "mother of God" only by reason of the unity of the divine Word with the human son which she bears. Now a prudent man does not barge into a long-established liturgical custom and simply declare that a long-familiar part of it is henceforth forbidden. One just does not do that sort of thing, but Nestorius did it.

Immediately, those who were inclined to affirm that this term is not only poetically but theologically right took occasion to defend it against Nestorius' protest; and among these, unfortunately for him, was the very able, very influential, very unscrupulous bishop, Cyril of Alexandria.[7] At that moment Cyril was himself in some difficulty, having been accused to the emperor, and to Nestorius himself as patriarch of Constantinople, of dictatorial and improper conduct of his office as bishop. Cyril not unnaturally welcomed the chance to step forward as the champion of orthodoxy. Nestorius had given him an opening for diversionary action, and he was quick to take advantage of it. He declared that Nestorius was a heretic in thus rejecting the traditional affirmation about Mary, the mother of our Lord, and bringing into question the Lord's divinity itself.

The position that Cyril was prepared to maintain was that in the person of Jesus Christ, the Logos is united with a complete human nature, which is, however, generic rather than individual. That is to say, the Logos, without giving up any of his own proper being, assumes in addition the general characteristics of humanity. In this sense Cyril used often the Apollinarian phrase (which he attributed to Athanasius): "one nature

---

7. Whether Cyril fully deserves the dark picture of his character that prevailed when Calhoun lectured on him is open to dispute. The facts connected with the Council of Ephesus in 431 that Calhoun later describes are not in dispute, but the political tensions— to defend the prestige of Alexandria against the upstart see of Constantinople—were enormous. For a glimpse of a very different side of Cyril, see Robert L. Wilken, *The Spirit of Early Christian Thought* (New Haven: Yale University Press, 2003) 115–21[ed.].

of the Word of God incarnate" (*mia physis tou theou logou sesarkomene*). Jesus Christ, then, is one who can be called fully God and fully, but not individually, man. Thus two natures are present in him, although one of them is present in such fashion that its presence is logical, shall we say, rather than dynamic; and the unification of these two, so Cyril insisted, constituted physical or natural unity (*henosis physike* or *henosis kath' hypostasin*).

Cyril urged this position against Nestorius, and Nestorius struck back. Cyril sent to Nestorius a list of twelve anathemas, insisting that not simply *synathea* but also *henosis physike*, *krasis*, and so on shall be affirmed.[8] Nestorius brushed off Cyril's warning, talking very tactlessly about children's arrows that can't hurt him and about the carelessness of a good shepherd with respect to what the wolves may think about him.[9] But the dispute had already been brought to the notice of Coelestine, bishop of Rome; and in this particular stage of the controversy, Rome sided with Alexandria. In 430 a Roman synod rejected the position of Nestorius, and Coelestine wrote to him indicating that he appeared to be a wolf and a hireling, and that he had ten days in which to recant or be excommunicated. At the same time, he directed Cyril to see that his decision was carried out. Pretty clearly, the dispute called for some higher authority to intervene, and a general council was summoned to meet in 431 at Ephesus, which was about halfway between Constantinople and Alexandria. Cyril and Nestorius alike were called to be present and to offer their respective views for decision.

Ephesus had the great disadvantage for Nestorius that the route by water from Alexandria could be covered in very quick time, whereas the land route his supporters would use from Palestine and Syria was likely to take a good while longer. As a result, Cyril arrived early, long before most of Nestorius' supporters from the region of Antioch could get there. Fifty bishops were in his party. He had come by ship from Alexandria, and the sailors and the stevedores went ashore, paraded in the streets of Ephesus, and announced the truth in respect to the theological issues which were at stake. Nestorius and ten bishops friendly to him were also on the ground. The members of the Alexandrine delegation were invited

---

8. Cyril's works are found in PG 68–77 and in numerous critical editions. English translation in *LFC* [?] 43 (1874), 47 (1881), and 48 (1885). For a critical edition of Epistle 17 and the anathemas, see E. Schwartz, *ACO* I.1.33–42.

9. For Nestorius' letters, see Schwartz, *ACO* I.

to speak in the Churches of Ephesus while the Nestorians were excluded, because Memnon, bishop of Ephesus, was strongly in favor of the position of Cyril. The council itself opened late because the most important of Nestorius' supporters were delayed in their overland travels and had not arrived. John of Antioch and Theodoret were indispensable people for the presentation of Nestorius' case. The opening session was postponed from June 7 for a week and then another week, but still the Syrians did not come. Instead of waiting any longer, and in spite of the official protest of the emperor's representative, on June 22 the council was called into session with about two hundred members present—and with Cyril in the chair. Nestorius was summoned to appear before the council and he refused to do so. Consequently, writings attributed to him were read before the council; and in a single day's session, the council decided on the basis of these excerpts that Nestorius was a heretic and "with many tears" he was deposed and excommunicated.

Four days later, John of Antioch and his contingent from Syria arrived. After hearing what had been done, they forthwith held a counter-council, attended by forty three bishops and Count Candidianus, the emperor's legate, who had also arrived late. They deposed, excommunicated, and anathematized Cyril of Alexandria and Memnon of Ephesus, and excommunicated all who did not repudiate the twelve anathemas which Cyril had circulated against Nestorius. When Pope Coelestine's legates arrived, they accorded papal confirmation to what had been done by Cyril and his confederates. The main body of the council resumed sessions on July 10 and enlarged the scope of their excommunications to include John of Antioch and all his party.

These irregularities were reported in due course to the emperor, who, however, decided to confirm the action of both parties. It seemed to him that both Nestorius and Cyril had been properly read out of the Church. Nestorius was sent into exile according to the unhappy precedent set at Nicaea. Cyril was also banished, but his sentence was lifted after a very few months. He found suitable ways of appealing to the emperor and hence his questionable theological opinions, whatever they may have been, were overlooked. In consequence, he was restored to his position in Alexandria on condition that he and John of Antioch must agree on a formula which would obviate further controversy. Cyril apparently was in a chastened mood, and John of Antioch was a little bothered by Nestorius' obstinacy regarding a liturgical phrase; consequently, John proposed a formula (the

"Symbol of Union") in which the admissibility of the term *theotokos* was declared and in which the position of the Antiochenes was set forth in more general and conciliatory terms. The text of this formulary of re-union becomes of great importance for the later decision at Chalcedon.[10] Cyril subscribed to it in 433, though much to the disgruntlement of some of his more extreme supporters. It reads in part:

> We confess our Lord Jesus Christ, the son of God, only-begotten, perfect God and perfect man, of rational soul and body [thus excluding Apollinarian thought]; on the one hand, begotten of the Father before the ages according to the Godhead, but in the last days the same one for us and our salvation begotten of Mary the Virgin according to humanity, *homoousion* with the Father according to his Godhead and *homoousion* with us according to his humanity . . .

Identical in essential being with us and with his mother because according to the Antiochene view, it is impossible for a mother to give birth to one who is not essentially of the same nature as herself

> For a union of two natures came about . . .

Notice how very wide open a way is left by that phrase, which gives no indication of what kind of *henosis* but simply states that a union was effected,

> Thus one Christ, one Son, one Lord, we confess, [and then later on in the statement] in one *prosopon*, two natures can be discerned.

Cyril was quite ready to regard this as concordant with his own understanding of the Alexandrine tradition so long as one does not understand it to suggest a separation of divine and human in Jesus Christ. "In thought" one recognizes that he is both human and divine, and that is in a way distinguishing the natures. But any suggestion of the natures operating independently of one another must be thwarted. And it seemed to him that the Antiochene view led precisely to that sort of double or parallel action. This statement, then, he was quite ready to accept, despite the scandal the compromise created for certain of the extremists in his party.

---

10. Schwartz, *ACO*, I.4; Hahn, *Bibliothek*, §170. English translation in Hardy and Richardson, eds., *Christology of the Later Fathers*, LCC 3 (London: SCM, 1954) 355–58.

On the other side, however, the supporters of Nestorius were also scandalized because he was condemned by both John and Cyril and his deposition confirmed. Theodoret in particular was offended, and he became a kind of attorney for the Antiochene defense through the whole controversy, which continued on during the rest of his lifetime. He refused to anathematize Nestorius, who, as it seemed to him, had been teaching what the tradition of Antioch required all the while. So this phase of the controversy ended in a kind of armed truce declared by both sides. The next time the argument arose, it was in a much more virulent form.

Nestorius remained in exile in the desert area of the upper Nile in spite of his repeated and pathetic protests that his were views which later decisions heartily regarded as orthodox. His most extended defense of these views is in a very curious work, which we have now only in a Syriac version. It has the strange title *The Bazar of Heraclides*. The work became available in an English translation only in 1925.[11] As a matter of fact, it is difficult to tell even with that work in hand whether Nestorius is or is not orthodox in the sense of the Chalcedonian definition.[12]

11. Critical edition by Bedjan, *Nestorius: Le Livre d'Heraclide de Damas* (Paris, 1910). English translation by Driver and Hodgson, *Nestorius: the Bazar of Heracleides. Newly Translated from the Syriac* (Oxford: Clarendon, 1925).

12. Professor Calhoun had an aversion to detailed lecturing on texts which he could not read (and quote!) in the original, and so it is not surprising that he discussed Nestorius' *Bazar* at length only once (in the 1948 LHCD II:186–87). We have omitted this discussion from the main text, but as it is not without interest even to specialists, it is reproduced in what follows:

> In Nestorius' presentation of his doctrine in the *Bazar*, which he claims to have held all the while, the key word is *prosopon*. And the position which he seems to defend in this work is that before the incarnation, one can recognize two *prosopa*, one divine and one human; but after the incarnation there is but one *prosopon*. The union, then, on this view is labeled in the textbooks a prosopic union rather than—following Cyril's terminology—a hypostatic union. So in the God-man there are not two persons, there are not two sons, there are not two individual beings; there is only one. In other passages Nestorius speaks of two natures, using sometimes the term *physis*, sometimes the term *ousia*. He ascribes to the divine *ousia* its appropriate character and to the human *ousia* its appropriate and different character, and declares that they are united in one *prosopon*. As you will recall, that is very close indeed to Tertullian's formulation: *duae naturae, una persona*.
>
> The term *prosopon*, as the editors of this translation are at great pains to point out, refers in the first sense to that which is perceptible as an individual being. That means the phenomenon that we call a human person—the appearance, the visible body, that by which we judge that there is an individual here. Then the term is contracted in meaning until it refers to the face by which we distinguish

one individual from another. Then by extension it is assigned to the mask by which a role on the stage is indicated. In any of these cases, the term *prosopon* refers to that which is superficial or manifest rather than to that which is fundamental or essential. But metaphysically it means something more extensive than that. It means the observable properties and behavior of a real entity, so that we have a kind of sequence of this sort: *ousia* is fundamental being; *hypostasis*, as the Origenists and especially the Cappadocians have sought to distinguish that word from *ousia,* means fundamental being determined in a specific way; and *prosopon* means the manifestation of that distinctiveness of being. One can't then have a *prosopon* apart from a *hypostasis; prosopon* is that by which one recognizes a hypostatic being. Now what Nestorius is saying in effect is that it is possible to recognize deity in Jesus Christ in the works of wonder, in the manifestations of power; and it is possible to recognize humanity in him in the indications of weakness, weariness, of hunger, of sorrow, and the like; but it is also possible to recognize that there is a single, unitary manifestation which combines both human and divine attributes made manifest. The prosopic unity therefore which he is urging is discovered by reading the stories in the Gospels, by reading the references in the prophets on the one hand and in the apostles on the other. But what they tell us refers to what he observably was and did, and it is plainly one personal life about which they are talking—but one personal life in which we can recognize the presence of some activities which are used for humanity. But the choice of this word *prosopon* by Nestorius still leaves the inner nature of his beliefs in some doubt. That there is but one appearance in Jesus Christ is perfectly plain. But what lies back of that one appearance is precisely what is here in question, and on that point one gets the impression that Nestorius is thinking in relatively primitive rather than in relatively subtle and sophisticated terms.

Take another passage. "In that which concerns the humanity he is not by nature divine but by revelation. But in the nature of the divinity there exists a great difference between those who are called gods or lords or christs, but in the humanity he is like them all, and there is one *prosopon* in two natures." That is Tertullian's formulation without any change at all as regards the wording. "He is God and he is Lord and he is Christ; for he makes not use of a *prosopon* which has undergone a division but makes use of it as of his own *prosopon.*" The man's mind simply labors and belabors these repetitive terms rather than working out a precise and systematic analysis that would make plain the meaning of the terms. "For all the things appertaining to the *ousia* are his by virtue of the union and not by nature" (*Bazar,* II.i.287; Driver and Hodgson, 206). That is to say, the properties which we regard as divine properties are assumed by the human nature in virtue of its union to the divine. It is not that the human nature is a special human nature already divine; rather, it acquires its divinity by reason of its unity with the Logos. Again, as far as Nestorius goes, he is saying what the Church eventually declares must be said. "He was not transformed and changed from his divinity, just as also the humanity of Christ is not changed in nature from [that of] men except in honor and in *prosopon:* for he is God of all and Lord and Son; and in all the things which are the divinity in *ousia,* in them exists the humanity in honour, not by another honour but by the same as that of him who took the *prosopon*": (that is, the human nature becomes worthy of the same honor which we pay properly

His effort to vindicate himself from the charge of subversive teaching enlists one's sympathy, but a part of his trouble was his own inability to make sufficiently sharp and definite the thing that he is trying to say. He is caught in the toils of a theological subtlety which his mind grips hard but without very much precision. At all events, whereas Cyril was recalled from exile and restored to his place in Alexandria within two months, Nestorius, surely no more culpable than Cyril, remained to bear the burden of his error until his death about 452. After the Council of Chalcedon in 451, his confidence that he had been vindicated by the decisions of the Church was even stronger; and the cry that comes from his barbarous place of banishment in Upper Egypt appealed to the decision of the universal church as evidence that he had been right all the while. Instead his name became for everyone, except for such staunch supporters as Theodoret, a label for a heresy to be disapproved throughout the church, and which it is not clear he ever held.

Now I think there may be some point in pausing here in the course of narrative for a few further comments on the doctrinal significance of the positions which were involved. In the first place, if we say in Jesus Christ both deity and humanity are present, we need to raise the question how far the humanity is genuine and complete. Apollinaris was interpreted as saying that it is not complete. Cyril rejects this view expressly, emphatically, and repeatedly, insisting that so far as he is concerned, when it is said Jesus Christ is a composite being of two natures, that means of two complete natures; he is complete Godhead united with complete humanity. But if we say complete humanity, just how much does that imply with respect to the independence of being of the human side of Jesus' life? Both of these groups were prepared to say that the human nature is permitted to develop according to its own laws; and that this involves a kind of *kenosis*, a kind of self-restraint on the part of the deity. For if the human nature were completely overwhelmed by its union with deity, obviously enough it would not be able to grow as human nature does grow. The Alexandrines, however, wanted to restrict this growth to physical development. They argued that the full mind of God is present

---

to the divine being, and that in virtue of his union therewith). "The humanity making use of the *prosopon* of the divinity and the divinity of the *prosopon* of the humanity, since for this it has been taken and for this he has taken it, not indeed so that we should not confess him who was taken but that we might confess him" (*Bazar*, II.i.287; Driver and Hodgson, 207) [ed].

in Jesus Christ from the beginning, but that the self-restraint which is exercised voluntarily by the divine nature in him is such that he can properly enough speak of himself as ignorant of certain events without really lacking perfect knowledge. The Antiochenes want to go much further. They contend that the development applies both to body and to mind, so that the human nature on their showing has initiative, makes its own choices—always in harmony with the divine nature that is present, always in harmony with the will of the Father—and therefore always displays the image of God which Adam had lost but which in Christ is for the first time being perfectly restored. There is at this point, then, it seems to me, a crucial difference between the two ways of thinking. Both say Jesus Christ embraces full humanity as well as genuine deity. Both say the human nature is permitted by self-restraint on the part of the divine nature to grow in its own proper way. But the one group desires to keep this growth restricted to the physical sphere; the other desires to have it characterize also the mental sphere. And it is for this reason that the Antiochenes were prepared to argue that the full and complete image of God is to be seen in Jesus Christ only at the resurrection. Up to that time, there have always been other decisions still to be made, other possibilities not yet closed. But once the Lord had obeyed the will of his Father completely to the very last moment of his life, and once the Father's approval is made plain in his rising from the dead, then one can see the image of God now for the first time since Adam fully realized in human form.

In the second place, a term which in the earlier part of the controversy had been somewhat less prominent than *ousia*, *hypostasis*, and *prosopon* comes to be crucial: *physis*, which means "nature" and which like *ousia* and *hypostasis* could be interpreted as either a nature shared by members of a natural group or a concrete individual member of such a group. One could talk of *physis* then as meaning an individual being, or one could talk of *physis* as meaning a sharable essential character. Obviously, it would make a very great difference whether one were understanding the term in the one sense or the other. Now as the controversy continued, two phrases come to be watchwords of the two contesting groups. On the one hand, the Alexandrines insisted that although it is proper enough to think of Jesus Christ as "of two natures," i.e., one who is a composite being in whom both humanity and deity are included, it should not be said that after the union he still is to be thought of as "in two natures." To say he is "in two natures," they said, is Nestorianism. It leads directly to the affirmation that there are two Sons or two persons; it splits the unity of the Savior's being and so lands one directly in the heresy that had been condemned. On the other hand, if we say he is "of two natures," we may be willing to go further as Cyril himself had done and to say "in thought alone one can distinguish two natures in him." We will not say he exists in two natures, but we can say deity and humanity are both recognizable and so distinguishable but never divisible. "Of two natures," then, for the Alexandrines and "in two natures" for the Antiochenes.

Thus to summarize, we have a theological debate between two schools. One, the school of Antioch, as we saw, is largely historical in its presuppositions. It insists that the right understanding of Jesus Christ requires painstaking, literal-minded study of the scriptural record. What emerges from such a study is a concrete, vivid picture of the man Jesus of Nazareth, and what is to be said about his divinity must be harmonized with what is here recorded about his humanity. On the other hand, there is the school of Alexandria, in which scriptural study had long been carried on with the principles of allegorical or spiritual interpretation as a guide. Moreover, mystical and metaphysical rather than historical and ethical emphases had helped to shape theological thinking in Alexandria. Therefore, Alexandrine Christological thought is likely to tend toward a stress on the divinity rather than on the humanity of the Lord. This emphasis was central for Athanasius and for the Cappadocians, and now is championed especially by these Alexandrines. In their concept of redemption, *theopoiesis* or deification understood metaphysically is central. But how is that deification of the believer to be brought about, unless the redeemer himself is primarily God, who appears in the midst of human life but is not himself human in any such way as to compromise his ability to transform human life? On the other hand, the thinkers of Antioch, without excluding deification, stress historical and ethical considerations in interpreting the person of Jesus Christ. This theological controversy between two great schools is therefore one primary factor in the growing conflict.

## After Ephesus: Alexandria vs. Rome

The Council of Ephesus of 431 is commonly listed as one of the ecumenical councils, but in point of fact the sessions were highly inconclusive. Doctrinally, the most important thing that came out of it was a statement of policy that no new creed was to be framed or taught other than that which the fathers had adopted at Nicaea. A decision of that kind, however, was not going to leave anyone very well satisfied, excepting those who were concerned above everything else for papering over the cracks in the life of the church. There were supporters of Cyril and of the Alexandrine Christology who insisted that people like Theodoret and Andrew of Samosata who were still supporting Nestorius must be compelled to denounce him. On the other hand, Theodoret, who was the ablest theologian still living in the Antiochene group, insisted that those twelve anathemas which Cyril had pronounced against Nestorius must be disapproved, if possible by Cyril himself; but if not by Cyril, at any rate by the rest of the church.

Temporarily the argument quieted down, but in 444 Cyril died and was succeeded as bishop of Alexandria by the more violent Dioscurus, who followed the line not simply of defending Cyril but also of seeking to destroy the whole Antiochene theological tradition. He agreed with the more extreme supporters of Cyril that Theodore and Diodore as well as Nestorius deserved to be condemned. Two years later, the place of Nestorius' successor in Constantinople was filled by Flavian, a much milder member of the Antiochene faction. The Antiochenes from their side accused their opponents of being Apollinarian; that was a customary term of abuse on the one side, just as Nestorianism was a customary term of abuse from the other side.

Yet the factors which enter into the continuing controversy were quite as largely political as theological. Constantinople had only recently moved up to a position of political preeminence. It was after Constantine had made himself emperor of the whole Roman world that he turned Byzantium into a second Rome; and since he chose Constantinople rather than Rome as his imperial seat, the city even professed to have a certain primacy in comparison with Rome itself. By common consent before this time, Rome had been given the number one position, Alexandria the number two position, and Antioch the number three position. The older churches had been ranked according to the traditions of their apostolic foundation. Rome claimed first place because two apostles of the top rank were supposed to have had a hand in the founding of that church; both Peter and Paul had helped to establish the Christian community in Rome. Alexandria claimed Philip as founder. Antioch is the place where, according to records in Acts, Christians were first called by that name;

and both Peter and Paul had been there. Constantinople had no claim at all to apostolic foundation, and Byzantium was not one of the missionary churches of the apostolic age. But because of its political dominance, Constantinople was now laying claim to ecclesiastical preeminence in the very top rank. It was not Rome which was chiefly endangered by that claim, for by now the primacy of Rome was everywhere acknowledged. Not that Rome exerted authority over the other churches, but Rome was commonly given first rank. Alexandria and Antioch, however, were very seriously concerned over the new claims put forward on behalf of Constantinople. Curiously enough, these claims worked in opposite directions. The bishops of Constantinople for a considerable period of time were drawn from the Antiochene school. Consequently, there was a theological affinity between Antioch and Constantinople. For that reason Alexandria regarded both Antioch and Constantinople with aversion and was likely to seek the support of Rome against both of them. On the other hand, the Western theology, which had been formulated by Tertullian, agrees much better with the Christological thought of Antioch than with that of Alexandria. Consequently, we find the bishop of Rome taking now one side and now the other side in the course of the controversy. When Nestorius and Cyril appealed to Coelestine, Rome took the side of Cyril. But now when the controversy breaks out all over again, we shall find Leo, bishop of Rome, taking the side of Flavian, bishop of Constantinople.

About 448 an elderly monk, Eutyches, who had achieved eminence as head of a monastic community near Constantinople, and who took pride in his own theological acumen and orthodoxy, began teaching a very strange doctrine.[13] He said that in Jesus Christ there is a fully divine nature so that he is *homoousios* with the Father, but he is not *homoousios* with us. In other words, there is in him no genuine human nature at all. There is "one" nature after the incarnation. When pressed, Eutyches was forced to say that before the incarnation there were two natures, one divine and one human, so that one may say of the Lord, he is of two natures (*ek duo physeon*); but one must not say of him that after the incarnation he exists in two natures (*en duo physesin*). After the incarnation, the divine and the human fuse so that there is but one nature and it is divine. In the course of the controversy, that position comes to be labeled Monophysite, which means "only one nature."

---

13. See Hahn, *Bibliothek*, §222.34, 319–20.

Now Eutyches had the misfortune to come under the scrutiny of a man who had taken part in the earlier controversy—a man who prided himself as much as Eutyches on being a vigorous defender of the faith. He was Eusebius of Dorylaeum, a man of no historical importance as far as I know, save as he succeeds in precipitating a major dispute in the church over the position taken by Eutyches. Eusebius of Dorylaeum declared that Eutyches was teaching heretical doctrine; and Eutyches appealed to Dioscorus of Alexandria, feeling rightly enough that his conception of one nature in Jesus Christ was in line with the Alexandrine rather than with the Constantinopolitan or Antiochene Christology. Dioscorus immediately rallied to his side against Eusebius of Dorylaeum. Since Eutyches was within the jurisdiction of Constantinople, Flavian had to take account of this new development in the dispute, and with his Antiochene background it seemed to him that Eutyches was completely off the road and was teaching a conception which has no justification in Christian teaching or in the Scripture.

Although Flavian had no enthusiasm for taking issue with so highly influential and popular a figure as this aged ally, there was no way really to avoid it. In 448 he called a home synod to meet in Constantinople in order to examine the view which Eutyches was accused of teaching. Eutyches pleaded illness and declined to present himself for examination. A succession of representatives of the synod was sent to interrogate him, but they got only evasive replies. Among other things, they asked him whether he held that Jesus Christ is *homoousios* with us as regards his human nature. And he said, "I've not read any such statement as that in the fathers; if you say so, doubtless it must be so." They asked him whether he regarded the human nature of Jesus Christ as in the full and proper sense human. "Well, yes, it is a human body, but not the body of a man." Obviously he was trying to avoid the Nestorian alternative here that would suggest a man alongside a divine being. Well, is Jesus Christ *homoousios* with his mother? And again, Eutyches pleaded theological naïveté. He just was not expert in these matters and he would prefer not to be pressed. What he did do was to insist that he stood by the Creed of Nicaea—which, of course, has no particular relevance to the issues that are now involved. He held with the decision taken at Ephesus not to prepare another statement of faith other than the one which had been approved by the 318 fathers. It was impossible then to get Eutyches to give a clear account of what he himself believed; he tended always to turn the issues back on his interrogators, asking them what they believed. So they had to report back to the home synod that they got nowhere with him, and that he still refused to appear.

Now by canon law, if after a third summons an accused refuses to appear to examination, he can be condemned on grounds of contumacy without any necessary reference to his orthodoxy or unorthodoxy. So the home synod declared that Eutyches is to be brought under condemnation, and the synod went on to say that on the ground of some of his answers, it seems clear his teaching was in fact unorthodox. He was teaching that there is only one nature in the person of Jesus Christ, and that one is the divine nature.

So in conjunction with the synod in Constantinople in 448, Flavian declared Eutyches heretical and excommunicated him. Eutyches appealed to Cyril's writings, as pretty much everybody did on occasion; and to a statement which Cyril himself had thought was a statement of Athanasius, that after the incarnation we must speak of one incarnate nature of God the Word.

Actually, as we have noted, that statement appears in a creed which is probably Apollinarian; we never find Athanasius using that particular sort of language.[14] But it is important, I think, to see exactly what it does and what it does not say. It does not say that in Jesus Christ there is only one nature, namely deity; what it says rather is that there is in him one incarnate nature. The term *physis* can here be understood in the sense of concrete individual being. He is one incarnate person, if you will, and this you can say of the Logos only as incarnate. This is not then a statement which denies the humanity; it is a statement which denies any division within the incarnate Word. But Eutyches appealed to it as a kind of justification for his own very different way of thinking which slurred over the humanity of the Lord without using either Apollinarian or Docetic terms.

When both parties appealed to Rome, Leo I recognized the position which Flavian was defending as in line with Western tradition. (Interestingly, Flavian did not send word to Dioscorus in Alexandria or to Juvenal in Jerusalem. Domnus in Antioch and Leo in Rome would approve what the synod had done, and they got official notification.) In June 449, Leo wrote to Flavian a long, careful theological letter in which

---

14. See n 3 above.

he defined very precisely the Western Christology, which holds that in the person of Jesus Christ there are two complete natures, one divine and one human; that they are united in him without confusion yet inseparably, without division, in such fashion that in him we recognize one person in whom two natures are present inseparably and perpetually. This document became known as the Tome of Leo, and is a simple, clear, assured, and moderate though uncompromising statement of a position which later at Chalcedon is affirmed to be the position of the church.[15] Part of Leo's concern in setting forth this view was for the right interpretation of the sacramental practice of the church. What Eutyches affirmed would make impossible the proper understanding of the Eucharist. If you say that the Lord is not of the same essential being with us, then there is no natural or physical basis upon which the Eucharist can be rightly interpreted. In a letter to the emperor's sister Pulcheria, Leo made a similar point about baptism. This sacramental and legal emphasis is characteristic of his thinking. His concern was for the tradition which was regarded as correct everywhere in the West, not for one Eastern theological-philosophical conception of the incarnation as against another. It is not primarily Antiochene but Western thought that he is defending.

Leo's attitude toward Eutyches was uncompromising though not unsympathetic. He recognized that he was an elderly and rather dim-witted person who prided himself unduly on his theological acumen. If he is ready to recognize and acknowledge his error and submit to the teaching of those who are better qualified than he to decide upon the truth, then let him come back in. But if he is going to remain obdurate, there is nothing that the church can do but to recognize and affirm that he is out of bounds.

Eventually this was done in the formula of Chalcedon, but that decision was still two years in the future. In 449 the supporters of Eutyches had the upper hand. Dioscorus saw a chance to come to the support of a man who is holding a view which he regarded as properly the traditional one. He therefore received Eutyches into communion, although the synod had condemned him and excluded him from reception as a fellow cleric. Flavian had hoped that Leo's intervention might settle the issue without the need for a general council, but Eutyches and his friends were

---

15. Schwartz, *ACO*, II.2.1; Hahn, *Bibliothek*, §224.36, 321–30. An English translation may be found in Hardy and Richardson, LCC 3:359–70.

obdurate, and correspondence with Rome was interrupted by more than one delay.

So the emperor summoned a council to meet at Ephesus in August 449. Dioscorus and his Alexandrines arrived in full force; and following the bad precedent set by Cyril, had himself installed as chairman of the council. Leo was unable to be present but was represented by a bishop, a priest, and a deacon as legates, whose instructions were set forth in the Tome. Theodosius was represented by two noblemen of the court. Flavian was present as one of the parties to the controversy; Eutyches also was there in a total assembly of 135.

Dioscorus' program was simple: to confine discussion to the positions affirmed at Nicaea and at the earlier council of Ephesus in 431, where Nestorius had been condemned; and to insist that Eutyches' assertions were in accord with these earlier decisions. If Eutyches was acknowledged on this basis to be orthodox, it followed that those who sought his condemnation were themselves to be condemned. The Tome of Leo was handed to Dioscorus but not read to the council. Antiochene representatives like Theodoret were refused seats in the assembly. The proceedings from start to finish were one-sided. Leo's delegates made no effective protest at the suppression of his doctrinal letter by the hostile presiding officer. Harnack says of the council "that it was guided by one vigorous and determined will, that of Dioscorus."[16]

Dioscorus focused the attention of this council of 449 in Ephesus on the one feature of Eutyches' position that had most widespread support: that after the incarnation there was but "one nature of the divine Word incarnate and made man." This affirmation, it will be recalled, had been strongly urged by Cyril of Alexandria, who appealed to the (Apollinarian) creed which he and others took to be a statement of Athanasius. Dioscurus had therefore impressive support for this particular item in Eutyches' faith. Even the Roman legates were not ready to fight against tradition on this issue. Eutyches therefore was declared orthodox, without any explicit approval of the more novel and dubious tenets referred to in Flavian's letters.[17] Hilary the deacon, one of Leo's legates, made his escape from

16. As the German edition from which Professor Calhoun translated the above quotation has not been located, the reference here is to an English translation somewhat different from his: Adolf Harnack, *History of Dogma* (New York: Dover, 1961 reprint of the ET of the 3rd German edition "that appeared circa 1900") 4:208 [ed.].

17. The position of Eutyches that had been condemned by a synod at Constantinople

the council to avoid being forced to subscribe to a decree exonerating Eutyches and by implication censuring both Flavian and Leo. Leo says the Roman legates protested strongly against the decision; but whether from conviction or fear or both, the council decreed as Dioscorus directed.

From this decision, practical consequences followed. Eutyches was restored to communion and to his monastic dignities. Flavian and Eusebius of Dorylaeum, his accusers, were deposed and excommunicated. Similar action was taken against Ibas of Edessa and Theodoret, men of the Antiochene school; various lesser churchmen; and finally Domnus, bishop of Antioch, who opposed the further measures demanded by Dioscorus. It is hard to know how to appraise the stories of overt violence that Gibbon has recited from sixth-century historians: the bursting-in of the church doors by a partisan mob; the hustling and trampling of the elderly Flavian, so that he died shortly afterward; the panic-stricken cringing and wholesale surrender of the opponents of Dioscorus. Harnack accepts as fact the terrorizing of the council by Barsumas and his wild monks, but he regards it as "not at all certain" that Flavian was "trodden half to death." Loofs enters a cautious verdict of "not proven." What nobody doubts is that Dioscorus was from first to last the unqualified master of the situation and emerged as the first Eastern patriarch who had successfully defied and defeated Rome. When at some time after the council he excommunicated Leo himself, the act was symbolic of the completeness of his victory.

## THE COUNCIL OF CHALCEDON

Leo, however, was far too stubborn and resourceful an antagonist to be written off in spite of his grievous loss of prestige in defeat. The condem-

---

in 448 was thus described by Flavian in two letters to Leo: "... he persisted in saying that our Lord Jesus Christ ought not to be understood by us as having two natures after his incarnation in one substance (*hypostasis*) and one person (*prosopon*): nor yet that the Lord's flesh was of one substance (*homoousion*) with us, as if assumed from us and united to God the Word hypostatically: but he said that the Virgin who bare him was indeed of the same substance with us according to the flesh, but the Lord himself did not assume from her flesh of the same substance with us." And again: "... that before the incarnation, indeed, our Savior Jesus Christ had two natures, Godhead and manhood: but that after the union they became one nature; not knowing what he says, or on what he is speaking so decidedly." T. A. Lacey, ed., *Appellatio Flaviani: The letters of appeal from the Council of Ephesus, A.D.449, addressed by Flavian and Eusebius to St. Leo of Rome* (London: SPCK, 1903) n.p.

nation of Flavian and the obvious one-sidedness of the decision left him in a highly irate frame of mind. He had been simply and insultingly ignored, even though he was the first of the whole series of Roman bishops, as far as I know, who had expressingly and emphatically claimed doctrinal authority over the decisions in non-Western parts of the church.

Theodoret and other victims of the *Latrocinium*, the "Robber Band," as Leo promptly named the Ephesian synod, turned to the Roman pontiff for help. His dogmatic letter, the Tome, that had been unheard at Ephesus, now circulated widely in the East and found numerous adherents. Leo wrote urgently to Theodosius and to Pulcheria, his older sister, who was favorable to Leo and to the Antiochene point of view, seeking a new general council to be convened in Italy, under the closer influence of Rome. Theodosius, however, was wholly disinclined to do anything to upset the decision which had been taken in 449 and nothing came of Leo's urging until Theodosius died in 450. Pulcheria succeeded to the throne, and her husband Marcian called another council to meet at Nicaea in 451. A shift of plans transferred the meeting place to Chalcedon, across the Bosporus from Constantinople under the very eyes of the imperial court. There, in October 451, some six hundred churchmen gathered in the largest ecumenical council of antiquity. And this time it was Leo and his supporters of the imperial court who had the advantage. The imperial commissars acted as presiding officers. Leo had been pressed by Marcian and Pulcheria to attend in person and take the first seat among the churchmen present, but declining to leave Italy, he sent two bishops and a priest as his legates. They, not Dioscorus, this time had the place of honor and the first vote on roll calls. Dioscorus had been enjoined by the emperor to come from Alexandria alone, without his company of monks and bravos, and even before the first session was convened, it was evident that he was regarded as a culprit, condemned in advance.

Although his position was hopeless, Dioscorus appears to have borne himself with defiant self-respect. When the council was opened, Paschasinus and Lucentius, the Roman legates, challenged the right of the Alexandrine patriarch to sit as a member of the council at all since he had "come to be judged," not to sit in judgment. The referees of the discussion, the lay commissioners representing the emperor, decided that temporarily at any rate, pending a decision from the emperor himself, both Dioscurus and the other five men who had been with him at the council of 449 should be suspended from active participation in the council. Dioscorus, as a matter of fact, was put into custody. The other five, curiously enough, beginning with Juvenal of Jerusalem who quite blatantly crossed over from Dioscorus' side of the table to Leo's side, were given a kind of unacknowledged remission of sentence. But Dioscorus was kept in seclusion from the conference. Then Eusebius of Dorylaeum, the original accuser of Eutyches, presented a petition, and the Acts of the Councils of Ephesus in 449 and of Constantinople in 448 were reviewed. Since the latter had been held under Flavian's jurisdiction, and his exposition of the Christological issue was in its records, the question of the orthodoxy of Flavian "of blessed memory" was directly posed and the delegates were asked to vote. Paschasinus, the chief Roman legate, and Anatolius, patriarch of Constantinople, voted in approval of Flavian's words. Lucentius quickly cut in with a declaration that if Flavian were thus approved, those who condemned him should be condemned. The voting continued, with Antioch and Caesarea likewise voting approval of Flavian. They were followed by the legates of lesser churches, with all but complete unanimity, in spite of the fact that two years earlier many of these same men had voted with Dioscorus and in all likelihood still believed with him. When Dioscorus himself was given a chance to speak on the decision affirmed by the council of 448 in Constantinople, whose Acts were now under review, he said bluntly, "The phrase 'of two (natures)', I accept; the 'two (natures)', I do not accept" (*to ek duo, dechomai; to duo, ou dechomai*). I am forced to be impudent, but the matter is one that touches my soul."[18] He could agree that the life of Jesus Christ had a twofold origin, divine and human. He could not and would not agree that duality of nature persisted in that life itself. "I can prove from Athanasius, Gregory, and Cyril that one should speak only of one incarnate nature of the Word after the union."[19] He was a man who was not prepared to compromise on what appeared to him to be genuinely the tradition to which he was committed.

It had become clear in the first session that the papal legates and the imperial commissars had the council well in hand; and in due course, a directed verdict of guilty was pronounced on Dioscorus by six hundred churchmen, most of whom believed as he did. Flavian, Eusebius, Theodoret, and the rest were now rehabilitated. It remained to issue a

18. *NPNF2* 14:248 [ed.].
19. Ibid.

confessional statement to settle the debate, and formally to condemn Dioscorus and Eutyches. Many of the bishops, understandably enough, had no desire for a new statement that would affirm what they did not believe. They much preferred to rest on the decisions of Nicaea (325), I Constantinople (381), and Ephesus (431). Especially they did not want Leo's Tome adopted as a dogmatic definition. But the papal legates—and apparently the emperor's commissioners—were inflexible. The old statements had not prevented this controversy, and only a new statement would settle it. The upshot was the drafting and presentation of a confessional formula which, in its decisive passages, followed the Tome of Leo in substance and professed to be in accord with the synodical letters of Cyril (letters to John of Antioch and to Nestorius, the latter including the twelve anathemas, the former including the text of the Formulary of Reunion). In the end, the Eastern churchmen were not forced to accept the Tome of Leo as the dogmatic statement of the council, but the formula proposed and adopted was based on Leo's statement and defines as dogma the doctrine he had set forth:

> Following the holy Fathers we all, with one voice, define that there is to be confessed one self-same Son our Lord Jesus Christ, perfect in godhead and perfect in manhood, truly God and truly man, of rational soul and body, [thus Apollinaris and Eutyches are excluded] *homoousion* with the Father according to the godhead and *homoousion* with us [against Eutyches] according to the manhood, like us in all respects excepting sin; before time (*pro aionon*) begotten of the Father according to the Godhead, in the last days for us and our salvation (born) of Mary the Virgin, Mother of God (*tes theotokou*), according to the manhood, one self-same Christ, Son, Lord, Only-begotten, made known in two natures: (*en duo physesin, in duabus naturis* [though one Greek source has "of two natures," which would nullify the point of the council's decision], inconfusedly, immutably [*atreptos*; that is to say, the Godhead, being incapable of change, must not be supposed to have altered its character in the incarnation—against Eutychean and Apollinarian views], indivisibly, inseparably [against the Nestorians]; the differences of the natures by no means being anulled through the union, but rather the peculiarity of each nature being preserved and (both) concurring into one person and one substantial individual (*hen prosopon kai mian hypostasin*), not divided or separated into two persons, but one self-same and only Son, (one) divine Word (*theon logon*),

(one) Lord Jesus Christ, as from of old the prophets taught concerning him and as the Lord Jesus Christ himself taught us and the creed of the fathers has transmitted to us.[20]

What we have then is a statement that the unity in Jesus Christ is a unity which manifests itself to the observers in the guise of a single person who acts both as man and as divine Word, and this unity must be thought of as hypostatic; that is to say, it is a unity that goes deeper than appearance. It manifests itself in observable actions and qualities, but those actions and qualities are grounded in a genuinely extant individual being.

In view of the immense complications of the discussion that followed Chalcedon, I think it may be worthwhile to spend a minute or two considering the nature of the formula which was adopted there, taking note of the intent as far as one can make it out of those who agreed to this formula. In the first place, it is not called a new *creed*. We recall that, as at Ephesus in 431, so at Chalcedon, it is reiterated that the faith adopted at Nicaea is sufficient and that no one is to introduce a new statement of faith. This formula then is supposed to interpret rather than to extend what was earlier decided. In the second place, it is chiefly a reaction against the teaching of Nestorius; he was regarded as the chief of sinners in the matter of theological doctrine, whereas his opponent Cyril was viewed on all sides as a spokesman for the genuine tradition. Rejecting a Nestorianism which was supposed to be a teaching that in Jesus Christ there were two persons or two sons—one human and one divine, this formula represents Cyrillian doctrine at the same time that it leaves room for a more moderate version of the Antiochene Christology. It also, of course, reflected the influence of Western Christology as represented in Leo's dogmatic letters to Flavian.

## After Chalcedon: Monophysitism and Compromise

It is not inaccurate to speak of the decisions of Chalcedon in 451 as roughly comparable to the decisions at Nicaea in 325, in the sense that the creed adopted became forthwith a bone of contention rather than an accepted settlement. The West was happy enough because Leo's doctrine had got a fair enough statement; but among the Easterners, who only two

---

20. Text of creed in Schwartz, *ACO* II.1.322–26; in Hahn, *Bibliothek*, §146.1, 166–67 (Greek) and §147.2, 167–68 (Latin). English translation in *NPNF2* 14:262–65; and in Hardy and Richardson, LCC 3:371–74.

years before (in 449) had nearly unanimously concurred with Dioscorus in repudiating Flavian's and the home council of Constantinople's condemnation of Eutyches, there were still to be found men—some of them extremely able theologians—who said this formula simply will not do, not primarily because of what it affirmed but because of what it did *not* affirm. During the controversy, a great many Eastern churchmen were most concerned to stress the incorruptible, immutable character of Jesus Christ. It seemed to them that this could best be assured if one declared that in him there is one dominant nature after the incarnation and that the nature is divine. Although he is to be declared in some sense man, that affirmation must not in any way prejudice the judgment that he is completely and impregnably perfect. If they call him human in the ordinary sense, one is in danger of saying that he is liable to sin. That was a point on which the Monophysite theorists were continually insisting. There is no way of regarding human nature as invulnerably sinless; and if one is to speak of the redeemer as sinless, then he cannot be in the ordinary sense human.

On the other hand, their opponents were convinced that a redeemer who was simply divine could not be a redeemer of humankind. Both parties were thinking in the categories of Greek metaphysical theology, and the redemption upon which they were intent was the deification of the fallible, corruptible, mortal human nature. As far as they could see, the only way in which that deification could be brought about was through the entrance of the divine creative power into the nature of man. To one group it seemed necessary to minimize the Savior's humanity, to avoid any possible diminution or contamination of his deity. To the other group, it seemed clear that if the redeemer were a divine being but not genuinely human, then he could bring about no real transformation of human nature.

The issue between the two groups, therefore, was one that involved fundamental religious principles, although the terms in which the issue had been stated thus far were terms which tended to obscure that issue. The participants were arguing about the metaphysical concept of *ousia* or *physis*, which was construed in relatively impersonal terms. When one uses the terms *essence* or *substance*, one is speaking in terms which are applicable not merely to personal existence but also to the existence of things. When one talks of the essential being of a tree or a stone, or of an irrational animal or of a human being, or of God, one is using the same vocabulary all the way through. Later on, the medieval schoolmen are going to insist that the term *being* cannot be used of Creator and creatures in the same sense (univocally) but at best in an analogical sense. The way to that conclusion had already been opened by Neoplatonic thought. But that distinction has not yet been clearly made in theological debate. Consequently, when we find these thinkers talking of a divine substance or nature, or a human substance or nature, we find them talking of an essentially nonpersonal base of existence. But the issue as regards the redeemer's sinlessness or changeability can be stated in terms that are religiously and ethically meaningful only if one recognizes that what one is concerned about is the Redeemer's status *as person*. Some impersonal substance present in him is hardly to be taken as the subject of either right or wrong conduct, good or bad choice. As long as the issue was posed in terms of this conception of essence or substance, it was posed in terms that tended to obscure the fundamental question over which the debate was raging.

The formula adopted in 451, based as we have seen on a statement of Leo that was forensic and practical rather than metaphysically precise and analytical, served merely to rule out views that were disapproved, not to solve the central problem. (This indeed is the proper function of dogmatic formulae; but to say so is to underscore the need for continual reexamination of the issues, even after a dogma has been decreed.) In the debate that followed 451, the strength of Monophysite views in the East became more and more evident. The collapse of the Western empire, the increasing difficulty of communication between East and West, a widening of the breach between patriarchs and popes that had been opened during the contest of Dioscorus against Leo, and the desire of a succession of Eastern emperors to reestablish unity among their Eastern subjects contributed to strengthen the Monophysite position. The position which the Antiochene school shared, at least verbally, with theologians of the West was at best a minority view in the East; and though Eutyches' inexpert fumbling was recognized as out of bounds, and Dioscorus had lost any title to theological importance, the position of Cyril of Alexandria was a rallying point for both moderate and extreme Monophysites. The formula of Chalcedon, moreover, could be interpreted in a Cyrillian sense; and although many Monophysites would have been glad to see it abrogated, much of the effort over the long period of controversy was directed to establishing a Cyrillian version of Chalcedonian orthodoxy.

Not unnaturally, theology and ecclesiastical maneuver were inseparable from imperial politics. Just as the attitude of Constantius had very
much to do with the rise of Arianizing views in the east after Nicaea, so now
the attitude of emperors who succeeded Marcian, himself a proponent of
the Chalcedonian settlement, gave aid and comfort to the opponents of
Chalcedon. Two emperors, indeed, made early attempts to rescind or to
bypass the formula. In 476, the emperor Basiliscus condemned it; and in
482 his successor Zeno published a compromising formula of unity, the
*Henotikon*, in which the two natures are acknowledged but the unity of
the God-man is chiefly emphasized, and anathema is pronounced against
all who have thought otherwise, "whether in Chalcedon or in any such
Synod." This so-called *Henotikon* of Zeno pleased nobody. It bypassed
practically all of the distinctive terminology in the Chalcedonian formula: stressing the unity, slurring over the distinctiveness of the natures that
remain even after the union, and encouraged the non-Chalcedonians to
press still harder for a rejection of the creed. Instead of being, as its name
suggested, a basis for union, it became a basis for still more determined
disunion. Thus the more skillful statesmen such as Justinian, a very powerful ruler who became sole emperor in 527 and reigned until 565, sought
rather to use the Chalcedonian formula itself, suitably interpreted, as a
basis of union.

This task was complicated by divisions within the Monophysite
movement as well as by denunciations from Rome. Before Justinian came
to the throne, two conspicuous Monophysite leaders had become recognized as heads of a moderate and an extreme wing. Severus of Antioch
led the moderates, who followed Cyril in affirming the true and complete humanity but insisted that the redeemer is in the strictest sense
one. "We confess one divine-human nature and subsistence (*mian. . . .
physin kai hypostasin theandriken*), as also one nature of the divine Word
incarnate"—the old watchword of Cyril. The Chalcedonian phrase "in
two natures" (*en duo physesin*) and all similar phrases were rejected. At
the same time it was affirmed that the earthly body of the Lord was a real
human body, subject to growth and hunger, weariness and pain, whereas
only after the resurrection did it become incorruptible and impassible.
Some of the Severians were ready to make similar assertions even about
the mind of the Lord, conceding that he grew in wisdom as well as in stature and therefore was not from the beginning omniscient. In sharp contrast to this moderation, the followers of Julian of Halicarnassus declared

that from the very moment of his conception, the body of the Lord was incorruptible. It was not, therefore, in the proper sense frail flesh at all. It was made susceptible to pain, fatigue, suffering, and death only through the free act of his will. In its own proper being it was a miraculous body, not vulnerable or mortal. There was bitter disagreement between various Julianist subgroups on how exactly to characterize Christ's body, but the Severians accused them all of Docetism—called them, with scrupulous and picturesque precision, aphthartodocetists ("those who think the incorruptibility is merely make-believe"). The Julianists retorted by accusing the Severians of phthartolatry (of worshipping a corruptible being, a creature). With passionate conviction and with mouth-filling epithets, these and many more fractional Monophysite groups carried on fierce controversy both against the diophysite orthodoxy of Chalcedon and against one another.

It is important to note that from one point of view these people were not really what the textbooks call them: Monophysites. Sometimes a distinction is made between *monophysis* and *henophysis*, rightly enough grammatically. The former is a term which means solitary or alone; the latter, internally undivided. Now if these people were Monophysites, they would be saying, "There is only one nature in Jesus Christ and that is a divine nature separate from all humanity." What they rather say is, "The incarnate nature in him is so internally unified that it is impossible to name division or separation so as to assign some of his works and acts to one nature and some to another." Thus the sense in which they were non-Chalcedonian was that they saw the formula as selling out to the Nestorians and as adding to what traditionally has been required in statements about Jesus Christ.

Outside these aggressive Monophysite parties but within the tradition of Cyrillian Christology, a school of Scythian monks worked at the task of interpreting the Chalcedonian formula in a manner inoffensive to the moderate Monophysites. The chief theologian of this school was Leontius of Byzantium (d. 543), who devised an ingenious compromise proposal. The formula affirms that there are and remain two natures in the incarnate Lord. Cyril had held that one of these, the human nature, was present in generic and abstract rather than in individual, concrete status. He had described the human nature as anhypostatic (*anhypostatos*), devoid of concrete individual being. It was generally agreed that this was a difficult conception because wherever there is a nature (*physis*), it is necessary that there be some *hypostasis* or subsistence, some individual being, with which that *physis* or essential character is united. To have a generic nature that does not characterize any individual being is not readily conceivable. So to acknowledge, even as far as Cyril did, that the Logos assumed real humanity seemed to require a second hypostasis characterized by that human nature; or else it seemed necessary to say that there is present in Jesus Christ a generic human nature with nothing which it characterizes, a nature which has no solid locus in the person of Jesus Christ at all. The alternatives seemed to be either Monophysitism or the frank duality of Western Christology, which prevailing opinion in the East found unsatisfactory.

Now Leontius' suggestion is one of those brilliantly deceptive proposals that seem to effect a major result by a trifling change to which nobody should object. Leontius employs a concept which Severus of Antioch had already used—the concept that if we say two natures are distinguishable in thought in the person of Jesus Christ, it is not necessary to suppose that each of these natures must have a separate *hypostasis*. He proposes that instead of speaking of the human nature in Jesus Christ as *anhypostatos*—that is, as abstract, generic, devoid of individual ground, one may speak of it as *enhypostatos*—that is, as internally individuated, and affirm that the individual being characterized by human nature is nothing other than the divine Logos. One fully concrete nature, it is held, can be the *hypostasis* for another; thus we have in the person of Jesus Christ the divine Logos to serve as *hypostasis* for both of the natures which are declared to be discernible as we contemplate his personal life. Two natures, then, but a single *hypostasis* for both of the natures, which are declared to be discernible as we contemplate his personal life. If this proposal be adopted, the person of Jesus Christ involves the presence of the Logos as a full hypostatic reality, and generic humanity as characterizing the Logos himself as incarnate. If the formula of Chalcedon were understood in this way, it would avoid the appearance of saying that two *hypostases* are present in the redeemer. At the same time, if Cyril's statements—so widely popular in the East—be understood in this way, they would avoid the suspicion of implying that the human nature is not really complete in every respect. It *is* complete—a nature with its own proper *hypostasis*. But the *hypostasis* is, in Cyril's language, "the one nature of the divine Word incarnate," not a separate *hypostasis* within the divine-human person. Therefore, there is full hypostatic union of the two natures. Both the letter of the formula and the spirit of Cyrillian Christology are preserved. The only thinkers who could find no comfort in it were the extreme Monophysites and the Westerners and the Antiochenes. The latter, who since Chalcedon had seemed to have authoritative opinion on their side, Leontius is quite prepared to condemn.[21]

Moreover, the policy of the powerful emperor Justinian from his accession in 527 was to unite the East on a Cyrillian reading of the formula of Chalcedon—the policy of the Scythian monks represented by Leontius. Very early he gave public approval to one of their favorite liturgical formulae: "One of the Holy Trinity suffered in the flesh."[22] He promulgated (in 543 or 544) an edict generally known as the *Three Chapters*,[23] that condemned in detail three of the Antiochene leaders: Theodore of Mopsuestia, Ibas of Edessa, and Theodoret. (He condemned incidentally—on political rather than theological grounds—the great progenitor of so much Eastern theology, of whom both Cyril and Leontius thought highly, and who was not directly involved in the current debate on Christology: Origen, hitherto frequently attacked but never authoritatively condemned.)

Pope Vigilius of Rome in 548, with serious misgivings and with some explicit reservations, but in deference to the emperor, approved the imperial edict on the *Three Chapters* with its indictment of the Eastern thinkers with whom the West most nearly agreed. His action resulted at once in the revolt of the bishops of three major provinces of the West; and in 550, the bishops of Africa excommunicated Vigilius himself. The reactions of his Western colleagues must have caused him some very sober second thoughts. For when Justinian summoned a new general council in 552— the fifth ecumenical council and the second of Constantinople—Vigilius went to the place of meeting but declined to attend the sessions, and issued a statement reversing his former stand. The council, however, carried out in detail the program which the emperor had himself marked out. In

---

21. See PG 86:1194–1768 for Leontius' works, especially *Against the Nestorians and Eutychians*, PG 86:1267–1358. (Leontius' version of the enhypostatic union of the two natures was replaced in orthodox Eastern Chalcedonianism by a different understanding, largely through the influence of Maximus the Confessor (d.662). See Pelikan, op. cit., 2:88–89.

22. This theopaschite formula originated with a Scythian monk, John Maxentius [ed.].

23. The edict is no longer extant [ed.].

a lengthy *Sentence* it echoed his condemnation of the Antiochene leaders in the *Three Chapters* with explicit and detailed reference to that edict.[24] On the grounds that *henosis* can be taken in many senses, it condemns "those who follow the impiety of Apollinarius and Eutyches, confusing the unity, and those who think the things of Theodore and Nestorius, since they favor a division (*diairisis*) and bring in a *schetic* unity. (Once again, I don't know how to translate that term; it is usually translated *relative* but that seems to me to be so vague that it means almost nothing; it is dispositional or habitual; it is an acquired unity rather than an innate and substantive unity. Both of these sorts of error are to be excluded.) And then by name, Theodore of Mopsuestia is condemned at great length together with his writing: in this instance both the man and his works. Then certain of the writings of Theodoret are condemned, specifically those which were directed against the orthodoxy of Cyril. And, finally, a letter of Ibas to Maris (or Mari) the Persian is anathematized.[25]

24. For English translation, see *NPNF2* 14:306–11.

25. In one listing of the heretics who are declared to be out of court, Origen's name appears at the end: Arius, Eunomius, Macedonius, Apollinarius, Nestorius, Eutyches, and Origen (*NPNF2* 14:314.11). In this statement there is no clear rationale for Origen's inclusion. We have a list of what purport to be fifteen anathematisms directed against Origen by this council, but the scholars are in hot debate as to whether this list actually was adopted by this council or whether it represents the judgment of the earlier and local synod which Justinian had convened among the clergy of Constantinople in 543, at which the emperor's own nine anathematisms against Origen were considered. In any event, there seems little doubt that they represent the judgment of the effective majority in 553.

Some of the doctrines which are anathematized are highly interesting (*NPNF2* 14:318–20). Here is the anathema of Justinian himself against Origen: "Whoever thinks that human souls preexisted, i.e. that they have previously been spirits and holy powers, but that, satiated with the vision of God, they had turned to evil, and in this way the divine love in them had died out (*appsygeisas*) and they had therefore become souls, (*psychas*—cooling down, you see) and had been condemned to punishment in bodies, shall be anathema" (*NPNF2* 14:320.1). "If anyone says or thinks that the soul of the Lord pre-existed and was united with God the Word before the Incarnation and Conception of the Virgin, let him be anathema" (*NPNF2* 14:320.2). That, of course, is central to Origen's Christology. "If anyone says or thinks that the body of our Lord Jesus Christ was first formed in the womb of the Holy Virgin and that afterwards there was united with it God the Word and the pre-existing soul, let him be anathema" (*NPNF2* 14:320.3). Neither before nor after the conception of the body but rather at the very moment of the conception the union must be affirmed. "If anyone says or thinks that the Word of God has become like to all heavenly orders, so that for the cherubim he was a cherub, for the seraphim a seraph: in short, like all the superior powers, let him be anathema" (*NPNF2* 14:320.4). Nowhere so far as I know in the extant writings of Origen is that said. "If anyone says or

Vigilius of Rome, who was present in the city but did not attend the council, as already noted, sought to block the action desired by the emperor by preparing a doctrinal statement of his own, independently of the council. In it he rested on the authority of the Council of Chalcedon, in which Ibas and Theodoret had been accepted as members, affirming that while any doctrinal errors of the three Antiochene leaders must of course be rejected, they should not themselves be condemned; and that the letter of Ibas in particular could be interpreted in a quite orthodox sense. He went so far as to declare that his present view must be accepted as binding on all churchmen, and that if any other view had been set forth "by anyone whomsoever, this we declare void by the authority of the Apostolic See."[26]

Needless to say, Justinian was not the man to be intimidated, and the council was fully under his control. He refused to receive the new statement prepared and addressed to him by Vigilius, instead sending a memorandum to the council bidding that Vigilius' name should be removed from the diptychs, the records of the orthodox—in short, that he be excommunicated as a heretic—on account of the "impieties" which he defended.[27] This apparently was done, although there was no question of severing communion with the Roman Church itself. There exists a letter that purports to have been written by Vigilius in December 553, after the adjournment of the council, in which he changes ground again. If the letter is genuine, it is an abject surrender to the council and the emperor: ". . . we annul and evacuate by this present written definition of ours whatever has been said by me or by others in defense of the aforesaid

---

thinks that, at the resurrection, human bodies will rise spherical in form and unlike our present form, let him be anathema" (*NPNF2* 14:320.5). Well, once again, nowhere in the extant writings of Origen are resurrected bodies called spherical. The stars are spherical, and maybe somebody did say that we are going to be like them, but there is no clear indication that Origen said it. "If anyone says the heaven, the sun, the moon, the stars, and the waters that are above heaven, have souls, and are reasonable beings, let him be anathema" (*NPNF2* 14:320.6).

There are also additional doctrinal anathemas; yet what we have here, so far as I can see, is a condemnation, not of the writings of Origen by one who was familiar with those writings, but of what certain sixth-century Origenists were teaching and representing as the teaching of their master. Origen's name, at any rate, is for the first time formally included among heretics condemned by an ecumenical council.

26. See *NPNF2* 14:323, note 2.

27. *NPNF2* 14:303.

Three Chapters."[28] He died about a year later, during his return to Rome. Rebellious groups in the West held out for another century and a half, and the bonds between East and West were subjected to unremitting strain.

## MONOTHELETISM AND THE END OF THE CONTROVERSY

Meanwhile, in spite of the Cyrillian victory, the thorough Monophysites were not reconciled. As Loofs points out, even the relatively moderate Severus had recognized in the Tome of Leo, which had dictated the crucial Chalcedonian phrase "in two natures," an as yet unresolved source of difficulty for Monophysites: the declaration that "Each nature in communion with the other does what is proper to itself." The divine nature works miracles, the human nature suffers. But to speak thus of two natural actions or operations (*duo physikai energeiai*) is to imply two individual beings (*hypostaseis* or *prosopa*), two wills (*duas thelematon*). Even if the question concerning *physis* were settled in favor of Cyril's formula, the implications of affirming that the human nature has its own mode of acting continued to keep the issue in doubt.

Shortly after 600, when the rising threat of Islamic expansion was pressing upon the Eastern Empire, it seemed desirable to make further efforts to win over the Severians. The patriarch Sergius of Constantinople shrewdly advised the Emperor Heraclius to offer a new statement respecting the issue of unity or duality of action or operation in Jesus Christ. The way to a possible agreement on this point with the Severians was suggested by a phrase in the writings of the widely venerated mystic known as Dionysius the Areopagite, of whom we shall hear more later. A hundred years earlier, Dionysius had written that "one selfsame Christ and Son works divine and human deeds by one divine-human act" (or operation —*mia theandrike[i], energeia[i]* ).[29] Sergius believed that agreement could perhaps be reached on this basis. The patriarch Cyrus of Alexandria concurred, and in 633 issued a proposed formula of union centering around that phrase. But Sophronius of Jerusalem strongly protested in a long and careful doctrinal statement of 634, in which he stresses again the duality of the God-man's works.

Sergius was prepared to concede the difficulties of discussing *energeia* in this context but suggests that if it seems improper to talk of one

28. *NPNF2* 14:323.
29. Reference uncertain [ed.].

*energeia* in Jesus Christ, at least it is no better to talk of two, for that immediately implies (as Severus had insisted) two wills that may be contrary to one another. This shifting of the ground of discussion to the Biblical and moral concept of will seemed to offer real hope of agreement. Surely in Jesus Christ there must be one will, even if it be the joint operation of two natures? Can we not say there is one theandric will in him and develop a Christology which comes to be called *monothelite* or *monothelete*? This view, when Sergius offered it to Pope Honorius, won the approval of the Roman prelate: "We confess one will (*hen thelema*) of the Lord Jesus Christ." With such support, the emperor promulgated in 638 a statement of faith which rejected the possibility of correctly affirming two wills that may be in conflict, and goes on: "Whence, following the holy Fathers in all things and also in this, we confess one will (*hen thelema*—Honorius' phrase) of our Lord Jesus Christ the true God."[30]

But in spite of the formidable backing given to this statement, it did not after all settle anything. One may judge that it was a clear advantage to have the discussion shifted now from impersonal terms like *nature* and *substance* to such personal terms as *act* and *will*. But the interest of the emperor was not in fruitful discussion; it was in political stability. This was made harshly clear by a new emperor, Constans II, who in 648 forbade under severe penalties any further debate. The reason was that the successors of Honorius in Rome refused to accept the statement of 638, and the old specter of political strife was rising once more from the field of theological discussion.

The ablest theologian who took part, Maximus the Confessor, a Greek monk devoted to the Chalcedonian doctrine, strongly supported the dyothelete position of the West. Since human nature consists essentially in moral will, he urged, to affirm that there are two natures in Jesus Christ implies that there are two wills, not indeed conflicting but really distinct. Conversely, to say that in Jesus Christ there was but one will, that of the Logos, is in effect to say that he was not essentially human at all. But we hear him pray: "Not my will, but thine be done," and say to his hearers, "I am come not to do my will, but to do the will of the Father who sent me." Such statements would be meaningless if he had no human will, distinct from—though not conflicting with—the will of God.

---

30. Hahn, *Bibliothek*, §234.46:343–44.

The controversy dragged on under the shadow of the imperial prohibition until Constans was murdered in 668. Strife between the East and Rome continued without remission until the new emperor, Constantine Pogonatus, summoned a sixth ecumenical council (as it turned out) to Constantinople in 680–81. In this council, attended by representatives of all the great sees, Pope Agatho plays a part like that of Leo I at Chalcedon. On the basis of the decisions by a Roman synod under one of his more vigorous predecessors, Martin I, in 649, he sends a long doctrinal letter to the council of 680, considering and rejecting in detail, with numerous citations of authority, all forms of Monophysite and Monothelete doctrine. His own position is that of Maximus. To affirm two natures requires that we affirm two wills, in perfect harmony but not simply one. To this view the council gave dogmatic status:

> After we had reconsidered, according to our promise . . . the doctrinal letters of Sergius, at one time patriarch of this royal God-protected city, to Cyrus, who was then bishop of Phasis and to Honorius some time Pope of Old Rome, as well as the letter of the latter to the same Sergius, we find that these documents are quite foreign to the apostolic dogmas, to the declarations of the holy Councils, and to all the accepted Fathers, and that they follow the false teachings of the heretics; therefore we entirely reject them, and execrate them as hurtful to the soul.[31]

The decree proceeds to condemn by name Sergius, Cyrus of Alexandria, Honorius, Macarius the present bishop of Antioch, and various others; and to approve Sophronius of Jerusalem, who had been the first to oppose Sergius' efforts to appease the Monophysites. Then, in a positive definition of faith, the council proceeds:

> . . . defining all this we likewise declare that in him are two natural wills and two natural operations indivisibly, inconvertibly, inseparably, inconfusedly, according to the teachings of the holy Fathers. And these two natural wills are not contrary the one to the other (God forbid!) as the impious heretics assert, but his human will follows and that not as resisting and reluctant, but rather as subject to his divine and omnipotent will.

---

31. *NPNF2* 14:342–43.

So too there are two natural operations, one divine, one human, similarly described. "Wherefore we confess two wills and two operations, concurring most fitly in him for the salvation of the human race."[32]

That was the end of the long, weary, and at many stages arid controversy. One of the outstanding characteristics of this dispute is the absence from it of any single figure who is comparable to Athanasius in the dispute over the Nicene decrees. For Athanasius, the primary issue was one of profound religious concern. To his mind the discovery of technical terms was entirely subordinate to the preserving of the essential religious emphasis. He was quite ready to concede differences of terminology if only he were assured that folk other than himself were intent upon the right fundamental view. And the right fundamental view must be that our redemption is of God and cannot be from a created being.

Now as the controversies over the person of Jesus Christ continued, the disputants increasingly give the impression, as far as my reading would indicate, of concern for political expediency or metaphysical subtleties rather than for fundamental religious values. They lack a genuine desire to understand what opponents using other language intended to mean. In contrast, let us keep in mind what Athanasius succeeded in doing with respect to the conservatives under Basil of Ancyra, when he said "Let's argue with these men as brothers and not reject them as enemies; they're afraid of our terminology, but we know our terminology is best for the purpose which they also have in mind. Since their purpose is the same as ours, let's urge that the folk on our side regard them as friends and potential allies and let the folk on the other side be persuaded rather than rejected." Had anybody in the course of this later Christological debate been prepared to ask whether the statement of Chalcedon is genuinely Nestorianizing or whether it is not in point of fact a very generous sort of statement leaving room for Cyril's Christology, for Theodore's Christology, and for Leo's Christology (and it seems to me that that is in fact the case), the course of the discussion might conceivably have been different. But as it was, Nestorius was a heresy-hunting and intransigent man; Cyril was intent upon breaking the prestige of Nestorius; and even Cyril's agreement with John of Antioch left extremists on both sides continuing the battle. Once we get on beyond that point to Dioscorus and Flavian, we find ourselves in the presence of emotions that are becoming more and more exacerbated and debates that are less and less intent on discovering

32. Ibid., 345–46.

possible common ground. The issues were vital for both an understanding and a practice of Christian conviction, but the way in which they were dealt with is deplorable. If one accepts Leo's description of the Ephesian council of 449 as the Robber Synod, one has to recognize that a similar sort of violence marked Chalcedon. It is an unhappy fact but an inescapable one. These theological decisions which were of the very life of the Church at the time were being made in an atmosphere of determined hostility and rivalry rather than an attempt to find a basis for common life.

These statements must be modified, at least to this extent: the later debate between sincere Monophysites and dyophysites is over a genuinely religious issue. Both groups were concerned for an interpretation of Jesus Christ which will do justice to his redemptive power. The one group believed that to admit the corruptibility of a creature in any essential way into his person is to undermine his dependability as Savior. The other is equally convinced that the Docetic tendency which the church had steadily rejected from the beginning must continue to be rejected. The issue is still between those who tend toward a mystical Docetism and those who insist on a historical and ethical understanding of the human nature of Jesus Christ—and who affirm that that human nature must be genuinely and fully the nature of a finite person, associated with divine power in such fashion that it is transformed, yet not in such fashion that it ceases to have its own personal essential character.

In the further thought of the church, the Christological problem has continued to be one of the most difficult and baffling with which theologians have sought to deal. I am inclined to think that the shift to the use of personal rather than impersonal categories in the latter part of this controversy was a shift in the right direction. But we are still struggling to get straight in our thinking about the difference between personal existence and nonpersonal existence. Since Kant, I suppose we are inclined to construe the essential difference in terms of responsible moral decision. A being capable of such responsible decision is a personal being; one incapable of such decision is not. If we transfer that sort of analysis to the Christological debate, I think we may find that the issues take on new life and import. The difficulties are not noticeably simplified, but at least they are vivified. It may be that out of our more concrete and realistic understanding of human nature will come a fresh and profound development of Christology.

# CHAPTER 14

# Doctrinal Closure in the East[1]

THUS FAR WE HAVE been discussing a period in which Christian doctrine was in process of formation, a creative time in the history of Christian self-definition. Now we find ourselves on the edge of an era in which developments are for the most part practical rather than theoretic.[2] In the East, that period began in the eighth century and lasted until recent years. In the West, it began shortly after the death of Augustine in the fifth century and lasted through the period ordinarily called the Dark Ages—roughly, until the eleventh century. We shall look first at a final doctrinal development and a systematization of orthodox faith in the Eastern Church, and then turn our sights to the West.

## SACRAMENTAL RELIGION AND ICONOCLASM

In the center of the liturgy of the Eastern Church are the so-called *mysteria*, the ritual acts which in the West are called sacraments. The connotations of the terms are rather different. A sacrament is in the first instance a pledge or an oath. *Sacramentum* for centuries had meant the oath of loyalty which the Roman legionary took on the standard of his legion, with the Senate and Roman people as the objects of his devotion. In the Church, the sacraments have somewhat the same signification for Latin-speaking Western Christians. They are in part pledges of loyal membership in the community, of devotion to the Lord Jesus Christ, and

1. The first section of this chapter and the Appendix on the Pseudo-Dionysius are drawn from the 1948 LHCD (II:201–6), but much the greater part of Section B, on John of Damascus, is taken from lectures Professor Calhoun delivered in later years.

2. Although, as Calhoun notes in the concluding paragraph of Section B, "Theological reflection of high quality continued in the East from time to time in later centuries, but as far as dogma is concerned, development ceased" [ed.].

of hope for the life to come. But the suggestion conveyed by the term *mysterion* is plainly different. It does not have primarily an ethical and social connotation but an ontological connotation. One takes part in the central mysteries of Eastern Christian ritual in order to participate in the eternal order of being. One is perpetually renewed by taking part in the Eucharist, as one has been permanently changed through the mystery of baptism. Through baptism one is made in principle a participant in the life of the risen Lord, and in the Eucharist one is continually renewing that status.

Along with the sacraments or mysteries at the center of the practical life of the church, there went a great multitude of popular practices in both West and East which had a kind of tacit recognition on the part of the ecclesiastical leaders. From the second century there had been widespread veneration of martyrs, not merely during their time of active confession, but also after their death. The tombs of the martyrs became shrines. Their relics, the bones or the ashes that remained of their bodies, distributed around perhaps in more than one place, were regarded as full of miracle-working powers. The same was true also of other sacred objects—physical mementos which had been used by the saints, associated with the history or the legends of the churches concerned, or connected with the companions and the heroic followers of the Lord in some manner or other. And the power which was present in these sacred objects was thought of as working not merely for physical restoration of those who were ill or maimed but also as working for moral restoration, for the salvation of the soul. One prayed to the saints and received divine help through their mediation. One carried amulets which had been brought into contact with the relics of the saints and had acquired through that contact something of the *mana* (to bring in that modern anthropological term), the wonder-working energy which had been present in the holy men and women.

[Unlike what happened in the West, where the mode of celebration of even the church's central rites was greatly altered by barbarian influence, official liturgical patterns remained relatively stable in the East and did not occasion doctrinally significant debate. There was, however, one exception]: a fierce controversy developed over the propriety of using images of Jesus Christ and the apostles—either as pictures painted on a flat surface, or bas-reliefs, or actual three-dimensional statues—in the life of the church, and specifically in the practice of its worship. In the first four centuries, there seem to have been repeated, though by no means unanimous, protests against the portrayal of Jesus Christ, but the practice grew. Early in the eighth century, however, the propriety of employing means of this sort was sharply and officially challenged. In 726, the Eastern emperor, Leo the Syrian (or Isaurian), banned the making and use of images for Christian worship. His son, Constantine V, was still more severe in his efforts to stamp out the practice. A synod at Constantinople in 754 declared the use of images "heresy and idolatry." But the practice was defended by Popes Gregory II and Gregory III, and by the chief Eastern theologian of the eighth century, John of Damascus. The argument of the Damascene was addressed to Leo in three public orations and summarized in his work *On the Orthodox Faith*.[3] The chapter "Concerning Images" in this work follows a chapter "Concerning the Honor Due to the Saints and Their Remains," in which it is held that the heroes of the faith should be honored as those in whom the image of God was truly preserved, over whom death has no power, and through whose bodies— once living temples of God, and even now "fountains of salvation"—the power of God works wonders. "Let us raise monuments to them and visible images, and let us ourselves become, through imitation of their virtues, living monuments and images of them."[4]

With respect to the use of images, it should be remembered first of all that God himself created man "after his own image," and it is for this reason that we may properly honor one another. "For as Basil, that much-versed expounder of divine things, says, the honour given to the image passes over to the prototype." We are indeed forbidden to portray in works of art "the invisible, incorporeal, uncircumscribed, formless God."[5] This is the point of the Old Testament prohibition. But after God himself took flesh and revealed himself in visible form, the true significance of the visible body as medium of invisible grace was made plain. The written word of Scripture, likewise, is a record and reminder of the earthly life of the incarnate Word; and for unlettered or unleisured people, pictorial images serve as records and reminders of Jesus Christ and the saints, to turn to their thoughts to God.

3. Critical edition of *De fide orthodoxa* (f.o.) by Kotter, ed., "Die Schriften des Johannes von Damaskos." *Patristische Texte und Studien*, vii (Berlin: de Gruyter, 1969 ff.). English translation by Salmond, *NPNF2* 9.

4. *NPNF2* 9, chapter 15, 87.

5. Ibid., chapter 16, 88.

In an earlier chapter near the beginning of the treatise, the Damascene had developed a conception of the ubiquity of God that later became very influential. In his proper Being, God

> . . . has not place. For he is his own place, filling all things and being above all things. . . . Yet we speak of God having place and the place of God where his energy becomes manifest. For he penetrates everything without mixing with it, and imparts to all his energy in proportion to the fitness and receptive power of each. . . . Wherefore by the place of God is meant that which has a greater share in his energy and grace.

Thus, heaven, earth, "his sacred flesh," the church—in a word, "the places in which his energy becomes manifest to us, whether through the flesh or apart from flesh, are spoken of as the places of God."[6]

These principles guided the decision reached at the Second Council of Nicaea in 787—the seventh in the usual listing of the ecumenical councils of the Church. The iconoclastic emperors had been succeeded by Constantine VI and his mother, the Empress Irene, and there was an interlude in the destruction of images and the persecution of the churchmen, especially the monks, who clung to their use. This council of 350 members rejected the decision of 754, affirmed its own accord with the orthodox councils, the fathers, and the catholic tradition of the past, and proceeded to decree that

> . . . just as the figure of the precious and life-giving Cross, so also the venerable and holy images, as well as in painting and mosaic as of other fit materials, should be set forth in the holy churches of God, [and elsewhere, in public and private]. For by so much more frequently as they are seen in artistic representation, by so much more readily are men lifted up to the memory of their prototypes, and to a longing after them; and to these should be given the salutation and honorable reverence (*aspasmon kai timetiken proskunesin*), not indeed that true worship (*latreian*) of faith which pertains alone to the divine nature; but to these, as to the figure of the precious and life-giving Cross and to the Book of the Gospels and to the other holy objects, incense and lights may be offered according to ancient pious custom. For the honour which is paid to the image passes on to that which the image represents, and he who reveres the image reveres in it the subject represented.

6. Ibid., chapter 13, 15.

Those who held otherwise were condemned, the entire membership of the council subscribed the decree, and the usual shouts of anathema were voiced against all the iconoclasts and traducers, all who refuse such veneration (*proskunesis*) on the ground that it is idolatry (*eidolatreia*)—offering to idols the adoration (*latreia*) that is due to God alone.[7]

This decision was rejected in the Frankish churches under Karl the Great (Charlemagne), and in the East also iconoclasm was renewed for a time. But by 850, both East and West generally concurred in the action of Nicaea II. It goes without saying that the nice distinctions which could be made by participants in a theological congress were unlikely to be kept very clear in the popular employment of the means that were thus approved, and the specter of dependence upon magical power played a very large part indeed in the popular life of the Christian church.

## SYSTEMATIZATION IN JOHN OF DAMASCUS

[John of Damascus, whom we have just met as an opponent of iconoclasm, is best known as the major systematizer of Eastern Orthodox thought as this developed up through the first seven ecumenical councils.] I am not sure, however, that this justifies calling his work, as has been done by Loofs, a primary example of scholastic thinking. I do not find in the writings of the Damascene what seems to me the dominant problem of Western scholasticism as we know it in the high Middle Ages: the problem of harmonizing the affirmations of faith with the findings of natural reason. What prompts the Western schoolmen, whether within the community of the church, of Judaism, or of Islam, is in each instance the same difficulty: the difficulty posed for faithful members of a religious community by the discovery or the popularization of an intellectual understanding of the natural world which appears to conflict with the demands of faith. The scholastic task is the task of working out the reconciliation of the findings of natural reason on the one hand and the affirmations of religious tradition on the other.

So far as I can see, no such problem confronts John of Damascus. What he does rather is to systematize the dogmatic conclusions already arrived at; and the title of the concluding part of his chief work, *An Exposition of the Orthodox Faith*, seems to me to state very precisely what he undertook. What he is saying is that the orthodox faith has now in its

---

7. *NPNF2* 14:550–51.

major outlines been established. There are two great foci of that faith: the doctrine of God on the one hand and the doctrine of the person of Jesus Christ on the other hand. With these two foci, one can work out an understanding of the Christian faith which in principle is not subject to further change.

The chief difference between the conception of God that one finds in the work of John of Damascus and that which we found in the later stages of the Nicene controversy, in the thought of Cappadocians like Basil of Caesarea and Gregory of Nyssa, can be stated thus: they began with Platonic presuppositions and tended on the whole to stress the triplicity of the divine being, finding unity as a theoretic insight which supervenes upon a first impression of trinality. The Father, Son, and Holy Spirit are ostensibly three; but we discover that they are one, as we recognize that Peter and James and John appear to be three, but really are one if we understand their being in Platonic terms.[8] John of Damascus starts with different presuppositions: philosophically he is more Aristotelian than Platonic, and it appears to him necessary to begin with the affirmation of divine unity and then to discern trinality in the Godhead by a further process of inquiry. The results that he reaches are virtually like the results which the Cappadocians reach, in that he affirms a single divine *ousia* and three divine *hypostases*. And he adds the concept of interpenetration of the three members of the Godhead in such fashion that each is dynamically involved in all the activities of each of the others. One may say that they are distinguishable as regards their status in the Godhead, but they are identical in the direction of their functioning. Their activity is completely harmonized, and in that sense each is present in each and in both of the others.

Book One in the work on *The Orthodox Faith* deals with the nature of God. God is declared to be completely beyond human comprehension; he is beyond not only all the categories by which existing things can be described; he is beyond existence itself. He is *hyperousios*—a term which is taken directly from Dionysius' writings and which occurs there again and again. To say God is superessential is not to say he is without being; rather, it is to say that it is improper to ascribe to him *ousia* as though it

---

8. A rather different understanding of the structure of Nicene thought as represented by Athanasius and the Cappadocians is now developing as a result of greater attention to their exegetical work. Behr, *op. cit.* 2:1–2; and for summaries of the argument, 1–17, 475–481[ed.].

were a simple or descriptive term, even though we must use that word in talking of the essential being of God since we have none that is better.

Yet even though we cannot conceive accurately the being of God, nevertheless we can demonstrate that God exists. And here arguments are employed by the Damascene that became characteristic of later scholasticism in the West. In arguments of this sort, we distinguish between things that are created and things that are not created by noting that whatever is susceptible of change in all of the modes that Aristotle had recognized must have come into being and in due course will pass out of being. Now if all things were subject to change in these ways, it would be impossible to account for the fact that they are here at all. It is necessary to recognize that whatever is susceptible of change in this multiple manner must depend for its being, for its very coming into existence, upon another than itself. But if this antecedent is itself subject to change and therefore brought into being, and so on in an indefinite sequence until one comes to one who is Creator but not created—one who thus becomes the basic source for all that comes into being although he himself does not come into being. Thus John proves that there must be God as the creative source of all the things that must change.

Consider next the way in which opposites are held in the world as we know it—a world of perpetual flux—in a kind of fluid order; they are held in such wise that fire and water, each of which is antithetic to the other, nevertheless operate side by side. How shall we account for the maintenance of such a world? Having come into being, why does it not simply pass out of being, ceasing to exist? The opposites continually tend to encroach upon one another. And the persistence of a world in which many pairs of opposites work one upon another argues for a sustaining power—a governing, ordering, provident power, if you will. So we say, God is required not only to account for the coming into being of the things that change but also for their persistence in being.

Does this tell us who or what God is? It does not. We are using a concept which we shall have to apply to God and especially to the Father within the Godhead—*archon*, or cause: Here *cause* must be taken in a much broader sense than the way in which, for example, in the physical disciplines, we speak of a uniform antecedent to a particular observable event. As John uses the term *cause*, it means what we would ordinarily call, I suppose, *ground*— the basic presupposition of the being of whatever is dependent and not self-sufficient. As cause, God then has to be described in terms most of which are negations. We say God is incorporeal, invisible, incomprehensible, immeasurable; we say God is not contained in any place but is himself rather everywhere present and containing all things. We say many negative things about God, and these are more likely to be true than if we tried to apply affirmative predicates to a nature which is, once again, beyond all nature and therefore not susceptible of accurate positive description.

But we know God not merely by reason of the created order which is maintained in a kind of perpetual balance. Knowledge of God in some sense has been implanted in each rational being; knowledge of God is involved in the surrounding environment, and knowledge of God is available through revelation (in the Scriptures and in the tradition of the church). When we turn from the world around us to these sources of revelation, we discover that God himself has affirmed certain truths with respect to his own being which we could not have discovered unaided. Among these is the truth which is set out plainly in Scripture and is in some sense supported also by philosophical requirements—i.e., that given the sort of Creator and sustainer that we need, we are talking about a being utterly simple and unitary. There cannot be many gods because if there were many gods, they would differ one from another. When we say *God*, we are speaking of a being that is perfect; but if there be differences, then some must fall short of perfection in the sense of completeness in one way or another. And consequently, it becomes impossible to talk of a distinguishable plurality of beings in God. There must be one God, and his being must be noncomposite being. If God's being were made up of components like created beings, whether mind or body, forthwith it would lose perfection and become susceptible of change.

God is characterized then by utter simplicity and unity, and yet out of unity it is necessary that duality arise. (Here we come upon what Lovejoy has called picturesquely "the principle of plenitude," i.e. the principle that whatever is possible must at some time become real.[9]) Now given the utterly unitary perfection of God, from such perfection an othering of God is called for. And this is what is intended in the Fourth Gospel when the Prologue speaks of God's Word, the Word which is God and yet which is in some sense other than the primary cause of being. If we

---

9. Lovejoy, *The Great Chain of Being: A Study of the History of an Idea* (Cambridge: Harvard University Press, 1936).

distinguish Father and Son, we are not distinguishing a divine being from a non-divine being—and here the difference between a being "un-originate" that has not come to be (*agenaton*), and, on the other hand, one which is "unbegotten" (*agennaton*) is spelled out in considerable length by this author. God by his very nature is to be called "without beginning"; he is one who has not come to be. But it does not follow that God by his very nature must be called "unbegotten." The Father is unbegotten, the Son is begotten, and both are equally God. The one sense in which we can say the Son differs from the Father is that the Father is the ground of being of the Son and of the possession by the Son of that very deity which belongs to the Father. But when we add that the Son is present eternally with the Father, we are saying God is not merely always God—he is always Father, and the Son is always with him. We must not suppose that this begetting, therefore, involves a succession of time; there is no process involved here. If there were process, there would be genesis and that is precisely what is incompatible with deity.

The Son then is the Father's Word, which is the thought or the will of the Father, but not like the word of human beings which, once spoken, vanishes like an empty breath of air. Rather, the Word of God is like God, whose Word thus spoken is subsistent and perpetually real. The Word of God is—and here is a curious use of the term which had been employed in Christological debate—*enhypostasis,* which is to say, having *hyposta-sis* or determinate being in himself. I suppose one could call the Father equally *enhypostasis,* but it would be rather silly to do so because we have already described the Father as the source of all existence. Therefore, the difference between Father and Son consists not in the presence in the one and the absence in the other of deity (which we can call for lack of a better term the divine *ousia*). It consists rather in the fact that they are different modes (*hyparksis*) of being or concrete existence; they differ, that is, in *hypostasis,* not in *ousia.* Once again, this is not a new idea; it is simply spelling out with complete explicitness what had been affirmed during the debate that began at Nicaea. (This phrase is, by the way, characteristic of the Cappadocians; it is their way of talking of distinctions within the Godhead; the *ousia* is one but the modes of being are distinguishable.)

Now just as the Father always begets the Son, and just as a word requires breath or a putting forth of energy, so we can say the Holy Spirit perpetually, eternally proceeds from the Father not, says John, from the Son, but through the Son from the Father. John wants a conception of a triune Godhead in which the Father retains a kind of primacy, not a primacy of temporal priority but primacy as the indispensable and ultimate ground—ground for the being of the Son and for the being of the Holy Spirit. We must recognize that the term *pneuma* is used in a great variety of ways: of the Holy Spirit, of the holy angels who are called spirits, even of the demons who are likewise spiritual beings, of created mind in man, and even of breath and air. And we must of course recognize that when we are talking of the Holy Spirit in the Godhead, we are using *spirit* in a very special way—not meaning breath or air, but power, energy, or divine act.

If we try to think of God in such fashion as this, we raise in a different way the question whether it is proper to give God names at all. And in a sense, the negative answer has already been determined. But still there are names of God; and here again, Dionysius is the proximate source; there are names of God which are less inappropriate than other names. And perhaps the most appropriate or the least inappropriate is to call God "he who is" (*ho on*), or to call God, as Dionysius following the line of succession from Plotinus had called him, "the Good." We must not suppose again that *the Good* used in this context is intended to stand for an Absolute of being more fundamental than itself, as if goodness were secondary. Rather, we must recognize that the very being of God is what we mean when we say *Good*, and conversely, that if we know what we mean we say Good in itself, we are talking about the perfect which stands in contrast to all dependent and changeable realities.

Another name which is not wholly inappropriate with respect to God is *ho theos*. And we get here a little venture into etymology, which is more picturesque than persuasive. *Theo* means to move; now God is the one who, while remaining unmoved, moves everything, although he remains "in one place." If we ask what is the "one place," we have to remember that although the being of God obviously cannot be in one place rather than another, yet we must recognize that there are as it were places in which minds operate in distinction from places in which bodies operate. You can say that the range of thought of the one thinker differs from the range of thought characteristic of another. We can say then of God also that the term *place* can be implied, not as if he were contained, but rather as recognizing that though he pervades all things, he is more fully present in some things than in others. Thus we can say he is more fully present in the body of the incarnate Word than in other human bodies;

we can say he is more fully present in the church than in other human communities, and so forth. Where is the place of God, then? Well, if you want to say heaven is God's throne and the earth is his footstool, recognizing that you're using figurative language, you are right because God, of course, is both in heaven and throughout the whole panorama of events on earth. So far then with respect to what we can say and what we must not try to say about the being of God, as John outlines it in the first book of *The Orthodox Faith*.

Book Two deals with the created world, the nature of man, providence, foreknowledge, and predestination. There are those, Gregory Nazianzen, for instance, who think that the first of created beings were the angels. Others think that the first heaven was created as a place into which the angels were subsequently introduced as inhabitants. John concurs with Gregory on this point, for it seems to him that the first creation should be pure mind, and that the second step in creation should be the creation of visible, phenomenal corporeal things, and that the third step should be the creation of human beings in whom mind and body are brought together. From the perspective of our earthly experience, angels must be regarded as pure spirits, but when viewed from the perspective of God's wholly incorporeal being, we have to say that they have a kind of body—not the kind of body that we know here, but a kind of body which the philosophers have tried to point to by using the term *ethereal*, suggesting that they are made of a fifth element (not earth, air, fire, and water, such as our bodies are made of), viz., that heavenly fire of which the celestial globes are made. At all events, the angels are intelligent and since intelligent, free: capable of acting in the way of decision and choice. They are not immortal by nature since they are created, having come into being; but they are granted immortality by divine grace provided they continue to make the right choices and serve God as faithful messengers. Some of them continually choose rightly and in course of time, they come to be immune to the making of wrong choices. But some of them do not. The one whom we call the Devil was himself a created angel, and it was only when he decided to set himself up on a throne rivaling the throne of God that calamity overtook him. Unhappily, he persuaded a multitude of fellow angels to align themselves with him, and so they all suffered what for an angelic being corresponds to death for human beings, i.e., an irrevocable fall. The consequences for angels and for human beings who get into trouble for the same reason and in much the same way—through disobedience to the will of God—are, however, different; because human beings are corporeal, they are susceptible of repentance whereas the angels are not. (Now if you press me hard on the question why precisely this should be true, I will confess I don't know; this is what one reads, however, and it was, one must say, characteristic of virtually all Christian theologians with the exception of people like Origen, who hoped for the restoration even of the demons and the prince of the devils himself.)

The angels then are created and the heavens are created; "heavens" rather than "a" heaven. One may perhaps find value in the view of the Greek metaphysicians that beyond the firmament there is a starless heaven, which is perhaps the "first heaven." And then the firmament, with its stars and planets, is the "second heaven." The air in which the birds of the air fly about is a "third heaven." When Paul was caught up into the third heaven, he of course started from here on earth; and consequently it was the starless heaven beyond the firmament to which he was presumably caught away. The heavens and the earth are corporeal; the heavens above have an eternal body. (Incidentally, this author goes into a good deal of astronomical detail: there are seven zones of the firmament that is thought of as a sphere surrounding the earth and carrying with it the sun, the moon, the other visible planets, and ultimately of course the constellations of the fixed stars.) John does not undertake to decide between views of the cosmos as firmament or as hemisphere. When one speaks of the heavens as spread out like a tent, that suggests a hemisphere. But it makes it a good deal easier if one thinks in terms of a complete surrounding of the earth by the firmament that carries the heavenly bodies along. Things on the earth, earth itself, its atmosphere, are made (as Aristotle had said) of prime matter elaborated into the simple elements: earth, air, fire, and water. And of these simple bodies, such complex bodies as the seeds of plants and animals and the organs and bodies of plants and animals are composed. The difference between Aristotle's view and the Christian view is that for the latter, the prime matter is itself created, i.e., God is the source not only of the elaboration and ordering of the world, but of the existence of anything that is susceptible to being ordered.

Into the midst of this world of bodies was set paradise, the garden which was on a high plateau somewhere in the east, where the climate was perfect and where all things grew in profusion. There the first man was placed with permission to eat of every tree of the garden except of the tree of the knowledge of good and evil. The tree of knowledge is primarily self-knowledge—knowledge of our own composition and capacity and possible objectives. And this, says John, is knowledge that is good for one who is mature but dangerous for one who is immature. Adam and Eve were as children in the garden, and that was why God prohibited their eating from the tree of knowledge. Now the tree of life is the glory of God himself; to eat of this tree is to become a participant in divine glory. If only God's commandment had been obeyed, it would not have been necessary for Adam and Eve to die, just as the angels are granted immortality by an act of divine favor, so they would likewise have been granted immortality, not by reason of their nature which is, once again, susceptible of passing away, but by an overplus of divine grace. But when they break the prohibition by eating of the tree of knowledge and become aware of themselves, then shame and remorse are the subjective results; and exclusion from the garden of innocency is the objective result. Fig leaves and garments of skin stand respectively for their remorse and for the penalty of death—the incorporating of their minds into a body which will be subjected to destruction. It is at this point that God acts on behalf of his rebellious creatures. And in so acting, God must manifest both his goodness and his justice: his goodness in the familiar sense of mercy, taking pity upon those who do not deserve to be pitied and helped, and his justice in that the help which is extended will not take the form of violent intrusion. God, of course, could simply have overpowered the Devil and his angels, but that would not have been to act justly; after all, human beings have gotten themselves into this scrape, and it is necessary that they shall in some fashion have a part in removing the shackles which bind them.

Book Three thus deals with human salvation, God's care for us, the incarnation on our behalf, and the way in which atonement is effected. The most fitting way, says John, that salvation could be brought about was for the Word of God to become man so that in what he suffers and what he achieves, both God and man are acting together. We must regard the union of deity and humanity in Jesus Christ not as a part-for-part correspondence so that this part of deity corresponds to this part of humanity; rather, as a whole in the whole, Jesus Christ is in every respect human and in every respect God so far as regards the permeation of his unique personal life by the characters of both Godhead and manhood. It will not do, says John, to try to find a class to which Jesus Christ belongs, for he is unique; he is the one genuinely new thing. The writer in Ecclesiastes who doubted that there was anything new under the sun had not foreseen what God eventually would do on our behalf; this is a fresh departure, and a departure made once for all. If we ask once again in what matter we are to think of deity and humanity as united in Christ, we must not make the mistake of supposing that deity changes into humanity or humanity into deity; instead, we must say there is in him one *hypostasis*—one subsistent, concrete, determinant, personal being in whom both human and divine wills and energies operate. We must declare that Christ is not *of* two natures because before the incarnation there was only one—the discarnate eternal nature of the Word. We must say "*in* two natures."

And we must not make another kind of mistake, supposing that the coming together into one of God and man changes the humanity into deity or changes the deity into humanity. If we find that in the scriptural accounts things are said of Christ that are appropriately to be said of God, or appropriately to be said of man, let us use our common sense in reading these scriptural affirmations and see that some of them apply to deity, some to humanity, and some to the unique union of the two in Jesus Christ. That is by reason of the fact that he is through and through human, that he has voluntarily made himself capable of suffering and of death. If we read that he grows in wisdom and stature, we must understand this not as meaning that at any point in his life he was less than fully cognizant of all that God knows; rather, we must say that in this manifestation to those around him, he presents a picture of growth. At this point, I confess it seems to me the account is less satisfactory than it is at many other points; the section devoted to this question is very brief and almost noncommittal. At all events, omniscience is to be affirmed at the same time as full humanity is affirmed—and once again appeal is made to the incomprehensibility to us of this sort of work of God.

The results of Christ taking upon himself our nature, suffering and dying on our behalf, and being raised and sitting at the right hand of his Father, are to be found practically in the making available for us at baptism—baptism with water, and along with it an anointing with olive oil—olive oil, because when the dove came back bringing Noah the word that the flood had gone down, it was an olive leaf that was the sign of renewed divine favor. So, water and oil for baptism which cleanses the one baptized of all prior sins; and then the Eucharist in which, says John, we must say not that the heavenly body of the Lord comes down but rather that the elements on the altar are changed so that they become the body and blood of the Lord. Again, all is incomprehensible; there is no attempt made to spell out as, e.g., the Latin schoolmen tried to spell out a metaphysical doctrine; it is simply affirmed as mystery. The assistance of the church, then, with baptism and the Eucharist as the signs of God's saving grace, will involve certain practices which John ascribes to the unwritten tradition. There is worshipping facing toward the east; this is not enjoined anywhere in Scripture, but the fathers have handed it down as good practice because it is in the east, of course, that the light first appears and overcomes the darkness. Similarly with respect to the veneration of saints; this must be carefully distinguished from worship, which is properly offered only to God.

Finally, Book Four is eschatological. Beginning with the resurrection, it examines speculatively what is to follow until at length the entire purpose of God is completely worked out. This book, like the three preceding ones, is scholastic only in the sense that it is systematic and retrospective. The truth has been found, and here is the way in which it can be set out in convenient order, once for all.

Theological reflection of high quality continued in the East from time to time in later centuries, but as far as dogma is concerned, development ceased. The increasing divisions within the church help to account for this. The Greeks, unlike the Latins, did not recognize merely Western (or merely Eastern) assemblies as truly ecumenical and competent to decide dogmatic issues. For them, the last ecumenical council was the seventh, Nicaea II, which condemned iconoclasm in 787. The modern ecumenical movement has awakened hopes in some quarters for church reunion and further doctrinal development, but what the possibilities are for these hopes to be actualized is, needless to say, beyond the competence of historians to assess.

## Appendix: Pseudo-Dionysius and the Rise of Mysticism[10]

Another stream of development [besides the systematizing tendency we have seen in John of Damascus] was the rise of speculative mysticism

---

10. The following extended section on the Pseudo-Dionysius is taken from the 1948 LHCD (II:203–206) where it precedes a brief discussion of John of Damascus. Professor Calhoun reversed the proportions in later years. The Pseudo-Dionysius tended to disappear from his lectures on Eastern (though not medieval Western) theology, while his attention to the Damascene increased because of the latter's importance for Orthodox communal and doctrinal self-definition. Moreover, Calhoun became aware that the

into a position of central influence. We have already noticed the recur-
rence of mystical tendencies in various Eastern thinkers. The conception
of *gnosis* in the Alexandrine fathers included a mild sort of cognitive
mysticism. The conception of deification of believers, stressing the practical assimilation of human to divine life, was taught by Irenaeus and
Athanasius, repeated by the Cappadocian thinkers, and elaborated into
full-bloom mysticism by Maximus the Confessor, the foe of Monophysite
and Monothelete doctrines in the seventh century. He was a commentator on Gregory Nazianzen but also the popularizer of the extraordinary
mystical writings of the man whom we now find ourselves forced to describe as Pseudo-Dionysius Areopagita. No fewer than four treatises and
ten letters attributed to Dionysius of the Areopagus (the man referred to
in Acts 17:34 as having been converted by St. Paul's address upon Mars'
Hill) became widely current and influential in the Eastern Church. It will
be recalled that early Monotheletes like the patriarchs Sergius and Cyrus
gave a prominent place to Dionysius' phrase, "one theandric operation,"
but the phrase had been cited by Severus of Antioch a full century earlier.
The Severians used Dionysius as a major authority in defending their
views in a synod at Constantinople in 533. At that time, the authenticity of the works was questioned on the ground that the fathers had not
quoted nor even mentioned them. This shrewd doubt was quickly forgotten, however, and until Renaissance scholarship revived and proved it
well founded, the writings were accepted as genuine first-century works
of high authority. Indeed, writings of a man thus closely related to St.
Paul were inevitably regarded as having a status almost Scriptural, since
the acknowledged basis of selection of the New Testament writings was
that they were thought to be the works either of apostles or of immediate
companions of apostles. If, then, the "Dionysian" works *On the Celestial
Hierarchy, On the Ecclesiastical Hierarchy, On the Divine Names,* and *On*

---

Pseudo-Dionysius can be read, not only as one in whom "Christian language is used for
the expression of Neoplatonic thought" (as he here puts it), but also, in the opposite direction, as one who employed Neoplatonic language to express Christian thought. He probably would not have wanted to publish the following material without changes indicating
the doctrinal (though not theological) marginality and ambiguity of Dionysian influence. This, however, is his fullest exposition of what he calls "intellectualistic" mysticism,
of which Plotinus is the type; and which he contrasts unfavorably with "voluntaristic"
mysticism, of which Bernard of Clairvaux is a type (1948 LHCD II:289). For this reason
it is included in this volume but relegated to the following appendix [ed.].

*Mystical Theology* had come from a convert of St. Paul, their authority must be very high indeed.[11]

It is unanimously agreed now that the language, style, and content of the writings make it impossible to assign them to a first-century author. The vocabulary includes many late theological and philosophical terms. The style is elaborate, self-conscious, and oracular. There is a quotation from Ignatius' letter to the Romans and a reference to "Clement the Philosopher"—presumably Clement of Alexandria. The thought is said by the experts to be fifth-century Neoplatonism—the thought of Iamblichus and Proclus rather than that of Plotinus. Since the first recognizable references to the writings occur early in the sixth century, it seems safe to judge that they were written around AD 500.

The late Neoplatonism of "Dionysius" is in many ways the culmination of a process of development from the *Republic* and the *Timaeus* of Plato (in which the principles of the Good, Reason, and Soul are presented as basic factors in and beyond reality) through Plotinus, Iamblichus, and Proclus, with increasing complication of causal claims and growing emphasis on the remoteness or inaccessibility of the ultimate principle from which all reality proceeds. Plotinus called it the One, or the Good, or God. Proclus uses the same terms and adds that from the One or God spring a definite number of unities (henads) or gods, of different ranks or degrees of inclusiveness, each of which is the source of further diversities and at the same time the indwelling principle of their requisite unity. The One itself remains aloof. Plotinus holds that from the One flows forth *Nous* (variously rendered by the translators as Mind, Spirit, Intellectual Principle). Proclus agrees in the general conception, but complicates it in two ways: *Nous* (which springs from certain of the "divine Henads") is in itself a triad of Being, Life, Mind, and from it spring a plurality of minds of different grades, each of which again is the source of still other chains of entities, all of whose members participate in being, some in life, and still fewer in consciousness. Plotinus holds that from *Nous* flows *Psyche* (Soul, the principle of life and motion), which unlike *Nous* becomes indi-

11. Migne, PG 3 and 4. English translation by Parker, *The Works of Dionysius the Areopagite*, 2 vols. (London and Oxford: Parker, 1897–99). Critical edition of *On the Celestial Hierarchy* by G. Heil, M. de Gandilloc, R. Roques, SC, 58,1958. Other English translations: Rolt, translator, *Dionysius the Areopagite: On the Divine Names and the Mystical Theology* (London: SPCK, 1920); Campbell, translator and editor, *Dionysius the Pseudo-Areopagite: The Ecclesiastical Hierarchy* (Washington DC: Catholic University Press of America, 1955).

viduated into particular souls, each with its body. Again, Proclus agrees, but again he complicates the pattern by specifying (besides Soul as unitary principle) divine souls thinking timelessly; lesser souls that think temporally but perpetually; and souls that vary between consciousness and unconsciousness. Bodies are a further step down in the scale since they are divisible into parts, being spread out spatially as souls and minds are not. The theoretic limit of plurality would be sheer manyness without unity—but that would be nonbeing. Plotinus sometimes writes as though nonbeing were synonymous with evil. Proclus, on the contrary, holds that evil is misconduct, not mere privation. Both agree that the work of God is unification and that salvation for individual souls is return toward unity, apprehended now in mystical intuition.

The radical differences between such a view and the Judaeo-Christian way of thinking need scarcely be pointed out. Instead of voluntary creation and discontinuity between God and world, Neoplatonism stresses with all emphasis the continuous and inevitable flow of the world from God. Instead of human corruption and the need of divine grace for redemption, Neoplatonism usually thinks of evil as a deficiency—as a shadow is the absence of light—and of a gradual return of human beings through moral and mental discipline to unification, best apprehended in ecstatic vision. It is this Neoplatonic religious thought that is set forth, partly in Christian language, partly in the vocabulary of speculative mysticism, by Pseudo-Dionysius.

First of all, God is described as the One completely beyond articulate description—One that may be spoken of only in some such fashion as this: "Superessential Essence and mindless Mind and unuttered Word (*hyperousios ousia kai nous anoetos kai logos arretos*) . . . the all-transcending hiddenness of the all-transcending superessentially superexisting superdeity (*ten hyper panta kruphioteta tes hyper panta hyperousios hyperouses hypertheot . . .*").[12] Phrases of that sort are employed in the struggle to suggest that the being of God is not a being in any sense that we can recognize and that the effort to say what God is must be a negative effort which literally says what God is not. Yet it so negates the negatives as to make it apparent that what one is talking about is not the absence

---

12. Inge, *Christian Mysticism, Considered in Eight Lectures Delivered before the University of Oxford* (New York: Scribners, 1899) 106, n. 1 and 2.

of being but the superabundance of being. God is "not," just because he is more than anything that can be specified.

The Trinitarian conception is applied somewhat perfunctorily to the nature of this God. God the Father is this utterly transcendent Source. He can be known through his Logos eternally manifesting him throughout the universe. The Spirit also is mentioned. But these are only three among countless divine names. The truth, as far as words can indicate it, is the unity of the divine nature. The many divine names serve symbolically to remind one who has had the ecstatic vision of God that that vision stands for what one may point toward but never comprehend in any articulate thought. The divine names are always of this kind: symbols pointing toward what cannot be grasped and described. On this way of thinking, the incarnation of the Logos (called Jesus) could be a purely universal incarnation. The universe is the embodiment of the divine principle, so that the God who is wholly transcendent is also immanent in a way that entitles one to point to Jesus Christ and say, Here God is made manifest.

Yet salvation is represented not as mediated uniquely by Jesus Christ but in a quite different way. The God who is the Source of the universe and who pervades it has his power mediated through nine divine orders of celestial beings. There are three ranks in heaven with three orders in each rank. Nearest to the Godhead are seraphim, cherubim, and thrones; next below them come dominations, virtues, powers; then principalities, archangels, angels. Those in the lowest rank are purifying powers. In the highest rank are perfecting powers. The grace of God is mediated down through these successive levels of emanation and picked up on earth by corresponding levels of ecclesiastical hierarchy which mirror precisely the organization in heaven. Corresponding to the lowest rank are the deacons, to the second rank the priests, and to the highest rank the bishops. The fountainhead of this hierarchy is Jesus Christ. Through the mediations of grace through the sacraments by the bishops, priests, and deacons, the connection is made between the unifying power of God and the dispersed life of human beings. For that from which they have to be freed is primarily pluralization, disunity. The way in which they are to be freed, plainly enough, is through being drawn into a unifying fellowship, being made subject to integrating power, and being lifted at length to the point at which distractions and diversities of ordinary life are left behind and unifying contemplation becomes possible.

That is the end to be sought in moral and intellectual discipline: the capacity for the contemplation of the unifying reality which makes the world real and good. And this contemplation must have the character of ecstasy (literally, standing outside one's self—a being carried out of one's ordinary rational personality, so that the vision which thus comes is not susceptible of rational statement at all). Such vision rises above the level of reason. One can work toward it through intellectual discipline, but one cannot achieve it through intellectual discipline. If it comes at all, it comes as a gift mediated from God through all of his ministers, celestial and ecclesiastical. The ultimate goal of the whole mediating process is not precisely the restoration of unity, for unity has been here all the while, but restoration of awareness of that perpetual unity in minds which have temporarily lost that consciousness.

In this sort of conception of the nature of the religious problem and of the solution of that problem, one can see the difference which has been so often insisted upon between mystical and prophetic insight. In prophetic insight, the invasion of the individual's mind lays open to him truth of which he is not ordinarily conscious or fills him with power which is not ordinarily available for him; the insight then leaves him, and he becomes once again his everyday self. The prophetic experience is a transient, almost a spasmodic experience. Mystical ecstasy is also transient, but what that ecstasy reveals is a state of affairs which is permanent. What the mystic sees is that he is at no time separated from God; he is at no time an isolated individual. Once he has fully grasped that truth about himself, in principle he can live perpetually on a level of realization that what is, is good, and that his life is secure because it is identified at its root with the principle of unity which pervades the whole. That is Dionysius' conception of the message of Christianity, and I think that one need hardly dwell on its differences from Pauline and Johannine conceptions of the Christian Gospel. Here we have Neoplatonism using the language of Christian dogma rather than Christian theology influenced by Neoplatonic philosophy. When we come to Augustine, we shall find an instance of this latter sort. In the thought of Augustine, Neoplatonism is transformed into Christian faith. In that of the Dionysian writer, Christian language is used for the expression of Neoplatonic thought.

CHAPTER 15

# Augustine of Hippo[1]

WHEN WE TURN FROM the East to the West, we focus our attention first on St. Augustine, who was, after St. Paul, the most important and the most influential theologian of the first five centuries. He combined in a quite extraordinary way factors which had hitherto been presented in different individuals. We find in him something of the tragic and profound religious insights of St. Paul joined with the constructive philosophical breadth and taste for systematic organization we have previously seen illustrated best in the work of Origen. Augustine was both a theologian of faith in something like the Pauline sense and a defender of the proper use of reason, not merely for critical but for constructive purposes in theology. More specifically, to borrow a phrase Paul Tillich applies to himself, Augustine lived "on the boundaries" between different historical epochs, geographical areas, and intellectual traditions. He became the ancestor both of medieval scholasticism and of Reformation thought. This could not have happened except for the extraordinary richness of the material which he took up, assimilated, and reshaped in the course of his own thought and life.

The first and most superficial sense in which he lived on the boundary is geographic. He was born in the province of Numidia in North Africa. There and in Carthage where he studied, as well as in the adjoining territory, the Phoenician language and culture were still alive, although Latin was dominant. According to his own account, he detested foreign languages when he was in school; consequently, he learned only so much Greek as the coercion of his masters compelled him to learn. He always

1. This chapter consists in approximately equal amounts of material from chapter 22 of the 1948 transcript (II:208–34) and from lectures of later years [ed.].

resented being forced into a linguistic territory that was not native to him. He picked up Latin by listening to conversations, by talking with his playmates, and eventually developed a kind of love for Virgil which arises on the part of one whose concern is spontaneous and not forced. But as for Homer, who told stories which were as good as Virgil's, Augustine just never could get up any enthusiasm. Although he learned enough Greek to make out phrases here and there, he was at home only in Latin. And Hebrew he never learned at all.

The impact of Punic culture on his own thinking shows up clearly in the influence of a certain Numidian Christian, Tychonius, who in his commentary on the Apocalypse uses the concept of two rival common-wealths: *civitates dei* on the one hand, *civitates diaboli* on the other. In the work which commonly is regarded as his outstanding masterpiece, Augustine uses that concept, softening the edges of Tychonius' highly apocalyptical mode of thought, but nevertheless showing something of the harsh dualism which comes through in that thought pattern. He lived not only in his native North Africa, however, but also a part of the time on the other side of the Mediterranean, in Rome and in Milan where he came into contact with another sort of society and of thought patterns different from those which he had known at home. All of this became grist for his very active mind.

Augustine also stood on the boundary between paganism and Christianity. He was a child of a divided home; his father, Patricius, was a minor Roman official who was a pagan until the very end of his life. His mother, Monica, was a naive, insistent, and somewhat unimaginative Christian who worked untiringly for Augustine's own conversion and eventually brought about the conversion of her husband also. While Augustine was at home, however, Patricius' conception of advancement in pagan culture, and Monica's hope that her child would become a son of the Church were continually in conflict. Augustine himself went through a considerable period while he was in school—both in Tagaste, in Madaura and then in Carthage—in which it was pagan insight that most attracted him. All these details come from the very elaborate spiritual autobiography we know as his *Confessions*. Even though in retrospect some of the emphases and some of the colorings undoubtedly have undergone change, so far as regards the basic facts I see no reason to question the correctness of Augustine's autobiographical recollections. He for a time pursued that vocation which was called in the ancient world *rhetor—*

a public orator and teacher of public address to those who desired to go into political life or who, for whatever reason wanted to increase their capacity to influence people by means of effective speech. As a rhetor Augustine developed a style which is much more nearly Ciceronian than that of his rugged predecessor, the lawyer Tertullian, who writes as if with the end of a crowbar. Augustine's pen was that of a man who seeks the nice balancing of clauses and the subtlety of figure which was the mark of the educated *literatus* in his society.

At this point, I would like to suggest perhaps too briefly and brashly what seem to me some of the basic differences between Christian and pagan understandings of human existence and the world we inhabit. In the first place, it was characteristic of pagan thought, especially in the pre-Christian era, to regard this world as *not* having come into being. Things in it come into being and pass away but the world as a whole has always been here. Any thought of radical creation was foreign to any of the Greek thinkers with whom I am at all familiar. After Plato had left the *Timaeus* for his successors to study, a question was raised in the Academy as to whether or not he had meant to teach a true beginning of the world soul and the shaping of the polygamal stuffs of which this is made. The answer of the majority was no, he did not—he used the narrative form, speaking as if there were a beginning simply for convenience; but really what he had in mind was to say that if we abstract from the world its guiding principle of rational control, this is what would be the remainder. He did not intend to argue that the world began with that remainder at some time and then was shaped by the intervention of a rational *demiourgos*. There is then no creation in pagan thought. On the other hand, it was characteristic of Christian thought in its mature form—that is to say, after the time of Irenaeus when the Gnostics had been confronted and after Marcion had been rejected—to insist that everything in this world is dependent for its very being upon the creative power and act of God. God is not to be thought of as one who operates in the midst of a given order of being; he is to be thought of rather as the source of being of everything other than himself. He is not simply *demiourgos*; he is not simply the ruler and guide. He is the indispensable ground.

A related difference between pagan and Christian thinking has reference to the understanding of time. In pagan thought, time is characteristically regarded as cyclical. I suppose the pattern of the recurrent seasons carried over into the mythical concept of the succession of ages, which in some fashion or other will be repeated. Even so sophisticated a group of thinkers as the Stoics talked about a world epoch which ends in a universal conflagration, out of which there will come a new age in which every detail of the present age will be repeated, and so on and so on without ultimate end. Over against that cyclical concept of time, the Hebrew and Christian concept of time as linear is a familiar enough notion, but some of its significations have not always been clearly recognized. If we think of time as cyclical, we are thinking of a pattern which is appropriate to a world which has neither beginning nor end but perpetually repeats a sequence of events which are, if you will, native to the world and not controlled from beyond it. But in the Hebrew-Christian understanding, just as the world depends upon God for its existence, so the sequence of events in time rests upon the eternal being and the eternal knowing of God; and no simple repetition is to be affirmed at all. Time thus understood can have a center, and of course it was characteristic of Christian thought that the center is the incarnation of the Word in Jesus Christ. So that what has gone before is in some sense preamble, and what has followed is in some sense development to the point of culmination. And we understand human life as set within this sort of context.

A third difference between the pagan and Christian worldviews lies in the understanding of the nature of the human person. It was characteristic of the Greek thought that I know best that the inner conflict which a human person undergoes is a conflict between a rational component and various subrational components in his makeup. Reason is the highest human faculty in principle and should be so in fact. But when sense perception and appetite get the upper hand, or when emotional drive takes over and subordinates rational insight to its own requirements, we go astray. Now reason in and of itself is often thought of as infallible. If you see what is so you cannot be mistaken. And if you see what is good—really see it in its full significance—you cannot do other than to seek it. But the Christian conception of human nature as Paul and now Augustine defined it locates the center of personal existence not in intellect but in will. Will is the supreme factor in the makeup of human beings; and will is by its very character ambivalent. Reason is in some sense an instrument through which we seek to make decisions, but decisions are made not by the mind as such; they are made rather by a capacity for choice which can go either toward God or away from God. Now if one thinks thus of human beings in volitional rather than fundamentally intellectual terms, and if one thinks of the will as thus intrinsically equivocal or ambivalent, plainly enough that which is supreme in human nature has lost any claim to infallibility. There is nothing in us which is proof against deviation, so that human nature now becomes in a sense different from anything that we find in pagan wisdom—dependent upon God for guidance, and ultimately for competence to do what should be done.

With persons conceived in this fashion, history comes to be thought of in a new and different way by Christians. History consists of decisions and their consequences; it is not a natural process which can be assimilated in some fashion to the ongoing of the stars and planets and the seasons, the alternation of warm and cold and of damp and dry. History now is shot through with ambiguity just as each human mind is ambivalent at its very center; moreover, set in the linear time scheme which is characteristic of this mode of thought, history has a beginning and middle and goal, so that instead of thinking of history as though it were something like a natural process under the control perhaps of the movements of the planets, history now too is made subject to the presence of God and to the ambivalent decisions of persons. This is what constitutes the fabric of the ongoing panorama of human life on earth.

Finally, I suppose the concept of the Good has undergone a drastic change in the direction of definition in concrete, personal terms. For Plato, the Good is a supreme principle; it is beyond being and beyond thought; it is a principle which is neither comprehensible nor definable, for that would mean placing it in a class. But it is the source of all classes; one cannot thus catch in a net that which is itself a presupposition of any and all nets with which human thought can operate. But the Good is itself not personal. Now with the concept of God as one who has made himself known to us in Jesus Christ, the Good which is in good Platonic fashion still declared to be beyond our reach, beyond our comprehension, is nonetheless regarded as coming to where we are and enabling us to participate through obedience, through faith—not simply in a sovereign principle but rather in a new mode of personal life.

In these respects (and you can no doubt recognize others), Christian thought about the human situation differs from pagan thought. Augustine once again stands on both sides of the dividing line; he learned first to think in pagan terms, and only thereafter did he begin to translate those pagan categories into the categories of Christian tradition and teaching.

A third sort of boundary which his life spans is that between Eastern and Western modes of thought. We said earlier on that Augustine testifies that he never was sufficiently well acquainted with Greek to be able to read readily material that was available only in Greek. He knew first of all, then, the writings of the Latin classics, and among Christian authors, particularly Tertullian and Cyprian, who were his own fellow-countrymen. But at a late period in his pre-Christian career, one of his fellow rhetors, Victorinus, who had been converted to Christianity, had made available for those who read only Latin a good working translation of the *Enneads* of Plotinus. And hence at a critical point in his own development, Augustine became acquainted with this Latin version of Neoplatonic thought. Hence there is worked into the fabric of his understanding of human beauty, human destiny, and human existence the most mature, the most comprehensive, the most subtle of all the versions of Greek philosophy—at the same time as there persists in him the stern Latin insistence on moral responsibility. The ethical and legal strata which we are accustomed to associate with Latin thought are there for Augustine, but he puts them into a metaphysical, ontological context which was not Latin but Greek.

There was still a fourth boundary for one who was living in the West—the boundary between the independent political entity that we know as the Roman Empire of the West and its overthrow by Teutonic tribesmen. Augustine stood literally on the borderline between the period when the old Western Empire was still in full power and the beginning of a new age without the Caesars. That happened in Augustine's lifetime. In 408, Alaric and his East Goths laid siege to Rome, returned for a second try, and in 410 actually broke through the Roman defenses and captured the city. From that time until 476 (which is the date usually assigned for the end of the Roman *imperium* in the West), the Roman emperor carried on at Ravenna a kind of theatrical existence, signing decrees with a gold penholder when decrees were no longer of imperial significance. The power in Rome had passed into the hands of tribesmen who had neither the technological nor the political ability to operate a complex society. Now once again, Augustine lives on both sides of that boundary line; he lives at the end of an age, and his own thinking is in obvious ways shaped by the shock which one supposes he shared with those Romans, both pagan and Christian, who found the ground slipping from under their feet when *Roma aeterna* had fallen into the hands of the barbarian.

Augustine saw the end coming, and he saw in part why the end was coming. From his vantage ground between the supposedly permanent order of the classical world and an unforeseeable new age, his thinking and his writing dealt in large measure with the problem: What ground of security can there be in a time like this?

Augustine is then peculiarly a man who lives on both sides of various boundaries, and the richness of his thought arises out of this fact. We ought to note one final boundary: in some sense, he lives at the end of antiquity in the West. He has been called by William James the first modern man, I suppose primarily because he is the first man in antiquity who became so preoccupied with his own inner life that one of his major works is a detailed spiritual autobiography. The *Confessions* have no counterpart in ancient literature as an effort to explore the subject instead of exploring primarily the objective world, as most of the Greek schools had undertaken to do.[2] I realize that Socrates had implored the Greeks to know themselves, but "know thyself" meant fundamentally to see oneself as subject to obligations that arise from beyond. For Augustine, "knowing thyself" is something very different. Obligations do arise from beyond, but the response to them, whether for good or for ill, is itself subject to the most intricate and sensitive examination and description. He had a genius for introspective observation and analysis, and this peculiarly modern character has a deep bearing on the shaping of his theology.

### AUGUSTINE'S INTELLECTUAL DEVELOPMENT: MANICHAEISM AND NEOPLATONISM

After his birth in 354 in the relatively unimportant Numidian town of Tagaste in North Africa, Augustine had gone through the best sort of schooling that could be provided for a Roman boy. The meager fortune of his father was supplemented by the aid of a wealthy patron, Romanianus, so that he could be sent to school not only in Tagaste and the neighboring Madaura but also in the metropolis, Carthage. While there from the age of seventeen to nineteen, he took a mistress with whom he lived for thirteen years. They had a son whom he named imaginatively Atheodotus—a gift of God—and the boy seems to have been a brilliant lad, if one can judge from the dialogue which Augustine later wrote called *On the Teacher* (*De*

---

2. Augustine's works in PL 32–45; critical editions in CCSL and CSEL. Critical edition of the *Confessions* in CSEL 38. A convenient and reliable English translation is that of Pine-Coffin, *Saint Augustine: Confessions* (New York: Penguin, 1961).

*magistro*), in which he represented himself as carrying on a conversation with his sixteen-year-old son about the character of symbols and the relation of language to the process of discovery and of knowing—a pretty fast pace for a sixteen-year-old to maintain!

At the end of two years in Carthage, when Augustine was theoretically ready to engage in the profession of rhetor, he got his hands on a dialogue of Cicero, the *Hortensius*; it is no longer extant, but we have enough excerpts from it to recognize that it was in effect a duplication of Aristotle's early eulogy on the theoretic life called *Peri philosophias* (*On Philosophy*). He read also a translation of Aristotle's *On the Categories*, but both these works supplied stimulus and method rather than content.

Then he thought for a while that he had found the intellectual outlook for which he was seeking when he came into contact with some Western representatives of Manichean thought, who presented a view which professed to be a version of Christianity for intellectuals. The Christianity that one hears from the preacher in the parish church is really pretty simple stuff in comparison; it is not really the kind of thing that a proud graduate of the Academy of Carthage would find interesting. The teaching of these Manichees had come from Babylonia, where their founder Mani had absorbed, it would appear, a great deal of ancient Babylonian and Persian dualism and had undertaken to combine that with what he understood of Christianity. It was a materialistic dualism setting in contrast a realm of Light and a realm of Darkness that have always existed side by side, the Light above and the Dark below. The Light is the dominant component, occupying, say, three-quarters of the total realm of existence, and the Dark occupying the remaining quarter.

Mani interpreted cosmic history in terms of a succession of three ages—the past, the present, and the future. In the past—the first age of the world—the Light and the Dark were at first sharply separated, save that they were in contact throughout a horizontal surface of limitless extent. But the prince of Darkness broke over this frontier to seize and hold prisoner a beam of light, and when the Primordial Man armed with five bright powers was sent by the King of Light as a rescuer, he too was overcome and his weapons taken away. Prompt countermeasures by the good King checked the rebellion, but light was now imprisoned in the darkness and needed to be set free. This light is the "suffering Jesus" and exists in many parts of the mixed (sensible) world that results from the mingling of light and darkness. The sun and moon are bright vessels that sail in the expanse of heaven. Bright fruits and flowers, likewise, have their special share of light and so are proper food for the children of light. But meanwhile something has to be done to recover the particles of light which have got all mixed up in the past with the encroaching powers of the dark. And so an elaborate machinery for reclamation of the light is set up. It involves a great chandelier suspended from the firmament; it involves the operations of the moon, which gradually collects light particles and waxes from a sliver to a full sphere and then hands over the collected light to the sun, which is a ship that traverses the heavens and unloads its cargo of light in a device hanging from heaven—which serves as the receptacle for the light particles on the way back as the moon is squeezed down again into an empty shell, comes round once more and fills up again with light particles which it takes back, and so forth. Adam and Eve come into being as the offspring of the Dark Ruler, and in their descendants the light and dark elements are intricately tangled in varying proportions.

The Manichees of North Africa at least held a view of man which affirms that there are in each individual two souls, one naturally good and one bad, one light and one dark. These two souls exert stress upon the conduct of the individual, and what he does is the result of these two opposing tendencies. It is a mechanical view of human conduct like that of earlier Gnostic teachers, though set now in a context of ultimate dualism. Man is a participant in the warfare that still goes on between light and darkness, and in that warfare he can perform his part only if he steadily resists any sort of action that will result in the further entangling of light in the region of darkness. This means that he must avoid procreation of his own kind (which would carry on the mingling of light and darkness and thus postpone the ultimate return); he should avoid animal food; and he should practice other sorts of carefully prescribed asceticism. The "hearers" were a kind of lay congregation, while the "perfect" or leaders were supposed to practice the full discipline, and thus help restore light to its proper domain and open a way of redemption for all who are the present victims of the struggle. The future is a time in which this restoration will be completed: the dark powers will be pushed back into their original place, and the light will occupy the whole of the territory which properly belongs to it.

For eight years Augustine counted himself one of the hearers in this Western Manichean group. What appealed to him in its teaching appears to have been on the one hand its proclamation of a superior intellectual understanding of the world and of human life, which nevertheless had something of the prestige of the Christian tradition; and on the other hand, its moral code, which spoke directly to his adolescent problems. It appeared to him that as an adherent of Manicheism, he could find a way of life in which both his moral and his intellectual demands would be fulfilled. But after eight years' experience, he expressed his disappointment. He was puzzled by some of the things the Manicheans taught. They were not in accord with the natural philosophy (science) of his day. The sun, for example, is not really a fiery ship but a red-hot stone moving in the firmament. When he raised embarrassing questions, his Manichean tutors always said, "Wait 'til Faustus comes; he knows the answers." And eventually Faustus came, and Augustine had a chance to subject him to a period of questions; but he discovered that the only difference between Faustus and the others was that he admitted his ignorance whereas they did not. Faustus did not really know more about these things than the popular evangelists. Neither morally nor intellectually could the Manichees do what they promised. It seemed to him that the Academics who said that it is impossible to have certain knowledge of reality were probably right.

In the meantime, he decided to go from Carthage to Rome and practice his vocation there. Characteristically, he left without saying anything to his mother; she and the girl who had become his companion never got along very well together, and so Augustine just found it more convenient to slip away quietly. He did that kind of thing again and again in the course of his life. He had difficulty making hard practical decisions, whereas at the very same time, in intellectual controversy, he was both skillful and aggressive until what appeared to him the right conclusion had been reached.[3] Augustine had a lack of practical assurance in himself.

In Rome, his impracticality showed up in another form: he could not collect fees from his students. He had heard of a great preacher in Milan—Ambrose—and he had heard also of a post as public orator which was to be filled there, so he applied for the post and got it, moving from Rome to Milan. Monica, meanwhile, had found out where he had gone and followed him; and she, his mistress, and his son all went together to the place where Ambrose was the great preacher. Augustine had intended to pick up pointers on the task of rhetor listening to this man's public

3. At this point I am drawing upon an unpublished dissertation by Evor Evan, who has, I think, thrown light on Augustine's personality that has not appeared in any printed sources known to me.

speech; but somewhat to his surprise, he found himself more and more fascinated by what Ambrose had to say.

But before speaking of that, we must mention the influence of the recent translation of Plotinus' *Enneads*, which he had begun to read with increasing interest along with the works of certain other teachers whom Augustine usually referred to merely as "the Platonists." (The dialogues of Plato himself were not available in Latin.) With the utmost enthusiasm, Augustine now absorbed a teaching with respect to the universe which was as nearly as possible the opposite of that materialistic dualism that Manichean thought had presented. It affirmed a spiritualistic monism with respect to all reality, and understood the proper place and real nature of human beings in the world of spirit as fundamentally that of a unitary, rational soul. Evil is deficiency and not an opposing substance or power with which the Good must contend. Our human problem is that of rediscovering what we are—cleansing that which is basic and real within us, and becoming restored to that unity which is the principle of all reality in the universe. This seemed to Augustine to be at last genuine truth.

## Conversion to Christianity

But a difficulty still remained for him: he found himself unable to practice the high-minded way of life which the Neoplatonists preached. His discontent was made more acute because his friends knew illiterate Christian monks who had achieved the sort of self-mastery which he with all his intellectual superiority was unable to achieve. Christianity, however, was not yet acceptable to him. His mother had taught him Bible stories when he was a boy, and her influence had followed him through the intervening years of his career; but when he had actually read the letters of St. Paul in Latin, the apostle's style seemed to him so barbarous in comparison to that of Cicero that he quickly turned away from it. The naïveté of Christian teaching had so far always repelled him, even though it had also attracted him. But now Ambrose showed how to understand the crudities of Scripture by allegorical interpretation in such fashion that they no longer gave offense to his university-trained intellect.

Yet the moral problem remained. His mother decided it was time for Augustine to get rid of his mistress, the mother of his son, whom he obviously loved with depth and sincerity. And she undertook to find a suitable wife for him—a wife with social status and property which would accord with the dignity she hoped Augustine eventually would attain. So Augustine sent his mistress back to Africa; and she withdrew, swearing she would never have anything to do with another man. He promised himself that he would follow the same rule regarding women until his marriage. Meanwhile, however, the fiancée his mother found for him would not be of marriageable age for another two years; and during those years, Augustine found to his utter self-disgust that he could not follow out the pattern which he, like his mistress, had set for himself. He fell into a kind of promiscuity which, so far as one can tell, he had not practiced since his early student days. This accorded badly with the high teachings of Neoplatonism and with the high teachings he heard from the mouth of the bishop of Milan.

Indeed, what was far more important, I suspect, for Augustine's conversion than Ambrose's scriptural interpretation was the moral energy and authority which he saw vested in this man who stood as the representative of the Christian church and proved himself able to oppose even the weight of imperial power in virtue of this status as spokesman for the organized Christian community. The refusal of Ambrose to let the Emperor Theodosius receive Communion until he had done penance for his brutality at Thessalonica was a kind of symbol for what, to Augustine's mind, Ambrose stood for. As man and as churchman, he had the kind of security and force that Augustine craved and so far had lacked. Under his teaching and influence, Augustine now found when he was thirty-two years old the answer which satisfied him on both the intellectual and the practical side.

One day he was in the garden of the home he and his mother had taken in Milan. He had been talking with his Christian friend Alypius, and he left a scroll of the Pauline letters lying on a bench in the garden. As he recalled the episode, he thought he heard the voice of a child from a nearby house saying *Tolle lege*—"take, read." He tried to remember whether he knew any childhood game which had this kind of formulary but he couldn't think of one. So he went over to the place where this scroll was lying and looked at the first verse on which his eye lighted, and it read: "Not in chambering and in wantonness, but put on the Lord Jesus Christ." Forthwith, he says, the sense of helplessness which had frustrated him for so long disappeared. He had tried to get himself under control, and he had failed again and again. Now suddenly the problem was solved. Alypius of course was overjoyed, as was Monica. For a time, Augustine and some of his contemporaries and students went off to a country house of one his friends at Cassiciacum, not far from Milan, for a reading party or an informal seminar, and Monica went along as a kind of referee and housemother. After the summer of 386, when Augustine was thirty-two years old, he applied to Ambrose for baptism for himself and his son, and received it in the spring of 387.

We need not dwell here on the controversy over how prompt and complete was Augustine's conversion to Christianity. His first writings after 386 are philosophical dialogues of a rather artificial kind, rhetorical in form and cool and studied in style. The question has been raised whether Augustine could possibly have written in this academic fashion so soon after passing through such a tumultuous experience as the one he describes eleven years later in his *Confessions*; yet there are hints he was feeling still something of the emotional backwash of an experience which had been for him, as a similar experience had been for St. Paul, emotionally harrowing in a very high degree. He speaks of lying awake in tears; he speaks of a sense of fierce urgency which still was not completely subsided in his mind. There are indications that the story told in the *Confessions* is not so far out of accord with the facts as the texts of the dialogues taken by themselves might suggest. At any rate, after Cassiciacum, baptism, and the death of his son, Augustine and his mother started on a journey to Africa; but at Ostia, the port just north of Rome, she fell ill of a fever and died; and Augustine went back to Tagaste alone.

By 391 Augustine had attracted the attention of nearby clergy by the acuteness and power of his interpretations of Scripture, and he was ordained in that year to the priesthood. In 395 he became bishop of the important seaport town of Hyporegius (or Hippo Regius) on the coast of Numidia. And that is where he spent the rest of his life until his death in 430.

### The Problem of Knowledge and the Discovery of God

Since our concern here is with Augustine's theology rather than with his further career as a churchman, I think we may turn rather abruptly to the question: What is the starting point from which Augustine sets out in shaping a specifically Christian understanding of the world and of human nature? It would be easier if Augustine had been what is now spoken of as a systematic theologian; if at some time he had written a single great work in which his outlook is put together in logical order—a *Summa theologiae* or *Kirchliche Dogmatik.* The nearest approach to that sort of work, I presume, is the *City of God*—great indeed but not systematic. His only *summa* is the *Enchiridion*, a small manual or summary, something you could hold in the hand or slip in the pocket, which he wrote for one of his friends and which does in fact give a succinct conspectus of his mature outlook in about forty pages—a scant outline. In the work *On the City of God*, a larger variety of aspects of his thought are brought together than in any other single work. But the fact is that Augustine, like St. Paul, wrote for the most part occasional controversial works directed to specific issues, and did not attempt to put together in architectonic form a complete theology. Nevertheless, it is not improper to look for a system of thought because, as a matter of fact, his mind was working always with certain presuppositions that are usually discernible.

We may begin with certain early works in which a philosophical interest is still uppermost. Augustine had only recently moved from a period in which skepticism had appealed to him into assurance with respect to the accessibility of truth, and the question had to be faced whether there is good ground for such assurance. In certain of his early dialogues, he faces that question, and the answer which he works out is repeated in later works such as *On the Trinity*. In the Middle Academy, under Arcesilaus and Carneades, the issue had been put in terms of this sort: The application of the sternest kind of logical analysis leads to the conclusion that certain knowledge of objective reality appears to be inaccessible to us. We may no doubt distinguish degrees of probability with reference to judgments about the nature of the real world, but certain knowledge of it we cannot have. It seems clear to Augustine, once he has emerged from the skeptical mood himself, that to say even so much as this is to imply more. In his work *Against the Academics*, Augustine argued that to say that we can distinguish more probable from less probable judgments implies that we have a standard which must itself be dependable: a standard of comparison which enables us to say one judgment approaches nearer to certainty than does this other. But if we can make that kind of judgment, plainly enough we must have some kind of conception, however dim, of what truth and certainty would be; and we must be able to apply that insight in judging that one affirmation is more or less probable than another. It appears, then, that if we are to be able to affirm even as much as these skeptics are ready to affirm, we do have a criterion.

But can we specify an instance of this criterion? Is there anything that can be certainly known? At this point, Augustine called upon his reading of the works of the Platonists and points to the possibility of having certain knowledge of purely formal entities, logical and mathematical. The numbers and magnitudes with which the mathematicians are concerned and the relations among these can be certainly known. In these areas, we can have what is not really probable belief but certain, indubitable knowledge of such a sort that to contradict it is to involve oneself in further contradiction. The forms likewise can be certainly known. Here is an instance of knowledge which even the skeptics are not prepared to throw overboard. But plainly enough, to know abstract form is of itself not to go very far in refuting the skeptical position; it is with respect to actual reality that their doubts are primarily raised. So it becomes necessary to inquire whether with respect to actual reality we can have knowledge as certain as the knowledge we have regarding formal terms and relations. Is it possible to know with equal certainty matters of fact?

In several works, early and late, Augustine offers the self as a first instance of what can be certainly known. If I find myself able to raise questions as the skeptics do about the possibility of having knowledge of objective reality, I find that in raising the question I am tacitly affirming my own existence as the questioner, the doubter. As a matter of fact, doubting is a very complex mental operation, for in doubt I affirm that I am doubtful—and that is not doubtful. "If I am deceived, I am." *Si fallor, sum*—he puts it into a little aphorism. Descartes later formulates a somewhat similar principle: *Je pense, donc je suis—cogito, ergo sum*; he is, in effect, following this Augustinian line. It takes its start, as far as Augustine is concerned, precisely from that extraordinary capacity of his for introspective observation, interpretation, and reporting. He discovers in the simplest act of judgment a whole array of mental acts. So in the very act of raising the question whether I can have knowledge, it turns out that I already do have knowledge of a rather complex kind with respect to my own being. I can be certain of my own existence.

But is it possible to have similarly certain knowledge—knowledge which cannot be doubted successfully—about beings other than myself? Augustine says yes. The simplest road to the recognition of this objective reality whose being is as certain as the existence of the soul itself is the recognition that when the soul undertakes to distinguish between true and false judgments, it submits to a standard which it acknowledges to be superior to itself. The forms and formal relationships of which we have already spoken are in a certain sense other-than-I and lay obligation upon me to think in accordance with the patterns which they actually display. I am aware, that is, of an ingrained order—Augustine calls it sometimes measure (*mensura*), sometimes form (*forma* or *ratio*), sometimes order (*ordo*)—which I cannot change by any amount of wishing or willing. What is the locus of those structured forms, which we have declared to be the subject matter of certain knowledge? Are they, so to say, produced by the mind that knows them? Plato had already given the answer, which is accepted by his successors. These forms are objective too, not produced by the finite mind that knows them. Where then are they located? Once again Plotinus has the answer. They are located in the ultimate Principle of being. This Principle is the source on the one hand of content which is rationally discernible; and on the other, of a medium, an intellectual light, in which such content can be discerned. (I need scarcely remind you of Plato's metaphor of the sun which makes things in the sensible world visible by the dispersion of its light, and the form of the Good which in the intelligible realm similarly supplies intelligibility to whatever turns out to be intelligible. That metaphor has come down through all the intervening generations of Platonic thought. Plotinus and his successors made full use of it; and Augustine is thinking here in essentially Neoplatonic terms.)

Now if I try to find this Principle somewhere inside myself, I fail. Augustine has a lengthy passage in the *Confessions* in which he speaks of the way in which he sought to explore the immense storehouse of memory, passing from sense perception to the records that such experience leaves. He became aware of a perfectly extraordinary container in which vestiges of past experience are preserved in such wise that I can call up at will one and another although others elude me. Is memory then capacious enough to include God? The answer has to be no. What I do discover, however, in trying to explore the heights and depths of memory is that my mind is in some sense greater than itself. There is a kind of self-transcendence, a kind of personal self-consciousness. I am able to think of the stars in heaven; I am able to think of events that happened before I was born; I am able to anticipate what will come to pass after I am no longer here. And it is memory that supplies the images in terms of which I can thus range the panorama of space and the whole sequence of time. My mind is then able to observe itself engaged in this kind of exploring. My mind is able to stand apart and view itself as though from outside—this I discover in undertaking to examine what goes on inside me. What I do not discover there is the source of this obligation that rests upon me to think in accordance with an order that is given. I must then say the way my mind works and the demands that are laid upon it convey to me a ground for the certain affirmation that God exists. Over against the skeptics, then, by this kind of natural reasoning, I can be assured that God is.

Can I know anything more about what God is? Yes, says Augustine in a number of passages—one of which is, I think, worth noting because of the part it later plays in Anselm's effort to establish a sure ground for affirming the being of God. The passage is located in the work called the *On the Morals of the Manichees*, in which Augustine is arguing that whatever God is and has made is good.[4] He raises the question: what is it we mean when we say *God*? And his answer is: "The utterly supreme Good, than which nothing better can be or can be thought, must be understood or believed to be God" (*summum bonum omnino, quo melius nihil est aut cogitari possit, aut intelligendum aut credendum Deum est*). Anselm is going to talk not quite in these terms of the Supreme Good—he's going to speak of the supremely great, the *summum ens*—but his argument starts precisely from this way of conceiving God. If I know what I mean when I use the term *Deus*, I recognize that it is this that I should mean: a being than which nothing better can be thought (or imaged, or apprehended as form or meaning—all this is implied by *cogitari*). I cannot think of God as anything other or less than the utterly Good. Hence whatever stems from God is good. We must distinguish between what is from God (*ex Deo*) and what is of God (*de Deo*). Now everything is from God but not everything is of God, and what is from God, insofar as it is at all, is to be regarded as a good and not an ill. Hence the rejection of the Manichean dualism, which treats evil as being just as radically existent as good.

Thus far we've been talking of rational knowledge of God; but for Augustine, of course, there is another way toward the apprehension of God: the way of belief. He uses as a kind of motto—again, Anselm follows him—*fides quaerens intellectum* (faith seeking understanding). It is impossible to love what one does not in some manner cognitively apprehend. One must either know what one loves, or one must believe. And to believe [within] the cognitive region [i.e., what is cognitively ap-

---

4. Augustine, *Mor. Manich.* (PL 32:1309). English translation in *NPNF1* 4:68–89.

prehended] is to be regarded as a starting point toward knowledge or understanding. We must not suppose that we can in point of fact achieve knowledge of everything that here and now we're called upon to believe; but on the other hand, we must not be content to rest idly in belief as if that were sufficient. We must try continually to expand the range of what we believe with clear insight; and that is what understanding means.

The Scriptures will provide us with a great range of material which is in the first instance to be accepted on the authoritative word of the Church, but which is to be studied with a view to recognizing the order of things shining through it in such wise that Scripture becomes, not a mass of aggregate single statements but an ordered body of revealed truth. Augustine's *On Christian Doctrine* is in effect a more or less systematic exposition of methods to be employed in interpreting Scripture.[5] He starts with the rules that his fellow countryman, Tychonius, had laid down, and then amends them in his own way. As was true for most of the tradition, allegorical or spiritual interpretation is an indispensable part of this way to pass from simple belief to understanding.

## The Being of God: Time and Eternity

If we say then that the whole of mathematical knowledge and of logical knowledge is possible only by reason of the grounding of the terms and relations which we must explore in the fundamental Reality, we are saying of that Reality: it is the basis of all truth, the basis of all rational order. But if we say that of it, then we may without too much violence go on to say a further thing. Since these forms are themselves timeless, that Reality in which they are grounded is itself then of a different order from the whole realm of time and change. Its being must be eternal being.

This raises the question of the nature of time and the meaning of eternity. Augustine deals with this question most extensively in the concluding books of the *Confessions*, in which he examines the opening verses of the first chapter of Genesis, the story of the creation of the world. And he confronts at once the very difficult problem of trying to define the nature of time and of succession. The upshot of his inquiry, which is philosophical rather than directly theological, is that the only

---

5. Augustine, *Doctr. chr.* (PL 34:15); critical edition in CSEL 80. English translation by D. W. Robertson, Jr., *On Christian Doctrine*, Library of Liberal Arts 80 (New York: Liberal Arts, 1958).

consistent account that can be given of time is an account which locates
it in consciousness. If we try to locate time outside of mind, we run into
quite unmanageable contradiction. For the only segment of time which
can be called real at any moment is an instantaneous segment—which is
a contradiction in terms. The only time which is presently real is that moment which can be called *now*, and if I try to extend the moment so that it
includes more than a single instant, I am getting into not merely the present but also the past, which by definition has ceased to be, and the future,
which is not yet. If I try then to locate time with reference to things, I find
that I am compelled to define time as at once a point and a continuum;
and it cannot be both in a real world in which only the present can be
said to be. On the other hand, if I locate time in consciousness, then in
terms of memory, present experience, and anticipation, I have a suitable
context in which *before* and *after* can be placed. But what, then, will be
the relation of time to the Being in whom formal terms and relations are
grounded? The answer must be that time as I experience it as a succession
from *before* to *after* cannot characterize that ultimate Being. Rather, the
nature of that Being must stand in a relation to time and succession of
such a sort that I can say that time depends upon eternity. My experience
unrolls, but the experience of an eternal Being would be simultaneous in
its full reach.

If I am prepared now to speak of this eternal Ground of number and
of form and of time as God, I can say perhaps that God is able to view the
whole span of time in a single moment, somewhat as I am able so to view
the contents of what I call my present. For God, the whole sweep of history is present. That does not mean that God is a temporal being. It means
that the temporality of the world that I know is dependent upon and
maintained by the consciousness of God, which is of a different order.
When that affirmation has been made of God, what has been said thus
far is enough to entitle one to say that God is perfect, in the sense that he
is self-sufficient and lacks nothing. Since he is the ground of the being of
both formal and temporal reality, his own being must be regarded as not
dependent upon something else for its ground, but rather as self-existent
and self-sufficient.

Augustine is confident that one can in principle have this much
knowledge about God as a matter of entire certainty. This is involved in
any kind of thinking that one undertakes to carry on. There are certain
other purely Christian affirmations about God which are not thus deriv-

able from the operations of pure reason but can be affirmed only as matters of faith, most especially the dogmatic Trinitarian formula which had been reaffirmed in Constantinople five years before Augustine became a Christian. His work *On the Trinity* we noted when we were examining the maturing and final formulation of Trinitarian thought. We recall that Augustine did not believe it was possible to show that the dogma's content is demonstrable by reason, but rather that its content is conformable to the requirements of reason, and that reason can call attention to certain positive experiences in the order of human life which will support the position set forth regarding the triunity of God.

## The Created World and the Fall

Next we concern ourselves with the created world. We have already commented on the difference made by holding that the world is created and hence not an emanation from God; and now turn immediately to the strategic position of human beings and of angels, who alone of all created beings are at once rational and free. Only they have the sort of freedom which would enable them to affirm anything other than the good order which God himself has established. Unhappily, the angels first and then the parents of the human race did precisely that. Confronted by the reality which stems perpetually from God, certain of the angels, instead of acknowledging fully and freely that both their being and their good comes only from God, claimed for themselves the self-sufficiency which comes from God alone; and in that affirmation there came for the first time the jarring note of falsity. This first impulse to turn away from God, whether on the part of angels or of human beings, arises from self-assertion; *superbia* or pride is the source of all other sins. The proud mind views nonbeing not simply as a shadowing possibility or a logical limit of thought; it professes nonbeing to be what it is *not*—namely, reality itself. When a creature professes to be of the same status as the Creator, a self-sufficient source of good, then that creature is permitting evil to become (we can hardly say real or actual) at least effective. Evil is now here.

Out of the creatures' initial revolt there followed at once two lamentable consequences, loss of knowledge and loss of satisfaction. The creature, cut off by its own act from the source of its truth and its good, is fated to ignorance and to insatiable craving or lust. Ignorance takes the place of that measure of knowledge which one may have had before;

on the one hand, cutting oneself off from the very ground of truth is to condemn oneself to a bondage of error; and on the other, cutting oneself off from the proper ground of good condemns one to a perpetually insatiable craving. It is *amor* all right, but is love directed to the wrong ends and consequently self-defeating. Augustine calls this debased form of love *concupiscentia*. These secondary consequences of the initial sin carry with them a state of inescapable emotional tumult instead of the initial tranquility of the one living in close communion with God. Fallen man now lives in alternation between depression (*tristitia, timor*) and false elation (*laetitia falsa*)—the mood swings of one like Augustine himself, who finds himself on some occasions utterly downcast and on other occasions deceptively inflated with a sense of power and self-sufficiency. So the result of the creature's revolt against the Creator is a state of affairs which closely corresponds with what St. Paul had declared to be the human plight. The motto of the *Confessions*—"O God, thou hast made us for thyself, and our hearts are unquiet until they find quiet in thee"—is in a sense the pattern of Augustine's theology. We have been made by one who is the only ground for our fulfillment; we seek that fulfillment elsewhere and otherwise. The result is the kind of disquiet which all of us know all too well. And it will continue until somehow we are enabled to return and find our good in God. As we shall see, Augustine's conception of that plight is morally just as pessimistic and metaphysically more gloomy on the whole than was that of St. Paul.

I think it may be well to dwell for a bit on this conception of a kind of evil which is defect but which has a kind of aggressiveness and destructiveness. The first thing is to say that, as far as I know, Augustine nowhere speaks of nonbeing as itself evil. Nonbeing as an abstract principle is a logical limit for thought concerning a universe that depends for all its being upon God and his creative power—a universe that is suspended, so to say, over an abyss of nonbeing which cannot be called either good or bad precisely because it has no determinate existence. Evil is therefore not to be equated with nonbeing but rather is to be equated with the intrusion of nonbeing into the realm of being. Evil is in a proper sense privation of being: it is to be equated with failure on the part of what is real, a defect or decline or lapse in the direction of nonbeing on the part of something which was created to occupy a definite status in the order of God.

A word is used by Professor Tsarnoff in his book *On the Nature of Evil* which seems to me to hit this point very precisely.[6] Evil, he says, is *degradatio,* loss of rank or status—degradation in the very literal meaning of a demotion from (*de*) one's proper *gradus*. God has created the world, and everything in it is good as regards its relation to nature and to other natural beings. There is no evil in nature. That is a principle from which Augustine never wavers after he has once learned it from his Neoplatonic teachers. In nature, there is nothing bad. If you point to the swine or the beasts of prey, to the noxious insects or poisonous snakes, you have to say that in their proper places in the natural order they all contribute to a very intricate totality which, in the judgment of God, is as he has willed it to be. But suppose you find a rational person, capable of self-control as a beast is not, behaving like a hog or like a tiger. Then you have evil. And the evil consists not in swinishness, which is a natural status, but in the decline from personal status to the level of the swine. For a pig to be swinish is natural and right, but for a man to be swinish is unnatural and wrong. It is the loss of one's proper place, not the occupying of one's proper place, in which evil consists. Once again, only beings who are gifted with imagination and freedom of will are susceptible of that kind of dislocation. The trees cannot leave their proper place in the natural order and sink to a lower one. Neither can the unreasoning animals. They continue to occupy the places which God has intended for them, and to make their contributions to the complex symphony of God's world.

It is only angels and human beings who are capable of being something less than God has intended them to be. When there is that kind of lapse or loss of level, one can speak in a paradoxical way of nonbeing encroaching upon being—not in the sense that nonbeing is an opposing being which has irrupted into the midst of the real order, but rather in the sense that in declining toward nonbeing, the real order has suffered a kind of revaluation for the worse.

The view that evil is a function of free will and of nothing else at all is a view to which Augustine came in the earliest period of his theological writing—the period in which he was primarily in revolt against Manichaeism. One of the points at which that outlook was most completely wrong was in supposing that there is an evil principle in nature—in the very existence of the world—and that the sins of rational beings are

6. Tsarnoff, Radoslav A., *The Nature of Evil* (New York: Macmillan, 1931).

performed by reason of an essentially natural operation upon them. To locate evil, and specifically to locate sin, in the order of nature seems to him quite intolerable; and in his early work on free will, *De libero arbitrio*, directed against the Manicheans, he takes a position from which he never thereafter recedes.[7] Evil can be thought of only as a function of free choice, and only a being of free choice is capable of evil acts. It appeared to him later that in this early tract he had stressed the extent of human freedom a little too strongly, but in principle he maintains for the rest of his career the position which here he takes: evil, and specifically sin, is not to be traced to any natural principle which is itself bad; rather, sin arises from the operation of a natural principle which is in itself good. The will is the supreme function or attribute of personal existence. Rational choice is the very finest manifestation in human beings of the beneficence of God, yet it is precisely our capacity for rational choice which is our chief peril. If it were not for that, we would be locked in the natural order as plants and animals are, and could do no wrong.

Here, as we noted earlier, is the point at which Augustine's judgment breaks completely with the whole classical philosophical tradition about human nature and human wrongdoing. In the classical tradition as we find it in the Platonic school, wrongdoing results from a conflict between rational insights and subrational capacities—appetites on the one hand and such driving factors as anger on the other. When a subrational factor gets the upper hand and revolts against reason, then a person deviates from the steady line toward good. But any suggestion that reason in itself can do wrong I find nowhere in the Platonic literature. Reason is *ipso facto* intent upon good, it is so by definition. Reason can be overborne by the subrational parts of our makeup, but in itself reason cannot go astray. It is too little reason that makes trouble, not too much. "To see the good is to follow it." That is a Socratic and Platonic principle that is never rejected. There are hints in Plato's latest dialogues, particularly in the *Laws*, that another kind of insight is beginning to bother him: the insight that one may see, perhaps not the perfect good, but at least a better, and find oneself choosing a worse. But even so, it seems to me that the choice of the worse is thought of as resulting from the operation of some inferior principle.

7. Augustine, *Lib.* (PL 32:1221; 43:93). Critical edition in CSEL 74. English translation by Benjamin and Hackstaff, *On Free Choice of the Will*, Library of Liberal Arts 150 (Indianapolis: Bobbs-Merrill, 1964).

By contrast with that, Augustine is perfectly uncompromising in affirming that the choice of the worse is the act of the highest human principle. It is not appetites that choose; appetites can only prompt this or that choice. It is not emotional drives that choose; they simply influence in this direction or that. It is rational will that chooses, and this is the very core and seat of human existence as personal. So far as I can see, here is a genuinely new departure in the understanding of man. We shall shortly have occasion to note the views of some of Augustine's predecessors who were paving the way for his thought at this point, but as far as I know, none of them moved clear out to the completed statement which we find in his thought.

## RESULTS OF THE FALL

Now consider another aspect of this view of evil as the outcome of rational choice. The effect of self-glorification on the part of either angels or human beings is pervasive and corrupting. It is not merely that one has made a wrong choice which one can regret and correct thenceforward. Rather, one has made a wrong choice that has altered one's status in the order of being. By lapsing to a lower level, one has put oneself in a position from which one cannot recover by one's own effort. One can specify on the one hand a psychological, and on the other hand a metaphysical, reason for this. Psychologically, one cannot recover because all one's acts, all one's strivings henceforth, issue out of a will which has already been warped; consequently, the strivings are themselves warped by the distortion that has entered into the capacity which one has for choosing. I have broken the law; I have been disobedient, but more than that I have made it impossible for myself henceforth to be obedient. Once the mind has deviated from its proper goal, any effort to get back on the track will result in further deviation because that effort is itself an expression of aggressive self-centeredness. What I am trying to do is to improve my lot, but in trying to improve my lot, I have my attention fixed still on myself. And so my effort is doomed to failure.

Metaphysically, the reason that one cannot recover is that once one has lost a level of being, that level can be regained only by a fresh creative act, for what is required is the actual production of being. Now God can create being, but no creature can. Consequently, though an angel or a man is free to slide down in the scale of being, he is not able by any effort of his own to climb back up. Once he has lapsed, anything that he does henceforward must be done with that lowered position as a starting point. He can fall still lower but he can never climb higher. Augustine's way of putting this is to say that when angels and human beings were created, they were able both to sin (*posse peccare*) and not to sin (*posse non peccare*). Their freedom consisted in their genuine ability to choose either to maintain their attention upon God and their devotion to him as the source of their being good; or instead of God, to affirm some other source of being and of good. Once they had gone this second way, their better capacity was lost. Everything they did from this point on would fall under the head of sin, because never again would a fallen creature be able with complete surety to maintain that selflessness which would unambiguously affirm complete dependence upon God. When one has put *oneself* in the center, there is no chance that one can by taking thought work oneself out of the center. Again, one can see psychologically why this is the case. Suppose I say to myself: I will be unselfish; I will forget myself. The harder I try to forget myself, obviously the more I am underlining the self that I am insisting on trying to forget. My actions have now come to be wrongly motivated, and that wrong motivation is not superficial but central. I am now a person who has become an egoist, and an egoist trying to be something else is still an egoist trying to be something else; there is no chance of success.

Human beings are still free then in an unhappy way—free to sin, free to sink lower. But they have lost their original freedom to turn wholly to God. What one must say is that personal nature is depraved. It is not merely that one has made a mistake or that one has acquired a wrong habit. What one has done is to poison the well from which the water of one's living proceeds; and all water that springs from it henceforth will be poisoned water. So the sin which separates one from God and condemns one to that turbulent life of depression and exaltation pervaded by ignorance (the inability to see things clearly because oneself is forever getting in the way) condemns one also to insatiable cravings because one wants always those things which will not satisfy. Fundamentally, what one needs is the status of being wholly open to God; but one tries to achieve satisfaction by seeking this or that pleasure, by seeking the security which comes with the possession of wealth, by seeking popular acclaim and the power to exercise authority over others; and one tries in these ways to gain security and satisfaction. But in principle that kind of effort is condemned in advance. If only sensualists could see what it really is they are trying to get, if only power-hungry despots could see what it is that drives them so frantically to seek more and more and more power for themselves, they would see that what they want at bottom is tranquility, security. But that is to be had only through the love of God.

We have not used the word *love* so far, but in Augustine's position, and especially in his later works, it is a very important term. The term that he uses is sometimes *amor* and sometimes *caritas*. It seems to me that *amor* corresponds pretty closely to the Platonic *eros*—an ambiguous, dynamic drive which, says Augustine, is the gravitation of the soul. Now in classical physics, especially in Aristotelian physics, every body has a place in the natural order, and it tends to seek that place. Heavy bodies tend toward the center of the massive spheres which make up the universe while light bodies tend toward the circumference. If a heavy body is lifted above the earth, its tendency is to go down toward the earth; if a lighter body is held down, its tendency is to rise. Bubbles rise upward in water, and fire rises upward even in air, seeking the place where the fires are at home. That intrinsic tendency of a body to seek its own level is its *gravitas*. That is the dynamic which pervades all of the physical universe. Now, says Augustine, souls are like that too; they have a natural tendency to seek that which they take to be their good. And this love for what attracts me is what guides my actions this way or that. In practice, there are just two sorts of objects to which I can thus be drawn. There is God, perfect Being, on the one hand and there is created being on the other. In as far as my love has been fixed upon created being instead of upon God, I am seeking to satisfy an infinite craving with finite sops. It is for that reason that I can never regain the tranquility of one whose love is set unambiguously upon God. The faithful angels still have that status. Theirs has become the perfect freedom of inability to sin (*posse non peccare*). Filled with concupiscence, fallen angels and human beings have the status of those whose love has been fixed upon unsatisfying objects; consequently, they will be perpetually unsatisfied so far as their own efforts are concerned.

## Original Sin

The third thing to say about the nature and consequences of sin is that so far as regards the human race, it is not only Adam himself who was corrupted; all of his descendants are corrupted likewise. It is not merely that they are corrupted in the sense that they desire the wrong things. Augustine affirms further that this wrong desire is itself blameworthy, so that they inherit from Adam not only a tendency to do wrong, but the guilt which attaches to that tendency. Therefore, the sins committed by Adam's descendants are on the one hand sins like his own, which are manifestations of egoistic pride—self-assertion as over against God—but they are on the other hand sins which are symptoms of an underlying body or seedbed of sin which is present in every human being and in the whole race collectively. It is necessary to say that the whole race after Adam is a mass of sin (*massa peccati*) or a mass of damnation (*massa perditionis*), which is simply another way of saying: Here is God's judgment upon the results of Adam's wrongdoing.

As far as I know, this is another idea which Augustine is the first to work out in quite uncompromising fashion. In Latin theology as far back as Tertullian, we have the beginnings of the suggestion that there is a carryover from our forebears in terms of an evil tendency. Tertullian speaks of each soul as affected by a certain vice of its origin (*vitium originis*). But in the one context in which Tertullian uses the phrase, that vice appears to be simply the lust associated with human procreation. Tertullian shares the Stoic traducianist understanding of the origin of each individual soul. Stoic metaphysics spoke of a seminal principle (*logos spermatikos*) which in each plant and in each animal is the vehicle of transmission from parents to offspring of the characteristic type of the plant or the animal species. According to the Stoics, when the corporeal human soul is conceived and physically transmitted, it is affirmable that the soul of the child is derived directly and physically from the souls of its parents. In as far as at the moment of conception the souls of the parents are pervaded by lust, that lust carries over into the soul of the child, as Tertullian understands the matter. However, it is not a situation in which Adam's sin has somehow mystically affected the whole human race. It is rather a piecemeal transmission from each generation to the next of a human status which is universal but which does not have the character of massive and all-inclusive depravity.

Somewhat similarly, Cyprian and Ambrose, who are in the succession of Latin thinkers between Tertullian and Augustine, refer to this hereditary taint. Ambrose even speaks of it as inherited sin. But for the most part he talks of it as though it were a disability which is inherited, rather than guilt which is inherited, so that it is more like a disease. And that is precisely the metaphor which these thinkers often employ. They speak of it as a contagion, so that what I have as a member of the succession of sinful human generations is a weakness, a tendency to evil.

But now Augustine takes the final step, affirming that what is inherited is not only a tendency to evil but guilt. Therefore, in the proper sense I am a sinner from the moment of my conception, subject to punishment, and not merely subject to pity for my sad lot. Tertullian shows the limited extent to which he was willing to think in terms of a carryover of culpability by his opposition to the practice of infant baptism. He was inclined to say, Wait until you are thirty years old before you use up your one chance to have your life washed clean. Why baptize infants? After all, they are not sinners and do not have anything to gain by having their lives washed clean. On the other hand, Augustine says: No, what they tell me of my behavior in the cradle makes it clear to me that I was a sinner then and there. When the infant kicks and bites and screams to get what he wants, he is displaying sinful propensities, and these propensities are punishable by eternal damnation unless the infant is brought into the Church and cleansed by God's grace.

Now if one raises the question how and why Adam's sin thus affects all his successors, one finds Augustine debating the question whether traducianism or creationism, with respect to the emergence of each new individual soul, is the more probable view. He does not explicitly take sides on the issue, but at least he does make it clear that he is not, like Tertullian, ready to affirm the traducianist view. It has seemed to a great many critics that traducianism would have made his own position simpler and easier to defend, but he is not persuaded of the truth of an essentially materialistic metaphysic, and Stoicism is materialistic. Traducianism belongs most readily in that context. Augustine, however, is Neoplatonist as far as he thinks metaphysically, and the spiritualism of Neoplatonic thought does not lend itself to traducianist theory. Creationism is the view that each new individual soul is the result of a fresh creative act on the part of God, so that the soul of the child is not directly derived from the soul of its parents. It is a new being. On the whole, Augustine tends to that side.

How then can we think of Adam's progeny as affected by his act? Augustine used language which on the face of it is metaphorical, and yet he used it in a way which appears to be realistic in intent. We are all somehow present in Adam when he sinned. And we were present in Adam, I take it, not in the sense of Aristotelian potentiality; rather, we were present in him partly in the sense that as the first man, he was the bearer of the full nature or essential character of human existence. He is all of humanity there is when he alone lives as a human person. And when Eve is put by his side, they two between them share the whole character of humanity. Therefore, in them the essential character of humanity has been polluted. But there are other times when Augustine seems to think in terms of a kind of mystical organic view. The whole race is present in Adam seminally, but also in the sense that there is an unbroken continuity between him and all of his successors of such a sort that the character which he displayed is not merely similar to theirs, but it *is* theirs. They are present in him; and in some sense what he does, they do. Obviously that is an extremely difficult position, and yet it is one which in the Pauline tradition is a familiar and essential one. All sinned in the first Adam; all are saved in the second Adam. It is impossible to tell how in any scientific way, but poetic or mystical or religious insight can sense somehow what happened. What happened is that the whole human race is bound together and stands or falls together. If that were not the case, the elaborate interrelations among men and the far-reaching effect of the acts of some men, whether for evil or for good, would not be understandable at all. We were present in Adam and in his fall we all had our share.

## Controversy with Pelagius

These views Augustine developed in the greatest detail and with the sharpest emphasis during a relatively late controversy in his career as a theologian. The controversy was precipitated by the vigorous attack of a British monk, Pelagius, who came to Rome in the early years of the fifth century and there was very warmly welcomed. He went, moreover, to the East and had an equally warm reception there because he was defending, against the novelty of Augustinian doctrine, that freedom of choice which had been characteristic of Greek theology from the start. The central principle in Pelagius' moral theology is that God would not have commanded us to do what we are unable to do. If we confront the law of God which says, "Thou shalt not kill, Thou shalt not commit adultery, Thou shalt not steal," we have the ability to obey these commandments; even that tenth commandment which had made most trouble for St. Paul, "Thou shalt not covet"—even this, God would not have commanded unless he had granted the power to obey. What we ought to do, we can do.

Pelagius has the utmost impatience with people who say "Oh, I want to. I'm trying hard, but I just cannot do as I ought." That seems to him a completely intolerable evasion.

Pelagius had been brought up in a monastic community in which disciplined life was taken as a matter of course and in which doing the things that the rule prescribed was something that every member of the community assumed that he was capable of doing. He himself was not a systematic thinker. Working out his theory in cold order was the work of two Italian disciples, Caelestius and Julian of Eclanum. The brilliant young bishop of Eclanum was the most acute systematic mind in the Pelagian school, and a good deal of what we know as Pelagianism was what he worked out. However, we have Pelagius' own commentaries on the Pauline epistles, and I am inclined to think that there are indications in his reading of some of the more difficult verses in the letter to the Romans that throw a great deal of light on his understanding of the issues which are here at stake.[8]

Let me preface any reference to his interpretation of Pauline material by a brief summary indication of the direction of his thinking. On the principle that human beings can do what they ought to do, Pelagius affirms that they are created with free will which they can never lose. Because their wills are free, they can make either right or wrong choices. If they make wrong choices, they make it more difficult for themselves to choose rightly the next time because whatever choice is made leaves prints in the framework of life; it establishes habits which are either virtuous or vicious. If a person establishes good habits, virtuous conduct is more difficult although never impossible. It would seem to follow that there must have been those who actually have obeyed the law of God perfectly, if in principle a person never loses the ability to do that which is right. Pelagius affirmed that Abel had been sinless; and Coelestius is declared to have said "that there were sinless men before the coming of Christ."

Now with respect to the very dark fact to which Augustine points— the pervasiveness, the massiveness, the obstinacy of human evil—Pelagius has one recourse. All this he is inclined to regard as the accumulation of bad habits in individuals and social groups. I am indeed predisposed to

---

8. Critical edition by Souter, *Pelagius's Exposition of Thirteen Epistles of St. Paul*. 3 vols. (I. Introduction, II. Text, III. Pseudo-Jerome Interpolations), Texts and Studies 9:1–3 (Cambridge: Cambridge University Press, 1931).

wrong conduct if my parents, from the time when I am an infant, set before me examples of imperfect lives, and if my companions in school and the adults in the community are committed to deception and aggression as ways of getting what they want. In short, Pelagius is willing to depend upon the misuse of freedom, the development of bad habits, and the influence of bad examples for his explanation of all the darker aspects of human behavior.

Now let us see what, with these presuppositions, he makes of certain passages in the Epistle to the Romans. In the seventh chapter, St. Paul speaks of the extraordinary difficulty of acknowledging the righteousness of God's commandments and then doing something else. St. Paul says, "It is not I who do thus," and Pelagius comments, "Before (I have established) a habit, I myself was acting willingly," and implies, "but now that I have established a habit I no longer act freely, in the sense of acting as I could act before this difficulty had been put in my way." But St. Paul went on to say, "It is not I who do thus, but sin that dwells in me." Pelagius is careful to say: "Dwells in me as a sojourner and an alien, not as if one (with me), as an accident, an acquired trait (*accidens*), not as a natural trait." St. Paul writes, "But I know that there does not dwell in me, that is in my flesh, any good." Pelagius notes: "He does not say, 'My flesh is not good.'" Then St. Paul says: "I consent to the law of God according to the inner man," and Pelagius says, "The inner man is the rational and intelligent soul which consents the law of God, for his law is to live rationally and not to be led by the passions of irrational animals." Pelagius' conception, as many critics have urged, is the classical conception. Our body is exterior, while our mind is the inner man; and in as far as we are rational, we recognize the propriety of living in accordance with the law. But, says Paul, "I see another law in my members, which opposes the insight of my mind." Pelagius comments: "Habitual desires, or the persuasion of the enemy" of God. "Opposing the law of my mind." "That is, says Pelagius, "natural conscience, or the divine law which has its place in the mind." Paul writes, "I am led captive to the law of sin which is in my members," and Pelagius comments, "In the habit (*consuetudine*) of sins." *Habit* may not be the best word to use here; it is perhaps *custom* or *disposition*; it is my familiar and repeated manner of acting, and in that consists the law of my members. I have built up in myself this way of behavior, and it is that which opposes now the insight of my rational mind. "Unhappy man that I am! Who shall set me free from the body of this death?" Pelagius says, "I who am thus detained, who shall set me free from this deadly corporeal disposition (*consuetudine mortifera corporali*)?[9] That is the character of Pelagius' understanding of St. Paul all the way along.

Augustine finds it infuriating. It seems to him that the rational outcome of Pelagius' view is that we can after all save ourselves if only we will, and that therefore divine grace is not needed. (We shall examine Augustine's doctrine of grace a little later.) Pelagius says, No, divine grace is necessary for salvation. But upon being pressed, it turns out that what he understands as divine grace (*gratia*, divine liberality or largesse) is (a) the granting of a freedom of the will which is unalienable; (b) the giving of the law as a guide to conduct; and (c) the sending of Jesus Christ as a good example. The grace of God operates in these rational and moralistic ways. "But," says Augustine, "what you have said when you say that freedom of choice has never been lost is that in any situation, however beclouded by previous acts, a person can in principle do what he ought to do. Then God's grace is not really necessary. It only makes easier what apart from God's help would be more difficult." And of course Augustine rejects that conception of human ability and human independence of God as just unchristian. The Pelagian view is a Pythagorean view, so he says on occasion. This is the view of classic philosophy masquerading as Christian theology. The true Christian position affirms that as the result of sin, human nature has been ruined. I think that word is not too strong. It is not that the image of God in man has been totally destroyed, for that would be impossible except by an act of God himself. But it has been so far distorted that actions which proceed from the remaining human nature are actions which make matters steadily worse rather than better. Augustine uses extremely emphatic and vigorous language to say what he here has in mind. The whole mass of sin rests upon every newborn human child, so that everyone is a debtor before God, culpable before the bar of God's judgment in respect of his participation in this stifling and poisonous bulk.

At one point we must be extremely careful: Augustine does not mean to deny that the freedom with which humanity was originally created is in a sense still there, but he distinguishes between free will as capacity and free will as active decision. The capacity remains: we can confront alternatives and make a choice. But the trouble is that our choice now

9. Souter, *op. cit.* II:58–60.

will always be wrong because it is made for the wrong motives, with the wrong end in view. We are free in the sense that we are neither sticks nor stones nor trees. But our freedom has lost that integrity without which the acts that arise from the capacity for free choice will not direct us back toward God.

One suggestion which seems to me very illuminating is that what Pelagius was teaching was in essence an atomistic conception of human conduct. Each act tends to stand alone, and the acts that I have performed up to this moment do not in principle destroy my ability to make the next choice as if I had not hitherto chosen at all. Now that is an exaggeration in view of Pelagius' doctrine of habit, but fundamentally it is right: each new choice is in principle a choice which I can make either way. Augustine, on the other hand, largely on the basis of his own personal experience of growing aspiration and helplessness in the face of his effort to bring his pride and appetites under control—and then having the problem solved not by his own effort which was getting nowhere but rather by an intervention from beyond himself—sees each act as an expression of an organically unitary and growing self which at every fresh moment is different from what it was before—different by reason of the fact that each decision functions to alter the pattern of the self who makes the decision. And neither man could really understand what the other found to be most fundamental. Pelagius, it would seem, simply did not have this kind of experience; he had the experience of life in a simplified environment in the monastery, with a regularized pattern of conduct according to which the calendar for each day was laid out and was carried through with a sense that this is what God desires of us. Anything like Augustine's sense of helplessness was foreign to the life that Pelagius had lived. Augustine, on the other hand, could not understand how anyone could be so optimistic. The two men just went past one another: they were not talking from the same sort of perspective on these issues. Of the two, I think it is necessary to say that Augustine's is clearly the more profound and the more realistic, certainly closer to what Paul had gone through and to the interpretation which Paul put upon his experience; he like Augustine had found himself jerked out of a course of action which he had chosen in all good faith and was unable himself to alter.

## Redemptive Grace: The Renewal of the Believer

How in that situation is there any hope for human beings? Augustine's answer is essentially the Pauline answer: there is no hope in us; there is hope only in God. And such hope is inseparable from—indeed may be almost identified with—faith. If one comes to recognize one's helplessness—and this will be genuine *humilitas*—and comes to trust God rather than oneself, then the healing process can go forward. But just as we have to distinguish more than one meaning for free will, so we have to distinguish more than one meaning for faith. Faith can mean simply *assensus*, i.e., cognitive acceptance of a statement as true or of a fact as existent. In this sense, I can say *credo omnia*, but that is not the faith which has any saving significance for me. Another sense of faith is trust, *fiducia*. If I say *credo Deum*, I mean no more necessarily than that I believe there is a God, and that is of no fundamental benefit to me as sinner. But if I say *credo Deo*, I am saying "I trust God." This is precisely the point at which my salvation starts.

But is this trust in God an act of my own or is it a gift which comes to me from God? The answer to this question depends upon recognition that a created being can operate only with the measure of existence that he has; he cannot provide himself, so to say, with an additional measure of existence, and therefore of good. The word which Augustine uses to refer to the redemptive work of God is *grace*. The very word itself (*gratia*) makes it perfectly clear to his mind that it must be regarded as free (*gratis*) and unconditioned. To suppose that God grants redemption to this or that person because of merit is to violate the fundamental conception of the freely granted power which God can justly offer or withhold.

Augustine is clear that the first move toward the salvation of the individual sinner must necessarily come from God and that therefore grace is to be called, in the first instance, prevenient, or as later English-speaking Protestant theologians like to say, "preventing grace." It is not that the sinner seeks to turn toward God in faith and in love, and then God grants the power to do so. The very first beginning must necessarily await the prompting of God. If we say that redemption for the individual depends on faith in God, it is necessary at once to add, faith is first God's gift. Faith is not something which I can achieve; in fact, it is precisely what I cannot achieve. When my twisted, egotistic, self-centered will tries to trust God, it finds that of all things, that is the most impossible. I have my attention fixed now on myself, and my chief trouble is precisely that I am unable to get myself out of the focus of my vision. Faith itself then is to be regarded as a gift from God, so that I cannot believe except as God enables me to believe.

The next thing to be said about grace is that the power which God puts forth to enable me to begin a life on the right line needs to be perpetually continued; if grace is prevenient, it is likewise "following." Fallen human beings need assisting grace, *gratia adjuvans*. It is necessary that the grace of God not merely turn them about in the way but accompany them at every step of the way. Augustine speaks sometimes of *gratia cooperans*, meaning essentially the same thing. If grace brings it about that I can turn toward God, grace continually upholds my will and enables me to live steadily the new life, so that I am dependent upon God at every single point for the life of redemption. The distinction between operating grace and cooperating grace is made rather more sharply in scholastic thought. Yet Augustine does use those two phrases, distinguishing between the initial emphasis and the sustaining power, and both are one act of God. For the individual then, grace in this sense is absolutely indispensable to the smallest beginning and to the continuing of a life of love properly directed toward God. This view is developed in proper contrast to the Pelagian view of a grace necessary to salvation which is after all hardly distinguishable from nature. For the Pelagian thinker, creation and redemption are far more closely identified than they are for Augustine. Grace for the Pelagian thinker is to be found in the first instance, we recall, in the giving of freedom; and then in the giving of the law, which is after all written into human nature as created; and then the giving of the perfect example in Jesus Christ. Only at that point does something supernatural come into the picture. Otherwise, Pelagian grace is a natural endowment. Now Augustine rejects that in principle. Creation is indeed a manifestation of the goodness of God, but redemption is quite another matter. That is a manifestation of the goodness of God in a radically different context: God is not now granting the status of being but is renewing a status of being which has been lost.

That brings us to a third comment on the nature of God's redemptive act for the individual. What is done at the core is precisely the restitution of personal existence, and that for Augustine means centrally restitution of personal will. This is why, once again, it is necessary that God and no created being be the Savior. What God does is to restore that ability not to sin (*posse non peccare*) which human beings had originally possessed but lost. They could never get it back for themselves, but God gives it back to them. So grace in Augustine's thought is not simply a personal or moral transaction or relationship between God and human beings. It is indeed forgiveness, but it is more than forgiveness. It is restitution, renewal. He uses a variety of words to underscore the genuine creative regeneration of the inner person. The one who is saved has full freedom, and not merely that paradoxical freedom of the unregenerate—freedom only to make matters worse. Moreover, he may look forward to the freedom which is the highest freedom of all. Here again we have the Christian principle that what God does for the believer is not merely to put him back where he was before, but to make him better than he was before. For now the one who is restored to full freedom in faith and in love toward God is enabled to look forward to the highest sort of freedom, which consists in being unable to sin (*non posse peccare*). That is the freedom of the faithful angels. Once having passed the test of loyalty to God, they are now secure forever and forever. That is the freedom of Jesus Christ within history—and within history, of him only. Even Adam did not have that sort of freedom. The promise of such freedom is now a further gift, and it looks to the future life.

The simplest and clearest psychological indication of this change—this fundamental reorientation of the believer's life—is the manifestation in him of trust in God, which was impossible before, and of love toward God. These two things, of course, come pretty much to the same point. This does not mean that the believer has become completely purged of the old life. He is completely cleansed of guilt. There remains over from his previous status the bodily appetites which are, says Augustine, a kind of raw material for sin (*fomes peccati*). The phrase is a very picturesque one. It means the tinder with which one can start a fire; the bodily appetites which are still present even in the believer are material out of which the fires of sin could be rekindled. But they are not themselves sin. The guilt is gone; the believer is genuinely justified. That is to say, he is made righteous in the reckoning of God.

It is extremely difficult for me to tell here how far we are dealing with fundamentally Pauline ideas and how far we are dealing with metaphysical ideas of a kind which are foreign to what I understand to be St. Paul's outlook. It seems to me that the two are so closely blended that to try to draw a line and say, "Thus far Augustine is following Paul, and over here he is adding something of his own," is extremely unsatisfactory. This notion of a recreation of the will, a redirection of human life, so that whereas before the gravitation of the soul was pulling downward, and now the gravitation in the soul pulls toward God—this resetting of the whole of human life is clearly in accord with St. Paul's conception of what happens when God intervenes and makes a person righteous. Yet the specific reference to the creative restoration of existence, the premise that existence is itself good, that loss of being and loss of goodness are interchangeable concepts, and that the restoration of goodness means restoration of being—all that, as far as I can see, is definitely non-Pauline. Yet it is so closely tied in with the moral and religious conception that it seems to me that the whole complex may stay rather closely unified in an integrated body of thought.

We noted above that for Augustine, creation and redemption are not identical as they are for the most part in Pelagian thought. Yet it is obviously necessary to say that they are closely related. They do not stand in sharp antithesis. Redemption is a creative act. Creation is for the sake of the City of God, and the carrying out of the divine will involves the setting up both of the initial framework and personnel of what is to be the whole cosmic drama and the carrying through of that drama in the face of the problems posed by the angelic and human fall. So creation and redemption are intimately connected although they are to be kept carefully distinguished as regards the occasion for each and as regards their specific characters.

Thus far we have spoken of grace as it affects the individual. But it is characteristic of Augustine's thought that he never for long speaks or thinks of the individual apart from the social context. That appears to me to be characteristic, even though in his *Confessions* and in various specific passages in his writing he talks as though he were a modern individualist. He insists on the fullness of the inner life as it is open to the inspection of the subject itself, so that, as we earlier mentioned, William James talks of him as the first modern man—that is to say, the first man known to us who was fully self-conscious, self-analytical, self-interpretative. But the self that he discovers is a self in social relations, and this is to be affirmed very rigorously with regard to his understanding of both sin and grace.

We have seen how that comment applies to his understanding of the status of being in sin. It is a common status; nobody escapes it. The Pelagian account of the matter, which spoke of bad social examples, seems to him to be wholly inadequate. It is not merely bad example which, from generation to generation, produces the wave of sinfulness. Rather it is the corruption of the whole social body. The behavior of corporate groups as well as the behavior of individual persons displays aggressiveness and deceptive and predatory patterns. Each member of such a corporate group acts not as though he were an isolated individual alongside other isolated individuals. He is acting as one in whom the patterns of behavior of the group are themselves brought to individual focus.

So too with respect to redemption. When God offers his grace to individual persons, it is true that each of these persons is redeemed in himself. Yet it is no less true that each is redeemed by God as a member of a chosen group. Augustine indulges in a bit of speculative fancy which, for the most part, he puts aside. Following the line of Platonic tradition, he suggests that the number of the fallen angels has left a gap in the heavenly choir. God created a definite number of spirits to praise him and now that that number has been depleted, it must be brought back to its original perfection. Hence he chooses out of the number of mankind enough individuals to recruit once again the heavenly community to its full strength.

## ELECTION AND PREDESTINATION

Here we come upon the very troublous question of election as one phase of divine predestination. Just as it is true that grace for the individual is prevenient, in the sense that it is not conditioned upon anything that this person has done or even wanted to do but is wholly free, so it is true with respect to the entire body of the saved in history. One must say that the difference between those who are chosen for salvation and those who are rejected is a difference which depends solely upon the arbitrary choice of God. Now it is good Pauline doctrine to state that God predestines those whom he foreknows, and Augustine affirms that; but he is very careful to specify that what God knows about those whom he chooses is not that they will of themselves become virtuous people. That is simply not the case. What he foreknows is that it is these whom he will redeem. So the predestination of some to salvation is bound up with God's eternal vision.

Augustine recognizes that to speak of foreknowledge with respect to God is a kind of anomaly; it is an anthropomorphism which is not really descriptive of God's nature. Just so, it is not accurate to speak of God's grace as coming preveniently and then subsequently. These are words which apply to our view of the matter and not to God's action. It is not as though in my individual life, God for a time withholds his grace and then grants it. God's grace flows eternally from his very being. But viewed from our side, the results which God's grace produces are successive in time. Therefore we can say, up to a certain point in his life this individual was sheer sinner; and then God intervened, and he became a redeemed person. That is a human account of the matter rather than a suggestion that there is mutability in God. If we are to say that first God does not do this and then he does do it, we are saying in effect that God changes from day to day and from year to year, and that obviously is improper. So when we speak of God in terms that suggest *before* and *after* in time, we must continually remind ourselves that these are humanly convenient metaphors rather than accurate descriptions of the eternal reality and activity of God. God's election of some to be saved, then, is an eternal decree and it has no specifiable ground other than God's own choice.

This means that the beginning of faith, even the desire for faith, comes from God. Augustine at first was not as clear about this as he later became. "I myself was wrong on this point in certain of my earlier writings, but I reread what the apostle says: 'What hast thou that thou hast not received?'—well, surely that includes the very first movement of confidence toward God; and 'of him are all things'—well, that surely must include the beginning of faith in the one who hitherto did not have faith."[10] So if one takes these words of Paul quite literally and quite seriously, one has to say it is not as though I found myself desiring to trust God, and then he enabled me to trust him, and then I am able to obey his commandments. Rather, it is necessary to say the very first stirring in me of a desire to trust God is itself God's doing and not mine.

But that obviously raises the very difficult question: why then in some and not in all? We read elsewhere, "God wills that all men shall be saved." Are we constrained then to say that God is not omnipotent so that his will in some respects is not effectual? Or are we constrained to say that the Scripture contradicts itself? Well, Augustine struggles to make these two sets of passages go together, and I must confess it seems to me he is more ingenious than persuasive with respect to the passage "God wills

10. The exact locus of this passage is Augustine is unknown [ed.].

that all men shall be saved." He says this means not all numerically, but all sorts of human beings—of every country, of every age, both male and female, of every calling. Similarly, when Scripture speaks of those who tithed "every herb," the reference is not to hunting through the woods and finding all the herbs there are and setting aside a tenth part of each of them, but rather to subjecting whatever herbs one has in one's garden to the rule of the tithe. So Paul then means all sorts and conditions of human beings. But as I say, it seems to me that that interpretation misses by a fairly wide margin the simple and plain sense of Scripture.

At any rate, if from God come all things, it seems to me we are on the edge here of a metaphysical determinism which Paul, if I read him rightly, never bothered his head about, and which Augustine, at first following the religious concern of Paul, did not try to explore. But now at the end of his career, he was confronted by the challenge not only of Pelagians but also of defenders of the ancient tradition of human responsibility and freedom, who are often spoken of as semi-Pelagians. Against them he came close to saying every event that comes to pass God has ordained. He doesn't want to say that: God does not ordain sin. But, you see, since he has described sin as a defect or privation rather than a positive action or a positive substance or a reality, he can say God does not ordain defects. But if he is prepared to say that God ordains the beginning of faith, and that this is true with respect to some but not with respect to others, then he has a doctrine of predestination which divides humankind into what he thinks is a minority who receive God's grace unto salvation and a majority who probably do not receive it. The difference, says he, between predestination and grace is that predestination prepares the way for grace; predestination is the determining of God before the foundation of the world that certain people will be chosen, will be called, will be saved, through the gift of saving grace. And what about the rest? Well, God does not ordain that they shall be lost; he simply leaves them to their own devices. So it is impossible to accuse God of injustice; after all, human beings have gotten themselves into this jam, and God would have been perfectly just if he had left them all to end in the "second death"— which is everlasting punishment. But if he chooses to save some, that is not to derogate from his justice; it is rather to underscore his mercy. So he acts in mercy to choose some who will be granted saving grace. It is not then that God foresees that some will believe and therefore chooses them; rather, he chooses some so that they will believe in due course. Whether

Augustine ever taught what is popularly called "irresistible grace" is a question over which argument will continue for a long time. As far as I know, he never uses the phrase: *gratia irresistibilis* is just not to be found even in his latest and most stringent treatises. But he does say at one point it is inconceivable that one whom God has elected and called should not be saved, and that does seem to imply that grace is irresistible.

The question whether Augustine teaches "single" or "double" predestination is one which I suppose will continue to be debated. Single predestination is the label for a theory which says merely that God chooses some for salvation, letting the rest go their own way. Double predestination labels a theory which says, God chooses some who shall be saved and others who shall be damned. It is not simply as though God withheld from the second group the aid by which they might have been led into the other path. It is that God has determined that the elect shall be saved and that these others shall be lost.

The question whether Augustine clearly supported one or the other of these views rests on extraordinarily tantalizing evidence. Ordinarily it has been said, and I myself have said it more than once, that throughout his earlier years Augustine taught a doctrine of single predestination, affirming that God saves those whom he really chooses to save and simply leaves the rest to follow their own devices. In his later years (say the last three years of his life from 428 until 430), when he was engaged in controversy with the conservatives we have already mentioned, he moved to the more drastic and less compromising position, and in such late works as On the Perseverance of the Saints and On the Gift of Perseverance he seems to teach straightforward double predestination.[11] The more I examine these late passages, the more I am inclined to recognize a measure of unsatisfactoriness in the evidence. Hitherto his concern has been primarily with the religious problem: How is it that I may be brought back from the way of sin? He has not been concerned with the problem of how the world is ordered to the end that some are brought back and others left. But in these last two treatises that is the question which gets pushed out into the foreground, and double predestination is involved in principle. Augustine by this time was teaching that every event that transpires is controlled by the decrees of God. So one may clearly infer

11. Augustine, *Praed.* (PL 44:959ff.); *Persev.* (PL 45:993ff.). English translation in *NPNF1* 5:497–552.

from that more inclusive metaphysical position that God decrees that some shall be saved, and that what happens to the others is likewise the outcome of divine decree. But I do not find anywhere that Augustine says in so many words (as Calvin later very frankly and emphatically does say) that when we are talking about an omnipotent Creator and Governor, any distinction between permitting and commanding is a meaningless distinction. Calvin says that; Augustine, as far as I can make out, does not. On the contrary, he says repeatedly that God does not foreordain "sins." It seems to me that there is a kind of reticence on his part here which is comparable to his distaste for affirming forthrightly the damnation of unbaptized infants. The damnation of infants follows inexorably from his conception of the participation of all human persons in the common guilt of sin. That guilt is moral guilt; and for an individual who has not been cleansed of it, clearly no possible future can be thought of save a future of separation from God. Yet Augustine shows the warmth of his own personal nature in struggling and squirming and twisting to try to find a way to avoid making that kind of repulsive affirmation. He writes to his friend Jerome to see whether Jerome can suggest some ground on which unbaptized infants might conceivably be given some sort of little chance. But Jerome cannot. It is an inference that is hard to escape, but it is an assertion that Augustine does not want to set down. It seems to me that his treatment of this doctrine of double predestination is of the same order. The hard doctrine is involved in the position which has been taken. The explicit statement of the doctrine in its baldest form is something which he avoids.

## CHRISTOLOGY

Now we turn to an aspect of the whole situation which I have postponed thus far precisely because in Augustine's thought it has so little prominence. This is the role of Jesus Christ. We have spoken of redemption as involving the awakening of faith and love for God. How is this brought about? Augustine says in so many words that it is brought about through the revelation of God in Jesus Christ. Yet the references to the actual, concrete, historical life of the Savior and to the centrality which St. Paul, for example, so emphatically gave to him in the process of redemption, we do not find in Augustine's writings. Professor Outler has developed an interpretation which I have not seen specifically worked out elsewhere, but which seems to me to be highly suggestive and probably sound. It is that Augustine's conception of God, in as far as it appears to be inadequate—verging toward Sabellianism, or toward Neoplatonic metaphysical speculation—has this defective character in central part because of Augustine's lack of an adequate Christology. I think that is right.

It has frequently been noticed that in Augustine's writings references with respect to human salvation are almost always to God. In his early dialogue, the *Soliloquies*, Truth puts the question to Augustine: What is it that you desire to know? The answer is the soul and God. Truth asks, Nothing else? And Augustine replies, Nothing else at all.[12] Here is a simple dipolar relationship—a relationship which would have been recognizable thus far to a Neoplatonist. Now when Augustine refers to his emancipation from Neoplatonism, he says in effect: I found all other Christian insights in the work of the Platonists save this one—the Word made flesh found I not among them. I found among them a conception of God as Spirit. I found among them an understanding of the Word as cosmic Reason and Law, the mind and the will of God. But what I did not find was any conception that God, who is the Eternal, perfect in his Being, stoops down to the level of needy creatures. The Word made flesh, in contrast to the Word in the heavens, was something that Platonism, which is to say classic wisdom, never had affirmed. So in principle Augustine is aware of the differentia of Christian teaching. Yet it appears to me that in his writings that differentia remains a difference of principle, which he did not succeed in articulating as a factor of concrete and central, personally felt experience. His Christology remains sketchy, shadowy, verbally affirmed but not concretely developed.

Now one modification of that statement seems called for. It is in his sermons rather than in his theological writings that one gets most of the signs of a growing awareness of the concrete meaning of Jesus Christ for the life of the believer. That is not to be wondered at. It is in relationships with a congregation that a Christian preacher is most likely to find the experiential material which then can be worked into a systematic theory. It looks as though Augustine had started along that way, but he never did get a full-blown and centrally focused Christology into his theological structure as a whole. Nevertheless, it is to be said

---

12. Augustine, *Solil.* (PL 32:869); Migne text with English translation in Gilligan, *The Soliloquies of Saint Augustine* (New York: Cosmopolitan Science & Art Service, 1943).

that faith which saves is, from one point of view, faith in God, and from another point of view faith in Christ. He uses both phrases. One may speak of believing God or Christ; one may speak of believing in God or in Christ. As far as I can make out, the distinction is between belief as an intellectual affirmation and belief as personal trust. One believes in God who affirms the reality and significance of the life of Christ. But one fully trusts God in the Christ for whom those intellectual affirmations are fulfilled in volitional devotion.

## CHURCH AND SACRAMENTS

We turn finally to that great work in which Augustine comes closer to drawing together all the threads of his thought than in any other, his work *On the City of God.*[13] One may say that the work was prepared for on its social side by certain controversies in which Augustine had debated the nature of the Church with the Donatist schismatics who had their strength solely in the provinces of North Africa. One of his relatively early controversial feats was arguing against the Donatists at a council in Carthage about 411. For just about a century an effort had been made to heal a breach in the Church which had broken out early in the fourth century when Donatus had led a party of rebels against the conformity of so many clergy who handed over to Diocletian's agents the books of their churches with or without protest. We remember that Donatus professed to be a true successor to Cyprian in this matter, and insisted that those clergy alone are true clergy who stand fast by their obligations. Those who followed Donatus' lead organized separate sectarian groups professing to be the true church; and the Catholic Church—the more secularized and conforming *ecclesia*—was repudiated as a false church. Therefore, the Donatists were in the habit of requiring that anybody who sought to transfer his membership from the Catholic Church into a Donatist group must be baptized again and that any clergyman who wanted to transfer had to be reordained. That is, they denied the validity of baptism and ordination in the Catholic Church, which they declared to be not a true church at all. On the other hand, with respect to the Donatists, the Catholic Church had held the opposite practice. The

13. Augustine, *Civ.* (PL 41:13); critical edition in CCSL 40. For a convenient and reliable English translation, see Knowles, editor, and Bettenson, translator, *Augustine: Concerning the City of God against the Pagans* (New York: Penguin, 1972).

Catholic view was that rebaptism is a contradiction in terms and the one who has been baptized in a Donatist group has been genuinely baptized. The Donatists are not heretics; they are simply a separatist sect. The difference between them and the Catholics are primarily differences over practical behavior and not over the fundamental nature of the Gospel. Similarly, Donatist ordination is valid ordination, and a Donatist clergyman who seeks to become a priest in the Catholic Church can be received without reordination.

From the time of Constantine up until the Council of Carthage in 411, the Donatists had retained their separate position. They appear to have had more than their share of strenuous, turbulent proponents of a highly active kind of Christian life, so that not infrequently they seized church property by force, established themselves and maintained themselves against the efforts of their more easy-going Catholic brethren; and one of their factions, the *Circumcelliones* (vagabonds), were quite ready to start riots when it appeared that that would further their ends. Although Augustine was not at his best in dealing with such overt violence, he was quite prepared to meet the Donatists in argument, whether by letters, sermons, or conferences face to face. In dialectic he felt at home, and he was able to meet the difficult and rather elusive issues which were presented by the sort of contrary practice to which reference has been made. How could one defend the Catholic Church against the position of the Donatists without admitting that the Donatists were after all the true church? If the Catholics say Donatist sacraments are valid sacraments, and the Donatists say Catholic sacraments are not valid sacraments, what account can be given of the rights and wrongs involved? It seems to me that Augustine met that test triumphantly, not simply in terms of verbal subtleties, but in terms of human insight.

The position that he took was this: the sacraments of ordination and of baptism have two distinguishable effects. On the one hand, each of them confers upon the recipient a certain indelible character which, once implanted, can never be obliterated or renewed. A baptized person is for all time a baptized person. An ordained person is an ordained person. If you say that Donatist sacraments are valid sacraments, then you must say that this indelible character has been affixed to the one baptized or ordained. But if that character is to develop into full-blown Christian reality, it must develop in a suitable environment, in a community of faith and of love. Now most unhappily, the Donatist communities are remarkable rather for vigor than for charity. So one baptized as a Donatist, who lives and learns Christian life in that environment, will fall far short of developing the sort of Christian life that he would have developed if the same baptism had been followed by nurture in a Catholic community. The same thing is true for ordination. The conception of the life of a minister—the duties of priests and of bishops held by the Donatists—is such as to insure that the possession of the status of the one ordained will be frustrated of that full achievement that would be possible only in a more favorable atmosphere. Hence the Catholic Church is right both in affirming the validity of Donatist sacraments and refusing to repeat them, and in denying that the schismatic Donatist communities are genuinely communities of Christian living. So the effort to persuade or compel Donatists to come into the Catholic Church is fully justified, and the affirmation that the Catholic Church is the true church as against the Donatist churches is likewise justified.

Now what do we mean by the Catholic Church? How can it be regarded as strictly universal when here in North Africa the Donatists have comparable numbers in their schismatic groups? The Catholic Church can properly be called catholic, says Augustine, in view of the fact that geographically it has members in all the known world. The Donatist sects have members only in the provinces of Africa. Secondly, the Catholic Church is universal in that it is cross-sectional. It has in it all the ranks of society, all nations and kinds and conditions of human life. It is therefore genuinely inclusive in principle, whereas the Donatist groups are separatist in principle. Therefore, one may say that the Catholic Church is the truly universal Church even though numerically the sectaries have been able to mislead a lamentably large number.

Apparently Augustine's arguments contributed to bringing about the breakdown of the appeal that Donatism had hitherto been able to make, so that after this Synod of Carthage in 411–412, the power of Donatism receded. Unluckily, another feature in the recession was the exercise of the political arm on behalf of the Catholic group. Augustine gradually came to accept and justify appeals for police help in dealing with these recalcitrant fellow Christians.

With this experience as a background, Augustine's later understanding of the nature of the Christian community was worked out in the *City of God* and elsewhere. He noted that in the Creed, the church comes after the article dealing with faith in the Trinity, and this obviously is because the Church is a community of created beings and should not of course be confused in any way with the Creator. But the church is the temple in which God dwells, and not merely, says Augustine, the Holy Spirit, but also the Father and the Son—because the works of the Trinity *ad extra* are indivisible. One can distinguish Father, Son, and Spirit within the Godhead, but when God acts toward the created world, it is the whole of God who acts. Now the church properly understood exists partly here and now on earth, but it includes the many who have trusted God in generations past. It will include of course also those in generations to come who are among the elect and for that reason will trust God. The signs of the presence of the church here on earth are the sacraments, but Augustine is inclined to be very free and easy in his enumeration of what the sacraments are. He offers a kind of generic definition: a sacrament is an outward and visible sign of the presence and working of the Holy Spirit; or otherwise, a symbol and an occasion of the working of the Holy Spirit. The fundamental religious reality is the inward work of the Spirit on the human heart. Since this may come about when the Word is preached, the preaching of the Word is then a sacrament. It may come about in any of a great variety of human situations, and if one understands *sacrament* to have this sense, then to try to enumerate a list of sacraments is rather idle; nevertheless, baptism and the Lord's Supper are plainly set apart in the customary life of the church; and with respect to each of these, Augustine is careful to say it is not the water as such or the bread and the wine as such but the divine promise which is specified in the Word that accompanies the water of baptism and the elements of the Eucharist that makes each a sacramental act. Like Paul, it seems to me that Augustine too is somewhat ambivalent in respect to the question whether the act of baptism or the celebration of the Eucharist has a kind of intrinsic power, or whether it is the total situation centering around the baptism of the convert or this infant in this Christian home, centering around this celebration of the Eucharist, in which the Spirit is present and active. It seems to me that some passages point one way and some point the other. In any case, the holy church is an environment in which God makes men and women holy. It is not as though this were already a New Jerusalem; it isn't; it's the life of very imperfect human beings still on earth. And if we call it catholic, what we mean is it seeks its membership everywhere among people of every sort. (Think once again that "God wills all men to be saved"—no distinctions now of geographic boundaries or vocational classes or color or sex or any other divisive condition among people.) The Catholic Church is a home for them all.

## THEOLOGY OF HISTORY

We turn finally to the expansion of Augustine's conception of human community into what has been called a theology or philosophy of history. This of course is to be found in his greatest work, *On the City of God*, which was begun after the sacking of Rome in 410 by Alaric and the Goths, as a kind of apologia defending the Christians against the charges of having been responsible for the impending collapse of civilization itself. But it goes on from defense against the specific charges of that time to an impressive examination of the meaning of all history.

The first part of the treatise we can dismiss briefly. You have in mind the line of Augustine's argument and the occasion which called it forth. I presume it is difficult for folk like ourselves to envisage the degree of shock which went through the Roman world when the capital city itself was invaded. The reason for the profound disquiet which accompanied that event was the deep-seated and largely unconscious assumption that Rome was a literally eternal city. The whole Greco-Roman conception of civilization was based upon the idea of security, maintaining an adequate clearing in the midst of chaos. I am following here the brilliant interpretation worked out by Charles N. Cochrane in his *Christianity and Classical Culture* and in a later set of unpublished lectures which he delivered at Yale on "Augustine and the Problem of Power."[14] The classical understanding of the meaning of civilization was that it consists in the maintaining of an oasis or order in the midst of a world in which that stronghold is surrounded by disorderly and hostile forces. The possibility of maintaining such an area depends upon a fortunate concurrence of circumstances, some having the nature of fate or destiny and some having the nature of moral character and intellectual resourcefulness. It is necessary that there be a prince in whom virtue and insight are combined and that such a prince be blessed with happy fortune. It is a rather precarious combination, but one with which it was thought civilization might be expected to hold its own. But to do more than hold its own was scarcely to be expected, for the very conception of the humanized

---

14. Charles N. Cochrane, *Christianity and Classical Culture* (New York: Oxford University Press, 1944).

world, as over against the unpredictable and uncontrollable forces of nature on the one hand and the disorderly habits of the barbarians on the other hand, was a conception of a hard-won and barely defensible area of felicity. Nevertheless, the success that the Roman emperors had had in maintaining a kind of humane civilization over a considerable period of time had gradually established the idea that Rome had finally solved the problem, that here was an order that would be permanent.

Now in 410 Rome itself was pillaged. The forces of disorder had broken in from the outside and the very basis of security was undermined. The sort of deep shudder that went through those Romans who looked around immediately for someone to blame is the shudder not of a folk who are annoyed, but of a folk who are in terror over what this first break in the structure of civilization may portend. When they looked for someone to blame, the most obvious possible target was the Christian church. Here was an organization which up to a century earlier had been a disapproved minority group. By devious means it had succeeded in gaining power, prestige, property, and then imperial favor, so that Constantine had established Christianity as the approved religion of the empire. And now see what has come about. Plainly enough, the old gods were angry. They had been deserted, and the punishment was now coming.

Augustine's answer in the first, apologetic part of the treatise (about ten of the twenty-two books) was to point out that this was not the first time misfortune had come upon the Roman people. Long before Christianity appeared on the scene, droughts, famine, military disasters, and misfortunes of various sorts had come again and again. This was not really something unprecedented; it was simply that people had been lulled into a false sense of security because such disasters had been intermitted for a considerable period of time. But a second part of his answer (the final twelve books), and a very much more fundamental part, was to say that it is quite true that the old order faced destruction. Of these twelve books, the first four deal with the issuance of human history out of the eternity of God; the middle four deal with the development side by side on earth of two kinds of human community, of God and of this earth; and the last four finally deal with the end toward which these two communities are moving side by side. The destruction falling upon Rome results primarily because of a deep-seated dichotomy in the whole order of existence. This dichotomy can be described by saying there are in essence two, and only two, kinds of human communities: those which are intent upon God and those which are intent upon themselves.

To label these two sorts of communities, it will be recalled, Augustine borrowed from his countryman, Tychonius, the terminology of the City or Commonwealth of God (*civitas Dei*—that is, the city which was coming down out of heaven), and the City or Commonwealth of Earth (*civitas terrene*—presented as on its way to destruction). This later he was prepared also to call the City of the Devil (*civitas diaboli*). Augustine took over this archaic North African or perhaps even Donatist scheme and turned it to his own uses.

These uses were influenced by the ways in which *civitas* had been used by classical thinkers. It was the usual term for denoting a political or social community,[15] and it had both factual and axiological connotations. Augustine makes this very plain by quoting from a now lost work of Cicero called *De Romano republica* (*On the Roman Commonwealth*), in which he represents some of the heroes of antiquity, and first of all Scipio, the great leader against Carthage, as engaging in a conversation respecting what one should mean when one says *res publica*. And the agreed answer is: one should mean the commonweal: *res publica* is *res populi*, it is the welfare of the people where justice is enforced as the pattern of social behavior. If then this is what we mean by a *res publica*, we have to raise the question whether there ever has been a community in pagan times which genuinely fulfilled those requirements, for righteousness (*justitia*), so Augustine is prepared to argue, is to be found nowhere apart from

15. In the background of that word is the Greek concept of the *polis*, which we translate as *city-state*, and that is correct enough. But the point is the Greek *polis* was at once a sociohistorical fact and a center of value. The *polis* differed in kind from, let us say, the great empires of the East over against which the inhabitants of the Greek city set the kind of culture which had been built up among them and in which they found themselves at home. The *polis* is a politically ordered community, no doubt. But it is at the same time a neighborhood; it is the sort of political entity in which all of the free participants can find fulfillment. *Civitas* carries over into the Latin much of that same significance. In the West, republican Rome had come as close as any other community to being like a Greek *polis*, and *urbs* came to carry much of the value connotation that *polis* also had, so that *urbanitas* is not merely the location of one's residence in the city; it is a way of life which is civilized as over against the disorder, the irresponsibility, the crudity, of the world outside. *Rusticitas* is the life of people from the back country who have not learned the graces of the city; *urbanitas*, *Romanitas*, that is something like *politeia*. Cicero had specified that one may properly talk of a *civitas* where, and only where, justice is enforced as the pattern of social behavior. (This material was originally an integral part of one of Professor Calhoun's lectures, but it fits better as a footnote in the present recension [ed.].)

the revelation of God in Jesus Christ. So we have to question whether this definition of a republic is not so exacting that historically we should have to say there has been no instance of it. Yet without justice, political sovereignty stands on the same footing as brigandage. This means that a certain pirate chief had justification for his alleged retort to Alexander the Great when the pirate was taken prisoner. Alexander asked why he sought to rule the sea by violence, and the pirate said in effect: "For the same reason that you seek to rule the whole earth. Because I do it with one small ship, I am a robber. But you, because you have a great navy, are an emperor." That seemed to Augustine a fair reply. Nevertheless, it seemed necessary to get a more inclusive definition of *community* if it is to be usable as generally as we want to employ it.

Augustine's suggestion, also borrowed from Cicero, is that we mean by a *people* something different from just any and every multitude; rather, it is "a multitude united by acknowledgment of law (*legis consensu*), though not necessarily of justice, and by community of interest (*utilitates communione*). *Civitas* then will mean that. Now interest, in this sense, is another way of referring to what Augustine had previously spoken of as the psychical gravitation called love. That which I love determines the direction of my behavior; that is true whether I am speaking of an individual or of a group. Now given groups of persons sharing a common direction of interest or of love, of desire, of aspiration, it is possible then to say that there are only two directions that love can turn. It turns either upward or downward. A community, then, whose aim is the knowledge and service of God may be spoken of appropriately enough as a community or commonwealth or city (*civitas*) of God. On the other hand, a community intent primarily on creaturely satisfaction, and most especially on power, is properly to be spoken of as a community defined by earthly rather than heavenly objectives.

Now, says Augustine, from the very beginning of life on earth, even before human beings were created, in the angelic order which preceded their coming, these two opposing commonwealths have been recognizable. The fallen angels are the heavenly counterpart of fallen humanity. And once the earthly drama began, we see the two cities developing side by side. Among Adam's sons Cain is the founder of the city of the world, and Abel and Seth carry on the line which will lead into an expanding city of God. The whole of the Old Testament is the story of the parallel development of the two opposing communities. The type of the one has been the great political empires, and there have been two such empires par excellence: Assyria in the old days of the East, and Rome in the newer West. These are merely the chief instances of such communities intent primarily upon gaining, holding, and increasing their own power. This is sovereignty without any primary concern for justice, and it is in effect large-scale and legalized banditry.

A distinction, however, must here be drawn. In Augustine's mind it is not true that political government is as such bad. As a matter of fact, sinful human nature requires government to keep it under control. Therefore, political order is to be regarded as itself a work of God. It is a pattern for created being which, in God's providence, has its function to perform. But when the men in whose hands government use their power for self-aggrandizement rather than for the common good, we have to say that political sovereignty has been made a tool in the service of the commonwealth of the Devil. In the great empires full of power lust, that sort of distortion becomes the dominant pattern. So that even though one acknowledges the need for political order, one must say that political power corrupts; and the greater the power the greater the corruption. In the course of history, especially in its earliest stages, the earthly city had the upper hand: the true servants of God have been not merely a minority, they have been all too frequently an oppressed minority. All efforts to crush it out have resulted instead in its further propagation, and therein the providence of God has been discernible.

With the coming of Jesus Christ, the City of God is defined in a new way. We can specify its character, not merely in terms of a general allegiance to God, a seeking of one's good in him. One can define it in terms of the Christian church. One can say, here now is the earthly manifestation, visible and growing, of that community of true servants who have been known to God before all ages and who are beginning at last to emerge into a recognizable social institution. What Augustine has in mind is neither an organization that one joins voluntarily nor a community into which one can work one's way by doing good; it is the divine decree which determines once-for-all whether I am a member of this commonwealth or a member of that one. Nothing that I can do can alter fundamentally that basic line of division.

Thus the distinction which has been made in regard to civil government must be made again with regard to ecclesiastical order. Augustine is not ready to do what, e.g., Eusebius of Caesarea had done in his panegyric on Constantine, and say: "Ah, now the government is Christian and everything is according to the will of God"—not a bit of it! The government is nominally Christian; so too the church is nominally Christian. The ecclesiastical institution is not as such the City of God. Rather, we find within the organized church those who are faithful servants and members of this heavenly commonwealth, but also those whom we can judge by their behavior to be members of the commonwealth of the Devil. The City of God and the institutional church stand in a relationship of tension and partial identity. The outline of that overlapping can be indicated by saying that the City of God contains, first, the faithful angels; secondly, the persons of the Old Testament who have served God through antiquity; thirdly, the faithful members of the Church who are now living; and finally, faithful members of the church who now are in heaven, or who will find their place in heaven in due course. All of these groups are included among the predestined, so that the City of God consists roughly of the faithful angels and the elect among humankind, who will eventually make that perfect choir upon which God's purpose is fixed. On the other hand, the City of the World includes the fallen angels and the non-elect among human beings in all ages, including those who are now members of the institutional church.

One may recognize the difficulty of maintaining a scheme of this sort with nice distinctions on each side. The distinctions are quite indispensable, and yet they are subject to continual warping and blurring in one way or another. We find Augustine talking in some passages as if the church were in fact the very embodiment of the City of God, so that the identification of the heavenly commonwealth with the angels in heaven and the whole ecclesiastical institution on earth can be used for purposes of propaganda and apologetic when that kind of argument seems appropriate. Sometimes he seems to identify secular organization itself with the earthly commonwealth. But when he is thinking most precisely, he always makes it clear that we have here orders within orders. What determines the place of an individual or group is not this or that particular earthly pattern or organization, but rather the direction of one's primary or controlling love. If one is intent primarily upon God, then one is a member of the commonwealth of God. if one is intent primarily upon oneself, then one is a member of the commonwealth of the Devil. And that fundamental dichotomy is everywhere recognizable.

Now in the course of history we have reached a stage, Augustine argues, at which the city of the world is on the point of final collapse. That is what we see in the tottering of the Roman Empire. In it the seeds of corruption, which have been present in a self-centered, power-hungry city all the while, have begun to reach their final fruition, and the imminent collapse of that secular order could not be a matter for surprise to those who really understand what God has been doing all this while. It should be rather a vindication of their faith in God. The City of God will come out of this collapsing world not weakened but strengthened through its new freedom from entanglement.

The culmination will be the ending of this present age and the glorification of those who have been chosen by God for eternal life. Here Augustine employs exceedingly picturesque language. As regards each individual who lives and dies on the earth, he will pass after death, Augustine thinks, to a place of waiting: a place either of tranquility or of temporal punishment. He is quite prepared to think in terms of a kind of purgatory. (That, we recall, had been a factor in Roman thought as far back as the time when Hermas had written *The Shepherd* and had worked out a kind of tariff or table of equivalents between a time of pleasure on earth and a time of punishment which will offset it later on.) Then at the time of final judgment and the general resurrection, the two cities will be separated out; then there will be no more ambiguity about who belongs where. Those who are members of the condemned city will suffer, as their primary punishment, eternal separation from God, and therefore the eternal insatiable craving which only association with God can satisfy. But Augustine is quite ready to represent that torment in terms of perpetually burning flames. This is the second death—not the death of the body that we all have to go through, but the death of the spirit. It is not annihilation, for annihilation would not be punishment. In the inexorable judgment of God, those who have been intent upon themselves will be kept in being to experience the consequences of that corruption. On the other hand, those who are elect will pass into eternal life in which the chief beatitude is the vision of God. Now they have that which makes their whole range of powers and possibilities fulfilled.

This will be a physical life. Augustine thinks the resurrection bodies will be all beautiful and all perfect. They will have the character of bodies of men and women at thirty years of age. The baptized elect who die in infancy will appear in heaven as mature persons. On the other hand, those who die in tottering old age will be restored to vigorous youthful maturity. So the heavenly city will be a place of beauty and of joy in which both body and spirit are in perfect harmony. One has to add unhappily that it appears to Augustine that the felicity of the blessed will be increased by recognition of the character of the punishment which they have escaped. They will be aware of the second death of the reprobates, and that will heighten their own gratitude and joy.

It is possible to say in summary that the *civitas Dei*, even while it was hidden, even while its membership was so small and obscure that no one would have known it was there, was steadily growing. Now it has come out into the open; and although it must not be identified with the institutional church, nevertheless the church among human institutions is the one which best testifies to the presence of this dynamic movement guided by God's providence. And eventually when earthly rule will be superseded, then "the commonwealth of God" will endure.

## SUMMARY: A CHRISTIAN WORLDVIEW

What we have here, so Cochrane argues, is an essentially new understanding of the ground for human security—not new with Augustine, although he has worked it out with fresh elaboration, but new with Christianity. By contrast with the classical conception of an earthly order which may be expected to endure, given fortunate circumstances, so that one may speak of Rome as eternal, the whole Christian conception is that of man and all human history as essentially non-permanent. The only permanence is God. He alone is eternal. Everything earthly is transient. Therefore, whoever seeks his security in what is creaturely is by that very fact displaying the distortion of his judgment and of his love. On the other hand, one who recognizes that his security is in God alone can view with equanimity the inevitable passing of any and every earthly order. He can look even upon the downfall of Rome itself without any of that inward dread felt by those faithful Romans who supposed that what was happening was the crumbling of the very ground under their feet. To recognize that one is a pilgrim and a stranger upon earth and that one's home is in heaven, that the whole course of earthly existence must be a perpetual transition, is to find a completely secure way of facing earthly tribulations.

But more than that, one is thus enabled to understand what has been happening and what will continue to happen here on earth. To understand what has happened to Rome, to understand what has been happening in the Church, one must set all these events in a cosmic perspective, cosmic not merely in the sense of the perspective of this created world but rather in the perspective of God's creative and providential rule. What Augustine has done now beyond that which his predecessors had been seeking in principle to do, is to show a way in which one can regard the whole course of history as a progressive revelation of God. Now we see from the vantage point of Christian faith the hand of God working from the beginning straight through till the end of time. The entire drama of human existence upon earth is a disclosure of God's providence. In that sense, we have a theology of history in which time is taken seriously, as against the classical conception of time as cyclical, continually repeating itself as the processes of nature repeat their own course. Here we have a conception of time and the events which constitute history as linear, with a beginning, a climactic middle, and a goal toward which the whole creation moves. This is a conception which makes it possible to think of human events as unique and unrepeatable; to think of individual lives similarly as something other than instances of general types. Here we have a conception of history as the concrete fabric of unique personal careers, personal relationships. And in that fabric the working of the presence of God, on the one hand, and the diversity of human response, on the other hand, make a massive and intelligible pattern.

# CHAPTER 16

# The End of the Era: Orange, Leo, and Gregory the Great[1]

[Theology declined as did the old imperial order during the two hundred years which separate St. Augustine from Gregory the Great. Yet these centuries were crucial. Through them was transmitted the doctrinal heritage of the past, and they influenced the way that heritage was understood. Of particular importance were the semi-Pelagian controversy; the Second Council of Orange; and two popes—Leo I and above all Gregory the Great.]

## SEMI-PELAGIANISM AND THE VINCENTIAN CANON

In the very last years of his life, as I previously noted in passing, Augustine confronted opposition that was in some degree like that of the Pelagians, and that is generally spoken of as semi-Pelagian. That label is an unfortunate one, because the character of this late opposition to Augustine seems to be simply the perduring of an archaic traditional conception of human nature, of the import of sin, and of the meaning of grace. Opposition centered in southern Gaul. Massilia (now Marseilles) was an ancient Greek colony, where an excellent university of Greek studies had existed in the later days of imperial culture. Around Massilia monastic houses had been built, particularly the monastery of Lérins on an island just off the coast. Certain of the inmates of this monastery insisted that Augustine's conception of the human condition was pessimistic beyond what Christian tradition warranted. We have the names of some of these men. Vincent of Lérins and John Cassian are perhaps the best known.

---

1. This chapter combines portions from chapters 23, 24, and 25 of the 1948 transcript (II:235–65) with material from lectures Professor Calhoun delivered in later years [ed.].

At two points in particular these semi-Pelagians or conservatives dissented from the drastic predestinarian views which Augustine had developed. The first point had reference to prevenient grace. Augustine had maintained that no one can make so much as the first preliminary beginning of repentance and turn toward God except as God enables him to do so. These men said that does not tally with what the church has taught; rather, the church has taught that when someone turns toward God, then God will grant him the grace required to carry out the new life. The second point had reference to the effect of God's grace when it is granted. These men said that if we follow the teaching of the church, we must say that people are able to resist it if they will. We have to safeguard human freedom at both those points.

The position taken by these theologians is set forth in a letter of one of Augustine's Gallic friends, Prosper of Aquitaine, who describes the arguments of the conservatives.[2] Augustine replied, as we mentioned earlier, in two treatises written in the last years of his life called *On the Predestination of the Saints* and *On the Gift of Perseverance*. In these treatises, he restated even more uncompromisingly the position which he had held hitherto. About as concise a statement as I have found of that position is a sentence or two in a slightly earlier treatise *On Correction and Grace*: "Whosoever, therefore, in God's most providential ordering, are foreknown, predestinated, called, justified, glorified,—I say not, even though not yet born again, but even although not yet born at all, are already children of God, and absolutely cannot perish."[3] Here we have the unqualified affirmation that the decrees of God have once for all determined who shall be saved. Those who are included among the elect have their fate completely fixed even before they appear on earth as human beings. The question with respect to prevenient grace Augustine answers by affirming over again that the beginning of faith is itself God's gift, and it is quite impossible for anyone to make so much as a beginning save as God enables him to do so. As regards the possibility of being lost in spite of God's grace, the work *On the Gift of Perseverance* holds the inevitable position that what God has decreed must come to pass. "Let not men say, then, that perseverance is given to anyone to the end, except when the end itself has come, and he to whom it has been given has been found to have

---

2. Prosper of Aquitaine (PL 51:1–868; Epistle to Augustine, PL 51:67–74); English translation of works in defense of Augustine in P. De Letter, *ACW* 32 (1963).

3. Augustine, *Corrept.*, *NPNF2* 5:23, 481.

persevered unto the end."[4] That is a proper caution. We must not attempt to decide which of the folk whom we know are of the elect. But in principle we can say that whoever is of the elect will have this gift of perseverance granted. And if we ask, Why should this gift be granted to some and not to others? Augustine's answer is: I do not know. "If you ask wherefore; because I confess that I can find no answer to make. And if you further ask why this is, it is because in this matter, even as his anger is righteous and as his mercy is great, so his judgments are unsearchable."[5] That is the note upon which Augustine ends his treatment of this mystery.

The conservatives were not satisfied. Some five years after Augustine's death in 430, Vincent of Lérins published a work which he called a reminder (*Commonitorium*) of the nature and proper tests of true Christian teaching.[6] Against all innovations it is necessary to be on guard. There are two tests, primarily, by which we distinguish true Christian teaching. One is the test of Scripture; but the other, made necessary by the ambiguities of Scripture, is the appeal to tradition in the church. Primarily, tradition has the function of showing us how Scripture should be interpreted. It is not, as far as I can make out, that this treatise presents tradition as a new source of truth, but rather that by following the lead of the acknowledged leaders of the church, we discover how properly to understand the Word of God. This is a safeguard, Vincent argues, which will enable us to recognize the error not only of the grosser heretics—the Arians and Pelagians—but of those men like Origen and Tertullian who were in many instances teachers of the truth, but who at some point or other introduced novel ideas and so got off the proper ground. The test which can be put most succinctly, in the mind of Vincent, is the one that has been quoted out of the treatise over and over again: "In the Catholic Church itself, all possible care must be taken, that we hold that faith which has been believed everywhere, always, and by all" (*Quod ubique, quod semper, quod ab omnibus creditum est*).[7] Universality, continuity, unanimity—these are

4. Augustine, *Persev., NPNF1* 5:10, 529.

5. Augustine, *Persev., NPNF1* 5:18, 531; *NPNF2* 11: chapter 2, 6, 132. Jülicher, ed., *Vincenz von Lerinum, Commonitorium* (Tübingen, 1925) 2.3, 3.

6. Vincent of Lérins, (PL 50:637–86); critical editions by Moxon, *Vincent of Lerins. Commonitorium* (Cambridge: Cambridge University Press, 1915); Jülicher, *Vincenz von Lerinum. Commonitorium* (Tübingen, 1925). English translation in *NPNF1* 11:131–56.

7. Augustine, *NPNF*, 2d ser., XI, chapter II:6, p.132; Jülicher, chapter II:6, p.132. *Comm.*, 3.3, p.

the marks of a belief which is rightly held. Later in the work, he appeals to the words at the end of 1 Timothy: "O Timothy, guard the *depositum*, he says, "that which has been given you in trust; and avoid deviating novelties" (1 Tim 6:20).[8] He spells out the meaning which he finds in the warning, ostensibly from Paul, in such a fashion as to make it [appear] that to his mind, the faith of the church is a fixed body of truth like a treasure put in a safe deposit box and guarded with the utmost care.[9] The marks of the heretics are the marks of mere locality, such as characterized the Donatists; of novelty, such as characterized all of the great heresiarchs; and of sectarianism, so that each of them won the assent of only a fraction of the folk who called themselves Christians. He goes through the list—one after another, after another, after another—and indicates how and why the church has condemned them.

Now Vincent thinks in his own day a view has developed (he does not name Augustine) which must be judged to come under the head of innovation. There are folk who are prepared to quote from the Scriptures, produce

> ... a thousand testimonies, a thousand examples, a thousand authorities from the Law, from the Psalms, from the apostles, from the Prophets, by means of which, interpreted on a new and wrong principle, the unhappy soul may be precipitated from the height of Catholic truth to the lowest abyss of heresy. ... For they dare to teach and promise, that in their church, that is, in the conventicle of their communion, [in their little sectarian offshoot] there is a certain great and special and altogether personal grace of God, so that whosoever pertain to their number, without any labor, without any effort, without any industry, even though they neither ask, nor seek, nor knock, have such a dispensation from God, that, borne up by angel hands, that is, preserved by the protection of angels, it is impossible they should ever dash their feet against a stone, that is, that they should ever be offended.[10]

Here is one of those poisonous novelties against which the faithful must be on guard. Now two Popes, Sixtus and Coelestinus, have been induced to write to certain of our friends, so Vincent goes on to say, that

8. Jülicher, *Vincenz von Lerinum, Commonitorium* 33, 52; Vincent of Lérins, *Comm.*, *NPNF2* 11: chapter 33, 156.

9. Vincent of Lérins, *NPNF2* 11: chapters 21–22, 146–49; 24, 149.

10. Vincent of Lérins, *Comm., NPNF2* 11: chapter 26, 151.

they must take care how they seek to oppose views of this kind. It is quite clear that these popes do not understand the situation. If it were as they believe it to be, if there were danger of folk going astray in these parts, it seems necessary to us who understand the matter to say that those who are in danger of going astray are these innovators who are bringing in a conception of grace which is morally unacceptable. It takes away the stress on the need for human effort.

Prosper of Aquitaine undertakes to answer Vincent in a series of theses (*Responsiones*) on behalf of Augustine.[11] And Prosper's answers seem to me by and large about as heavy-handed as Vincent's condemnation. Both of them eventually end up among the canonized saints, so the judgment of the Church was that each of them had meant well and each of them had told at least an essential part of the truth. But the question remained troubled for a hundred years.

## The Second Council of Orange

In 529, a small group of clergy came together to dedicate a church in the city of Orange. For some reason, Pope Boniface II sent them a letter suggesting that while they were gathered for the ceremonies, they might have a discussion among themselves of theses about grace and free choice which were still troubling the Church. Apparently he included a list of these for their consideration. Out of this list, they seem to have chosen eight for subscription and recommendation, and then they added some seventeen of their own. So we have a list of twenty-five *capitula* (theses or decrees, literally "chapters"). They are intended to be an examination of those things which pertain *ad ecclesiasticum regulam* (the rule of the Church) and later *fidei catholicae regulam* (the familiar phrase: the norm of catholic, that is, the orthodox, faith).[12]

The first eight of these theses support Augustine as against either the Pelagians on the one hand or the conservatives of Lérins on the other

---

11. See fn. 2.

12. Munier, ed., *Concilia Galliae*, A.511–A.695; CCSL, 148A (1963), 53–76; also in Hahn, *Bibliothek*, §74:220–27. Professor Calhoun usually translated into English on sight at his normal and somewhat rapid lecturing speed. The wording, needless to say, is not the same as that in the standard published translations, but despite occasional infelicities, his versions are generally reliable. With rare exceptions, they have been left unchanged [ed.].

hand, in insisting that God makes the first move; we do not. Some of the early headings run:

> That Through the Sin of Adam Not Only the Body But the Soul Was Damaged (Cap. I); That the Sin of Adam Hurt Not Only Himself But That It Is Transmitted Also in His Descendants (Cap. II); That the Grace of God Is Given Not on Condition of Prayer, But Itself Enables One to Ask (Cap. III); That God in Order to Cleanse Us from Sin Does Not Await Our Will But Prepares Our Will (Cap. IV); That the Beginning of Faith Is Not from Us But from the Grace of God (Cap. V).

The fifth *capitulum* continues:

> If anyone holds that just as the increase of faith, so the beginning of faith, i.e. that feeling of belief-fulness (*credulitatis affectum*) by which we believe in him who justifies the impious and come to the rebirth of holy baptism, is not by a gift of grace, that is, through the inspiration of the Holy Spirit correcting our will from unfaith to faith, from impiety to piety, but that this is in us *naturaliter*, he shows himself adverse to the apostolic teaching.

After quoting Paul, the *capitulum* continues: "For whoever in regard to the faith by which we believe in God (*qua in Deum credimus*—by which we are totally devoted to God) says that this faith is natural define all those who are in fact alien from the church of Christ as in some sense *fideles* (believers)."[13] This seems to me a very shrewd bit of analysis. If this faith is by nature, all persons have that which is by nature; and so all persons, whether in fact they trust God or not, are by this account to be regarded as numbered among those who can properly be called believers. And the sixth *capitulum*: "That without the grace of God, mercy is not granted to us in our believing and in our teaching,—since that grace itself brings it about that we believe and that we seek."

I will not go into the detail of that section because it simply spells out what the heading has laid down: we cannot make the first move except as God enables us to make it. We cannot talk about the assistance of grace as granted to human humility and obedience; rather, we should talk about the gift of grace as enabling us to be obedient and humble. It seems to me that that is supporting Augustine right down the line, and at the essential points that he had tried to make. The twenty-fifth of these

---

13. Hahn, *Bibliothek*, §74:222.

theses is interesting because it defines what is needed as love of God: "Fundamentally, the gift of God is to love God, for he himself has given that he may be loved, who loves though he has not been loved." This follows the Augustinian emphasis: not that God loved us because Christ died for us, but rather Christ died for us because God loved us; we are loved even while we are displeasing to him, that that might be brought about in us whence we could be pleasing to him.

So far that is good Augustinian doctrine. But then we come to a recapitulation at the end, and what we find, to our considerable astonishment if we have taken these earlier sections as a forthright statement of Augustinian views, is:

> That through the sin of the first man, free will was so inclined and weakened (*ita inclinatum et attenuatum fuerit*) that no one thereafter was able to love God as he ought, or to believe in God, or to do with respect to God what is good unless the grace of divine mercy prevene [come first].[14]

"The free will of man is so inclined and attenuated"—that phrase almost jumps out of the page in its non-Augustinianism. What is said here is not that man is depraved, corrupted through and through, so that his freedom to follow God is wholly lost, but rather that his free will is diminished and distorted.

> This we believe according to the Catholic faith, that with the grace received through baptism aiding and cooperating (*auxiliante et cooperante*), all who are baptized in Christ can and ought, if they will strive faithfully, to fulfill what pertains to the salvation of the soul.[15]

"Through grace received in baptism"—another deviation from Augustine's most characteristic conceptions. For him, baptism is necessary to the remission of sins, but cooperating grace comes to the believer in continuous inward personal communion with God.

The statement of the council closes with the affirmation that if there are folk who believe that some are predestined to evil by divine power, they shall be anathema: "We do not believe that some by divine power have been predestined to evil, and this we not only do not believe but if

---

14. *Capitulum* 25 in Hahn, *Bibliothek*, §74:226.
15. Ibid., 227.

there are those who are willing to believe such evil we pronounce anathema upon them with utter detestation."[16] Double predestination is out. So far, once again, Augustine might have agreed. But it is interesting that the one point at which a stark condemnation is pronounced is the one which would have made Augustinianism into the stern determinism which many later interpreters of Augustine took it to be.

The signatures to this statement include those of fourteen bishops, and interesting enough, eight laymen. The notion that laymen would be permitted to sign a dogmatic statement would have been simply unthinkable to the earlier church. What obviously we have here is a situation in which a rather informal conversation on the occasion of the dedication of a church has led to the framing of a statement which, it was thought, would carry greater weight if some influential people in the community put their names to it. We get something like this once again in the Reformation, when the *Augsburg Confession* is presented in 1530 with the sponsorship of princes of the German realm, but here we have a much earlier deviation from ancient practice.

## LEO I AND EFFORTS TO EXALT THE PAPACY

We come now to a development in the Western Church which corresponds roughly to a change which, as we noted earlier, also took place in the East. Attention shifted from primarily theoretical to primarily practical concerns. It will be recalled that before the death of Augustine, the threat of collapse of the structure of civilization in the West had become plain. As the fifth century goes on, the desire for security and the effort to consolidate a basis for continuity of life became increasingly evident.

Within the church, that effort to strengthen and centralize has a typical expression in the exertions of Pope Leo I, who, we remember, took an active part in the controversies over the person of Jesus Christ, and after a discouraging start succeeded in dominating the decisions of the Council of Chalcedon. Leo seems to have been one of those strenuous and intrepid Western churchmen on the pattern of Ambrose who actually embodied the force and authority of a great institution. The favorite example of Leo's exemplification of the authority and grandeur of the church is the story of his meeting with Attila, king of the Huns from the plains of central Asia, who had swept across central Europe down into the

16. Ibid.

regions of northern Italy, until he was met in the open field by an imperial embassy headed by the Pope in full panoply and persuaded to come no farther. Gibbon lists a dozen good reasons for Attila's yielding, and among them, the mysterious authority of the church as represented in Leo has a prominent place. Supernatural terrors seem to have exerted a real influence on the Hunnish king. But it seems no less plain that the threat of divine displeasure had to be presented by a man through whom divine power was convincingly symbolized by reason of his own psychological stability, confidence, and moral integrity.

Leo's theory in respect to the nature of the church turns rather strongly toward claiming for the bishop of Rome not merely the status of elder brother among brothers, but the status of superior authority over the bishops of other churches. In sermons, letters, and systematic writings Leo developed a theory which appears to have been suggested earlier in the century by Innocent I. Leo maintained that among the apostles, Peter had been given a place not merely of superior prestige but of superior authority with respect to the rest. And what was thus true of Peter and his colleagues was true also of Peter's successors in Rome and their fellow bishops elsewhere. Rome had an indisputable primacy. This does not mean that bishops differ with respect to status or dignity. The episcopal status is the same whether one be bishop of a large church or a small one. But in respect of rank and authority bishops are not equal. In the Roman succession there is a central line in which there has descended from generation to generation the title which was conferred first of all upon Peter by the Lord himself.

The question is by no means settled by these writings of Leo. In fact, we find Gregory I. still debating the issue a century and a half later and not claiming for himself the disputed title of universal bishop, which he steadily refuses to the patriarch of Constantinople. But Leo's claim, on the threshold of imperial collapse in the West, foreshadows the rise of the medieval papacy.

## POLITICAL AND SOCIAL BREAKDOWN

In the course of the century and a half after Leo I, the face of the Western world changed almost beyond recognition. The records we have refer to specific places and specific institutions. We know something of the fate of the Roman schools in the province of Gaul, the population decline in Rome itself, the collapse of the economic system, the ruin of military roads and public works. The details piece together to form a consistent and very shocking picture.

When Gregory I, the next theologically important person, came into a position of authority toward the end of the sixth century, the decline of the machinery of civilization in the West was about complete. The classic description of Rome in 590, "the lowest period of her depression," when Gregory became pope, is in Gibbon's work and based on the writings of Gregory himself. As far as I know, later research fills out rather than alters the main lines of his account. As regards the population of the capital city, Gibbon estimates that in its prime, the city may have held a million and a quarter of people. Other estimates put the total at two million. Ancient statistics are pretty ambiguous, and trying to define the odds and ends which come from various sources requires recognition of a wide margin of error. But there were somewhere between one million and two million people in Rome during the Golden Age. When Gregory became pope, somewhere between forty thousand and sixty thousand people are thought to have remained in Rome. That is somewhere between 2 and 6 percent of its maximum population. Ancient writers tell how one could stand on the ramparts of the old city, look out across the countryside, and see for miles deserted estates of the old Roman nobility—marble villas now inhabited by jackals and bats. The reason for this was, of course, not ill will on the part of the new conquerors: it was stark ignorance and inability on their part with respect to the mechanics of keeping a complex civilization alive. Tough, strenuous, enthusiastic, but technically untrained barbarians had no idea of the need to keep the sewer system of Rome in good repair. They knew nothing of the desirability of draining the malarial swamps of Latium, and paid no attention to the aqueducts built to bring pure water down from the Apennine slopes. Malaria, which had been the scourge of that part of the world, now came back in force. The swamps had been drained by Roman engineers, not to get rid of mosquitoes but to get rid of the dampness which was supposed to bring the disease. But ditching the swamps reduced the mosquitoes also, and the incidence of malaria had dropped off. Now the drainage ditches silted up, the swamps refilled, the mosquitoes came back, and malaria once again became a deadly killer in the Roman territory. The pollution of the city's life by undisposed sewage and the loss of suitable drinking water had its inevitable effect. Floods and epidemics added to the miseries of the ravaged city.

To feed the population of Rome, which for a very long time had ceased to be self-supporting, it had been necessary to arrange for great fleets of grain ships to bring wheat from the Black Sea and from Egypt and Sicily. That called for elaborate bookkeeping, for systematic planning, for the technology of shipbuilding and ship repair. Again, the new masters had no competence even to understand the need, and the food supply failed. Think of the Goths in their wolf skins and with their battle axes trying to maintain that kind of grain trade—impossible!

To maintain order in the old empire, a system of military roads had been kept in good condition so that imperial messengers could report quickly points at which disorders needed quelling, and legions could be moved quickly from place to place. Now the roads fell into disrepair, the organization of the messenger system lapsed, there was no basis for quick intelligence to come to the center of political administration, and consequently government at a distance became impossible. It is not difficult to understand why the life of the Western world declined so abruptly. The physical conditions for elastic, cultivated, organized, and disciplined living were no longer there. The collapse of the Roman kind of civilization in the West was a consequence not of deliberate destructiveness but rather of sheer technological incompetence on the part of extremely vigorous, able, and aggressive new peoples—but new peoples who needed to learn what they had not yet learned: how to keep a complex culture going.

What was true of political and economic life was true also of the intellectual life of the empire. I referred above to the school system of Gaul. At one time it had been the pride of the Roman world. Even the schools of Italy itself had not been superior. Many wealthy parents sent their sons by preference to Massilia or Lyons. By 550 the schools of Gaul were in complete stagnation. The study of the Greek language and literature, which had been a commonplace in the earlier centuries, had now become a curiosity. The ease of intercommunication which is essential to lively and diversified intellectual inquiry is no longer to be found.

Only in certain secluded nooks was it possible to maintain collections of manuscripts on which work could go on in a quiet, cumulative way. These backwaters of learning were largely to be found in monasteries established by choice in out-of-the-way places, which had become repositories of some of the technical knowledge, architectural and agricultural, of the old Roman world. But in the ebb and flow of tribal movement even the monasteries ceased to be places of real security. I have heard

Professor Bainton speak of the monasteries of Gaul, which had now become Merovingian Frankland, as dens of robbers. The study of Greek seems to have been carried on chiefly in Ireland, in monasteries on islands in the Irish Sea, and to some extent in the north of England after the disorders on the Continent had upset the possibility of leisurely work. So if, in the ninth or tenth century, you came upon a Western European who could read Greek, you were pretty confident that he came from Ireland or had studied under a teacher who did. The rarity of such modest learning is a mark of the extent to which Roman culture had been destroyed. When Gregory comes to the papal throne in 590, he speaks of himself with rueful picturesqueness as taking command of a ship so battered and with so many rotten planks that it was a question whether it could be kept afloat at all.

## Gregory the Great: The Last of the Fathers

Pope Gregory the Great was a towering figure who did marvels in temporarily slowing this steady decline of civilized life in the West. As a major transmitter of the classic heritage to the next age, he in some ways belongs more to the Middle Ages than to the patristic era. Indeed, he is sometimes called the first of the schoolmen. But it is more accurate to name him the last of the Fathers. However barbarous the times in which he lived, his education and outlook were those of a Roman patrician.

He had been a Roman courtier, and had distinguished himself in diplomatic missions, but he wanted to retire for the rest of his life into a Benedictine monastery. The establishment of the Rule of St. Benedict in 529 had regularized monastic life in the West and humanized it to a considerable extent, putting a premium not upon isolation or ascetic excesses but rather upon ordered life in a community. Useful work was scheduled for not less than seven hours a day, with periods of devotion so spaced as to safeguard the physical and mental health of the members of the community, and with a special place made for intellectual effort. Life in such an institution appealed strongly to Gregory, who had become wary of the stress and turmoil and futility of the secular world. Instead of being permitted to go quietly into a Benedictine house, however, he found himself in 590 under relentless pressure to accept the post of Bishop of Rome. He resisted unsuccessfully and took up the burden with reluctance, but with devotion and with the really impressive competence which he had shown in his early career.

For a period of fourteen years until his death in 604, Gregory headed the Roman Church. His talents, as he himself was the first to point out, were not primarily intellectual. He was neither a scholar nor a systematic thinker. He had steeped himself in the writings of Augustine, and he counted himself a humble follower of the Augustinian line. But his primary talents were those of the administrator and preacher. He would have been glad to become a monastic missionary, one who presented the Gospel in an outpost where the touch of moralizing, civilizing, humanizing insight was most needed and perhaps would be most readily welcome. But to the problems which the church as a whole now had to face, he brought driving energy, amazing resourcefulness, and sagacity— the kind of humane common sense which enabled him to acquire and maintain a quite surprising degree of understanding of local problems all over Europe, and of wisdom in counseling those who were trying to meet those problems on the ground.

## Administration

If one were to try to specify Gregory's chief accomplishment, I think I should say: the achievement of making the church the guardian of what remained of the old culture and the focal point for the construction of foundations for the new culture—the medieval European culture which was still to come. Gregory saw that the only institution which could with any hope at all take on that responsibility was the church. It alone had come through the wreck of the Western empire without destruction. A prime necessity, as it seemed to him, was to man strategic posts in the organization with representatives who were trained and then trusted by the central authorities. So he undertook to pick such men and to put them in clerical posts in Egypt, in Gaul, in the British Isles, where they could keep him informed as to the resources and the needs of their territory and where they could represent him in carrying out a gradually developing plan. He undertook to reestablish a system for importation of grain from Sicily and from Egypt. The church had estates in Sicily which could produce a very sizable crop of wheat, but things had fallen apart there largely because the peasants were being exploited by the representatives of the church; because false weights and measures were in customary use; and

because prices were so far down that there was no incentive to the peasants to raise more crops than they needed for their own use. So Gregory
sent one of his archdeacons, Peter, to Sicily to take charge of things there,
giving him detailed instructions in a series of letters with respect to decent
treatment for the *rustici*—the people who were actually doing the work
in the fields: destroy the oversized weights and the overlarge baskets, the
weights which are cheating the peasants, and replace them with weights
and measures of suitable sorts. Do away with the unfair requirement of
extra measures in each seventy that are provided by the peasants. Weed
out the unproductive herds and distribute the actually useful cows so that
they will be a source of many dairy herds on the land of a variety of
growers. And get the grain flowing to Rome once more. His own clergy
kept the books; no one else could. They reported to him the plans for
harvesting, for transporting, for distributing the grain that was needed as
the basis for restoring physical life at the center of the old Roman world.
Thus the church began work at the economic level as a spiritual service
to a needy continent.

He made the church responsible also for attempting a restoration of
political order and social discipline. He wrote on behalf of people who
were being unjustly treated by the secular magistrates. He wrote letters to
great nobles on the one hand, and to Teutonic chieftains and their wives
on the other hand, urging fair dealing for the poor as well as for the rich.
He allocated funds of the church to ransom captives who had been held
by bandit groups. whether in Italy or elsewhere. He wrote numerous letters urging fair treatment for Jews who, as he had heard, were prevented
from worshipping in their accustomed way and in various places. So
long as the Jews did not interfere with Christian worship, the Christians
should not interfere with Jewish worship. He recognized that social discipline in the British Isles could not be patterned after the social discipline
of the patrician circles in Rome with which he was familiar. Instead, he
got from his clerical outposts on the frontier specifications of the problems that they had to face in their parish work. It was he, of course, who
sent a mission to Britain in 596 headed by the monk Augustinus, with
whom incidentally there went Theodore of Tarsus, a Greek who established in the British Isles a tradition of Greek letters which persisted after
Greek learning on the Continent had pretty thoroughly died out. And
when this Augustinus wrote back to Gregory with practical questions
concerning the treatment of barbarians who had not been brought up

in the Christian tradition, Gregory answered with a degree of practical sagacity and humaneness and understanding which is, it seems to me, beyond praise. What shall be done with this chieftain who was polygamous in the older order and now has been baptized as a Christian but is reluctant to give up his plurality of wives? That is a problem which requires tact and shrewdness as well as firmness if it is to be soundly handled. What shall we do about admitting to Communion this tribesman who has continued the predatory habits which, in the old days, were regarded not merely as admissible but admirable? Shall we simply shut him out and say that he cannot come to church any more, or shall we try to gentle him by subjecting him to penance? (The latter course will be very difficult to enforce on a man who has been accustomed to the big open spaces and the freedom of life which the forests of central Europe had provided.)

Gregory's letters to those inquirers are, as it seems to me, models of a kind of ecclesiastical statesmanship that is grounded in understanding of and sympathy for human beings.[17] Their author had the kind of imagination that enabled him to recognize the differences of cultural background, of economic and social status or mores which will affect the very definition of each present problem, and which must be taken into account in proposing a way of dealing with it. The result is that during his fourteen years as the head of the Roman Church, he actually succeeded in making the church the senior partner in an effort to revive a civilized world order. We recall that the church had begun in the Roman world as a disapproved minority group. It had advanced under Constantine (if advanced be the right word) to the status of an established junior partner in a relationship in which the empire took primary responsibility for ordering the life of the Roman world, but the church was accepted as an assistant. Now the Empire in the West had gone to smash and under Gregory, the church stepped into the place of primary cultural responsibility. It was not, in the first instance, a theoretical development—it was an attempt to meet a quite inescapable present danger. And the effort to meet the demands of the crisis situation made of the church willy-nilly an institution taking responsibility that was not only spiritual but also secular. Grain shipments have an ultimate bearing on the well-being of the souls of men and women, but arranging for grain shipments is a temporal

17. For Gregory's works, see PL 75–78. English translations of selected epistles may be found in *NPNF2* 12 and 13.

job. The reestablishment of disciplinary machinery for the maintenance of social order has a bearing upon spiritual welfare, but fundamentally it is a task for the secular arm. To be sure, Gregory forbade his churchmen to become involved in secular politics: that is to say, they were not to try to hold office under a political as well as under an ecclesiastical rule. Yet the church had to take the initiative in reestablishing a basis for the performance of these temporal tasks, and the pattern which was suggested was fatefully maintained and theoretically rationalized as the Middle Ages went on. The doctrine of the two swords, of spiritual and of secular authority, with the sword of spiritual authority in the hand of the church as superior, was already implicit in the actual state of affairs beginning to take shape under Gregory's leadership.

## Folk Religion

As a theologian, Gregory was very human, very fallible, very devoted, and very unoriginal save for the less intellectual parts of his total outlook. This is illustrated by one of his particularly characteristic writings, a little work *On Pastoral Care* which is novel, not in its ideas, but in its practical good sense. When selecting a person for ecclesiastical office, do not choose someone who is overeager for this kind of preferment; on the other hand, do not choose one who is so reluctant that you cannot count on him to do the job if he is in fact chosen. One has to say that the pope is projecting a little self-image here; he was reluctant but not so reluctant that he refused when the choice fell upon him to take the unwanted load of practical responsibility. He would have preferred the life of a simplified monastic pattern, but he was ready to postpone to the next life the leisure which he could not have here. And he goes through a list of virtues which should be looked for when one is making appointments to the clergy, and they add up to a persuasive and convincing picture.[18] His originality also showed itself in another way through the introduction into approved theological doctrine of many elements of what had hitherto been popular folklore. Those aspects of Augustine's thought which had been kept in the background—a readiness, for example, to set store by miracles attributed to the relics of the saints—Gregory brings into the foreground. The evidence for this sort of dislocation of emphasis is to be found partly in his letters. He writes, for example, to the Empress Constantina, who

---

18. Gregory, *Liber regulae pastoralis,* English translation in *NPNF2* 12:1–72.

asked for the head of St. Paul to make the center of a great new church which is being built in the apostle's honor in Constantinople. Gregory says, "I'm sorry, I can't send you St. Paul's head nor any other part of his body because it has proved dangerous to fool around with the graves of those great men." He has stories of things of what had happened to people who, digging more or less at random, had stumbled upon graves and had suffered serious damage thereby. A crew of men inadvertently uncovered the body of a lesser saint, St. Lawrence, but didn't do a thing to move or even to touch it; nevertheless, all died within ten days. So Gregory says, "Sorry, we just have to settle for something a good deal more modest." His favorite miraculous gift on occasions of this sort consisted of filings of the chain with which St. Peter had been bound in prison, "provided," says he, "we can manage to get some filings off"—sometimes the chains yield readily and then the filings can be inserted into a replica of the key to St. Peter's tomb, but sometimes they turn the edge of a file and you can't get any filings.

But the great source of insight into his delight in wondrous tales is his four books of *Dialogues*.[19] The *Dialogues* constituted a quarry for medieval preachers for centuries to come. The illustrations in one set of handbooks for medieval preachers are almost always taken from one or another of the books of Gregory's *Dialogues*. One of those medieval manuals, incidentally, has the very engaging title *Dormi bene* ("Sleep Well"), addressed no doubt to the preacher, not to the congregation. With the help of this manual, the preacher will find his sermon ready and waiting for him on Sunday morning so he does not need to worry on Saturday night.

Gregory's *Four Books of Dialogues* consist almost entirely of miracle tales. Something of the contents is suggested by the titles: The first book, *Clergy in the Various Parts of Italy*; the second book, *St. Benedict Himself and Wonders Which He Worked on Behalf of Those Who Were in Need*; the third book, *Miscellaneous Miracles by Various Monks*. The fourth book goes into the very difficult question of the body of one who has died and the life after death, and earthly conditions which bear upon the later fate of the one who has died. The book dealing with St. Benedict has him rescuing a boy who has fallen carelessly into a swift-flowing stream and

19. Critical edition in SC, nos. 251, 260, and 265. English translation by Zimmerman, *Dialogues.*, FC 5 (Washington DC: Catholic University of America Press, 1959).

would surely have drowned except for the intervention of the saint. It tells of him repairing a glass vessel which the housekeeper had carelessly left on the edge of a table; it had toppled off and was broken, but he touches it and puts it together again so one cannot tell where the join is. On the other hand, by making the sign of the cross, he breaks a vase in which somebody has put a drink of poison; Benedict is the one who recognizes it—no one else would have—and so the dangerous vessel is shattered.

One of my favorite stories comes in the first book and concerns a monastic gardener of great age. A thief was accustomed to climb over the wall and secretly carry off vegetables. The gardener decided something must be done. Seeing a snake, he said "Follow me." And going to the place where the thief came in, he commanded the serpent, "In the name of Jesus, I order you that you guard this entrance." At the noon hour when all the brothers were sleeping, the thief climbed the wall, but when he was about to put his foot into the garden, suddenly he saw the snake, was frightened and caught his leather sandal on one of the stakes on the wall, so that he hung head downward. At the customary hour the gardener came and found him hanging on the fence, and he said to the serpent, "Thanks be to God, you have done what I ordered you; you can go now." So the snake went away. Then turning to the thief he said, "What is it, brother? God has given you into my hands. Why have you presumed so often to steal away what the labor of the monks has produced?" So saying he loosed his foot and set him down without any injury, led him to the entrance of the garden, and gave him vegetables with great generosity, saying, "Go, and after this do not do any more thieving, but when you are in need, then come to me and what with so much trouble you have labored to carry away I will give you freely."[20] Obviously a tale with a moral, and not merely with a miracle; such is the sort of thing which Gregory and a great many generations of Christians thereafter found edifying.

When we turn to the problem of what the church can do for the departed, we find that Gregory is quite clear that Masses said on behalf of those who have died are useful to their souls. The question is raised whether their being buried in the church will be good for them and the answer is yes, if they have been buried without a burden of serious sin. When their relatives come to church, they will be reminded of the one whose grave is there before their eyes, and they will pray for him. But

20. Gregory, *Dialogues*, 1:3.

if anyone has died with unforgiven serious sins on his conscience, then to be buried in the church is going to be worse. And of course Gregory has illustrations. A woman who had lived chastely but was an irresponsible gossip was buried in the church, and when the sexton came the next morning, he discovered that a part of the stone which had been laid over her grave was scorched and smoky and a part of it was clean. The fire had blazed up to clear away that part of her being which had been tainted with sin, and that part which profited from her virtue was left untouched. In the case of a man who was buried in a state of mortal sin, the sexton saw two terrifying figures open the grave and tie a rope around the corpse's feet, and drag him out of the church. The next morning, he told his colleagues what he had seen, and they came and found that the grave was in fact empty. Then they hunted around outside and discovered that the man had been carried to another place and buried in a more suitable environment. So on and so on—four books of such tales.

### God and Human Salvation

When we turn from Gregory's passion for the marvelous to his concern for doctrine and theology, we find that for the most part, it seemed to him that the teachings of Augustine were right and that he could do no better than to interpret them as best he knew how for the people of his own day.

With respect to God, his thought was conventional in the highest degree. In reference to the Trinity, for example, he says as one would expect that the three participants in the divine *substantia* are describable as *personae*. But the very subtle attempt Augustine had made to suggest a relationship among these *personae* that laid a special stress on their fundamental unity is quite beyond Gregory's reach. The three persons share one divine substance, but how that is he does not attempt to puzzle out at all. Similarly, he is content to say in relation to the world that this God is its Creator, Providential Sovereign, and Preserver. Much less than Augustine is Gregory concerned with the metaphysical status of the created order. The subtlety of Augustine's mind trained in Neoplatonism is simply beyond Gregory's comprehension. The created world depends upon God, and that is the primary thing to be said about it.

[In his treatment of human salvation, Gregory at times misunderstood rather than simply failed to understand Augustine.] We recall that for Augustine, human beings are so fully dependent upon God that they can do nothing save what God grants them the power to do. Gregory, in contrast, seems to say that once God has granted sinners the grace to turn them in the right direction they can by their own effort cooperate with the grace of God in working out the full realization of redemption. Original sin Gregory understands primarily as weakness and disease, as did Ambrose and Augustine's predecessors for whom human beings inherit a tendency to evil rather than the actual status of guilt. (Augustine's modification of that view had been to declare that what is inherited is the actual status of an indicted criminal. *Reatus*, as I understand it, is the actual condition of being under condemnation; and it is that, and not merely an evil tendency which is ours by birth. That is more than Gregory is willing to affirm.)

The person of Jesus Christ Gregory construes as the person of an eternal being who has become temporal in a rather restricted way. The divine Word takes upon itself human weakness rather more in the way of expediency than in the way of fundamental or essential being. He does not abandon divine power; there is a partial emptying of the status of deity. This partial emptying shows itself in the several grades of finiteness that one can recognize in the incarnate Savior. As far as regards his physical finiteness, this he assumes by a voluntary act. As far as regards his intellectual finiteness, it is denied. He has all wisdom; it is not necessary for him to learn and to grow, and he is incapable of making erroneous judgments. As regards his moral status, Gregory applies a distinction which he regards as proper for all human conduct. In every instance of sin there is first the outward stimulus which affects the body; next, the pleasure with which the body responds to a tempting stimulus; then last of all, the positive consent of the will. In a complete act of sin, all of these factors are present. Now as far as regards Jesus' life, only the first is recognizable. He was subjected to temptations, but they were purely external circumstances and there was not the slightest yielding on his part even in the way of the natural susceptibility of the flesh. And as regards consent which would make an act sinful, that of course is excluded by the very definition of his being, since he himself was perfect and immutable. Being God, he could not possibly take any step which would corrupt his being. Pretty obviously what we confront here is a Christology which is just on the edge of Docetism. The physical body is real enough, though its characteristics do not define the nature of the person. Rather, the nature of the person is defined by the immutable indwelling Logos, who temporarily and voluntarily takes for his own purposes the limitations of fleshly embodiment. But he completely controls the limitations at every moment, so that his needs for food or for rest are themselves voluntary affirmations on his part rather than genuine acknowledgement of human weakness. Gregory uses the term *exhibitive* for the situation which is thus involved. The Logos employs the flesh as a phenomenal manifestation and does not depend upon the flesh in any way for his own being, even during the period of incarnation.

The redeeming work which Jesus Christ effects on behalf of humanity Gregory construes in fairly complex but very crude fashion. In the first place, men and women are to be freed from the power of the Devil; and here the very ancient conception of the breaking of the power of evil is transformed into metaphors so vivid and so violent that one almost hesitates to put them into the record at all. The essential transaction which has been wrought is the deception of the Devil by the resources of God. The divinity of the incarnate Word was hidden in his human nature, and the Devil supposed that he was dealing with another ordinary man. He undertook therefore to seize hold upon Jesus Christ and to drag him down into his prison house. But then he discovered that he had been tricked, for the one whom he had thus carried off captive was an omnipotent champion with whom he could not deal. In one of his sermons Gregory uses the archaic conception of the devil as the chaotic power, the great fish (Tiamat), the one who is the abyss of chaos. But now the great fish had been caught, with the human nature of the Lord used as bait with the hook of the divine nature embedded in it, so that when the Devil snapped at the human nature, he was caught upon the divine nature and was therefore himself taken prisoner. That is the first aspect of the redemption which is brought about on our behalf.

Next we needed to be saved from the wrath of God; and this too the Savior has effected, making satisfaction on our behalf and achieving the propitiation of God. Here the emergence of the forensic patterns of thought which we have noted more than once in Latin theology scarcely needs to be pointed out. *Satisfactio* is the technical term for the recompense which balances the account. I have offended God and it is necessary that my offense shall be balanced by a work of merit which will put the relationship between God and myself straight. But that satisfaction is offered on our behalf by the Redeemer, and offering that satisfaction brings about the propitiation of the Judge who else could not take the attitude of one prepared to acquit or forgive.

The most profound insight in Gregory's conception of atonement comes in a third aspect. We need to be saved from the power of sin itself. Being freed from the Devil is an external transaction; being freed from the wrath of God is essentially a legal transaction; being freed from sin in one's own heart is on another level. Here Gregory makes use as best he can of Augustine's conception of illumination which comes from the indwelling of the Spirit; in this instance referring the illumination primarily to the teaching and example of Jesus Christ, and the referring, in Augustinian fashion again, to the mystical assimilation of the believer to the risen Lord. Here we have genuinely religious insight. It is not original, but it is perceptive.

By and large, Gregory conceives the whole process of atonement in a way that has something in it for everybody: for the simple believer who needs to have a vivid dramatic presentation of the work wrought on his behalf, and for the sensitive religious devotee who needs to be freed from the gnawing of his own sense of guilt. What Jesus has done is to effect salvation at all these various levels.

## Doctrine of the Church and the Means of Grace

Those who thus are saved become the members of the Christian community, and here for the first time, as far as I can judge, Gregory begins to move out upon a ground of theory in which he feels himself able to speak somewhat independently. Augustine had set the framework for a sound interpretation of the church; but Gregory, as one who knows the church from the inside, having had much to do with giving it its present status, was able to work out details which he did not simply take over from his predecessor. First of all, there are four distinctive marks or notes of the church by which it is to be distinguished from all other human institutions. Gregory's definition, it will be observed, is still employed very widely. The first note is its *unity*. As over against the diversities and inconsistencies of the heresies and schismatic sects, the Church has the character of an integral body. Its oneness is not simply uniformity. It is a unity which exists in the midst of diversity: one body, many members, many gifts, many sorts of contributions to be made. Its unity is the unanimity of faith and of love which pervades and integrates the whole diversified company.

A second note is *holiness*. In line with his Roman predecessors, Gregory conceived the holiness of the church primarily in sacramental rather than moral terms. The holiness of the church consists in its custody of the means of grace, the sacraments which are the instruments through which God works to make men and women holy. Yet he is prepared to parallel that sacramental concept by specifying a sense in which the church may be regarded as ethically holy, set apart from the world. There are in it now, and there have been in previous generations, actual saints whose presence has helped to characterize the church as a community. There will be more such saints whose lives act within the church to improve the virtues of those who come into contact with them directly or indirectly. And the church has the potentiality of becoming, at the last day, genuinely a communion of saints whose members are all holy. The holiness of the church is therefore partly actual and partly potential or prospective, partly sacramental and partly moral. It seems to me that what Gregory has done is to appraise very realistically what may suitably be said about the actual company of Christians at any given time.

A third note is *catholicity*. This is interpreted largely in Augustine's manner as inclusiveness of a geographical and a social kind. The Catholic Church has members in all parts of the world. It is not a regional organization. Moreover, it makes room in its membership for all sorts and conditions of human beings. It is not a class organization; it is not restricted to persons of wealth or education or whatnot. It is in fact an inclusive fellowship.

Its fourth mark is *apostolicity*, with regard to both doctrine on the one hand and succession within the church on the other. To say that the church is apostolic is to affirm, in the first instance, that it still preaches and disseminates the faith of the apostles. But the assurance of such apostolicity in doctrine is provided by an actual transmission from generation to generation from the beginning to authorized successors of Peter as the first bishop of Rome of that doctrine which Peter as eyewitness had in his possession and handed to his successors. But in Gregory's view, there is more than simply this succession of those who are in possession of transmitted truth. That was the basis of the importance that Irenaeus had ascribed to the known continuity of the bishopric in Rome. Gregory shares in a moderate way the view that we noted in speaking of Leo I—that Peter had the primacy among the apostles, and the successors of Peter in Rome have therefore a proper basis for exercising a degree of authority over other bishops in the territory that is dependent upon Rome.

We have an interesting correspondence on this issue between Gregory and John of Constantinople and his successor Cyriacus—the patriarchs contemporary with Gregory. John had assumed in his correspondence the title Ecumenical Bishop, which seemed pretty clearly to suggest that he was affirming universal supremacy now for New Rome. The Western world had collapsed, the old empire was no more, but the Eastern Empire had continued. So John was professing to be entitled to the first place among all the bishops of the existent world. The character of Gregory's exchange of letters with him over this issue is very interesting, because Gregory argues the impropriety of this claim on the part of the Constantinopolitan patriarch but disavows a similar claim on his own behalf. It seems to him rather that the fellowship of bishops within the church is of such sort that for any one of them to assert clear title to dictatorial authority over the others is wrong. In the West, it seems to him that the bishop of Rome should have such authority, and in the East the patriarch of Constantinople. But any effort to assert unique supremacy of any of the bishops is at present neither realistic nor right.

The church, then, is marked by these four distinctive notes. It is one, holy, catholic, and apostolic. And the institution which is thus recognizable may claim doctrinal authority to define right beliefs for its members and to enforce acceptance of such defined belief. The authority of the church as a teaching church (*ecclesia docens*), definer of dogma, arises out of the direct instruction of the Holy Spirit. The impartation of the Holy Spirit, especially to the clergy and most of all to the higher clergy, gives them access to a unique and ultimate source of guidance in making dogmatic judgments and definitions. The interesting feature of Gregory's dictum on this point also is its moderation. There is no secret teaching; there is no such thing as an esoteric unwritten tradition which the higher clergy have but which is not accessible to the people at large. It is rather that the higher clergy may be expected to have superior insight in interpreting the material that is available to everyone. The revelation is written down in Scripture. How to interpret that revelation will depend upon the Spirit of God, for it is God who knows ultimately what that revelation means. So Gregory is prepared to say that because the Spirit is at work within the church, and especially within the hierarchy, the hierarchy has the right to define doctrine and interpret the meaning of divine revelation. It may properly demand acceptance of its teachings so long as the teachings are in accord with reason. It has no right to demand that people shall believe absurdities. Yet its teaching is to be accepted not because it is rationally demonstrable but upon the ground of a faith which is presupposed by any attempt to show the accord of dogma with the demands of rational coherence. That faith is itself an act of obedience; it is not the outcome of a logical demonstration. It is a volitional commitment. Once again, it seems to me that Gregory is occupying a realistic middle ground, neither rationalism on the one hand nor fideism on the other hand. A teaching of the church is to be regarded as testable both by the demand for fundamental personal commitment and by the proviso that one is committing oneself to affirmations which are not self-contradictory.

With respect to the present status of the church, Gregory took full account of its alliance with the state. The precise terms in which the effort to define the relationship of the Empire to the church would be worked out in the next centuries were not yet present. We shall have occasion later to note the specific ground of the clash between those who held to the Roman conception of the church as authoritatively based upon the Word of God and those chieftains who understood religion as simply a social function of the folk, the tribal community. But for Gregory that is not an issue, for the people with whom he is dealing are, as far as regards their direct relations with him, committed to recognition of the importance of the old Roman civilization. What had happened in Rome under Gregory's leadership was that the church had made itself responsible for preserving *Romanitas*. Something like the Stoic humanity which had guided Ambrose in his ethical writing guides Gregory likewise. The church is itself custodian of that kind of civilized living which in the West the state had ceased to guarantee. Now the church in a way is coming to be the nurturing guardian of a new political power, and to Gregory's mind, the relation between the two sorts of power should be cooperative.

We spoke of the church as the custodian of the means of grace. These are the sacraments. And it appears that Gregory used the term for only two: baptism and the Lord's Supper. The other ordinances of the church he does not himself define as sacraments. Augustine had spoken of sacraments as symbols and occasions of the working of the Holy Spirit; and he described under that rubric a rather indefinite list of such means of grace, including the preaching of the Word. When he saw people moved to righteousness by a preacher who was interpreting for them the Word of God, that seemed to him a sacramental occasion. Such inclusiveness in the use of *sacrament* now seems to give place to a sharpening and narrowing of the term to the two specific occasions of introduction into membership in the church and the central rite of worship from which all except full members of the church are excluded.

There is no discussion by Gregory of the general character of the sacraments. He simply takes over Augustine's discussion at that point. Baptism has primarily a negative effect—the effect of cleansing away of original sin and any previous actual sin, freeing one, therefore, to enter upon the Christian life. But it thus also has a positive effect: it is the point at which there is a beginning of faith, which is effected by the Holy Spirit acting in and through the baptismal rite.

The Eucharist is regarded as a sacrament both in the sense of Augustine, and as a repeatable sacrifice. For Gregory the Lord's Supper is the Mass, and as such it is properly interpreted as a continual offering to God on behalf of believers of a gift which then is returned to believers with the grace of God infused, so that what we first offer to God we then receive back for our own benefit. There is no assertion that the sacrifice thus offered is a repetition of the sacrifice on Calvary. The language used is not unambiguous, but it most naturally suggests the repetition rather of that giving of himself which characterized the relation of Jesus to his friends the night before Calvary. At the Lord's Supper he offered to them his body and his blood, and in that self-giving he was indeed foreshadowing the more tragic offering on the Cross. Now what the church is able to do in repeating the Lord's Supper is to repeat not merely a symbolic sharing of food in token of fellowship but also the self-giving which characterized the act of the Lord in that first celebration of the Lord's Supper. And this is properly to be thought of as a hieratic and efficacious offering to God for the benefit of human beings, who must then complete the offering by a willing sacrifice of themselves also. It redounds, moreover, to the benefit not merely of living church members but of the dead. For Gregory is committed to what had before been a chiefly popular conception of a purgatorial state in which the souls of those who have departed this life with their moral accounts not fully in balance will be held for a time until they are completely cleansed. For them, as well as for the members of the church who are now living, the sacrifice of the Mass is beneficial.

Along with this conception of purgatory go two other conceptions which Gregory does not work out in detail but which became of great significance in medieval Christianity: the conception of the intercession of the saints and the conception of the efficacy of works of penance. The intercession may be asked not only on behalf of oneself or of one's living fellow Christians, but on behalf likewise of those who are now departed and are awaiting their fate in purgatory. Penitential works, likewise, are associated with the notion of purgatory and of benefit to those who are detained therein. A complete work of penance begins with an act of contrition, the acknowledgment by the sinner of the wrong he has done and of the regret that he feels. Contrition will normally be followed by confession. This, if it be regarded by the priest as genuine, will be followed by a pronouncement of absolution, which means that the one who has confessed his sins is entitled to work off his debit account by doing penitential works assigned to him by the confessor. Penitential works do not remove the guilt of the sins confessed; the guilt is removed solely by repentance. God forgives the repentant sinner because he is penitent and not because he has done something in addition to penitence. The works of penance have the effect of lightening the load of correction which otherwise one would have to bear in purgatory. Penitential works, or *satisfactio*, bring about temporal rather than eternal forgiveness; and Gregory is beginning a line of thought which in later medieval theology bulks very large indeed. The specification of repentance as a sacrament was still far away in the future. Yet the beginnings of lines which are later worked out in such elaborate fashion are recognizable here.

## Conclusion: Collapse before Regrowth

When the old structure of secular society in the West collapsed, anything like unified control even in the church was made exceedingly difficult. We have spoken of Gregory as beginning the reestablishment of such centralized control, but even genius like his can operate only within finite limits. It was quite impossible for him to restore within fourteen years what had been breaking down during a hundred and fifty years. The peoples who had settled in the old provinces of the Roman empire, in as far as they had been Christianized at all, had developed regional types of Christian belief and practice. In Gaul, the conversion of the Frankish king Clovis through his wife brought adherence to the Nicene type of Christian faith. In many other parts of Europe, conversion of the Teutonic folk had been to Arian rather than to Nicene Christianity. In Spain, the West Goths who had moved across the Pyrenees and settled in the peninsula found themselves struggling against an invasion from the south which brought Mohammedan Arabs into Spain in the seventh century. By the time the Arabs had settled and consolidated their position, Gothic and Arab folk-ways and folk beliefs were having a strange effect upon Christian teachings. In Britain, there was likewise a regional church. I hesitate to speak, as do some historians, of national churches because the nation-state as we understand it today was far in the future. We are dealing here with loose conglomerations of tribes with tribal thought and tribal folkways as their familiar manner of understanding the universe and responding to it. Under the leadership of Gregory, the church centered in Rome had begun trying to make headway against this regionalism by developing a conception of the church which, as Seeberg in the fourth edition of his *Dogmengeschichte* clearly and illuminatingly points out, was antithetic to that of any of these tribal peoples.

So far as the tribesmen were concerned, religion was an affair of the group. Their priests, who represented the religious interests of the folk, were responsible to and conditioned by the mores of the tribe. The chieftain was head of the secular society, and he was head also of whatever religious interests were involved in the life of the society. Religion was a function of the folk group. Now the Roman conception of the church in relation to society was in principle opposed to this one. The ecclesial conception which had developed in the old Roman world was that of an independent order, a spiritual commonwealth, whose pattern of government and source of authority was the Word of God, standing over against all secular society, all secular customs, all secular folk beliefs, and undertaking to judge and to transform rather than simply to represent and give expression to these folkways. If you conceive religion as an expression of the existing communal outlook, then plainly enough the principle that a change of ruler and of policy should bring about a change of religion is sound. If, on the other hand, you regard religion as not emerging out of the life of the group but rather confronting and judging its life, then you have a very different conception of the nature of the church and its proper relation to the community. In effect, the long conflict between the Papacy and the Empire that went on through the Middle Ages and that, I should say, continues right through our own day under various new guises, is an elaborate prolongation and development of this fundamental conflict.

The conception of the church as a function of secular society seemed to the people of the tribally organized regions of the new Europe quite obvious and inescapable. Religion is something the group does of its own will, and the group can at will change the pattern and direction of its religious expression. Over against that, the conception of religion as coming from God, not from man; of the church as speaking for God, not for the chieftain and the tribesmen; of the Christian life as a drastic correction, not a further expression of the existing patterns of folk living was an entirely foreign conception. And when those two conceptions of the nature of religion and the nature of the church and the relation of each to the secular order met face to face, there was no way to reconcile them. They are in principle irreconcilable. And what happened during the period we are speaking of is that those who were convinced of the correctness of the Roman hierarchical understanding of the church and of its task sought all sorts of ways to increase the measure of influence they could exert in trying to alter the view maintained against them by those tribal leaders who viewed with resentment the efforts of representatives of an alien organization to take power away from them.

The Roman Church had a sort of advantage in this contest in view of the fact that it possessed cultural and technological knowledge out of the old civilization that was not in possession of the tribesmen. The monasteries of the church were the outposts not simply of classical learning but also of superior agricultural, architectural, and mechanical techniques. They were outposts of civilized living, and the methods which they practiced they could teach to the surrounding tribesmen to the advantage of the latter and with added prestige for the former. We have then constant local struggles between secular rulers who, though influenced by the Christianity they had adopted, tried to use the church for their own purposes and ecclesiasts who sought to assert the church's independence and primacy. Those among the ecclesiasts who recognized the need to win over the new peoples to acceptance of the authority of the church as not something they had made and could discard or transform at will, but as something which confronted them with a word of authority, resorted at times to some strange devices to consolidate the influence they were seeking to exert.

Among these devices was the fabrication in the eighth and ninth centuries of such spurious documents as the *Donation of Constantine*[21] and the *Decretals of Isidore*.[22] The *Donation* purported to be the last will and testament of Constantine I making over to Pope Sylvester I and his successors the imperial Lateran palace in Rome, and in addition transferring to the pope authority over "all provinces, places and cities of Italy or of the western regions" (the exact extent of the territory is left conveniently vague). The chief intent of the *Decretals*, in partial contrast, was not to exalt the power of the Papacy but to emphasize the independence of the episcopacy: something like the so-called Gallican theory of the church in which the *collegium episcoporum* rather than the transalpine curia is regarded as the prime seat of authority may reflect the thinking of those who produced the *Decretals*. They were contesting secular control and worked to establish the bishops in their independency. (To be sure, the document could also be used as a weapon in the hands of a powerful and ambitious pope, as in fact it was by Nicholas I.)

The authenticity of the *Decretals* as of the *Donation* seems to have gone unchallenged for an amazingly long time, and they were employed in controversies not only between Church and state but also between local bishops and their metropolitans. We can smile or frown over the bizarre devices employed to break the secular grip, while at the same time sympathizing with the clerics who were trying to make an impression upon the tough habits of the representatives of tribal ways. As far as I can judge, this development of thought about the nature of the church and its relations to the secular order was by all odds the most important for the future of theology during the period from the death of Gregory in 604 until about the middle of the eleventh century.

[This interval is the great hiatus in the history of Christian thought.] There was, to be sure, a brief revival of learning during the Carolingian interlude of the eighth and ninth centuries, but its rootage was shallow,

---

21. For the text of the *Donation*, C. Mirbt, *Quellen zur Geschichte des Papstums* (4th ed., 1924), no. 228, 107–12; for an English translation, see Ehler and Morrall, trans. and eds., *Church and State Through the Centuries* (Westminster, MD: Newman, 1954) 16–22.

22. Critical edition by Hinschius, *Decretales Pseudo-Isidorianae et Capitula Angilramni* (Leipzig, 1863). It professes to be Isidore's compilation of canons and decretals from various councils and popes from Clement of Rome to the early eighth century. There are different levels of interpolated material in the work, ancient and recent, genuine, garbled, spurious. The result is an extraordinary and impressive farrago well calculated to deceive an uncritical age.

and it was destroyed by the Viking, Magyar, and Saracen incursions which reached a crescendo in the tenth century. The Dark Ages, as they are often called, were never darker. What was happening on the practical and popular levels during these four hundred years was important for the later history of theology, but it was not until the eleventh-century beginnings of scholasticism that intellectual developments of doctrinal importance once again got under way. [Since then, theological learning and reflection have continued down to the present without any comparable interruptions, but in worlds very different from the classic one. Gregory the Great marks the end of an era; but he is also as we have seen the harbinger of a new epoch.]

# Bibliography

Augustine. *Concerning the City of God Against the Pagans*. Translated by Henry Betten-son. Harmondsworth, UK: Penguin, 1972.

————. *Confessions*. Translated by R. S. Pine-Coffin. Baltimore: Penguin, 1961.

————. *On Christian Doctrine*. Translated by D. W. Robertson Jr. New York: Bobbs-Merrill, 1958.

————. *On Free Choice of the Will*. Translated by Anna S. Benjamin and L. H. Hackstaff. Indianapolis: Bobbs-Merrill, 1964.

————. *The Soliloquies of Saint Augustine*. Translated by Thomas F. Gilligan. New York: Cosmopolitan Science and Art Service, 1943.

Bardy, Gustave. *Paul de Samosate: étude historique*. Paris: Champion, 1923.

————. *Recherches sur saint Lucien d'Antioche et son école*. Paris: Beauchesne, 1936.

————. "La Thalie d'Arius." *Revue de Philologie* 53 (1927) 211–33.

Barth, Karl. *Protestant Thought: From Rousseau to Ritschl; Being the Translation of Eleven Chapters of* Die protestantische Theologie im 19. Jahrhundert. Translated by Brian Cozens. New York: Simon & Schuster, 1959.

————. *Der Römerbrief*. Zürich: EVZ, 1940.

Bauer, Walter. *Orthodoxy and Heresy in Earliest Christianity*. Translated by a team from the Philadelphia Seminar on Christian Origins and edited by Robert A. Kraft and Gerhard Krodel. Philadelphia: Fortress, 1971.

Baur, C. "Drei unedierte Festpredigten aus der Zeit der nestorianischen Stretigkeiten." *Traditio* 9 (1953) 101–26.

Bedjan, Paul, editor. *Nestorius, le livre d'Héraclide de Damas*. Paris: Letouzey et Ane, 1910.

Bethune-Baker, J. F. *The Meaning of Homoousios in the "Constantinopolitan" Creed*. Texts and Studies. Cambridge: Cambridge University Press, 1901.

Bright, William, editor. *Kata Areianōn logoi. The Orations of St. Athanasius against the Arians according to the Benedictine Text, with an Account of His Life*. Oxford: Clarendon, 1873.

Brooke, A. E., editor. *The Commentary of Origen on S. John's Gospel: The Text Revised with a Critical Introduction and Notes*. 2 vols. Cambridge: Cambridge University Press, 1896.

Burrows, Millar. *The Dead Sea Scrolls*. New York: Viking, 1955.

Butterworth, G. W., editor. *Origen on First Principles, Being Koetschau's Text of the "De Principiis."* London: SPCK, 1936.

Calhoun, Robert L. "The Role of Historical Theology." *Journal of Religion* 21 (1941) 444–54.

Campbell, Thomas L., editor. *Dionysius the Pseudo-Areopagite: The Ecclesiastical Hierarchy.* Translated by Thomas L. Campbell. Washington, DC: Catholic University of America Press, 1955.

Caspari, Karl Paul. *Alte und neue Quellen zur Geschichte des Taufsymbols und der Glaubensregel.* 1879. Reprint, Brussels: Brepols, 1991.

Clement, of Alexandria. *Clemens Alexandrinus.* 4 vols. Edited by Otto Stählin. Leipzig: Hinrichs, 1905–1936.

Cochrane, Charles Norris. *Christianity and Classical Culture: A Study of Thought and Action from Augustus to Augustine.* New York: Oxford University Press, 1944.

Cross, F. L., editor. *Athanasius De incarnatione: An Edition of the Greek Text.* London: SPCK, 1939.

Daley, Brian. *Gregory of Nazianzus.* Early Church Fathers. London: Routledge, 2006.

Driver, G. R., and L. Hodgson, editors. *Nestorius, the Bazaar of Heracleides.* Oxford: Clarendon, 1925.

Ehler, Sidney Z., and John B. Morrall, editors. *Church and State through the Centuries: A Collection of Historic Documents with Commentaries.* Westminster, MD: Newman, 1954.

Faye, Eugène de. *Clément d'Alexandrie, étude sur les rapports du christianisme et de la philosophie grecque au IIe siècle.* 2nd ed. Paris: Leroux, 1906.

Feltoe, Charles Lett, editor. *DIONYSIOU LEIPSANA: The Letters and Other Remains of Alexander.* Cambridge: Cambridge University Press, 1904.

———. *St. Dionysius of Alexandria: Letters and Treatises.* London: SPCK, 1918.

Flavian, Saint. *Appellatio Flaviani: The Letters of Appeal from the Council of Ephesus, A.D. 449, Addressed by Flavian and Eusebius to St. Leo of Rome.* Edited by T. A. Lacey. London: SPCK, 1903.

Frei, Hans W. "Barth and Schleiermacher: Divergence and Convergence." In *Theology and Narrative: Selected Essays,* edited by George Hunsinger and William C. Placher, 177–99. New York: Oxford University Press, 1993.

Gonzales, Justo L. *A History of Christian Thought.* 2nd ed. Nashville: Abingdon, 1987.

Gregory the Great. *Dialogues.* Translated by Odo John Zimmermann. Fathers of the Church 39. Washington, DC: Catholic University of America Press, 1959.

Greer, Rowan A., editor. *Origen.* Translated by Rowan A. Greer. New York: Paulist, 1979.

Gwatkin, Henry M. *The Arian Controversy.* New York: Longmans, Green, 1898.

Hahn, August. *Bibliothek der Symbole und Glaubensregehen der Alten Kirche.* 3rd ed. 1897. Reprint, Hildesheim: Olms, 1962.

Hardy, Edward Rochie, and Cyril C. Richardson, editors. *Christology of the Later Fathers.* Philadelphia: Westminster, 1954.

Harnack, Adolf von. *Geschichte der altchristlichen Literatur bis Eusebius.* 2 vols. Leipzig: Hinrichs, 1893–1904.

———. *History of Dogma.* Translated from the 3rd German ed. by Neil Buchanan. 7 vols. London: Williams & Norgate, 1896–1899.

———. *Lehrbuch der Dogmengeschichte.* 4th ed. Tübingen: Mohr/Siebeck, 1909.

———. *Marcion: das Evangelium vom fremden Gott, eine Monographie zur Geschichte der Grundlegung der katholischen Kirche.* 2nd ed. Leipzig: Hinrichs, 1924.

———. *Neue Studien zu Marcion.* Texte und Untersuchungen zur Geschichte der altchristlichen Literatur 44. Leipzig: Hinrichs, 1923.

Harvey, W. Wigan. *Sancti Irenaei, episcopi Lugdunensis, Libros quinque adversus haereses.* Cambridge: Cambridge University Press, 1857.

Herzog, J. J. *Realencyklopädie für protestantische Theologie und Kirche.* 3rd ed. Edited by Albert Hauck. Leipzig: Hinrichs, 1896–1913.

Hinschius, Paulus, editor. *Decretales Pseudo-Isidorianae et Capitula Angilramni.* Leipzig: Tauchnitz, 1863.

Hort, Fenton John Anthony. *Two Dissertations.* London: Macmillan, 1876.

Inge, William Ralph. *Christian Mysticism, Considered in Eight Lectures Delivered before the University of Oxford.* New York: Scribners, 1899.

Irenaeus, of Lyon. *Contre les hérésies.* 10 vols. Edited by Adelin Rousseau. Sources chrétiennes. Paris: Cerf, 1965–1982.

Jay, Eric George. *Origen's Treatise on Prayer: Translation and Notes with an Account of the Practice and Doctrine of Prayer from New Testament Times to Origen.* London: SPCK, 1954.

John, of Damascus, Saint. *Die Schriften des Johannes von Damaskos.* 7 vols. Edited by Bonifatius Kotter. Patristische Texte und Studien. Berlin: de Gruyter, 1969–.

Jülicher, Adolf, editor. *Vincenz von Lerinum: Commonitorium pro catholicae fidei antiquitate et universitate adversus profanes omnium haereticorum novitates.* 2nd ed. 1925. Reprint, Frankfurt: Minerva, 1968.

Kelly, J. N. D. *Early Christian Creeds.* 3rd ed. New York: McKay, 1972.

Koch, Hal. *Pronoia und Paideusis: Studien über Origenes und sein Verhältnis zum Platonismus.* Berlin: de Gruyter, 1932.

Lawlor, H. J. "The Sayings of Paul of Samosata." *Journal of Theological Studies* 19 (1917–1918) 20–120.

Lear, Jonathan. *Aristotle: The Desire to Understand.* New York: Cambridge University Press, 1988.

Lietzmann, Hans. *Apollinaris von Laodicea und seine Schule: Texte und Untersuchungen.* Tübingen: Mohr/Siebeck, 1904.

Lovejoy, Arthur O. *The Great Chain of Being: A Study of the History of an Idea.* Cambridge: Harvard University Press, 1936.

McGiffert, A. C. *The Apostles' Creed: Its Origin, Its Purpose, and Its Historical Interpretation.* New York: Scribners, 1902.

Mirbt, Carl. *Quellen zur Geschichte des Papstums und des römischen Katholizismus.* 4th ed. Tübingen: Mohr/Siebeck, 1924.

Munier, Charles, editor. *Concilia Galliae, A.314–A.506.* Turnhout: Brepols, 1963.

Nau, F. *Le livre d'Héraclide de Damas, suivi du texte grec des trios homélies de Nestorius sur les tentations de Notre-Seigneur.*

Nestorius. *Nestoriana: Die Fragmenta des Nestorius.* Edited by Friedrich Loofs. Halle: Niemeyer, 1905.

Opitz, Hans-Georg. *Athanasius, über die Entscheidungen des Konzils von Nicaea.*

———. *Urkunden zur Geschichte des Arianischen Streites 318-328.* 3 vols. Berlin: Brandenburgischen Akademie der Wissenschaften, 1934-1935.

Origen. *Contra Celsum.* Translated by Henry Chadwick. New York: Cambridge University Press, 1953.

———. *Origenes Werke.* Edited by P. Koetschau et al. Leipzig: Hinrichs, 1899-1955.

———. *Origenis Opera omnia quae Graece vel Latine tantum exstant et ejus nomine circumferentur.* 25 vols. Edited by Eduard Lommatsch. Berlin: Haude & Spener, 1831-1848.

Pelagious. *Pelagius's Exposition of Thirteen Epistles of St. Paul.* 3 vols. Translated by Alexander Souter. Cambridge: Cambridge University Press, 1931.

Pelikan, Jaroslav, *The Christian Tradition.* 5 vols. Chicago: University of Chicago Press, 1971–1989.

Pelikan, Jaroslav, and Valerie Hotchkiss, editors. *Creeds and Confessions of Faith in the Christian Tradition.* New Haven: Yale University Press, 2003.

Pseudo-Dionysius, the Areopagite. *Dionysius, the Areopagite, The Divine Names and, Mystical Theology.* Translated by C. E. Holt. New York: Macmillan, 1951.

———. *The Works of Dionysius the Areopagite.* 2 vols. Translated by John Parker. London: Parker, 1897–1899.

Robinson, James M., editor. *The Nag Hammadi Library in English.* San Francisco: Harper & Row, 1977.

Routh, Martin Joseph. *Reliquiae Sacrae: sive auctorum fere iam perditorum secundi tertiique saeculi post Christum natum quae supersunt.* 2d ed. 5 vols. 1846–1848. Reprint, New York: Olms, 1974.

Rusch, William G., editor and translator. *The Trinitarian Controversy.* Sources of Early Christian Thought. Philadelphia: Fortress, 1980.

Schaff, Philip. *The Creeds of Christendom.* New York: Harper, 1877.

Schweitzer, Albert. *Quest of the Historical Jesus: A Critical Study of Its Progress from Reimarus to Wrede.* Translated by William Montgomery. New York: Macmillan, 1910.

Seeberg, Reinhold. *Lehrbuch der Dogmengeschichte.* 4th ed. 4 vols. Akademische Druck-u. Verlagsanstalt, 1953–1954.

Stead, Christopher. *Divine Substance.* Oxford: Clarendon, 1977.

Tsarnoff, Radoslav Andrea. *The Nature of Evil.* New York: Macmillan, 1931.

Turner, C. H. "A Critical Text of the *Quicunque vult.*" *Journal of Theological Studies* 11 (1910) 401–11.

Vincent, of Lerins. *The Commonitorium of Vincentius of Lerins.* Edited by Reginald Stewart Moxon. Cambridge: Cambridge University Press, 1915.

Williams, Rowan. *Arius: Heresy and Tradition.* 2nd ed. Grand Rapids: Eerdmans, 2002.

Zeller, Eduard. *Die Philosophie der Griechen in ihrer geschichtliche Entwicklung dargestellt.* 6 vols. Leipzig: Reisland, 1903–1922.

# Name Index

Made in the USA
Middletown, DE
19 January 2016